Brookings Papers
ON ECONOMIC ACTIVITY

FALL 2008

DOUGLAS W. ELMENDORF
N. GREGORY MANKIW
LAWRENCE H. SUMMERS
Editors

BROOKINGS INSTITUTION PRESS
Washington, D.C.

ISSN 0007-2303
ISBN-13: 978-0-8157-0299-3

Brookings Papers
ON ECONOMIC ACTIVITY

FALL 2008

PURPOSE The *Brookings Papers on Economic Activity* publishes research on current issues in macroeconomics, broadly defined. The journal emphasizes innovative analysis that has an empirical orientation, takes real-world institutions seriously, and is relevant to economic policy. Papers are presented and discussed at conferences held twice each year, and the papers and discussant remarks from each conference are published in the journal several months later. Research findings are described in a clear and accessible style to maximize their impact on economic understanding and economic policymaking; the intended audience includes analysts from universities, governments, and businesses. Topics covered by the journal include fiscal and monetary policy, consumption and saving behavior, business investment, housing, asset pricing, labor markets, wage- and price-setting, business cycles, long-run economic growth, the distribution of income and wealth, international capital flows and exchange rates, international trade and development, and the macroeconomic implications of health costs, energy supply and demand, environmental issues, and the education system.

The conference and the journal are based upon the work partially supported by the National Science Foundation under Grant No. 0752779.

The papers and discussant remarks reflect the views of the authors and not necessarily the views of the funding organizations or the staff members, officers, or trustees of the Brookings Institution.

CALL FOR PAPERS Most papers that appear in the *Brookings Papers on Economic Activity* are solicited by the editors, but the editors also consider submitted proposals. Editorial decisions are generally made about a year in advance of each conference. Therefore, proposals should be received by September 1 for the following fall conference and by April 1 for the following spring conference. Proposals should be no more than three double-spaced pages and should be sent to brookingspapers@brookings.edu or to William Gale, Brookings Institution, 1775 Massachusetts Ave., NW, Washington, D.C. 20036.

ACCESSING THE JOURNAL For information about previous issues of the journal, participants in this conference, and agendas for upcoming conferences, visit www.brookings.edu/economics/bpea/bpea.aspx. To purchase subscriptions or single copies, visit www.brookings.edu/press, or contact the Brookings Institution Press at 866-698-0010 or P.O. Box 465, Hanover, PA 17331-0465. Brookings periodicals are available online through both the Online Computer Library Center (contact OCLC subscription department at 800-848-5878) and Project Muse (http://muse.jhu.edu). Archived issues of the *Brookings Papers on Economic Activity* are available through JSTOR (www.jstor.org).

EDITORS, PANEL ADVISERS, AND STAFF FOR THE EIGHTY-SIXTH CONFERENCE

Daron Acemoglu *Massachusetts Institute of Technology*
George A. Akerlof *University of California, Berkeley*
Olivier J. Blanchard *Massachusetts Institute of Technology*
William C. Brainard *Yale University*
Ricardo J. Caballero *Massachusetts Institute of Technology*
Karl E. Case *Wellesley College*
Kathryn M. Dominguez *University of Michigan*
Douglas W. Elmendorf *Brookings Institution*
Emmanuel Farhi *Harvard University*
Kristopher Gerardi *Federal Reserve Bank of Atlanta*
Pierre-Olivier Gourinchas *University of California, Berkeley*
Robert E. Hall *Stanford University*
Jan Hatzius *Goldman Sachs*
Peter Blair Henry *Stanford University*
Charles I. Jones *Stanford University*
Donald L. Kohn *Board of Governors of the Federal Reserve*
Rafael La Porta *Dartmouth College*
Andreas Lehnert *Board of Governors of the Federal Reserve*
Deborah Lucas *Northwestern University*
N. Gregory Mankiw *Harvard University*
Stephen Morris *Princeton University*
William D. Nordhaus *Yale University*
George L. Perry *Brookings Institution*
Carmen M. Reinhart *University of Maryland*
Vincent R. Reinhart *American Enterprise Institute*
Dani Rodrik *Harvard University*
David Romer *University of California, Berkeley*
Shane M. Sherlund *Board of Governors of the Federal Reserve*
Hyun Song Shin *Princeton University*
Andrei Shleifer *Harvard University*
Nicholas S. Souleles *University of Pennsylvania*
Lawrence H. Summers *Harvard University*
Paul Willen *Federal Reserve Bank of Boston*
Michael Woodford *Columbia University*

Rebecca N. Mintz *Brookings Institution*
Michael Treadway *Brookings Institution*
Lindsey B. Wilson *Brookings Institution*

GUESTS WHOSE WRITINGS OR COMMENTS APPEAR IN THIS ISSUE

Martin Neil Baily *Brookings Institution*
Alan S. Blinder *Princeton University*
Christopher D. Carroll *Johns Hopkins University*
Richard N. Cooper *Harvard University*
J. Bradford DeLong *University of California, Berkeley*
Eduardo M. Engel *Yale University*
Kristin J. Forbes *Massachusetts Institute of Technology*
Benjamin A. Friedman *Harvard University*
Linda Goldberg *Federal Reserve Bank of New York*
Austan D. Goolsbee *University of Chicago*
Robert J. Gordon *Northwestern University*
Chang-Tai Hsieh *University of Chicago*
Frederic S. Mishkin *Columbia University*
Hélène Rey *London Business School*
Paul Romer *Stanford University*
Charles L. Schultze *Brookings Institution*

Editors' Summary

THE BROOKINGS PANEL ON ECONOMIC ACTIVITY held its eighty-sixth conference in Washington, D.C., on September 11 and 12, 2008. Several of the conference papers examine aspects of the current financial crisis: the relationships among recent global financial imbalances, mortgage lending, and volatile commodity prices; the errors made by lenders in judging subprime mortgages and instruments derived from them to have fairly low credit risk; the effect of mortgage foreclosures on the dynamics of home prices; the impact of mortgage credit losses on the supply of credit; and the implications for financial regulation of spillovers from failing financial institutions. The remaining papers deal with the role of the unofficial economy in economic development, and the effect of an undervalued currency on economic growth in developing countries. This issue of the *Brookings Papers on Economic Activity* presents the seven papers from the conference, comments by the formal discussants, and synopses of the discussions of the papers by conference participants.

In the first paper, Ricardo Caballero, Emmanuel Farhi, and Pierre-Olivier Gourinchas make the case that outsized international capital flows, the U.S. subprime crisis, and recent swings in oil and other commodity prices are interrelated phenomena. They argue that the root cause of all of these developments is a global scarcity of sound and liquid financial assets relative to the demand for such assets. As emerging market and commodity-producing nations searched for ways to invest their newfound wealth, they focused on U.S. financial markets, their own being relatively underdeveloped. The strong demand for U.S. assets pushed down required rates of return and created an environment conducive to asset bubbles, with the expansion of subprime lending and the rapid rise in home prices among the consequences.

However, market attempts to accommodate this excess demand for U.S. assets contained the seeds of their own demise, because U.S. assets became "stretched" to an unsustainable degree. Ultimately, the housing and financial bubbles collapsed. At that point, according to the authors, the continued search for investment opportunities generated the dramatic run-up in commodity prices, especially oil. These new bubbles persisted until they weakened global economic activity to the point that the underlying demand for commodities receded.

In the view of the authors, these patterns will recur in some form as long as rapidly growing developing economies remain financially underdeveloped and the chronic shortage of financial assets persists. Only when the world economy generates enough safe and profitable stores of value to meet the demand by savers will this cycle end.

The second paper asks why sophisticated analysts did not anticipate that so many of the subprime mortgage loans and related assets they were holding would perform badly. Kristopher Gerardi, Andreas Lehnert, Shane Sherlund, and Paul Willen begin by showing that lenders made riskier loans in 2005 and 2006 than earlier, with the key difference being an increase in borrower leverage. However, they find that the change in mortgage characteristics was too small by itself to explain the recent surge in defaults. Instead, defaults have been spurred by the collapse in home price appreciation since early 2006.

To have misjudged the riskiness of subprime mortgages, then, lenders must have been mistaken about future trends in home prices, the sensitivity of foreclosures to changes in home prices, or some combination of both. Using data through 2004 only, the authors show that if analysts had known the future trajectory of home prices, they could have predicted the large rise in foreclosures with reasonable accuracy. Indeed, the authors' reading of research reports and media commentary by mortgage market analysts between 2004 and 2006 suggests that these analysts had a reasonable sense of the potential impact on the subprime market of home price declines. However, these analysts generally assigned a substantial price decline a very low probability, apparently putting more weight on the historical rarity of such events than on the risk posed by the unprecedented jump in home prices during the preceding decade.

In the third paper, Karl Case explores the mechanisms through which home prices are adjusting to restore equilibrium in the housing market. He explains that two different mechanisms are at work today. One is the traditional process in which prospective buyers search deliberately for homes that best suit them, while homeowners are reluctant to sell at a loss and thus tend to wait for better offers. This process generally restores equilibrium slowly, through growth in the quantity of housing demanded, with relatively small changes in prices. The other equilibrating mechanism is auctions of homes acquired by banks and mortgage servicers through default and foreclosure. This process leads to more abrupt price declines, because institutional sellers are eager to move the properties off their balance sheets.

Case notes that both auctions and the traditional search mechanism have played important roles in previous, regional housing slumps. With housing demand now falling sharply in many parts of the country, auctions are becoming more common: between the third quarter of 2006 and November 2008, auctions climbed from 9 percent to 27 percent of total existing-home sales. Case concludes that home prices may well decline substantially further during the next few years, but he holds out hope that a faster turnaround is possible.

Jan Hatzius, in the fourth paper, analyzes the implications of mortgage losses for new lending. He estimates that if home prices fall an additional 15 percent from their level in mid-2008, total losses on residential mortgages will ultimately exceed $750 billion. About half of those losses will likely be borne by leveraged financial institutions in the United States, greatly reducing those institutions' equity capital. In addition, banks generally trim their desired leverage ratios when financial and economic conditions sour. All in all, Hatzius calculates that financial institutions might reduce their outstanding loans by more than $2 trillion from what they would have been otherwise.

The supply of credit will take a further hit from the sharp drop in issuance of asset-backed securities. Much-larger-than-expected losses on existing securities have undermined confidence in the firms that bundle individual loans, and in the rating agencies that evaluate the risk of those securities, so demand has tumbled. Taking together the different channels of reduced credit supply, Hatzius estimates that growth in aggregate demand could be reduced (before allowing for any multiplier effects) by roughly 2.5 percentage points on average in 2008 and 2009. He emphasizes the importance of government policies to boost private lending and to ensure continued lending by the government-sponsored mortgage enterprises Fannie Mae and Freddie Mac.

In the fifth paper, Stephen Morris and Hyun Song Shin reconsider the basic strategy of financial regulation. They explain that the traditional rationale for regulating financial institutions is to ensure their solvency and thereby protect the interests of retail depositors. This rationale has encouraged a focus on capital regulation in which the required capital buffer depends on the riskiness of an institution's assets. However, events of the past year show that this approach does not ensure the stability of the financial system as a whole. The key problem is that actions taken by financial institutions to protect their own solvency can have spillover effects on other institutions; thus actions that are rational for individual firms can be counterproductive for the overall economy.

Therefore, the goal of financial regulation should be to mitigate these spillovers. One important type of spillover arises with assets that are not risky themselves but are systemically important because of the way they connect institutions. Drawing on an analysis of this interconnectedness, the authors recommend two new elements of financial regulation: a simple (non-risk-adjusted) leverage constraint, and a liquidity requirement that regulates the composition of asset portfolios rather than just their size.

In the sixth paper, Rafael La Porta and Andrei Shleifer examine the "unofficial" or "informal" sector in developing economies. Unofficial firms, which generally do not pay taxes or abide by regulations, account for up to about half of economic activity in poor countries. However, experts disagree about their role. In the "romantic" view, as defined by La Porta and Shleifer, unofficial firms are similar to official firms but are held back by legal barriers to official recognition and by lack of access to finance. Government policy that aims at helping these firms enter the formal sector would boost economic growth. In contrast, the "parasite" view holds that unofficial firms are too small to produce efficiently, but that the cost advantage of avoiding taxes and regulations allows them to undercut more-productive formal firms. From this perspective, eliminating unofficial firms would boost economic growth. Lastly, the "dual economy" view agrees that unofficial firms are inefficient but does not view them as threatening formal firms, because they are led by less-able entrepreneurs and sell to different customers. If this is the correct view, government tax and regulatory policy should support the formation of official firms but should neither foster nor discourage unofficial firms.

La Porta and Shleifer present evidence that supports the dual view over the romantic and parasite views. According to their data, unofficial firms are small and unproductive relative to official firms. In addition, unofficial firms employ managers with significantly less human capital, tend to use less physical capital, exploit external finance to a lesser extent, and pay their workers substantially less. Informal firms do not tend to become formal as they grow, but instead remain in their separate markets. The authors conclude that the existence of informal firms is important for poverty alleviation as long as the economy remains underdeveloped, but does not contribute much to productivity gains or economic growth.

The final paper in this issue is an evaluation by Dani Rodrik of the effect of the real exchange rate on economic growth. Rodrik observes that significant overvaluation of a currency is widely viewed as a detriment to growth, but that little consensus exists about the effects of undervaluation. His empirical analysis finds that undervaluation boosts economic growth just as strongly as overvaluation diminishes it. Noteworthy examples of this positive relationship between undervaluation and growth include China, India, some other Asian countries, and several African countries. However, undervaluation appears to be correlated with economic growth only for developing countries and not for rich ones.

Rodrik proposes the following explanation for his results: Developing countries suffer from institutional and market failures that hinder economic activity in general and production of tradable goods in particular. Currency undervaluation raises the domestic price of tradables relative to nontradables, which provides an offsetting boost to the tradable goods sector. By undoing the distortion away from tradable goods, undervaluation thus increases economic growth. Eliminating the distortion directly would avoid the costs of undervaluation but is often not feasible; an exchange rate policy of deliberate undervaluation appears to provide a feasible alternative.

RICARDO J. CABALLERO
Massachusetts Institute of Technology

EMMANUEL FARHI
Harvard University

PIERRE-OLIVIER GOURINCHAS
University of California, Berkeley

Financial Crash, Commodity Prices, and Global Imbalances

ABSTRACT The current financial crisis has its origins in global asset scarcity, which led to large capital flows toward the United States and to the creation of asset bubbles that eventually burst. In its first phase the crash exacerbated the shortage of assets in the world economy, which triggered a partial re-creation of the bubble in commodities markets, and oil markets in particular. This bubble in turn led to an increase in petrodollars seeking financial assets in the United States, which became a source of stability for the U.S. external balance. The second phase of the crisis is more conventional and began to emerge in the summer of 2008, when it became apparent that the financial crisis would permeate the real economy and sharply slow global growth. This slowdown worked to reverse the tight commodity market conditions required for a bubble to develop, ultimately destroying the commodity bubble.

In this paper we argue that the persistent global imbalances of recent decades, the subprime crisis, and the volatile oil and asset prices that followed it are tightly interconnected. All stem from a global environment where sound and liquid financial assets are in scarce supply.

Our story goes as follows: Global asset scarcity led to large capital flows toward the United States and to the creation of asset bubbles that eventually burst. The crash in the real estate market was particularly complex from the point of view of asset shortages, since it compromised the whole financial sector and, by so doing, closed many of the alternative saving vehicles. Thus, in its first phase, the crisis exacerbated the shortage of assets in the world economy, which triggered a partial re-creation of the

Figure 1. Current Account Balances, 1990–2008

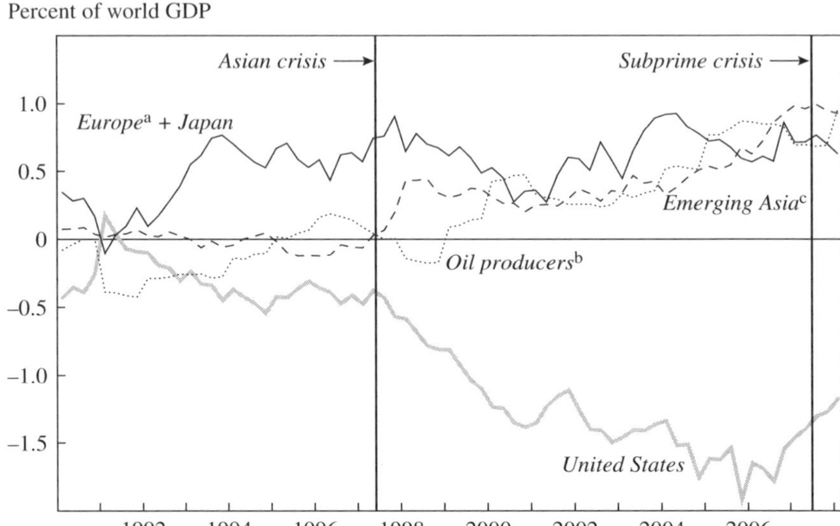

Sources: World Bank, *World Development Indicators*; International Monetary Fund, *World Economic Outlook* and *International Financial Statistics*; Organization for Economic Cooperation and Development; authors' calculations.

a. Austria, Belgium, Denmark, France, Germany, Iceland, Ireland, Italy, Netherlands, Spain, Sweden, and Switzerland.

b. Bahrain, Canada, Iran, Kuwait, Libya, Mexico, Norway, Oman, Russia, Saudi Arabia, and Venezuela.

c. China, Hong Kong, Indonesia, Malaysia, the Philippines, Singapore, South Korea, Taiwan, and Thailand.

bubble in commodities, and in oil markets in particular. Rising oil prices in turn led to an increase in petrodollars seeking financial assets in the United States. In contrast to the typical, destabilizing role played by capital outflows during financial crises, petrodollar flows became a stabilizing factor for the U.S. economy. The second phase of the crisis is more conventional and began to emerge during the summer of 2008. It became apparent then that the financial crisis would permeate the real economy and sharply slow global growth. This slowdown worked to reverse the tight commodity market conditions required for a bubble to develop, ultimately destroying the commodity bubble.

We now develop some of these steps, starting from the underlying structural force fueling U.S. asset appreciation. Figure 1 displays the main patterns of global imbalances since 1990 as revealed in the current accounts of the United States, Europe and Japan (combined), emerging Asia, and the oil-producing economies, all relative to world GDP. The facts are well known: Starting in 1991 the U.S. current account deficit worsened continuously, reaching 6.4 percent of U.S. GDP in the fourth quarter of 2005, then falling back to 5 percent of GDP by early 2008. The current account surpluses that were the counterpart of the U.S. deficits initially emerged in Japan and Europe and were bolstered by surpluses in emerging Asia and the commodity-producing countries after 1997.

In a previous paper we showed how this buildup in global imbalances could be understood as the consequence of asymmetries in financial development and growth prospects across different regions of the world.[1] In particular, we argued that the emerging market crises at the end of the 1990s, the subsequent rapid growth of China and other East Asian economies, and the associated rise in commodity prices in recent years reoriented capital flows *from* emerging markets *toward* the United States. In effect, emerging markets and commodity producers in need of sound and liquid financial instruments to store their newfound wealth turned to the U.S. financial markets, which were perceived as uniquely positioned to provide these instruments.[2]

As we explained then, a by-product of this reallocation of capital flows was a necessary decline in U.S. and world real interest rates and a boom in U.S. asset markets. Ex ante real interest rates on 10-year U.S. government bonds fell below 2 percent a year in 2002 (figure 2), and the rate on a 30-year fixed-rate conventional mortgage reached 5.23 percent in June 2003 (figure 3), with annual inflation at 2.9 percent. As foretold by Ben Bernanke, then a governor of the Federal Reserve, in his influential "savings glut" speech,[3] it is now apparent that this boom was located in no small part in a rise in U.S. housing markets and the related markets for structured credit instruments (figures 4 and 5). In the context of low real interest rates, U.S. households were encouraged to take on more housing risk than they could bear, risks that then disappeared as if by magic from the mortgage-backed securities and other structured investment vehicles whose supply exploded over the same period (figure 5). The catastrophic and systemic failures of this originate-to-distribute model are now well documented.[4]

1. Caballero, Farhi, and Gourinchas (2008).

2. In recent years a significant portion of the capital flows from emerging markets to the United States took the form of official reserve accumulation. The composition of capital flows is not the focus of our analysis. Nonetheless, we observe that especially in the case of China, most of these reserves are indirectly held by local investors through low-return sterilization bonds.

3. Bernanke (2005).

4. See Brunnermeier (2009) and Greenlaw and others (2008) for detailed recent accounts of the subprime crisis.

Figure 2. Real Interest Rates, 1990–2008

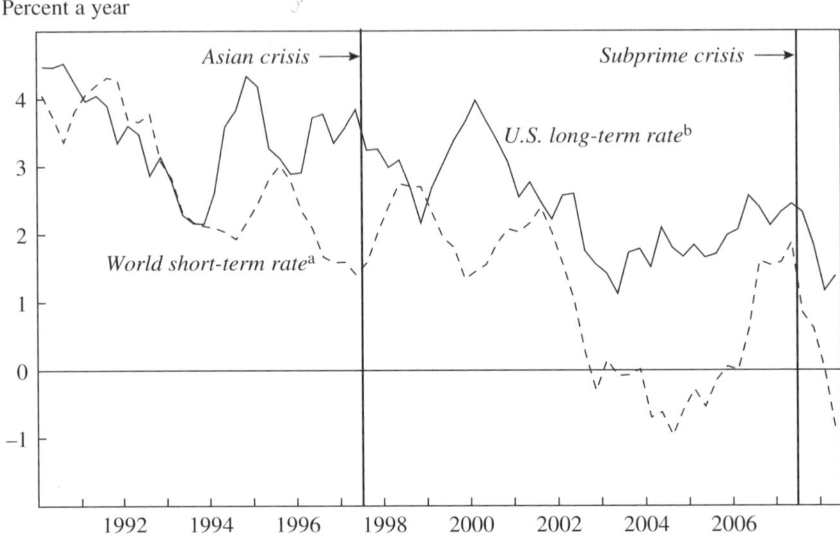

Sources: World Bank, *World Development Indicators*; International Monetary Fund, *International Financial Statistics*; Organization for Economic Cooperation and Development; Survey of Professional Forecasters; authors' calculations.

a. Average ex post rate for the previous four quarters on three-month national treasury bills of the Group of Seven countries. Averages across countries are weighted by GDP. Each country's nominal interest rate is deflated by its consumer price index.

b. Rate on 10-year U.S. Treasury bonds minus 10-year expected inflation from the Survey of Professional Forecasters.

By sometime in 2006, the rise in U.S. real estate prices had come to a halt, and the U.S. current account deficit began to turn around (see figures 1 and 4). Starting in earnest in June 2007, with the bailout of two hedge funds operated by the investment bank Bear Stearns that could not meet their margin calls, the world economy entered, with a certain fracas, into a period of significant global adjustment. Within weeks, funding dried up for entire segments of both the U.S. and the international banking sectors, especially asset-backed commercial paper (see figure 5), leading to major convulsions of credit and money markets, including the dramatic collapse and rescue of several major U.S. and European commercial and investment banking institutions. More than 12 months after the onset of the crisis, financial markets appear nowhere near stabilized. In fact, by the beginning of the summer of 2008, financial distress in major players had begun to accelerate, a process that started with the government rescue of the government-sponsored enterprises Fannie Mae and Freddie Mac in July and culminated

Figure 3. Contract Interest Rate on 30-Year Fixed-Rate Conventional Home Mortgage Commitments, 1990–2008

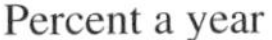
Percent a year

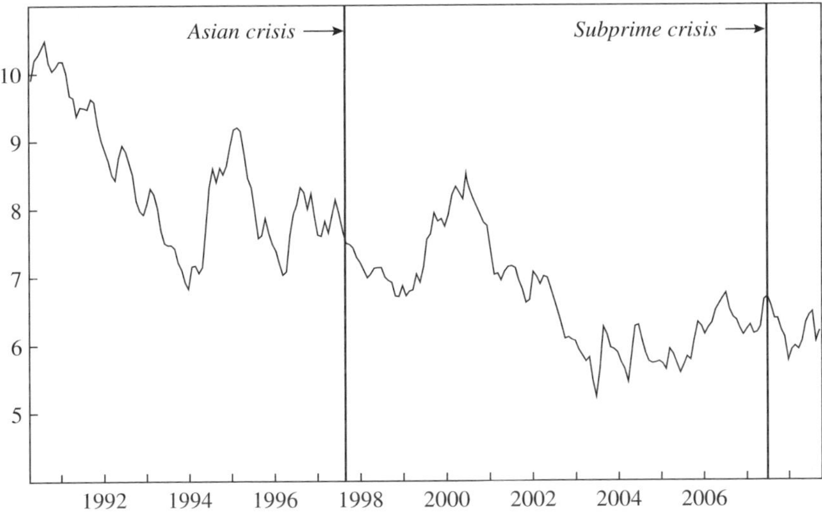

Source: Federal Reserve Statistical Release H.15, "Selected Interest Rates."

Figure 4. Real S&P/Case-Shiller Composite 10 Home Price Index, 1990–2008

January 2000 = 100

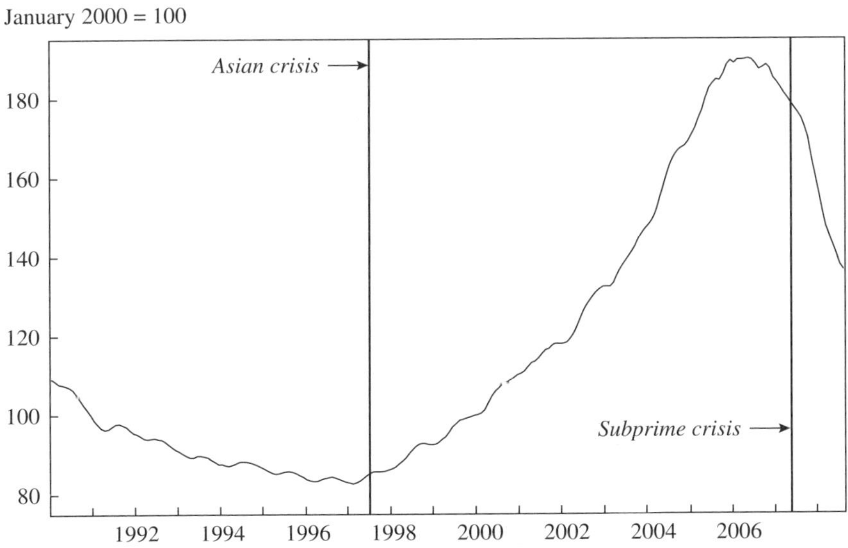

Sources: Standard & Poor's; International Monetary Fund, *International Financial Statistics*; authors' calculations.

Figure 5. Commercial Paper Outstanding, 2003–08

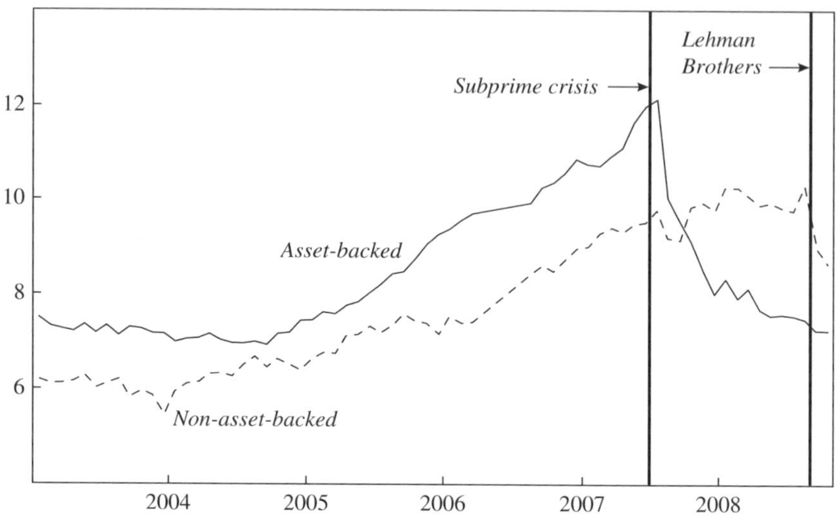

Source: Federal Reserve Board.

with the failure of the investment bank Lehman Brothers on September 15. This was a watershed moment. Until then, the crisis had been severe but largely contained within the financial sector. Following the collapse of Fannie and Freddie and of the entire U.S. broker-dealer industry, the seizing up of wholesale money markets reached unprecedented proportions. Figure 6 decomposes the spread between the three-month London interbank offer rate (LIBOR) and the three-month Treasury yield (the TED spread) into two parts: a LIBOR-overnight index swap (OIS) spread, which measures interbank credit risk, and a Treasury-OIS spread, which captures the flight to liquidity. In the weeks following the collapse of Lehman Brothers, both components of the spread increased dramatically, with the Treasury-OIS spread reaching 165 basis points on September 17 and the LIBOR-OIS spread reaching 365 basis points on October 10. With credit markets on life support, the crisis quickly spread to the rest of the economy.

It is most likely that the strong U.S. capital inflows of the last few years contributed to the significant weakening of U.S. credit markets. The eventual recognition of their degraded performance was one of the triggers of the current crisis. However, this weakening is in itself part of the endogenous

Figure 6. Components of the TED Spread, January 2007–November 2008

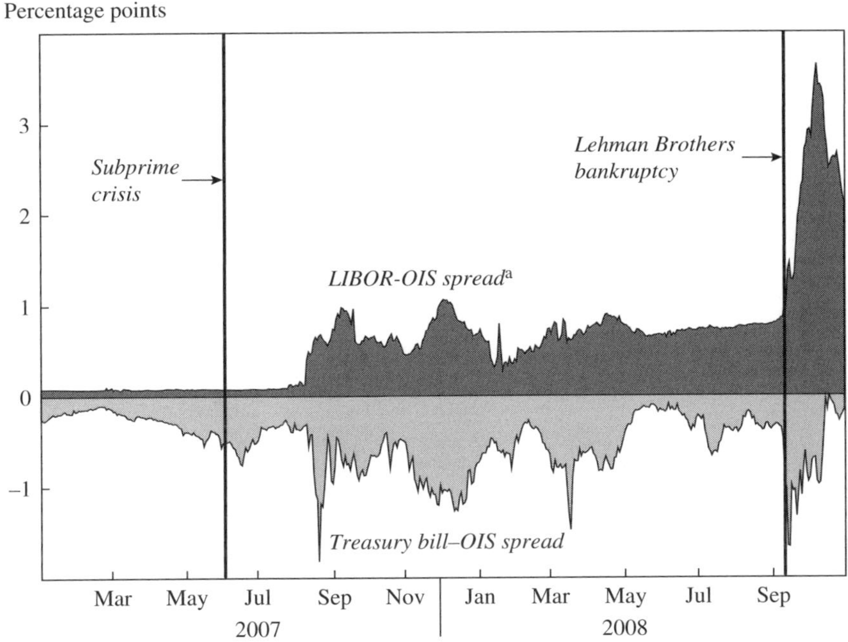

Source: MorganMarkets; authors' calculations.
a. OIS, overnight index swap.

response of U.S. financial markets to world financial conditions. In effect, U.S. assets became stretched as U.S. markets tried to accommodate the world's excess demand for assets. Therein lies the structural problem. This chronic excess demand for assets derives from financial underdevelopment in emerging markets and most commodity-producing economies, rather than from macroeconomic imbalances. Excess asset demand leaves an unmistakable signature in low real interest rates, which in turn provide a fertile ground for bubbles to emerge. Thus an alternative, if perhaps metaphorical, interpretation of the sequence of events is that the bubble located in emerging markets during the 1990s migrated to the U.S. housing and credit markets (and before that the NASDAQ) following the emerging market crisis of the late 1990s and the coming on line of capitalist China.[5]

5. See Caballero and Krishnamurthy (2006) for a model of bubbles and capital flows in emerging markets based on financial underdevelopment.

Figure 7. Price of West Texas Intermediate Oil, 1970–2008

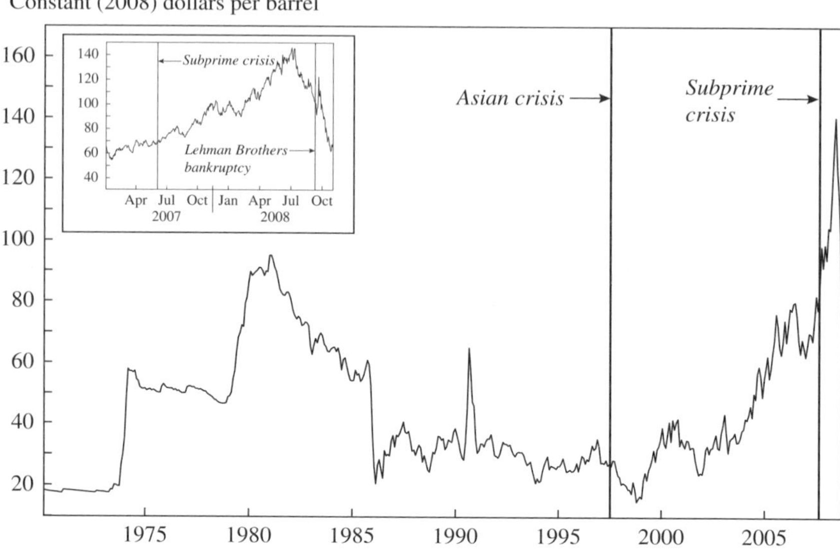

Sources: Global Financial Data; International Monetary Fund, *International Financial Statistics*; authors' calculations.

With the U.S. financial crisis, that bubble collapsed as well. Initially, the excess asset demand that produced it did not. Indeed, emerging markets and commodity producers found themselves more than ever in search of investment opportunities—witness the long list of sovereign wealth funds that have recently been formed in many emerging markets and the enormous financial means at their disposal. According to Deutsche Bank,[6] these state-owned funds managed $3 trillion in assets as of September 2007 and were expected to be managing an additional $7 trillion within 10 years. (These figures are now being revised downward as a result of the brutal slowdown in world economic growth.) Another bubble was likely to appear as the endogenous response of a world economy seeking to increase the global supply of financial assets. We argue that it did so quickly, in the form of a commodity bubble. Figure 7 tracks the real price of a barrel of West Texas Intermediate (WTI) crude oil since 1970, in 2008 dollars. Between June 2007 and June 2008, the real price of WTI increased by almost 100 percent. During the summer of 2008, however, as the financial

6. Deutsche Bank (2007).

crisis spread and economic growth started to decline, commodity prices suffered a dramatic collapse. Between July 2008 and October 2008, the real WTI price declined by almost 53 percent, bringing it back to its level of June 2007.[7]

Essentially, in the first phase of the crisis the *combination* of tight commodities markets and the decline in equilibrium real interest rates made it worthwhile, from the point of view of private economic agents, to transform commodities into an asset (or even a new bubble). The mechanism is related (but not identical) to that described by Harold Hotelling more than 70 years ago:[8] Sufficiently low real interest rates make inventory accumulation profitable and drive up the price of exhaustible resources. However, in the second phase the market tightness precondition disappeared, which in turn destroyed the asset accumulation incentive behind the feverish rise in commodity prices, triggering their collapse.

A scatterplot of daily observations of WTI prices against the S&P500 index from 2004 to 2008 (figure 8) clearly illustrates the different phases of the crisis. Before June 2007 the correlation between oil prices and U.S. stock prices was positive. During the first phase of the crisis, from July 2007 to June 2008, the correlation turned strongly negative. Finally, since July 2008, the correlation has again become strongly positive. The negative correlation during the first phase of the crisis is especially interesting from our point of view. Explanations of the surge in commodity prices driven purely by demand for commodities would predict a positive correlation between stock and commodity prices. Later in this paper we provide evidence from instrumental variables estimations to support the claim that the negative correlation in this phase is due not to oil supply shocks but to the financial mechanism we describe.

Let us now return to the implications of these developments for global imbalances. According to the framework developed in our earlier paper, the sharp contraction in U.S. asset supply caused by the subprime crisis

7. This price pattern is quite general across commodities. It is apparent for energy commodities (coal, gasoline, heating oil) and for foodstuffs used as biofuels, such as corn. It is also present for most metals (aluminum, copper, gold, and silver) with the exception of lead, zinc, and nickel, whose prices peaked earlier in 2007. We find it also for most food prices (wheat, soybeans, coffee, tea, cocoa, barley, rice, palm oil, groundnuts, and rapeseed oil, less so for sugar, cattle, and hogs). Our model provides a broad-brush picture of the general evolution of commodity prices. Yet individual commodities might also be affected by other factors—supply disruptions, weather, and commodity-specific demand shocks. We also note that high energy prices generally push up food prices through higher production costs and stronger competition for acreage from biofuels.

8. Hotelling (1931).

Figure 8. West Texas Intermediate Oil Price and S&P500 Index, 2004–08

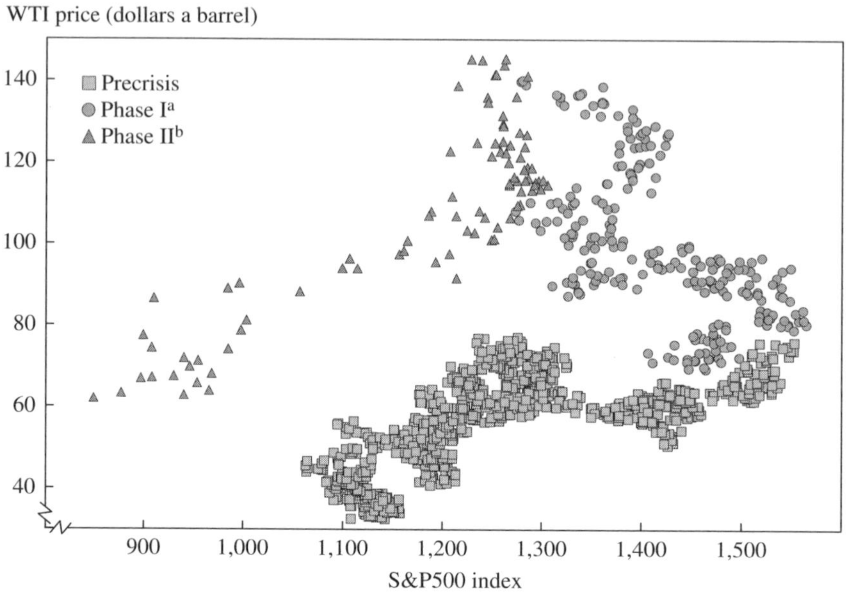

Sources: Global Financial Data; authors' calculations.
a. July 1, 2007, to June 30, 2008.
b. July 1, 2008, to November 8, 2008.

should lower equilibrium interest rates and trigger a rebalancing away from now-"toxic" U.S. assets.[9] The resulting decline in U.S. wealth reduces domestic consumption and improves the trade balance and the current account. This is in line with what has happened since June 2007: annual U.S. long-term real interest rates fell from 2.3 percent to 1.4 percent by June 2008 (figure 2). The current account deficit improved from 5.6 percent of GDP to 5.0 percent, and the trade deficit from 5.2 percent of GDP to 5.0 percent, from June 2007 to 2008.

Although our prediction is qualitatively correct, the initial response of the trade balance and the current account was muted relative to what our basic view implies. That is, if the relative financial appeal of the United States is what is behind the initial imbalances, the subprime crisis should have led to a sharper turnaround in the U.S. current account. Why didn't it? Again, we argue that the answer lies in the *endogenous* response of commodity prices. Because commodity inventories were initially very low, a

9. Caballero, Farhi, and Gourinchas (2008). The model also predicts a simultaneous move toward "safe" U.S. assets. This flight to quality is an important feature of our analysis.

by-product of the strong demand arising from the robust growth of emerging economies, net asset creation from the commodity mechanism was initially small. In contrast, the strong impact of the price rise on the income of commodity-producing economies led to a sharp rise in their demand for stores of value, which further depressed real interest rates and stabilized capital outflows to the United States in the short run.[10]

In the current, second phase of the crisis, external imbalances may or may not increase. Two offsetting forces are at play. On the one hand, the decline in economic growth reduces asset supply. This increases capital outflows to the United States. Simultaneously, the collapse in commodity prices makes commodity producers poorer, hence reducing asset demand. For low levels of inventories, we find that this second effect dominates, so that external imbalances fall.

The rest of this paper provides a model and a quantitative assessment of the story and mechanisms just described. The model adds commodities to our earlier framework. It has two regions, U and M. We interpret U as the United States and M as the rest of the world, with an emphasis on emerging market economies and commodity producers. The model features two goods: a nonstorable good X, produced by both regions, and a storable commodity Z, produced by M only. The supply of X grows exogenously whereas the supply of Z is constant. This feature is meant to capture the growing demand pressures on commodities that arise from robust world economic growth. We set up the model so that a bubble develops initially in U. As discussed above, we interpret this bubble metaphorically as the extent to which asset markets in U are stretched to provide financial assets to the rest of the world. With the bubble, the United States runs a larger current account deficit and world interest rates are low.

The original event in our model is the U.S. financial crisis: The bubble bursts at $t = 0$, leaving savers scrambling for alternative stores of value. The resulting decline in real interest rates has two effects. First, it increases the value of "good" U assets. This translates into a flight to quality, from the bubble assets to the "good" U asset. Second, and more important, it triggers the commodity markets into action. As speculative hoarding takes place, the prices of commodities jump, resulting in a wealth transfer from U to M. But M needs good stores of value. Thus a significant portion of that newfound wealth finds its way back into U. The resulting capital inflows

10. The reader may wonder why the rise in the price of oil is not simply a transfer of income from oil consumers to producers and hence has no impact on asset demand. The answer is in our choice of numeraire, which is the noncommodity good. This will be clearer once we describe the model but, as with all normalizations, it has no substantive implications.

further boost the value of U assets and cushion the impact of the bubble's bursting. Eventually, and gradually, the increase in asset supply due to growing commodity inventories pushes up interest rates, which forces rebalancing in U. To capture the second phase of the crisis, we assume that somewhere along this process the financial crisis compromises global growth. The decline in global growth removes the excess demand in asset markets, leading to a decumulation of inventories and a rapid collapse in commodity prices along with asset prices.

Before turning to the details, it is worth clarifying two modeling subtleties that are important in interpreting our formal discussion. First, although the commodity side of our model shares some of Hotelling's seminal insights, our model does not rely on his key stock constraint (an exhaustible resource). Instead, the model includes a flow extraction constraint which is insufficient to meet demand growth. This mismatch is the main factor behind the structural trend in commodity prices. In this context the subprime collapse superimposes on the previous trend a speculative reason for rising commodity prices. The collapse in global growth in the second phase of the crisis undermines the structural reason (the trend) supporting the bubble. Second, this speculative factor raises the effective opportunity cost of resource extraction for producers, since there is now an asset opportunity cost, as in Hotelling's model, which reduces their extraction incentives. The latter response means that, in equilibrium, there need not be any rise in measured inventories, and hence inventories throughout this paper are defined to include previously unextracted commodities.

The rest of the paper is organized as follows. The first section describes the basic mechanism connecting the financial crisis to commodity prices. The second section focuses on long-run global imbalances, and the third discusses short-run imbalances and presents some back-of-the-envelope estimates of the effects we describe. The fourth section calibrates the model and explores its dynamic implications. The fifth section presents evidence supporting the speculative nature of the rise in oil prices following the subprime crisis and of the recent drop in these prices. The final section offers some conclusions. Appendices A and B expand the discussion in the penultimate section to explore further the possible role of futures markets and antispeculative policies, and of inventory trends, respectively. Appendices C and D present formal derivations of some of the equations in the second, third, and fourth sections.[11]

11. Appendices C and D may be found online via the Brookings Papers website (www.brookings.edu/economics/bpea/bpea.aspx).

Global Capital and Commodity Markets

We begin by describing the main features of our model for the world economy.

The Model for the World Economy

In our model, time evolves continuously. Infinitesimal agents (households or traders) are born at a rate θ per unit of time and die at the same rate; population mass is constant and equal to one. Agents receive some endowment at birth, which, for simplicity, they save in its entirety until they die. Denote by W_t the savings accumulated by households at date t. In every period, aggregate consumption C_t is then a constant fraction θ of these accumulated savings:[12]

$$C_t = \theta W_t. \tag{1}$$

Households consume a basket of two goods: an X good (the numeraire) and a Z good. Intratemporal preferences over these two goods are of the constant-elasticity-of-substitution type:

$$C_t = \left[C_{X,t}^{(\sigma-1)/\sigma} + \alpha^{\frac{1}{\sigma}} C_{Z,t}^{(\sigma-1)/\sigma}\right]^{\sigma/(\sigma-1)}. \tag{2}$$

Here $\sigma > 0$ is the elasticity of substitution, and $\alpha > 0$ controls the equilibrium share of expenditure on the Z good.

Given a relative price p_t of the Z good, households split their consumption between the two goods as follows:

$$C_{X,t} = \frac{\theta W_t}{1 + \alpha p_t^{1-\sigma}} \text{ and } C_{Z,t} = \frac{\alpha p_t^{-\sigma} \theta W_t}{1 + \alpha p_t^{1-\sigma}}. \tag{3}$$

The X good is a conventional nonstorable good, whereas the Z good is a storable commodity. Denote by $I_t \geq 0$ the outstanding inventories of the Z good. Storing the commodity imposes an iceberg storage cost $d \geq 0$ per unit of time and good stored. Denote by r_t the instantaneous interest rate (in terms of the X good). By arbitrage, p_t must satisfy

$$\frac{\dot{p}_t}{p_t} \leq r_t + d, \tag{4}$$

12. As we show in our earlier paper (Caballero, Farhi, and Gourinchas 2008), this can be interpreted equivalently as log-preferences over consumption streams.

with equality if $I_t > 0$ or $\dot{I}_t > 0$, where a dot above a variable indicates its time derivative. This arbitrage equation is central to the analysis of storable commodities, as in Hotelling's analysis. It states that the rate of capital gains on commodities cannot exceed the interest rate, net of any convenience yield or carrying cost.

The endowment of the X good, denoted X_t, grows at rate $g > 0$ over time. By contrast, we assume that the endowment of the Z good is constant through time ($Z_t = Z$); this assumption allows us to capture the idea that demand pressures on commodities are growing over time.[13]

The Z good is assumed to be noncapitalizable unless it is transformed into inventories (below or above the ground). In contrast, a fraction δ of the X good is capitalizable. We capture this feature as follows. At every point in time, there is a number X_t of identical trees with an aggregate market value of V_t. Each tree yields one unit of X good per unit of time, a fraction δ of which is distributed to its current owners. Since the number of trees grows at rate g, the total value of new trees is gV_t per unit of time. The fraction of the output that is not capitalized is distributed to newborns, as are the new trees. Hence, the total endowment received by newborns per unit of time comprises $(1 - \delta)X_t$ units of the X good, Z units of the Z good, and gX_t new trees. The value of this endowment is $(1 - \delta)X_t + p_t Z + gV_t$.

The return on existing trees is the dividend-price ratio $\delta X_t/V_t$ plus the capital gain $\dot{V}_t/V_t - g$, which, in equilibrium, must equal the instantaneous interest rate in the economy r_t:

$$r_t V_t = \delta X_t + \dot{V}_t - gV_t. \tag{5}$$

In addition to the tree asset, some of our equilibria will exhibit rational bubbles, B_t, which must satisfy the arbitrage condition

$$\dot{B}_t = (r_t + \lambda)B_t, \tag{6}$$

where $\lambda > 0$ is the hazard that the bubble will burst in the next instant. For simplicity we analyze the limit case as λ goes to zero and $d > \lambda$. These assumptions allow us to approximate the solution with the perfect-foresight case and to reduce the number of subcases we need to discuss.

13. Note that our model differs from Hotelling's in that we replace his stock constraint with a flow constraint on commodity production. This has important implications later, since it allows us to separate more cleanly the asset aspect of commodities from their goods aspect. Moreover, in our framework macroeconomic conditions determine whether one aspect or the other dominates in price determination. See Jovanovic (2007) for a Hotelling-based model of bubbles in exhaustible resources.

Savings decrease with withdrawals (deaths) and increase with the endowment allocated to new generations and the return on accumulated savings:

$$\dot{W}_t = -\theta W_t + (1-\delta)X_t + p_t Z + gV_t + r_t W_t. \tag{7}$$

In equilibrium, savings must be equal to the value of all the assets in the economy:

$$W_t = V_t + p_t I_t + B_t. \tag{8}$$

Using equation 3 and imposing market clearing in the market for X goods, we obtain

$$\frac{\theta W_t}{1+\alpha p_t^{1-\sigma}} = X_t \text{ and } \frac{\alpha p_t^{-\sigma}\theta W_t}{1+\alpha p_t^{1-\sigma}} = Z - \dot{I}_t - dI_t. \tag{9}$$

In equilibrium, replacing equation 9 back into equation 7 yields the equilibrium interest rate (for the case with inventories; that is, when max $\langle I_t, \dot{I}_t \rangle > 0$):

$$r_t = \theta \frac{\left(\delta + g\dfrac{B_t + p_t I_t}{X_t}\right) - \left(\dfrac{p_t z}{x_t} - \alpha p_t^{1-\sigma}\right)}{1+\alpha\sigma p_t^{1-\sigma}} + \varepsilon_d, \tag{10}$$

where ε_d is an expression that plays no role in our main discussion.[14]

The interest rate rises as θ rises, because a higher θ increases consumption and reduces asset demand. The two terms in parentheses in the numerator are central to our discussion below. The first of these terms represents asset supply: the interest rate rises with δ and with $B_t + p_t I_t$ because they increase asset supply. The second term represents the "petrodollar" effect and is present when inventories are being accumulated: when the price of commodities rises, the income of commodity producers rises more than the effective income of commodity consumers falls. This net income effect lowers interest rates because it raises asset demand.

Later on we will show that for plausible parameter values, the asset demand effect dominates the asset supply effect in the short run, so that an increase in the price of commodities puts downward pressure on real interest rates. Since commodity prices also rise when interest rates fall (see expression 4), the interaction between commodity prices and real interest rates gives rise to potentially large feedbacks.

14. $\varepsilon_d \equiv -d(\sigma-1)\alpha p_t^{1-\sigma}/(1+\alpha\,\sigma p_t^{1-\sigma})$.

The $\sigma = 1$ *Case*

Although in practice the short-run elasticity of demand for the Z good is significantly smaller than one, it is useful to start with the case $\sigma = 1$, since it allows us to characterize explicitly the main mechanisms at work. We simplify things further by studying the case where d converges to zero (while preserving the assumption $d > \lambda$).

Assume momentarily that the equilibrium has neither inventories nor bubbles. Then equation 10 yields a reference interest rate, $r^{ref} = \theta\delta/(1 + \alpha)$. Henceforth we shall assume that financial assets are sufficiently scarce (δ is low) for the economy to be dynamically inefficient ($r^{ref} < g$):

Assumption 1: The economy is dynamically inefficient: $\delta < g(1 + \alpha)/\theta$.

BUBBLELESS EQUILIBRIUM. Suppose for now that there are no bubbles; then the equilibrium *must have inventories.* To see this, note that if there are no inventories, $r = r^{ref} < g$. But in this case equation 9 requires $p_t = \alpha X_t/Z$, so the price of commodities grows at a rate g, which exceeds the equilibrium interest rate. Thus, there is a clear incentive to accumulate inventories, which contradicts the no-inventories premise.

From expression 4 and equation 9, the dynamics of the economy can be summarized in a simple system with variables I_t and $q_t \equiv p_t/X_t$:

(11)
$$\begin{cases} \dot{I}_t = Z - \alpha q_t^{-1} \\ \dot{q}_t = (r_t - g)q_t \end{cases}$$

where r_t is given by

(12)
$$r_t = \theta\frac{\delta + \alpha - q_t\left(Z - gI_t\right)}{1 + \alpha}.$$

Asymptotically, the level of inventories stabilizes at a strictly positive level, which is proportional to the degree of dynamic inefficiency in the economy:

(13)
$$\lim_{t\to\infty} I_t = \bar{I} = \frac{1 + \alpha}{\alpha\theta g}\left(g - r^{ref}\right)Z > 0.$$

The price p_t of the Z good grows at rate g, and the interest rate r_t converges to the growth rate g of the X good.

Figure 9. The Model with Inventories When $\sigma = 1$

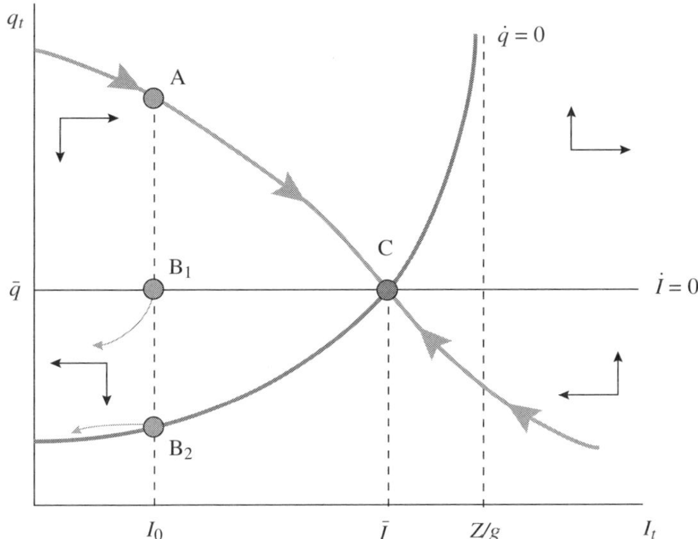

Source: Authors' model described in the text.

Figure 9 depicts the phase diagram associated with the dynamic system 11. The system exhibits the saddle path property.[15] This saddle path is downward sloping: when inventories are low ($I_t < \bar{I}$), the price of commodities is high ($q_t > \bar{q} \equiv \alpha/Z$) and decreasing ($r_t < g$). Conversely, when inventories are abundant ($I_t > \bar{I}$), the price of commodities is low ($q_t < \bar{q}$) and increasing ($r_t > g$).

A key element of our model lies in the slope of this saddle path. To understand why it is downward sloping, consider an initial inventory position $I_0 < \bar{I}$ and suppose that the price is such that the commodity market is initially in equilibrium at that inventory level ($\dot{I}_0 = 0$, or $q_0 = \bar{q}$). This is point B_1 in figure 9. It is immediately apparent that the interest rate r_0 that clears the asset markets at point B_1 must be *below* the growth rate g. The economic intuition is that at $q = \bar{q}$, too few assets are created through inventories (whose value is $\bar{q}I_0$). Equilibrium in global asset markets then requires a

15. Figure 9 is drawn for the case where $\theta\delta/(1 + \alpha) < g < \theta\,(\delta + \alpha)/(1 + \alpha)$, where the first inequality is a consequence of assumption 1. The case where $g > \theta\,(\delta + \alpha)/(1 + \alpha)$ is similar and also features a downward-sloping saddle path, but the $\dot{q} = 0$ schedule is downward sloping.

low interest rate. But when $r_0 < g$, the (normalized) price of commodities declines over time, and this increases demand for commodities and reduces inventories ($\dot{I}_0 < 0$). Instead, the equilibrium requires that the price of commodities be sufficiently high initially to depress the demand for commodities and allow inventory accumulation ($\dot{I}_0 > 0$). Equivalently, the price of commodities needs to rise sufficiently to depress equilibrium interest rates and make inventory accumulation profitable. This is represented by point A in figure 9. This high initial price depresses interest rates *below* r_0. Over time, since $r_t < g$, (normalized) commodity prices decrease, and this increases demand for commodities and slows inventory accumulation. The steady state is reached at point C.

The price of commodities performs a dual role in the model with inventories: it influences the demand for the Z good on the spot market, and it influences the global supply of assets in the economy ($V_t + p_t I_t$). As in traditional models of portfolio balance, it is the tension between these two functions that generates interesting dynamics.[16]

BUBBLES. Now let us turn to the opposite extreme, where bubbles exist and do not vanish asymptotically relative to the size of the economy. In the limit, since we assumed $d > \lambda$, there are no inventories. Without inventories, the Z good is for consumption only, and its price rises at rate g. The interest rate r_t converges to g, and the bubble converges to

$$B_t \underset{t\to\infty}{\sim} \frac{1+\alpha}{\theta g}\left(g - r^{ref}\right)X_t. \tag{14}$$

The size of the asymptotic bubble in expression 14 is the same as that of the asymptotic equilibrium inventories pI in the bubbleless equilibrium (equation 13). In both cases the endogenous increase in asset supply is just sufficient to increase the equilibrium interest rate to g.

THE NO-INVENTORY ECONOMY (A BENCHMARK). In our model the price of the Z good is both a relative price and, when inventories are nonzero, an asset price. To illustrate the importance of this dual role, we describe a benchmark economy where the inventory channel is turned off. That is, we assume that storage costs are prohibitive (d is very large), so the Z good cannot be stored.

This benchmark economy has two long-run steady states: a bubbly one and a bubbleless one. The bubbly steady state is exactly as above, with the same equilibrium prices and quantities. However, the bubbleless equilib-

16. See Kouri (1983) and, more recently, Blanchard, Giavazzi, and Sa (2005) for examples of portfolio balance models.

rium is different, since inventories cannot be accumulated. In the bubbleless equilibrium, market clearing for the Z good implies that p_t grows at rate g. Equilibrium in asset markets implies that the interest rate r_t is equal to $r^{ref} < g$.

Note that assumption 1 implies that the interest rate r^{ref} in the bubbleless equilibrium of the no-inventory economy is lower than the interest rate g in the bubbleless equilibrium of the economy with inventories. The reason for this difference is that total asset supply is smaller in the economy without inventories. Note also that p_t is the *same* in the bubbly equilibrium and in the bubbleless equilibrium without inventories. That is, the price is entirely determined by the relative endowments of the X good and the Z good and is completely decoupled from the asset market.

The Financial Crash and Commodity Boom (Phase I)

Suppose now that a "subprime" shock takes place. This can be interpreted as the realization that financial instruments are less sound than they were previously perceived to be. It could result, inter alia, from the realization that corporate governance is less benign than once thought (excessive risk taking and poor risk management by investment banks) or that securitization and certification by rating agencies involve important agency problems; or from a significant loss of informed and intermediation capital (deleveraging of commercial and investment banks hit by losses); and so on. All of these factors and more have been mentioned in the events surrounding the recent subprime crisis.[17] We assume that this shock is completely unanticipated, but this is not crucial to our analysis as long as there is some degree of market incompleteness, preventing agents from fully hedging away their risk.

In the model we capture this shock with a bursting of the bubble B at date t_0. The dynamics that follow are described by those in the bubbleless system and are illustrated in figure 10 for the case where $\sigma = 1$. Right before the shock, the economy is at point A with $q_{t_0} = \bar{q}$ and no inventories ($I_{t_0} = 0$). When the crisis erupts, the price of commodities jumps to point B on the saddle path. With decreased demand in the spot market, the economy immediately begins to build inventories (which could be kept under the ground). The price of commodities remains high until the economy converges to the new steady state (point C).

The collapse of the bubble reduces asset supply and leads to a drop in the interest rate. Lower interest rates make more attractive the strategy

17. See Greenlaw and others (2008) and Brunnermeier (2009).

Figure 10. Subprime Crisis at t_0 When $\sigma = 1$

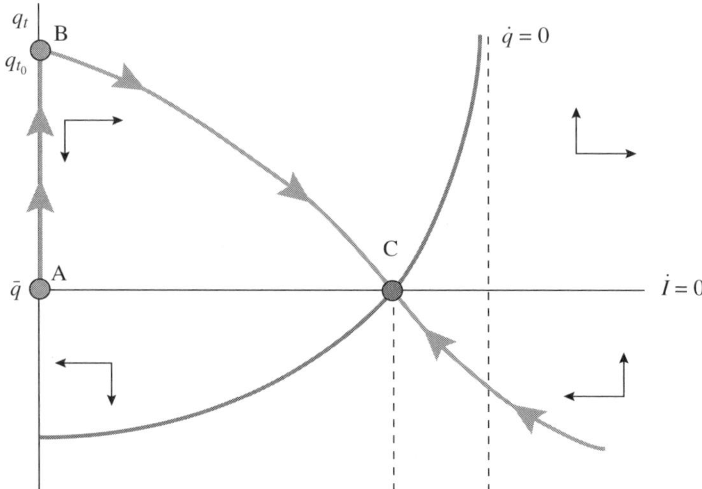

Source: Authors' model described in the text.

of storing the Z good so as to sell it in the future, which validates the buildup in inventories. Higher commodity prices during the transition to the new long-run equilibrium are required to lower demand and restore equilibrium in the Z good market. The commodity price jumps at $t = t_0$ and then declines asymptotically from above to the same path as in the pre-crash economy.

The interest rate initially drops by

$$(15) \qquad r_{t_0^+} - r_{t_0^-} = -g\frac{B_{t_0^-}}{W_{t_0^-}} - \frac{\theta\alpha}{1+\alpha}\left(\frac{p_{t_0^+}}{p_{t_0^-}} - 1\right) < 0$$

and then converges smoothly back to the asymptotic level g. There are two terms on the right-hand side of equation 15. The first, "bubble-burst" term, $-gB_{t_0^-}/W_{t_0^-}$, is directly due to the collapse of the bubble. The second, "commodity-price-jump" term follows from the increase in the price of the Z good, which raises the rate of wealth accumulation. Since inventories are only gradually accumulated, an additional gap opens between asset supply and asset demand, which requires a further decline in interest rates.

In the benchmark no-inventory economy, the normalized price of commodities stays constant and equal to $\bar{q}$, so the economy remains indefinitely at point A in figure 10. Since the price of commodities does not jump, the second term in equation 15 would equal zero, and the interest rate drop would be entirely given by the bubble-burst term.[18]

Note that there is a strong *flight-to-quality* feature in the model, since both the value of accumulated savings and the *total* value of assets are continuous at $t = t_0$:

$$W_{t_0^-} = (V_{t_0^-} + B_{t_0^-}) = W_{t_0^+} = V_{t_0^+} = \frac{1+\alpha}{\theta} X_{t_0}.$$

This means that the decline in interest rates raises the value of the trees (the "good" asset) enough to fully offset the loss in value due to the collapse of the bubble. Later we will show that when $\sigma < 1$, the decline in the interest rate is more pronounced than in the $\sigma = 1$ case, which further raises the value of the remaining "good" assets.[19]

The Growth Slowdown (Phase II)

Eventually, the financial crisis starts to hurt global growth prospects. We capture this turn of events by assuming that at $t = t_1$, global growth slows unexpectedly and permanently from g to $\hat{g} < g$. In the long run the slowdown reduces inventories $\bar{I}$. In fact, from equation 13 we see that if the growth slowdown is sufficiently severe as to reverse assumption 1, the commodity bubble ultimately bursts, and $\bar{I} = 0$. We formalize this with the following assumption:

Assumption 2: A severe growth slowdown occurs: $\hat{g} < \delta\theta/(1 + \alpha)$.

Under assumption 2, inventories are not sustainable in the long run. The dynamics that follow the growth slowdown are illustrated in figure 11. At time t_1 the economy is at point D, with inventory levels I_{t_1} and a commodity price q_{t_1}. Following the shock, the price of commodities needs to collapse so as to pick up the slack from the decreased rate of inventory accumulation. Equivalently, the collapse in commodity prices from point D to point E pushes equilibrium interest rates to $r_t > \hat{g}$, making inventory accumulation

18. We know from the previous analysis that the interest rate would drop to $r^{ref} = \delta\theta/(1 + \alpha)$.

19. Note that if we were to use a true consumer price index (rather than the price of good X) to deflate quantities, wealth would always drop in real terms after a crash. This alternative numeraire formulation, which we develop in appendix C (online), modifies the "language" but none of our substantive conclusions.

Figure 11. Growth Slowdown at t_1 When $\sigma = 1$

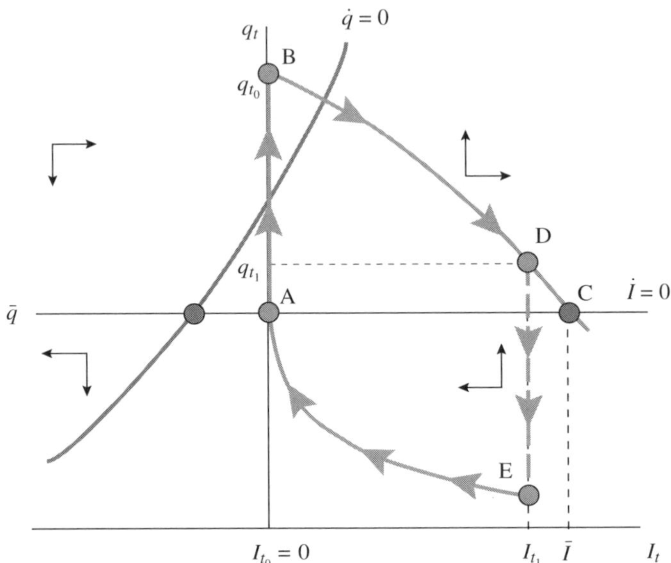

Source: Authors' model described in the text.

less profitable.[20] Over time, inventories converge to $\bar{I} = 0$, while commodity prices increase back to $\bar{q}$ (point A), and the interest rate converges to r^{ref}.

By contrast, in the no-inventory economy, the commodity price and the interest rate would not be impacted at $t = t_1$. The economy would remain indefinitely at point A in figure 11.

Global Imbalances in the Long Run

Let us now examine global equilibrium in a world with two large regions, $i = \{U,M\}$. We interpret region U as the United States, with initially good but perhaps fragile financial conditions, and region M as the set of emerg-

20. Note that although $r_{t_1^+} > \hat{g}$, the interest rate can increase or decrease when the growth shock hits, depending on the level of inventories I_{t_1}, because a decrease in commodity prices reduces both asset supply (the value of inventories decreases) and asset demand (the value of the flow of Z goods decreases). When I_{t_1} is small, the asset supply curve shifts less than the asset demand curve, requiring an increase in the interest rate to clear the asset market. We can compute the increase in interest rates, $r_{t_1^+} - r_{t_1^-} = \frac{\theta}{1+\alpha}\frac{Z}{X_{t_1}}\left(p_{t_1^-} - p_{t_1^+}\right) + \frac{\theta}{1+\alpha}\frac{I_{t_1}}{X_{t_1}}\left(p_{t_1^+}\hat{g} - p_{t_1^-}g\right)$, where the second term on the right-hand side is negligible if I_{t_1} is small. Note that despite this potential increase at impact, the interest rate eventually converges to a lower level, since $r^{ref} < g$ under assumption 1.

ing and commodity-producing economies whose current account surpluses offset the U.S. deficit.

Each of the regions is described by the same setup as the world economy, with an instantaneous return r_t from hoarding a unit of either region's trees; r_t is common across both regions and satisfies

$$r_t V_t^i = \delta X_t^i + \dot{V}_t^i - g V_t^i, \tag{16}$$

where V_t^i is the value of region i's trees at time t. We assume initially that both regions have common parameters g, δ, and θ, but that the initial bubble is concentrated in the U region. The latter assumption captures the idea that the U region has more attractive assets than the M region. Moreover, we assume that the Z good is produced only in the M economy and that the potential inventories are held in this region (perhaps under the ground; see the later discussion). These two features are all that differentiates the two regions, aside from scale.

Let W_t^i denote the savings accumulated by agents in region i at date t. By analogy with equation 7:

$$\dot{W}_t^i = -\theta W_t^i + (1-\delta) X_t^i + g V_t^i + r_t W_t^i + 1_{\{i=M\}} p_t Z, \tag{17}$$

where $1_{\{i=M\}}$ is an indicator for region M. Adding equations 16 and 17 for U and M shows that the world economy is exactly that described in the first section, with

$$W_t = W_t^U + W_t^M; \quad V_t = V_t^U + V_t^M; \quad X_t = X_t^U + X_t^M.$$

The current account balance CA_t^U of region U represents the net accumulation of assets by region U and is given by

$$CA_t^U = \dot{W}_t^U - \dot{V}_t^U - \dot{B}_t^U. \tag{18}$$

Let us start from the steady state with bubbles and $\sigma = 1$ as described in the preceding section. Figure 12 represents graphically the external equilibrium in U in a Metzler diagram.[21] The curve labeled V^U/X^U represents the long-run value of the U tree, relative to output. It is equal to δ/r and decreases with the interest rate r. The curve labeled W^U/X^U represents the long-run value of the savings-to-output ratio, as a function of the equilibrium

21. Metzler (1968).

Figure 12. Metzler Diagram When $\sigma = 1$

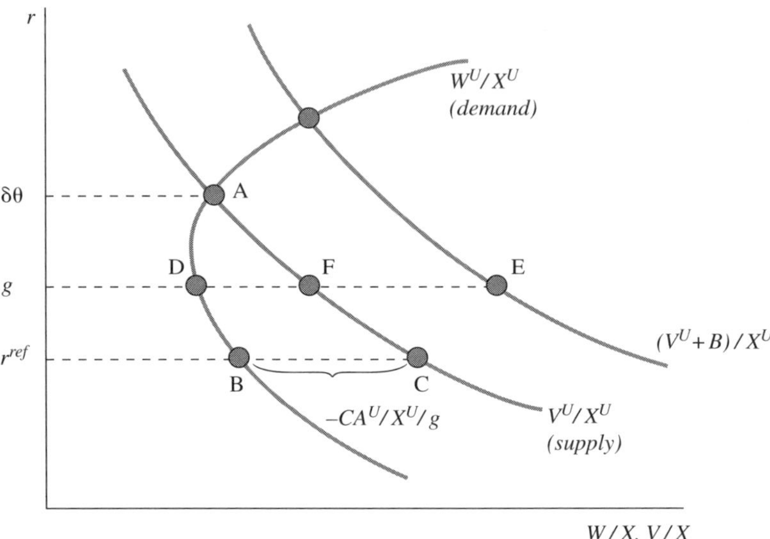

Source: Authors' model described in the text.

interest rate. It is equal to $(1 - \delta + g\delta/r)/(\theta + g - r)$. It first decreases and then increases with r.[22]

Without bubbles or inventories, long-run financial autarky is achieved at point A, with $r = \delta\theta$. Under financial integration, but still without bubbles or inventories, the interest rate is lower, at $r^{ref} = \delta\theta/(1 + \alpha)$. The reason for the lower equilibrium interest rate is that a larger fraction of global output is not capitalized when there are commodities. The lower interest rate allows U to supply more assets to M and to run a current account deficit that is proportional to the distance between points B and C in figure 12.

In the presence of the bubble, the supply of assets increases from $V^U/X^U = \delta/g$ to

$$\frac{V^U + B}{X^U} = \frac{\delta}{g} + \left(\frac{1+\alpha}{\theta} - \frac{\delta}{g}\right)\frac{X_{t_0}}{X^U_{t_0}}$$

22. Although the asset demand schedule W^U/X^U can be downward sloping, the gap between W^U/X^U and V^U/X^U, equal to $(1 - \delta\theta/r)/(\theta + g - r)$, is always increasing with the interest rate. The downward-sloping part of the W^U/X^U curve comes from the impact of interest rates on asset demand through the new trees gV^U. When $g < \delta\theta$, the W^U/X^U curve has the shape shown in figure 12. When $g > \delta\theta$, the asset and demand curves cross on the downward-sloping part of the asset demand curve W^U/X^U.

so as to eliminate the dynamic inefficiency of assumption 1. The increase is such that the world equilibrium interest rate increases from r^{ref} to g. The current account deficit in the bubble equilibrium (proportional to the distance between points D and E) is always larger than in the no-bubble, no-inventories case (the distance between points B and C).[23] The reason for this larger current account deficit is that a disproportionate share of M's income is noncapitalizable (because its commodity income, pZ, is noncapitalizable unless it is transformed into inventories), whereas U produces a disproportionate share of global assets.

Long-Run Imbalances with No Growth Slowdown

As before, the subprime shock takes place at $t = t_0$. In the long run the presence of commodities leads to a larger global rebalancing in response to a subprime shock in the United States (region U). Consider first what happens if there is no growth slowdown. In this case, since the asymptotic interest rate in the absence of bubbles is still $r = g$, the asymptotic current account deficit of the U region following the collapse of the bubble is smaller by *exactly* the size of the bubble:

$$\frac{CA_t^U}{X_t^U} \underset{t\to\infty}{\sim} g\left[\frac{1}{\theta} - \frac{\delta}{g}\right].$$

This asymptotic current account will be in deficit if the degree of dynamic inefficiency in the global economy is not too severe ($\delta\theta > g$), as is assumed in figure 12. Otherwise the buildup in inventories is significant, which increases the supply of assets in region M and reduces its need to buy foreign assets as a store of value.

This buildup of inventories implies that endogenous commodity prices lead to *more* rebalancing in the long run. The reason is that inventories contribute to increasing asset supply in region M and hence endogenously reduce the effective asymmetry between the two regions. In terms of figure 12, the current account deficit contracts from D – E to D – F, as the bubble collapses and inventories are accumulated, whereas it would contract from D – E to B – C in the benchmark no-inventory economy. Therefore,

23. Indeed, the increase in the current account deficit in the presence of the bubble can be computed as

$$CA^{U,no-bubble} - CA^U = \frac{g - r^{ref}}{\theta/(1+\alpha)}\left[\frac{\alpha g}{(1+\alpha)(\theta + g - r^{ref})} + \frac{X}{X^U} - 1\right],$$

which is always positive under assumption 1.

Figure 13. Long-Run External Imbalances When $\sigma = 1$

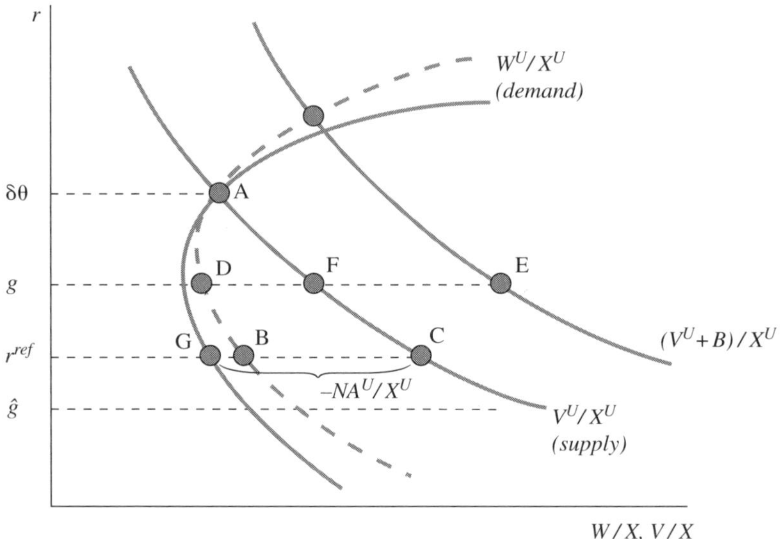

Source: Authors' model described in the text.

the inventory channel unambiguously leads to more rebalancing in the long run. We will see in the next section that this result can be overturned in the short run when $\sigma < 1$.

Long-Run Imbalances with a Growth Slowdown

Let us now reintroduce the slowdown in growth. Under assumption 2 the asymptotic interest rate drops to r^{ref}. Figure 13 describes what happens to *U's* asymptotic external imbalances as growth declines. The asset demand curve rotates clockwise around point A, so that asset demand decreases in the relevant range ($r < \delta\theta$).

The asymptotic net foreign asset position $NA^U/X^U = (W^U - V^U)/X^U$ can be read as the distance G – C. Since there are no inventories and $r = r^{ref}$, it is the same as in the benchmark no-inventory economy and worsens as the growth rate $\hat{g}$ declines. Further, this asymptotic net foreign asset position is more negative with the growth slowdown (G – C) than without it (D – F). The reason is that slower growth eliminates the buildup in commodity inventories and hence curtails the expansion in asset supply in the *M* region. The inventory channel analyzed above, which reduces the asymmetry between the two regions, is now dampened, and the economy experiences less rebalancing in the long run. However, since growth is also slower in the former case, the current account may or may not worsen asymptotically with a growth slowdown.[24]

Global Imbalances in the Short Run

We now turn to a phase-by-phase analysis of the model's implications for short-run global imbalances.

Phase I: The Financial Crisis

The behavior of the current account in the short run depends on the initial portfolios, the degree of home portfolio bias, and the degree of substitution between the commodity and the general consumption good. As in our earlier paper,[25] we assume an extreme form of home bias: at $t = t_0$ all the assets held by agents in the U region are U assets. Moreover, we assume that domestic residents' portfolios are proportional to the relative value of trees and bubbles. The assumption of extreme portfolio home bias is a good approximation of actual conditions. As of 2005, Piet Sercu and Rosanne Vanpée found that the degree of home bias for equities varied between 0.31 for the Netherlands and 0.91 for Japan.[26] The assumption that domestic residents' portfolios are proportional to the relative value of trees and bubbles implies that M has a significant exposure to U's bubble asset. Again, this is a reasonable assumption. The onset of the U.S. subprime crisis was marked by the failure of a small German bank, IKB, and a few months later by the collapse of Northern Rock, a U.K. bank, highlighting the exposure of foreign investors to tainted U.S. assets.[27]

Under these assumptions the degree of rebalancing on impact, $CA^U_{t_0^+} - CA^U_{t_0^-}$, is given by the sum of two terms: the adjustment in the trade balance $X^U_t - \theta W^U_t$, and the change in payments on external debt, through asset

24. The asymptotic current account deficit is now $\frac{CA^U_t}{X^U_t} \underset{t\to\infty}{\sim} \frac{-\alpha\hat{g}}{\theta + \hat{g} - r^{ref}}$ and decreases with $\hat{g}$.

25. Caballero, Farhi, and Gourinchas (2008).

26. Sercu and Vanpée (2007). The degree of home equity bias is defined as one minus the ratio of the share of foreign equities in the domestic and world portfolios. It varies between zero (when the weight on foreign equities is given by their relative market capitalization) and one (when investors hold no foreign equities). It has declined in recent years but remains very high for most countries.

27. According to Beltran, Pounder, and Thomas (2008, table 6), foreigners hold 40 percent ($2.4 trillion out of $6 trillion) of outstanding U.S.-asset-backed securities and about 16 percent of all U.S. credit market instruments.

valuations and interest rates. The adjustment in payments on external debt is swamped by the adjustment in the trade balance when the external debt is initially small, so we focus on the trade balance. This is always positive and given by

$$(19) \qquad TB^U_{t_0^+} - TB^U_{t_0^-} = -\theta\left(W^U_{t_0^+} - W^U_{t_0^-}\right) = \theta\mu_{t_0^-}\left(B_{t_0^-} + V^U_{t_0^-} - V^U_{t_0^+}\right),$$

where $\mu_{t_0^-} = W^U_{t_0^-}/(V^U_{t_0^-} + B_{t_0^-})$ represents the share invested in the domestic tree and the domestic bubble before the crash; $\mu_{t_0^-} < 1$ when U is a net debtor at time t_0. At impact, the direct effect of the bubble collapse is a reduction in wealth $W^U_{t_0}$, which lowers consumption and improves the trade balance.[28] Note that there is always less trade rebalancing in this economy than in the benchmark no-inventory economy.[29] The change in the trade balance and the drop in $W^U_{t_0^-} - W^U_{t_0^+}$ are exactly proportional to the change in the value of the U assets, $V^U_{t_0^-} + B_{t_0^-} - V^U_{t_0^+}$. As a starting point, note that when $\sigma = 1$, the decline in asset prices is exactly the same in the economy with endogenous commodity prices as in the economy without:

$$(20) \qquad V^U_{t_0^-} + B_{t_0^-} - V^U_{t_0^+} = B_{t_0^-}\left(1 - x^U_{t_0}\right) \geq 0,$$

where $x^U_{t_0} = X^U_{t_0}/X_{t_0}$ is the share of U in world output. This result is peculiar to the case $\sigma = 1$ because the share of X goods in consumption is invariant to the price p_t of Z goods.[30]

Phase II: The Growth Slowdown

Consider now the effects of the growth slowdown shock. We maintain the assumption of extreme home bias, so that immediately before the

28. However, in equilibrium the drop in wealth is dampened because interest rates plummet, raising the value of the "good" U asset and making up for part of the drop in wealth.

29. In appendix D (online) we show that the difference in trade rebalancing between these two economies is strictly less than the direct effect of the change in the terms of trade resulting from speculation in commodities, holding imports and exports constant. In other words, imported and exported quantities adjust by more in the economy with endogenous commodity prices than in the no-inventory economy.

30. In contrast, we show in appendix C (online) that in the more realistic $\sigma < 1$ case, the increase in the price of U assets in response to the subprime shock, $V^U_{t_0^+} - V^U_{t_0^-}$, is larger when commodity prices are endogenous than when they are not. The reason for the larger increase in the value of U assets is that the share of X goods in value added decreases, which raises asset demand relative to asset supply. As a result of this gap, asset supply has to increase by more in equilibrium. This "petrodollar" channel will prove crucial later in our quantitative exercises. This effect is absent in the benchmark no-inventory economy, which would as a result experience a greater amount of rebalancing in the short run.

growth slowdown shock hits, all of U's wealth is invested in U assets. The adjustment in the trade balance is always positive:

$$TB^U_{t_1^+} - TB^U_{t_1^-} = -\theta\left(W^U_{t_1^+} - W^U_{t_1^-}\right) = \theta\mu_{t_1^-}\left(V^U_{t_1^-} - V^U_{t_1^+}\right),$$

where $\mu_{t_1^-} = W^U_{t_1^-}/V^U_{t_1^-}$. The change in the value of U assets can be computed as above. We show in appendix C (online) that when I_{t_1} is small and $\sigma = 1$, the impact of the growth slowdown on the trade balance is negligible. By contrast, when $\sigma < 1$, the decline in the value of U assets is accentuated, and the trade balance improves at impact. We show in the calibration section that most of this improvement originates in an improvement in the commodity component of the trade balance.

Back-of-the-Envelope Calculations

This section gauges the order of magnitude of the effects discussed above. We focus here on the impact effect of the financial crisis, which we can develop analytically, and discuss the full dynamics in the next section. We find from this back-of-the-envelope exercise that our model can explain much of the observed decline in real interest rates and rise in the price of oil in the first phase of the financial crisis, as well as the sharp collapse in the price of oil in the second phase. The model also goes a long way toward explaining why the U.S. current account adjustment has been only modest so far, but it forecasts that the decline in the price of oil will reduce the trade deficit significantly in the future.

PHASE I: THE FINANCIAL CRISIS. We begin with the impact of the crisis on interest rates. According to figure 2, real interest rates declined by about 1.75 percentage points between September 2006, when home prices started to decline and the current account turned around, and June 2008.[31] With a unit elasticity of substitution, $\sigma = 1$, the change in interest rates is given by equation 15; when this elasticity is smaller than one, the drop in interest rates $r_{t_0^+} - r_{t_0^-}$ can still be expressed as the sum of two terms: a bubble-burst term reflecting the direct impact of the collapse of the bubble on asset supply, and a commodity-price-jump term reflecting the impact of the increase in the price of commodities on global asset supply and demand.[32]

The starting point in assessing the role of the two terms is an estimate of the size of the perceived losses generated by the financial crisis, in relation to the world's financial wealth: $B_{t_0^-}/W_{t_0^-}$. Estimates of the perceived size of

31. The world short-term real interest rate dropped from 1.6 percent to –0.9 percent. The U.S. long-term real rate dropped from 2.4 percent to 1.4 percent.

32. See appendix C (online) for an expression for the commodity-price-jump term.

the initial collapse of the bubble are difficult to come by and necessarily imprecise. A key issue is that the endogenous response of interest rates offsets the impact of the crash in B_t on global wealth.[33] Empirically, this means that the estimates of the size of the initial bubble that we obtain are likely to be biased downward.

Direct losses in U.S. mortgage markets alone are estimated to be in the vicinity of $500 billion.[34] In its April 2008 *Global Financial Stability Report,*[35] the International Monetary Fund reaches a similar estimate of aggregate losses in the U.S. residential mortgage market. Adding to this the potential losses to broader credit markets, the IMF calculates aggregate losses from writedowns of U.S. loans and securitized assets of about $945 billion.[36] To these losses we add the declines in asset values generated by the broad process of deleveraging and the associated contraction in lending across markets. For instance, David Greenlaw and coauthors estimate an overall contraction of $2.3 trillion in intermediaries' balance sheets.[37] Moreover, mortgage market losses reflect only the increased rate of delinquencies on prime mortgages and commercial real estate (as well as the declining value of foreclosed properties). To this we add the decline in housing wealth for residential borrowers that remain in good standing on their mortgages. Estimates of the latter significantly exceed the direct losses in mortgage markets. For instance, the Federal Reserve estimates households' housing wealth at $19.4 trillion as of June 2006.[38] In terms of the Case-Shiller U.S. Composite 10 home price index, U.S. housing prices declined 19.8 percent in nominal terms between September 2006 and June 2008 (see figure 4). If this decline is across the board, it implies that at least an additional $3.8 trillion was wiped out in U.S. housing wealth alone.[39]

Adding these estimates yields a total loss in U.S. housing wealth and mortgage markets in the range of $2 trillion to $4 trillion. What is relevant in our calculation is the ratio of these initial losses to the world's financial wealth $W_{t_0^-}$. We construct a crude estimate of the latter at the onset of the

33. For instance, we have seen that in the case of a unit elasticity ($\sigma = 1$), aggregate wealth remains unchanged at impact.

34. Greenlaw and others (2008).

35. IMF (2008a).

36. In its October 2008 report (IMF 2008b), the IMF revised its estimate of U.S. declared losses on loans and securitized assets to $1.4 trillion.

37. Greenlaw and others (2008).

38. See table B.100 of the March 2008 release of the Flow of Funds Accounts.

39. This figure is calculated under the extreme assumption that all mortgage market losses are housing market losses. Of course, foreclosures and repossessions generate additional losses beyond the decline in housing values.

Table 1. Predicted Change in World Interest Rates for Different Parameter Values[a]
Percentage points

	Change in commodity prices, $p_{t_0^+}/p_{t_0^-}$				
Elasticity of substitution σ	1.0	1.2	1.5	*2.0*	3.0
0.05	–2.22	–2.23	–2.25	–2.28	–2.37
0.1	–1.02	–1.04	–1.08	*–1.16*	–1.33
0.2	–0.44	–0.48	–0.55	–0.69	–1.00
0.5	–0.12	–0.21	–0.37	–0.66	–1.27
1.0	–0.06	–0.23	–0.50	–0.93	–1.80

Source: Authors' calculations based on the model described in the text.

a. Each cell reports the model-predicted initial change in the world interest rate $r_{t_0^+} - r_{t_0^-}$ associated with the indicated change in commodity prices at the indicated value of σ. Italicized numbers correspond to the authors' preferred calibration.

crisis as the sum of U.S. household net worth of $51.7 trillion at the end of 2005, and an estimate of the financial wealth of the rest of the world of $80.7 trillion.[40] This indicates an initial size of the bubble of between 1.5 and 3.0 percent of the world's financial wealth. In what follows we assume an initial bubble equal to 2 percent of the world's financial wealth.

It is immediately apparent that the bubble-burst term in equation 15, equal to $-gB_{t_0^-}/W_{t_0^-}$, is relatively small: at an output growth rate of around 3 percent, it is equal to only –0.06 percent. On the other hand, the commodity-price-jump term can be substantial. To show this, table 1 reports estimates of the decline in r for different values of the elasticity of substitution σ and different estimates of the increase in commodity prices. The calculation of the commodity-price-jump term requires an estimate of the average expenditure share of commodities $s_{zt_0^-}$. In constructing the table we assume that $s_{zt_0^-} = 0.04$, which corresponds to the average share of oil expenditure in world GDP in 2005 and 2006.[41]

40. See table B.100 of the June 2008 issue of the Federal Reserve's Flow of Funds Accounts for the U.S. figure. To obtain an estimate of the financial wealth of the rest of the world in 2006, we calculate the ratio of output to financial wealth for the United States, the European Union, and Japan between 1982 and 2004. We find a GDP-weighted average of 2.48 (see Caballero, Farhi, and Gourinchas 2008 for additional details). Applying this ratio to the GDP of the rest of the world in 2005, we obtain $80.7 trillion. To the extent that many countries are less financially developed than the United States, Europe, or Japan, this estimate likely overstates the world's financial wealth. This would further bias downward our estimate of B_{t_0}/W_{t_0}.

41. According to the Energy Information Administration's *International Petroleum Monthly* (table 2.4, World Petroleum Demand), world demand for oil in 2005 was 83.8 million barrels a day. At a WTI price of $56.64 a barrel, this corresponds to $1.7 trillion a year, or 3.8 percent of world GDP. In 2006 the share of oil in total expenditure was 4.16 percent. The remaining parameters are discussed in more detail in a later section.

Between September 2006 and June 2008 the price of a barrel of WTI in constant 2008 dollars increased from \$67.81 to \$140.82 (figure 7). Interpreting this surge as the direct effect of the crisis yields $p_{t_0^+}/p_{t_0^-} = 2.08$. The associated decrease in real interest rates in table 1 is consistent with what we see in the data. For a realistically low level of the short-term price elasticity of demand $\sigma = 0.1$, we find a decline in interest rates of 1.16 percentage points, smaller than the 1.75 percentage points observed over that period, but much larger than the 0.06-percentage-point decline associated with the direct effect of the collapse of the bubble. Most of the decline in interest rates comes from the indirect effect of higher commodity prices, hinting that the endogenous response of commodity prices to the subprime crisis is critical in understanding the global macroeconomic environment.

We now turn to the effect of the crash on commodity prices. We can compute the decline in *U's* financial wealth and find an expression for the jump in commodity prices as a function of the decline in *U's* wealth and the size of the original collapse of the bubble (see online appendix C):

$$(21) \qquad \frac{p_{t_0^+}}{p_{t_0^-}} = \left[1 + \frac{W^U_{t_0^+} - W^U_{t_0^-}}{X^U_{t_0}} \frac{\theta}{\mu_{t_0^-}} \frac{1 - s_{zt_0^-}}{s_{zt_0^-}} + \frac{1}{s_{zt_0^-}}\left(\frac{1}{x^U_{t_0}} - 1\right)\frac{B_{t_0^-}}{W_{t_0^-}}\right]^{1/(1-\sigma)}.$$

We already have estimates for $B_{t_0^-}/W_{t_0^-}$ and $s_{zt_0^-}$. We estimate the decline in U.S. financial wealth $W^U_{t_0^+} - W^U_{t_0^-}$ from the Federal Reserve Flow of Funds Accounts. Between June 2007 and March 2008, U.S. households' financial wealth declined by \$1.65 trillion, or 11.5 percent of output.[42] Next we construct an estimate of $\mu_{t_0^-}$, the share of domestic financial wealth invested in the domestic tree and the domestic bubble before the crash. In 2005 the net foreign liabilities of the United States amounted to \$1.85 trillion, or 15 percent of U.S. GDP.[43] This corresponds to $(W^U_{t_0^-} - V^U_{t_0^-} - B_{t_0^-})/X^U_{t_0}$. Substituting the expression for $\mu_{t_0^-}$, and using the fact that $W^U_{t_0^-}/X^U_{t_0^-} = 4.16$, we obtain $\mu_{t_0^-} = 0.96$.[44] Finally, we set the ratio of U.S. to world output in 2005 at approximately 0.25.[45] Table 2 reports estimates of the increase in com-

42. See table B.100 of the June 2008 Federal Reserve Flow of Funds estimates. Household net worth was \$57.6 trillion in June 2007 at the onset of the crisis and only \$55.9 trillion in March 2008.

43. From table 2 of the Bureau of Economic Analysis's International Investment Position. The net asset position is estimated at market value.

44. This represents an overestimate of the share of U.S. assets held by U.S. investors, since we assume an extreme form of home bias.

45. U.S. GDP in 2005 was \$12.4 trillion, and world GDP was about \$45 trillion, for a ratio of 0.276. Although the theoretical model refers only to *U* and *M*, in this back-of-the-envelope exercise and the simulations that follow, it is natural to include other countries as part of *M*.

Table 2. Predicted Effect of the Subprime Crisis on Commodity Prices[a]
Percentage points

	Initial size of the financial bubble as share of world financial wealth, $B_{t_0^-}/W_{t_0^-}$ *(percent)*				
Elasticity of substitution σ	1	2	3	4	5
0.05	1.11	1.91	2.73	3.57	4.42
0.1	1.11	*1.98*	2.89	3.83	4.80
0.2	1.13	2.16	3.30	4.53	5.83
0.5	1.21	3.42	6.76	11.22	16.81

Source: Authors' calculations based on the model described in the text.
a. Each cell reports the model-predicted change in commodity prices $p_{t_0^+} - p_{t_0^-}$ associated with the indicated size of the original bubble at the indicated value of σ. Italicized numbers correspond to the authors' preferred calibration.

modity prices as a function of the elasticity σ and the size of the initial bubble collapse $B_{t_0^-}/W_{t_0^-}$.

The results in table 2 support our view that the collapse in the U.S. housing market and the contraction in credit markets played a significant role in explaining the surge in commodity prices that followed the subprime crisis. We find that for our benchmark estimate of the size of the bubble of 2 percent, commodity prices increase by 98 percent when the short-run elasticity of substitution equals 0.1, which is very close to the 108 percent observed in the data. Recall that without an asset channel (in the benchmark no-inventories economy), commodity prices would not jump when the crisis occurs.

Turning to the external accounts, between September 2006 and June 2008 the U.S. trade deficit on goods and services decreased from –5.96 percent of U.S. GDP to –4.94 percent, a 1.02-percentage-point improvement.[46] Can the model explain this very limited rebalancing? We answer this question by rewriting the trade balance equation (equation 19) as

$$\frac{TB^U_{t_0^+} - TB^U_{t_0^-}}{X^U_{t_0}} = \frac{\mu_{t_0^-}}{1 - s_{zt_0^-}} \left\{ \frac{B_{t_0^-}}{W_{t_0^-}} \left(\frac{1}{x^U_{t_0}} - 1 \right) - s_{zt_0^-} \left[\left(\frac{p_{t_0^+}}{p_{t_0^-}} \right)^{1-\sigma} - 1 \right] \right\}.$$

The first term inside the curved brackets represents the direct impact of the collapse of the bubble on the trade balance. It contributes positively to global rebalancing. The second term reflects the contribution of commodity

46. See the Bureau of Economic Analysis's National Income and Product Accounts, table 4.1.

Table 3. Predicted Effect of the Subprime Crisis on the Region *U* Trade Balance[a]
Percent of GDP

Change in commodity prices, $p_{t_0^+}/p_{t_0^-}$	*Initial size of the financial bubble as share of world financial wealth,* $B_{t_0^-}/W_{t_0^-}$ *(percent)* 1	2	3	4	5
1.0	3.01	6.02	9.04	12.05	15.06
1.2	2.30	5.31	8.32	11.33	14.34
1.5	1.24	4.26	7.27	10.28	13.29
2.0	–0.47	*2.55*	5.56	8.57	11.58
3.0	–3.77	–0.75	2.26	5.27	8.28

Source: Authors' calculations based on the model described in the text.

a. Each cell reports the model-predicted change in the region *U* trade balance relative to the region's output $(TB^U_{t_0^+} - TB^U_{t_0^-}) / X^U_{t_0}$ associated with the indicated size of the original bubble and the indicated change in commodity prices, at an assumed elasticity of substitution $\sigma = 0.1$. Italicized numbers correspond to the authors' preferred calibration.

prices. Table 3 reports the sum of the direct and indirect impacts of the subprime crisis on the trade balance as a function of the commodity price surge $p_{t_0^+}/p_{t_0^-}$ and the size of the initial bubble $B_{t_0^-}/W_{t_0^-}$ for an elasticity of substitution σ equal to 0.1.

The first line of the table reports the change in the trade balance in the benchmark no-inventory economy (which coincides with the direct effect). We find a large and implausible improvement in the trade balance. For instance, for an initial bubble equal to 2 percent of world financial wealth, the no-inventory economy predicts an improvement in the trade balance equal to 6.02 percent of output. This is a far cry from the 1.02 percent observed in the data. Again, once we introduce the "petrodollar" channel, the required rebalancing drops significantly. For instance, the trade balance improves by "only" 2.55 percent of output, instead of 6.02 percent when commodity prices double. If instead we consider a tripling of commodity prices, or a smaller initial bubble collapse, it is possible for the trade balance to worsen on impact. Although our preferred numbers are on the high side (2.5 percent of output compared with 1.02 percent), it is apparent that the model has the capacity to rationalize the very limited global rebalancing that we are witnessing.[47]

All in all, we conclude that the model is in the right ballpark and can account for the broad features of the global economy in the first phase of the crisis.

47. Calculations for the current account are very similar since when μ_{t_0} is close to 1, interest payments remain small.

Table 4. Predicted Effect of the Growth Slowdown on Commodity Prices[a]
Percent

	Change in region U *financial wealth,* $(W^U_{t_1^+} - W^U_{t_1^-}) / X^U_{t_1}$ *(percent)*			
Elasticity of substitution σ	–0.05	*–0.10*	–0.15	–0.17
0.05	0.72	0.44	0.17	0.07
0.1	0.70	*0.42*	0.16	0.06
0.2	0.67	0.38	0.12	0.04
0.5	0.53	0.21	0.03	0.01

Source: Authors' calculations based on the model described in the text.

a. Each cell reports the model-predicted change in commodity prices $p_{t_0^+} / p_{t_0^-}$ associated with the indicated change in region *U* financial wealth at the indicated value of σ. Italicized numbers correspond to the authors' preferred calibration.

PHASE II: THE GROWTH SLOWDOWN. We now ask whether the model can account for the broad features of the data following the slowdown in economic activity. In real terms, between July and November 2008 oil prices declined by 53 percent (see figure 7). We can use equation 21 to write the change in commodity prices as

$$\frac{p_{t_1^+}}{p_{t_1^-}} = \left[1 + \frac{W^U_{t_1^+} - W^U_{t_1^-}}{X^U_{t_1}} \frac{\theta}{\mu_{t_1^-}} \frac{1 - s_{zt_1^-}}{s_{zt_1^-}} \right]^{1/(1-\sigma)}. \quad (22)$$

The change in commodity prices is a function of the drop in *U*'s financial wealth. Reasonable estimates of the financial losses incurred since July 2008 are not available yet. Instead, table 4 reports predicted declines for a range of estimates of $(W^U_{t_1^+} - W^U_{t_1^-})/X^U_{t_1}$ and different values of the short-run demand elasticity for commodities.

It is immediately apparent that commodity prices are extremely sensitive to the drop in financial wealth. For $\sigma = 0.1$, a modest decline in U.S. financial wealth equal to 10 percent of output triggers a staggering 58 percent (0.42 – 1) decline in commodity prices. This is remarkably close to the 53 percent decline observed in the data.

Table 5 reports the predicted change in the trade balance as a function of the decline in U.S. financial wealth. Since $TB^U = X^U - \theta W^U$, this calculation is independent of σ. This part of the analysis is necessarily more speculative. It indicates that the model predicts a significant rebalancing of the trade balance, equal to about 2.2 percent of output, as a consequence of the growth slowdown.

Table 5. Predicted Effect of a Growth Slowdown on the Region *U* Trade Balance[a]
Percent of GDP

	Change in region U *financial wealth,* $(W^U_{t_1^+} - W^U_{t_1^-}) / X^U_{t_1}$ *(percent of GDP)*			
	–0.05	*–0.10*	–0.15	–0.17
Change in region *U* trade balance, $(TB^U_{t_1^+} - TB^U_{t_1^-}) / X^U_{t_1}$	1.09	*2.18*	3.27	3.70

Source: Authors' calculations based on the model described in the text.
a. Each cell reports the model-predicted change in the region *U* trade balance relative to the region's output associated with the indicated change in region *U* financial wealth. Italicized numbers correspond to the authors' preferred calibration.

Calibration and Dynamics

We now turn to an analysis of full general-equilibrium dynamic simulations. We begin with a discussion of plausible short- and long-run elasticities of demand for commodities. We then present the results from dynamic simulations of the financial crisis with and without a growth slowdown.

Short- and Long-Run Elasticities

A key parameter of our model is the elasticity of substitution σ. William Nordhaus finds low "apparent" short-run price elasticities of demand of around 0.3 at the time of the 1973 oil price shock.[48] Long-run elasticities are typically higher, since with time, energy users can substitute away from energy-intensive technology. Nordhaus notes that for many components of the physical capital stock, energy substitution is possible only when the existing capital is scrapped. In the transportation sector, for instance, in which energy consumption depends in large part on the fuel efficiency of the outstanding stock of vehicles, energy consumption responds gradually as old vehicles are slowly replaced with more-fuel-efficient ones. Similarly, in the case of electric power generation, there is almost no possibility for substitution in the short run, but in the long run utilities can switch to other sources such as nuclear or wind power.

More recent studies confirm the "crude" estimates in Nordhaus's analysis for the short run while finding higher long-run estimates.[49] The typical estimates for short-run price elasticities vary between 0.05 and 0.35; long-run estimates vary between 0.21 and 0.86.[50]

48. Nordhaus (1980).
49. See Roy and others (2006) and Dahl and Sterner (1991) for older surveys.
50. See Hamilton (2008) for a recent discussion of crude oil prices, and the references therein.

Table 6. Apparent Price Elasticity of U.S. Petroleum Demand[a]
Percent a year

	1988–2003	*2003–07*
Change in real price of petroleum products[b]	1.44	8.55
Change in U.S. demand for petroleum products	0.84	0.61
Apparent elasticity[c]	0.04	
Memorandum: average change in U.S. real GDP	2.83	2.90

Sources: Energy Information Administration, *Annual Energy Review,* tables 3.1 and 3.3; *Monthly Energy Review,* tables 2.2–2.6.

a. All data are compound annual averages.

b. Consumer price estimate through 2005; fossil fuel composite price after 2005.

c. Assumes a sectoral elasticity with respect to GDP of unity.

Table 6 provides an update on Nordhaus's "apparent" price elasticity estimates for the period around the recent increase in oil prices. The table reports recent data on U.S. petroleum consumption and prices before and after 2003, where the break in oil prices is apparent in figure 7. Between 2003 and 2007, petroleum prices increased by an average of 8.55 percent a year, a sharp break from the 1.44 percent average annual increase between 1988 and 2003. Nevertheless, annual growth in demand for petroleum products slowed only from 0.84 percent to 0.61 percent. The "apparent" price elasticity is calculated as by Nordhaus, under the assumption of a unit elasticity of petroleum product demand to GDP, as the (opposite of the) percentage slowdown in energy demand corrected for the percentage change in real output growth, divided by the percentage acceleration in prices.[51] We obtain an estimate of 0.04, on the low end of available empirical estimates.[52] This is consistent with recent empirical estimates that find an even smaller short-run price elasticity now than in the 1970s.[53]

A simple way of capturing this time variation in σ is to assume that the elasticity of substitution remains significantly smaller than 1 until the share of expenditure on the Z good reaches a certain exogenous level $\bar{s}_z$. When

51. The income elasticity of petroleum demand is largely irrelevant in these calculations, since output growth was essentially the same over both subperiods. This elasticity in industrial countries has declined significantly since the oil price shocks of the 1970s and is now closer to 0.5. However, the income elasticities of emerging markets and oil-producing countries appear to be much closer to, or even above, unity. See Gately and Huntington (2002) and the discussion in Hamilton (2008).

52. Interestingly, the same calculations for residential demand for petroleum products (not reported here) yield a much larger apparent elasticity of 0.78. The price elasticity is lowest for the industrial and transport sectors, for which it is close to zero.

53. Hughes, Knittel, and Sperling (2008) find a short-run price elasticity of between 0.03 and 0.08 between 2001 and 2006.

that level is reached, we assume that the elasticity of substitution becomes equal to 1. This transition is fully anticipated by economic agents. Continuity of the demand schedule also requires that α differ as the economy transitions from $\sigma < 1$ to $\sigma = 1$.[54] We denote α' as the preference parameter after the switch to $\sigma = 1$.

The Dynamic System and the U.S. Financial Shock

We now characterize the full dynamic path of the economy in response to a U.S. financial collapse. We start the economy on the dynamic path of the bubble equilibrium with $\sigma < 1$ and a given level of global imbalances. At $t = t_0$, the bubble collapses and the economy jumps to the dynamic path of the bubbleless equilibrium. Appendix D (online) provides a complete exposition of the dynamic system and the transitions that occur between the different regimes.

Calibration of the dynamic path requires that we provide values for the following parameters: the capitalization ratio δ, the growth rate of the economy g, the relative sizes of U and M, the elasticity of substitution σ, the propensity to consume out of financial wealth θ, and the share of commodity expenditures $\bar{s}_z$ when the elasticity of substitution becomes unitary. We adopt a mixed approach, setting the values of some parameters on the basis of plausible values and calibrating others so as to reproduce key features of the data.

We start by setting the growth rate of the X good to $g = 0.03$, which is close to the average annual real growth rate of output in the United States between 1950 and 2007 (3.28 percent). As discussed above, we assume that U represents a quarter of the world's output. We set σ equal to 0.3. This is significantly higher than the apparent elasticity estimate in table 6. Nonetheless, as argued above, it is well within the range of estimates in the empirical literature. Furthermore, this value of σ produces realistic levels of adjustment in commodity prices in the model. It also implies that the price of commodities increases initially at $g/\sigma = 10$ percent in the equilibrium with bubble, accounting for some of the rapid increase in commodity prices observed *before* the U.S. financial crisis.

We set $\bar{s}_z = 0.1$, so that the long-run model takes over when the expenditure share of commodities reaches 10 percent. This seems a reasonably high value. In the data the share of oil in world output reached 4.16 percent in 2006, up from 1.29 percent in 1998. In the simulation it would take

54. To see this, suppose that the transition occurs at some time T. Aggregate demand for X goods right before T is given by $W_{T-} = [(1 + \alpha p_T^{1-\sigma}) X_T]/\theta$. Right after the switch, it is equal to $W_{T+} = [(1 + \alpha') X_T]/\theta$. Continuity of commodity prices and wealth requires that $\alpha p_T^{1-\sigma} = \alpha'$.

around 10 years before the expenditure share reached 10 percent. This yields $\alpha' = 11.11$ percent. Finally, we set the value of the world capitalization index δ to 0.15, which corresponds to about half of the share of capital in national accounts. As discussed in our previous paper, δ should be substantially lower than the capital share, since many forms of capital do not generate capitalizable streams of revenue.[55] We then calibrate each region's δ so as to stabilize global imbalances before the crisis erupts. We obtain $\delta^U = 0.144$ and $\delta^M = 0.152$.[56]

The two remaining parameters to calibrate are θ and α. We set their values so as to control both the size of the initial bubble relative to aggregate wealth at $t = 0$, $B_0/W_0 = \beta_0$, and the limit size of the bubble that would emerge in the bubbly equilibrium under $\sigma = 1$, $\beta_1 \equiv \lim_{t\to\infty} B_t/W_t$. From equation D2 in appendix D (online), we obtain $\lim_{t\to\infty} B_t/W_t = 1 - \delta\theta/g(1 + \alpha')$. For given values of β_0 and β_1, we infer back the corresponding values of θ and α.

In practice we set $\beta_0 = 0.02$, so that the collapse of the bubble represents roughly 2 percent of the world's wealth, as estimated in the previous section. We set $\beta_1 = 1.01\beta_0$, so that the economy is not far from its long-run steady state when the bubble collapses. (This ensures that the share of commodities in expenditure is not too small.) We obtain $\theta = 0.22$ and $\alpha = 0.40$. We view these values as plausible. As a point of reference, our earlier paper, using data on U.S. household sector net worth and U.S. GDP, computed a value of $\theta = 0.25$. (θ can be interpreted as the output–to–financial wealth ratio.) These values imply that the economy is slightly dynamically inefficient, since $\delta\theta/(1 + \alpha') = 2.94$ percent $< g = 3$ percent. Finally, we set the initial net foreign asset position relative to U.S. output $\eta = -0.15$, in line with estimates of the U.S. net external debt position in 2006. Table 7 summarizes the parameter values.

Figure 14 reports the simulation obtained with these parameter values. Before the crisis the real interest rate is slightly above 3.4 percent and increasing, commodity prices (normalized) are equal to their steady-state value $\hat{q} \equiv (\alpha/Z)^{1/\sigma}$, and both the trade balance and the current account are in deficit and improving (–3.5 percent and –4 percent of output, respectively).

At $t = 0$ the financial crisis hits, wiping out 2 percent of aggregate financial wealth. The response of interest rates is quite stark (top left panel of figure 14): they drop from about 3.5 percent to 2.7 percent. This decline is

55. Our earlier paper (Caballero and others, 2008) assumed $\delta = 0.12$, at which the results are largely unchanged.

56. Although the calibration sets δ^U slightly lower than δ^M, the "perceived" capitalization index in U in the presence of the bubble B is much larger, equal to $\hat{\delta}^U = [\delta - (1 - x^U_{t_0})\delta^M] / x^U_{t_0} = 0.156$. In that sense the calibration is extreme in that it assumes that U has no fundamental advantage in supplying stores of value.

Table 7. Parameter Values Used in the Simulation

Parameter	*Value*
Growth rate of output g	0.03
Elasticity of substitution σ	0.3
Share of U region output in world output X^U/X	0.25
Long-run expenditure share of commodities in output $\bar{s}_x$	0.1
Capitalization ratio δ	0.15
Initial value of financial bubble as a fraction of world financial wealth at time of financial crisis β_0	2 percent
Long-term value of financial bubble as a fraction of world financial wealth in the bubbly equilibrium β_1	2.02 percent
Initial net foreign asset position in U region as a fraction of region's output η	–0.15
Inferred parameters	
Preference for commodities α	0.40
Propensity to consume out of financial wealth θ	0.22
Capitalization ratio in the U region δ_U	0.144
Capitalization ratio in the M region δ_M	0.152

much larger than the mere 6 basis points in the benchmark economy (dashed line in the top left panel). The fall in interest rates in the simulated economy is strong enough to trigger inventory accumulation. As the top right panel shows, the normalized price of commodities $\hat{q}_t = p_t/X_t^{1/\sigma}$ jumps 2.3-fold and gradually converges back over the next 12 years. By contrast, in the benchmark economy, the (normalized) price of commodities remains unchanged and equal to $\hat{q}$.[57] The jump in prices lowers the demand for commodities and allows inventory accumulation. We find that starting from $I_{t_0} = 0$, inventories rise relatively slowly: it takes 12 years before their market value pI peaks at 3.2 percent of world financial wealth (middle left panel). In the initial periods after the shock, in particular, inventories remain very low, contributing little to the global supply of assets.

The middle right panel of figure 14 reports the current account balance relative to output in the simulated economy and in the benchmark economy. In both cases the current account improves as a result of the collapse of the bubble. However, as conjectured in the previous section, the rebalancing is much smaller in the economy with inventories. In the benchmark economy the current account balance jumps from –4 percent of output to +2 percent, an instant rebalancing of 6 percentage points. This is not surprising, given that the bubble is located in the United States: the reduction in asset supply

57. This still implies that in the benchmark economy, p_t increases at the rate g/σ, faster than the rate of economic growth.

Figure 14. Dynamics of the Subprime Crisis Response in the Short and the Long Run without a Growth Slowdown

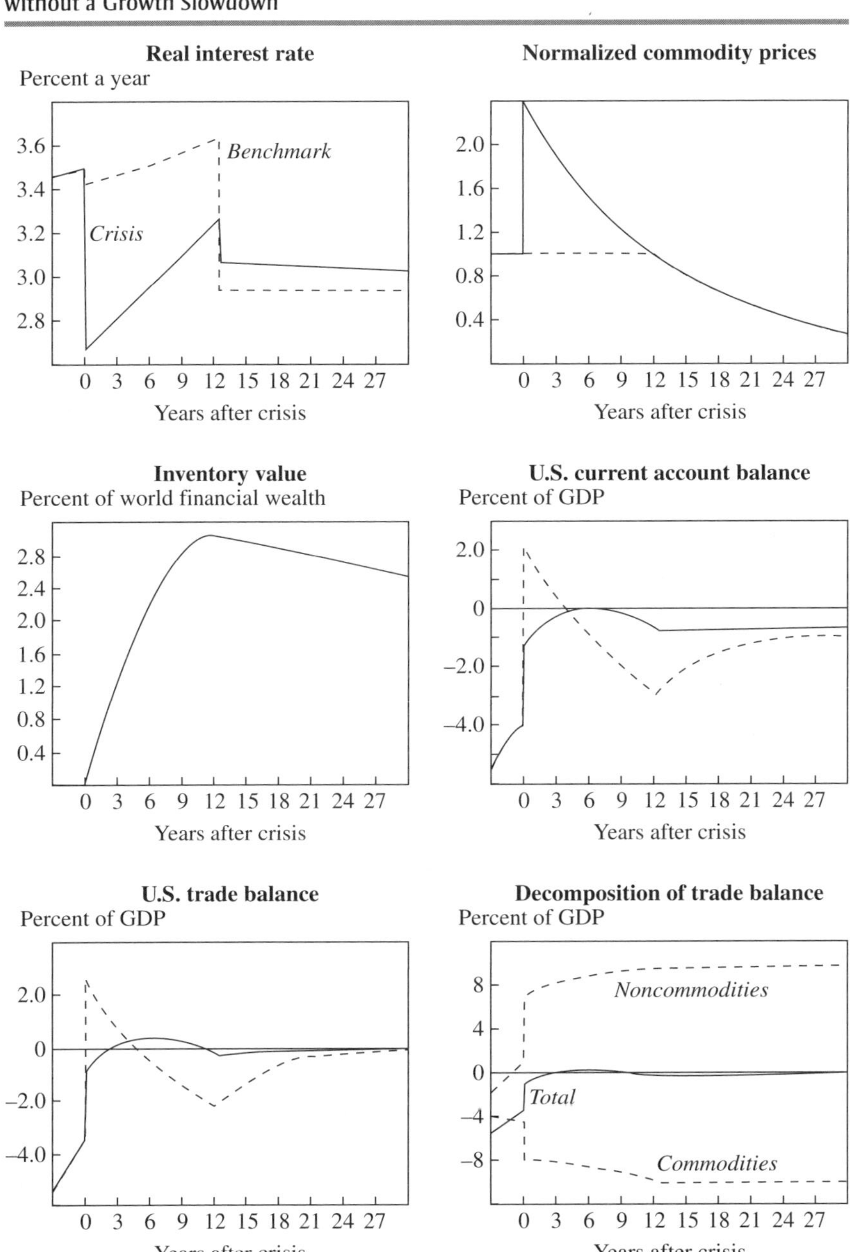

Source: Authors' calculations.

Table 8. Change in the U.S. Trade Balance, Selected Periods
Percent of GDP

	1980–89		*1999–2008*	
	1980–87	*1987–89*	*1999–2006*	*2006–08*
Total change in the trade balance	−2.5	1.5	−2.8	0.8
Of which:				
Change in balance of nonoil goods and services	−4.4	1.5	−1.4	1.5
Change in oil balance	1.9	0.0	−1.4	−0.7

Source: Authors' calculations from Bureau of Economic Analysis data.

leads agents to move part of their financial investments to *M*. By contrast, in the simulated economy the rebalancing is "only" from −4 percent to −1.4 percent of GDP. As we discussed earlier, this is larger than the rebalancing observed in the data, but of a similar order of magnitude.

Eventually, the rebalancing must become larger in the simulated economy, to achieve a long-run current account balance of −0.6 percent compared with −0.9 percent in the benchmark no-inventory economy. Nevertheless, the role of commodities is to stabilize capital outflows for the first four years after the initial shock. The bottom left panel of figure 14 shows that the implications for the trade balance are very similar, as discussed earlier. The bottom right panel further decomposes the trade balance into its noncommodity component, $X_t^U - \theta W_t^U/(1 + \alpha p_t^{1-\sigma})$, and its commodity component, $-\alpha p_t^{1-\sigma}\theta W_t^U/(1 + \alpha p_t^{1-\sigma})$. Underlying the muted response of the trade balance, both the commodity and the noncommodity trade balances adjust sharply. The commodity balance falls from −4.6 percent to −7.9 percent of output, while the noncommodity balance jumps from 1.0 percent to 6.9 percent of output.

This asymmetric response of the commodity and noncommodity components of the trade balance is consistent with the empirical evidence. Table 8 reports the change in the U.S. trade balance during the last two rebalancing episodes: 1987–89 and 2006–08.[58] The table shows that the recent improvement in the U.S. trade balance comes entirely from the nonoil component, which improved by more than 1.5 percent of GDP. By contrast, the oil balance worsened by 0.7 percent of GDP. When this rebalancing episode is compared with the previous episode, centered around 1987, it is striking to note that oil prices played no role in attenuating the external

58. Milesi-Ferretti (2008) presents additional evidence on the contrast between the two episodes.

rebalancing then: the deficit of the oil balance did not change between 1987 and 1989.

The Dynamic System and a Global Slowdown

The preceding results account for the negative correlation between U.S. financial assets and commodity prices that emerged in the first phase of the U.S. financial crisis. Starting in July 2008, however, commodity prices retreated dramatically. Bad news for commodities was also bad news for U.S. and world financial markets.

Of course, this global collapse has many causes, and a host of overshooting mechanisms are at work, from balance sheet multipliers, to margin calls, to Knightian uncertainty, all of which contribute to the overall process of deleveraging. Our framework is not suited to addressing the role of each of these factors. Instead, we emphasize here the dramatic impact of a global economic slowdown. To do so, we recalibrate our model assuming that a moderate slowdown—a fall in annual global output growth from 3 percent to 2 percent—takes place unexpectedly one year after the beginning of the U.S. financial crisis.

Such a decline in global growth is sufficiently large to ensure that assumption 2 is satisfied, so that the tightness in global asset markets is relieved. Figure 15 presents the results. In each panel the solid line reports the simulation with a growth slowdown, and the dashed line reports the simulation from figure 14, without a growth slowdown. The collapse in global growth at $t = 1$ has dramatic consequences for asset and commodity prices. First, slower growth reduces asset values. In the short run, however, it leads to an even larger decline in asset demand. The result is an *increase* in interest rates (top left panel) and a decline in asset prices (bottom right panel).[59] This decline in asset demand arises from the sudden decline in commodity prices (top right panel), which makes commodity producers poorer. As discussed previously, this collapse in commodity prices arises from a downward adjustment in sustainable long-run equilibrium inventories (middle left panel). The growth slowdown eliminates the dynamic inefficiency of the economy and thus the need to hold inventories in the long run. Inventory holders immediately reduce the rate of accumulation of inventories, which leads to a collapse in the price of commodities. As before, the decline in commodity prices is reinforced by the short-run increase in interest rates that makes commodity accumulation less profitable.

59. The bottom right panel reports the total value of U assets, including the bubble for $t \leq 0$, both in the case with and in the case without a growth slowdown. It also reports the value of the "good" U asset in the case with a growth slowdown.

Figure 15. Dynamics of the Subprime Crisis Response in the Short and the Long Run with a Growth Slowdown

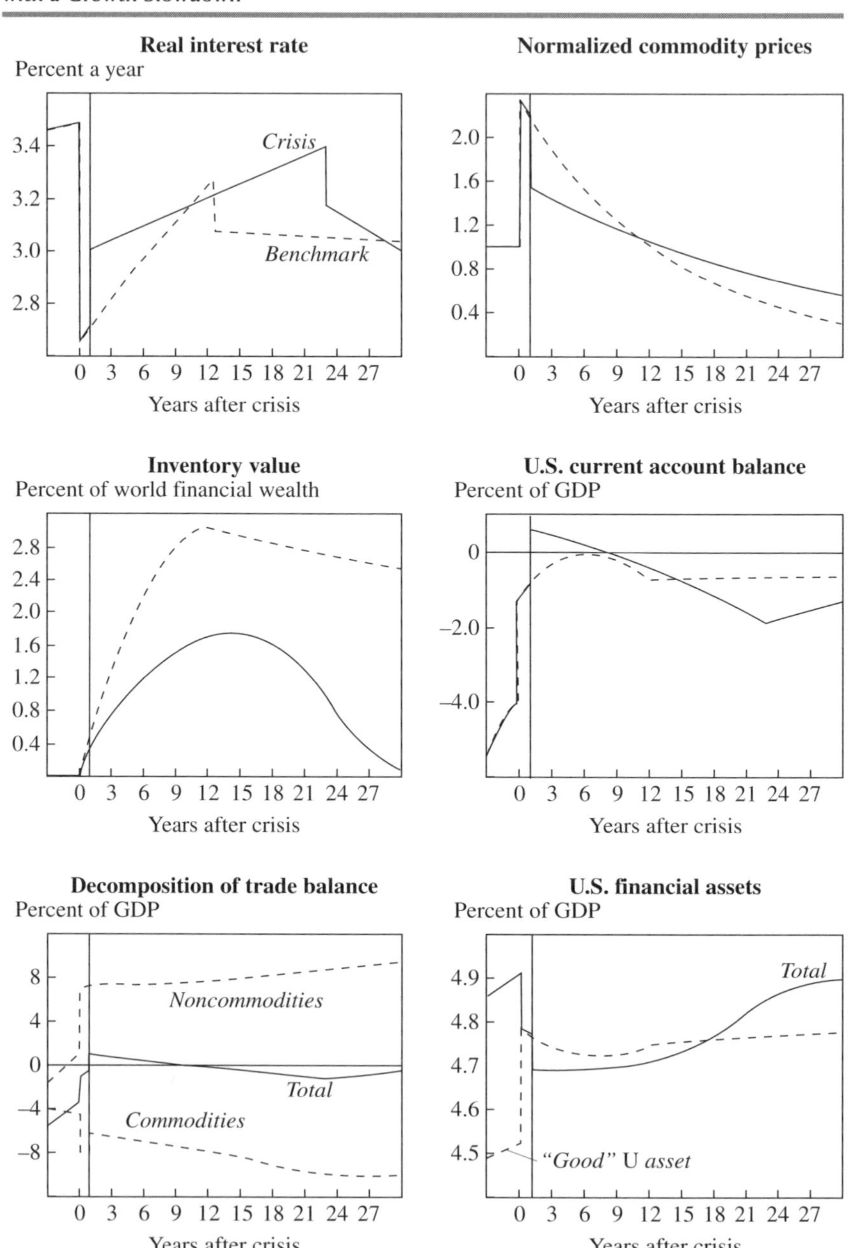

Source: Authors' calculations.

The impact on external imbalances is also interesting. Whereas the previous discussion indicated that external imbalances could increase or decrease when growth slows down, we find that for these parameter values, the decline in commodity prices accelerates the process of global rebalancing (middle right panel), largely through an improvement in the commodity component of the trade balance (bottom left panel).

The growth slowdown generates a pattern of positive co-movements for asset prices and commodities that closely matches what the world economy has experienced since July 2008. In our framework the decline in global economic growth shrinks or even eliminates the bubble by reducing global asset demand. However, it is important to recall that this experiment assumes that the growth slowdown is permanent, a highly unlikely situation. Once real economic conditions recover, our model predicts that asset demand will rebound, re-creating the chronic shortage of assets, and the cycle will start again.

Inventories, Oil Prices, and Asset Supply: Some Evidence

We now examine in more detail the role of inventories and the empirical evidence on the linkage between financial factors and commodity prices.

Inventories

One objection to stories like ours, where asset demand for oil plays an important role in price determination, is that measured oil inventories did not rise during the recent price spike. Petroleum inventories in the OECD countries increased from 3.74 billion barrels in January 2000 to 4.08 billion barrels in April 2008. However, this increase mostly occurred between 2000 and 2006. After the onset of the subprime crisis, OECD petroleum inventories declined from 4.25 billion barrels in September 2006 to 4.08 billion barrels across the board.[60]

60. In the United States, petroleum and crude oil stocks increased between January 2000 and September 2006 by 307 million and 168 million barrels, respectively. Between September 2006 and April 2008, U.S. petroleum stocks declined from 1.79 billion to 1.67 billion barrels, while crude oil inventories remained relatively constant at around 1 billion barrels. A closer look, however, reveals that nonstrategic crude oil inventories decreased by 13.6 million barrels. The only component of U.S. petroleum stocks that increased between September 2006 and April 2008 is the Strategic Petroleum Reserve (SPR; see Energy Information Administration, *Monthly Energy Review,* tables 3.4 and 11.3). This change in the SPR is a consequence of the Energy Policy Act of 2005, which mandated a gradual increase in the reserve from 700 million to 1 billion barrels. In May 2008, in response to the rapid increase in oil prices, Congress voted to stop depositing oil in the SPR.

Yet there are at least two reasons why the absence of a rise in measured inventories need not be a serious concern. First, observed inventories are the result of two opposing forces: the asset market force, which leads to an increase in inventories, and a demand force, which does the opposite. In appendix B we show that if the long-run elasticity of substitution exceeds 1, inventories follow a nonmonotonic path—rising first and afterward declining—in response to speculation.

Second, as argued by Jeffrey Frankel and others,[61] producers are the most efficient inventory holders, since they do not need to extract the oil in order to hold it. In our model this amounts to assuming $d^{oilproducer} < d$, which implies that *all* inventories are held under ground.

Our model is amenable to several interpretations where inventories are just oil in the ground. Suppose, for example, that new reserves of the *Z* good are discovered every period. More precisely, the stock of discovered reserves increases by *Z* per unit of time. The economy cannot consume resources that have not been discovered yet. In addition, suppose that the rights to these new reserves are not capitalized, either because they accrue to new entrants, or because they are likely to be expropriated, or because they embody unmodeled uncertainty. This economy would be exactly equivalent to our simulated economy. Under this interpretation there are no physical inventories of *Z* goods. Inventories reflect only discovered and not-yet-consumed reserves of the *Z* good.

Another, more abstract interpretation is that of a social contract in region *M*. This (implicit) contract specifies that each generation is entitled to an endowment *Z* of *Z* goods. They can decide when to sell it. If they do not sell it immediately, they can store it. Moreover, they can trade rights to future consumption claims on their endowment; that is, they can sell the *Z* good forward. They can also acquire the *Z* good from agents of the same or a different generation in *M:* they can then treat these newly acquired goods exactly as their own endowment. This economy is once again completely isomorphic to our economy. Inventories are just goods in the ground. As we show in appendix A, the underground inventory holding view has important implications for the effectiveness of recent proposals to tax speculative transactions in commodities.

The Empirical Link between Oil Prices and Asset Supply

The asset role of oil suggests a negative correlation between oil prices and the value of assets negatively affected by financial shocks, and a posi-

61. Frankel (2006).

tive correlation between oil prices and economic growth. As a starting point for investigating this question, we run the following simple regression using ordinary least squares (OLS):

$$\Delta p_t = \alpha + \beta \Delta S{+}P_t + \gamma \Delta y_t + \varepsilon_t, \tag{23}$$

where all variables are in logarithms, p_t denotes the spot price of crude oil, $S{+}P_t$ is the S&P500 index, and y_t is the monthly U.S. industrial production index. In the model a decline in the value of bubble assets that lowers stock prices leads to a reallocation of assets toward commodities, and so we expect to find $\beta < 0$. A decline in growth should also push down commodity prices, and so we expect $\gamma > 0$. Table 9 reports the results of this simple regression for the period from January 1984 to November 2008. We find a negative but statistically insignificant link between oil prices and stock market performance, and a positive and mostly insignificant link between growth and oil prices.

There are two obvious issues with the OLS regression. First, as shown in figure 8, the apparent correlation is strongly negative only in the first phase of the crisis. In the second phase, as explained above, the collapse in global growth reduces both asset and commodity prices. Second, there is an obvious reverse causality concern. For instance, an exogenous increase in oil prices could increase the chances of a recession, leading to a decline in stock returns, or push up inflation rates, leading to a tightening of monetary policy, which would also send equities tumbling. To control for this we use two instruments: the price of gold and the performance of financial stocks relative to the broader market. Increases in the price of gold are often associated with flight-to-quality episodes. In fact, since gold itself provides little services or yield, it is the perfect example of an asset held for speculative reasons. The relative performance of financials captures the fact that financial crises impact the financial sector more directly, whereas there is no reason for oil shocks to affect this service sector more than, for example, the energy-intensive transportation or manufacturing sectors.

The top panel of table 10 presents our instrumental variables estimates. Notice that the coefficient on equities is much larger than in the OLS estimate and strongly significant at the daily, weekly, monthly, and quarterly frequencies. The elasticity is always in excess of one. The coefficient on growth has the correct sign at the quarterly and annual frequencies but appears to be insignificant. The bottom panel reports the first stage of the instrumental variables regression.

Table 9. OLS Regressions of Oil Prices on U.S. Stock Prices and Industrial Production[a]

	Regression									
Independent variable	*9-1*	*9-2*	*9-3*	*9-4*	*9-5*	*9-6*	*9-7*	*9-8*	*9-9*	*9-10*
Change in log S&P500 index	–0.06	–0.01	–0.07	–0.45	–0.44	–0.06	–0.02	–0.11	–0.50	–0.63
	(1.41)	(0.13)	(0.37)	(1.59)	(1.42)	(1.39)	(0.17)	(0.72)	(1.73)	(2.57)
Change in industrial production index			1.30	3.10	1.81			1.03	2.23	–0.59
			(1.25)	(2.04)	(1.23)			(1.05)	(1.11)	(0.27)
Change in log S&P500 index, lagged one period						0.06	–0.07	–0.07	0.67	0.22
						(1.58)	(0.83)	(0.43)	(0.29)	(0.67)
Change in industrial production index, lagged one period								2.68	1.07	2.43
								(2.02)	(0.57)	(0.97)
Data frequency	Daily	Weekly	Monthly	Quarterly	Annual	Daily	Weekly	Monthly	Quarterly	Annual
No. of observations	6,233	1,296	297	295	286	6,232	1,295	296	294	285
R^2	0.000	0.000	0.001	NA	NA	0.001	0.001	0.004	NA	NA

Source: Authors' regressions.

a. The dependent variable is the change in the logarithm of the spot price in dollars of a barrel of West Texas Intermediate oil. The sample period is January 1, 1984, to November 8, 2008. Changes at all intervals are measured from the end of one period to the end of the next. Quarterly and annual regressions are run on overlapping monthly data. Eicker-White robust t statistics are reported in parentheses for the daily, weekly, and monthly regressions and Newey-West t statistics for the quarterly and annual regressions, with windows of 2 and 11 months, respectively. Constant terms are included in all regressions (results not reported).

Table 10. Instrumental Variables Regressions of Oil Prices on U.S. Stock Prices and Industrial Production[a]

	Regression				
Independent variable	*10-1*	*10-2*	*10-3*	*10-4*	*10-5*
			Second-stage regressions		
Change in log S&P500 index	−1.14	−1.52	−2.96	−3.08	−3.74
	(4.95)	(3.45)	(3.12)	(3.71)	(1.98)
Change in industrial production index			−0.94	3.86	7.99
			(0.40)	(1.25)	(1.39)
			First-stage regressions		
Log change in S&P500 financials index less change in overall S&P500	0.29	0.28	0.29	0.29	−0.01
	(8.55)	(5.56)	(2.96)	(2.75)	(0.06)
Log change in price of gold	−0.11	−0.08	−0.09	−0.11	−0.28
	(3.87)	(1.91)	(0.94)	(1.21)	(1.83)
Data frequency	Daily	Weekly	Monthly	Quarterly	Annual
No. of observations	6,098	1,296	297	295	286
R^2	0.06	0.06	0.06	NA	NA

Source: Authors' regressions.

a. The dependent variable in the second-stage regressions is the change in the logarithm of the spot price in dollars of a barrel of West Texas Intermediate oil. The dependent variable in the first-stage regressions is the change in the logarithm of the S&P500 index. Changes at all intervals are measured from the end of one period to the end of the next. Quarterly and annual regressions are run on overlapping monthly data. Eicker-White robust t statistics are reported in parentheses for the daily, weekly, and monthly regressions and Newey-West t statistics for the quarterly and annual regressions, with windows of 2 and 11 months, respectively. Constant terms are included in all regressions (results not reported).

Financial relative performance has the right impact on equilibrium asset values at all frequencies but annual: conditional on growth, bad news in U.S. financial markets is good news for oil as an asset. Conversely, good news in U.S. financial markets is bad news for oil.[62]

Discussion

The prevailing view of financial disruptions is one of central bank excesses and mistakes leading to excess liquidity, speculative bubbles, and unavoidable crises. This seems overstated: central banks, when reasonable, are not nearly that powerful. In this paper we take a contrarian view and provide an entirely private sector account of the main facts, without any role for monetary factors. Reality is probably in between.

62. The results are similar if we restrict the sample to the period before July 2008, preceding the second phase of the crisis.

Our framework builds on the idea that the world economy entered the present crisis with chronic excess demand for financial assets; the subprime market developments may have been merely a (failed) market attempt to bridge this gap. Within this perspective we argue that the sharp rise in oil prices following the subprime crisis—nearly 100 percent in just a matter of months, and in the face of recessionary shocks—was the result of a speculative response to the financial crisis itself, in an attempt to rebuild asset supply. That is, the global economy was subjected to one shock with multiple implications rather than to two separate shocks (financial and oil).

Eventually, the persistent financial crisis and its many multipliers severely hurt growth prospects, and recognition of this fact triggered an implosion in commodity prices and asset demand more broadly. However, by the same token, when real conditions recover, our model predicts that asset demand is likely to rebound, re-creating the chronic shortage of assets, and the cycle will start again. Regulation, unless distortionary enough to depress growth, is no match for these market forces. The real problem is more macroeconomic in nature and unlikely to go away until the world economy's ability to generate sound stores of value catches up with its potential income growth. In other words, like so much else these days, the outcome depends largely on developments within China and other emerging markets.

ACKNOWLEDGMENTS We thank Kathryn Dominguez and Carmen Reinhart for their comments and Gabriel Chodorow-Reich for excellent research assistance. Ricardo Caballero and Pierre-Olivier Gourinchas thank the National Science Foundation for financial support. Gourinchas acknowledges the support of the Coleman-Fung risk management research center.

APPENDIX A

Speculation and Policy

In this appendix we expand on the paper's penultimate section and analyze the effect of introducing futures markets, as well as the effects of policies aimed at curtailing "speculation."

Futures

Let us start by introducing (fully collateralized) futures contracts on the Z good. We make two simple and related points: first, the payoff of the strategy that consists in buying the Z good and storing it can be replicated by simple futures positions; second, in our model the introduction of a futures market has no impact on the equilibrium.

By covered interest parity, the forward rate f_{t+s} is equal to

$$f_{t+s} = p_t \exp^{\int_t^{t+s} (r_u + d)du}.$$

Consider the strategy of buying a forward contract at t with maturity $t + s$ and reselling it at date $t + s' < t + s$. The payoff at $t + s'$ is

$$p_{t+s'} - p_t \exp^{\int_t^{t+s} (r_u + d)du} \exp^{-\int_{t+s'}^{t+s} (r_u + d)du} = p_{t+s'} - p_t \exp^{\int_t^{t+s'} (r_u + d)du},$$

which, in net present value, is exactly the same as that from buying one unit of the Z good at t, storing it until $t + s'$, and then selling it on the spot market. To the extent that there is heterogeneity in the cost of storing the Z good, all the inventories will be held by the agents with the lowest storage costs—typically the producers, who can leave at least some of the Z good in the ground. Agents with higher storage costs will prefer to buy futures contracts from the producers.

Equilibrium and Policy

However, the introduction of futures contracts has absolutely no effect on the equilibrium of our economy. Futures do not increase asset supply: every long position is offset by a corresponding short position, and there are no agents with biased beliefs deviating from the perfect-foresight price path. As a result, the imposition of a tax on futures trading, or the prohibition of such trading, would have absolutely no moderating effect on commodity prices.

In order for a tax to have any consequence in our model, it must affect the agents with the lowest storage costs, that is, those who actually hold the inventories. Thus, let us consider the effect of taxing producers for holding inventories. Although in practice this is extremely hard to do, since producers are likely to hold most of their inventories under ground, it is a useful positive exercise to gauge the potential impact of this type of policy.

It turns out that taxes on the value of inventory holdings are almost isomorphic with the holding cost parameter d, except that under the tax interpretation, the proceeds can be rebated as a lump sum to the agents at no resource cost. We take the latter route here and let τ denote the tax rate per unit of value of inventories (that is, the tax per unit of inventory is τp_t).

We maintain the assumption that $\sigma = 1$ but strengthen the dynamic inefficiency assumption (assumption 1 in the text) to the following:

Assumption 3: $g - \tau > \dfrac{\theta\delta}{1+\alpha}$.

Under assumption 3, the bubbleless steady state of the economy is now such that the interest rate is given by

$$r_t = g - \tau,$$

the price grows at rate g:

$$p_t = \alpha \frac{X_t}{Z},$$

and long-run inventories are constant:

$$I_t = \frac{1+\alpha}{\alpha} \frac{1}{\theta(g-\tau)} \left[g - \tau - r^{ref}\right] Z.$$

The long-run level inventory function $I(\tau)$ is decreasing with respect to τ, whereas the price of oil is unaffected, since the relative consumption of X and Z goods is unchanged in the long run. However, in the short run the imposition of a tax τ lowers inventories and the price of oil, which is equal to $p_t = \alpha X_t/(Z - \dot{I}_t)$.

In summary, a tax on inventories reduces inventories and succeeds in temporarily depressing the price of the Z good but does not affect it in the long run. Note also that the tax reduces the equilibrium interest rate and aggravates dynamic inefficiency in the bubbleless equilibrium, at a cost to the economy. The intuition is transparent. A dynamically inefficient economy is characterized by a scarcity of assets. A tax on inventories discourages the accumulation of inventories and hence reduces asset supply. The interest rate has to adjust downward to clear the asset market.[63]

APPENDIX B

Declining Inventories

In this appendix we expand on a remark in the paper's penultimate section and analyze formally the consequences for inventory accumulation of allowing the short-run and the long-run elasticities of substitution between

63. Note that the bubbly equilibrium of the economy is not affected by τ. Moreover, if assumption 3 is violated, then the bubbleless equilibrium becomes identical to that of the benchmark no-inventory economy.

good X and good Z to differ. In most analyses of commodity price and inventory dynamics, the forward curve for commodity prices plays a central role. In our model, after the shock, the world is deterministic and risk-neutral. At date t the forward price s periods ahead, f_{t+s}, is simply the future spot price p_{t+s}. In our case it will prove more convenient to reason in terms of the log-forward curve, which traces $\log f_{t+s} = \log p_{t+s}$ as a function of maturity s.

The decision to accumulate inventories is determined by comparing the slope of the log-forward curve $\frac{\dot{p}_t}{p_t}$ of the price for the Z good with the interest rate r_t. The steeper that slope, the higher the expected increase in price of the Z good, and the more attractive storage becomes. Similarly, the lower the interest rate, the more attractive storage becomes. The elasticity σ of the demand for the Z good is a key parameter governing the slope of the log-forward curve. The higher σ, the flatter the log-forward curve.

Key to our analysis is the basic idea that the short-run elasticity of demand for commodities σ is low in the short run but high in the long run. Let us denote the short- and long-run elasticities by σ^{short} and σ^{long}, respectively, with $\sigma^{short} < 1 < \sigma^{long}$. The switch from σ^{short} to σ^{long} is typically gradual and potentially governed by a number of time- and state-dependent factors. If σ^{long} for the Z good is high enough, then inventories will eventually be undone. This is formalized by the following assumption:

Assumption 4: $\frac{g}{\sigma^{long}} < \delta\theta.$

This assumption is more likely to be verified, the higher is σ^{long}. When it is verified, the long-run steady state of the economy features no inventories. In the long-run steady state, the interest rate is $\delta\theta$. The price of the Z good is given by $\left(\alpha X_t / Z\right)^{\frac{1}{\sigma^{long}}} = p_t$ and rises at a rate g/σ^{long}, which is too low to make the accumulation of inventories worthwhile. The share of the Z good in total consumption converges to zero, and the economy effectively behaves as an economy without commodities.

Turning to transitional dynamics, imagine that the economy enters the region where $\sigma = \sigma^{long} > 1$ with positive inventories $I_t > 0$. The presence of inventories affects both the goods market and the asset market: the total intertemporal supply of the Z good is higher, which depresses the price p_t of the Z good. Asset supply is higher, since inventories act as a store of value, resulting in a higher interest rate r_t. These two forces trigger a process of inventory reduction, and the economy eventually converges to a steady state with no inventories.

References

Beltran, Daniel O., Laurie Pounder, and Charles Thomas. 2008. "Foreign Exposure to Asset-Backed Securities of U.S. Origin." International Finance Discussion Paper 939. Washington: Board of Governors of the Federal Reserve System.

Bernanke, Ben. 2005. "The Global Saving Glut and the U.S. Current Account Deficit." Sandridge Lecture, Virginia Association of Economics, Richmond, Va. (March).

Blanchard, Olivier, Francesco Giavazzi, and Filipa Sa. 2005. "International Investors, the U.S. Current Account, and the Dollar." *BPEA,* no. 1, pp. 1–49.

Brunnermeier, Markus K. 2009. "Deciphering the Liquidity and Credit Crunch 2007–08." *Journal of Economic Perspectives* 23, no 1.

Caballero, Ricardo J., and Arvind Krishnamurthy. 2006. "Bubbles and Capital Flow Volatility: Causes and Risk Management." *Journal of Monetary Economics* 53, no. 1: 35–53.

Caballero, Ricardo J., Emmanuel Farhi, and Pierre-Olivier Gourinchas. 2008. "An Equilibrium Model of 'Global Imbalances' and Low Interest Rates." *American Economic Review* 98, no. 1: 358–93.

Dahl, Carol, and Thomas Sterner. 1991. "Analysing Gasoline Demand Elasticities: A Survey." *Energy Economics* 13, no. 3: 203–10.

Deutsche Bank. 2007. "Sovereign Wealth Funds—State Investments on the Rise." *Current Issues* (September 10).

Frankel, Jeffrey A. 2006. "The Effect of Monetary Policy on Real Commodity Prices." Working Paper 12713. Cambridge, Mass.: National Bureau of Economic Research (December).

Gately, Dermot, and Hillard G. Huntington. 2002. "The Asymmetric Effects of Changes in Price and Income on Energy and Oil Demand." *Energy Journal* 23, no. 1: 19–55.

Greenlaw, David, Jan Hatzius, Anil K Kashyap, and Hyun Song Shin. 2008. "Leveraged Losses: Lessons from the Mortgage Market Meltdown." U.S. Monetary Policy Forum Report No. 2. Initiative on Global Markets, University of Chicago Graduate School of Business, and Rosenberg Institute for Global Finance, Brandeis International Business School.

Hamilton, James. 2008. "Understanding Crude Oil Prices." University of California, San Diego (May).

Hotelling, Harold. 1931. "The Economics of Exhaustible Resources." *Journal of Political Economy* 39, no. 2: 137–75.

Hughes, Jonathan E., Christopher R. Knittel, and Daniel Sperling. 2008. "Evidence of a Shift in the Short-Run Price Elasticity of Gasoline Demand." *Energy Journal* 29, no. 1: 113–34.

International Monetary Fund. 2008a. *Global Financial Stability Report: Containing Systemic Risks and Restoring Financial Soundness.* Washington (April).

———. 2008b. *Global Financial Stability Report: Financial Stress and Deleveraging: Macrofinancial Implications and Policy.* Washington (October).

Jovanovic, Boyan. 2007. "Bubbles in Prices of Exhaustible Resources." Working Paper 13320. Cambridge, Mass.: National Bureau of Economic Research (August).

Kouri, Pentti. 1983. "Balance of Payment and the Foreign Exchange Market: A Dynamic Partial Equilibrium Model." In *Economic Interdependence and Flexible Exchange Rates,* edited by Jagdeep Bhandari and Bluford Putnam. MIT Press.

Metzler, Lloyd A. 1968. "The Process of International Adjustment under Conditions of Full Employment. A Keynesian View." In *Readings in International Economics,* edited by Richard Caves and Harry G. Johnson. Homewood, Ill.: Irwin.

Milesi-Ferretti, Gian Maria. 2008. "Fundamentals at Odds? The Dollar and the U.S. Current Account Deficit." Prepared for the Siena Conference on the Impact of Global Financial Imbalances, Siena, Italy, September.

Nordhaus, William D. 1980. "Oil and Economic Performance in Industrial Countries." *BPEA,* no. 2: 341–88.

Roy, Joyashree, Alan H. Sanstad, Jayant A. Sathaye, and Raman Khaddaria. 2006. "Substitution and Price Elasticity Estimates Using Inter-Country Pooled Data in a Translog Cost Model." *Energy Economics* 28, no. 5–6: 706–19.

Sercu, Piet M., and Rosanne Vanpée. 2007. "Home Bias in International Equity Portfolios: A Review." Katholieke Universiteit Leuven.

Comments and Discussion

COMMENT BY

KATHRYN M. DOMINGUEZ This ambitious paper by Ricardo Caballero, Emmanuel Farhi, and Pierre-Olivier Gourinchas seeks to explain, in one model, all that is wrong in the global economy. The culprit is underdeveloped financial markets in emerging Asia and the oil-producing countries. U.S. fiscal and monetary policies play no role. The three stylized phenomena explained and linked in the model are the large U.S. current account deficits (and the counterbalancing large surpluses in emerging Asia and oil-producing countries), financial bubbles, and volatile commodity prices. The model intriguingly suggests that all three features can persist in equilibrium.

The model begins by dividing the world into two regions, one with developed financial markets, which the authors label *U* (for the United States), and one with underdeveloped financial markets, labeled *M*. The *M* countries extract and consume commodities *Z*, while *U* only consumes *Z*. The model starts with the formation and bursting of a financial bubble in *U* (although where the bubble starts turns out to be unimportant). With the bursting of the bubble, global savers flee the bubble assets in search of new stores of value in *U*. Note that savers flee to safer assets in *U* and not to the *M* countries, because financial markets are more developed in *U*. These capital flows (from *M* to *U*) lead to a decline in real interest rates in *U*. Low real interest rates, in turn, lead to speculative commodity hoarding and commodity price jumps, resulting in wealth transfers from *U* to *M*. *M*'s new wealth, however, again finds its way to *U*, which has comparative advantage in quality asset creation. These capital inflows further lower real interest rates in *U* and allow *U* to run ever larger current account deficits.

Changes in interest rates are the driving force in this model. The bursting of the initial financial bubble and the consequent scramble by global savers to place their wealth in higher-quality assets in *U* lead to lower real interest rates. It is these low interest rates that make commodity inventory accumulation profitable, driving up commodity prices and leading in turn to wealth transfers from *U* (the consumers of commodities) to *M* (the commodity producers). The link between low real interest rates and high commodity prices comes from Harold Hotelling's insight that for resources in fixed supply with zero extraction costs, extraction in equilibrium is characterized by resource prices that increase at the interest rate.[1] If a resource is in fixed supply and its future price is expected to be high, then low interest rates drive up current prices in order to induce owners to sell.

In the authors' model the resource, *Z*, is *not* assumed to be in fixed supply, but instead there is a flow extraction constraint that is insufficient to meet demand growth and acts to limit supply. The tricky aspect of this assumption is that expectation formation in this sort of model is less straightforward than in the standard Hotelling fixed-supply setup. The link between the interest rate and the commodity price posited by Hotelling will be broken if expectations of future commodity prices systematically change with the same forces that affect interest rates. The paper suggests that the rise in commodity prices in early 2008 and the more recent precipitous decline in oil prices (and many other commodity prices) fit well with their model, in that when demand for these commodities was high, the flow extraction constraint was binding, and when demand growth declined, so did commodity prices as the flow constraint ceased to bind. What is more difficult to connect in this version of Hotelling's model is the role of interest rates. At the same time that global demand growth declined, countercyclical policies in the United States were targeted at reducing real interest rates, so that interest rates remained low, while commodity prices first spiked and then fell. In the first seven months of 2008, commodities posted their best performance in 35 years, rising by 35 percent; then, in August, they had their worst month in 28 years, falling by 11 percent, followed by an even more precipitous decline of 41 percent in the four months through November. These extreme movements suggest that expectations, rather than interest rates, have played a dominant role.

The version of this paper presented at the September 2008 Brookings Panel conference was written before commodity prices collapsed, so this

1. Harold Hotelling, "The Economics of Exhaustible Resources," *Journal of Political Economy* 39, no. 2 (1931): 137–75.

aspect of the story (which the paper terms the "second phase" of the crisis) is new. Whereas in the earlier version the bursting of the financial bubble did not lead to a fall in global growth, but only a slowdown in *U,* in the new version it is this global slowdown that removes the excess demand in asset markets, leading to a decumulation of commodity inventories and a fall in commodity prices. Interestingly, in the earlier version commodity prices were predicted to fall only if the U.S. financial crisis subsided. In this version it is the ongoing crisis and its effects on global economic growth that lead to a collapse in commodity prices and asset prices more generally.

Wealth transfers play another key role in this paper. Savers always prefer to invest in *U,* where financial markets are more developed. Consequently, even when the *M* countries are doing well (that is, when commodity prices are high), capital flows to *U.* The focus in the paper is exclusively on the private sector, so that, strictly speaking, these wealth transfers do not include government flows. Data from the International Monetary Fund's *Balance of Payments Statistics,* however, suggest that foreign governments and official institutions have dramatically increased their role in U.S. capital inflows in recent years through their foreign reserve accumulations. Interestingly, in a recent paper I report evidence that it is precisely those countries with less developed financial markets that hold high levels of foreign reserves, the bulk of which are invested in U.S. assets.[2] This suggests that including the government sector in the model might well strengthen the results (more on this to come).

Is there evidence that *U* has comparative advantage over *M* in creating high-quality financial assets, as the authors' model assumes? One testable hypothesis that follows from this assumption is that countries with higher-quality financial markets pay lower premiums on their assets. Joseph Gruber and Steven Kamin examine this hypothesis and find that real long-term interest rates and expected earnings yields on bonds and equities are no lower in the United States than in other industrial countries.[3] Their paper does not examine asset premiums in *M* countries, which are surely

2. Kathryn M. Dominguez, "International Reserves and Underdeveloped Capital Markets," University of Michigan (September 2008).

3. Joseph Gruber and Steven Kamin, "Do Differences in Financial Development Explain the Global Pattern of Current Account Imbalances?" International Finance Discussion Papers 2008-923 (Washington: Board of Governors of the Federal Reserve System, March 2008).

higher than those in industrial countries, but this evidence does suggest there is little reason for capital to flow to the United States in preference over other industrial countries.

Along with providing an intriguing model that connects the present financial crisis with commodity price movements and global imbalances, this paper also presents some suggestive empirical work, consisting of back-of-the-envelope impact estimates as well as a calibration exercise to work through the implications of the model dynamics. The paper marshals an impressive array of estimates from the literature, starting with the size of the perceived losses generated by the financial crisis, to explore what the model can explain (and what it misses). The results of these exercises suggest that although the model does a fairly good job of explaining the first phase of the crisis (through the summer of 2008), harder work is needed to connect the crisis with the global slowdown, the consequent dramatic reversal in commodity prices, and the implications of both for global imbalances. To be fair, few economists predicted the downward spiral of events of the past year, with or without the aid of a model, and the authors of this paper do not claim to be clairvoyant.

In its conclusion the paper notes that by taking a "contrarian view" and assuming no role for government policy, it is likely to overstate the role of the private sector in the current global crisis. It seems incumbent on the discussant, therefore, to describe some alternative explanations that the model ignores.

One of the stylized facts that the model attempts to explain is the sustained U.S. current account deficit. A country's current account balance is equivalent to the difference between its domestic saving and its investment. Private saving and public saving in the United States have been unusually low in recent years, relative to other industrial countries and relative to U.S. history. Since 2000 the U.S. personal saving rate has averaged 2 percent of personal disposable income (in the 1980s it was 9 percent, and in the 1990s it was 5 percent; currently it is close to zero), and U.S. net national saving, at negative 2 percent of GDP, is at its lowest rate since the Great Depression. One explanation for the low private saving rate, at least through 2007, was that rapid increases in the stock market and in residential property led to a wealth effect. In the paper this wealth effect is driven by capital inflows from *M* countries, due to the scarcity of quality financial assets outside of *U*. The model, however, does not include a rationale (or a role) for low *public* saving. Historically, when private saving has been low, public saving has tended to provide an offsetting force.

That this is not true in the current context works in the model's favor, although it begs the question of whether fiscal policy can in the future provide a stabilizing role.

There is no money in the model, and therefore no banks and no role for central bank monetary or exchange rate policy. Although recently banks seem not to be playing their usual role as intermediaries, their absence in a model of financial crises is jarring. Likewise, although the role of expansionary monetary policy during the Greenspan era may be overplayed, it seems likely that the low real interest rates that are at the heart of the paper's commodity price story are driven at least in part by U.S. central bank policy decisions. Further, the desire on the part of many *M* countries to keep their currencies stable against the dollar can provide an additional rationale for why capital has continued to flow from *M* to *U* even as asset prices in *U* have deteriorated.

The paper purposely ignores the role of money and government policy in order to highlight the role of differences in financial market development. The argument is that the lack of financial development in *M* countries, in and of itself, can lead to global financial market dislocation. The key implication is that as long as financial development lags in *M,* the current patterns of global imbalances will persist. One reason to be a bit suspicious of this dire prediction is that this asymmetry in financial market development existed long before global imbalances ballooned after 1998. If one measures financial development according to the relative size of bond and equity markets, the gap between industrial countries and developing countries is apparent starting in the late 1980s, yet the U.S. current account ran small deficits in those years—and even a small surplus in 1991. Of course, if the current financial crisis continues for much longer, financial markets in *U* may well shrink to such an extent that financial markets in *M* will finally catch up.

This paper attempts to provide a "one model fits all" explanation of recent global economic events. This is a tall order. Policymakers are likely to have mixed views on the paper's message. On the one hand, by focusing on financial market development rather than policy mistakes, the paper may seem to give monetary and fiscal authorities an opportunity to dodge responsibility for the current mess. On the other hand, the impotence of policy in the model is unlikely to make it popular in current policy circles. The contribution of the paper, therefore, is less in its lessons for policy and more in the insights it provides regarding the critical role of private sector capital flows in a world of differentially imperfect financial markets.

COMMENT BY

CARMEN M. REINHART I appreciate the opportunity to discuss this paper by Ricardo Caballero, Emmanuel Farhi, and Pierre-Olivier Gourinchas. This paper was described to me as a mix of theoretical and empirical work that attempts a hat trick: explaining the joint combination of global imbalances, the deflation of the housing price bubble that created the subprime crisis, and volatile oil prices. Given the scope of this undertaking, it is not really surprising that the authors deliver only on the theoretical part—the empirical analysis takes up only about 5 of the paper's 55 pages. Because this is a paper mainly about theory, I will devote my comments mostly to the framework the authors present, with particular emphasis on the basic assumptions made.

The paper rests on two building blocks familiar from the authors' earlier work. First, emerging market economies are increasing their demand for sound and liquid financial assets over time. Essentially, the residents of those countries want a safe store for their newfound wealth. This demand is treated by the authors entirely as a private sector phenomenon, but governments play a role because safe, liquid assets are in scarce supply. Indeed, one government alone, that of the United States, creates the Treasury instruments that are especially prized in investors' portfolios.[1] Second, fluctuations in commodity prices (or oil prices—the authors refer to both interchangeably) are explained to an important extent by speculative hoarding.

The model that the authors build to explain these features can be described succinctly. There are two regions. One, the United States, is endowed with "trees." The other, the emerging market economies, has a fixed endowment of an unspecified commodity. Only these two goods exist, and people in both regions consume both. Little trees grow at a positive rate. Commodity supplies do not grow at all. The last two assumptions imply a secular increase in the stock of trees relative to that of the commodity, so that the price of the latter rises over time.

The inconvenient fact, however, is that the actual run-up in world commodity prices relative to the prices of other goods is a very recent phenom-

1. An influential paper by Gourinchas and Hélène Rey, "From World Banker to World Venture Capitalist: US External Adjustment and the Exorbitant Privilege," Working Paper 11563 (Cambridge, Mass.: National Bureau of Economic Research, 2005), examines the consequences of this "exorbitant privilege" (a phrase that, the authors note, originated not with Charles de Gaulle, as is commonly held, but with his then-finance minister Valéry Giscard d'Estaing) whereby the United States alone is able to issue what are viewed as the safest of assets.

Figure 1. Real Commodity Prices, 1790–2007

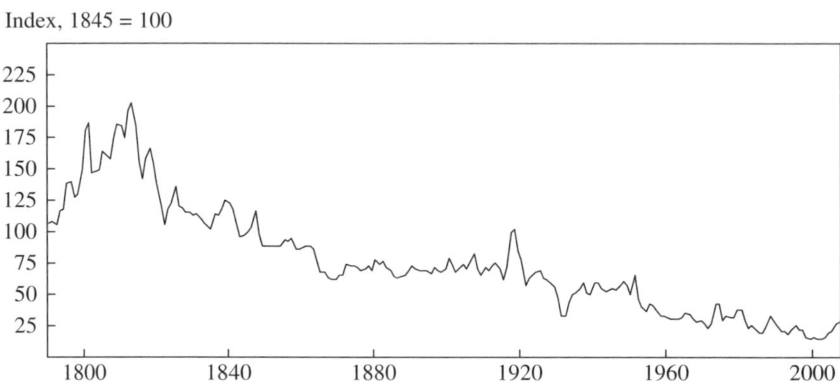

Source: Carmen M. Reinhart and Kenneth Rogoff, *This Time Is Different: Eight Centuries of Financial Folly* (Princeton University Press, forthcoming), drawing on various sources.

enon (which in recent months has abruptly unraveled). In fact, since about the turn of the eighteenth century, real commodity prices have been on a secular decline, as shown in my figure 1, taken from a recent paper I co-wrote with Kenneth Rogoff.[2] Thus, the model is broadly at odds with the big picture that emerges from this roughly two-and-a-quarter-century history. However, since this implication of the model fits well with the *cyclical* pattern of commodity prices between about 2000 and 2007 (the period the authors are most interested in explaining), I will focus my remarks on some of the core model's other simplifying assumptions that I find more problematic.

THE MODEL LACKS A FINANCIAL SECTOR. The paper purports to examine a financial crash, and the word "financial" is used liberally throughout. Dictionary.com defines "financial" as "1. pertaining to monetary receipts and expenditures; pertaining or relating to money matters; pecuniary: financial operations; 2. of or pertaining to those commonly engaged in dealing with money and credit." Thus, the authors' use of the word is difficult to reconcile with the fact that their model is a real model, with neither money, nor credit, nor financial intermediaries, nor exchange rates—in short, without a financial sector.

THE MODEL LACKS AN OFFICIAL SECTOR. Further, lacking a financial sector, the model has no scope for the stockpiling of international reserves by the

2. Carmen M. Reinhart and Kenneth Rogoff, *This Time Is Different: Eight Centuries of Financial Folly* (Princeton University Press, forthcoming).

Figure 2. Foreign Purchases of U.S. Government Securities, 1948–2008[a]

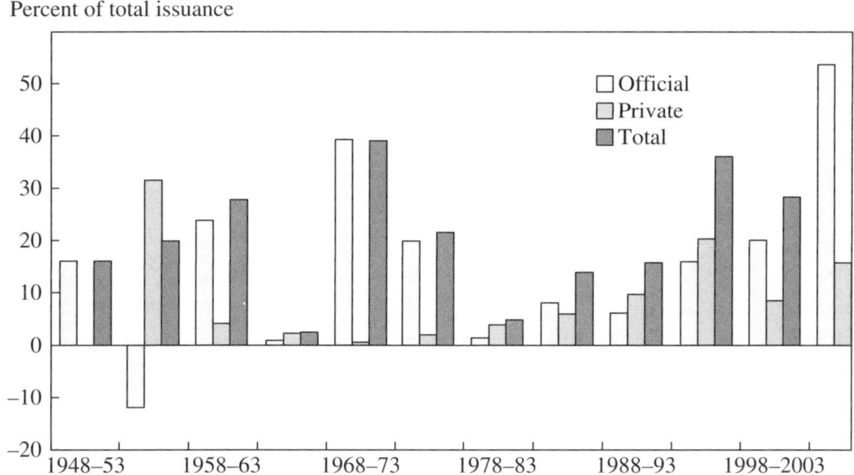

Source: Carmen M. Reinhart and Vincent Reinhart, "Is the US Too Big to Fail?" (VoxEU, 2008). www.voxeu.com/index.php?q=node/2568.

a. As reported in the Federal Reserve's Flow of Funds Accounts.

central banks of emerging market economies. Yet given that the worst financial crises of the late 1990s originated in emerging markets (followed in the next decade by crises in Argentina and Uruguay), it is worth noting that the key driver of the demand for U.S. Treasury securities *from emerging markets* has been the official sector (central banks trying to build a war chest), not the private sector as stressed in the model. Private demand for U.S. assets in the run-up to the 2007 crisis came primarily from other developed economies. The clear manifestation of the United States' "exorbitant privilege" can be seen in the fact that foreign official acquisitions of U.S. government securities have accounted for an increasing share of total issuance (figure 2).

This massive accumulation of foreign exchange reserves would seem central to understanding recent developments regarding the global imbalances between the developed economies and emerging markets—notably in Asia, as Vincent Reinhart and I have discussed elsewhere.[3] This role for the official sector is something that the authors may want to incorporate in

3. Carmen M. Reinhart and Vincent Reinhart, "Is the US Too Big to Fail?" (VoxEU, 2008). www.voxeu.com/index.php?q=node/2568.

a future variant of their framework, as it provides another important argument for one of their central premises, namely, that "safe assets" are in short supply in emerging markets.

THE DETERMINANTS OF SAVING ARE OVERSIMPLIFIED. To explain aggregate saving, the authors have to assume that it results from the birth of new generations and the return on accumulated savings. There is no role for financial liberalization (and the related issue of liquidity constraints) or wealth effects.[4] Specifically, the only way the saving rate can decrease in the model is with an increase in the death rate. How can such a model possibly explain the roughly 7-percentage-point reduction in the U.S. saving rate over the past two decades? In light of the model's emphasis on cross-border saving differentials and asset demands, revisiting this rather restrictive premise is called for.

THERE IS NO UNCERTAINTY IN THE MODEL. Lastly, there is no uncertainty in the authors' model, and thus no reason for a risk premium to exist, let alone to rise during a crisis, and the value of the nonstorable good as collateral should always be known. Hence the key event analyzed in the model is hard to reconcile with the model. We are told that a subprime shock "can be interpreted as the realization that financial instruments are less sound than they were previously perceived to be." In the absence of financial instruments and uncertainty, it is hard to imagine how such a shock would take place.

In fact, the subprime crisis as depicted in the model is an exogenous and adverse terms-of-trade shock. The structure of the model precludes overborrowing, leveraging, or excessive risk taking. Similarly ruled out are herding behavior by investors and the nonlinearities that produce self-fulfilling prophecies. Thus, absent in this framework are any of the mechanisms crucial to this or any other financial crisis. As for the key mechanism, the U.S. terms of trade, its decline began in 1999, and so it matches neither the timing nor the magnitude of the current financial crisis.

I find this an important paper that offers two key insights. The first is the importance of understanding the scarcity of safe "saving vehicles" in the emerging (and the not-so-emerging) world, and of the United States as the provider of such assets. (The stampede into U.S. Treasury securities

4. See Klaus Schmidt-Hebbel and Luis Servén, "Saving across the World: Puzzles and Policies," Discussion Paper 354 (Washington: World Bank, 1997), for cross-country evidence on these issues.

in the fall of 2008 attests to this scarcity.)[5] The second is that this scarcity is related to the commodity price dynamics of recent years. This is not, however, a framework that lends itself to explaining or understanding *financial crashes* in general. In particular, it does not add to our understanding of traditional banking crises or the problems that produced the current subprime crisis.

My preferred diagnosis of the subprime financial crisis in the United States is spelled out simply in the following quotation: "[Overindebtedness] may be started by many causes, of which the most common appears to be *new opportunities to invest at a big prospective profit* . . . such as through new inventions, new industries, development of new resources, opening of new lands or new markets. Easy money is the great cause of over-borrowing." That the essence of the problem can be captured so simply is encouraging. What is discouraging is that this insight was made by Irving Fisher in 1933.[6] Crises recur, but the best explanations are eternal.

GENERAL DISCUSSION Lawrence Summers noted that the idea is already widely accepted that high rates of saving in emerging markets have pushed real interest rates down in the rest of the world, leading to the large U.S. current account deficit and a series of market bubbles. What is of interest in the paper is its development of a coherent, consistent, and well-designed intertemporal general equilibrium model that articulates this idea. Of even greater interest is determining whether this model is the appropriate way to think about the performance of the U.S. and world economies over the past five years. The central argument in the paper is not new; it goes back to Harold Hotelling, was used by Summers himself and Robert Barsky in the 1980s to explain the behavior of gold and other commodities, and was recently used by Jeffrey Frankel in analyzing the commodities boom. The paper would be more convincing, Summers

5. See Reinhart and Reinhart, "Is the US Too Big to Fail?" on this episode: "If this had happened to any other government in the world whose national financial institutions were in as deep disarray as those of the US, investors would have run for the hills—cutting off the offending nation from global capital markets. But for the US, just the opposite has happened. Rather than facing prohibitive costs of raising funds, US Treasury Bills have seen yields *fall* in absolute terms and markedly in relative terms to the yields on private instruments. This has been called a 'flight to safety.' But why do global investors rush into a burning building at the first sign of smoke?"

6. Irving Fisher, "The Debt-Deflation Theory of Great Depressions," *Econometrica* 1, no. 4 (1933): 348 (italics in original).

argued, if it engaged more definitively with the dynamics of commodity markets. He suggested that rather than simply demonstrating the consistency of their explanation with the observed facts, the authors should place more emphasis on proving that the factors they identify are indeed the central ones in accounting for this complex phenomenon.

Bradford DeLong contended that it was reserve accumulation by central banks that had pushed real interest rates down from a dynamically efficient to a dynamically inefficient level. He admired the authors' model for its simplicity but thought it would be of even greater value if it incorporated more factors into a five- or six-dimensional system rather than the present two-dimensional system of equations. He felt that the recent behavior of foreign central banks fit with the authors' model but that the recent actions of the Federal Reserve and the Treasury with respect to the financial crisis did not. A larger, more elaborate model might do a better job.

Robert Hall suggested that the United States was experiencing not a major financial crisis but rather the popping of a huge housing bubble. He, too, praised the authors' model for the simplicity with which it modeled the bubble. He noted that monetary policy cannot deal with asset price bubbles directly but rather must provide a nominal anchor, such as an interest rate. He also wished the model were more comprehensive, in order to better address the level of U.S. saving relative to the world economy, even in situations without asset price bubbles.

Richard Cooper remarked that the authors' model is primarily about private behavior and assumes that the private sector faces a shortage of financial assets. He objected to that idea, noting that there is plenty of money, a financial asset, available, although he conceded that assets offering high yields may be in short supply. He suggested revising the model's assumptions so as to deemphasize the shortage of assets and instead focus on the excess saving that has led to low real interest rates. He suggested further that the model include the rest of the developed world, as well as the demographic factors that have contributed to a decline in investment, focusing primarily on the private sector, which accounts for the large majority of foreign investment in the United States.

Kristin Forbes complimented the authors on the richness of their model but questioned its fidelity to certain accepted stylized facts. In the model, oil supplies are somewhat elastic with respect to interest rates, but in the real world, oil supplies are not responsive to movements in interest rates since exploration and drilling take time and old wells become less productive over time. She proposed an alternative model that could explain the stylized facts in a manner consistent with the short-term inelasticity of oil supply. Like the authors' model, hers would assume that emerging markets have a limited supply of financial assets and want to invest in the United States, and that foreigners withdraw their money when a financial crisis occurs in the United States. In her model, the dollar would depreciate as a result of the withdrawal, and since oil is priced in dollars, demand for oil in foreign countries would increase, and oil prices would rise substantially. She believed her model would better explain the pattern in oil prices seen in the weeks before the conference, when a decline in oil prices followed an appreciation of the dollar.

Frederic Mishkin recommended that the authors consider the financial crisis in its historical context, particularly with respect to financial innovation. In the long run such innovation produces better and more efficient financial systems, but in the short run it can cause major problems. He believed that the massive interventions of the Federal Reserve and the Treasury had mitigated the current crisis and prevented it from becoming another Great Depression or worse.

Michael Woodford was intrigued by the paper's implication that the subprime crisis had caused the large increase in oil prices. He recommended that the authors stress the impact on oil, rather than on commodities in general, since it is unlikely that the mechanism works identically for all commodities. He wondered about the necessity of using a model based on the notion of a persistent rational bubble. He believed the model includes a structural situation where, in the absence of bubbles or inventories, the equilibrium real interest rate is lower than the growth rate, allowing for the possibility of a rational bubble that could last forever. Yet it is not necessary to invoke rational bubbles in order to explain the current financial crisis; the bubble could be an irrational one yet still have the same effects as the story told in the model.

Hélène Rey commented on the model's interesting implication regarding the adjustment of the U.S. current account deficit: in the model, the bursting of the bubble in the United States moves the current account toward balance, while at the same time rising commodity prices lead to massive wealth transfers to commodity-producing economies, which in turn reinvest part of their gains in the U.S. financial markets, thus slowing the adjustment process. Since the model is essentially a two-country model, she suggested that the authors discuss the more complex real-world situation more thoroughly elsewhere in the paper. In the recent past, the Asian economies were the United States' main creditors, but as the increase in commodity prices has transferred wealth to the commodity producers, the latter have become the major creditors. These economies tend to have different investment preferences than the Asian countries, which could affect the adjustment process—a consequence not considered in the model's benchmark case.

William Nordhaus further addressed the oil dimension. He argued that the presence of oil-related assets in a hedge fund's portfolio is evidence either of incompetence or of a bubble. In the context of the Hotelling model, the idea presented in the paper that price growth equals a risk-adjusted interest rate would not hold for a commodity unless there are zero extraction costs, zero unproduced reserves, and only one grade of the commodity. He also pointed out that hedge funds do not actually hold the underlying asset. Commenting on the increase in oil price volatility over the past forty years, he ascribed that volatility to two factors: the shift from a situation of excess supply to one of scarcity and inelastic supply, and the low short-run price elasticity of demand for crude oil. The only ways to reduce that volatility are to find a more elastic source of production or to return to a situation of excess capacity.

Christopher Carroll, citing a recent article in *The Onion* titled "Recession-Plagued Nation Demands New Bubble to Invest In," questioned the authors' choice of a limited time frame. The recent period has been characterized by a series of bubbles: the tech bubble, the linked housing and subprime bubbles, and the oil bubble. He wondered whether the authors thought the economy would ever make the transition from the present state of affairs, where low interest rates translate into bubbles, to one where they translate into higher investment in real productive capital.

KRISTOPHER GERARDI
Federal Reserve Bank of Atlanta

ANDREAS LEHNERT
Board of Governors of the Federal Reserve System

SHANE M. SHERLUND
Board of Governors of the Federal Reserve System

PAUL WILLEN
Federal Reserve Bank of Boston

Making Sense of the Subprime Crisis

ABSTRACT Should market participants have anticipated the large increase in home foreclosures in 2007 and 2008? Most of these foreclosures stemmed from mortgage loans originated in 2005 and 2006, raising suspicions that lenders originated many extremely risky loans during this period. We show that although these loans did carry extra risk factors, particularly increased leverage, reduced underwriting standards alone cannot explain the dramatic rise in foreclosures. We also investigate whether market participants underestimated the likelihood of a fall in home prices or the sensitivity of foreclosures to falling prices. We show that given available data, they should have understood that a significant price drop would raise foreclosures sharply, although loan-level (as opposed to ownership-level) models would have predicted a smaller rise than occurred. Analyst reports and other contemporary discussions reveal that analysts generally understood that falling prices would have disastrous consequences but assigned that outcome a low probability.

Had market participants anticipated the increase in defaults on subprime mortgages originated in 2005 and 2006, the nature and extent of the current financial market disruptions would be very different. Ex ante, investors in subprime mortgage-backed securities (MBSs) would have demanded higher returns and greater capital cushions. As a result, borrowers would not have found credit as cheap or as easy to obtain as it became during the subprime credit boom of those years. Rating agencies would have reacted similarly, rating a much smaller fraction of each deal investment grade. As a result, the subsequent increase in foreclosures would have been significantly smaller, with fewer attendant disruptions in the housing market, and investors would not have suffered such outsized, and unexpected, losses. To make sense of the subprime crisis, one needs to understand why, when accepting significant exposure to the creditworthiness of subprime borrowers, so many smart analysts, armed with advanced degrees, data on the past performance of subprime borrowers, and state-of-the-art modeling technology, did not anticipate that so many of the loans they were buying, either directly or indirectly, would go bad.

Our bottom line is that the problem largely had to do with expectations about home prices. Had investors known the future trajectory of home prices, they would have predicted large increases in delinquency and default and losses on subprime MBSs roughly consistent with what has occurred. We show this by using two different methods to travel back to 2005, when the subprime market was still thriving, and look forward from there. The first method is to forecast performance using only data available in 2005, and the second is to look at what market participants wrote at the time. The latter, "narrative" analysis provides strong evidence against the claim that investors lost money because they purchased loans that, because they were originated by others, could not be evaluated properly.

Our first order of business, however, is to address the more basic question of whether the subprime mortgages that defaulted were themselves unreasonable ex ante—an explanation commonly offered for the crisis. We show that the problem loans, most of which were originated in 2005 and 2006, were not that different from loans made earlier, which had performed well despite carrying a variety of serious risk factors. That said, we document that loans in the 2005–06 cohort were riskier, and we describe in detail the dimensions along which risk increased. In particular, we find that borrower leverage increased and, further, did so in a way that was relatively opaque to investors. However, we also find that the change in the mix of mortgages originated is too slight to explain the huge increase in defaults. Put simply, the average default rate on loans originated in 2006 exceeds the default rate on the riskiest category of loans originated in 2004.

We then turn to the role of the collapse in home price appreciation (HPA) that started in the spring of 2006.[1] To have invested large sums in subprime mortgages in 2005 and 2006, lenders must have expected either that HPA would remain high (or at least not collapse) or that subprime defaults would be insensitive to a big drop in HPA. More formally, letting

1. The relationship between foreclosures and HPA in the subprime crisis is well documented. See Gerardi, Shapiro, and Willen (2007), Mayer, Pence, and Sherlund (forthcoming), Demyanyk and van Hemert (2007), Doms, Furlong, and Krainer (2007), and Danis and Pennington-Cross (2005).

f represent foreclosures, *p* prices, and *t* time, we can decompose the growth in foreclosures over time, d*f*/d*t*, into a part corresponding to the sensitivity of foreclosures to price changes and a part reflecting the change in prices over time:

$$\mathrm{d}f/\mathrm{d}t = \mathrm{d}f/\mathrm{d}p \times \mathrm{d}p/\mathrm{d}t.$$

Our goal is to determine whether market participants underestimated d*f*/d*p*, the sensitivity of foreclosures to price changes, or whether d*p*/d*t*, the trajectory of home prices, came out much worse than they expected.

Our first time-travel exercise, as mentioned, uses data that were available to investors ex ante on mortgage performance, to determine whether it was possible at the time to estimate d*f*/d*p* on subprime mortgages accurately. Because severe home price declines are relatively rare and the subprime market is relatively new, one plausible theory is that the data lacked sufficient variation to allow d*f*/d*p* to be estimated in scenarios in which d*p*/d*t* is negative and large. We put ourselves in the place of analysts in 2005, using data through 2004 to estimate the type of hazard models commonly used in the industry to predict mortgage defaults. We use two datasets. The first is a loan-level dataset from First American LoanPerfomance that is used extensively in the industry to track the performance of mortgages packaged in MBSs; it has sparse information on loans originated before 1999. The second is a dataset from the Warren Group, which has tracked the fates of homebuyers in Massachusetts since the late 1980s. These data are not loan-level but rather ownership-level data; that is, the unit of observation is a homeowner's tenure in a property, which may encompass more than one mortgage loan. The Warren Group data were not (so far as we can tell) widely used by the industry but were, at least in theory, available and, unlike the loan-level data, do contain information on the behavior of homeowners in an environment of falling prices.

We find that it was possible, although not necessarily easy, to measure d*f*/d*p* with some degree of accuracy. Essentially, a researcher with perfect foresight about the trajectory of prices from 2005 forward would have forecast a large increase in foreclosures starting in 2007. Perhaps the most interesting result is that despite the absence of negative HPA in 1998–2004, when almost all subprime loans were originated, we could still determine, albeit not exactly, the likely behavior of subprime borrowers in an environment of falling home prices. In effect, the out-of-sample (and out-of-support) performance of default models was sufficiently good to have predicted large losses in such an environment.

Although it was thus possible to estimate d*f*/d*p*, we also find that the relationship was less exact when using the data on *loans* rather than the data on *ownerships*. A given borrower might refinance his or her original loan several times before defaulting. Each of these successive loans except the final one would have been seen by lenders as successful. An ownership, in contrast, terminates only when the homeowner sells and moves, or is foreclosed upon and evicted. Thus, although the same foreclosure would appear as a default in both loan-level and ownership-level data, the intermediate refinancings between purchase and foreclosure—the "happy endings"—would not appear in an ownership-level database.

Our second time-travel exercise explores what analysts of the mortgage market said in 2004, 2005, and 2006 about the loans that eventually got into trouble. Our conclusion is that investment analysts had a good sense of d*f*/d*p* and understood, with remarkable accuracy, how falling d*p*/d*t* would affect the performance of subprime mortgages and the securities backed by them. As an illustrative example, consider a 2005 analyst report published by a large investment bank:[2] analyzing a representative deal composed of 2005 vintage loans, the report argued it would face 17 percent cumulative losses in a "meltdown" scenario in which house prices fell 5 percent over the life of the deal. That analysis was prescient: the ABX index, a widely used price index of asset-backed securities, currently implies that such a deal will actually face losses of 18.3 percent over its life. The problem was that the report assigned only a 5 percent probability to the meltdown scenario, where home prices fell 5 percent, whereas it assigned probabilities of 15 percent and 50 percent to scenarios in which home prices rose 11 percent and 5 percent, respectively, over the life of the deal.

We argue that the fall in home prices outweighs other changes in driving up foreclosures in the recent period. However, we do not take a position on why prices rose so rapidly, why they fell so fast, or why they peaked in mid-2006. Other researchers have examined whether factors such as lending standards can affect home prices.[3] Broadly speaking, we maintain the assumption that although, in the aggregate, lending standards may indeed have affected home price dynamics (we are agnostic on this

2. This is the bank designated Bank B in our discussion of analyst reports below, in a report dated August 15, 2005.

3. Examples include Pavlov and Wachter (2006), Coleman, LaCour-Little, and Vandell (2008), Wheaton and Lee (2008), Wheaton and Nechayev (2008), and Sanders and others (2008).

point), no individual market participant felt that his or her actions could affect prices. Nor do we analyze whether housing was overvalued in 2005 and 2006, such that a fall in prices was to some extent predictable. There was a lively debate during that period, with some arguing that housing was reasonably valued and others that it was overvalued.[4]

Our results suggest that some borrowers were more sensitive to a single macro risk factor, namely, home prices. This comports well with the findings of David Musto and Nicholas Souleles, who argue that average default rates are only half the story: correlations across borrowers, perhaps driven by macroeconomic forces, are also an important factor in valuing portfolios of consumer loans.[5]

In this paper we focus almost exclusively on subprime mortgages. However, many of the same arguments might also apply to prime mortgages. Deborah Lucas and Robert McDonald compute the price volatility of the assets underlying securities issued by the housing-related government-sponsored enterprises (GSEs).[6] Concentrating mainly on prime and near-prime mortgages and using information on the firms' leverage and their stock prices, these authors find that risk was quite high (and, as a result, that the value of the implicit government guarantee on GSE debt was quite high).

Many have argued that a major driver of the subprime crisis was the increased use of securitization.[7] In this view, the "originate to distribute" business model of many mortgage finance companies separated the underwriter making the credit extension decision from exposure to the ultimate credit quality of the borrower, and thus created an incentive to maximize lending volume without concern for default rates. At the same time, information asymmetries, unfamiliarity with the market, or other factors prevented investors, who were accepting the credit risk, from putting in place effective controls on these incentives. Although this argument is intuitively persuasive, our results are not consistent with such an explanation. One of our key findings is that most of the uncertainty about losses stemmed from uncertainty about the future direction of home prices, not from uncertainty about the quality of the underwriting. All that said, our

4. Among the first group were Himmelberg, Mayer, and Sinai (2005) and McCarthy and Peach (2004); the pessimists included Gallin (2006, 2008) and Davis, Lehnert, and Martin (2008).

5. Musto and Souleles (2006).

6. Lucas and McDonald (2006).

7. See, for example, Keys and others (2008) and Calomiris (2008).

models do not perfectly predict the defaults that occurred, and they often underestimate the number of defaults. One possible explanation is that there was an unobservable deterioration of underwriting standards in 2005 and 2006.[8] But another is that our model of the highly nonlinear relationship between prices and foreclosures is wanting. No existing research has successfully distinguished between these two explanations.

The endogeneity of prices does present a problem for our estimation. One common theory is that foreclosures drive price declines by increasing the supply of homes for sale, in effect introducing a new term into the decomposition of df/dt, namely, dp/df. However, our estimation techniques are to a large extent robust to this issue. As discussed by Gerardi, Adam Shapiro, and Willen,[9] most of the variation in the key explanatory variable, homeowner's equity, is within-town (or, more precisely, within-metropolitan-statistical-area), within-quarter variation and thus could not be driven by differences in foreclosures over time or across towns. In fact, as we will show, one can estimate the effect of home prices on foreclosures even in periods when there were very few foreclosures, and in periods in which foreclosed properties sold quickly.

No discussion of the subprime crisis is complete without mention of the interest rate resets built into many subprime mortgages, which virtually guaranteed large increases in monthly payments. Many commentators have attributed the crisis to the payment shock associated with the first reset of subprime 2/28 adjustable-rate mortgages (these are 30-year ARMs with 2-year teaser rates). However, the evidence from loan-level data shows that resets cannot account for a significant portion of the increase in foreclosures. Christopher Mayer, Karen Pence, and Sherlund, as well as Christopher Foote and coauthors, show that the overwhelming majority of defaults on subprime ARMs occur long before the first reset.[10] In effect, many lenders would have been lucky had borrowers waited until the first reset to default.

The rest of the paper is organized as follows. We begin in the next section by documenting changes in underwriting standards on mortgages. The following section explores what researchers could have learned with the data they had in 2005. In the penultimate section we review contemporary analyst reports. The final section presents some conclusions.

8. This explanation is favored by Demyanyk and van Hemert (2007).

9. Gerardi, Shapiro, and Willen (2007).

10. Mayer, Pence, and Sherlund (forthcoming); Foote and others (2008a).

Underwriting Standards in the Subprime Market

We begin with a brief background on subprime mortgages, including a discussion of the competing definitions of "subprime." We then discuss changes in the apparent credit risk of subprime mortgages originated from 1999 to 2007, and we link those changes to the actual performance of those loans. We argue that the increased number of subprime loans that were originated with high loan-to-value (LTV) ratios was the most important observable risk factor that increased over the period. Further, we argue that the increases in leverage were to some extent masked from investors in MBSs. Loans originated with less than complete documentation of income or assets, and particularly loans originated with both high leverage and incomplete documentation, exhibited sharper subsequent rises in default rates than other loans. A more formal decomposition exercise, however, confirms that the rise in defaults can only partly be explained by observed changes in underwriting standards.

Some Background on Subprime Mortgages

One of the first notable features encountered by researchers working on subprime mortgages is the dense thicket of jargon surrounding the field, particularly the multiple competing definitions of "subprime." This hampers attempts to estimate the importance of subprime lending. There are, effectively, four useful ways to categorize a loan as subprime. First, mortgage servicers themselves recognize that certain borrowers require more frequent contact in order to ensure timely payment, and they charge higher fees to service these loans; thus, one definition of a subprime loan is one that is classified as subprime by the servicer. Second, some lenders specialize in loans to financially troubled borrowers, and the Department of Housing and Urban Development maintains a list of such lenders; loans originated by these "HUD list" lenders are often taken as a proxy for subprime loans. Third, "high-cost" loans are defined as loans that carry fees and interest rates significantly above those charged to typical borrowers. Fourth, a subprime loan is sometimes defined as any loan packaged into an MBS that is marketed as containing subprime loans.

Table 1 reports two measures of the importance of subprime lending in the United States. The first is the percent of loans in the Mortgage Bankers Association (MBA) delinquency survey that are classified as "subprime." Because the MBA surveys mortgage servicers, this measure is based on the first definition above. As the table shows, over the past few years, subprime mortgages by this definition have accounted for about 12 to

Table 1. Subprime Share of the Mortgage Market, 2004–08[a]
Percent

Period	Mortgage loans outstanding[b]	New originations[c]: Home purchases	New originations[c]: Refinancings
	Subprime loans as a share of		
2004	12.3	11.5	15.5
2005	13.4	24.6	25.7
2006	13.7	25.3	31.0
2007	12.7	14.0	21.7
2008Q2	12.2	n.a.	n.a.

Sources: Mortgage Bankers Association; Avery, Canner, and Cook (2005); Avery, Brevoort, and Canner (2006, 2007, 2008).

a. Only first liens are counted; shares are not weighted by loan value.

b. From MBA national delinquency surveys; data are as of the end of the period (end of fourth quarter except for 2008).

c. Share of loans used for the indicated purpose that were classified as "high cost" (roughly speaking, those carrying annual percentage rates at least 3 percentage points above the yield on the 30-year Treasury bond).

14 percent of outstanding mortgages. The second and third columns show the percent of loans tracked by the Federal Financial Institutions Examination Council under the Home Mortgage Disclosure Act (HMDA) that are classified as "high cost"—the third definition. In 2005 and 2006 roughly 25 percent of loan originations were subprime by this measure.[11]

These two measures point to an important discrepancy between the *stock* and the *flow* of subprime mortgages (source data and definitions also account for some of the difference). Subprime mortgages were a growing part of the mortgage market during this period, and therefore the flow of new subprime mortgages will naturally exceed their presence in the stock of outstanding mortgages. In addition, subprime mortgages, for a variety of reasons, tend not to last as long as prime mortgages, and for this reason, too, they form a larger fraction of the flow of new mortgages than of the stock of outstanding mortgages. Furthermore, until the mid-2000s most subprime mortgages were used to refinance an existing loan and, simultaneously, to increase the principal balance (thus allowing the homeowner to borrow against accumulated equity), rather than to finance the purchase of a home.

11. The high-cost measure was introduced in the HMDA data only in 2004; for operational and technical reasons, the reported share of high-cost loans in 2004 may be depressed relative to later years.

In this section we will focus on changes in the kinds of loans made over the period 1999–2007. We will use loan-level data on mortgages sold into private-label MBSs marketed as subprime. These data (known as the TrueStandings Securities ABS data) are provided by First American LoanPerformance and were widely used in the financial services industry before and during the subprime boom. We further limit the set of loans analyzed to the three most popular products: those carrying fixed interest rates to maturity and the so-called 2/28s and 3/27s. As alluded to above, a 2/28 is a 30-year mortgage in which the contract rate is fixed at an initial, teaser rate for two years; after that it adjusts to the six-month LIBOR (London interbank offer rate) plus a predetermined margin (often around 6 percentage points). A 3/27 is defined analogously. Together these three loan categories account for more than 98 percent of loans in the original data.

In this section the outcome variable of interest is whether a mortgage defaults within 12 months of its first payment due date. There are several competing definitions of "default"; here we define a mortgage as having defaulted by month 12 if, as of its 12th month of life, it had terminated following a foreclosure notice, or if the loan was listed as real estate owned by the servicer (indicating a transfer of title from the borrower), or if the loan was still active but foreclosure proceedings had been initiated, or if payments on the loan were 90 or more days past due. Note that some of the loans we count as defaults might subsequently have reverted to "current" status, if the borrower made up missed payments. In effect, any borrower who manages to make 10 of the first 12 mortgage payments, or who refinances or sells without a formal notice of default having been filed, is assumed to have *not* defaulted.

Figure 1 tracks the default rate in the ABS data under this definition from 1999 through 2006. Conceptually, default rates differ from delinquency rates in that they track the fate of mortgages originated in a given month by their 12th month of life; in effect, the default rate tracks the proportion of mortgages originated at a given point that are "dead" by month 12. Delinquency rates, by contrast, track the proportion of all active mortgages that are "sick" at a given point in calendar time. Further, because we close our dataset in December 2007, we can track the fate of only those mortgages originated through December 2006. The continued steep increase in mortgage distress is not reflected in these data, nor is the fate of mortgages originated in 2007, although we do track the underwriting characteristics of these mortgages.

Note that this measure of default is designed to allow one to compare the ex ante credit risk of various underwriting terms. It is of limited

Figure 1. Twelve-Month Default Rate on Subprime Mortgages[a]

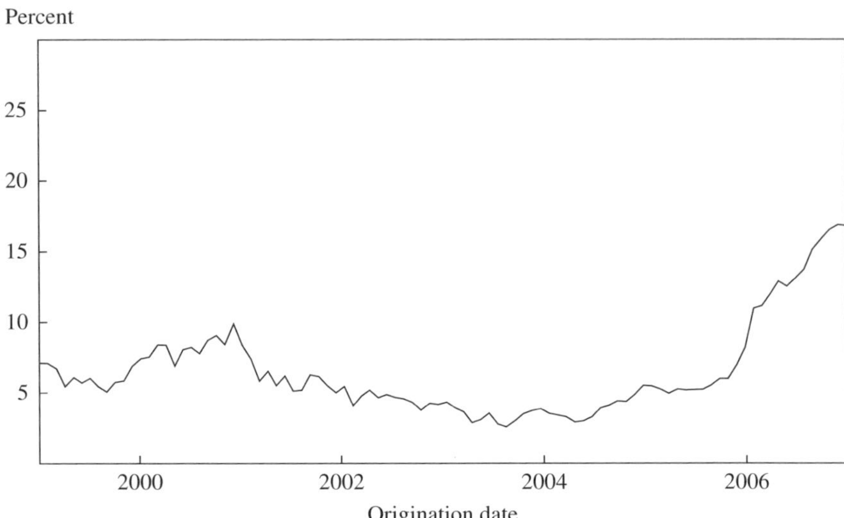

Sources: First American LoanPerformance; authors' calculations.
a. Share of all subprime mortgages originated in the indicated month that default within 12 months of origination.

usefulness as a predictor of defaults, because it considers only what happens by the 12th month of a mortgage, and it does not consider changes in the home prices, interest rates, or the overall economic environment faced by households. Further, this measure does not consider the changing incentives to refinance. The competing-risks duration models we estimate in a later section are, for these reasons, far better suited to determining the credit and prepayment outlook for a group of mortgages.

Changes in Underwriting Standards

During the credit boom, lenders published daily "rate sheets" showing, for various combinations of loan risk characteristics, the interest rates they would charge to make such loans. A simple rate sheet, for example, might be a matrix of credit scores and LTV ratios; borrowers with lower credit scores or higher LTV ratios would be charged higher interest rates or be required to pay larger fees up front. Loans for certain cells of the matrix representing combinations of low credit scores and high LTV ratios might not be available at all.

Unfortunately, we do not have access to information on changes in rate sheets over time, but underwriting standards can change in ways that are observable in the ABS data. Of course, underwriting standards can also change in ways observable to the loan originator but not reflected in the ABS data, or in ways largely unobservable even by the loan originator (for example, an increase in borrowers getting home equity lines of credit after origination). In this section we consider the evidence that more loans with ex ante observable risky characteristics were originated during the boom. Throughout we use loans from the ABS database described earlier.

We consider trends over time in borrower credit scores, loan documentation, leverage, and other factors associated with risk, such as the purpose of the loan, non-owner-occupancy, and amortization schedules. We find that from 1999 to 2007, borrower leverage, loans with incomplete documentation, loans used to purchase homes (as opposed to refinancing an existing loan), and loans with nontraditional amortization schedules all grew. Borrower credit scores increased, while loans to non-owner-occupants remained essentially flat. Of these variables, the increase in borrower leverage appears to have contributed the most to the increase in defaults, and we find some evidence that leverage was, in the ABS data at least, opaque.

CREDIT SCORES. Credit scores, which essentially summarize a borrower's history of missing debt payments, are the most obvious indicator of prime or subprime status. The most commonly used scalar credit score is the FICO score originally developed by Fair, Isaac & Co. It is the only score contained in the ABS data, although subprime lenders often used scores and other information from all three credit reporting bureaus.

Under widely accepted industry rules of thumb, borrowers with FICO scores of 680 or above are not usually considered subprime without some other accompanying risk factor, borrowers with credit scores between 620 and 680 may be considered subprime, and those with credit scores below 620 are rarely eligible for prime loans. Subprime pricing models typically used more information than just a borrower's credit score; they also considered the nature of the missed payment that led a borrower to have a low credit score. For example, a pricing system might weight missed mortgage payments more than missed credit card payments.

Figure 2 shows the proportions of newly originated subprime loans falling into each of these three categories. The proportion of such loans to borrowers with FICO scores of 680 and above grew over the sample period, while loans to traditionally subprime borrowers (those with scores below 620) accounted for a smaller share of originations.

LOAN DOCUMENTATION. Borrowers (or their mortgage brokers) submit a file with each mortgage application documenting the borrower's income,

Figure 2. Distribution of Subprime Mortgages by FICO Score at Origination

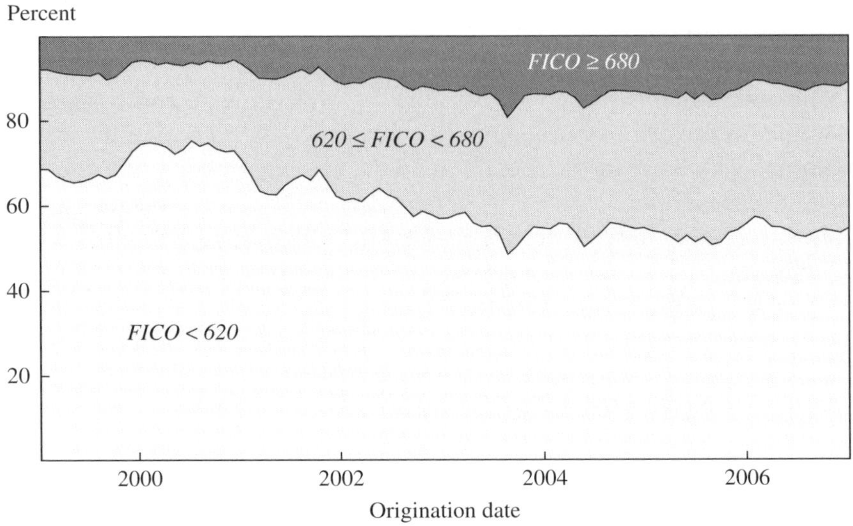

Sources: First American LoanPerformance; authors' calculations.

liquid assets, and other debts, and the value of the property being used as collateral. Media attention has focused on the rise of so-called low-doc or no-doc loans, for which documentation of income or assets was incomplete. (These include the infamous "stated-income" loans.) The top left panel of figure 3 shows that the proportion of newly originated subprime loans carrying less than full documentation rose from around 20 percent in 1999 to a high of more than 35 percent by mid-2006. Thus, although reduced-documentation lending was a part of subprime lending, it was by no means the majority of the business, nor did it increase dramatically during the credit boom.

As we discuss in greater detail below, until about 2004, subprime loans were generally backed by substantial equity in the property. This was especially true for subprime loans with less than complete documentation. Thus, in some sense the lender accepted less complete documentation in exchange for a greater security interest in the underlying property.

LEVERAGE. The leverage of a property is, in principle, the total value of all liens on the property divided by its value. This is often referred to as the property's combined loan-to-value, or CLTV, ratio. Both the numerator and the denominator of the CLTV ratio will fluctuate over a borrower's tenure in the property: the borrower may amortize the original loan, refi-

Figure 3. Shares of Subprime Mortgages with Various Risk Factors

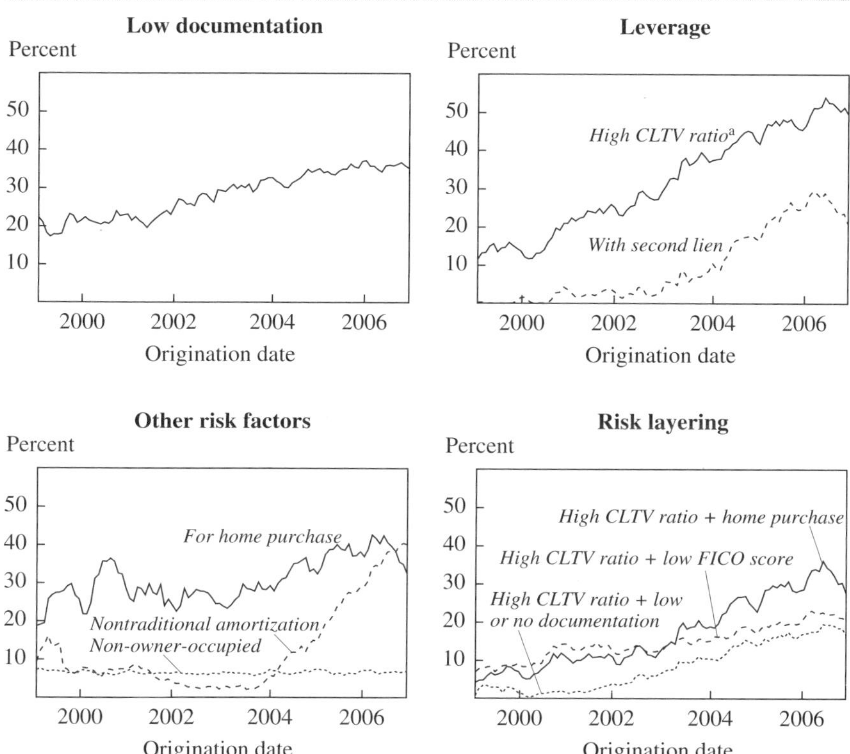

Sources: First American LoanPerformance; authors' calculations.
a. CLTV ratio ≥ 90 percent or including a junior lien.

nance, or take on junior liens, and the potential sale price of the home will change over time. However, the current values of all of these variables ought to be known at the time of a loan's origination. The lender undertakes a title search to check for the presence of other liens and hires an appraiser to confirm either the price paid (when the loan is used to purchase a home) or the potential sale price of the property (when the loan is used to refinance an existing loan).

In practice, high leverage during the boom was also accompanied by additional complications and opacity. Rather than originate a single loan for the desired amount, originators often preferred to originate two loans: one for 80 percent of the property's value, and the other for the remaining desired loan balance. In the event of a default, the holder of the first lien would be paid first from the sale proceeds, with the junior lien holder getting the remaining proceeds, if any. Lenders may have split loans in this way for the same reason that asset-backed securities are tranched into an AAA-rated piece and a below-investment-grade piece. Some investors might specialize in credit risk evaluation and hence prefer the riskier piece, while others might prefer to forgo credit analysis and purchase the less risky loan.

The reporting of these junior liens in the ABS data appears spotty. This could be the case if, for example, the junior lien was originated by a different lender than the first lien, because the first-lien lender might not properly report the second lien, and the second lien lender might not report the loan at all. If the junior lien was an open-ended loan, such as a home equity line of credit, it appears not to have been reported in the ABS data at all, perhaps because the amount drawn was unknown at origination.

Further, there is no comprehensive national system for tracking liens on any given property. Thus, homeowners could take out a second lien shortly after purchasing or refinancing, raising their CLTV ratio. Although such borrowing should not affect the original lender's recovery, it does increase the probability of a default and thus lowers the value of the original loan.

The top right panel of figure 3 shows the growth in the number of loans originated with high CLTV ratios (defined as those with CLTV ratios of 90 percent or more or including a junior lien); the panel also shows the proportion of loans originated for which a junior lien was recorded.[12] Both measures of leverage rose sharply over the past decade. High-CLTV-ratio lending accounted for roughly 10 percent of originations in 2000, rising to over 50 percent by 2006. The incidence of junior liens also rose.

The presence of a junior lien has a powerful effect on the CLTV ratio of the first lien. As table 2 shows, loans without a second lien reported an average CLTV ratio of 79.9 percent, whereas those with a second lien reported an average CLTV ratio of 98.8 percent. Moreover, loans with reported CLTV ratios of 90 percent or above were much likelier to have associated junior liens, suggesting that lenders were leery of originating single mortgages with LTV ratios greater than 90 percent. We will discuss later the evidence that there was even more leverage than reported in the ABS data.

OTHER RISK FACTORS. A variety of other loan and borrower characteristics could have contributed to increased risk. The bottom left panel of

12. The figures shown here and elsewhere are based on first liens only; where there is an associated junior lien, that information is used in computing the CLTV ratio and for other purposes, but the junior loan itself is not counted.

Table 2. Distribution of New Originations by Combined Loan-to-Value Ratio, 2004–08
Percent

CLTV ratio	*Without second lien*	*With second lien*
Less than 80 percent	35	1
Exactly 80 percent	18	0
Between 80 and 90 percent	18	1
Exactly 90 percent	15	1
Between 90 and 100 percent	8	16
100 percent or greater	5	80
Memorandum: average CLTV ratio	79.92	98.84

Sources: First American LoanPeformance; authors' calculations.

figure 3 shows the proportions of subprime loans originated with a nontraditional amortization schedule, to non-owner-occupiers, and to borrowers who used the loan to purchase a property (as opposed to refinancing an existing loan).

A standard or "traditional" U.S. mortgage self-amortizes; that is, a portion of each month's payment is used to reduce the principal. As the bottom left panel of figure 3 shows, nontraditional amortization schedules became increasingly popular among subprime loans. These were mainly loans that did not require sufficient principal payments (at least in the early years of the loan) to amortize the loan completely over its 30-year term. Thus, some loans had interest-only periods, and others were amortized over 40 years, with a balloon payment due at the end of the 30-year term. The effect of these terms was to slightly lower the monthly payment, especially in the early years of the loan.

Subprime loans had traditionally been used to refinance an existing loan. As the bottom left panel of figure 3 also shows, subprime loans used to purchase homes also increased over the period, although not dramatically. Loans to non-owner-occupiers, which include loans backed by a property held for investment purposes, are, all else equal, riskier than loans to owner-occupiers because the borrower can default without facing eviction from his or her primary residence. As the figure shows, such loans never accounted for a large fraction of subprime originations, nor did they grow over the period.

RISK LAYERING. As we discuss below, leverage is a key risk factor for subprime mortgages. An interesting question is the extent to which high leverage was combined with other risk factors in a single loan; this practice was sometimes known as "risk layering." As the bottom right panel of figure 3 shows, risk layering grew over the sample period. Loans with incomplete documentation *and* high leverage had an especially notable rise, from essentially zero in 2001 to almost 20 percent of subprime originations by the end of 2006. Highly leveraged loans to borrowers purchasing homes also increased over the period.

Effect on Default Rates

We now consider the performance of loans with the various risk factors just outlined. We start with simple univariate descriptions before turning to a more formal decomposition exercise. We continue here to focus on 12-month default rates as the outcome of interest. In the next section we present results from dynamic models that consider the ability of borrowers to refinance as well as default.

DOCUMENTATION LEVEL. The top left panel of figure 4 shows default rates over time for loans with complete and those with incomplete documentation. The two loan types performed roughly in line with one another until the current cycle, when default rates on loans with incomplete documentation rose far more rapidly than default rates on loans with complete documentation.

LEVERAGE. The top right panel of figure 4 shows default rates on loans with and without high CLTV ratios (defined, again, as those with a CLTV ratio of at least 90 percent *or* with a junior lien present at origination). Again, loans with high leverage performed approximately in line with other loans until the most recent episode.

As we highlighted above, leverage is often opaque. To dig deeper into the correlation between leverage at origination and subsequent performance, we estimated a pair of simple regressions relating the CLTV ratio at origination to the subsequent probability of default and to the initial contract interest rate charged to the borrower. For all loans in the sample, we estimated a probit model of default and an ordinary least squares (OLS) model of the initial contract rate. Explanatory variables were various measures of leverage, including indicator (dummy) variables for various ranges of the reported CLTV ratio (one of which is for a CLTV ratio of *exactly* 80 percent) as well as for the presence of a second lien. We estimated two versions of each model: version 1 contains only the CLTV ratio measures, the second-lien indicator, and (in the default regressions) the initial contract rate; version 2 adds state and origination date fixed effects. These regressions are designed purely to highlight the correlation among variables of interest and not as fully fledged risk models. Version 1 can be thought of as the simple multivariate correlation across the entire sample, whereas version 2 compares loans originated in the same state at the

Figure 4. Twelve-Month Default Rates of Mortgages with Selected Characteristics

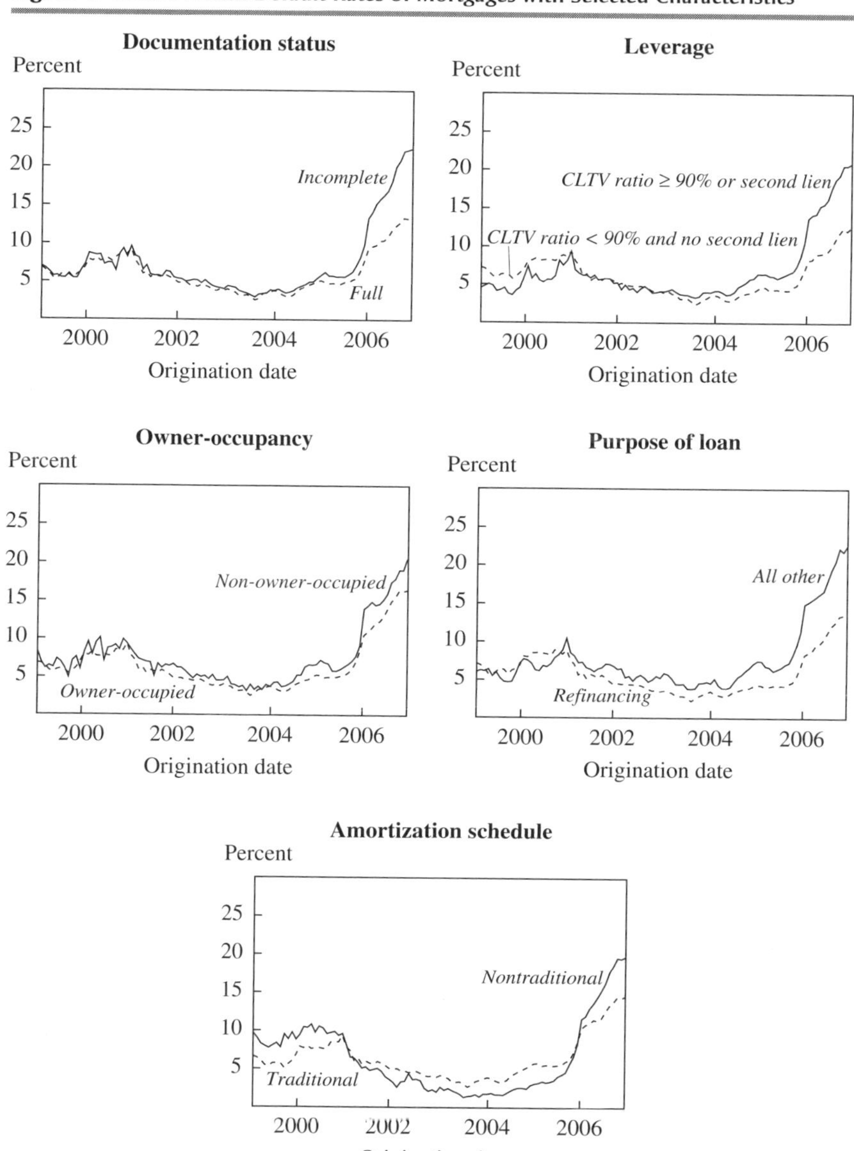

Sources: First American LoanPerformance; authors' calculations.

Table 3. Regressions Estimating the Effect of Leverage on Default Probability and Mortgage Interest Rates

Independent variable	*Marginal effect on probability of default within 12 months of origination*[a] *Version 1*	*Version 2*	*Marginal effect on initial contract interest rate*[b] *Version 1*	*Version 2*	*Variable mean*[c]
Constant			7.9825	10.4713	
CLTV ratio (percent)	0.00219	0.00223	0.0093	0.0083	82.6929
$CLTV^2/100$	–0.00103	–0.00103	–0.0063	–0.0082	70.3912
Initial contract interest rate (percent a year)	0.01940	0.02355			8.2037
Indicator variables					
CLTV ratio = 80 percent	0.00961	0.01036	–0.0127	–0.0817	15.72
CLTV ratio between 80 and 90 percent	0.00014	–0.00302	0.0430	0.1106	15.56
CLTV ratio = 90 percent	0.00724	–0.00041	0.1037	0.2266	12.86
CLTV ratio between 90 and 100 percent	0.00368	–0.00734	0.0202	0.3258	9.68
CLTV ratio 100 percent or greater	0.00901	–0.00740	0.0158	0.3777	16.20
Second lien recorded	0.05262	0.04500	–0.8522	–0.6491	14.52
Regression includes origination date effects	No	Yes	No	Yes	
Regression includes state effects	No	Yes	No	Yes	
No. of observations[d]	679,518	679,518	707,823	707,823	
Memorandum: mean default rate (percent)					6.55

Source: Authors' regressions.

a. Results are from a probit regression in which the dependent variable is an indicator equal to 1 when the mortgage has defaulted by its 12th month.

b. Results are from an ordinary least squares regression in which the dependent variable is the original contract interest rate on the mortgage.

c. Values for indicator variables are percent of the total sample for which the variable equals 1.

d. Sample is a 10 percent random sample of the ABS data.

same time. The results are shown in table 3; using the results from version 2, figure 5 plots the expected default probability against the CLTV ratio for loans originated in California in June 2005.

As the figure shows, default probabilities generally increase with leverage. Note, however, that loans with reported CLTV ratios of exactly 80 percent, which account for 15.7 percent of subprime loans, have a sub-

Figure 5. Effect of CLTV Ratio on Default Probability and Initial Interest Rate[a]

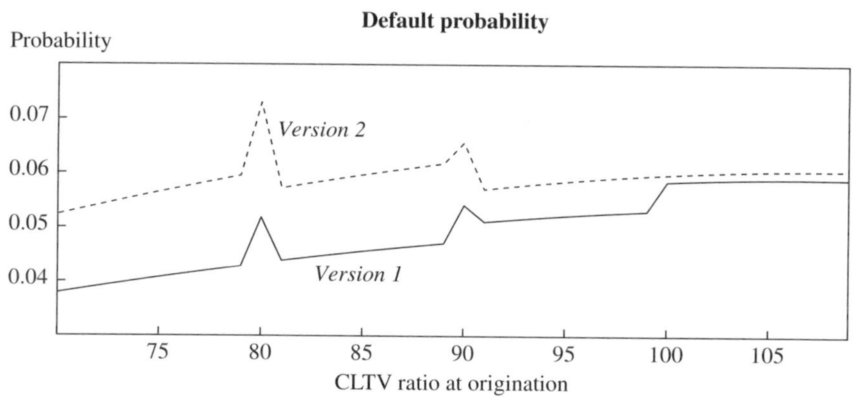

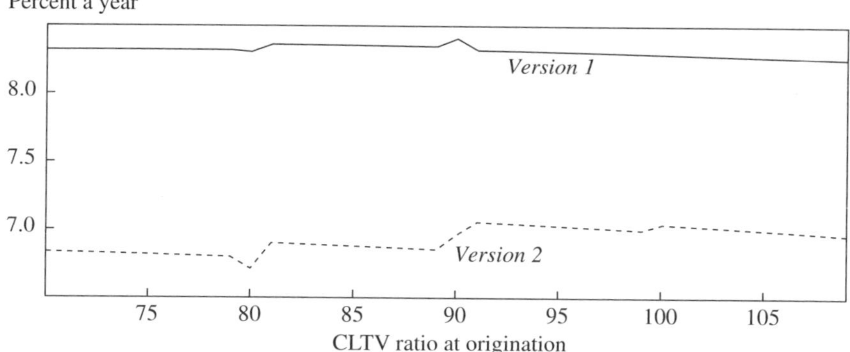

Sources: First American LoanPerformance; authors' calculations.
a. Estimation results of model versions 1 and 2 are reported in table 3.

stantially higher default probability than loans with slightly higher or lower CLTV ratios. Indeed, under version 2 such loans are among the riskiest originated. As the bottom panel of figure 5 shows, however, there is no compensating increase in the initial contract rate charged to the borrower, although the lender may have charged points and fees up front (not measured in this dataset) to compensate for the increased risk. This evidence suggests that borrowers with apparently reasonable CLTV ratios were in fact using junior liens to increase their leverage in a way that was neither easily visible to investors nor, apparently, compensated by higher mortgage interest rates.

OTHER RISK FACTORS. The bottom three panels of figure 4 show the default rates associated with the three other risk factors described earlier: non-owner-occupancy, loan purpose, and nontraditional amortization schedules. Loans to non-owner-occupiers were not (in this sample) markedly riskier than loans to owner-occupiers. The 12-month default rates on loans originated from 1999 to 2004 varied little between those originated for home purchase and those originated for refinancing, and between those carrying traditional and nontraditional amortization schedules. However, among loans originated in 2005 and 2006, purchase loans and loans with nontraditional amortization schedules defaulted at much higher rates than did refinancings and traditionally amortizing loans, respectively.

RISK LAYERING. Figure 6 shows the default rates on loans carrying the multiple risk factors discussed earlier. As the top panel shows, loans with high CLTV ratios *and* low FICO scores have nearly always defaulted at higher rates than other loans. High-CLTV-ratio loans that were used to purchase homes also had a worse track record (middle panel). In both cases, default rates for high-CLTV-ratio loans climbed sharply over the last two years of the sample. Loans with high CLTV ratios and incomplete documentation (bottom panel), however, showed the sharpest increase in defaults relative to other loans. This suggests that within the group of high-leverage loans, those with incomplete documentation were particularly prone to default.

Decomposing the Increase in Defaults

As figure 1 showed, subprime loans originated in 2005 and 2006 defaulted at a much higher rate than those originated earlier in the sample. The previous discussion suggests that this increase is not related to observable underwriting factors. For example, high-CLTV-ratio loans originated in 2002 defaulted at about the same rate as other loans originated that same year. However, high-CLTV-ratio loans originated in 2006 defaulted at much higher rates than other loans.

Decomposing the increase in defaults into a piece due to the mix of types of loans originated and a piece due to changes in home prices requires data on how all loan types behave under a wide range of price scenarios. If the loans originated in 2006 were truly novel, there would be no unique decomposition between home prices and underwriting standards. We showed that at least some of the riskiest loan types were being originated (albeit in low numbers) by 2004.

To test this idea more formally, we divide the sample into two groups: an "early" group of loans originated in 1999–2004, and a "late" group

Figure 6. Twelve-Month Default Rates on Mortgages with Risk Layering

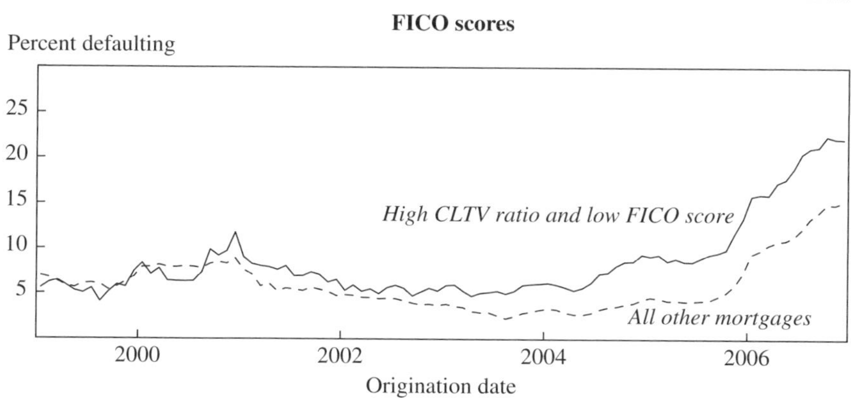

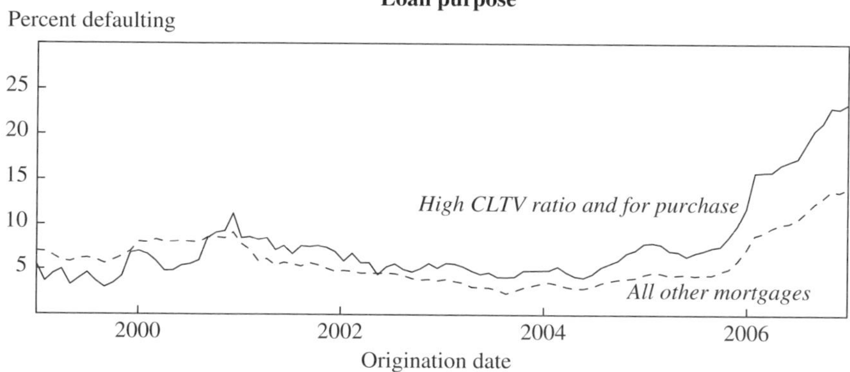

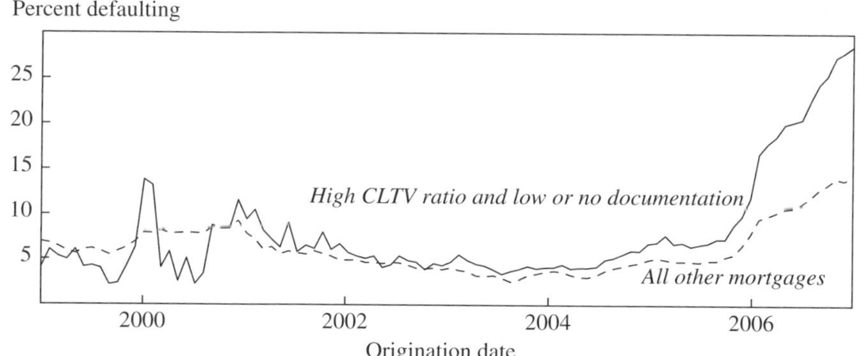

Sources: First American LoanPerformance; authors' calculations.

originated in 2005 and 2006. We estimate default models separately on each group, and we track changes in risk factors over the entire period. We then measure the changes in risk factors between the two groups and the changes in the coefficients of the risk model. We find that increases in high-leverage lending and risk layering can account for some, but by no means all, of the increase in defaults.

Table 4 reports the means of the relevant variables for the two groups and for the entire sample. The table shows that a much larger fraction of loans originated in the late group defaulted: 9.28 percent as opposed to 4.60 percent in the early group. The differences between the two groups on other risk factors are in line with the earlier discussion: FICO scores, CLTV ratios, the incidence of 2/28s, low-documentation loans, and loans with nontraditional amortization all rose from the early group to the late group, while the share of loans for refinancing fell (implying that the share for home purchase rose).

Table 5 reports the results of a loan-level probit model of the probability of default, estimated using data from the early group and the late group. The table shows marginal effects and standard errors for a number of loan and borrower characteristics; the model also includes a set of state fixed effects (results not reported). The differences in estimated marginal effects between the early and the late group are striking. Defaults are more sensitive in the late group to a variety of risk factors, such as leverage, credit score, loan purpose, and type of amortization schedule. The slopes in table 5 correspond roughly to the returns in a Blinder-Oaxaca decomposition, whereas the sample means in table 4 correspond to the differences in endowments between the two groups. However, because the underlying model is nonlinear, we cannot perform the familiar Blinder-Oaxaca decomposition.

As a first step toward our decomposition, table 6 reports the predicted default rate in the late group using the model estimated on data from the early group, as well as other combinations. Using early-group coefficients on the early group of loans, the model predicts a 4.60 percent default rate. Using the same coefficients on the late-group data, the model predicts a 4.55 percent default rate. Thus, the early-group model does not predict a significant rise in defaults based on the observable characteristics for the late group. These results are consistent with the view that a factor other than underwriting changes was primarily responsible for the increase in mortgage defaults. However, because these results mix changes in the distribution of risk factors between the two groups as well as changes in the riskiness of certain characteristics, it will be useful to consider the increase

Table 4. Summary Statistics for Variables from the ABS Data

Percent of total except where stated otherwise

	All mortgages		*Early group*[a]		*Late group*[b]	
Variable	*Mean*	*Standard deviation*	*Mean*	*Standard deviation*	*Mean*	*Standard deviation*
Outcome 12 months after origination						
Defaulted	6.57	24.78	4.60	20.95	9.28	29.01
Refinanced	16.22	36.86	15.96	36.63	16.57	37.18
Mortgage characteristics						
Contract interest rate (percent a year)	8.21	1.59	8.38	1.76	7.97	1.27
Margin over LIBOR (percentage points)	4.45	2.94	4.28	3.11	4.69	2.67
FICO score	610	60	607	61	615	58
CLTV ratio (percent)	83	14	81	14	85	15
Mortgage type						
Fixed rate	28.14	44.97	32.30	46.76	22.43	41.71
2/28[c]	58.54	49.27	53.40	49.88	65.58	47.51
3/27	13.33	33.99	14.30	35.01	11.99	32.48
Documentation status						
Complete	68.28	46.54	70.62	45.55	65.07	47.68
No documentation	0.31	5.58	0.38	6.12	0.23	4.75
Low documentation	30.71	46.13	27.82	44.81	34.68	47.60

(continued)

Table 4. Summary Statistics for Variables from the ABS Data (*Continued*)

Percent of total except where stated otherwise

	All mortgages		*Early group*[a]		*Late group*[b]	
Variable	*Mean*	*Standard deviation*	*Mean*	*Standard deviation*	*Mean*	*Standard deviation*
Other						
Nontraditional amortization[d]	16.04	36.69	6.93	25.40	28.53	45.15
Non-owner-occupied	6.57	24.78	6.51	24.68	6.66	24.93
Refinancing	67.00	47.02	70.95	45.40	61.58	48.64
Second lien present	14.59	35.30	7.50	26.34	24.32	42.90
Prepayment penalty	73.55	44.11	74.00	43.87	72.93	44.43
No. of observations	3,532,525		2,043,354		1,489,171	

Sources: First American LoanPeformance; authors' calculations.

a. Mortgages originated from 1999 to 2004.

b. Mortgages originated in 2005 and 2006.

c. A 30-year mortgage with a low initial ("teaser") rate in the first two years; a 3/27 is defined analogously.

d. Any mortgage that does not completely amortize or that does not amortize at a constant rate.

Table 5. Probit Regressions Estimating the Effect of Loan and Other Characteristics on Default Probability[a]

	Early group (1999–2004 originations)		*Late group (2005–06 originations)*	
Variable	*Marginal effect*	*Standard error*	*Marginal effect*	*Standard error*
Contract interest rate (percent a year)	0.0097	0.0001	0.0328	0.0002
Margin over LIBOR (percentage points)	0.0013	0.0001	0.0016	0.0003
Loan is a 2/28	0.0036	0.0009	0.0158	0.0016
Loan is a 3/27	0.0030	0.0010	0.0105	0.0020
CLTV ratio	0.0007	0.0001	0.0037	0.0002
$CLTV^2/100$	−0.0002	0.0001	−0.0018	0.0002
CLTV ratio = 80 percent	0.0035	0.0005	0.0225	0.0012
80 percent < CLTV ratio < 90 percent	−0.0017	0.0006	0.0119	0.0014
90 percent ≤ CLTV ratio < 100 percent	−0.0014	0.0008	0.0154	0.0022
CLTV ratio ≥ 100 percent	−0.0000	0.0015	0.0229	0.0029
Second lien present	0.0165	0.0008	0.0391	0.0009
FICO score	−0.0003	0.0000	−0.0003	0.0000
FICO < 620	−0.0015	0.0008	0.0202	0.0015
FICO = 620	−0.0012	0.0016	0.0194	0.0031
620 < FICO < 680	−0.0040	0.0006	0.0110	0.0010
High CLTV ratio and low FICO	−0.0004	0.0006	0.0013	0.0010
High CLTV ratio and purchase	0.0053	0.0006	−0.0143	0.0010
High CLTV ratio and low documentation	0.0059	0.0007	0.0129	0.0010
Loan is a refinancing	−0.0064	0.0004	−0.0223	0.0009
Non-owner-occupied	0.0113	0.0006	0.0158	0.0010
Low documentation	0.0127	0.0004	0.0160	0.0007
No documentation	0.0107	0.0027	0.0293	0.0059
Prepayment penalty	0.0012	0.0003	0.0087	0.0006
Payment-to-income ratio 1[b]	0.0003	0.0000	0.0008	0.0000
Payment-to-income ratio 2	0.0008	0.0008	0.0008	0.0001
Ratio 1 missing	0.0131	0.0007	0.0330	0.0014
Ratio 2 missing	0.0240	0.0006	0.0273	0.0017
Loan is from a retail lender	0.0036	0.0005	−0.0204	0.0012
Loan is from a wholesale lender	0.0050	0.0004	0.0044	0.0009
Loan is from a mortgage broker	0.0011	0.0011	−0.0055	0.0019
Nontraditional amortization	0.0043	0.0005	0.0218	0.0006
No. of observations	2,043,354		1,489,171	
Pseudo-R^2	0.0929		0.0971	

Source: Authors' regressions.

a. The dependent variable is the probability of default after 12 months. All regressions include a complete set of state fixed effects.

b. Ratios 1 and 2 are back- and front-end debt-to-income ratios, respectively.

Table 6. Predicted Default Rates
Percent

Data used in estimation	Default probability using model estimated on data from: Early period (1999–2004)	Late period (2005–06)
Early period	4.60	9.30
Late period	4.55	9.27
Origination year		
1999	6.66	15.37
2000	8.67	20.00
2001	6.52	14.34
2002	4.83	9.86
2003	3.49	6.42
2004	3.44	6.05
2005	3.96	7.50
2006	5.31	11.55

Source: Authors' calculations.

in riskiness of a typical loan after varying a few characteristics in turn. Again, because of the nonlinearity of the underlying model, we have to consider just one set of observable characteristics at a time.

To this end, we consider a typical 2/28 loan originated in California with observable characteristics set to their early-period sample means. We change each risk characteristic in turn to its late-period sample mean or to a value suggested by the experience in the late period. Table 7 shows that even for loans with the worst combination of underwriting characteristics, the predicted default rate is less than half the actual default rate experienced by this group of loans. The greatest increases in default probability are associated with higher-leverage scenarios. (Note that decreasing the CLTV ratio to exactly 80 percent increases the default probability, for reasons discussed earlier.)

What Can We Learn from the 2005 Data?

In this section we focus on whether market participants could reasonably have estimated the sensitivity of foreclosures to home price decreases. We estimate standard competing-risks duration models using data on the performance of loans originated through the end of 2004—presumably the information set available to lenders as they were making decisions about loans originated in 2005 and 2006. We produce out-of-sample forecasts of foreclosures assuming the home price outcomes that the economy actually experienced. Later we address the question of what home price expecta-

Table 7. Effects of Selected Mortgage Characteristics on Default Probability for a Generic 2/28 Mortgage
Percent

Loan characteristics	*Estimated 12-month default probability*[a]
Base case[b]	1.96
Base case except:	
CLTV ratio = 80 percent	2.28
High CLTV ratio (= 99.23 percent, with second lien)	3.76
Low FICO score (FICO = 573)	2.47
Low documentation	2.88
Nontraditional amortization	1.96
Home purchase	2.41
High CLTV ratio *and* low documentation	6.17
High CLTV ratio *and* low FICO score	3.76
High CLTV ratio *and* home purchase	5.22

Source: Authors' calculations.

a. Calculated using the model estimated from early-period (1999–2004) data.

b. The base case is a 2/28 mortgage originated in California for the purpose of refinancing and carrying an initial annual interest rate of 8.22 percent (and a margin over LIBOR of 6.22 percent), with a CLTV ratio of 81.3, a FICO score of 600, complete documentation, no second lien, and traditional amortization. Mortgages with these characteristics experienced an actual default probability of 11.36 percent. Each of the remaining cases differs from the base case only with respect to the characteristic(s) indicated. Values chosen for these characteristics are late-period (2005–06) sample means or otherwise suggested by the experience in that period.

tions investors had, but here we assume that market participants had perfect foresight about future HPA.

In conducting our forecasts, we use two primary data sources. The first is the ABS data discussed above. These data are national in scope and have been widely used by mortgage analysts to model both prepayment and default behavior in the subprime mortgage market, so it is not unreasonable to use these data as an approximation of market participants' information set. The second source of data is publicly available, individual-level data on both housing and mortgage transactions in the state of Massachusetts, from county-level registry of deeds offices. Although these data are not national in scope and lack the level of detail on mortgage and borrower characteristics that the ABS data have, their historical coverage is far superior. The deed registry data extend back to the early 1990s, a period in which the Northeast experienced a significant housing downturn. In contrast, the ABS data have very sparse coverage before 2000, as the non-agency, subprime MBS market did not become relevant until the turn of the century. Hence, for the vast majority of the period covered by the ABS data, the economy was in the midst of a significant housing boom. In the next section we discuss the potential implications of this data limitation for predicting mortgage defaults and foreclosures.

The Relationship between Housing Equity and Foreclosure

For a homeowner with positive equity who needs to terminate his or her mortgage, a strategy of either refinancing the mortgage or selling the home dominates defaulting and allowing foreclosure to occur. However, for an "underwater" homeowner (that is, one with negative equity, where the mortgage balance exceeds the home's market value), default and foreclosure are sometimes the optimal economic decision.[13] Thus, the theoretical relationship between equity and foreclosure is not linear. Rather, the sensitivity of default to equity should be approximately zero for positive values of equity, but negative for negative values. These observations imply that the relationship between housing prices and foreclosure is highly sensitive to the housing cycle. In a home price boom, even borrowers in extreme financial distress have more appealing options than foreclosure, because home price gains are expected to result in positive equity. However, when home prices are falling, highly leveraged borrowers will often find themselves in a position of negative equity, which implies fewer options for those experiencing financial distress.

As a result, estimating the empirical relationship between home prices and foreclosures requires, in principle, data that span a home price bust as well as a boom. In addition, analysts using loan-level data must account for the fact that even as foreclosures *rise* in a home price bust, prepayments will also *fall.*

Given that the ABS data do not contain a home price bust through the end of 2004, and that, as loan-level data, they could not track the experience of an individual borrower across many loans, we expect (and find) that models estimated using the ABS data through 2004 have a harder time predicting foreclosures in 2007 and 2008.

Forecasts Using the ABS Data

As described earlier, the ABS data are loan-level data that track mortgages held in securitized pools marketed as either alt-A or subprime. We restrict our attention to first-lien, 30-year subprime mortgages originated from 2000 to 2007.

A key difference between the model we estimate in this section and the decomposition exercise above is in the definitions of "default" and "pre-

13. See Foote and others (2008a) for a more detailed discussion.

payment." The data track the performance of these mortgages over time. Delinquency status (current, 30 days late, 60 days late, 90 days or more late, or in foreclosure) is recorded monthly for active loans. The data also differentiate between different types of mortgage termination: by foreclosure or by prepayment without a notice of foreclosure. Here we define a default as a mortgage that terminates after a notice of foreclosure has been served, and a prepayment as a mortgage that terminates without such a notice (presumably through refinancing or sale of the home). Thus, loans can cycle through various delinquency stages and can even have a notice of default served, but whether they are classed as happy endings (prepayments) or unhappy endings (defaults) will depend on their status at termination.

To model default and prepayment behavior, we augment the ABS data with metropolitan-area-level home price data from S&P/Case-Shiller, where available, and state-level house price data from the Office of Federal Housing Enterprise Oversight (OFHEO) otherwise. These data are used to construct mark-to-market CLTV ratios and measures of home price volatility. Further, we augment the data with state-level unemployment rates, monthly oil prices, and various interest rates to capture other pressures on household balance sheets. Finally, we include zip code-level data on average household income, share of minority households, share of households with a high school education or less, and the child share of the population, all from the Census Bureau.

EMPIRICAL MODEL. We now use the ABS data to estimate what an analyst with perfect foresight about home prices, interest rates, oil prices, and other variables would have predicted for prepayment and foreclosures in 2005–07, given information on mortgage performance available at the end of 2004. We estimate a competing-risks model over 2000–04 and simulate mortgage defaults and prepayments over 2005–07. The baseline hazard functions for prepayment and default are assumed to follow the Public Securities Association (PSA) guidelines, which are fairly standard in the mortgage industry.[14]

Factors that can affect prepayment and default include mortgage and borrower characteristics at loan origination, such as CLTV and payment-to-income ratios, the contractual mortgage interest rate, the borrower's credit score, the completeness of loan documentation, and occupancy status. We also include whether the loan has any prepayment penalties, interest-only features, or piggybacking; whether it is a refinancing or a purchase; and the type of property. Further, we include indicator variables to

14. For the specific forms of the PSA guidelines, see Sherlund (2008).

identify loans with risk layering of high leverage and poor documentation, loans to borrowers with credit scores below 600, and an interaction term between occupancy status and cumulative HPA over the life of the mortgage.

Similarly, we include dynamically updated mortgage and borrower characteristics that vary from month to month *after* loan origination. The most important of these is an estimate of the mark-to-market CLTV ratio; changes in home prices will primarily affect default and prepayment rates through this variable. In addition, we include the current contract interest rate, home price volatility, state-level unemployment rates, oil prices, and, for ARMs, the fully indexed mortgage interest rate (six-month LIBOR plus the loan margin).

Because of the focus on payment changes, we include three indicator variables to capture the effects of interest rate resets. The first is set to unity in the three months around (one month before, the month of, and the month after) the first reset. The second captures whether the loan has passed its first reset date. The third identifies changes in the monthly mortgage payment of more than 5 percent from the original monthly payment, to capture any large payment shocks. Variable names and definitions for our models using the ABS data are reported in table 8, and summary statistics in table 9.

ESTIMATION STRATEGY AND RESULTS. We estimate a competing-risks, proportional hazard model for six subsamples of our data. First, the data are broken down by subprime product type: hybrid 2/28s, hybrid 3/27s, and fixed-rate mortgages. Second, for each product type, estimation is carried out separately for purchase mortgages and refinancings.

Table 10 reports the estimation results for the default hazard functions.[15] These results are similar to those previously reported by Sherlund.[16] As one would expect, home prices (acting through the mark-to-market CLTV ratio term) are extremely important. In addition, non-owner-occupiers are, all else equal, likelier to default. The payment shock and reset window variables have relatively small effects, possibly because so many subprime borrowers defaulted in 2006 and 2007 ahead of their resets. Aggregate variables such as oil prices and unemployment rates do push up defaults, but by relatively small amounts, once we control for loan-level observables.

SIMULATION RESULTS. With the estimated parameters in hand, we turn to the question of how well the model performs over the 2005–07 period.

15. For brevity we do not report the parameter estimates for the prepayment hazard functions. They are available upon request from the authors.

16. Sherlund (2008).

Table 8. Variable Names and Definitions in the ABS Data

Variable name	*Definition*
cash	Indicator variable = 1 when mortgage is a refinancing with cash-out
cltvnow	Current mark-to-market CLTV ratio (percent)
cltvorig	CLTV ratio at origination (percent)
doc	Indicator variable = 1 when documentation is complete
educ	Share of population in zip code with high school education or less
ficoorig	FICO score at origination
frmnow	Current market interest rate on 30-year fixed-rate mortgages (percent a year)
frmorig	Market interest rate on 30-year fixed-rate mortgages at origination (percent a year)
hhincome	Average household income in zip code (dollars)
hpvol	Current home price volatility (2-year standard deviation of HPA, in percent)
hpvorig	Home price volatility at origination (2-year standard deviation of HPA, in percent)
indnow	Current fully indexed market interest rate on ARMs (6-month LIBOR plus margin, percent a year)
indorig	Fully indexed market interest rate on ARMs at origination (percent a year)
invhpa	Cumulative HPA if non-owner-occupied (percent)
kids	Share of population in zip code who are children
lngwind	Indicator variable = 1 when mortgage rate has previously reset
lofico	Indicator variable = 1 when FICO < 600
loqual	Indicator variable = 1 when CLTV ratio > 95 and no documentation
mratenow	Current mortgage interest rate (percent a year)
mrateorig	Contract interest rate at origination (percent a year)
nonowner	Indicator variable = 1 when home is non-owner-occupied
oil	Change in oil price since origination (percent)
origamt	Loan amount at origination (dollars)
piggyback	Indicator variable = 1 when a second lien is recorded at origination
pmi	Indicator variable = 1 when there is private mortgage insurance
pmt	Indicator variable = 1 when current monthly payment is more than 5 percent higher than original payment
ppnow	Indicator variable = 1 when prepayment penalty is still in effect
pporig	Indicator variable = 1 when prepayment penalty was in effect at origination
proptype	Indicator variable = 1 when the home is a single-family home
pti	Payment-to-income ratio at origination (percent)
race	Minority share of population in zip code
refi	Indicator variable = 1 when the loan is a refinancing (with or without cash-out)
rstwind	Indicator variable = 1 when the mortgage is in the reset period
unempnow	Change in state-level unemployment rate since origination (percentage points)
unorig	State-level unemployment rate at origination (percent)

Table 9. Sample Averages of Variables in the ABS Data[a]

	2000–04				2004	2005
Variable name	*At origination*	*Active mortgages*	*Mortgages in default*	*Mortgages prepaid*	*At origination*	*At origination*
cash	0.57	0.57	0.52	0.58	0.58	0.54
cltvnow	81.91	73.59	66.10	0.00	83.76	84.90
cltvorig	81.91	83.15	81.61	79.81	83.76	84.90
doc	0.70	0.69	0.74	0.70	0.66	0.64
educ	0.36	0.37	0.38	0.35	0.37	0.37
ficoorig	610	616	582	605	616	619
frmnow	6.28	5.75	5.75	5.75	5.88	5.85
frmorig	6.28	6.03	6.89	6.62	5.88	5.85
hhincome	43,110	42,421	39,116	44,945	43,007	42,379
hpvol	3.38	4.15	3.20	4.78	3.91	4.57
hpvorig	3.38	3.41	2.52	3.46	3.91	4.57
indnow	8.52	9.06	9.51	9.12	7.90	9.81
indorig	8.52	8.06	10.06	9.05	7.90	9.81
invhpa	1.63	1.14	2.31	2.38	0.55	0.16
kids	0.27	0.27	0.27	0.27	0.27	0.27
lngwind	0.00	0.09	0.20	0.11	0.00	0.00
loqual	0.05	0.07	0.03	0.03	0.09	0.12
mratenow	8.22	7.73	9.95	8.81	7.32	7.56
mrateorig	8.22	7.72	9.95	8.82	7.32	7.56

nonowner	0.08	0.09	0.10	0.07	0.09	0.08
oil	0.00	26.96	54.47	53.35	0.00	0.00
origamt	118,523	119,569	89,096	121,636	136,192	148,320
piggyback	0.08	0.11	0.05	0.04	0.14	0.23
pmi	0.27	0.24	0.35	0.31	0.19	0.23
pmt	0.00	0.04	0.03	0.00	0.00	0.00
ppnow	0.73	0.67	0.36	0.38	0.73	0.72
pporig	0.73	0.74	0.75	0.71	0.73	0.72
proptype	0.87	0.88	0.90	0.86	0.87	0.86
pti	38.99	38.87	39.09	39.18	39.41	40.07
race	0.31	0.30	0.32	0.31	0.31	0.31
refi	0.68	0.67	0.64	0.70	0.65	0.60
rstwind	0.00	0.02	0.06	0.09	0.00	0.00
unempnow	0.00	–4.50	13.47	2.95	0.00	0.00
unorig	5.58	5.69	5.06	5.48	5.63	5.06
No. of observations	3,654,683	2,195,233	183,586	1,275,864	1,267,866	1,794,953

Source: Authors' calculations.

a. See table 8 for variable definitions.

Table 10. Default Hazard Function Estimates from the ABS Data, 2000–04[a]

	Subprime 2/28		*Subprime 3/27*		*Subprime fixed-rate*	
Variable name	*Purchase*	*Refinancing*	*Purchase*	*Refinancing*	*Purchase*	*Refinancing*
Constant	7.519*	4.143*	5.819*	–0.842	7.826*	3.213*
cash	NA[b]	0.016	NA	0.087	NA	–0.110*
cltvnow	0.030*	0.008*	0.019*	0.025*	0.036*	0.028*
cltvorig	–0.032*	0.002	–0.010	–0.008	–0.027*	–0.011*
doc	–0.185*	–0.378*	–0.012	–0.272*	–0.271*	–0.194*
educ	–0.439	–0.125	–1.401*	–0.376	–0.075	0.227
ficoorig	–4.388*	–4.881*	–4.084*	–2.321*	–4.874*	–4.386*
frmnow	–0.124*	–0.179*	0.054	0.109	0.181*	0.113*
frmorig	–0.105*	0.105*	–0.310*	–0.025	–0.209*	–0.198*
hhincome	–0.575*	–0.256*	–0.758*	–0.223	–0.872*	–0.222*
hpvol	–0.034*	–0.038*	–0.046*	–0.029	–0.064*	–0.037*
indnow	0.291*	0.369*	0.217*	0.234*	NA	NA
indorig	–0.270*	–0.358*	–0.136*	–0.145*	NA	NA
invhpa	–0.032*	–0.012*	–0.064*	–0.015	–0.030*	–0.011*
kids	0.317	0.249	1.304	–0.635	0.521	–0.695
lngwind	0.139	0.059	0.683*	–0.027	NA	NA
lofico	–0.151*	–0.056	–0.256*	0.056	–0.085	0.128*
loqual	–0.039	–0.112	0.031	–0.331	–0.215	0.561*
mratenow	–0.031	0.044	1.071*	0.376	0.468	0.109

mrateorig	0.325*	0.273*	−0.786	−0.067	−0.255	0.159
nonowner	0.557*	0.281*	0.883*	0.351*	0.540*	0.431*
oil	0.002	0.000	0.001	−0.001	0.006*	0.005*
origamt	0.298*	0.115*	0.489*	0.234*	0.480*	0.148*
piggyback	0.287*	0.286*	0.300*	0.287	0.133	−0.329
pmi	0.075*	0.174*	0.212*	0.074	0.311*	0.160*
pmt	0.525*	−0.149	1.478*	0.707*	1.144*	0.393
ppnow	−0.156*	−0.056	0.148	−0.084	−0.141	−0.320*
pporig	0.033	0.115	−0.329	0.056	0.157	0.439*
proptype	0.143*	0.031	0.167	0.060	−0.128	−0.025
pti	0.005*	0.009*	0.009*	0.007*	−0.002	0.006*
race	0.690*	−0.302*	0.182	−0.082	0.593*	−0.324*
rstwind	−0.239*	−0.150*	0.100	0.143	NA	NA
unempnow	0.007*	0.009*	0.005*	0.004	0.000	−0.003*
unorig	−0.023	−0.040*	−0.028	−0.043	−0.080	−0.091*
Log-likelihood	−140,135	−297,352	−30,071	−50,544	−36,574	−170,927
No. of observations	1,095,227	2,015,104	241,511	373,976	324,431	1,582,146

Source: Authors' calculations.

a. Coefficient estimates are for the default hazard function from a competing-risks duration model. The model is estimated at a monthly frequency using the maximum likelihood method. Asterisks indicate statistical significance at the 5 percent level.

b. NA, not applicable.

Here we focus on the 2004 and 2005 vintages of subprime mortgages contained in the ABS data. To construct the forecasts, we use the estimated model parameters to calculate predicted foreclosure (and prepayment) probabilities for each mortgage in each month during 2005–07. These simulations assume perfect foresight, in that the assumed paths for home prices, unemployment rates, oil prices, and interest rates follow those that actually occurred. The average default propensity each month is used to determine the number of defaults each month, with mortgages with the highest propensities defaulting first (and similarly for prepayments). We then compare the cumulative incidence of simulated defaults with the actual incidence of defaults using cumulative default functions (that is, the percent of original loans that default by loan age *t*).

The 2004 and 2005 vintages differ on many dimensions: underwriting standards, the geographic mix of loans originated, oil price shocks experienced, and so on. However, the key difference is in the fraction of active loans in each vintage that experienced the home price bust that started, in some regions, as early as 2006. Loans from both vintages were tied to properties whose prices declined; however, loans from the later vintage were much more exposed. As we show, cumulative defaults on the 2004 vintage were reasonable, but those on the 2005 vintage skyrocketed. Thus, the comparison of the 2004 and 2005 vintages provides a tougher test of a model's ability to predict defaults. Any differences we find here would be larger when comparing vintages further apart; for example, the 2003 vintage experienced much greater and more sustained home price gains than did the 2006 vintage.

Figure 7 displays the results of this vintage simulation exercise. The model overpredicts defaults among the 2004 vintage and underpredicts defaults among the 2005 vintage. It estimates that after 36 months, 9.3 percent of the 2005 vintage would have defaulted, but only 7.9 percent of the 2004 vintage, an increase of 18 percent. Although this is fairly significant, it is dwarfed by the *actual* increase in defaults between vintages, both because the 2005 vintage performed so poorly, and because the 2004 vintage performed better than expected.

Cash flows from a pool of mortgages are greatly affected by prepayments. Loans that are prepaid (because the underlying borrower refinanced or moved) deliver all unpaid principal to the lender, as well as, in some cases, prepayment penalties. Further, loans that are prepaid are not at risk for future defaults. As the bottom panel of figure 7 shows, predicted prepayment rates fell dramatically from the 2004 to the 2005 vintage. The model predicted that 68 percent of loans originated in 2004, but only

Figure 7. Default and Prepayment Simulations for the 2004 and 2005 Mortgage Vintages Using ABS Data[a]

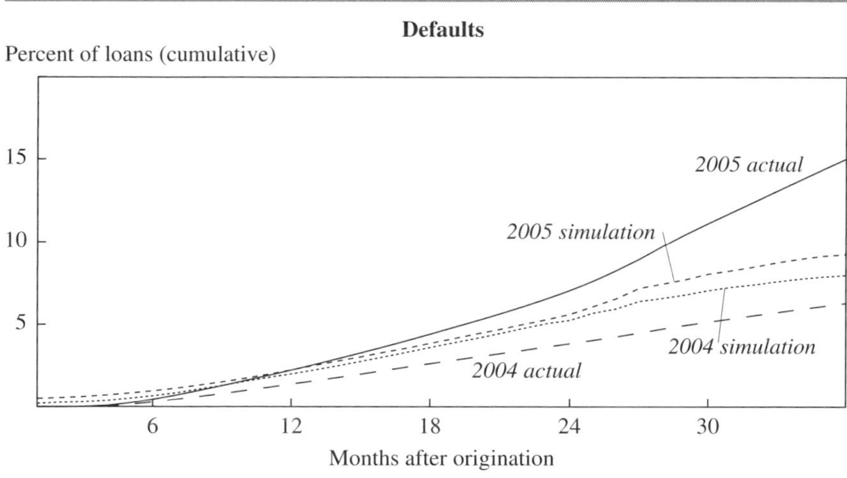

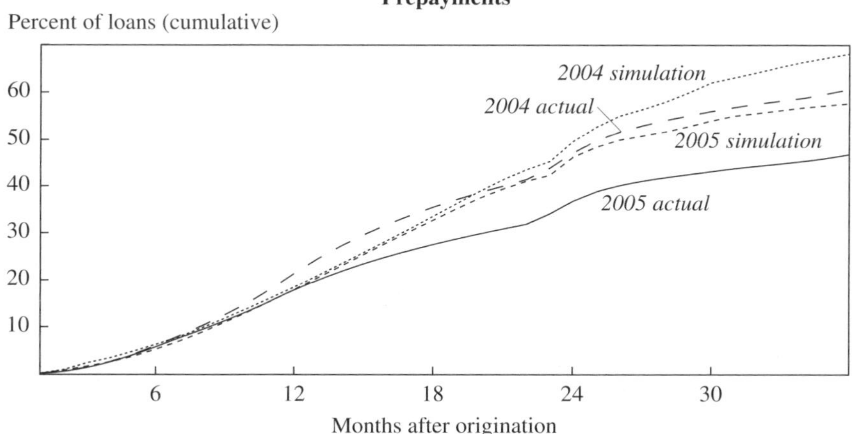

Sources: First American LoanPerformance; authors' calculations.

a. Simulations assume perfect foresight about home prices, interest rates, oil prices, and unemployment rates.

57 percent of loans originated in 2005, would have prepaid by month 36, a 16 percent drop. Thus, the simulations predict an 18 percent increase in cumulative defaults and a 16 percent drop in cumulative prepayments for the 2005 vintage of loans relative to the 2004 vintage. These swings would have had a large impact on the cash flows from the pool of loans.

To further investigate the effect of home prices on the model estimated here, we compute the conditional default and prepayment rates for the generic hybrid 2/28 mortgage analyzed in table 7. By focusing on a particular mortgage type, we eliminate the potentially confounding effects of changes in the mix of loans originated, oil prices, interest rates, and so on between the two vintages and isolate the pure effect of home prices. We let home prices, oil prices, unemployment rates, and so on proceed as they did in 2004–06. We then keep everything else constant but replace 2004–06 home prices with their 2006–08 trajectories. The resulting conditional default and prepayment rates are shown in figure 8. For this type of mortgage at least, the sensitivity to home price changes is extreme. The gap between the default probabilities increases over time because, again, home prices operate through the mark-to-market CLTV ratio, and this particular loan started with a CLTV ratio at origination of just over 80 percent. The gyrations in default and prepayment probabilities around month 24 are associated with the loan's first interest rate reset.

Forecasts Using the Registry of Deeds Data

In this subsection we use data from the Warren Group, which collects mortgage and housing transaction data from Massachusetts registry of deeds offices, to analyze the foreclosure crisis in Massachusetts and to determine whether a researcher armed with these data at the end of 2004 could have successfully predicted the rapid rise in foreclosures that followed. We focus on the state of Massachusetts mostly because of data availability. The Warren Group currently collects deed registry data for many of the Northeastern states, but their historical coverage of foreclosures is limited to Massachusetts. However, the underlying micro-level housing and mortgage historical data are publicly available in many states, and a motivated researcher certainly could have obtained the data had he or she been inclined to do so before the housing crisis occurred. Indeed, several vendors sell such data in an easy-to-use format for many states, albeit at significant cost.

The deed registry data include every residential sale deed, including foreclosure deeds, as well as every mortgage originated in the state of Massachusetts from January 1990 through December 2007. The data contain transaction amounts and dates for mortgages and property sales, but not mortgage terms or borrower characteristics. The data do identify the mortgage lender, which enables us to construct indicators for mortgages originated by subprime lenders.

These data allow us to construct a panel dataset of homeowners, each of whom we can follow from the date when they purchase the home to the date when they either sell the home, experience a foreclosure, or reach the end

Figure 8. Effect of Changing Home Prices on a Generic 2/28 Mortgage[a]

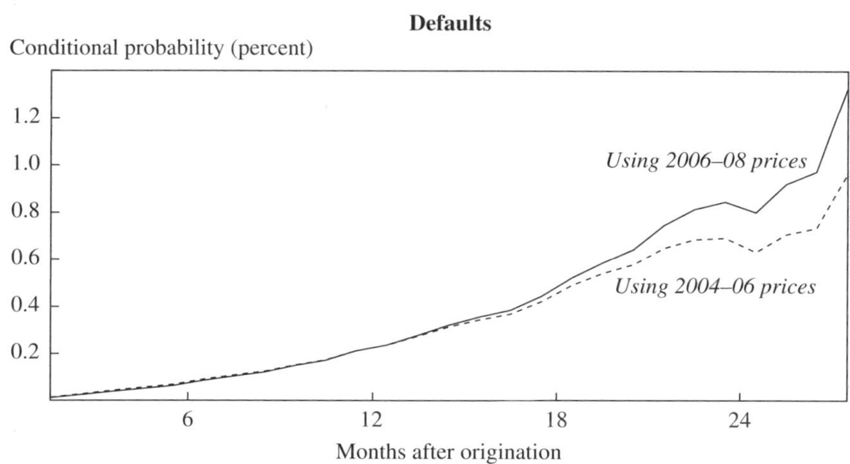

Prepayments

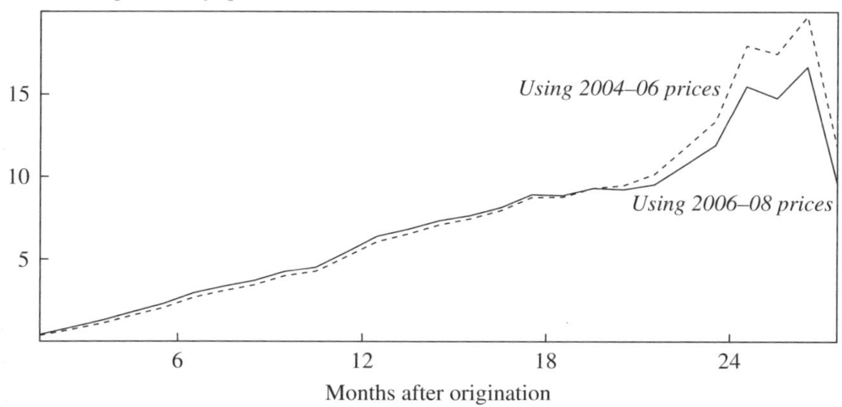

Source: Authors' calculations using the model described in the text.

a. Probabilities are those in month t conditional on surviving to month $t - 1$, estimated for a generic 2/28 subprime mortgage with the characteristics described in the base case in table 7. It is assumed that all dynamic variables follow their 2004–06 trajectories except for home prices, which follow either their 2004–06 or their 2006–08 trajectories as indicated.

of our sample. We use the term "ownership experience" to refer to this time period.[17] Since the data include all residential sale transactions, we are also able to construct a collection of town-level, quarterly, weighted repeat-sales indexes using the methodology of Karl Case and Robert Shiller.[18]

We use a slightly different definition of foreclosure in the deed registry data than in the loan-level analysis above. Here we identify foreclosure through the existence of a foreclosure deed, which signifies the very end of the foreclosure process, when the property is sold at auction to a private bidder or to the mortgage lender. This definition is not possible in the loan-level analysis, in part because state foreclosure laws vary greatly, resulting in significant heterogeneity in the time span between the beginning of the foreclosure process and the end.

COMPARISON WITH THE ABS DATA. The deed registry data differ significantly from the ABS data. Whereas the latter track individual mortgages over time, the deed registry data track homeowners in the same residence over time. Thus, with the deed registry data, the researcher can follow the same homeowner across different mortgages in the same residence and determine the eventual outcome of the ownership experience. In contrast, with the ABS data, if the mortgage terminated in a manner other than foreclosure, such as a refinancing or sale of the property, the borrower drops out of the dataset, and the outcome of the ownership experience is unknown. Gerardi, Shapiro, and Willen argue that analyzing ownership experiences rather than individual mortgages has certain advantages, depending on the question being addressed.[19]

As already noted, another major difference between the deed registry data and the ABS data is the period of coverage. The deed registry data encompass the housing bust of the early 1990s in the Northeast, in which there was a sharp decrease in nominal home prices as well as a significant foreclosure crisis. Figure 9 tracks HPA and the foreclosure rate in Massachusetts since 1987. Foreclosure deeds began to rise rapidly starting in 1991 and peaked in 1992 at approximately 9,300 statewide. The foreclosure rate remained high through the mid-1990s, until nominal HPA became positive in the late 1990s. The housing boom of the early 2000s is

17. See Gerardi, Shapiro, and Willen (2007) for more details regarding the construction of the dataset.

18. Many Massachusetts towns are too small to allow the construction of precise home price indexes. To deal with this issue, we group the smaller towns together based on both geographic and demographic criteria. Altogether, we are able to estimate just over 100 indexes for the state's 350 cities and towns.

19. Gerardi, Shapiro, and Willen (2007).

Figure 9. Massachusetts Foreclosure Rate and Home Prices, 1987–2007

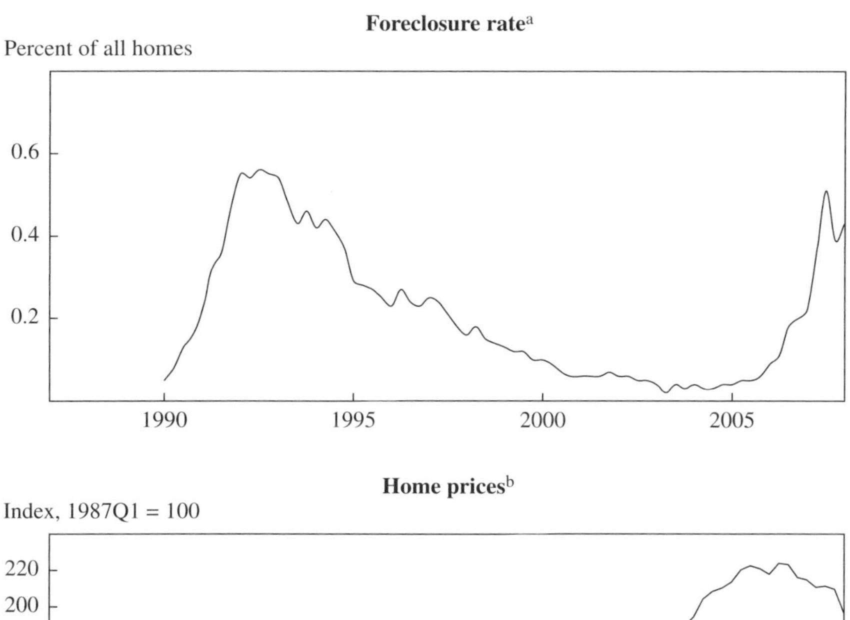

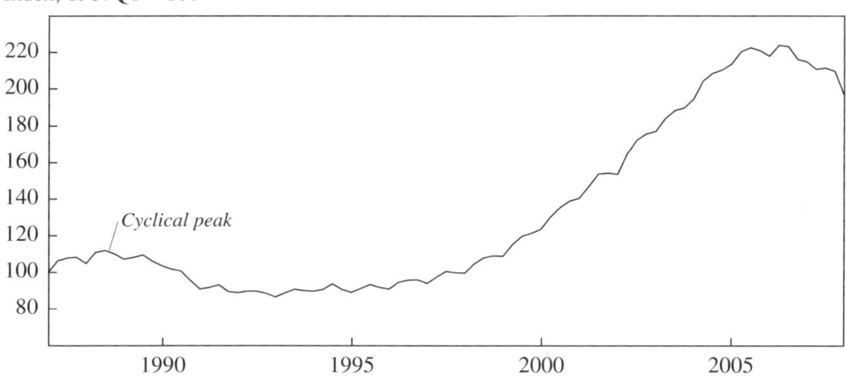

Sources: Warren Group; Massachusetts Department of Revenue.

a. Total foreclosures in a given quarter divided by the total number of residential parcels that year, where a parcel is any real unit of property used for the assessment of property taxes, and typically consists of a plot of land defined by a deed and any buildings on that land.

b. Calculated using the Case-Shiller weighted, repeat-sales methodology.

evident, with double-digit annual HPA and extremely few foreclosures. We see evidence of the current foreclosure crisis at the very end of our sample: the number of foreclosure deeds begins rising in 2006 and by 2007 is approaching the levels witnessed in the early 1990s.

The final major difference between the two data sources is in their coverage of the subprime mortgage market. Since the ABS data encompass pools of nonagency MBSs, a subprime mortgage is defined simply as any mortgage contained in a pool of mortgages labeled "subprime." The deed registry data do not reveal whether a mortgage is securitized or not, and thus, we cannot use the same subprime definition. Instead, we match each lender against a list of lenders who originate mainly subprime mortgages; the list is constructed by the Department of Housing and Urban Development (HUD) on an annual basis. The two definitions are largely consistent with each other.[20] Table 11 shows the top ten Massachusetts subprime lenders for each year going back to 1999, as well as the number of subprime loans originated by each lender and by all lenders. The composition of the list does change from year to year, but for the most part the same lenders consistently occupy a spot on the list. It is evident from the table that subprime lending in Massachusetts peaked in 2005 and fell sharply in 2007. The increasing importance of the subprime purchase mortgage market is also very clear. From 1999 to 2001 the subprime market consisted mostly of refinancings: in 1999 and 2000 home purchases with subprime mortgages made up only about 25 percent of the Massachusetts subprime market, and only about 30 percent in 2001. By 2004, however, purchases made up almost 78 percent of the subprime mortgage market, and in 2006 they accounted for 96 percent. This is certainly evidence supporting the idea that over time the subprime mortgage market opened up the opportunity of homeownership to many households, at least in the state of Massachusetts.

EMPIRICAL MODEL. The empirical model we implement is drawn from Gerardi, Shapiro, and Willen and resembles previous models of mortgage termination.[21] It is a duration model similar to the one used in the above analysis of the ABS data, with a few important differences. As in the loan-level analysis, we use a competing-risks, proportional hazard specification, which assumes that certain baseline hazards are common to all ownership experiences. However, because we are now analyzing ownership experiences rather than individual loans, the competing risks correspond to the two possible terminations of an ownership experience, sale and foreclosure, as opposed to the two possible terminations of a mortgage, prepayment and foreclosure. As discussed above, the major difference between the two specifications comes in the treatment of refinancings. In the loan-level analysis, a loan that is refinanced drops out of the dataset, because the

20. See Gerardi, Shapiro, and Willen (2007) for a more detailed comparison of different subprime mortgage definitions. Mayer and Pence (2008) also compare subprime definitions and reach similar conclusions.

21. Gerardi, Shapiro, and Willen (2007). Previous models include those of Deng, Quigley, and van Order (2000), Deng and Gabriel (2006), and Pennington-Cross and Ho (2006).

mortgage is terminated. However, in the ownership experience analysis, a borrower who refinances remains in the data. Thus, a borrower who defaults on a refinanced mortgage will show up as a foreclosure in the deed registry dataset, but that borrower's first mortgage will show up in the ABS data as a prepayment, and the second mortgage may or may not show up in the data at all (depending on whether the mortgage was sold into a private-label MBS), but either way, the two mortgages will not be linked together. Thus, for a given number of eventual foreclosures, the ABS data will always show a lower apparent foreclosure rate.

Unlike for mortgage terminations, there is no generally accepted standard baseline hazard for ownership terminations. Thus, we specify both the foreclosure and the sale baseline hazards in a nonparametric manner, using an indicator variable for each year after the purchase of the home. In effect, we model the baseline hazards with a set of age dummies.[22]

The list of explanatory variables is different from that in the loan-level analysis. We have detailed information regarding the CLTV ratio at the time of purchase for each homeowner in the data, and we include the CLTV ratio as a right-hand-side variable. We also combine the initial CLTV ratio with cumulative HPA experienced since purchase in the town where the home is located, to construct a measure of household equity, E_{it}:

$$E_{it} = \frac{\left(1 + C_{jt}^{HPA}\right) - CLTV_{i0}}{CLTV_{i0}}, \tag{1}$$

where $CLTV_{i0}$ corresponds to household i's initial CLTV ratio, and C_{jt}^{HPA} corresponds to the cumulative amount of HPA experienced in town j from the date of the home purchase through time t.[23] Based on our discussion above of the theory of default, an increase in equity for a borrower in a position of negative nominal home equity should have a significantly different effect from an increase in equity for a borrower with positive nominal equity. For this reason we assume a specification that allows the effect of equity on default to change depending on the borrower's equity. To do

22. Gerardi, Shapiro, and Willen (2007) and Foote, Gerardi, and Willen (2008) use a third-order polynomial in the age of the ownership. The nonparametric specification used here has the advantage of not being affected by the nonlinearities in the tails of the polynomials for old ownerships, but the results for both specifications are very similar.

23. This equity measure is somewhat crude as it does not take into account amortization, cash-out refinancings, or home improvements. See Foote and others (2008a) for a more detailed discussion of the implications of these omissions for the estimates.

Table 11. Top 10 Subprime Lenders in Massachusetts, 1999–2007

Lender	*Total originations*	*Purchase originations*	*Lender*	*Total originations*	*Purchase originations*	*Lender*	*Total originations*	*Purchase originations*
2007			*2004*			*2001*		
Summit	1,601	1,584	Option One	3,767	3,129	Option One	2,660	1,111
Option One	360	358	New Century	2,991	2,507	New Century	1,263	323
Equifirst	195	195	Freemont	2,895	2,461	Ameriquest	1,984	296
New Century	149	149	Argent	2,200	2,068	Citifinancial Services	1,040	140
Freemont	108	107	Fieldstone	1,131	1,023	Freemont	748	317
Accredited Home	75	74	Accredited Home	1,014	820	Household Financial Corp.	548	61
Argent	73	73	Mortgage Lender Net	972	536	Wells Fargo Finance	467	43
Aegis	54	53	Nation One	946	927	Argent	457	66
Wilmington Finance	46	43	WMC	888	586	First Franklin	367	251
Nation One	44	44	Long Beach	812	685	Meritage	349	333
Total[a]	3,021	2,956	Total	23,761	18,481	Total	15,308	4,595
2006			*2003*			*2000*		
Mortgage Lender Net	2,489	2,310	Option One	3,157	2,222	Option One	2,773	1,000
Summit	2,021	1,948	New Century	1,694	1,053	Ameriquest	2,047	287
Freemont	2,016	1,973	Freemont	1,519	1,089	Citifinancial Services	1,275	112
New Century	1,978	1,942	Ameriquest	1,288	436	New Century	1,251	336
WMC	1,888	1,860	First Franklin	922	917	Freemont	773	267
Option One	1,616	1,552	Argent	836	536	Household Financial Corp	761	55
Accredited Home	1,006	986	Mortgage Lender Net	802	381	Long Beach	470	289
Argent	640	626	Accredited Home	636	428	First Franklin	464	407
Southstar	632	624	Fieldstone	585	430	Mortgage Lender Net	464	36
Equifirst	598	564	Citifinancial Services	459	70	Argent	437	48
Total	18,211	17,489	Total	17,988	11,062	Total	15,870	3,982

2005			*2002*			*1999*		
Option One	4,409	4,152	Option One	2,822	1,502	Option One	2,828	1,013
Freemont	3,927	3,675	Ameriquest	1,713	526	Ameriquest	1,929	229
New Century	3,125	2,906	New Century	1,261	443	Citifinancial Services	1,303	108
Argent	2,253	2,195	Freemont	1,071	595	New Century	1,273	340
WMC	1,846	1,681	First Franklin	657	622	Freemont	738	233
Accredited Home	1,601	1,498	Citifinancial Services	656	97	Household Financial Corp	728	47
Long Beach	1,599	1,551	Mortgage Lender Net	627	170	Wells Fargo Finance	478	26
Summit	1,588	1,440	Argent	606	166	Mortgage Lender Net	452	44
Mortgage Leader Net	1,494	1,211	Wells Fargo Finance	411	27	Long Beach	413	202
Nation One	969	959	Accredited Home	358	184	Argent	410	38
Total	28,464	26,128	Total	15,296	6,459	Total	16,161	3,852

Sources: Warren Group; authors' calculations.

a. Totals are for all lenders.

this we specify equity as a linear spline with six intervals: $(-\infty, -10\%)$, $[-10\%, 0\%)$, $[0\%, 10\%)$, $[10\%, 25\%)$, and $[25\%, \infty)$.[24]

Since detailed mortgage and borrower characteristics are not available in the deed registry data, we instead use zip code–level demographic information from the 2000 Census, including median household income and the percentage of minority households in the zip code, and town-level unemployment rates from the Bureau of Labor Statistics. We also include the six-month LIBOR in the list of explanatory variables, to capture the effects of nominal interest rates on sale and foreclosure.[25] Finally, we include an indicator variable for whether the homeowner obtained financing from a lender on the HUD subprime lender list at the time of purchase. This variable is included as a proxy for the different mortgage and borrower characteristics that distinguish the subprime from the prime mortgage market. We emphasize that we do not assign a causal interpretation to this variable. Rather we interpret the estimated coefficient as a correlation that simply reveals the relative frequency of foreclosure for a subprime purchase borrower compared with a borrower who has a prime mortgage.

Table 12 reports summary statistics for the number of new Massachusetts ownership experiences initiated, and the number of sales and foreclosures broken down by vintage. The two most recent housing cycles are clearly evident. Almost 5 percent of ownerships initiated in 1990, but fewer than 1 percent of those in vintages between 1996 and 2002, eventually experienced a foreclosure. Despite a severe right-censoring problem for the 2005 vintage of ownerships, as of December 2007 more than 2 percent had already succumbed to foreclosure. The housing boom of the early 2000s can also be seen in the ownership statistics: between 80,000 and 100,000 ownerships were initiated each year between 1998 and 2006, almost double the number initiated each year in the early 1990s and 2007.

Table 13 reports summary statistics for the explanatory variables included in the model, also broken down by vintage. It is clear from the LTV ratio statistics that homeowners became more leveraged on average over the sample period: median initial CLTV ratios increased from 80 percent in 1990 to 90 percent in 2007. Even more striking, the percentage of CLTV ratios 90 percent or greater almost doubled, from approximately 22.5 percent in 1990 to 41.6 percent in 2007. The table also shows both

24. The intervals are chosen somewhat arbitrarily, but the results are not significantly affected by assuming different intervals.

25. We use the six-month LIBOR because the vast majority of subprime ARMs are indexed to this rate. However, using other nominal rates, such as the 10-year Treasury rate, does not significantly affect the results.

Table 12. Ownership Outcomes in the Massachusetts Deed Registry Data by Vintage

Vintage	*No. of new ownerships*	*Percent ending in foreclosure*	*Percent ending in sale*
1990	46,723	4.79	29.63
1991	48,609	2.18	31.56
1992	57,414	1.33	32.10
1993	63,494	1.17	32.63
1994	69,870	1.07	33.81
1995	65,193	1.05	35.79
1996	74,129	0.87	37.30
1997	79,205	0.77	38.32
1998	89,123	0.59	39.09
1999	90,350	0.74	39.75
2000	84,965	0.90	39.74
2001	83,184	0.82	36.09
2002	86,648	0.88	30.70
2003	88,824	1.09	23.12
2004	97,390	1.75	15.60
2005	95,177	2.19	8.49
2006	80,203	1.34	4.00
2007	48,911	0.07	1.36

Sources: Warren Group; authors' calculations.

direct and indirect evidence of the increased importance of the subprime purchase mortgage market. The last column of the table reports the percentage of borrowers who financed a home purchase with a subprime mortgage in Massachusetts: fewer than 4 percent of new owners did so before 2003, but in that year the share increased to almost 7 percent, and in 2005, at the peak of the subprime market, it reached almost 15 percent. The increased importance of the subprime purchase market is also apparent from the zip code–level income and demographic variables: the percentage of ownerships coming from zip codes with large minority populations (according to the 2000 Census) has increased over time, as has the number of ownerships coming from lower-income zip codes.

ESTIMATION STRATEGY. We use the deed registry data to estimate the proportional hazards model for three separate sample periods. We then use the estimates from each sample to predict foreclosure probabilities for the 2004 and 2005 vintages of subprime and prime borrowers, and we compare the predicted probabilities with the actual foreclosure outcomes of those vintages. The first sample encompasses the entire span of the data, from January 1990 to December 2007. This basically corresponds to an in-sample goodness-of-fit exercise, as some of the data being used would not have been available to a forecaster in real time when the 2004 and 2005

Table 13. Summary Statistics of the Massachusetts Deed Registry Data by Vintage[a]

	Initial CLTV ratio		*Percent minority borrowers*		*Median income of owner (dollars)*				
Vintage	*Median (percent)*	*Percent ≥ 90%*	*Median*	*Mean*	*Median*	*Mean*	*Percent condos (mean)*	*Percent multifamily (mean)*	*Percent of subprime loans for purchase (mean)*
1990	80.0	22.54	8.52	14.59	54,897	57,584	19.41	10.21	0.00
1991	80.0	24.20	7.98	13.39	56,563	59,784	17.08	7.69	0.00
1992	80.0	26.05	7.76	13.00	56,879	60,217	15.02	7.89	0.01
1993	84.9	30.47	7.77	13.33	56,605	59,714	14.77	8.86	0.10
1994	87.2	32.90	7.98	13.79	55,880	58,848	14.87	10.15	0.39
1995	87.4	35.29	8.26	14.49	55,364	58,089	16.01	10.97	0.43
1996	87.1	35.22	8.25	14.22	55,364	58,076	16.98	10.41	0.91
1997	85.0	33.87	8.26	14.39	55,358	57,864	17.64	10.59	1.92
1998	85.0	33.41	8.25	14.20	54,897	57,394	18.90	10.40	2.56
1999	85.0	33.28	8.63	14.88	54,677	56,742	20.15	11.11	2.43
2000	82.4	31.67	8.65	14.96	54,402	56,344	21.55	11.17	2.43
2001	85.0	34.42	8.63	14.98	53,294	55,524	21.34	11.46	2.89
2002	82.0	32.32	9.14	15.25	53,357	55,672	22.63	11.14	3.88
2003	85.0	34.47	9.14	15.51	53,122	55,337	22.68	11.20	6.86
2004	86.6	35.68	9.66	16.42	52,561	55,017	24.48	11.85	9.99
2005	89.9	39.40	10.19	17.07	52,030	54,231	28.29	11.83	14.81
2006	90.0	41.65	9.92	17.10	51,906	54,326	28.09	10.80	12.96
2007	90.0	41.62	9.92	16.64	53,122	55,917	29.95	8.54	3.95

Sources: Warren Group, U.S. Census Bureau, and authors' calculations.

a. All statistics except CLTV ratios are calculated from data at the zip code level. Medians and means reported are those of the median or the mean of all zip codes in the sample.

vintage ownerships were initiated. This period covers two housing downturns in the Northeast, and thus two periods in which many households found themselves with negative equity. From the peak of the market in 1988 to the trough in 1992, nominal housing prices (based on our index) fell by more than 20 percent statewide, implying that even some borrowers who put 20 percent down at the time of purchase found themselves with negative equity at some point in the early 1990s. For comparison, nominal Massachusetts housing prices fell by more than 10 percent from their peak in 2005 through December 2007.

The second sample includes homeowners who purchased homes between January 1990 and December 2004. This is an out-of-sample exercise, as we are using only data that would have been available to a researcher in 2004 to estimate the model. Thus, with this exercise we are asking whether a mortgage modeler in 2004 could have predicted the current foreclosure crisis using only data available at that time. This sample does include the housing downturn of the early 1990s, and thus a significant number of negative equity observations.[26] However, it includes a relatively small number of ownerships involving the purchase of a home with a subprime mortgage. It is clear from table 11 that the peak of the subprime purchase mortgage market occurred in 2004 and 2005. Thus, although the 1990–2004 sample period does include a significant housing price decline, it does not include the peak of the subprime market. Furthermore, we presented evidence earlier that the underlying mortgage and borrower characteristics of the subprime market evolved over time. Thus, the subprime purchase mortgages in the 1990–2004 sample are likely to have different characteristics than those originated after 2004, and this could have a significant effect on the fit of the model.

The final sample covers ownership experiences initiated between January 2000 and December 2004 and corresponds to the sample period used in the loan-level analysis above. This was a time of extremely rapid HPA, as can clearly be seen in figure 9. Home prices increased at an annual rate of more than 10 percent in Massachusetts during this period. Thus, the major difference between this sample and the 1990–2004 sample is the absence of a housing downturn.

ESTIMATION RESULTS. Unlike our loan-level analysis, which was estimated at a monthly frequency, our proportional hazard model is estimated at a quarterly frequency, because that is the frequency of the town-level

26. See Foote and others (2008a) for a more detailed analysis of Massachusetts homeowners with negative equity in the early 1990s.

home price indexes. The model is estimated using the maximum likelihood method. Since we are basically working with a panel dataset containing the entire population of Massachusetts homeowners, the number of observations is too large to conduct the estimation. Thus, to facilitate computation, we use a random sample of ownerships for each sample (10 percent for the 1990–2007 sample, 10 percent for the 1990–2004 sample, and 25 percent for the 2000–04 sample). Finally, we truncate ownerships that last longer than eight years, for two reasons. First, there are relatively few of these long ownerships, which would result in imprecise estimates of the baseline hazard. Second, because information regarding equity withdrawal upon refinancing is unavailable, the equity measure becomes more biased as the length of the ownership experience increases.[27]

Figure 10 displays the estimates of the baseline hazards for both foreclosures and sales. The foreclosure baseline is hump-shaped, reaching a peak between the fourth and fifth year of the ownership experience. The sale baseline rises sharply over the first three years of the ownership, then flattens until the seventh year, after which it resumes its rise. Table 14 reports the parameter estimates for the foreclosure hazard.[28] For the most part, the signs on the estimated coefficients are intuitive and consistent with economic theory. Higher interest and unemployment rates tend to raise foreclosures (the coefficients on these variables are positive), although the coefficient estimate associated with the LIBOR variable switches signs in the 1990–2004 sample. Homeowners who finance their home purchase from subprime lenders are more likely to experience a foreclosure than those who use prime lenders. In the full sample and in the 1990–2004 sample, borrowers who purchase a condominium or a multifamily property are more likely to experience a foreclosure than borrowers who purchase a single-family home. This likely reflects the fact that the Massachusetts condominium market was hit especially hard by the housing downturn in the early 1990s, and the fact that housing stocks in many of the economically depressed cities in Massachusetts are disproportionately made up of multifamily properties. In the 2000–04 sample homeowners in condominiums are actually less likely to experience a foreclosure. Finally, ownerships located in zip codes with relatively larger minority populations and lower median incomes are more likely to experience a foreclosure.

27. The estimation results are not very sensitive to this eight-year cutoff. A seven-year or a nine-year cutoff produces almost identical results.

28. For brevity we do not report the parameter estimates for the sale hazard. They are available upon request from the authors.

Figure 10. Estimates of Baseline Hazards

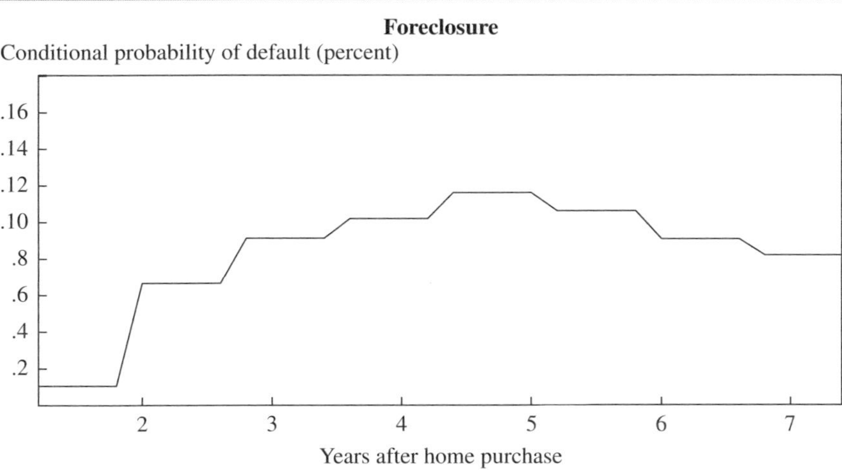

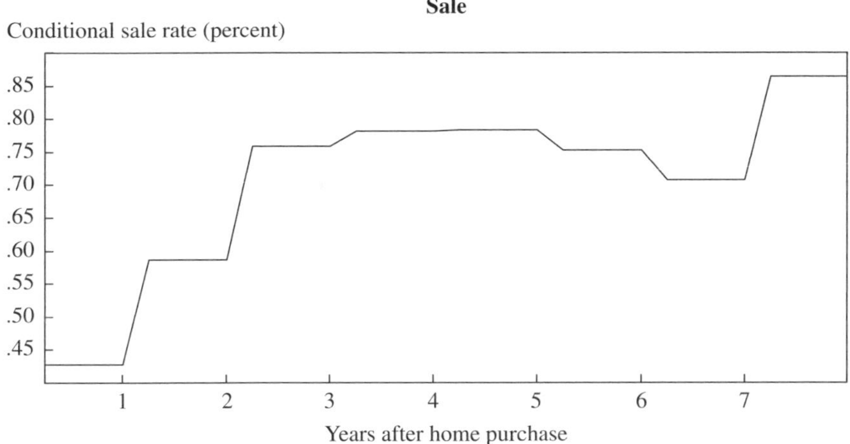

Source: Authors' calculations.

Table 15 explores the quantitative implications of the parameter estimates. The table reports the effect of a change in each of several selected variables (by one standard deviation for continuous variables, and from zero to one for dummies) on the probability of foreclosure. For example, the column for the 1990–2007 sample shows that a homeowner who purchased a home with a subprime mortgage is approximately 7.3 times as likely to default, all else equal, as a homeowner who purchased with a prime mortgage, and 1.1 times as likely to experience a foreclosure if the

Table 14. Regressions Estimating Foreclosure Hazard Using Massachusetts Deed Registry Data[a]

	1990–2007 sample		*1990–2004 sample*		*2000–04 sample*	
Independent variable	*Coefficient*	*Standard error*	*Coefficient*	*Standard error*	*Coefficient*	*Standard error*
Initial LTV ratio	−0.27	0.19	−1.40	0.22	−0.82	1.71
6-month LIBOR	$1.96e^{-02}$	$1.39e^{-02}$	$-3.09e^{-02}$	$1.52e^{-02}$	0.18	0.11
Unemployment rate	$4.74e^{-02}$	$6.00e^{-03}$	$5.03e^{-02}$	$6.14e^{-03}$	$7.70e^{-02}$	$5.24e^{-03}$
Percent minority[b]	$9.23e^{-03}$	$1.03e^{-03}$	$1.09e^{-02}$	$1.20e^{-03}$	$6.30e^{-03}$	$4.31e^{-.03}$
Median income[b]	$-1.60e^{-05}$	$1.82e^{-06}$	$-1.71e^{-05}$	$2.05e^{-06}$	$-6.90e^{-05}$	$1.03e^{-05}$
Indicator variables						
Condo	0.33	0.05	0.44	0.05	−1.19	0.35
Multifamily property	0.54	0.05	0.54	0.06	−0.24	0.20
Subprime purchase	1.99	0.06	1.21	0.19	1.70	0.21
No. of observations	3,005,137		2,365,999		813,802	

Source: Authors' regressions.

a. Coefficient estimates are for the foreclosure hazard function from a competing-risks duration model. The model is estimated at a quarterly frequency using the maximum likelihood method.

b. From 2000 Census zip code–level data.

Table 15. Standardized Elasticities Derived from Estimates Using Massachusetts Deed Registry Data

		Factor change in hazard		
Variable	*Change in the variable*	*1990–2007*	*1990–2004*	*2000–04*
Unemployment rate	+ 1 SD[a] (2.06)	1.10	1.12	1.17
Percent minority[b]	+ 1 SD (19.58)	1.20	1.24	1.13
Median income[b]	– 1 SD ($24,493)	1.49	1.53	5.60
Indicator variables				
Multifamily	From 0 to 1	1.72	1.72	0.79
Condo	From 0 to 1	1.39	1.55	0.30
Subprime purchase	From 0 to 1	7.32	3.35	5.47

Source: Authors' calculations.

a. SD, standard deviation.

b. From 2000 Census zip code-level data.

unemployment rate is 1 standard deviation above the average. The functional form of the proportional hazard model implies that the effects of these different changes affect the hazard multiplicatively. For example, the combined effect of a subprime purchase ownership and 1-standard-deviation-higher unemployment is $7.3 \times 1.1 = 8.0$.

The results for the different sample periods in table 15 differ in interesting ways, most notably associated with the estimate of the subprime purchase indicator. As noted, for the full sample period, subprime purchase ownerships are more than seven times as likely to end in foreclosure, but in the earlier subsample period (1990–2004), they are only 3.4 times as likely. Our analysis above suggests that this difference likely reflects differences in mortgage and borrower characteristics between the two samples. For example, increases in debt-to-income ratios and in low-documentation loans, as well as increases in mortgages with discrete payment jumps, have characterized the subprime market over the past few years. This has likely had a lot to do with the deterioration in the performance of the subprime purchase market. Of course, other explanations are possible, such as a deterioration in unobservable, lender-specific underwriting characteristics. Another possibility is a higher sensitivity to declining home prices relative to prime purchase ownerships. Although the subprime market existed in the early 1990s, most of the activity, as noted above, came in the form of refinancings. Thus, few subprime purchase ownerships from the 1990–2004 sample actually experienced a significant decline in home prices, whereas the vast majority of subprime ownerships took place in 2004 and 2005, and many of these were exposed to large price declines. Subprime purchases in the 2000–04 sample perform better than the full sample but worse than the 1990–2004 sample: they are approximately 5.5 times as likely to experience a foreclosure.

Since housing equity E_{it} is estimated with a spline, the estimates are not shown in table 15. Instead, figure 11 graphs the predicted foreclosure hazard as a function of equity relative to a baseline subprime purchase ownership. The covariates for the baseline ownership have been set to their full sample averages. There were virtually no equity values below zero in the 2000–04 sample from which to estimate the spline, so instead we were forced to use a single parameter.

What the figure reveals is that increases in E_{it} have a large and negative effect on foreclosures for the range of equity values between –50 and 25 percent of the purchase mortgage. For ownerships with nominal equity values above 25 percent, further increases in equity have a much smaller effect on the foreclosure hazard. This is consistent with the intuition presented above. Homeowners with positive equity who either are in financial distress or need to move for another reason are not likely to default, since they are better off selling their home instead. Thus, if a homeowner already has a significant amount of positive equity, additional equity is likely to matter little in the default decision. However, when one takes into account the potential transactions costs involved in selling a property, such as the real estate broker's commission (usually 6 percent of the sale price) and moving expenses, the equity threshold at which borrowers will default may be greater than zero. Therefore, the apparent kink in the foreclosure hazard at 25 percent equity is not necessarily inconsistent with the discussion above.

The estimated nonlinear relationship is similar for the full sample and for the 1990–2004 sample. The scale is higher and the nonlinearity more pronounced in the full sample, which includes the recent foreclosure crisis. But perhaps the most surprising observation from figure 11 is the shape of the predicted hazard from the 2000–04 sample (bottom panel). Although the predicted hazard is necessarily smooth because of the single parameter that governs the relationship, its shape and scale are very similar to those of the other samples. This is surprising because the sensitivity of foreclosure to equity is being estimated with only positive equity variation in this sample. On the face of things, the figure seems to suggest that one could estimate the sensitivity using the positive variation in equity, and then extrapolate to negative equity values and obtain findings that are similar to those obtained using a sample that includes housing price declines. This is, of course, in part due to the nonlinear functional form of

Figure 11. Estimated Effect of Equity Share on Foreclosure Rate

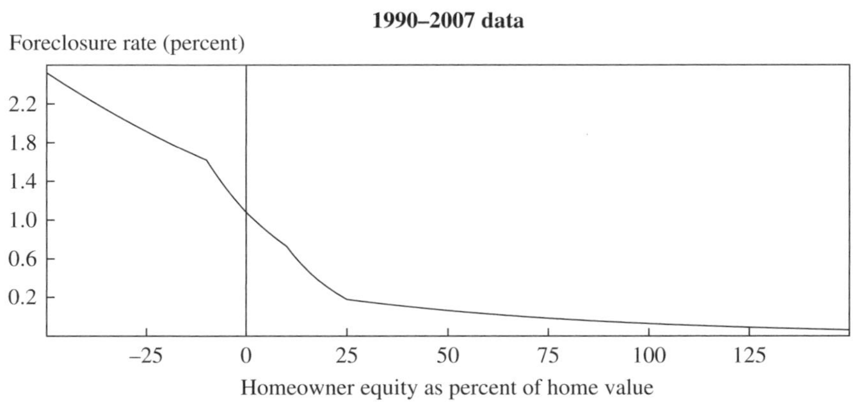

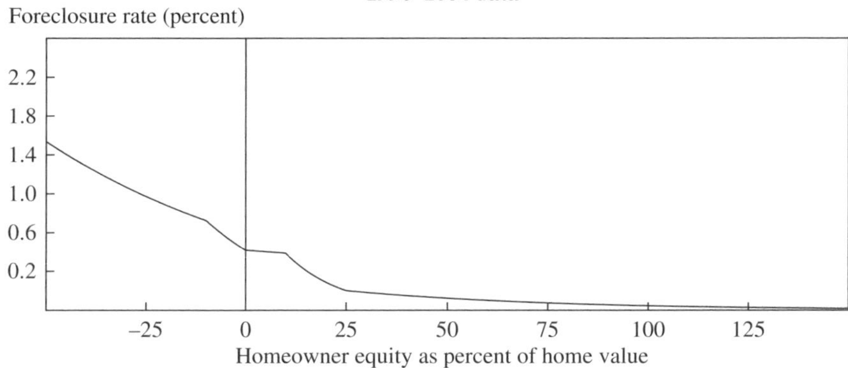

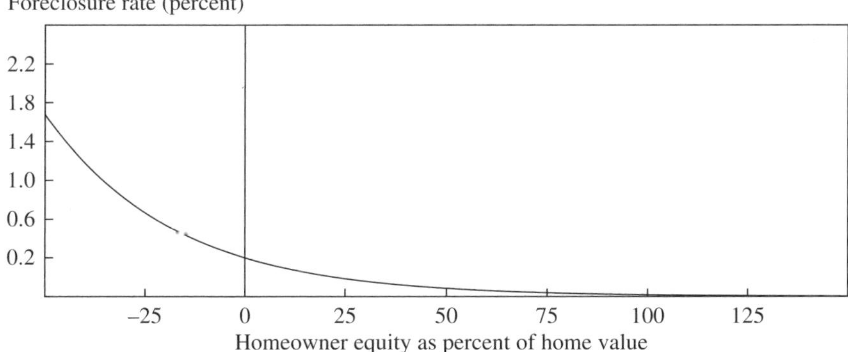

Source: Authors' calculations.

the proportional hazard model and would be impossible in a linear framework (for example, a linear probability model). The implications of this observation for forecasting ability are discussed below.

SIMULATION RESULTS. With the estimated parameters in hand, we turn to the question of how well the model performs, both in sample and out of sample. In this exercise we focus on the 2004 and 2005 vintages of subprime purchase borrowers—a choice motivated by performance as well as by data availability. The summary statistics in table 12 suggested that the 2004 vintage was the first to suffer elevated foreclosure levels in the current housing crisis, and the 2005 vintage is experiencing even higher foreclosure numbers. Unfortunately, we do not yet have enough data to conduct a thorough analysis of the 2006 or 2007 vintages.

To construct the forecasts, we use the estimated model parameters to calculate predicted foreclosure probabilities for each individual ownership in the vintages of interest between the time that the vintage was initiated and 2007Q4. We then aggregate the individual predicted probabilities to obtain cumulative foreclosure probabilities for each vintage, and we compare these with the probabilities that actually occurred.[29] Figures 12 and 13 display the results for the 2004 and 2005 subprime purchase vintages, respectively.

The model consistently overpredicts foreclosures for the 2004 subprime vintage (top panel in figure 12) in the full sample: approximately 9.2 percent of ownerships of that vintage had succumbed to foreclosure as of 2007Q4, whereas the model predicts 11.2 percent. For the out-of-sample forecasts, the model underpredicts Massachusetts foreclosures, but there are significant differences between the two sample periods. The model estimated using data from 1990 to 2004 (middle panel) is able to account for a little over half of the foreclosures experienced by the 2004 vintage, whereas the model estimated using data from 2000 to 2004 (bottom panel) accounts for almost 85 percent of the foreclosures. The better fit of the latter can likely be attributed to the larger coefficient estimate on the subprime purchase indicator variable for the 2000–04 sample than on that for the 1990–2004 sample (table 14). Figure 13 reveals similar patterns for the 2005 subprime vintage, although the in-sample forecast slightly underpredicts cumulative foreclosures, and the out-of-sample forecasts are markedly worse for both sample periods compared with the 2004 subprime vintage forecasts. The 1990–2004 out-of-sample forecast accounts for only

29. See Gerardi, Shapiro, and Willen (2007) for more details.

Figure 12. Foreclosure Simulations for the 2004 Subprime Purchase Vintage

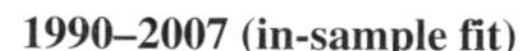

1990–2007 (in-sample fit)

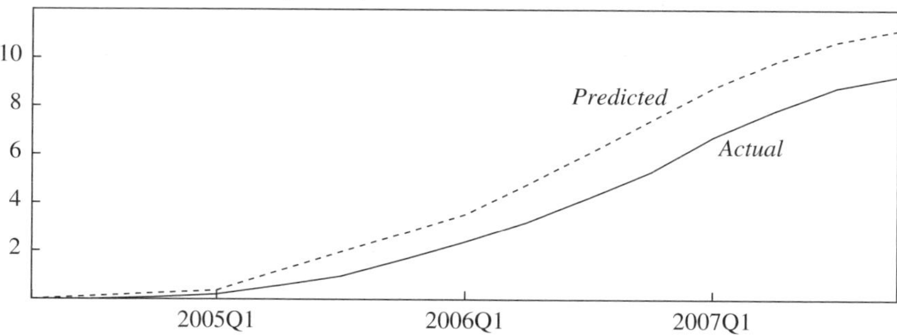

1990–2004 (out-of-sample fit)

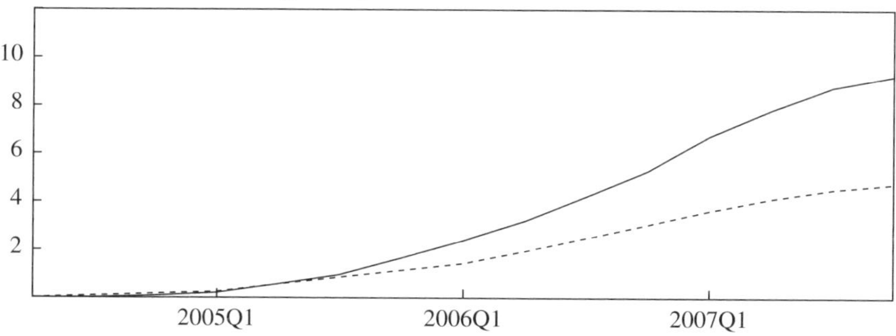

2000–04 (out-of-sample fit)

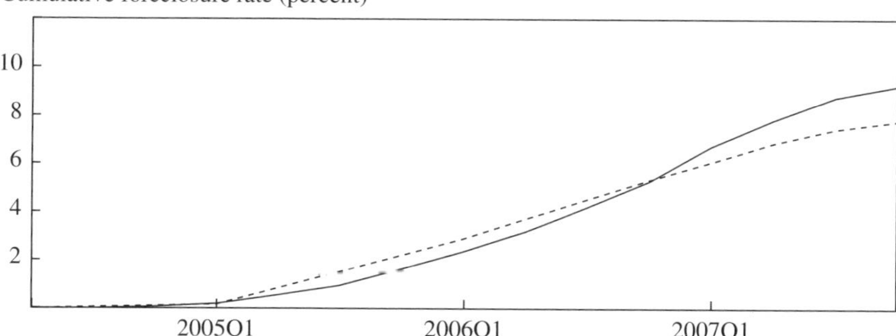

Source: Authors' calculations.

Figure 13. Foreclosure Simulations for the 2005 Subprime Purchase Vintage

1990–2007 (in-sample fit)

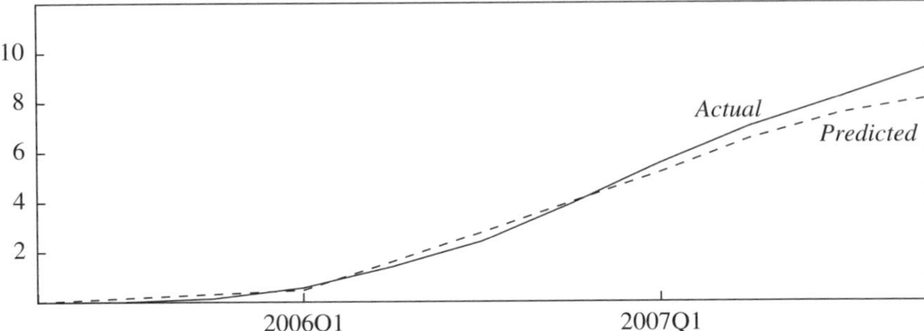

1990–2004 (out-of-sample fit)

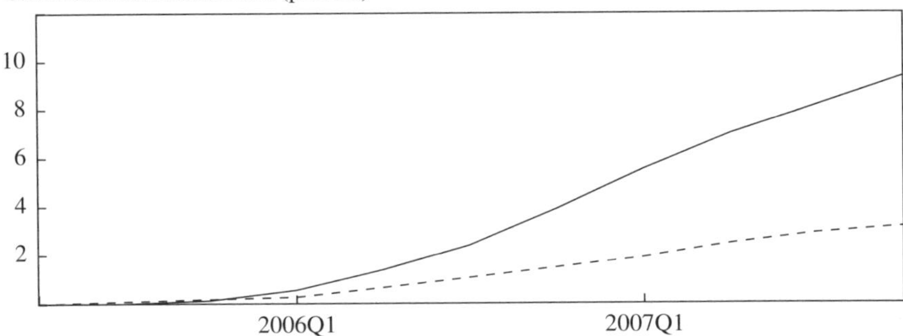

2000–04 (out-of-sample fit)

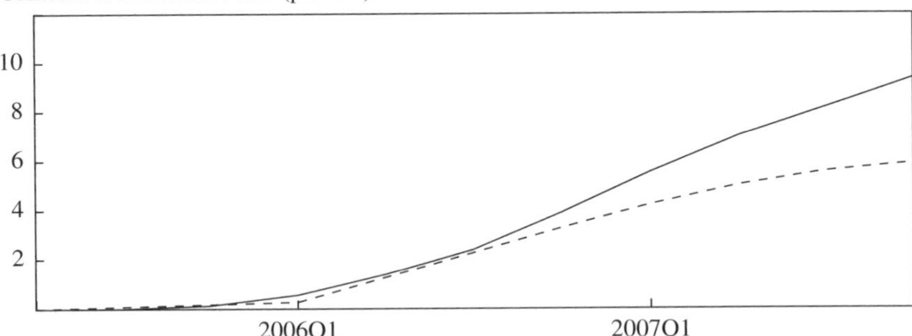

Source: Authors' calculations.

one-third of the foreclosures experienced by the 2005 subprime vintage; the 2000–04 forecast does better, accounting for more than 60 percent.

To summarize, the model estimated using data from the 2000–04 vintages does very well at predicting 2005–07 out-of-sample foreclosures for the 2004 vintage of subprime purchase borrowers, accounting for approximately 85 percent of cumulative foreclosures in 2007Q4. The model does not perform quite as well for the 2005 vintage, accounting for only 63 percent of cumulative foreclosures in 2007Q4. There are significant differences in the performance of the model estimated using data from different sample periods. The model estimated using the 2000–04 sample performs much better than the model estimated using the 1990–2004 sample, despite the fact that only the latter sample period includes a decline in housing prices. Figure 11 suggests that the proportional hazards model is able to estimate the nonlinear relationship between equity and foreclosure, even when there are no negative equity observations in the data. Thus, the primary explanation for the difference in the out-of-sample forecasts is the different coefficient estimates associated with the HUD subprime purchase indicator.

What Were Market Participants Saying in 2005 and 2006?

In this section we attempt to understand why the investment community did not anticipate the subprime mortgage crisis. We do this by looking at written records from market participants in the period from 2004 to 2006. These records include analyst reports from investment banks, publications by rating agencies, and discussions in the media. Because we are interested in the behavior of the investment community as a whole more than of individual institutions, we have chosen not to identify the five major banks we discuss (J. P. Morgan, Citigroup, Morgan Stanley, UBS, and Lehman Brothers) individually, but rather by alias (Bank A, Bank B, and so on).[30] Five basic themes emerge. First, market insiders viewed the subprime market as a great success story in 2005. Second, subprime mortgages were viewed, in some sense correctly, as actually posing lower risk than prime mortgages because of their more stable prepayment behavior. Third, analysts used fairly sophisticated tools to evaluate these mortgages but were hampered by the absence of episodes of falling prices in their data. Fourth, many analysts anticipated the possibility of a crisis in a qualitative way, laying out in various ways a roadmap of what could happen, but never

30. Researchers interested in verifying the sources should contact the authors.

Figure 14. Home Price Appreciation and Cost of Insuring Subprime-Backed Securities, 2006–08

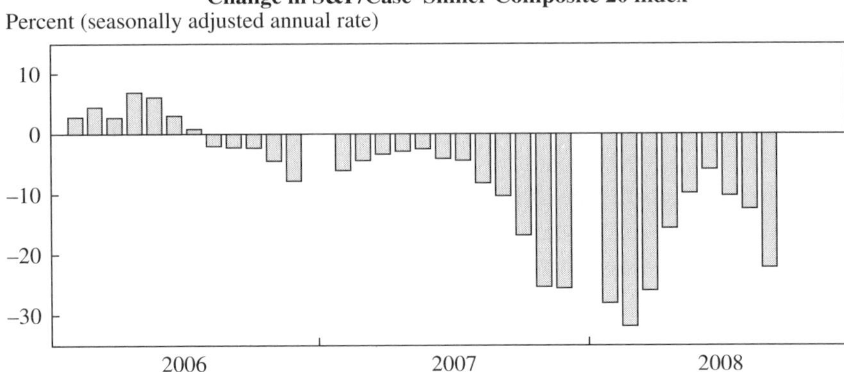

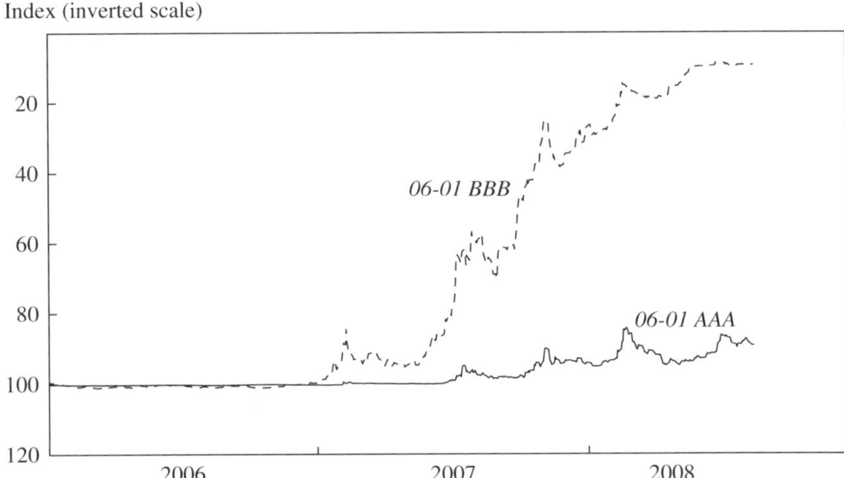

Sources: Haver Analytics; Markit.

a. ABX-HE indexes of AAA- and BBB-rated MBSs issued in late 2005.

fleshed out the quantitative implications. Finally, analysts were remarkably optimistic about HPA.

Figure 14 provides a timeline for this discussion. The top panel shows HPA during 2006–08 using the S&P/Case-Shiller Composite 20 index. In the first half of 2006, HPA for the nation as a whole was positive, but in the single digits, and so well below the record pace set in 2004 and 2005. By the end of the third quarter, however, HPA was negative, although given the reporting lag in the Case-Shiller numbers, market participants would not have had this data point until the end of the fourth quarter. The bottom panel tracks the prices of the ABX-HE 06-01-AAA and ABX-HE 06-01-BBB indexes, which measure the cost of insuring, respectively, AAA-rated and BBB-rated subprime MBSs issued in the second half of 2005 and containing mortgages originated throughout 2005. (The series are inverted so that a rise in the cost of insurance—a fall in the index—is plotted as a rise.) One can arguably date the subprime crisis to the first quarter of 2007, when the cost of insuring the BBB-rated securities, which had not changed throughout all of 2006, started to rise. The broader financial market crisis, which started in August 2007, coincides with another spike in the BBB index and the first signs of trouble in the AAA index. The purpose of this section is to try and understand why market participants did not appreciate the impending crisis, as evidenced by the behavior of the ABX indexes in 2006.

The General State of the Subprime Market

In 2005 market participants viewed the subprime market as a success story along many dimensions. Borrowers had become much more mainstream. Bank A analysts referred to the subprime borrower as "Classic Middle America," writing, "The subprime borrower today has a monthly income above the national median and a long tenure in his job and profession. His home is a three-bedroom, two-bathroom, typical American home, valued at the national median home price. Past credit problems are the main reason why the subprime borrower is ineligible for a prime mortgage loan."[31] Analysts also noted that the credit quality of the typical subprime borrower had improved: the average FICO score of subprime borrowers had risen consistently from 2000 to 2005.[32] But other aspects got better, too: "Collateral credit quality has been improving since 2000. FICO scores and loan balances increased significantly, implying a *mainstreaming of the subprime borrower.* The deeply subprime borrower of the late-1990s has been replaced by the average American homeowner."[33]

Lenders had improved as well. Participants drew a distinction between the somewhat disreputable subprime lenders of the mid- to late 1990s and the new generation of lending institutions, which they saw as well capitalized and well run: "The issuer and servicer landscape in the [home

31. Bank A, October 20, 2005.

32. Bank A, October 20, 2005, and Bank E, February 15, 2005.

33. Bank A, October 20, 2005 (emphasis in original).

equity loan] market has changed dramatically since the liquidity crisis of 1998. Large mortgage lenders or units of diversified financial services companies have replaced the small specialty finance companies of the 1990s."[34] The new lenders, analysts believed, could weather a storm: "Today's subprime issuers/servicers are in much better shape in terms of financial strength. . . . If and when the market hits some kind of turbulence, today's servicers are in a better position to ride out the adverse market conditions."[35] Another dimension along which the market had improved was the use of data. Many market participants were using loan-level data and modern statistical techniques. Bank A analysts expressed a widely held view when they wrote of "an increase in the sophistication of all market participants—from lenders to the underwriters to the rating agencies to investors. All of these participants now have access to quantitative models that analyze extensive historical data to estimate credit and prepayment risks."[36]

Contemporary observers placed a fair amount of faith in the role of credit scoring in improving the market. FICO scores did appear to have significant power to predict credit problems. In particular, statistical evidence showed that FICO scores, when combined with LTV ratios, could "explain a large part of the credit variation between deals and groups of sub-prime loans."[37] The use of risk-based pricing made origination decisions more consistent and transparent across originators, and thus resulted in more predictable performance for investors. "*We believe that this more consistent and sophisticated underwriting is showing up as more consistent performance for investors. An investor buying a sub-prime home equity security backed by 2001 and 2002 (or later vintage) loans is much more likely to get the advertised performance than via buying a deal from earlier years.*"[38] One has to remember that the use of credit scores such as the FICO model emerged as a crucial part of residential mortgage credit decisions only in the mid-1990s.[39] And as late as 1998, one observer points

34. Bank A, October 20, 2005. Here and elsewhere, "home equity loan" is the term typically used by market participants for either a junior lien to a prime borrower or a senior lien to a subprime borrower. Although the two loan types appear quite different, from a financial engineering standpoint both prepaid relatively quickly but were not that sensitive to prevailing interest rates on prime first-lien mortgages.

35. Bank E, January 31, 2006.

36. Bank A, October 20, 2005.

37. Bank E, February 15, 2005.

38. Bank E, February 15, 2005 (emphasis in original).

39. Mester (1997).

Table 16. Outcomes of S&P Ratings of Mortgage-Backed Securities, 1978–2004

Rating	*No. rated*	*Percent subsequently upgraded*	*Percent subsequently downgraded*	*Percent defaulting*
AAA	6,137	NA	0.5	0.07
AA	5,702	22.4	3.6	0.5
A	4,325	16.2	1.3	0.7
BBB	4,826	11.1	2.0	1.2
BB	2,042	17.9	2.3	1.4
B	1,687	14.1	4.1	3.1

Source: Standard & Poor's, "Rating Transitions 2004: U.S. RMBS Stellar Performance Continues to Set Records," January 21, 2005.

out, FICO scores were absent for more than 29 percent of the mortgages in their sample, but by 2002 this number had fallen to 6 percent.[40]

Other things had also made the market more mature. One reason given for the rise in average FICO scores was that "the proliferation of state and municipal predatory lending laws has made it more onerous to fund very low credit loans."[41]

Finally, market participants' experience with rating agencies through mid-2006 had been exceptionally good. Rating agencies had what appeared to be sophisticated models of credit performance using loan-level data and state-of-the-art statistical techniques. Standard & Poor's, for example, used a database "which compiles the loan level and performance characteristics for every RMBS [residential mortgage-backed securities] transaction that we have rated since 1998."[42] Market participants appeared to put a lot of weight on the historical stability of home equity loan credit ratings.[43] And indeed, through 2004 the record of the major rating agencies was solid. Table 16, which summarizes Standard & Poor's record from their first RMBS rating in 1978 to the end of 2004, shows that the probability of a downgrade was quite small and far smaller than the probability of an upgrade.

Prepayment Risk

Many investors allocated appreciable fractions of their portfolios to the subprime market because, in one key sense, it was considered less risky

40. Bank E, February 15, 2005.

41. Bank A, December 16, 2003.

42. "A More Stressful Test of a Housing Market Decline on U.S. RMBS," Standard & Poor's, May 15, 2006, p. 3.

43. Bank A, October 20, 2005.

than the prime market. The issue was prepayments, and the evidence showed that subprime borrowers prepaid much less efficiently than prime borrowers, meaning that they did not immediately exploit advantageous changes in interest rates to refinance into lower-interest-rate loans. Thus, the sensitivity to interest rate changes of the income stream from a pool of subprime loans was lower than that of a pool of prime mortgages. According to classical finance theory, one could even argue that subprime loans were less risky in an absolute sense. Although subprime borrowers had a lot of idiosyncratic risk, as evidenced by their problematic credit histories, such borrower-specific shocks can be diversified away in a large enough pool. In addition, the absolute level of prepayment (as distinct from its sensitivity to interest rate changes) of subprime loans is quite high, reflecting the fact that borrowers with such loans often either resolve their personal financial difficulties and graduate into a prime loan, or encounter further problems and refinance again into a new subprime loan, terminating the previous loan. However, this prepayment behavior was also thought to be effectively uncorrelated across borrowers and not tightly related to changes in the interest rate environment. Mortgage pricing revolved around the sensitivity of refinancing to interest rates; subprime loans appeared to be a useful class of assets whose cash flow was not particularly highly correlated with interest rate shocks. Thus, Bank A analysts wrote in 2005 that "[subprime] prepayments are more stable than prepayments on prime mortgages, adding appeal to [subprime] securities."[44]

A simple way to see the difference in prepayment behavior between prime and subprime borrowers is to look at variation in a commonly used mortgage industry measure, the so-called constant prepayment rate, or CPR, which is the annualized probability of prepayment. According to Bank A analysts,[45] the minimum CPR they reported was 18 percent for subprime fixed-rate mortgages and 29 percent for subprime ARMs. By contrast, for Fannie Mae mortgages the minimums were 7 percent and 15 percent, respectively. As mentioned above, this was attributed to the fact that even in a stable interest rate environment, subprime borrowers will refinance in response to household-level shocks. At the other end, however, the maximum CPRs for subprime fixed-rate and ARM borrowers were 41 percent and 54 percent, respectively, compared with 58 percent and 53 percent, respectively, for Fannie Mae borrowers. The lower CPR for subprime borrowers reflects, at least in part, the prevalence of prepayment penalties: more

44. Bank A, October 20, 2005.
45. Bank A, October 20, 2005.

than 66 percent of subprime borrowers face such penalties. Historically, the prepayment penalty period often lasted five years, but in most cases it had shortened to two for ARMs and three for fixed-rate mortgages by 2005.

Data

Correctly modeling (and thus pricing) prepayment and default risk requires good underlying data. Thus, market participants have every incentive to acquire data on loan performance. As mentioned above, analysts at every firm we looked at, including the rating agencies, had access to loan-level data, but these data, for the most part, did not include any examples of sustained price declines. The databases relied on by the analysts in their reports have relatively short histories. And the problems were particularly severe for subprime loans, since there essentially were none before 1998. To add to the problems, analysts believed that the experiences of pre- and post-2001 subprime loans were not necessarily comparable. In addition, in one sample analysts identified a major change in servicing, pointing in particular to a new rule that managers needed to have four-year college degrees, as explaining significant differences in default behavior before and after 2001.

Analysts recognized that their modeling was constrained by lack of data on the performance of loans through home price downturns. Some analysts simply focused on the cases for which they had data: high and low positive HPA experiences. In one Bank A report, the highest range of current LTV ratios examined was "> 70%."[46] The worst case examined in a Bank E analyst report in the fall of 2005 was one that assumed 0–5 percent annual HPA.[47]

In truth, most analysts appear to have been aware that the lack of examples of negative HPA was not ideal. Bank A analysts wrote in December 2003: "Because of the strong home price appreciation over the past five years, high LTV buckets of loans thin out fast, limiting the history."[48] And they knew this was a problem. A Bank A analyst wrote in June 2005: "We do not project losses with home appreciation rates below −2.5%, because the data set on which the model was fitted contained no meaningful home price declines, and few loans with LTVs in the high-90%. Therefore, model projections for scenarios that take LTVs well above 100% are subject to significant uncertainty."[49]

46. Bank A, March 17, 2004.
47. Bank E, December 13, 2005.
48. Bank A, December 16, 2003.
49. Bank A, June 3, 2005.

However, at some point some analysts overcame these problems. In a debate that we discuss in more detail below, Standard & Poor's and Bank A analysts considered scenarios with significant declines in home prices. A Standard & Poor's report in September 2005 considered a scenario in which home prices fell on the coasts by 30 percent and in the interior of the country by 10 percent.[50] Bank A analysts examined the same scenario, illustrating that by December they were able to overcome the lack of meaningful price declines identified in June.[51]

The Role of HPA

Market participants clearly understood that HPA played a central role in the dynamics of foreclosures. They identified at least four key facts about the interaction between HPA and foreclosures. First, HPA provided an "exit strategy" for troubled borrowers. Second, analysts identified a close relationship between refinancing activity and prepayment speeds for untroubled borrowers, which also reduced losses. Third, they knew that high HPA meant that even when borrowers did default, losses would be small. Finally, they understood that the exceptionally small losses on recent vintage subprime loans were due to exceptionally high HPA, and that a decline in HPA would lead to greater losses.

The role of HPA in preventing defaults was thus well understood. Essentially, high HPA meant borrowers were very unlikely to have negative equity, and this, in turn, implied that defaulting was never optimal for a borrower who could profitably sell the property. In addition, high HPA meant that lenders were willing to refinance. The following view was widely echoed in the industry: "Because of strong HPA, many delinquent borrowers have been able to sell their house and avoid foreclosure. Also, aggressive competition among lenders has meant that some delinquent borrowers have been able to refinance their loans on more favorable terms instead of defaulting."[52] The "double-trigger" theory of default was the prevailing wisdom: "Borrowers who are faced with an adverse economic event—loss of job, death, divorce, or large medical expense—and who have little equity in the property are more likely to default than borrowers who have larger equity stakes."[53]

50. "Simulated Housing Market Decline Reveals Defaults Only in Lowest-Rated US RMBS Transactions," Standard & Poor's, September 13, 2005.

51. Bank A, December 2, 2005.

52. Bank A, October 20, 2005; see also Bank E, December 13, 2005.

53. Bank A, December 2, 2005.

Participants also identified the interaction between HPA and prepayment as another way that HPA suppressed losses. As a Bank A analyst explained in the fall of 2005, "Prepayments on subprime hybrids are strongly dependent on equity build-up and therefore on home price appreciation. Slower prepayments extend the time a loan is outstanding and exposed to default risk."[54] The analyst claimed that a fall in HPA from 15 percent to –5 percent would reduce the CPR, the annualized prepayment rate of the loan pool, by 21 percentage points.

Analysts seem to have understood both that the high HPA of recent years accounted for the exceptionally strong performance of recent vintages, and that lower HPA represented a major risk going forward. As a Bank E analyst wrote in the fall of 2005, "Double-digit HPA is the major factor supporting why recent vintage mortgages have produced lower delinquencies and much lower losses."[55] A Bank C analyst wrote, "The boom in housing translated to a buildup of equity that benefited subprime borrowers, allowing them to refinance and/or avoid default. This has been directly reflected in the above average performance of the 2003 and 2004 [home equity loan] ABS vintages."[56] And in a different report, another Bank E analyst argued that investors did understand its importance: "If anyone questioned whether housing appreciation has joined interest rates as a key variable in mortgage analysis-attendance at a recent [industry] conference would have removed all doubts. Virtually every speaker, whether talking about prepayments or mortgage credit, focused on the impact of home prices."[57]

Analysts did attempt to measure the quantitative implications of slower HPA. In August 2005, analysts at Bank B evaluated the performance of 2005 deals in five HPA scenarios. In their "meltdown" scenario, which involved –5 percent HPA for the life of the deal, they concluded that cumulative losses on the deals would be 17.1 percent of the original principal balance. Because the "meltdown" is roughly what actually happened, we can compare their forecast with actual outcomes. Implied cumulative losses for the deals in the ABX-06-01 index, which are 2005 deals, are between 17 and 22 percent, depending on the assumptions.[58]

The lack of examples of price declines in their data thus did not prevent analysts from appreciating the importance of HPA, consistent with the

54. Bank A, December 2, 2005.
55. Bank E, December 13, 2005.
56. Bank C, April 11, 2006.
57. Bank E, November 1, 2005.
58. See Bank B, August 15, 2005, and Bank C, August 21, 2008.

results of the previous section. In an April 2006 report, analysts at Bank C pointed out that the cross section of metropolitan areas illustrated the importance of HPA: "The areas with the hottest real estate markets experienced low single-digit delinquencies, minimal . . . losses, [and] low loss severity . . . a sharp contrast to performance in areas at the low end of HPA growth."[59] At that time Greeley, Colorado, had 6 percent HPA since origination and 20 percent delinquency. At the other extreme was Bakersfield, California, with 88 percent HPA and 2 percent delinquency. Bank C's estimated relationships between delinquency rates and cumulative loss rates, on the one hand, and cumulative HPA since origination, on the other, using the 2003 vintage, are plotted in figure 15. Even in their sample, there was a dramatic difference between low and high levels of cumulative HPA. But if the analysts had looked at predicted values, they would have predicted dramatic increases in both delinquencies. If they had used the tables to forecast delinquencies in May 2008 with a 20 percent fall in house prices (roughly what happened), they would have predicted a 35 percent delinquency rate and a 4 percent cumulative loss rate. The actual numbers for the 2006-1 ABX are a 39 percent delinquency rate and a 4.27 percent cumulative loss rate.[60]

What is in some ways most interesting is that some analysts seem to have understood that the problems might extend beyond greater losses on some subprime MBSs. In the fall of 2005, Bank A analysts mapped out almost exactly what would happen in the summer of 2007, but the analysis is brief and not the centerpiece of their report. They start by noting, "As of November 2004, only three AAA-rated RMBS classes have ever defaulted. . . ."[61] And, indeed, as of this writing almost no AAA-rated MBSs have defaulted. But the analysts understood that even without such defaults, problems could be severe: "Even though highly rated certificates are unlikely to suffer losses, poor collateral or structural performance may subject them to a ratings downgrade. For mark-to-market portfolios the negative rating event may be disastrous, leading to large spread widening and trading losses. Further down the credit curve, the rating downgrades become slightly more common, and need to be considered in addition to the default risk."[62]

The only exception to the claim that analysts understood the magnitude of df/dp comes from the rating agencies. As a rating agency, Standard &

59. Bank C, April 11, 2006.

60. Citi, "ABX Monthly—September 2008 Remittance," October 1, 2008.

61. Bank A, October 20, 2005.

62. Bank A, October 20, 2005.

Figure 15. Bank C's Estimated Relationship between HPA and Delinquency Rates and Cumulative Losses, 2006

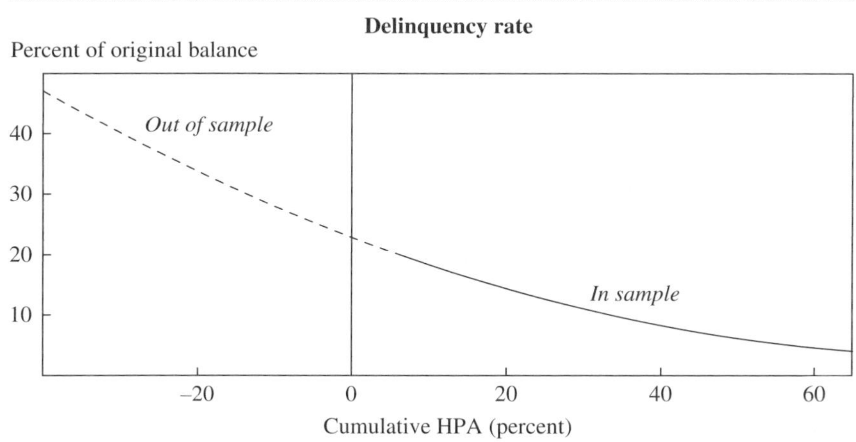

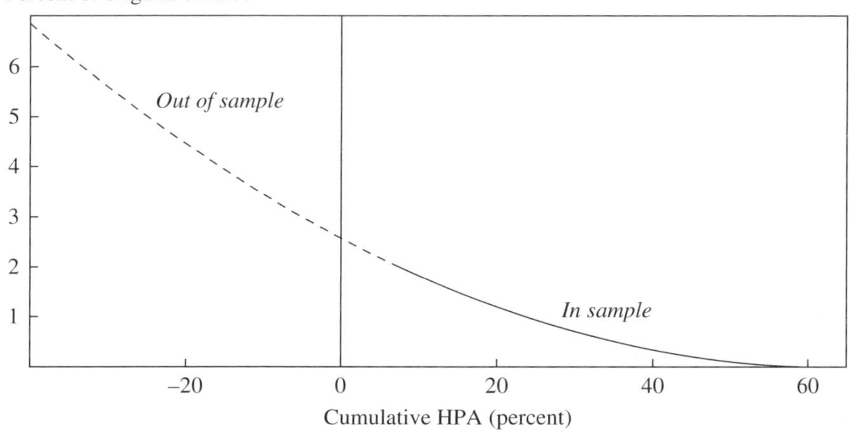

Source: Bank C.

Poor's was forced to focus on the worst possible scenario rather than the most likely one. And their worst-case scenario is remarkably close to what actually happened. In September 2005, they considered the following:[63]

—a 30 percent home price decline over two years for 50 percent of the pool

63. "Simulated Housing Market Decline Reveals Defaults Only in Lowest-Rated US RMBS Transactions," Standard & Poor's, September 13, 2005.

—a 10 percent home price decline over two years for 50 percent of the pool

—a "slowing but not recessionary economy"

—a cut in the federal funds rate to 2.75 percent, and

—a strong recovery in 2008.

In this scenario they concluded that cumulative losses would be 5.82 percent. Interestingly, their losses for the first three years are around 3.43 percent, which is in line with both of the estimates in figure 15 and the data from deals in the 2006-1 ABX. Their problem was in forecasting the major losses that would occur later. As a Bank C analyst recently said, "The steepest part of the loss ramp lies straight ahead."[64]

Standard & Poor's concluded that none of the investment-grade tranches of MBSs would be affected at all—no defaults or downgrades. In May 2006 they updated their scenario to include a minor recession in 2007, and they eliminated both the rate cut and the strong recovery.[65] They still saw no downgrades of any A-rated bonds or most of the BBB-rated bonds. They did expect widespread defaults, but this was, after all, a scenario they considered "highly unlikely." Although Standard & Poor's does not provide detailed information on their model of credit losses, it is impossible not to conclude that their estimates of df/dp were way off. They obviously appreciated that df/dp was not zero, but their estimates were clearly too low.

The problems with the Standard & Poor's analysis did not go unnoticed; Bank A analysts disagreed sharply with it, saying, "Our loss projections in the S&P scenario are vastly different from S&P's projections under the same scenario. For 2005 subprime loans, S&P predicts lifetime cumulative losses of 5.8%, which is less than half our number. . . . We believe that the S&P numbers greatly understate the risk of HPA declines."[66] The irony in this is that both Standard & Poor's and Bank A ended up quite bullish on the subprime market, but for different reasons. The rating agency apparently believed that df/dp was low, whereas most analysts appear to have believed that dp/dt was unlikely to fall substantially.

Home Price Appreciation

Virtually everyone agreed in 2005 that the record HPA pace of the immediately preceding years was unlikely to be repeated. However,

64. Bank C, September 2, 2008.

65. "A More Stressful Test of a Housing Market Decline on U.S. RMBS," Standard & Poor's, May 15, 2006.

66. Bank A, December 2, 2005.

many believed that price *growth* would simply revert to its long-run average, not that price *levels* or *valuations* would. At worst, some predicted a prolonged period of subpar nominal price growth.

A Bank A report in December 2005 expressed the prevailing view on home prices: "A slowdown of HPA seems assured."[67] The question was by how much. In that report, the Bank A analysts stated that "the risk of a national decline of home prices appears remote. The annual HPA has never been negative in the United States going back to at least 1972." The authors acknowledge that there had been regional falls but noted, "In each one of these regional corrections, the decline of home prices coincided with a deep regional recession."

The conclusion that prices were unlikely to fall followed from the fact that "few economists predict a near-term recession in the United States"[68] An analyst at Bank D described the future as a scenario in which house prices would "rust but not bust."[69]

In August 2005 Bank B analysts actually assigned probabilities to various home price outcomes.[70] They considered five scenarios:

—an *aggressive* scenario, in which HPA is 11 percent over the life of the pool (with an assigned probability of 15 percent)

—a *modestly aggressive* scenario, with 8 percent HPA over the life of the pool (15 percent)

—a *base* scenario, in which HPA slows to 5 percent by the end of 2005 (50 percent)

—a *pessimistic* scenario, with 0 percent HPA for the next three years and 5 percent HPA thereafter (15 percent), and

—a *meltdown* scenario, with –5 percent HPA for the next three years and 5 percent HPA thereafter (5 percent).

HPA over the relevant period (the three years after Bank B's report) actually came in a little below the –5 percent of the meltdown scenario, according to the S&P/Case-Shiller index. Reinforcing the idea that they viewed the meltdown scenario as implausible, the analysts devoted no time to discussing its consequences, even though it is clear from tables in the paper that it would lead to widespread defaults and downgrades, even among the highly rated investment-grade subprime MBSs.

67. Bank A, December 2, 2005.
68. Bank A, December 2, 2005.
69. Bank D, November 27, 2006.
70. Bank B, August 15, 2005.

The belief that home prices could not decline that much persisted even long after prices began to fall. The titles of a series of analyst reports entitled "HPA Update" from Bank C tell the story:[71]

—"More widespread declines with early stabilization signs" (December 8, 2006, reporting data from October 2006)

—"Continuing declines with stronger stabilization signs" (January 10, 2007, data from November 2006)

—"Tentative stabilization in HPA" (February 6, 2007, data from December 2006)

—"Continued stabilization in HPA" (March 12, 2007, data from January 2007)

—"Near the bottom on HPA" (September 20, 2007, data from July 2007)

—"UGLY! Double digit declines in August and September" (November 2, 2007, data from September 2007).

By 2008 Bank C analysts had swung to the opposite extreme, arguing in May, "We expect another 15% drop in home prices over the next 12 months."[72]

However, not everyone shared the belief that a national decline was unlikely. Bank E analysts took issue with the views expressed above, writing, "Those bullish on the housing market often cite the historic data . . . to make the point that only in three quarters since 1975 have U.S. home prices (on a national basis) turned negative, and for no individual year period have prices turned negative,"[73] and pointing out, correctly, that those claims are only true in nominal terms; home prices in real terms had fallen on many occasions.

What They Anticipated

With the exception of the S&P analysts, it seems everyone understood that a major fall in HPA would lead to a dramatic increase in problems in the subprime market. Thus, understanding df/dp does not appear to have been a problem. In a sense, that more or less implies that failure to accurately predict dp/dt was the problem, and the evidence confirms it. Most analysts simply thought that a 20 percent nationwide fall in prices was impossible, let alone the even larger falls since observed in certain states—Arizona, California, Florida, and Nevada—that accounted for a disproportionate share of subprime lending.

71. Bank C, "HPA Update," dates as noted.
72. Bank C, May 16, 2008.
73. Bank E, November 1, 2005.

One can argue that the basic pieces of the story were all there. Analysts seem to have understood that home prices could fall. They seem to have understood that HPA played a central role in the performance of subprime loans. Many seem to have understood how large that role was. Others seem to have understood that even downgrades of MBSs would have serious consequences for the market. However, none of the analyst reports that we have found seem to have put the whole story together in 2005 or 2006.

Conclusion

The subprime mortgage crisis leads one naturally to wonder how important and sophisticated market participants so badly underestimated the credit risk of heterodox mortgages. As we have shown, subprime lending added risk features only incrementally, and the underlying leverage of loans was, at least in some data sources, somewhat obscure. Thus, far from plunging them into uncharted waters, investors may have felt that each successive round of weaker underwriting standards was bringing them increasing comfort.

The buoyant home price environment that prevailed through mid-2006 certainly held down losses on subprime mortgages. Nonetheless, as we have also shown, even with just a few years of data on subprime mortgage performance, containing almost no episodes of outright price declines, loan-level models reflect the sensitivity of defaults to home prices. Loss models based on these data should have warned of a significant increase in losses, albeit smaller than the actual increase. Of course, making the effort to acquire property records from a region afflicted in the past by a major price drop, such as Massachusetts in the early 1990s, would have allowed market participants to derive significantly more precise estimates of the likely increase in foreclosures following a drop in home prices. Nonetheless, even off-the-shelf data and models, from the point of view of early 2005, would have predicted sharp increases in subprime defaults following such a decline. However, the results of these models are sensitive to the specification and to the assumptions chosen about the future, so by choosing the specification that gave the lowest default rates, one could have maintained a sanguine outlook for subprime mortgage performance.

In the end, one has to wonder whether market participants underestimated the probability of a home price collapse or misunderstood the consequences of such a collapse. Here our reading of the mountain of research reports, media commentary, and other written records left by market participants of the era sheds some light. Analysts were focused on issues such as small differences in prepayment speeds that, in hindsight, appear of secondary importance to the potential credit losses stemming from a home price downturn. When they did consider scenarios with home price declines, market participants, as a whole, appear to have correctly gauged the losses to be expected. However, such scenarios were labeled as "meltdowns" and ascribed very low probabilities. At the time, there was a lively debate over the future course of home prices, with analysts disagreeing over valuation metrics and even the correct index with which to measure home prices. Thus, at the start of 2005, it was genuinely possible to be convinced that nominal U.S. home prices would not fall substantially.

ACKNOWLEDGMENTS We thank Deborah Lucas and Nicholas Souleles for excellent discussions and the Brookings Panel and various other academic and nonacademic audiences for their helpful comments. We thank Christina Pinkston for valuable help in programming the First American Loan-Performance data. Any errors are our own responsibility. The opinions and analysis in this paper are solely the authors' and not the official position of the Federal Reserve System or any of the Reserve Banks.

References

Avery, Robert B., Kenneth P. Brevoort, and Glenn B. Canner. 2006. "Higher-Priced Home Lending and the 2005 HMDA Data." *Federal Reserve Bulletin* 92: A123–A166.

———. 2007. "The 2006 HMDA Data." *Federal Reserve Bulletin* 93: A73–A109.

———. 2008. "The 2007 HMDA Data." *Federal Reserve Bulletin* 94: A107–A146.

Avery, Robert B., Glenn B. Canner, and Robert E. Cook. 2005. "New Information Reported under HMDA and Its Application in Fair Lending Enforcement." *Federal Reserve Bulletin* 91: 344–94.

Calomiris, Charles. 2008. "The Subprime Turmoil: What's Old, What's New, and What's Next." Working paper. Columbia University.

Case, Karl, and Robert Shiller. 1987. "Prices of Single Family Homes since 1970: New Indexes for Four Cities." Working Paper 2393. Cambridge, Mass.: National Bureau of Economic Research.

Coleman, Major D., IV, Michael LaCour-Little, and Kerry D. Vandell. 2008. "Subprime Lending and the Housing Bubble: Tail Wags Dog?" Working paper. California State University at Fullerton and University of California, Irvine.

Danis, Michelle A., and Anthony N. Pennington-Cross. 2005. "The Delinquency of Subprime Mortgages." Working Paper 2005-022A. Federal Reserve Bank of St. Louis.

Davis, Morris A., Andreas Lehnert, and Robert F. Martin. 2008. "The Rent-Price Ratio for the Aggregate Stock of Owner-Occupied Housing." *Review of Income and Wealth* 54, no. 2: 279–84.

Demyanyk, Yuliya, and Otto van Hemert. 2007. "Understanding the Subprime Mortgage Crisis." Supervisory Policy Analysis Working Papers 2007-05. Federal Reserve Bank of St. Louis.

Deng, Yongheng, and Stuart Gabriel. 2006. "Risk-Based Pricing and the Enhancement of Mortgage Credit Availability among Underserved and Higher Credit-Risk Populations." *Journal of Money, Credit, and Banking* 38, no. 6: 1431–60.

Deng, Yongheng, John Quigley, and Robert van Order. 2000. "Mortgage Terminations, Heterogeneity and the Exercise of Mortgage Options." *Econometrica* 68, no. 2: 275–307.

Doms, Marla, Fred Furlong, and John Krainer. 2007. "Subprime Mortgage Delinquency Rates." Working Paper 2007-33. Federal Reserve Bank of San Francisco.

Foote, Christopher, Kristopher Gerardi, and Paul Willen. 2008a. "Negative Equity and Foreclosure: Theory and Evidence." *Journal of Urban Economics* 64, no. 2: 234–45.

Foote, Christopher L., Kristopher Gerardi, Lorenz Goette, and Paul S. Willen. 2008b. "Subprime Facts: What (We Think) We Know about the Subprime Crisis and What We Don't." Public Policy Discussion Paper 08-02. Federal Reserve Bank of Boston.

Gallin, Joshua. 2006. "The Long-Run Relationship between House Prices and Income: Evidence from Local Housing Markets." *Real Estate Economics* 34, no. 3: 417–38.

———. 2008. "The Long-Run Relationship between House Prices and Rents." *Real Estate Economics* 36, no. 4: 635–58.

Gerardi, Kristopher, Adam Shapiro, and Paul Willen. 2007. "Subprime Outcomes: Risky Mortgages, Homeownership Experiences, and Foreclosures." Working Paper 07-15. Federal Reserve Bank of Boston.

Haubrich, Joseph, and Deborah Lucas. 2006. "Who Holds the Toxic Waste? An Investigation of CMO Holdings." Working paper. Federal Reserve Bank of Cleveland and Northwestern University.

Himmelberg, Charles, Christopher Mayer, and Todd Sinai. 2005. "Assessing High House Prices: Bubbles, Fundamentals and Misperceptions." *Journal of Economic Perspectives* 19, no. 4: 67–92.

Keys, Benjamin J., Tanmoy K. Mukherjee, Amit Seru, and Vikrant Vig. 2008. "Did Securitization Lead to Lax Screening? Evidence from Subprime Loans." Working paper. University of Michigan, Sorin Capital Management, University of Chicago, and London Business School.

Lucas, Deborah, and Robert L. McDonald. 2006. "An Options-Based Approach to Evaluating the Risk of Fannie Mae and Freddie Mac." *Journal of Monetary Economics* 53, no. 1: 155–76.

Mayer, Christopher J., and Karen Pence. 2008. "Subprime Mortgages: What, Where, and To Whom?" Working Paper 14083. Cambridge, Mass.: National Bureau of Economic Research (June).

Mayer, Christopher, Karen Pence, and Shane M. Sherlund. Forthcoming. "The Rise in Mortgage Defaults: Facts and Myths." *Journal of Economic Perspectives.*

McCarthy, Jonathan, and Richard W. Peach. 2004. "Are Home Prices the Next 'Bubble'?" *FRBNY Economic Policy Review* 10, no. 3: 1–17.

Mester, Loretta. 1997. "What's the Point of Credit Scoring?" Federal Reserve Bank of Philadelphia *Business Review,* September/October, pp. 3–16.

Musto, David, and Nicholas Souleles. 2006. "A Portfolio View of Consumer Credit." *Journal of Monetary Economics* 53, no. 1: 59–84.

Pavlov, Andrey D., and Susan M. Wachter. 2006. "Underpriced Lending and Real Estate Markets." Working paper. University of Pennsylvania.

Pennington-Cross, Anthony, and Giang Ho. 2006. "The Termination of Subprime Hybrid and Fixed Rate Mortgages." Working Paper 2006-042A. Federal Reserve Bank of St. Louis.

Sanders, Anthony, Souphala Chomsisengphet, Sumit Agarwal, and Brent Ambrose. 2008. "Housing Prices and Alternative Mortgage Concentrations." Working paper. Ohio State University, Federal Reserve Bank of Chicago, Office of the Comptroller of the Currency, and Pennsylvania State University.

Sherlund, Shane. 2008. "The Past, Present, and Future of Subprime Mortgages." Finance and Economics Discussion Series 2008-63. Washington: Federal Reserve Board.

Wheaton, William C., and Nai J. Lee. 2008. "Do Housing Sales Drive Housing Prices or the Converse?" MIT Department of Economics Working Paper 08-01. Massachusetts Institute of Technology.

Wheaton, William C., and Gleb Nechayev. 2008. "The 1998–2005 Housing 'Bubble' and the Current 'Correction': What's Different This Time?" *Journal of Real Estate Research* 30, no. 1: 1–26.

Comments and Discussion

COMMENT BY

DEBORAH LUCAS In the wake of falling home prices and skyrocketing default rates, seemingly sophisticated investors have lost hundreds of billions of dollars on subprime mortgages. This paper by Kristopher Gerardi, Andreas Lehnert, Shane Sherlund, and Paul Willen provides new evidence on to what extent investors could have anticipated such severe losses, and whether they assigned a reasonable probability ex ante to the events that occurred. The authors also offer an interesting interpretation of their evidence, which is that investors probably understood the sensitivity of foreclosure rates to home price declines but placed a very low probability on a severe, marketwide decline.

What investors believed ex ante has been the subject of considerable debate. Some commentators have argued that it would have been very difficult to foresee the possibility of such large losses. They point to the short time series of available data on subprime performance and the benign default rates over the preceding period. Others claim that investors were poorly informed or even duped about the risk of what they were buying. Investors may not have realized the increased prevalence of highly leveraged properties and low-documentation loans. Further, complex securitization structures may have made the risks opaque to the ultimate investors, who were inclined to rely on credit ratings rather than a careful analysis of the underlying collateral. Reliance on securitization and complicated mechanisms to transfer risk also created agency problems by rewarding originators for increasing loan volumes rather than for prudently screening borrowers. A dissenting point of view, however, is that although investors in the triple-A-rated tranches of subprime mortgage-backed securities (MBSs) may have been genuinely surprised to be hit with losses, the risk-tolerant investors who bought the junior tranches were making a calculated bet that they understood to be quite risky.

These different viewpoints can be evaluated against the evidence provided in the paper's analysis. Such an evaluation is important because the appropriate policy response depends on whether the subprime losses were primarily attributable to unforeseeable circumstances, to bad information, or to purposeful risk taking. If the ex ante probability of a meltdown was objectively extremely low, then perhaps few fundamental regulatory changes are called for. If, on the other hand, a lack of transparency was the root of the collapse, the remedy likely rests on stronger disclosure requirements and greater regulatory oversight of the mortgage origination and securities markets. Finally, if the cause was deliberate risk taking that had systemic consequences, then enhanced controls, such as more stringent capital requirements and greater oversight of the over-the-counter market, are likely to be the most appropriate response.

In this discussion I briefly review the main findings of this analysis and consider whether the authors' conclusions are convincing in light of the data presented. I also consider some broader evidence about what investors were aware of before the crisis. To summarize, I am persuaded by the authors' argument that even in an environment of rising home prices, the sensitivity of foreclosures to home equity can be identified in publicly available cross-sectional data, and that this sensitivity was likely understood by many market participants. I also agree that the evidence points to weaker lending standards exacerbating the problems, but probably to a lesser extent than some observers have claimed. In fact, the authors make a plausible case that the riskier loans could have been expected to perform reasonably well had home prices not fallen. What is less convincing is their more speculative conclusion, based on investment analysts' published reports, that investors underappreciated the risk of a significant decline in home prices. Drawing on a variety of financial indicators, I argue that many investors must have recognized the possibility of large losses, but that apparently they did not have an incentive to avoid the risk. Thus I conclude that the evidence points more toward deliberate risk taking than to a lack of warning signs about the risks. Notwithstanding these differences in interpretation, this paper is the most substantive analysis of the subprime crisis that I have seen, and I think it will have a significant influence on how the crisis is understood.

EVALUATING THE FINDINGS. The central question addressed in this paper is to what extent investors could have anticipated the increase in foreclosure rates that occurred. The authors break the change in the foreclosure rate into two pieces: the sensitivity of the foreclosure rate to changes in home prices, df/dp, and the change in home prices over time, dp/dt. Combining the two components, the change in the foreclosure rate over time is given by $df/dt = (df/dp) \times (dp/dt)$.

This decomposition is useful empirically because better information is available for evaluating each component separately than for trying to explain changes in foreclosure rates directly. Nevertheless, investors and analysts may not have conceptualized risk in exactly this way, and so their statements may not map smoothly into this framework. This is an issue for how the authors interpret what the rating agencies were saying at the time, as discussed below.

Using publicly available data—both a nationwide sample and one that has a longer time series but is specific to Massachusetts—the authors are able to estimate the sensitivity of foreclosure rates to changing home prices. An important insight is that although the era of subprime lending coincides with a period of overall home price appreciation, it is possible to exploit regional variation in price changes to study the sensitivity of foreclosure rates to price declines. The authors make a convincing case, first, that this sensitivity is high, and second, that the relationship is nonlinear.

To see whether the historical sensitivity of foreclosure rates to price changes carries over to the environment of falling prices after 2005, the authors predict foreclosure rates for that period using models estimated with data from 2000 to 2004, but calibrated with the actual price changes for the later period. They find that had investors been endowed with perfect foresight about actual home price changes, they could have predicted a significant portion of the increase in foreclosure rates that ensued, although not all of it. This finding is particularly interesting because the incentive to default could have been significantly affected by whether price declines are local or broadly based, for instance because prices may be perceived as less likely to recover quickly when declines are more widespread.

Given the public availability of these data and the robustness of their results to different specifications, the authors conclude that investors were likely to have been aware of these historical relationships. Their extrapolations also suggest that historical experience was predictive of foreclosure sensitivity to home price changes during the crisis. I would emphasize that a further reason to believe that investors were aware of the nonlinear sensitivity of foreclosures to home prices is that it is consistent with basic economic theory—and with common sense. The right to default is a type of put option, and it is only worth exercising when the price of the home, plus various costs associated with defaulting such as loss of access to credit, falls below the principal balance on the mortgage. Further, whether or not market participants studied the same data that the authors use, it is likely that they observed a very similar pattern in any local data with which they were familiar.

The analysis also provides evidence about the extent to which underwriting standards had declined and how much that decline contributed to the increase in foreclosure rates. Consistent with most accounts of the crisis, the authors find increases over time in risk factors such as high loan-to-value ratios, the presence of second liens, low- or no-documentation loans, and loans with a combination of these risk factors, or "risk layering." Interestingly, they find that the increase in foreclosure rates during the crisis for riskier loans that had been originated several years before the crisis was not much above that for more tightly underwritten loans originated around the same time. Loans originated shortly before the crisis, however, had much higher overall foreclosure rates, and for this later group lower underwriting standards are more important. The authors conclude that weaker underwriting standards can account for only a portion of the increase in foreclosure rates.

Although this part of the authors' analysis provides very useful information that helps put the role of underwriting standards into perspective, it does not resolve the question of to what extent declining underwriting standards caused the crisis. Since the information provided is based on public data, it suggests that sophisticated investors should have known that standards were deteriorating, but it is not established that they did know. More critically, the data do not reveal whether the decline in standards was due to an increasing appetite for risk among investors, or instead to agency problems associated with the opaque nature of MBSs.

On the question of what investors perceived about the likely direction of home prices in the period leading up to the crisis, much less concrete information is available. The authors have chosen to examine the published reports of financial analysts, and they conclude that analysts assigned a small probability to a home price meltdown of the magnitude that occurred. I suspect that these reports are unreliable indicators of what market participants believed. After all, research reports are a sales tool, and it seems unlikely that investors view these reports as providing unbiased information. For instance, it is well known that the frequency of sell recommendations in stock analysts' reports is much lower than the fraction of stocks that subsequently fall in value. Reporting a high probability of a crash in the housing market would be tantamount to a sell recommendation on mortgage securities, so it is not surprising that such forecasts were difficult to find. Nor is it surprising that these same banks now support the idea that a price decline would have been extremely difficult to predict, since the alternative, which is that they were marketing as good investments securities that they perceived to be extremely risky, would be an invitation to litigation. A final point is that the occurrence of a crisis is not in itself evidence that analysts should have assigned any particular ex ante probability to its occurrence. The conclusion that the probabilities reported by analysts were unrealistically small can be established only if there is other evidence of greater risk, which, as I argue below, there appears to be.

Finally, the authors suggest that unlike the investment banks, the rating agency Standard & Poor's (S&P) did not understand the sensitivity of foreclosure rates to home price declines. This inference is based on their analytical framework, $df/dt = (df/dp) \times (dp/dt)$; on the fact that S&P used a scenario in its worst-case analysis that resembled the home price decline that actually occurred; and on the observation that S&P estimated the probability of losses in the senior tranches of MBSs to be close to zero. The reasoning is that if df/dt is reported to be close to zero and dp/dt is highly negative, then df/dp must have been thought to be close to zero. However, given the rest of the evidence in this paper, it seems quite unlikely that S&P was unaware that df/dp is significantly negative. A more plausible explanation, which has been suggested elsewhere,[1] is that the rating agencies understood the effect of home price risk on the performance of individual mortgages, but failed to properly model the effect of correlation between mortgages in a pool and how it would affect the losses on different tranches of MBSs. Figure 1, taken from a case study by Darrell Duffie and Erin Yurday,[2] shows that when the probability of default on each individual mortgage is held fixed, increasing the assumed default correlation in a portfolio changes the shape of the distribution of portfolio default rates in a way that increases expected losses on triple-A-rated tranches. Hence this could explain why S&P reported a low probability of losses on highly rated securities despite understanding that foreclosures are sensitive to home prices.

OTHER EVIDENCE. Although there is little direct evidence that investors understood the risk of a sharp decline in aggregate home prices before the subprime crisis, I believe that there were many indicators of heightened risk; I will describe these briefly here.

1. See, for example, Darrell Duffie and Erin Yurday, "Structured Credit Index Products and Default Correlation," case study no. F269 (Harvard Business School, 2004); Joshua D. Coval, Jakub W. Jurek, and Erik Stafford, "Economic Catastrophe Bonds," *American Economic Review* (forthcoming).

2. Duffie and Yurday, "Structured Credit Index Products and Default Correlation."

Figure 1. Distribution of Portfolio Default Rates under Different Assumed Default Correlations

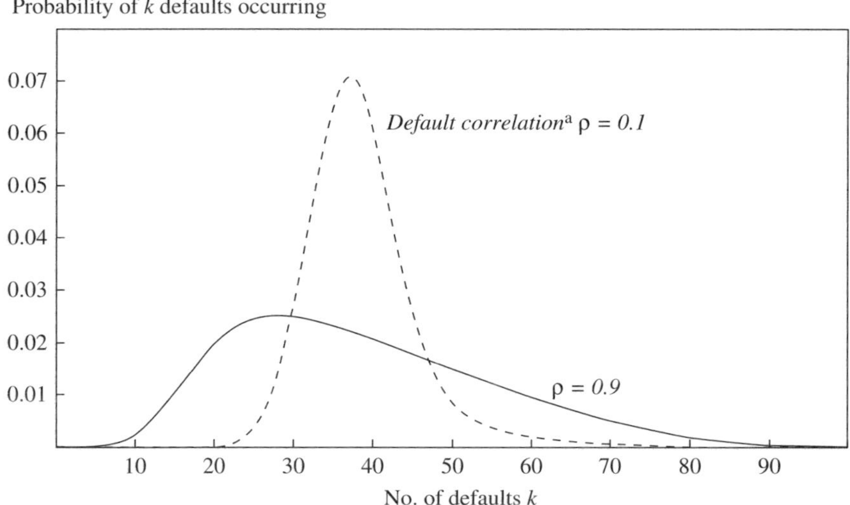

Source: Darrell Duffie and Erin Yurday, "Structured Credit Index Products and Default Correlation," case study F269 (Harvard Business School, 2004).

a. Pairwise correlation between firms in the portfolio of default events. The probability of an individual firm defaulting is held constant across the two cases.

It is important to realize that investors do not need to see a high frequency of defaults or home price declines to understand that there is a significant risk of such occurrences. Credit losses, because they arise from what are in effect written put options, should be expected to be low most of the time but on occasion to be very large. The historical pattern of default rates on corporate bonds is consistent with this prediction. Most years see very few defaults, but occasionally, and as recently as in 2001, default rates have been very high (see my figure 2). Although aggregate home price declines are very rare events in U.S. history, the rapid rate of home price appreciation that started in the late 1990s was also unprecedented. It seems reasonable to expect that a period of unprecedented price increases could be followed by one of unprecedented price declines (see figures 1 and 2 in the paper by Karl Case in this volume). The NASDAQ bubble of the late 1990s also should have served as a recent reminder to investors that rapid price increases can be quickly reversed.

An examination of credit spreads also reveals much about the degree of risk tolerance in credit markets before the crisis. The spread over Treasury rates on speculative-grade investments had fallen to less than half of its

Figure 2. Defaults on Corporate Bonds, 1980–2005

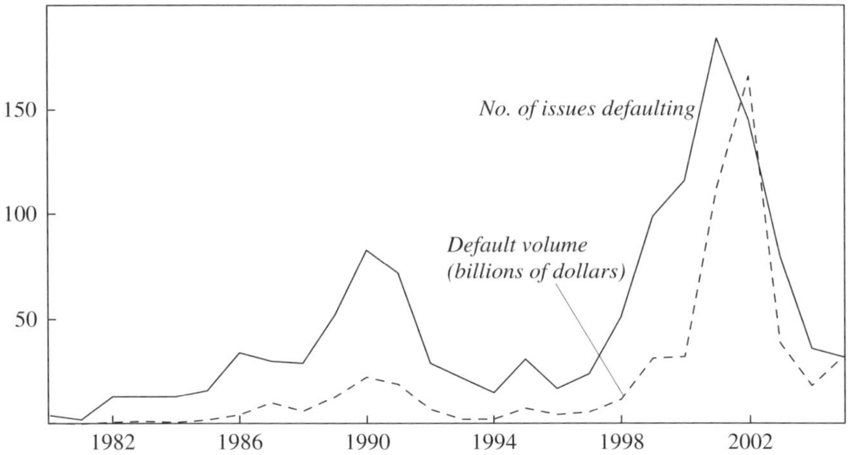

Source: Moody's.

historical average by 2004, and the narrow spreads persisted through the first half of 2007. This could be interpreted as indicating either low expectations of default or unusually high risk tolerance. A factor that points to the latter is the sharp increase in speculative-grade debt outstanding over the same period, suggesting that rating agencies expected higher default rates. As my figure 3 shows, speculative-grade corporate debt issuance is a lead-

Figure 3. Originations of and Default Rates on Speculative-Grade Debt, 1981–2008

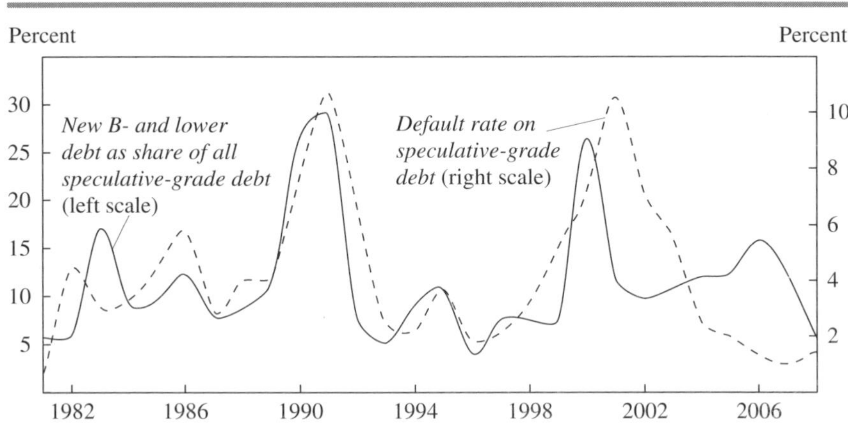

Sources: Standard & Poor's Global Fixed Income Research; Standard & Poor's CreditPro.

ing indicator of default rates on speculative debt generally. By analogy, investors should have been able to infer that the sharp increase in subprime originations would have a similar effect on defaults in the mortgage market. In fact, the emergence of a fully private subprime lending market can itself be interpreted as arising from increased risk tolerance, since before 2000 most subprime loans carried Federal Housing Administration guarantees.

This body of evidence, together with the findings in this paper, leads me to conclude that unusually high risk tolerance was likely to have been more important than a misperception of risk to the rapid growth in subprime lending and to the crisis that followed.

COMMENT BY

NICHOLAS S. SOULELES Kristopher Gerardi, Andreas Lehnert, Shane Sherlund, and Paul Willen have assembled a number of rich mortgage datasets and carefully analyzed them to address some important issues at the center of the current financial crisis. In particular, could (and should) analysts have predicted the recent surge in home foreclosures? The paper's answer to this question has three main parts. First, the declines in home prices and housing equity were the key drivers of the foreclosures; other factors such as underwriting standards did not deteriorate enough to explain them. Second, the strong sensitivity of foreclosures to home prices was predictable in advance. Third, analysts must therefore have believed that there was little chance of a large decline in home prices. I will start by discussing the first two arguments and the paper's empirical analysis of mortgage defaults. To summarize, although it is not necessary to run a "horserace" between home prices and underwriting standards, the empirical analysis provides compelling evidence that one could have predicted that a large decline in home prices would lead to a significant increase in defaults. This is an important result. But what the result implies for home price expectations is a more subtle issue.

THE ANALYSIS OF MORTGAGE DEFAULTS. First, underwriting standards could potentially have played a larger role than implied by the paper's results. Figure 3 of their paper shows that underwriting standards declined along numerous margins, and there could be important interactions across those and other margins. To illustrate, the top left panel of figure 4 shows that through 2005 the probability of default for low-documentation (low-doc) loans was similar to that for full-documentation loans, but after 2005 the probability of default rose much more for the low-doc loans. This suggests that some other factor that interacts with low-doc loans deteriorated after 2005. The key question is whether this factor is (mainly) the decrease in home prices. There are other, not mutually exclusive, possibilities. Suppose that before the housing boom, lenders were more likely to offset the risk associated with low documentation by reducing risk along other margins; for instance, by relying more on lower loan-to-value (LTV) ratios, or on higher credit scores, traditional amortization, or other positive risk factors. This would have reduced the overall risk of low-doc loans in the past. Conversely, there might have been more observations of bad combinations of risk factors (for example, low documentation and low scores) in recent years. The point is that underwriting standards have many components, and they can endogenously interact. In that case one cannot simply introduce the individual components separately into an empirical model. The paper recognizes this point and includes some interaction terms ("risk layering"), but only a few; these are mostly interactions with LTV and are mostly limited to the first default model, the probit model reported in their table 5. In this sense the results provide a lower bound on the importance of underwriting standards. It would be interesting to know what greater proportion of defaults could be explained by including more interaction terms—indeed, as saturated a set as possible.

Further, although the paper's datasets are rich in information about borrowers and their mortgages, this is still only a subset of the information available to lenders for assessing their loans. For instance, the datasets lack information on some contract terms, such as points and fees; some application data, such as the borrowers' financial wealth; and some credit bureau data, such as past mortgage payment problems. Such information, which is known by lenders, could potentially have been used to predict even more of the increase in defaults.[1]

Second, it is not necessary to think of the paper's exercise as a horserace between underwriting standards and home prices. To begin with, in nonlinear models generally there is no unique decomposition of the importance of individual explanatory variables. More substantively, if home prices interact with underwriting standards and other factors, it is inherently difficult to quantify the relative importance of home prices per se. For example, a number of studies have found that low equity interacts with

1. For example, David Gross and Nicholas Souleles, "An Empirical Analysis of Personal Bankruptcy and Delinquency," *Review of Financial Studies* 15, no. 1 (2002): 319–47, using an administrative dataset containing all the key variables tracked by credit card lenders, analyze the increase in consumer bankruptcy and credit card default in the late 1990s.

"triggers" such as unemployment spells.[2] Such triggers can also be correlated with underwriting standards; for example, unemployment risk could be correlated with a low credit score.

A larger role for declines in underwriting standards (or for other factors) can still be consistent with the overall argument of the paper, so long as these declines were largely observable or predictable, and so long as home prices were a predictably significant factor in generating default. If recent subprime mortgages were even more risky, and predictably so, the argument would be that this implied even more optimism about future home prices. Pushing the argument further, many of the subprime mortgages might have been unviable unless the borrowers could eventually refinance out of them, which presumes positive-enough net equity and high-enough home prices.[3]

The paper does provide compelling evidence about the predictable significance of housing equity for mortgage default. (One small quibble: The paper contends that analysts could have used the results for low-but-positive equity in 2000–04 to quantitatively extrapolate the effects of negative equity after 2004. This extrapolation depends, of course, on the assumed functional form, and analysts could not have known ex ante which functional form would have worked well.) As for the effects of underwriting standards, to the extent that there were few observations in the early data of some of the bad combinations of risk factors that became salient later (perhaps, for example, low documentation combined with low credit scores), it would have been more difficult to forecast future default rates with precision. In fact, the main default model applied to the ABS data (the competing-risks model reported in table 10) could not include some salient mortgage characteristics—not even the uninteracted effects of nontraditional amortization, or of negative equity (that is, a nonlinear

2. See, for example, Christopher Foote, Kristopher Gerardi, and Paul Willen, "Negative Equity and Foreclosure: Theory and Evidence," *Journal of Urban Economics* 64, no. 2(2008): 234–45. To illustrate, consider the polar case in which default occurs if and only if the borrower both has negative equity and becomes unemployed. Foote and his coauthors find that borrowers with negative equity in recent years are more likely to default than borrowers with negative equity were in 1991 (before the growth in subprime loans), ceteris paribus. Using the ABS data in this paper, but without ending the sample in 2004, Shane M. Sherlund, "The Past, Present, and Future of Subprime Mortgages," Staff Paper 2008-63 (Washington: Federal Reserve Board of Governors, 2008), finds that borrowers with fixed-rate mortgages were less significantly sensitive to negative equity than were borrowers with adjustable-rate mortgages, ceteris paribus. Such results suggest that net equity might interact with other factors, such as the characteristics of borrowers or their mortgage terms.

3. See, for example, Gary Gorton, "The Panic of 2007," working paper (Yale University, 2008).

effect for low equity, in addition to the included linear equity variables)—since there were too few observations of mortgages with those characteristics in the ABS data before 2004.

IMPLICATIONS FOR HOME PRICE EXPECTATIONS. Supposing it was predictable that large declines in home prices would lead to large increases in default rates, can one therefore conclude that lenders and other analysts must not have been expecting large declines in home prices? There are again alternative, not mutually exclusive, possibilities.

First, without complete information on the terms of the mortgage contracts, it remains possible that lenders thought they were offsetting somewhat more of the mortgage risk than implied by the analysis. Second, lenders and investors might have been willing to tolerate some nonnegligible risk of a large decline in home prices, if their risk aversion was low enough and they considered alternative outcomes (such as a period of stagnant home prices) sufficiently likely. Third, insofar as agency problems were important, some lenders might have thought that they would not fully bear the costs of the increased defaults, even if they could have predicted them.[4] To investigate this possibility, one would ideally like to distinguish the information set of the mortgage originators from the information sets of investors and other agents, which presumably are subsets of the former, to see whether the additional information available to the originators would have predicted significantly more of the defaults.

Finally, even if analysts should have been able to predict much of the increase in mortgage defaults, it would have been more difficult to forecast their spillover onto the rest of the financial system and the extent of the resulting crisis, and moreover to forecast how the crisis in turn would spill back into the mortgage market, further increasing defaults through even lower home prices and other mechanisms (such as higher unemployment).

Although the paper's competing-risks models explain much of the increase in defaults, in the end they still generally underpredict them, especially for the 2005 vintage of mortgages. The paper suggests that this could reflect the fact that the 2005 vintage was more exposed than the 2004 vintage to home price declines. However, the competing-risks models are

4. On this topic, see, for example, Adam Ashcraft and Til Schuermann, "Understanding the Securitization of Subprime Mortgage Credit," Staff Report 318 (Federal Reserve Bank of New York, 2008); Charles Calomiris, "The Subprime Turmoil: What's Old, What's New, and What's Next," working paper (Columbia University, 2008); Benjamin Keys and others, "Securitization and Screening: Evidence from Subprime Mortgage Backed Securities," working paper (University of Michigan, 2008); and Atif Mian and Amir Sufi, "The Consequences of Mortgage Credit Expansion: Evidence from the 2007 Mortgage Default Crisis," working paper (University of Chicago, 2008).

supposed to control for the effects of lower home prices through lower housing equity (and for the resulting decline in the borrower's ability to refinance the mortgage or sell the home instead of defaulting). How much larger a share of the observed defaults could be explained through improved measurement and modeling of housing equity remains an open question. Perhaps other relevant risk factors are still missing from the model, or perhaps the increase in defaults was to some degree inherently difficult to predict in advance, even given the path of home prices. Nonetheless, the paper has made a valuable contribution in showing that home prices were in any case a predictably significant contributor to the defaults.

GENERAL DISCUSSION Jan Hatzius remarked that the idea that people incorrectly guessed the direction of home prices but not the relationship between home prices and defaults was consistent with his impression from discussions he had had with market analysts over the past few years. Most refused to believe, despite a history of large regional declines in home prices, and of nationwide declines in other countries, that home prices in the United States could decline in nominal terms. This denial, he believed, was the essential problem that led to the crisis.

Karl Case stressed the importance of examining the data at the regional level. What was happening in Florida, Nevada, and Arizona, for example, was very different from what was occurring in the Midwest and the Northeast. California's situation was particularly notable since that state accounts for 25 percent of the nation's housing value and experienced a steep decline in prices. He added that the laws relevant to housing differ in important ways from state to state, and that markets clear at different rates in different areas.

Austan Goolsbee offered an airline analogy to illustrate how the crisis arose largely from the interaction of declining home prices and deteriorating lending standards, with the latter playing the lead role. To enable people with bad credit to buy homes, the financial markets had created subprime mortgages and other products that translated home price appreciation into broader home ownership. Just as flying on a budget airline is fine until something goes wrong, so these subprime mortgages were fine until prices started to fall. Goolsbee added that the securitization of those mortgages was much more complicated than what the paper portrayed, and that lending standards deteriorated not only through the relaxation of lending criteria but also through outright fraud: people were allowed to lie about the owner-occupier status of the home they purchased. This matters because people are more likely to walk away from a second home than from a primary residence as soon as they fall into negative equity. Lenders should have assumed that the market would go bad at some point and priced their loans accordingly.

Frederic Mishkin noted that the adjustable subprime contracts inherently assumed a rise in asset prices, because otherwise the loans would not continue to be serviced when the interest rate was reset. Lenders assumed that prices would continue to rise, turning subprime borrowers into prime borrowers, who could then refinance the loan on better terms. He indicated that loans made with the expectation that they would be refinanced may have been prompted by underlying principal-agent issues.

Robert Hall mentioned the work of John Campbell and Robert Shiller showing that overvaluation in a stock market can be detected by looking at the price-dividend ratio: the higher the ratio, the higher the likelihood of a price decline. He suggested incorporating this type of analysis into the paper by looking at price-rent or price-income ratios, noting that their unprecedentedly high levels in the mid-2000s signaled a high probability of future decline.

Martin Baily directed the Panel's attention to the prices of ABX securities—the collateralized debt obligations built on the mortgage-backed securities—and to delinquency rates, which, he argued, revealed a likely change in underwriting standards in the years before the crisis. ABX securities declined significantly in price between the first and the second quarters of 2006, too short an interval to be explained by a drastic change in the underlying mortgages. Delinquency rates, in contrast, increased sharply in the fourth quarter of 2005 and continued to rise in subsequent quarters. The dissimilarity between these two data series seems to indicate a change in something other than housing prices, such as underwriting standards.

Charles Schultze summarized the paper as saying that analysts did understand the nonlinear dependence of foreclosures on changes in home prices but were shocked by the idea that home prices would fall as much as they did. He attributed the unusual size of the price drop to the fact that there had not been an upward movement in home prices this large in the previous forty years. He blamed the incentive structure facing the managers and employees of financial firms: one's approach to risk management changes if one can expect bonuses for four or five years on the upside and only miss one or two on the inevitable downside. He cited a UBS report written after the bank lost the first $19 billion of $42 billion in eventual losses, in which the downplaying of risk management is noted. In addition, the lack of attention to risk evaluation by investors generated a surge in demand for subprime mortgage-backed securities that put pressure on mortgage originators for a substantial erosion of underwriting standards.

Lawrence Summers noted the long tradition of financial messes made because people observed that over a long period the strategy of writing out-of-the-money puts had proved consistently profitable, and so continued the strategy until inevitably a problem occurred. He seconded Goolsbee's comment on the interaction of factors deepening the crisis and asked the authors to try to tease out these different factors. He also suggested that the authors examine the strategies pursued by major builders, the stock prices of those builders, and the implied volatility in puts on their stocks, since builders are essentially betting their franchises on the housing business remaining strong. He guessed that such an examination of these factors would show that the builders shared in the euphoria of rising home prices yet did not share in the ignorance—an idea at odds with Schultze's emphasis on Wall Street's compensation structures.

Bradford DeLong came to the defense of those who had bought homes in California, Florida, and Boston, arguing that long-term interest rates will eventually decline, leading to an increase in home price–rent ratios. Also, rising population in the United States will eventually lead to increased congestion, so land will essentially become a Hotelling good with prices rising over time.

Richard Cooper remarked that one should not limit one's analysis of home price–income ratios to a period of worldwide decline in real long-term interest rates, because housing is a long-term asset. He also pointed out that, at least in the United States, the income elasticity of demand for housing is significantly greater than one, so that rising incomes would eventually lead to an increase in home price–income ratios. But it would be too simplistic to make an evaluation from this ratio alone.

KARL E. CASE
Wellesley College

The Central Role of Home Prices in the Current Financial Crisis: How Will the Market Clear?

ABSTRACT This paper begins by describing some patterns in home price movements over recent decades. It then discusses some distinguishing characteristics of housing markets that will contribute to determining prices going forward: Housing is heterogeneous, making prices hard to measure. Home prices are subject to inertia and are sticky downward. Housing markets have traditionally been quantity clearing markets, with excess inventories absorbed only as new households are formed. And housing markets depend critically on credit market conditions and monetary policy. Two opposite scenarios for future home prices are both plausible: The first, noting among other things the many "underwater" mortgages and unsold inventories and the likelihood of a severe recession, foresees a slow recovery. The second observes that the market clearing process has been orderly so far and that deep regional housing busts in the past have sometimes been followed by quick recoveries, suggesting that a more rapid turnaround is possible.

The housing market today lies at the heart of a potentially catastrophic collapse of the banking and financial system. By some measures, housing prices are down by more than even the most pessimistic forecasters were predicting a year ago. The collapse in value of the collateral behind the nation's $12 trillion portfolio of home mortgages has led to unprecedented rates of delinquency and foreclosure. The decline in home prices has also led investors to unwind the layers of risk created by and traded in new, complex contracts, which now threaten the foundation of the payment system.

This paper begins with an overview of changes in the value of residential capital and land over the last four decades. It then lays out some salient facts about how the housing market has operated in the past, with a focus on alternative market clearing mechanisms. Finally, while stopping short of a specific forecast, the paper presents both the case for a continuing severe decline, with prices falling well into 2010, and an argument that the market may begin to stabilize as early as 2009Q1.

Home Prices and Land Values in the United States, 1975–2007

One national index of home prices suggests that nominal prices never fell over any full quarter between 1975 and 2005. The national quarterly repeat sales index of the Office of Federal Housing Enterprise Oversight (OFHEO; top panel of figure 1) rose 532.4 percent, or more than sixfold, in nominal terms between 1975Q1 and 2007Q1. The bottom panel of figure 1 plots the S&P/Case-Shiller National Index, available back to 1987. Nominal home prices by this measure fell in a number of quarters, but the overall pattern is the same: prices were either rising or flat between 1987 and 2005. Nominal prices rose at an average annual rate of 6.0 percent over the whole period but began accelerating rapidly in 2000.

Table 1 compares increases in home prices with income growth and inflation. Between January 1975 and December 2006, the consumer price index (CPI) rose nearly fourfold, implying an average annual rate of increase of about 4.3 percent over the 32 years. Personal income per capita grew at the same rate as home prices, although median household income did not keep pace.

Figure 2, which shows the OFHEO index in real terms, reveals four time periods when real home prices fell. For purposes of understanding behavior in the housing and mortgage markets, this paper will focus mostly on nominal home price changes, since household debt is carried in nominal terms.

Although national-average nominal home prices rarely or never fell during 1975–2005, boom-bust cycles led to substantial periods of decline in a number of regions. Table 2 presents a rough chronology of these ups and downs based on repeat sales indexes produced by Fiserv CSW and OFHEO. Between 1975 and the late 1990s, major price booms occurred in California (twice) and in the Northeast. Major busts occurred in Texas, the Northeast, and California.

In 1975 the national economy was in recession. During the recovery, California experienced a substantial housing price boom, with nominal prices rising 138 percent between 1975 and 1980. During the same period home prices in the rest of the country rose by only 64 percent. The California boom ended during the deep double-dip recession of 1980–83. With the fixed-rate 30-year mortgage reaching 18 percent and the federal funds

Figure 1. National Nominal Home Price Indexes, Quarterly Data

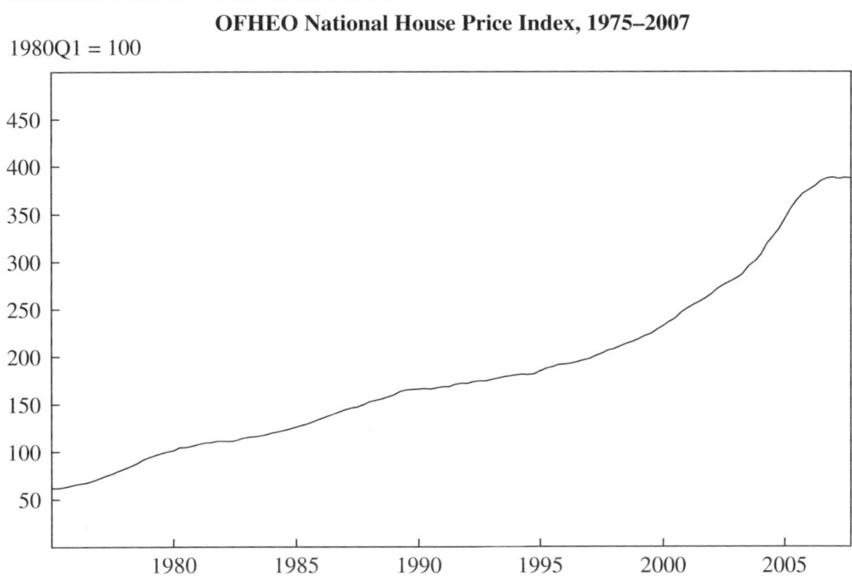

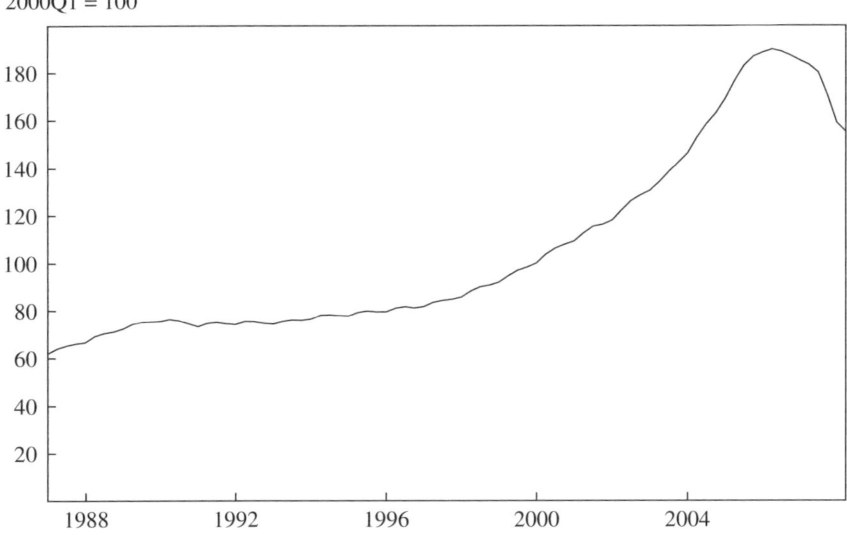

Sources: Office of Federal Housing Enterprise Oversight; Standard & Poor's.

Table 1. Changes in Home Prices, Income, and Consumer Prices, January 1975–December 2006
Percent

Indicator	*Total change*	*Annual average*
OFHEO basic index of house prices	528	5.9
Median household income	308	4.5
Personal income per capita	526	5.9
Average hourly earnings	270	4.2
Consumer price index for all urban consumers (CPI-U)	289	4.3

Sources: Office of Federal Housing Enterprise Oversight, Bureau of Economic Analysis, Bureau of Labor Statistics, and Moody's Economy.com.

rate peaking at 20 percent, demand dropped sharply, and many observers expected a sharp drop in home prices. Instead prices merely went flat from 1981 to late 1984, when the next boom began.

Between 1980 and 1985 the recession ended, inflation subsided, and interest rates fell. By the end of the period, national nominal home prices were up 24 percent, but prices remained substantially below their 1980 peaks in real terms.

Figure 2. Real Price of a Home Worth $100,000 in 2000, 1975–2007

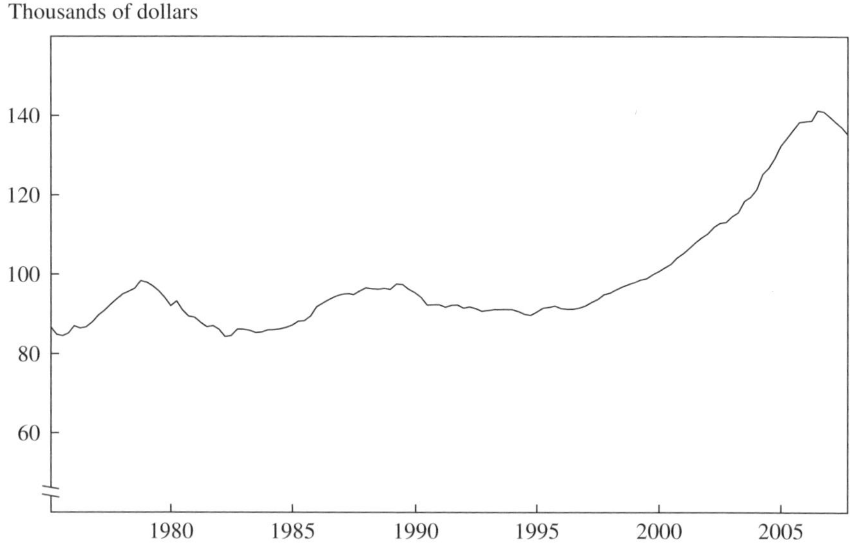

Sources: Office of Federal Housing Enterprise Oversight; author's calculations.

a. Values are calculated from the OFHEO National House Price Index adjusted for inflation using the consumer price index (CPI-U).

Table 2. Housing Booms and Busts since 1975

Period and episode	*Change in home prices (percent)*
1975–80	
First California boom, ending in recession	+138
U.S. national index	+64
1980–85	
Nominal prices in California hold	
Deep recession followed by recovery	
U.S. national index	+24
1985–90	
Texas bust (not preceded by boom), 1986–88	−14
Bottom reached after 10 quarters	
Oklahoma bust, 1983–88	−23
Bottom reached after 19 quarters	
New England-New York boom, 1984–88	+110[a]
New England-New York bust, 1988–92	−12
Bottom reached after 14 quarters	
Second California boom, 1984–90	+92
U.S. national index	+28
1990–95	
Second California bust	−13
Bottom reached after 19 quarters	
San Diego bust, 1990–96	−17
Bottom reached after 24 quarters	
U.S. national index	+14
1995–2000	
Housing prices rising nationwide	
U.S. national index	+29
2000–06	
U.S. national index	+89
Case-Shiller Composite 10	+126
Case-Shiller Composite 20	+107
Miami boom	+181
Bottom tier	+241
Los Angeles boom	+174
Bottom tier	+240
Washington, D.C., boom	+151
Bottom tier	+197
San Diego boom	+150
Bottom tier	+197
Las Vegas boom	+135
Bottom tier	+144
Phoenix boom	+127
Bottom tier	+139

Sources: Standard & Poor's and Office of Federal Housing Enterprise Oversight.
a. Figure is for Boston only.

From 1985 to 1990 the housing market took front and center. First, the oil patch states, which had never experienced a housing boom, saw a sharp decline in their economies, which felt the sting of oil prices falling to $10 a barrel and newly aggressive bank examiners.[1] Texas and the West South Central region saw home prices fall 14 percent in nominal terms, with a bottom after 10 quarters. A worse decline was felt in Oklahoma, where nominal prices fell 23 percent, and a bottom was not reached for 19 quarters. The impact on mortgage defaults was huge.

Precisely as Texas and the rest of the oil patch were in a bust, the Northeast and California housing markets were booming. Nominal home prices nearly doubled in the Northeast in the five years from 1984 to 1989. A second California boom, which also nearly doubled prices, was in full swing as the Northeast bubble burst in 1989.

Both the Northeast boom and the second California boom led to busts of significant magnitude. Nominal prices fell 12 percent in the Northeast, where a bottom was reached in 14 quarters. In California nominal prices fell 13 percent after their peak in 1990, and a bottom was not reached for 19 quarters. As in California a decade earlier, some areas did worse: in San Diego prices fell 17 percent and did not hit bottom for 24 quarters.

What came to be called the "rolling recession," with overlapping housing market cycles, kept national home price indexes rising steadily, with only modest cyclicality overall. There were no national booms or busts until 2000. Beginning in that year, regional housing markets suddenly began to move together. Over the next six years, a rapid acceleration occurred simultaneously in many regions, states, and metropolitan areas. Prices nationwide increased nearly 90 percent from 2000Q1 to 2006. The S&P/Case-Shiller Composite 10 and Composite 20 indexes both more than doubled.[2]

The last panel of table 2 shows how strong the boom was in many areas. The gold medal goes to Miami, where prices increased 181 percent between 2000 and 2006. Los Angeles was just behind at 174 percent, with Washington, D.C., and San Diego both recording increases of 150 percent. The sharpest increases in each market were observed in the lowest tier by value. In Miami and Los Angeles the average property in the bottom tier more than tripled. Just behind them were the bottom tiers of San Diego and Washington.

1. See Congressional Budget Office (1991).

2. The Composite 10 index is an index of home prices in Boston, Chicago, Denver, Las Vegas, Los Angeles, Miami, New York, San Diego, San Francisco, and Washington, D.C. The Composite 20 includes, in addition, Atlanta, Charlotte, Cleveland, Dallas, Detroit, Minneapolis, Phoenix, Portland, Ore., Seattle, and Tampa.

Table 3. Changes in Home Prices by Metropolitan Area through August 2008
Percent

		Change				
Metropolitan area[a]	*Peak*	*Since peak*	*Since one year before*	*July to August 2008*	*June to July 2008*	*January 2000 to August 2008*
Atlanta	Aug. 2006	−7.7	−8.5	−0.2	+0.3	+24.8
Boston	Sept. 2005	−10.8	−4.7	+0.1	+0.2	+62.8
Charlotte	Aug. 2007	−2.8	−2.8	−0.8	−0.2	+32.1
Chicago	Sept. 2006	−11.3	−9.8	0.0	−0.4	+49.5
Cleveland	July 2006	−10.5	−6.6	+1.1	−0.3	+10.5
Dallas	June 2007	−2.8	−2.7	−0.2	+0.6	+22.9
Denver	Aug. 2006	−5.4	−5.1	0.0	+0.8	+32.6
Detroit	Dec. 2005	−27.2	−17.2	0.8	+0.6	−7.6
Las Vegas	Aug. 2006	−35.9	−30.6	−2.4	−2.8	+50.5
Los Angeles	Sept. 2006	−30.9	−26.7	−1.8	−1.6	+89.2
Miami	Dec. 2006	−34.7	−28.1	−1.8	−1.6	+83.5
Minneapolis	Sept. 2006	−17.1	−13.8	−1.0	+1.3	+41.9
New York	June 2006	−10.7	−6.9	−0.2	−0.7	+92.8
Phoenix	June 2006	−36.3	−30.7	−2.9	−2.7	+44.8
Portland, Ore.	July 2007	−7.8	−7.6	−1.3	−0.5	+71.9
San Diego	Nov. 2005	−32.8	−25.8	−2.3	−1.8	+68.2
San Francisco	May 2006	−30.7	−27.3	−3.5	−1.8	+51.4
Seattle	July 2007	−8.9	−8.8	−0.7	−1.0	+75.2
Tampa	July 2006	−26.8	−18.1	−0.4	0.0	+74.3
Washington, D.C.	May 2006	−22.4	−15.4	−0.3	−1.1	+94.9
Composite 10	June 2006	−22.0	−17.7	−1.1	−1.1	+76.6
Composite 20	July 2006	−20.3	−16.6	−1.0	−0.9	+64.6

Source: Standard & Poor's, October 28, 2008.
a. Metropolitan areas are those tracked in the Case-Shiller Composite 20 index.

Not every city was as volatile on the upside. Atlanta, Charlotte, Cleveland, Dallas, Denver, and Detroit all saw healthy but unspectacular price growth ranging from 23 percent (Cleveland) to 40 percent (Denver). There was no hint of the kind of booms going on elsewhere.

Table 3 reports the most recent home price data as of this writing, released by Standard & Poor's on October 28, 2008, and covering the period through August. The new data show the declines since the peak of the market, which occurred at different times in different cities. In September 2005 Boston became the first market to peak, and by March 2008, prices there had fallen 13.1 percent. Prices in Boston have increased slightly each month since April, so that by August the total decline had moderated to 10.8 percent. From the peak through June 2008, prices in Boston had fallen for 11 quarters. The pattern thus resembles the bust that occurred there from 1988 to 1992, when prices fell for 14 quarters. Prices in New York show a similar pattern.

The most severe declines have occurred in Las Vegas, Miami, and Phoenix, which have all seen prices drop by about 35 percent from peaks in mid- to late 2006 to August 2008. Just behind them comes California, where Los Angeles, San Diego, and San Francisco are down more than 30 percent from peak. Next, with declines of over 20 percent, are Detroit, Tampa, and Washington, D.C. Minneapolis is down 17 percent, followed by Boston, Chicago, Cleveland, and New York, with declines of just over 10 percent.

Between 2005 and 2008, for the first time since regional data became available, U.S. housing prices fell virtually everywhere. The S&P/Case-Shiller National Index was down 18.2 percent through 2008Q2, and the Composite 10 and Composite 20 indexes were down 22.0 percent and 20.3 percent, respectively, through August.

Housing Prices and Income over the Cycle

How did home prices fluctuate relative to local income over these cycles? In our 2003 Brookings Paper, Robert Shiller and I used state data to explore the relationship between changes in home prices and one measure of income.[3] Using data including all 50 states and the District of Columbia from 1985 though 2002, we found a relatively stable relationship between personal income per capita and price in 43 states. In the remaining 8, this relationship was cyclical and volatile.

Similar plots for the three decades leading up to 2008, however, show volatility spreading. In 2008 all metropolitan-area housing markets fell into one of three regimes: flat markets, single-peak markets, and regular-cycle markets. The flat market category includes most of the country. Figures 3 and 4 show the typical pattern of these markets for five metropolitan areas: Dallas, Memphis, and Pittsburgh, and Charlotte and Chicago. In these cities home prices did not significantly outpace income; indeed, they fell relative to income in most periods. In all cities but Chicago, the ratio of home prices to income per capita drops in the early 1980s and stays flat through 2007, between 3 and 5. In Chicago the ratio stays flat between 5 and 6, rising to 7 after 2000.

3. Case and Shiller (2003).

Figure 3. Ratios of Home Prices to Personal Income per Capita in the Dallas, Memphis, and Pittsburgh Metropolitan Areas, 1976–2007[a]

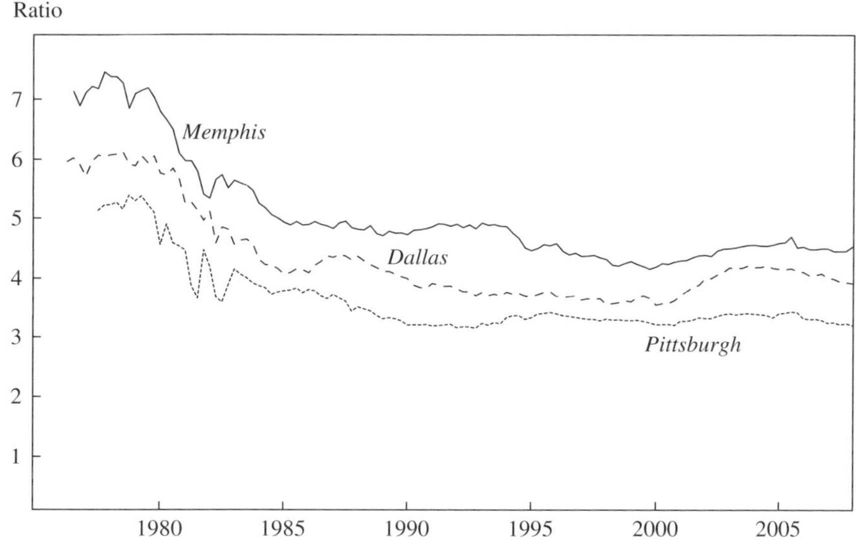

Sources: Office of Federal Housing Enterprise Oversight; author's calculations.

a. Median sales price of existing single-family houses in 2000 deflated with the OFHEO purchase-only price index for the indicated metropolitan area.

Figure 4. Ratios of Home Prices to Personal Income per Capita in the Chicago and Charlotte Metropolitan Areas, 1987–2008

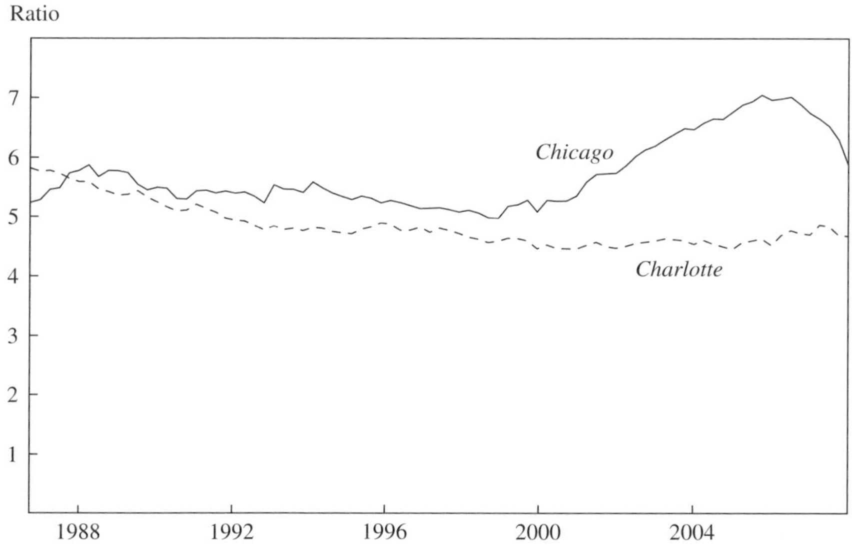

Sources: Standard & Poor's; U.S. Census Bureau; Bureau of Economic Analysis; Moody's Economy.com.

Figure 5. Ratio of Home Prices to Personal Income per Capita in the Phoenix and Miami Metropolitan Areas, 1989–2008

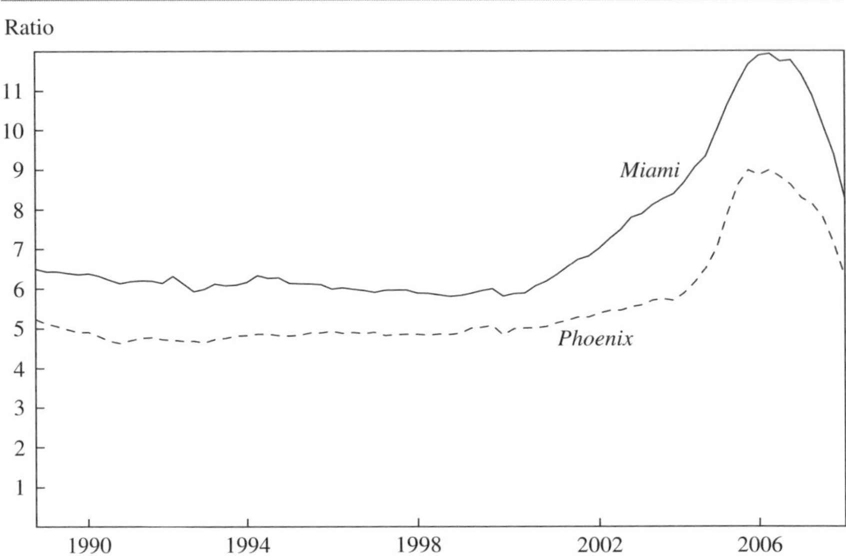

Sources: Standard & Poor's; U.S. Census Bureau; Bureau of Economic Analysis; Moody's Economy.com.

The single-peak markets are Las Vegas, Miami, and Phoenix. Figure 5 shows a remarkably similar pattern for the last two. The Phoenix market remained perfectly stable at a home price-income ratio of around 5 from 1989 through 2000. The ratio then rose slowly to 6 in 2004 before jumping up to 9 in 2006 and falling rapidly back to 6 in 2008. Miami's ratio was completely flat at about 6 until around 2000; it then accelerated upward to 12 by 2006 before dropping sharply.

In the regular-cycle markets of the Northeast and California, the boom-bust cycle has been virtually continuous. The ratio of home prices to income in Boston rose from 7 to over 11 during the boom that ended in 1988 (figure 6). This was followed by a drop back to just above 7 by the mid-1990s. Beginning in 1989 the ratio again rose sharply, peaking at 12 at the end of 2005. By the end of 2008Q1 it was back down to 10. A similar pattern can be found in data for the entire New York–New England region.

In Los Angeles the pattern is the same, but the ratios are higher. Starting at 7 in the mid-1980s, the ratio rose to almost 11 by 1990 before beginning a seven-year decline back to 6 by 1997. From 1997 to 2001 the ratio rose slowly and then accelerated, reaching 16 by the peak in 2006 before falling back to 11 by mid-2008.

Figure 6. Ratio of Home Prices to Personal Income per Capita in the Boston and Los Angeles Metropolitan Areas, 1987–2008

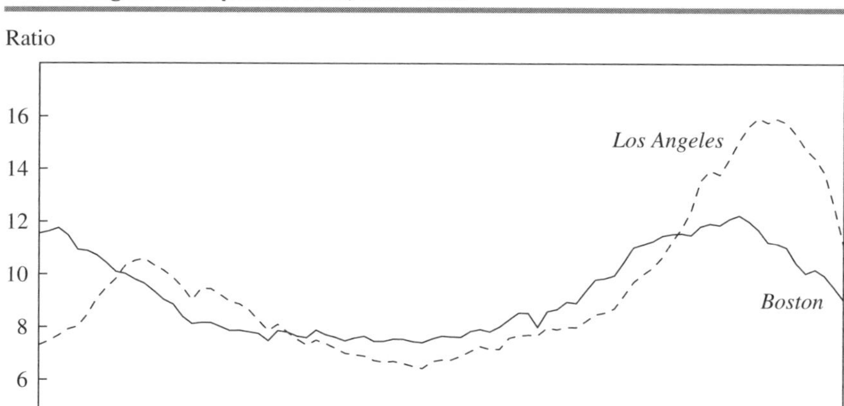

Sources: Standard & Poor's; U.S. Census Bureau; Bureau of Economic Analysis; Moody's Economy.com.

How Does the Housing Market Find a Bottom?

Thus far this paper has simply described the pattern of home price movement over the past few decades. The questions of interest today are, When will prices stop falling? And when will order be restored to the battered housing and mortgage markets? If prices continue to fall into 2010, as many have argued they will, the books of mortgage business written in 2008 to 2009 are not likely to be profitable. If prices stop falling today, default rates will moderate, and recovery will soon follow.

This section of the paper describes the ways in which the housing market differs from other markets. These differences raise some issues that are integral to the process that will determine home values going forward. Some of the distinguishing characteristics of the housing market are the following:

—Housing is heterogeneous and prices are hard to measure.

—Prices are subject to inertia (bubbles) and are sticky downward.

—Housing markets have traditionally been quantity clearing markets.

—Housing markets depend critically on credit markets and monetary policy.

Housing Is Heterogeneous and Prices Are Hard to Measure

The concept of a market price in the housing market is slippery, because every home is at least slightly different from every other. An individual home is a unique combination of both structural and neighborhood characteristics. The purchase of a home involves buying a bundle of attributes: living space, heating and other systems, usually a parcel of land of some dimension, a view, a number of rooms, various structural features (fireplaces, windows, appliances, and so on), and others. It also involves buying into a specific location with a specific natural environment, a school system, other amenities, a set of neighbors, a crime rate, and a tax rate. The purchased home may be of good or poor construction quality and (unless purchased new) may have been well or poorly maintained. Homes also differ in their degree of accessibility. All this makes it very difficult to look at a property, compare it with other properties, and know what it is worth.

The price of a home also includes the cost of the capital used to purchase it. Thinking about a home in this way highlights what makes it a potentially desirable investment. Consider a household buying a home outright, with no mortgage finance. The baseline yield on that investment (essentially the dividend) is the flow of housing services the household receives net of depreciation, maintenance, and taxes. The flow of dividends from an investment in corporate equity depends on profits and is taxable (albeit at a low rate). The flow of *real net imputed rent,* in contrast, is fixed and not taxable, and the costs of finance and property taxes are deductible. Thus, this component of yield has a stabilizing effect in downturns. Housing can therefore be seen as a substitute for equities in periods of uncertainty. In addition to the real services yield, there is the potential for capital gain, which for most households is also tax free. Housing is typically highly leveraged, however, so returns are volatile.

Forming reasonable expectations about gains is difficult, again because housing is heterogeneous. Much has been learned about how expectations are formed from extensive surveys of homebuyers in the Boston, Los Angeles, Milwaukee, and San Francisco metropolitan areas. These surveys were first conducted in 1988 and are now conducted annually.[4] They illustrate several points: that expectations are backward looking, that buyers perceive little risk in purchasing a home, and that the expected returns are unrealistic. For example, two-thirds of buyers surveyed as recently as the spring of 2008 in Boston and San Francisco believed that prices would rise, not fall, that year. That figure was 75 percent in Milwaukee and 54 percent

4. For examples see Case and Shiller (1988, 2003); Case (2009).

in Orange County, California. In the 2004 survey, 92 percent of respondents in Boston anticipated a one-year price rise, compared with over 95 percent in the other three sample sites. In the 2008 survey an even larger majority expected gains over 10 years, and the mean anticipated gain in three of the four cities was 10 percent a year (7.5 percent in again relatively pessimistic Boston).

At a minimum, measurements of changes in home prices must account for changes in physical attributes. There are two basic approaches, which both rely on arm's-length transactions: hedonic price indexes with time dummies, which require fine detail on changes in characteristics, and repeat sales indexes, which control for differences by looking only at properties with at least two observable sales during the relevant period. The advantages and disadvantages of these two approaches and the variations on them are the subject of much debate, which is beyond the scope of this paper. The important question, addressed below, is, How should these indexes be interpreted? What do they tell us about what is happening when they emerge from different market clearing processes taking place at the same time and in the same market?

Home Prices are Subject to Inertia (Bubbles) and Are Normally Sticky Downward

In 1957 Paul Samuelson wrote,

> I have long been struck by the fact, and puzzled by it too, that in all the arsenal of economic theory we have absolutely no way of predicting how long [a bubble] will last. To say that prices will fall back to earth after they reach ridiculous heights represents a safe but empty prediction. Why do some manias end when prices have been ridiculous by 10 per cent, while others persist until they are ridiculous to the tune of hundreds of per cent?[5]

A good deal of evidence indicates that the housing market is prone to bubbles. I argued in 1986 that the price boom in Boston that began in 1984 was not caused by fundamentals but was indeed a bubble.[6] A structural supply-and-demand model that had been reasonably successful at predicting home prices in 9 of the 11 cities in my sample suggested that fundamentals (income growth, interest rates, employment growth, demographics, and so forth) should have pushed Boston home prices up by 16 percent. Instead they increased by over 140 percent before peaking in late 1988.

5. Samuelson (1957, p. 216).
6. Case (1986).

Shiller and I constructed an accurate measure of price changes with transactions data obtained from Atlanta, Chicago, Dallas, and San Francisco.[7] We found evidence of substantial positive serial correlation in real home prices. Our 1989 paper showed that a change in price observed over one year tends to be followed by a change in the same direction the following year between 25 and 50 percent as large. We found evidence of serial correlation in excess returns as well. Subsequent work demonstrated that both California and Massachusetts experienced price bubbles in the 1980s and 1990s.[8]

Price booms like those observed over the past 30 years are more likely to occur where the elasticity of supply of land is low, as in California and Massachusetts. The work of Edward Glaeser and his colleagues has focused attention on zoning and land use regulation.[9] Markets with an elastic supply of developable land seemed to avoid price booms, Florida and Arizona being classic examples. From 1990 until 2000, home prices in these markets could be fully explained by income growth. Between 2000 and the first half of 2006, however, speculative demand boomed, driving prices up dramatically despite what remains a very elastic supply of land. As a result, prices accelerated and building increased faster than immigration and household formation could absorb the new inventory.

Another important aspect of housing market efficiency is that prices tend to be sticky downward. In most markets, when excess supply develops, prices fall quickly to clear the market. But housing downturns have been characterized by sticky prices. Sales and starts drop but prices are slow to respond.

Demand can drop for a variety of reasons: demographic pressures, a weak core economy with falling income or rising unemployment, home prices simply rising far faster than income, or a change in market psychology. On the other hand, there have been clear instances of overbuilding, where supply simply grew faster than demand. All these causal factors can be present in a single market, and they always interact. A decline in a regional economy or a glut of condominiums can drive up the number of listings, newspaper articles, and for-sale signs, which can trigger a shift in consumer psychology that may accelerate the demand decline.

Prices might be slow to respond to imbalances for various reasons. Since housing is heterogeneous, comparable sales do not represent identical units,

7. Case and Shiller (1987, 1989).

8. On the former period see Case and Shiller (1988, 1990).

9. Glaeser (2002); Glaeser and Gyourko (2002); Glaeser, Gyourko, and Saks (2005, 2006); Glaeser, Gyourko, and Saiz (2009).

so sellers are uncertain of the actual worth of their property. Value is determined in a stochastic process in which buyers and sellers search for terms that will lead to a sale. Also, sellers tend to view the worth of their property as embodied in comparable sales at the peak.

The dramatic rise in inventory of unsold homes at the beginning of every downturn is strong evidence of this stickiness. Responses to the survey questions discussed above also provide direct evidence. Buyers who had sold properties before buying in the four metropolitan areas surveyed (Boston, Orange County, San Francisco, and Milwaukee) were asked, "If you had been unable to sell your home for the price that you received, what would you have done?" Of the 254 respondents to the first survey in 1988, 95 (37 percent) said that they would have "left the price the same and waited for a buyer, knowing full well that it might take a long time." Another 70 respondents (28 percent) answered that they would have taken the house off the market or rented it, and 77 (30 percent) answered that they would have "lowered the price step by step hoping to find a buyer." Only 12 respondents (5 percent) answered that they would have "lowered the price until a buyer was found." Results tabulated for the spring 2008 version of the same survey show that individual sellers are more likely to reduce the price when demand drops. But even in this survey only 20 percent said they "would have lowered the price until they found a buyer."

Downward stickiness has been most evident when demand declines are triggered by mortgage rate increases and most homeowners are sitting on fixed-rate mortgages. The classic example occurred at the end of the California boom from 1975 to 1980. Home prices during that boom increased 147 percent. But in 1981 interest rates rose and the average mortgage rate settled between 16 and 18 percent. The combination of high interest rates and the recession caused the housing market to cool sharply, yet prices in California never fell in nominal terms during the ensuing period. Selling induced the enforcement of due-on-sale clauses, and with interest rates so high, potential sellers preferred to hold onto their low fixed-rate mortgages. Interestingly, Vancouver, Canada, experienced a very similar run-up in the late 1970s. However, Canadian law prohibits fixed-rate mortgages with terms exceeding 10 years. As a result, the increased rates led to higher payments, which homeowners could not afford. Many sold out or went into foreclosure. The average nominal price fell by about 60 percent.[10]

10. Repeat sales indexes for Canada were provided by Stanley Hamilton, University of British Columbia.

When demand declines and prices stick, agreements are still reached and properties do sell. Buyers with enough income or wealth can participate in the market and may strongly prefer specific units. Despite the market turmoil in late 2008, existing-home sales reported by the National Association of Realtors remained at a seasonally adjusted rate of 4.98 million as of October. Foreclosure sales reported by Realtytrac accounted for about 1.0 million, or 20 percent, of these sales.

The S&P/Case-Shiller indexes are based on essentially all arm's-length sales of property, but many observed sales are foreclosure sales. Although the indexes exclude bank *purchases,* which are usually made at the mortgage amount, they include bank *sales.* When a bank or other institution holding a property after a foreclosure puts the home on the market, its goal is to clear inventory. Hence there is little observed stickiness. In addition, most foreclosed properties in the recent episode were financed with variable-rate rather than fixed-rate mortgages, and the downturn in home prices was not triggered by a rate spike.

Some argue that the Case-Shiller indexes are biased in that auction sales at fire-sale prices do not represent the "real" market. Any metropolitan-area price index is, of course, subject to aggregation bias, because each metropolitan area is made up of many submarkets. A clearer picture of price movements across space requires submarket indexes, which are available (see table 6 below).

Many properties sold at auction had originally been purchased at the peak of the market. Lower-tier price indexes in the glut markets of Las Vegas, Los Angeles, Miami, Phoenix, and San Diego more than doubled (in some cases tripled) between 2000 and 2006. Excluding auction sales of the properties that inflated dramatically during the boom would present a biased view of where the market ultimately settled after the bust.

Housing Markets Have Traditionally Been Quantity Clearing Markets

Downwardly sticky prices lead to "quantity clearing markets" rather than "price clearing markets." In most markets with excess supply, prices and output fall immediately. If prices are slow to respond, however, the burden of adjustment falls on the quantity of production, prolonging the cycle.

Home prices have followed exactly that pattern over many years. Demand drops. The inventory of unsold homes rises. Prices stick. Output falls. The inventory of unsold property remains high (because a house is a durable good, not a consumable). But household formation rates remain positive, and the new households eventually absorb the excess inventory

Figure 7. Housing Starts, Monthly Data, 1972–2008[a]

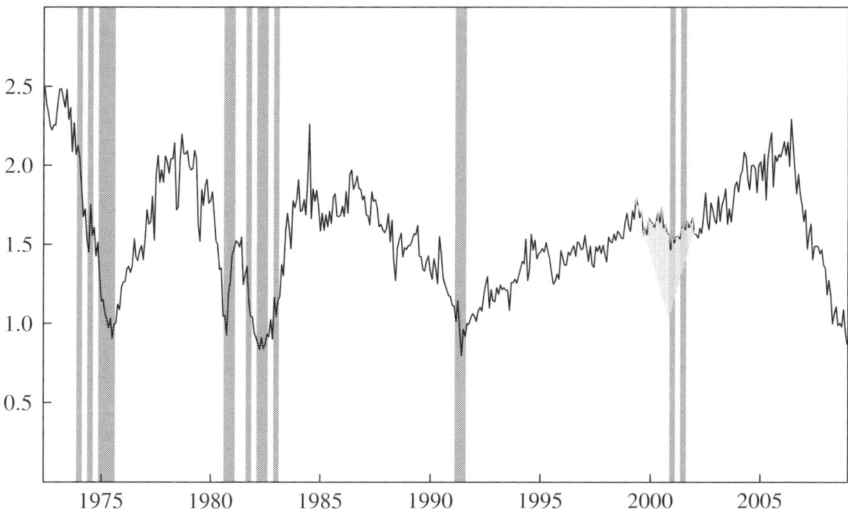

Source: U.S. Census Bureau.

a. Vertical bands indicate quarters of negative GDP growth. Shading indicates the decline in starts that would have been expected given the decline in economic activity in that period.

and output rebounds. Assuming there is upward inertia, prices then rise and ultimately overshoot; demand again slows, starting the next cycle.

The process is accelerated by the fact that housing production is a large part of aggregate demand. When production falls off, it slows the economy, which slows demand growth. John Quigley and I found large income effects from the contractions in housing production that the United States has experienced over the years.[11]

Figure 7 shows just how regular the cycle has been. Since the early 1970s, the United States has gone through four major housing cycles, with peaks in 1972, 1978, 1984, and 2006. Each time housing starts rose above 2 million on an annualized basis, the cycle turned. In the first three cycles, starts then fell by more than 60 percent, to less than a million, before turning up again. In the current cycle, starts hit exactly a million in December 2007 and then bounced up and down for a few months. October 2008, the most recent month for which data are available, was the slowest to date in this cycle, with 625,000 starts.

Table 4 further illustrates the amazing regularity of the cycle in the past. The top of every cycle finds real gross residential investment at about

11. Case and Quigley (2008).

Table 4. Gross Residential Investment and Housing Starts in Down Cycles, 1973–2008

Cycle	*Peak*	*Trough*	*Change (percent)*
1973–75			
Gross residential investment	1973Q1	1975Q1	
Billions of 2000 dollars	$308.3	$186.1	−40
As percent of GDP	7.2	4.4	
Housing starts	January 1973	February 1975	
Millions of units	2.481	0.904	−64
1978–82			
Gross residential investment	1978Q3	1982Q3	
Billions of 2000 dollars	$321.5	$175.6	−45
As percent of GDP	6.3	3.4	
Housing starts	December 1977	November 1981	
Millions of units	2.142	0.837	−61
1984–91			
Gross residential investment	1986Q3	1991Q1	
Billions of 2000 dollars	$341.3	$258.6	−24
As percent of GDP	5.4	3.7	
Housing starts	February 1984	January 1991	
Millions of units	2.260	0.798	−65
2005–08			
Gross residential investment	2005Q4	2008Q3	
Billions of 2000 dollars	$602.0	$353.7	−41
As percent of GDP	5.4	3.0	
Housing starts	January 2006	November 2008	
Millions of units	2.273	0.625	−73

Sources: Bureau of Economic Analysis, Census Bureau construction reports, and Federal Reserve Flow of Funds.

6 percent of real GDP. At the bottom of the last three cycles, the same ratio was on average 3.6 percent of real GDP. The Bureau of Economic Analysis's release of third-quarter GDP in October 2008, however, shows that real gross residential investment has fallen below this historic floor, to 3.0 percent. It shows no sign of rising soon.

Homebuilding is the only major industry that loses 60 percent of its business in a normal contraction. In 2007 the national average cost of a new home was roughly $300,000. After subtracting the value of land and imported building materials (based on data from a number of sources, including the National Association of Homebuilders, the Census Bureau's construction reports, and *Engineering News Record*), each start contributes roughly $240,000 in new residential construction to GDP. With starts down to 817,000 (again on an annualized basis), a total of 1.45 million units that would have been built will not be started; their absence represents a demand shock of roughly $348 billion. This number is confirmed by the reported decline in gross private residential investment from a peak of $808 billion in 2006Q1 to $480 billion in 2008Q3. Assuming a multiplier of 1.4, this is equivalent to a drop in aggregate demand of 3.2 percent.

Although past housing cycles have been regular in amplitude, their length has varied. For example, the recovery in housing starts following the recession of 1975 lasted from February 1975 through May 1978, and that following the recession of 1980–81, when housing starts bottomed out at 837,000 in November 1981, reached a new peak of 2.26 million by February 1984. In contrast, the housing expansion that began in the early 1990s was much longer. From a bottom of 798,000 in January 1991, starts took 15 years to climb back to 2.27 million (figure 7).

The data also show that although homebuilding paused in 1999–2000, the housing market "skipped" a cycle. The easy availability of credit that came with the slowdown in 2001 kept the housing market going: building continued to rise through the next slowdown in the economy in 2002–04. The shaded area in figure 7 simulates a typical decline in starts given the mild nature of the recession of 2000–01. Had the homebuilding sector responded typically, 1.2 million fewer housing units would have been built during that period. Census data show that between 2000 and 2004, new housing units exceeded household formations by just fewer than 4 million. With 1.2 million fewer units, the vacancy rate would have been about 30 percent lower in 2004.

Housing Market Performance Depends on Credit Markets and Monetary Policy

Housing is far more responsive to interest rate changes than any other sector. Historically, when the Federal Reserve has acted to stimulate or slow the economy, housing has shown the greatest first-order response of any sector. The affordability of a given house depends ultimately on the monthly payment, and that depends on the mortgage rate.

From 1970 until 2000, every recession was caused in part by a major rate shock. Between March 1973 and July 1974, the federal funds rate rose from 7 percent to 13 percent. From October 1978 to July 1981, the Federal Reserve pushed the funds rate from 9 percent to almost 20 percent. And from April 1988 to March 1989, it raised the funds rate from below 7 percent to just under 10 percent. In each case the Federal Reserve was responding to inflationary pressure. Similarly, toward the end of each recession, rates came down and helped kick off a housing sector rally. However, the relationship between monetary policy and the housing sector was different in a number of ways in the period beginning in 2000, as the next section describes.

The Roots of the Crash

The 21st century began with an investment-led slowdown and the bursting of the dot-com bubble. After a huge, investment-led expansion, including a 29 percent increase in gross private domestic investment in 2000Q2, investment dropped sharply for six quarters, dragging the economy into negative growth in 2001. The expansion was largely due to expenditure surrounding the Y2K problem, which led many firms to replace their entire computer systems. Investment that would have taken place in 2002 and 2003 was effectively shifted to 1999 and 2000.

This period also differed from the beginnings of the three previous recessions in its lack of inflationary pressure. The stock market peaked and began to drop in early 2000, and the tragedies of September 11 created a sense of real crisis late in 2001. In December 2001 the year-over-year change in the CPI was 1.6 percent. Thus, the way was clear for aggressive monetary policy to deal with the recession early, yet gross investment spending was unable to respond to the stimulus of lower interest rates. What responded were the mortgage market and, subsequently, the housing market.

Figure 8 chronicles this period, using data carefully developed by Alan Greenspan and James Kennedy,[12] who were able to reconcile the differences among the various confusing sources of origination data. Monetary policy began easing in January 2001, when the Federal Reserve cut the funds rate by 50 basis points, from 6.5 percent to 6.0 percent. By the end of the year, the central bank had cut rates 11 times, to 1.75 percent. At the time the easing began, the average 30-year fixed conventional mortgage rate was just below 7.2 percent, down slightly from an average of 8.2 percent for the first nine months of 2000. By the time the federal funds rate hit 1.75 percent in 2000Q4, the conventional fixed-rate mortgage was down to 6.8 percent. But rates were just starting their descent. The funds rate continued to decline until June 2003, when it hit 1 percent, by which time the average conventional 30-year fixed-rate mortgage carried a rate of 5.3 percent. The funds rate then stayed at 1 percent for over a year.

12. Greenspan and Kennedy (2005, 2007).

Figure 8. Mortgage Originations and the Target Federal Funds Rate, 2000–08

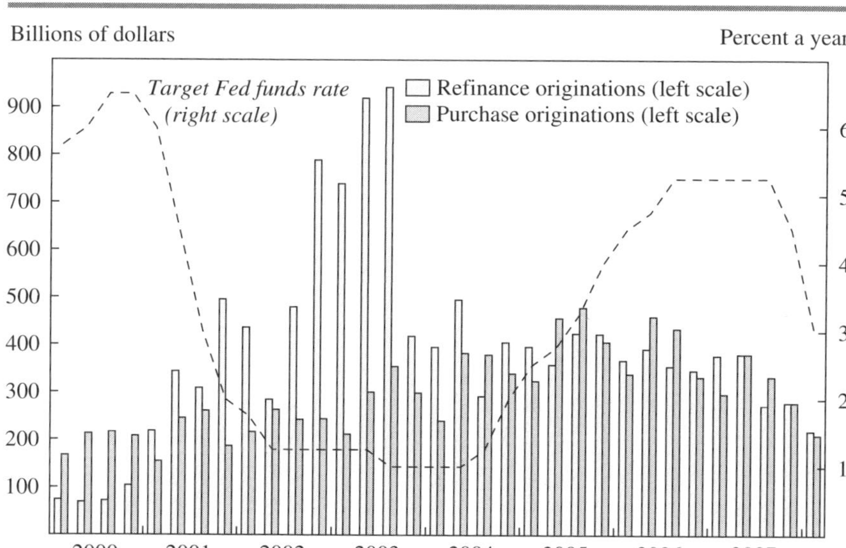

Sources: Greenspan and Kennedy (2005, with updates by James Kennedy); Board of Governors of the Federal Reserve; Standard & Poor's.

Lower rates made housing much more affordable. At a fixed rate of 8.2 percent, the monthly payment on a $300,000 conventional 30-year mortgage with 20 percent down is $1,795 before tax benefits. The monthly payment on the same mortgage with a fixed rate of 6.8 percent is $1,565, and with a 5.3 percent rate it is $1,333. Thus, expansionary policy cut the cost of buying a home by almost a third.

The sharply lower rates had a powerful effect on the mortgage and housing markets. The housing market kept the economy out of recession and helped it grow substantially through the turbulent early and mid-2000s. Figure 8 shows that the volume of mortgage lending exploded at the end of 2002, beginning with a huge refinancing boom. Between 2002Q4 and 2003Q4, $5.5 trillion in mortgages was originated and $3.7 trillion was paid off. Over five quarters the market's total originations were about the same as the total stock of mortgage debt outstanding in 2001. Seventy-five percent of originations were refinancings.

In June 2003 mortgage rates spiked and began to rise, jumping from 5.3 percent to 6.3 percent by August. The third quarter of 2003 saw the highest-ever volume of refinancings, with originations of $942 billion, as borrowers scrambled to catch the bottom. After that the "refi" boom was over: in 2003Q4 refinancings fell by 56 percent.

During the expansion of credit up to the end of 2003, the mortgage industry grew and became highly competitive. With fee income averaging about 2.5 percent on each transaction, the sector earned over $100 billion on total originations of $4 trillion in 2003. In addition, the book of business had very low default rates.

Armed with huge books of profitable business, booming home prices, very low default and foreclosure rates, and general prosperity, along with the federal government's continued push for the American dream of homeownership, lenders competed for homebuyers' business. Purchase originations doubled from $239 billion in 2004Q1 to $478 billion in 2005Q3. Much of the business was directed at low-cost neighborhoods and subprime borrowers. In all, between 2002Q4 and 2006Q4, the market originated a staggering $14.4 trillion in mortgage paper, paid off $10.3 trillion, and pushed the value of total one-to-four-family residential mortgage liabilities from $6.2 trillion to $10.3 trillion, according to the Greenspan-Kennedy data. Table 5 uses data collected by the Federal Financial Institutions Examination Council under the Home Mortgage Disclosure Act to show how lending shifted into low- and moderate-income tracts in virtually every metropolitan area.

Credit expansion of this magnitude had a major impact on the housing market. Prices rose across the board. As shown in table 2, between 2000 and 2006 bottom-tier prices increased the most, by 241 percent in Miami, 240 percent in Los Angeles, and just under 200 percent in Washington, D.C., and San Diego. The S&P/Case-Shiller Composite 10 and Composite 20 indexes more than doubled, and the national index was up nearly 90 percent.

Finally, at the end of 2005 and into 2006, the housing market began to soften for a variety of reasons. Interest rates rose, as Federal Reserve tightening pushed the federal funds rate back up to 5.4 percent and the 30-year mortgage rate followed to 6.6 percent by the second half of 2006. Gluts of speculative building occurred in Arizona, Florida, and Nevada. Housing in California and the Northeast became very expensive relative to incomes. The manufacturing base of the Midwest fell into recession. As expectations turned gloomy, 16 of the 20 Case-Shiller metro areas saw prices falling in 2005 or 2006. By 2007 all 20 were falling.

Inventories of housing rose. In the past, when markets had overshot, prices were sticky and adjustment was orderly. But with home prices falling nationally, and with virtually all of the current mortgage debt having been

Table 5. Originations in Low- and Moderate-Income Census Tracts by Metropolitan Area, 1999–2006
Percent of total purchase loans

								Price change (percent), lower tier	
Metropolitan area[a]	*1999*	*2000*	*2001*	*2002*	*2004*	*2005*	*2006*	*2000–peak*	*Peak to October 2008*
Detroit	10	11	12	13	25	28	30	...	...
Boston	17	18	18	19	26	29	30	119	–21
Miami	14	14	13	14	21	24	27	241	–46
Phoenix	13	14	13	15	20	24	26	139	–48
Los Angeles	11	13	13	16	23	24	25	240	–46
Chicago	9	14	14	16	20	22	23	84	–18
New York	9	9	10	12	18	21	23	160	–14
San Francisco	17	17	17	17	20	23	23	176	–58
San Diego	13	13	14	15	21	22	23	197	–46
Washington, D.C.	13	13	14	16	19	21	23	197	–36
Tampa	15	15	14	15	18	21	23	180	–34
Portland, Ore.	12	12	11	12	18	20	21	100	–9
Atlanta	12	13	13	14	18	20	21	38	–17
Seattle	12	12	12	13	18	19	20	102	–13
Denver	18	17	16	16	19	20	20	39	–15
Minneapolis	10	10	11	12	16	18	18	88	–26
Cleveland	15	14	13	13	16	18	17	33	–27
Dallas	12	11	10	10	12	13	13	...	...
Charlotte	9	9	9	9	12	11	12	...	...
Las Vegas	5	4	4	4	10	11	11	144	–45
United States	12	12	12	12	16	18	18		

Source: Federal Financial Institutions Examination Council, Standard & Poor's, and author's calculations.
a. Metropolitan areas are ordered by their 2006 values.

written since 2004, the bulk of it at high loan-to-value ratios, the default rate rose sharply.

Meanwhile underwriting practices had changed. Over the past 30 years, default and foreclosure models had been developed that seemed to "explain" differences in default and claim incidence as a function of borrower and loan characteristics. All market participants used these models, sometimes without even knowing it. Fannie Mae and Freddie Mac wrote the code for their ironically named automated underwriting systems, "Desktop Underwriter" (now sometimes called "Desktop Undertaker") and "Loan Prospector," by running thousands of regressions, which reported high explanatory power. Their specific purpose was to accurately price the risk that originators and secondary market participants were taking. Their low

Figure 9. Home Prices and Underwriting Credit Risk

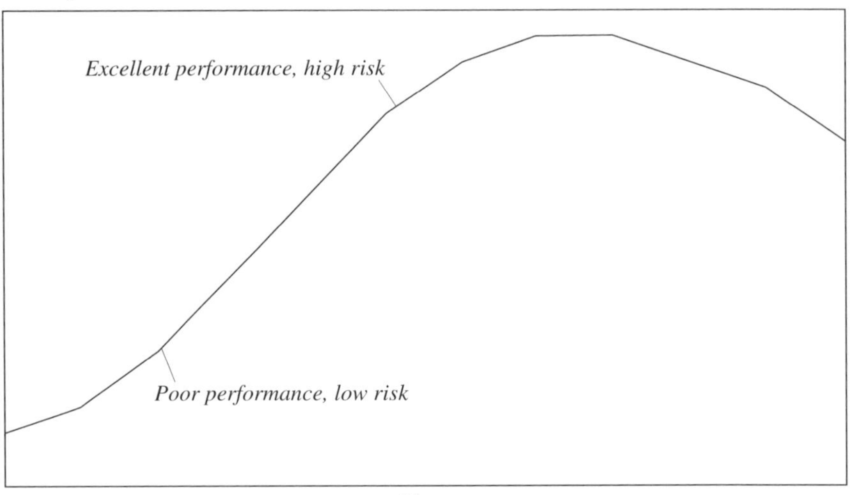

cost and ease of operation made them the industry standard, and originators and mortgage insurance companies that would not accept their decisions received no business.

The stated goal was to transform the current patchwork risk allocation process into a more efficient and accurate risk-based pricing system. The problem was that the regressions on which the automated systems were based had been run with data from a 30-year period of continuously rising national home prices, where regional price declines coincided with regional economic performance. Thus, the model concluded that as long as a portfolio was regionally diversified and pricing was based on credit scores, loan-to-value ratios, and so forth, the business would be profitable. When instead home prices declined everywhere and the regional cycles became more synchronized, the model no longer fit the data.

Another problem was that the timing of performance-based adjustments to underwriting standards was subject to the "fool in the shower" problem. Consider a city that experiences the time path of home values shown in figure 9. The timing of the turns is unknown ex ante. The optimal time to apply the brakes on writing risk is precisely when prices are rising. Paper written at the peak is the most vulnerable, but at that moment default rates are at a minimum. In the current downturn, the disastrous 2005 and 2006 books of business were written while the mortgage industry was enjoying excellent results with few defaults.

What Are the Indexes Telling Us Now?

The years between 2000 and 2005 witnessed a boom of historical proportions, as described in detail above. That boom enjoyed credit market underpinning unlike any other in history. Indeed, the period from 2000 to 2008 is among the truly important economic episodes of the last century. Today all eyes are still focused on home prices, to see what will happen next. How fast and how far will prices fall? And when will some sense of equilibrium be restored?

To a very large extent, the media, the regulators, and the public are all relying on the various indexes, including the S&P/Case-Shiller indexes, that are reported each month and, in at least one instance, each day. Some regulators and accounting firms are using the indexes on a metropolitan-area basis to value portfolios of distressed housing-backed assets. The indexes are meant to measure changes in the "market value" of housing, essentially single-family houses, in a given area. From a legal perspective, the market price for a property is what a willing buyer would agree to pay a willing seller in an arm's-length exchange, which implies that in calculating an index point, every available arm's-length sale should be considered. If this market were pricing a relatively homogeneous good, measuring price movements would be simple. But in the housing market today, two kinds of prices are being generated from two fundamentally different equilibrium processes. These two processes operate side by side, often neighborhood by neighborhood, within metropolitan areas.

The first is the traditional search process involving would-be homebuyers and individual homeowners wishing to sell; this process is characterized by downwardly sticky prices, high inventory, and aversion to loss on the part of sellers. Liquidity-constrained sellers are actually more reluctant to sell than unconstrained sellers, because selling may have high transactions costs. Evidence also suggests that homeowners do not like to sell at a loss. This type of market clearing is slow, usually resulting in an extended and costly period of quantity adjustment with relatively little price change. Second, and concurrently, banks, servicers, and other players are left holding portfolios of houses acquired through default and foreclosure. These properties are typically auctioned off to the highest bidder, often at very low prices.

The parallel operation of these two processes is not a new phenomenon. In every past regional decline, both processes worked together to clear the

Table 6. Changes in Home Prices in Massachusetts, Second Quarter 2008

	Percent change			
City or town	*One year*	*Five years*	*Ten years*	*Median price (dollars)*
Brockton	−14.85	+6.53	+137.06	230,000
Lawrence	−13.02	+14.01	+167.94	165,000
Worcester	−11.28	+6.76	+101.64	230,000
Lynn	−10.47	+5.40	+109.33	250,500
North Dartmouth	−10.15	+13.72	+123.90	258,000
Northborough	−9.09	+5.02	+83.97	372,000
North Andover	−7.48	+2.81	+77.53	500,000
Westborough	−6.43	+7.19	+82.55	350,000
Andover	−5.55	+3.63	+81.47	519,000
Lynnfield	−5.22	+10.45	+103.29	494,000
Southborough	−5.20	+9.75	+88.92	533,000
Springfield	−5.15	+46.53	+125.77	159,000
Weymouth	−5.00	+10.53	+127.50	285,000
Gloucester	−4.45	+8.31	+105.27	385,000
North Adams	−3.82	+40.14	+101.58	127,000
Walpole	−2.66	+11.68	+98.75	402,500
Billerica	−2.51	+9.87	+94.99	326,000
Weston	−0.94	+13.62	+95.45	1,202,500
Lexington	−0.45	+11.70	+98.29	839,000
Wellesley Hills	−0.29	+16.73	+101.76	1,210,000
Lincoln	−0.22	+12.03	+99.14	1,045,000
Dover	+0.21	+17.50	+105.37	932,500
Needham	+0.64	+16.10	+103.57	716,500
Belmont	+0.68	+17.21	+108.87	722,500
Waltham	+1.03	+16.26	+109.30	389,000
Newton	+2.74	+19.93	+110.01	895,500
Cambridge	+12.63	+40.75	+166.84	590,000

Source: Fiserv CSW.

market. In the New England decline of 1989–90, average single-family home prices were down roughly 11 percent, yet the glutted condominium markets had concentrations of ill-advised conversions that lost 75 percent of their original value when sold at auction.[13] Table 6 presents average sale prices for a nonrandom sample of zip codes in Massachusetts through 2008Q2, showing that prices in the areas of low and moderate income-price ratios are down significantly more than in areas with higher ratios. Evidence suggests that foreclosed properties in most cities trade at significantly larger losses than properties not in foreclosure. Fiserv CSW has calculated preliminary repeat sales indexes on cities with large quantities of foreclosed

13. Case (1991).

Figure 10. S&P/Case-Shiller Home Price Index for Miami, 1972–2008

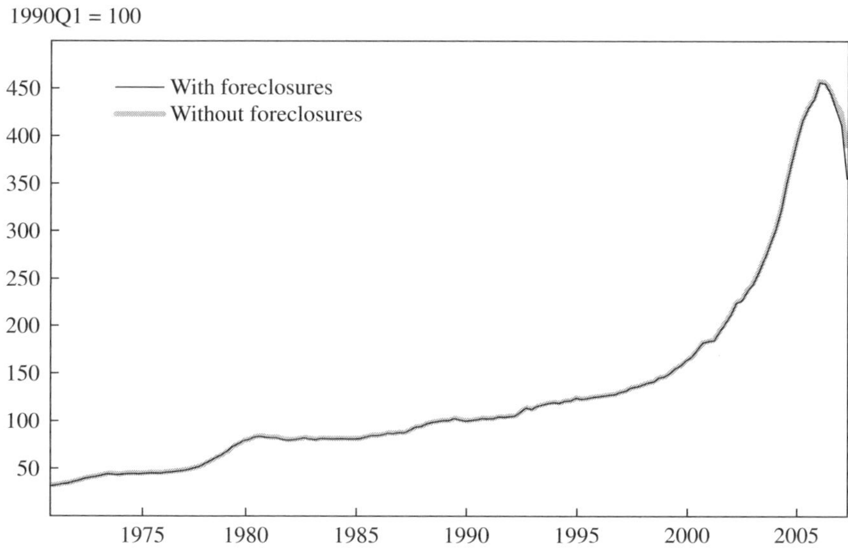

Source: Fiserv CSW.

properties both with and without the foreclosure sales in the data. In Miami as of 2008Q1, the index with the full sample showed a 22 percent decline since the peak of prices, whereas the index excluding auction sales showed only a 15 percent decline (figure 10). In Chicago the comparable figures are 10 percent and 7 percent. The difference is greater for Cleveland.

There are three potential explanations for these differences. First, the foreclosed properties are typically, although not exclusively, in neighborhoods in the lower tier that had experienced rapid run-ups and very high peaks in 2006 and 2007 (see table 2). Second, auction sales typically involve less "price discovery" and search. Although not all such sales are fire sales, most firms that hold foreclosed property prefer to move it off their balance sheets quickly. Third, many foreclosure properties are not properly maintained during the foreclosure process; thus, some substantial unobserved quality change can occur. The indexes have some remedies for these problems.

In using the indexes to value the stock of housing, it is important to understand that all are based on transactions. To the extent that these transactions do not represent the stock, the indexes may be a biased estimator of changes in the stock's value. The only way to deal with this problem is to

Table 7. Value of Owner-Occupied Housing in Selected States, Fourth Quarter 2005

State	*Billions of dollars*	*Percent of total U.S. housing value*
United States	18,336	100.0
California	4,554	24.8
Florida	1,389	7.6
New York	1,382	7.5
Connecticut	898	4.9
New Jersey	881	4.8
Illinois	762	4.2
Texas	715	3.9
Massachusetts	626	3.4
Michigan	495	2.7
Washington	491	2.7
Ohio	478	2.6
Arizona	415	2.3
Georgia	400	2.2
North Carolina	373	2.0
Minnesota	330	1.8
Colorado	318	1.7
Oregon	255	1.4
Nevada	184	1.0
District of Columbia	55	0.3
Above 19 states		81.8

Source: Case (2007); author's calculations.

carefully explore geographically disaggregated data such as the tier indexes or zip code–level data.

Finally, which states have the biggest problems? Table 7 gives a rough estimate of the value of owner-occupied housing by state.[14] The biggest area of concern, California, accounts for almost 25 percent of total home value nationwide. Florida and California, which together account for just under a third of the home value in the country, are experiencing the greatest declines in value.

Table 8 reports ratios of foreclosure sales (both "notice of trustee sales" and "notice of foreclosure sales") to total sales of existing homes for 2006Q3 to 2008Q1. (Total sales are from state data; a few states where the data are not consistent are excluded.) For the United States as a whole, this ratio doubled over the period, from 9.3 percent to 18.8 percent. The highest ratios are in Arizona (86 percent), Nevada (62 percent in 2007Q4; this figure fell in 2008Q1), and Georgia (46 percent). California and Florida

14. Case (2007).

Table 8. Foreclosure Sales as Share of Existing-Home Sales, by State, 2006–08[a]
Percent

State	*2006Q3*	*2006Q4*	*2007Q1*	*2007Q2*	*2007Q3*	*2007Q4*	*2008Q1*
United States	9.3	9.3	11.1	12.8	18.0	18.1	18.8
Arizona	19.6	24.4	32.8	46.1	81.0	70.0	86.3
Nevada	7.4	11.7	20.5	31.3	29.6	62.0	19.7
Georgia	19.8	25.8	29.3	29.3	39.6	45.5	45.6
Colorado	35.3	42.7	41.2	51.1	55.8	41.9	42.0
Michigan	26.6	24.6	22.5	37.6	47.8	41.7	44.3
California	4.3	6.3	10.2	19.5	30.9	39.9	32.4
Maryland	4.4	3.7	5.8	8.9	25.5	34.2	38.6
Utah	12.6	11.5	12.4	11.2	14.6	26.1	32.3
Ohio	15.8	15.9	18.6	19.2	30.4	25.7	17.7
Florida	5.6	4.9	12.8	11.8	21.3	24.6	24.3
Rhode Island	11.1	9.7	14.3	17.0	18.7	24.6	47.7
Virginia	3.2	2.6	4.9	8.6	21.1	20.7	33.0
Washington	10.6	11.5	14.1	14.1	16.3	19.4	20.9
Texas	24.1	20.0	21.5	13.7	23.3	19.0	18.2
Arkansas	11.3	11.3	12.9	16.3	15.4	17.9	18.0
Indiana	13.0	n.a.	15.3	11.8	20.3	16.0	14.7
Tennessee	10.0	12.3	12.3	15.2	17.2	14.5	15.8
Missouri	5.0	5.5	5.5	9.8	10.5	14.3	14.7
Minnesota	4.4	5.9	5.9	7.7	13.5	13.5	12.0
Nebraska	7.0	8.6	8.6	5.6	8.5	12.8	7.6
Pennsylvania	9.2	6.5	11.2	9.8	11.7	10.7	9.4
Dist. of Columbia	0.0	0.3	0.2	1.2	10	10.4	48.3
Alaska	3.1	3.4	2.9	3.6	4.8	9.5	4.5
Idaho	n.a.	n.a.	8.2	7.6	12.4	9.1	19.4
Massachusetts	8.4	5.0	6.1	12.8	16.2	8.8	27.5
Montana	3.0	4.9	4.5	4.6	4.9	6.8	7.1
Oregon	3.4	6.7	2.6	3.3	4.2	6.1	7.8
Illinois	4.4	3.1	2.8	3.5	3.9	6.1	3.4
Iowa	0.6	3.9	5.3	3.7	7.0	5.8	5.3
Wisconsin	2.0	2.5	2.9	3.2	5.3	5.8	7.9
Hawaii	1.3	2.0	2.3	3.6	4.7	5.4	5.3
New Jersey	4.4	4.6	6.0	5.5	9.3	5.2	7.8
Alabama	2.1	4.2	3.2	3.1	3.9	4.9	4.4
Kansas	3.6	4.1	4.5	4.6	4.8	4.8	4.8
Oklahoma	5.4	4.7	6.1	4.7	6.8	4.7	5.5
Connecticut	3.0	2.1	3.7	5.7	4.0	4.4	7.8
Kentucky	3.1	3.1	3.8	5.0	5.3	4.3	3.8
Maine	0.8	0.7	0.5	4.7	4.2	3.6	5.7
New York	5.1	4.1	2.3	2.5	3.7	2.6	3.7
Mississippi	0.9	1.9	2.3	2.2	2.2	2.4	2.2
West Virginia	2.3	3.1	2.8	6.3	4.0	1.7	1.6
South Dakota	1.3	1.3	1.6	1.8	1.6	1.3	1.4
South Carolina	1.0	0.9	1.0	1.1	1.1	0.9	1.0
Wyoming	2.1	2.4	1.0	0.5	3.7	0.9	0.3
New Mexico	1.2	1.6	1.5	0.5	0.1	0.3	0.2
Vermont	0.1	0.1	0.0	0.3	0.3	0.3	0.2
North Dakota	0.0	0.0	0.1	0.2	0.2	0.1	0.1

Sources: National Association of Realtors, Existing Home Sales; Realtytrac.

a. States are listed in descending order by values in 2007Q4. Delaware, Louisiana, New Hampshire, and North Carolina are omitted because of data inconsistencies.

Table 9. Distribution of Foreclosure Auctions by State, 2006–08

Foreclosure auctions as percent of existing-home sales	*No. of states with indicated share of foreclosure auctions*						
	2006Q3	*2006Q4*	*2007Q1*	*2007Q2*	*2007Q3*	*2007Q4*	*2008Q1*
Less than 5	27	27	22	21	18	15	14
≥5 and <10	9	8	9	10	7	10	11
≥10 and <15	5	5	9	7	5	6	3
≥15 and <20	3	2	2	5	6	5	7
≥20 and <25	1	2	3	0	4	3	2
≥25 and <30	1	1	1	1	2	2	1
30 or greater	2	3	2	4	6	7	10

Sources: Realtytrac and National Association of Realtors.

have ratios of 32.4 percent and 24.3, percent, respectively. Table 9 shows the shifting distribution of states by the extent of foreclosure sales. Foreclosures are fewer than 5 percent of total existing-home sales in only 14 states today, compared with 27 states in 2006Q3. At the other extreme, only two states had ratios of over 30 percent in 2006. That figure is now 10 states.

Updates through November 2008 show a substantial drop in total existing-home sales to 4.49 million, at a seasonally adjusted annual rate from a revised 4.91 million in October. Total existing-home sales had been essentially flat at 5 million for a year before the drop in November. Auction sales in November alone totaled 87,700, or about 27 percent of the unadjusted monthly total of 322,000 existing-home sales. California and Florida together accounted for 40 percent of all auction sales in the country in November.

How long will it take for prices to stabilize? The bulk of analysts say it will take a long time. Shiller argues, as does Mark Zandi, that it will take until well into 2010 or longer.[15] They point to the backlog of unresolved "underwater" mortgages, coming resets of interest rates, large inventories of unsold properties, and the legal delays entailed in unwinding the layers of risk and liabilities built into the new credit instruments. In addition, the crashing stock market and what appears to be a serious recession cast doubt on any overly confident forecast. Add to that uncertainty about the behavior of homebuyers and sellers in a down market nationwide, an environment for which little data are available, and it is no wonder that the futures and

15. Shiller (2008); Zandi (2009).

options markets based on home prices are so illiquid. The real danger is that a continued decline in prices could make the 2008 and 2009 books of mortgages unprofitable, prolonging the credit crunch.

Is there any good news? First, it is clear that the two market clearing processes described above are proceeding in a fairly orderly way. In November 2008 existing-home sales dropped, yet nearly 4.5 million homes (at a seasonally adjusted annual rate) were sold. Although auction sales accounted for 27 percent of the total, that means traditional sales still accounted for 73 percent. In cities like Boston, the current downturn has not been as severe as that of early 1990, from which the market recovered in a remarkably short time.

Second, the battle of the "plans" is under way. Economists and policymakers are focused on settling on a strategy to prevent foreclosures. Preventing foreclosures reduces moving costs, potential vandalism, and the litigation and high transactions costs that often follow foreclosures. In addition, as the number of auctions inevitably declines, traditional sales will gain strength in the home price indexes, and downward resistance will stabilize aggregate prices more quickly.

It is often said that prices will stop rising only when they return to "fundamentals." But what are the fundamentals in housing, and in particular in land? People will bid for locations as long as those with ability to pay are willing to pay for them. Only time will tell when that will be.

ACKNOWLEDGMENTS This paper could not have been written without the help of Rachel Hamilton, Milena Mereva, and Ratha Ly.

References

Case, Karl E. 1986. "The Market for Single Family Homes in Boston." *New England Economic Review* (May/June): 38–48.

———. 1991. "The Real Estate Cycle and the Economy: Consequences of the Massachusetts Boom of 1984–1987." *New England Economic Review* (Sept./Oct.): 37–46. Revised version in *Urban Studies* 29, no. 2: 171–83 (Spring 1992).

———. 2007. "The Value of Land in the United States: 1975–2005." In *Land Policies and Their Outcomes,* edited by Gregory K. Ingram and Yu-hung Hong. Cambridge, Mass.: Lincoln Institute of Land Policy.

———. 2009. "What Were They Thinking? The Behavior of Home Buyers in Boom and Post-Boom Markets 1988–2008." Paper presented at the annual meetings of the American Economics Association, San Francisco, January 3.

Case, Karl E., and John M. Quigley. 2008. "How Housing Booms Unwind: Income Effects, Wealth Effects and Feedbacks through Financial Markets." *European Journal of Housing Policy* 8, no. 2: 161–80.

Case, Karl E., and Robert J. Shiller. 1987. "Prices of Single Family Homes since 1970: New Indexes for Four Cities." *New England Economic Review* (Sept./Oct.): 45–56.

———. 1988. "The Behavior of Home Buyers in Boom and Post-Boom Markets." *New England Economic Review* (Nov./Dec.): 29–46.

———. 1989. "The Efficiency of the Market for Single-Family Homes." *American Economic Review* 79, no. 1: 125–37.

———. 1990. "Forecasting Prices and Excess Returns in the Housing Market." *Journal of the American Real Estate and Urban Economics Association* 18, no. 3: 253–73.

———. 2003. "Is There a Bubble in the Housing Market?" *BPEA,* no. 2: 299–342.

Congressional Budget Office. 1991. "The Cost of Forbearance during the Thrift Crisis." Staff memorandum. Washington (June).

Davis, Morris, and Jonathan Heathcote. 2005. "Housing and the Business Cycle." *International Economic Review* 46, no. 3: 751–84.

Davis, Morris, and Michael Palumbo. 2008. "The Price of Residential Land in Large U.S. Cities." *Journal of Urban Economics* 63, no. 1: 352–84.

Glaeser, Edward L. 2002. "Comment [on 'Tax Incentives and the City' by Teresa Garcia-Milá and Therese J. McGuire]." *Brookings-Wharton Papers on Urban Affairs* pp. 115–24.

Glaeser, Edward L., and Joseph E. Gyourko. 2002. "Zoning's Steep Price." *Regulation* 25, no. 3: 24–30.

Glaeser, Edward L., Joseph E. Gyourko, and Albert Saiz. 2009. "Housing Supply and Housing Bubbles." *Journal of Urban Economics* 64, no. 2: 198–217.

Glaeser, Edward L., Joseph E. Gyourko, and Raven E. Saks. 2005. "Why Have Housing Prices Gone Up?" *American Economic Review Papers and Proceedings* 95, no. 2: 329–33.

———. 2006. "Urban Growth and Housing Supply." *Journal of Economic Geography* 6, no. 1: 71–89.

Greenspan, Alan, and James Kennedy. 2005. "Estimates of Home Mortgage Originations, Repayments, and Debt on One-to-Four Family Residences." Federal Reserve Board Finance and Economic Discussion Series 2005-41. Washington.

———. 2007. "Sources and Uses of Equity Extracted from Homes." Federal Reserve Board Finance and Economic Discussion Series 2007–20. Washington.

Samuelson, Paul. 1957. "Intertemporal Price Equilibrium: A Prologue to the Theory of Speculation." *Weltwirtschaftliches Archiv* 79, no. 2: 181–221.

Shiller, Robert. 2008. *The Subprime Solution: How Today's Global Financial Crisis Happened and What to Do about It.* Princeton University Press.

Zandi, Mark. 2009. *Financial Shock: A 360° Look at the Subprime Mortgage Implosion and How to Avoid the Next Financial Crisis.* Upper Saddle River, N.J.: FT Press, Pearson Education.

JAN HATZIUS
Goldman Sachs

Beyond Leveraged Losses: The Balance Sheet Effects of the Home Price Downturn

ABSTRACT This paper quantifies the impact of declining home prices, increasing mortgage credit losses, and the associated reduction in credit supply on real GDP growth. Using a state-level panel analysis, I first estimate the link between home prices and foreclosures. I estimate that an additional 15 percent home price decline from mid-2008 levels would be consistent with total residential mortgage credit losses over 2007–12 of $750 billion, although the uncertainty is high. I then gauge the impact of such losses on the supply of credit from banks, asset-backed security markets, and the government-sponsored enterprises, and in turn on real GDP growth. In the central scenario, the crisis could lower real GDP growth in 2008 and 2009 by an average of 2.6 percentage points per year. This estimate excludes both adverse multiplier effects (labor market deterioration, global trade repercussions, and credit quality feedback) and policy offsets.

The current housing market downturn weighs on the economy in four main ways. First, the sharp decline in residential construction activity reduces aggregate output directly. From the fourth quarter of 2005 to the third quarter of 2008, declining real residential investment subtracted a cumulative total of 2.5 percentage points from real GDP growth.

Second, declining income in the housing sector in turn has effects on other parts of the economy. Laid-off construction workers and real estate agents cut back on consumer spending, homebuilders (and their subcontractors) invest less in construction equipment, and nonresidential construction firms see less demand for new commercial development. These second-round effects are harder to quantify because they are so spread out through the economy, but they are likely to be significant as well.

Third, declining home prices weigh on aggregate personal consumption through either a negative wealth effect or a mortgage liquidity effect, or both. Households who spent more than they earned during the boom by borrowing against the rising value of their home may be forced to cut back. Even households who did not outspend their income might reduce their consumption in response to a decline in their wealth or their permanent income, or both. Most studies analyzing this issue find evidence for a housing wealth effect, but its size varies widely depending on the time period and the empirical design.[1]

Fourth, losses on mortgage credit deplete the equity capital of leveraged financial institutions and persuade them to reduce their financial leverage. This reduces the supply of credit to households and nonfinancial businesses. David Greenlaw, Hatzius, Anil Kashyap, and Hyun Song Shin (henceforth GHKS) find that an assumed $500 billion in aggregate mortgage credit losses could cut real GDP growth by 1.5 percentage points over a year's time.[2]

This paper focuses on the fourth channel. Building on the study by GHKS, its main contributions are a more detailed empirical analysis of the link between home price declines and mortgage credit losses and a more systematic look at the role of the asset-backed security (ABS) markets. The first section analyzes the links between home prices and foreclosures, and ultimately between home prices and mortgage credit losses, using a state-level panel dataset for the period 1998–2008 to predict foreclosures. The second section discusses the impact of mortgage credit losses on the supply of credit to private nonfinancial borrowers, with a particular focus on on-balance-sheet lending by banks and other leveraged financial institutions, off-balance-sheet lending through the ABS markets, and lending backed by government-sponsored enterprises (GSEs) such as Fannie Mae and Freddie Mac. The third section discusses the potential impact on economic activity, using an instrumental variables approach to estimate the link between credit supply and real GDP growth. The fourth section concludes.

The Link between Home Prices and Credit Losses

The underlying cause of the recent financial crisis is the decline in home prices and the associated increase in foreclosures and credit losses. Fig-

1. For an overview, see Muellbauer (2007).
2. Greenlaw and others (2008).

Figure 1. Two Measures of the Decline in Home Prices, 1992–2008

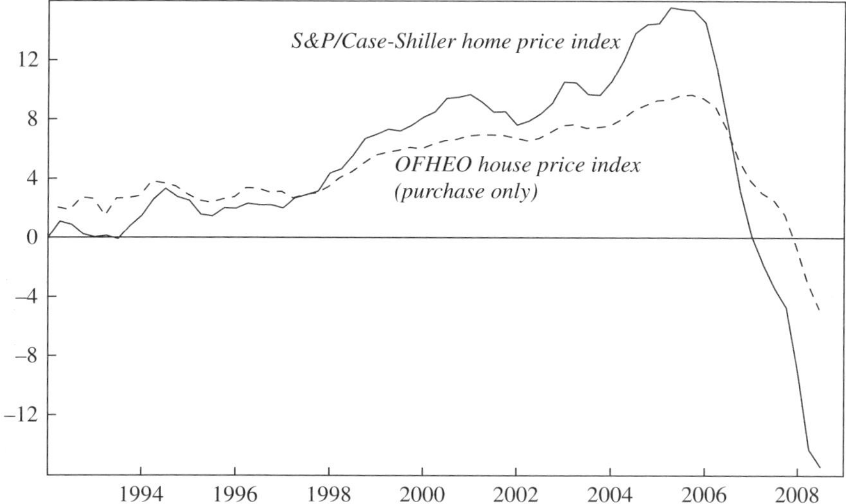

Sources: Office of Federal Housing Enterprise Oversight, Standard & Poor's, Fiserv, and MacroMarkets.

ure 1 shows the current pace of decline in home prices as measured by the two most widely used measures, the S&P/Case-Shiller U.S. National Index and the purchase-only OFHEO index, seasonally adjusted, constructed by the Office of Federal Housing Enterprise Oversight. As of the second quarter of 2008, home prices on a year-on-year basis were down 15.4 percent according to the Case-Shiller index and 4.8 percent according to the OFHEO index.[3]

3. The large difference between the two indexes is due to three main factors. First, the Case-Shiller index is weighted by market capitalization, whereas the OFHEO index is weighted by the number of households. This means that the Case-Shiller index gives more weight to regions with high average home values, in particular the coasts, which generally have seen larger home price swings. Second, the Case-Shiller index includes all home transactions, whereas the OFHEO index includes only transactions involving conforming mortgages. This means that the OFHEO index has missed the direct effects of the subprime mortgage boom and likely understates the rate of home price decline in the broad housing market. Third, the Case-Shiller index covers only 70 percent of the United States (by market value), whereas the OFHEO index has near-complete geographic coverage. Since the regions excluded by the Case-Shiller index are generally rural and relatively stable, the Case-Shiller index likely overstates the rate of home price decline in the broad housing market.

Existing Approaches to Measuring Mortgage Credit Losses

The key question this section of the paper asks is how large an aggregate mortgage credit loss will result from the decline in home prices. Analysts have attempted to answer this question in three main ways. First, some have estimated "market-implied" losses from indexes such as the ABX.HE index of prices of subprime credit derivatives.[4] But although such an estimate of market-implied losses is useful for gauging how much principal financial institutions that mark to market will need to write down in the near term, there is no particular reason to think that it will prove to be an accurate gauge of ultimate credit losses. Indeed, if analysts were to use market prices to forecast credit losses, and the market then relied on these forecasts to price assets, the cat would be chasing its own tail.

Second, many applied mortgage credit analysts use detailed vintage-by-vintage data to estimate credit losses by projecting forward historical delinquency, default, and loss curves. Here the key assumption is that although different mortgage vintages (a vintage is the set of mortgages initiated in a given year) have different default trajectories, the relative progression through time is stable, or at least highly predictable. For example, suppose that the cumulative default rate of the 2006 subprime vintage is 3 percent at the end of 2007. Suppose further that the 2004 vintage showed a cumulative default rate of 1 percent after one year and 4 percent after three years, for a fourfold increase over two years. In that case the model implies that the 2006 vintage should show a 12 percent default rate by 2009. The problem with this approach should be readily apparent, namely, that within-vintage patterns are unlikely to remain stable as one goes from a rising to a falling home price environment. At a minimum, one should adjust the curves for falling home prices, but this is difficult to do because the detailed data required for building these vintage-by-vintage models are available only back to the late 1990s, a period without a national housing downturn until very recently.

Third, one can use historical relationships among defaults, home prices, and perhaps other economic variables to estimate future default rates. For example, Adrian Blundell-Wignall estimates an equation that explains the subprime delinquency rate by GDP, home prices, and unemployment, using data from 1998 to 2007.[5] He then uses the resulting equation, along with assumptions about the relationships among delinquencies, defaults,

4. For example, Blundell-Wignall (2008), GHKS (2008), and Bank of England (2008).
5. Blundell-Wignall (2008).

and losses and trends in the explanatory variables, to forecast credit losses. The problem with this approach is that the underlying dataset is confined to 40 aggregate observations during a period that, again, saw no housing downturn except at the very end.

A State-Level Approach

Given these limitations, it is more promising to use disaggregated region-by-region information that includes at least some periods of declining home prices in each region to estimate the relationship between home prices and mortgage credit performance. For example, GHKS look at foreclosure data from the Texas, California, and Massachusetts housing downturns of the 1980s and 1990s to gauge what a significant nominal home price downturn could mean for foreclosures. Nominal home price declines in these episodes of 10 to 15 percent resulted in a tripling of the rate of foreclosure starts over a two-to-six-year period, with only a gradual decline thereafter. Extrapolating this observation to the post-2007 national housing market, and making assumptions about the percentage of foreclosure starts that result in repossessions and about average "severity" (the size of the loss associated with a default), GHKS argue that the regional precedents may be consistent with total losses of around $500 billion in the current episode.

However, this region-by-region approach is also subject to several limitations. One could argue, on the one hand, that it is too pessimistic, because the rise in foreclosures in the three regional downturns was undoubtedly partly due to the massive labor market deterioration recorded in all three cases. From the start of the downturn, the unemployment rate rose by a cumulative 3.3 percentage points in Texas, 4.8 percentage points in California, and as much as 6.0 percentage points in Massachusetts. For comparison, the biggest national increase in the postwar period totaled 4.4 percentage points, seen in the 1973–75 recession. Although the national labor market is clearly deteriorating quite sharply at present, using such a large decline as the baseline assumption may be too extreme.

On the other hand, one could argue that the region-by-region approach delivers overly optimistic results, because it cannot take account of the far-reaching structural changes in the housing and mortgage markets that have occurred since these regional episodes. In particular, the subprime mortgage market barely existed before the mid-1990s. Since a large share of the current problem is concentrated in the subprime market, this might suggest that the current downturn may be more severe. The behavior of mortgage borrowers may also have changed. As recently as the early 1990s, it seems that only a relatively small share of homeowners with negative equity ended up defaulting on their mortgage debt. For example, Christopher Foote, Kristopher Gerardi, and Paul Willen show that only 6.4 percent of Massachusetts homeowners who were estimated to be in negative equity at the end of 1991 defaulted over the next three years.[6] Now, however, anecdotal reports, at least, suggest that a significant number of borrowers walk away from their mortgage once they are in negative equity. This could imply that the impact of home price declines on defaults will be larger in the current national episode than in the three regional downturns.

The model presented in this paper instead uses more recent state-level information to estimate the link between home prices and foreclosures, and ultimately between home prices and credit losses. I use quarterly panel data from the Mortgage Bankers Association (MBA) for all 50 states and the District of Columbia over the period 1998Q1–2008Q2 to estimate the relationship between the logarithm of the state foreclosure rate and changes in nominal state home prices as measured by the purchase-only OFHEO index.[7] I estimate separate equations for prime adjustable-rate, prime fixed-rate, subprime adjustable-rate, and subprime fixed-rate loans and include state and time fixed effects as well as three lags of the dependent variable.[8]

I then use these equations to project state-level foreclosure rates for each type of mortgage for a given home price path and combine these projections with assumptions about the estimated foreclosure completion rate and mortgage loss severity to calculate a path for total mortgage credit losses. Finally, by summing up these period-by-period losses over 2007–12, I obtain a rough estimate of total credit losses on the currently outstanding stock of residential mortgage debt.

This approach has some important advantages compared with previous analyses. First, when combined with assumptions about foreclosure completions and severities, it allows the implications for foreclosures of a given change in the home price outlook to be estimated using a very simple and transparent method. Other approaches, including the regional approach of GHKS, do not allow such a calculation.

6. Foote, Gerardi, and Willen (2008b).

7. Unfortunately, the Case-Shiller home price index is not available at the state level. The purchase-only OFHEO index is generally viewed as the most reliable state-level home price measure.

8. It is well known that a simple fixed effects estimator leads to downwardly biased coefficient estimates on the lagged dependent variable. However, the results in Judson and Owen (1997) suggest that the bias should be very small given the dimensions of the panel, which covers all 50 states and the District of Columbia and 42 periods.

Second, this approach brings a large amount of state-by-state information to bear on the problem. Depending on the specification, almost 2,000 observations are available on the link between changes in home prices and foreclosures at the state level. This is especially noteworthy because the panel structure of the dataset ensures that the large sample does not include old data from periods when the behavior of borrowers and lenders may have been very different, such as the early-1990s downturn.

Third, this approach models foreclosures for different types of mortgages and can therefore take into account potential differences in the performance of subprime versus prime mortgages, and adjustable-rate (ARM) versus fixed-rate (FRM) mortgages.[9] Subprime borrowers are more vulnerable to default than prime borrowers, both because they tend to be financially weaker and because they have, in recent years, often taken out mortgages with higher loan-to-value ratios in particularly "frothy" parts of the country.

This analysis also has some clear limitations. First, and most important, it extrapolates a fairly recent event—the unprecedented downturn in mortgage credit quality that started in late 2006 or early 2007—into uncharted territory. Despite the large number of observations, it would be optimistic to believe that the analysis will reveal stable (let alone "structural") relationships between home prices and foreclosures. At best one can hope to provide an order-of-magnitude estimate of the likely amount of mortgage credit losses assuming a particular outcome for home prices.

Second, because the analysis is reduced-form in nature, one cannot be sure about the causal relationship between home prices and foreclosures. Although Foote and his coauthors argue persuasively that home prices have a bigger impact on foreclosures than foreclosures have on home prices, the arrows of causation surely run in both directions.[10] A good instrument for state-level home prices that might settle this issue is unavailable. However, this does not appear to be a serious problem, because much of the interest in the link between home prices and mortgage credit losses is of a "reduced-form" variety. That is, one would like to know what mortgage

9. The distinction between prime and subprime is not entirely clean. Participants who service both prime and subprime loans report the results of each separately for maximum precision in the classification. However, the prime sample contains some subprime loans, and the subprime sample some prime loans. Also, there is no separate category for so-called alt-A mortgages, which are loans to borrowers with high credit scores that are lower in quality on other metrics such as income documentation or loan-to-value ratios. My understanding is that alt-A loans are largely included in the "prime" sample.

10. Foote and others (2008a).

credit loss estimate is consistent with a given path for home prices, and the present analysis does provide an answer to this question.

Third, because the foreclosure data used here do not pertain to specific mortgage vintages, one cannot control directly for the effects of good versus bad underwriting standards in particular vintages, nor can one precisely estimate foreclosures on the currently outstanding stock of mortgages. The approach could lead to a higher or a lower number than a true "lifetime loss" analysis, depending on whether the losses on mortgages that have yet to be originated but will be realized in the 2008–12 period are greater or smaller than the losses on mortgages that have already been originated but will not be realized until after 2012. I suspect that the difference between these two numbers—whether positive or negative—is small relative to the range of potential estimates, but there is no way to be sure.

Estimates of the Impact of Home Price Changes on Foreclosures

The odd-numbered columns in table 1 report my baseline estimates of the effects of changes in home prices on foreclosures for subprime ARMs, subprime FRMs, prime ARMs, and prime FRMs. All equations include both state and time dummies. Although time dummies pose some problems for projection purposes, as it is difficult to be sure what number to use for future periods (see the discussion below), I found that equations without time dummies resulted in a significant overprediction of foreclosures in some of the boom-bust states toward the very end of the sample period. This problem was particularly severe for subprime ARMs. When time dummies are included, the overprediction problem is reduced significantly. One potential explanation is that part of the deterioration in the 2006–07 period reflects poor underwriting standards and mortgage fraud in the 2006 and 2007 vintages rather than the impact of home price declines per se. A specification without time dummies will miss such vintage effects. It will attribute all of the deterioration to the home price decline and therefore predict a closer relationship between home price declines and foreclosures than is appropriate if there are indeed important vintage effects.

The upshot of these results is that the link between home price changes and foreclosures is very close. For all four types of mortgages, the relationship is highly significant, with coefficients that sum to between −8.4 and −10.8. If the lagged dependent variables are ignored, this means that a 1 percent drop in home prices is associated with an 8.4 to 10.8 percent increase in foreclosures. Moreover, there is substantial persistence in all four equations, with coefficients on the lagged dependent variables that sum to between 0.49 and 0.76. In general, the equations show that prime and subprime mortgage foreclosures are quite similar in terms of their links with home prices. The level of foreclosure starts is much higher for subprime loans, and particularly for subprime ARMs, but the elasticity with respect to home prices is not too different. In fact, if anything the elasticity of foreclosure starts to home price declines is slightly higher in the prime market than in the subprime market.

These baseline estimates do not include state-specific economic variables such as the state unemployment rate.[11] I found little evidence that state unemployment rates have significant predictive power with respect to foreclosures, at least once the model includes the home price and the lagged dependent variable terms. This is illustrated in the regressions reported in the even-numbered columns in table 1, which add the current state unemployment rate and three lags to the baseline specifications. In all four cases the coefficients sum to around zero, with negative coefficients on the current unemployment rate and positive coefficients (in three of the four estimates) on the thrice-lagged unemployment rate. Taking this result seriously would imply that a rising unemployment rate was associated with *fewer* foreclosures. However, the effect is extremely small. For example, the equation for subprime ARMs implies that a 1-percentage-point increase in the unemployment rate—a very large move on a quarter-to-quarter basis—lowers foreclosure starts by just 3 percent (logarithmically). Hence, in what follows I ignore the unemployment rate and instead use the baseline results (the odd-numbered columns) to project alternative paths for overall mortgage credit losses for given home price paths. To be able to do this, one needs to make a number of assumptions, which I now discuss in turn.

Projecting Foreclosure Starts

To use the model to project foreclosure starts, one needs to choose assumptions for the explanatory variables, namely, state home prices and the time dummies. Regarding state home prices, I choose three paths that are each statistically consistent with one of the following assumptions: a further 5 percent (logarithmic) decline in nominal home prices from their 2008Q2 level, a further 15 percent decline, and a further 25 percent decline, all through the middle of 2009 and measured by the national Case-Shiller index. To translate these national-level home price assumptions to the state level, I use the predicted values from 51 simple regres-

11. National-level variables such as mortgage rates cannot be included because of the time fixed effects.

Table 1. Regressions of Foreclosure Starts on Changes in Home Prices[a]

	Type of mortgage							
	Prime ARMs		*Prime FRMs*		*Subprime ARMs*		*Subprime FRMs*	
Independent variable	*1-1*	*1-2*	*1-3*	*1-4*	*1-5*	*1-6*	*1-7*	*1-8*
Constant	–0.15	–0.18	–0.36	–0.44	0.50	0.46	0.30	0.32
	(0.02)	(0.08)	(0.05)	(0.15)	(0.03)	(0.07)	(0.02)	(0.09)
ln foreclosure ratio$_{t-1}$	0.41	0.41	0.38	0.38	0.40	0.39	0.30	0.30
	(0.04)	(0.04)	(0.05)	(0.05)	(0.04)	(0.04)	(0.04)	(0.04)
ln foreclosure ratio$_{t-2}$	0.18	0.19	0.17	0.17	0.15	0.15	0.17	0.17
	(0.04)	(0.04)	(0.04)	(0.04)	(0.04)	(0.04)	(0.04)	(0.04)
ln foreclosure ratio$_{t-3}$	0.10	0.09	0.21	0.21	0.04	0.04	0.02	0.02
	(0.03)	(0.03)	(0.05)	(0.05)	(0.02)	(0.02)	(0.03)	(0.03)
Change in ln home prices	–3.60	–3.66	–1.09	–1.15	–2.08	–2.18	–0.90	–1.03
	(0.73)	(0.71)	(0.92)	(0.92)	(0.67)	(0.67)	(0.94)	(0.94)
Change in ln home prices$_{t-1}$	–2.74	–2.88	–3.57	–3.61	–2.39	–2.47	–1.70	–1.81
	(0.66)	(0.66)	(0.97)	(0.99)	(0.57)	(0.57)	(0.92)	(0.93)
Change in ln home prices$_{t-2}$	–2.56	–2.62	–2.56	–2.58	–3.80	–3.81	–3.84	–4.00
	(0.74)	(0.72)	(0.86)	(0.84)	(0.76)	(0.76)	(0.97)	(0.98)

Change in ln home prices$_{t-3}$	−1.88	−1.79	−1.23	−1.15	−1.67	−1.59	−2.23	−2.28
	(0.84)	(0.83)	(0.96)	(0.95)	(0.71)	(0.71)	(0.98)	(0.97)
Unemployment rate		−0.07		−0.03		−0.03		−0.01
		(0.04)		(0.06)		(0.05)		(0.04)
Unemployment rate$_{t-1}$		0.01		−0.03		−0.01		−0.10
		(0.04)		(0.04)		(0.04)		(0.04)
Unemployment rate$_{t-2}$		0.10		0.06		0.03		0.06
		(0.05)		(0.07)		(0.05)		(0.05)
Unemployment rate$_{t-3}$		−0.03		0.01		0.02		0.04
		(0.03)		(0.06)		(0.03)		(0.03)
No. of observations	1,981	1,981	1,942	1,942	1,952	1,952	1,919	1,919
Adjusted R^2	0.87	0.87	0.84	0.84	0.82	0.82	0.74	0.74
Durbin-Watson statistic	2.02	2.01	1.96	1.95	2.04	2.04	1.90	1.90

Source: Author's regressions.

a. The dependent variable is the logarithm of the ratio of foreclosure starts to total mortgages serviced, in percent. The sample period is 1998Q4 to 2008Q2. All regressions include dummy variables for state and time. White standard errors are in parentheses.

sions (results not reported) of the quarter-to-quarter change in the regional purchase-only OFHEO index on the change in the national Case-Shiller index (both seasonally adjusted using the Census X-12 algorithm). This allows alternative expectations for national home prices, expressed in terms of the Case-Shiller index, to be translated into corresponding assumptions about state-level prices, which are available only from OFHEO. As one might expect, states with volatile housing markets, such as California and Florida, show much greater sensitivity to changes in national home prices than do states with more stable housing markets, such as Iowa and Missouri.[12]

I set the time dummies to zero, which indicates that the time effect is assumed equal to the average of the sample period, under the assumption that the positive time dummies in the 2006–07 period reflect vintage effects resulting from poor underwriting or mortgage fraud, and that these poorly underwritten or fraudulent mortgages have now largely defaulted. This is an important and relatively optimistic assumption, since the time dummies have been mostly positive in recent quarters.[13] Finally, to estimate the absolute number of foreclosure starts, I multiply all foreclosure rates by the number of mortgages serviced for each state and mortgage type, adjusted for the rising coverage of the MBA sample.[14]

Figure 2 shows actual foreclosure starts since the beginning of 2007 along with my projections through 2012, assuming a further 15 percent home price decline (my central scenario). The model predicts that foreclosure starts will peak at around 530,000 (not annualized) in the fourth quarter of 2008 before gradually falling back toward the levels seen in early 2007 (around 200,000). In total, the model predicts 8.3 million foreclosure starts from early 2007 to late 2012, with projected shares of 37 percent for subprime ARMs, 16 percent for subprime FRMs, 21 percent for prime ARMs, and 26 percent for prime FRMs.

12. Moreover, the predicted values for the national purchase-only OFHEO index that result from aggregating the 51 state predictions are very close to the actual national series, with an R^2 of 85 percent.

13. If one instead set the time dummies equal to the values estimated for 2008Q2, the projected foreclosure rates would be 15 percent higher for subprime ARMs, 21 percent higher for prime ARMs, 8 percent higher for subprime FRMs, and 15 percent higher for prime FRMs.

14. The total number of mortgages serviced in the MBA dataset as a share of all first-lien home mortgages outstanding according to the American Housing Survey has risen from 57 percent in 1998 to 88 percent in 2008.

Figure 2. Projected Foreclosure Starts Assuming a Further 15 Percent Home Price Decline, by Mortgage Type, 2007–2012

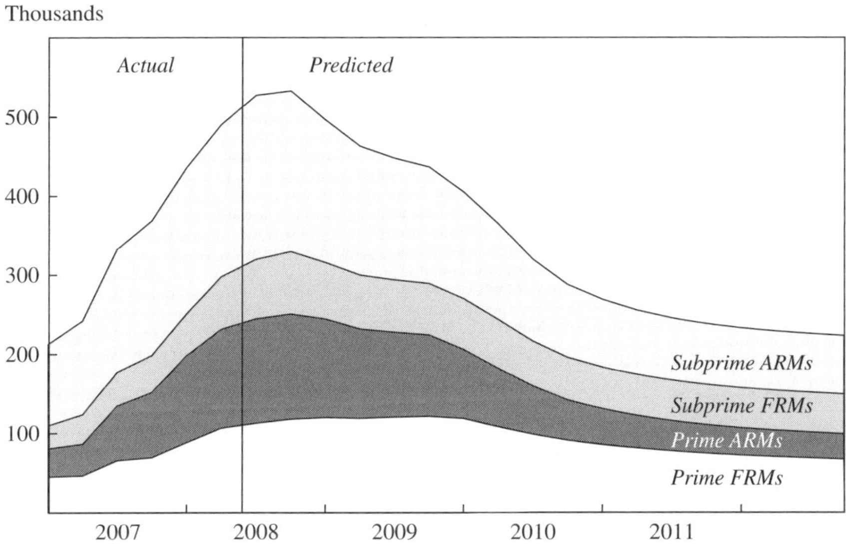

Sources: Standard & Poor's, Fiserv, MacroMarkets, Mortgage Bankers Association, and author's calculations.

Projecting Loss Incidence and Severity

The MBA data pertain to foreclosure starts rather than credit losses. Hence, to estimate the latter, one needs to make assumptions about the share of foreclosure starts that result in a loss to the lender, whether through seizure of a home (the "foreclosure completion rate") or not, and about the average size ("severity") of that loss.

Regarding the first issue, the question is what happens to borrowers against whom a foreclosure notice has been filed. In theory, there are a number of possibilities. They could again become current on their mortgage of their own volition (which implies no loss to the lender), lose their home in a sheriff's auction (a large loss to the lender), agree to a "short sale" in which the lender accepts the proceeds even though it falls short of the mortgage balance (usually a somewhat smaller loss), or agree to a repayment plan that may involve some debt forgiveness (an even smaller loss).

Unfortunately, no hard data are available on the relative frequencies of these ultimate outcomes. However, there is good reason to believe that a large proportion of the foreclosures started over the next couple of years

Table 2. Foreclosure Starts and Sales of Foreclosed Homes in Four States, 2007–08

	California		*Florida*		*Arizona*		*Nevada*	
Quarter	*Starts*	*Sales*	*Starts*	*Sales*	*Starts*	*Sales*	*Starts*	*Sales*
2007Q1	28,656	7,417	18,690	2,527	4,342	1,034	3,499	979
2007Q2	32,572	10,967	21,735	3,435	5,364	1,397	4,258	1,395
2007Q3	47,119	15,533	32,285	5,110	6,992	2,362	4,708	1,781
2007Q4	52,348	22,348	42,639	6,200	9,260	3,494	6,807	2,740
2008Q1	81,684	36,581	58,496	9,780	14,646	6,290	9,434	4,489
2008Q2	99,125	56,953	72,418	14,788	19,164	10,273	12,241	7,163

Source: Hope Now, "July State Data 2008."

will result in a significant cost to the lender, in most cases a sheriff's auction. This is partly for a priori reasons. Presumably, negative equity sharply decreases a homeowner's incentive to become current on the mortgage, which would suggest that the percentage of foreclosure starts that result in a cost to the lender will increase as home prices decline. Indeed, this is largely confirmed by data from Hope Now on recent foreclosure starts and sales in states that have already seen large-scale home price declines for several quarters, and where the impact of negative equity on borrower behavior should therefore be most readily apparent.[15] Table 2 shows that in three of these states (California, Arizona, and Nevada) the number of foreclosure *sales* is currently running about even with the number of foreclosure *starts* two quarters earlier. Given the usual foreclosure timeline, this suggests that the vast majority of foreclosure starts currently result in sheriff's auctions in these states. The exception to this pattern is Florida, where foreclosure sales are running at only about one-third the level of foreclosure starts two quarters earlier. However, Florida is a "judicial" state, where lenders need to obtain a court order to proceed with the foreclosure, and a serious logjam in processing foreclosures in the Florida court system has been widely reported. If this is so, most of the foreclosures currently started may still end up resulting in foreclosure sales, but the lag would be too long for this to show up in the foreclosure sales data in the near term.

Moreover, a longer perspective for the state of California confirms that the percentage of foreclosure starts that result in sales closely tracks

15. Hope Now is a coalition of mortgage servicers and other market participants that have committed themselves to preventing foreclosures in cooperation with the Treasury Department.

Figure 3. California: Foreclosure Starts and Sales of Foreclosed Homes, 1992–2008

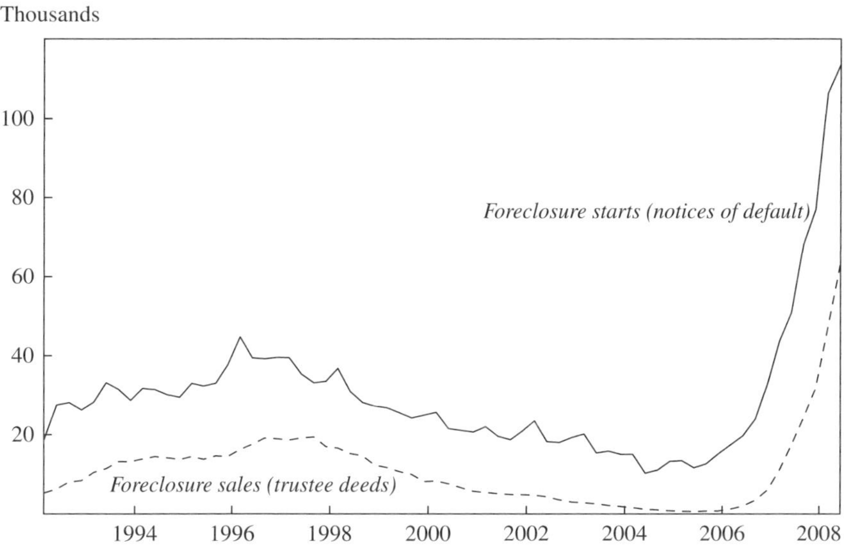

Source: DataQuick Information Systems.

overall housing and mortgage market developments. The real estate information company DataQuick has produced a quarterly time series on foreclosure starts (notices of default) and foreclosure sales (trustee deeds) for California since 1992 (figure 3).[16] In the downturn of the early to mid-1990s, when nominal home prices fell moderately, a sizable proportion of foreclosure starts turned into foreclosure sales. During the California real estate boom that started in the late 1990s, hardly any foreclosure starts turned into sales. Finally, in the home price plunge of the past 12 to 18 months, foreclosure sales have climbed essentially in lockstep with foreclosure starts one to two quarters earlier, confirming that a very large proportion of all new foreclosure starts now result in sales.

These observations suggest that a very large proportion of foreclosure starts in the current cycle will involve a significant loss to the lender, in most cases because a foreclosure start is followed by an eventual sheriff's auction. Moreover, the data suggest that loss incidence shows a strong

16. The absolute numbers are higher than those in table 2 because the DataQuick figures are a universe count whereas the Hope Now figures are based on a sample of servicers. However, the changes over time are quite similar for the (short) period during which both series overlap.

inverse relationship with changes in home prices. Unfortunately, this relationship cannot be estimated empirically from available data. Instead I assume a foreclosure completion rate of 75 percent if home prices drop another 5 percent from mid-2008 levels, 85 percent if prices drop another 15 percent, and 95 percent if prices drop another 25 percent.[17]

The predicted number of foreclosures must also be converted into dollar losses. Since the MBA foreclosure data are based on the number rather than the dollar value of loans, this requires making an assumption about the average mortgage balance by state. To do this, I use data from the Federal Reserve Bank of New York on the average balances of subprime and alt-A loans by state. I assume that the typical foreclosure in the MBA categories "subprime ARMs" and "subprime FRMs" involves an average-sized subprime loan, and that the typical foreclosure in the MBA categories "prime ARMs" and "prime FRMs" is an average-sized alt-A loan.[18]

The only remaining issue is what to assume for average severity. Severity depends inversely on home prices because a larger home price decline implies that the typical foreclosed home is more deeply in negative equity. Like the foreclosure completion rate, however, the relationship between home prices and severities cannot be estimated statistically from available data. Instead I assume that—depending on the home price outcome—severities vary between 58 and 68 percent for subprime mortgages and between 39 and 45 percent for prime and alt-A mortgages.[19]

17. One can loosely justify these assumptions by cross-sectionally correlating the 2008Q2 foreclosure completion rate from the Hope Now data (estimated using the ratio of foreclosure sales to foreclosure starts two quarters earlier) with the cumulative home price change from 2006Q2 to 2008Q2. An ordinary least squares regression with 51 observations yields a slope coefficient of −1.35 (with a t statistic of −5.6), meaning that an incremental 10-percentage-point home price drop implies an incremental 13.5-percentage-point rise in the foreclosure completion rate.

18. This is a relatively conservative assumption. The MBA subprime sample includes at least a small number of alt-A loans (which are generally larger than subprime loans), and the MBA prime sample includes most jumbo loans (which are generally larger than alt-A loans). Moreover, it is likely that the average foreclosure involves a larger-than-average mortgage balance, since an excessive amount of debt presumably is a key reason the borrower experienced problems in the first place.

19. This assumption is qualitatively consistent with the methodology of Standard & Poor's (2008), whose severity assumptions depend directly on the decline in home prices. A sampling of recent severity estimates for different mortgage types shows that Standard & Poor's (2008) assumes prime jumbo, alt-A, and subprime severities of 30, 40, and 50 percent, respectively; Freddie Mac (2008) assumes average alt-A severities of 45 percent; and Goldman Sachs (2007) assumes subprime severities of 60 percent.

Table 3. Projected Mortgage Credit Losses by Quarter and by Mortgage Type under Three Home Price Scenarios, 2007–12

Billions of dollars

Period or type of mortgage	*Loss assuming indicated decline in home prices from mid-2008 level*		
	5 percent	*15 percent*	*25 percent*
By quarter			
2007Q1	5	5	5
2007Q2	8	8	8
2007Q3	13	13	13
2007Q4	19	19	19
2008Q1	27	27	27
2008Q2	37	37	37
2008Q3	43	48	53
2008Q4	44	52	72
2009Q1	38	54	91
2009Q2	34	52	107
2009Q3	30	50	102
2009Q4	27	49	82
2010Q1	24	44	60
2010Q2	22	39	47
2010Q3	20	34	40
2010Q4	19	30	35
2011Q1	19	27	33
2011Q2	18	26	31
2011Q3	18	24	29
2011Q4	17	24	28
2012Q1	17	23	27
2012Q2	17	23	27
2012Q3	17	22	26
2012Q4	17	22	26
By type of mortgage			
Subprime ARMs	218	291	391
Subprime FRMs	87	110	134
Prime ARMs	119	173	264
Prime FRMs	126	175	234
Total, 2007–12	550	750	1,023

Source: Author's calculations.

Credit Loss Projections

I use the above assumptions to project total credit losses for three alternative price scenarios, as reported in the top panel of table 3. If nominal home prices fall another 5 percent before reverting to the previous trend, in which prices rose by an average of 3 percent a year, the model implies that mortgage credit losses realized in 2007–12 will total $550 billion. If instead nominal home prices fall another 15 percent through the middle of 2009, the model projects losses of $750 billion. Finally, if prices drop another 25 percent, predicted losses increase to $1.02 trillion. Moreover, the table suggests that losses peak in the fourth quarter of 2008 if home prices drop another 5 percent; in the first quarter of 2009 if prices drop another 15 percent; and in the second quarter of 2009 if prices drop another 25 percent.[20]

The bottom panel in table 3 reports total estimated losses in the above three home price scenarios for each type of mortgage. In the central scenario (home prices fall by 15 percent), the model implies that losses of $402 billion (with rounding), or just over half of all losses, will occur in the subprime sector. As it happens, this corresponds roughly to the subprime losses currently implied by prices of the ABX.HE family of subprime credit derivatives.[21] One could interpret this as saying that the market is currently discounting an implicit further home price decline of just under 15 percent. However, this statement is highly approximate because the ABX analysis is based on the stock of mortgages currently outstanding, whereas my analysis of the MBA foreclosure data is based on projected cumulative foreclosures over the 2007–12 period.

The Link between Credit Losses and Lending

The main reason why credit losses are important from a macroeconomic perspective is that they weigh on the supply of credit to nonfinancial borrowers. In this section I use the mortgage credit loss estimates of the previous section to quantify this link.

I start by documenting the facts about credit extension. About half of the nearly $50 trillion in total credit extended by U.S.-based entities consists of liabilities by domestic nonfinancial private borrowers; the rest is mainly financial and government debt. I focus here on the availability of credit to private nonfinancial borrowers because it is likely to have the most direct effect on overall economic activity.[22]

20. Losses are dated as of the foreclosure start, since this usually coincides roughly with the booking of a loss by the lender. If the date of foreclosure sale were used instead, the peaks would occur roughly two quarters later.

21. According to the model developed in Goldman Sachs (2007), the ABX.HE market was discounting total subprime losses of $388.5 billion as of November 3, 2008.

22. Reduced availability of financial credit may be important indirectly, but such an effect would usually work by way of a tightening of nonfinancial lending conditions. A reduction in credit availability to government borrowers is unlikely except in extreme cases.

Figure 4. Outstanding Debt of Private Nonfinancial Borrowers, Second Quarter 2008

Trillions of dollars

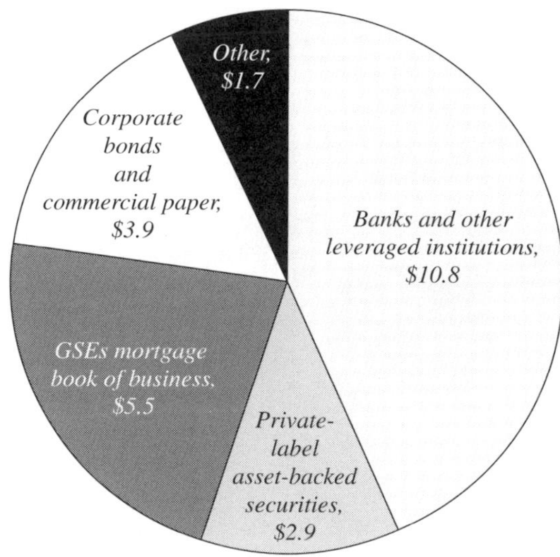

Source: Board of Governors of the Federal Reserve.

Using information from the Federal Reserve Board's flow of funds accounts as well as my own assumptions and interpolations, one can divide this debt into five main categories (figure 4):

—*On-balance-sheet lending by leveraged private entities* ($10.8 trillion as of the second quarter of 2008). These include banks, broker-dealers, savings institutions, and finance companies. The largest categories are residential and commercial mortgages held on balance sheet, followed by other bank loans and consumer credit held on balance sheet. (This measure of on-balance-sheet lending does not include GSE-backed mortgage-backed securities, or MBSs, for which the credit risk ultimately resides with a government agency.)

—*Lending in the ABS markets* ($2.9 trillion). This category mostly consists of nonconforming mortgage-backed securities, but it also includes securities backed by consumer credit and corporate loans. This figure excludes ABSs held on the balance sheets of leveraged institutions.

—*Debt owned or guaranteed by a GSE* ($5.5 trillion). This category consists almost entirely of the mortgage books of business of Fannie Mae and Freddie Mac, which include mortgages or MBSs on their balance sheets as well as MBSs for which those institutions bear the credit risk. I

Figure 5. Accounting for Growth in Nonfinancial Private Credit, 1991–2008

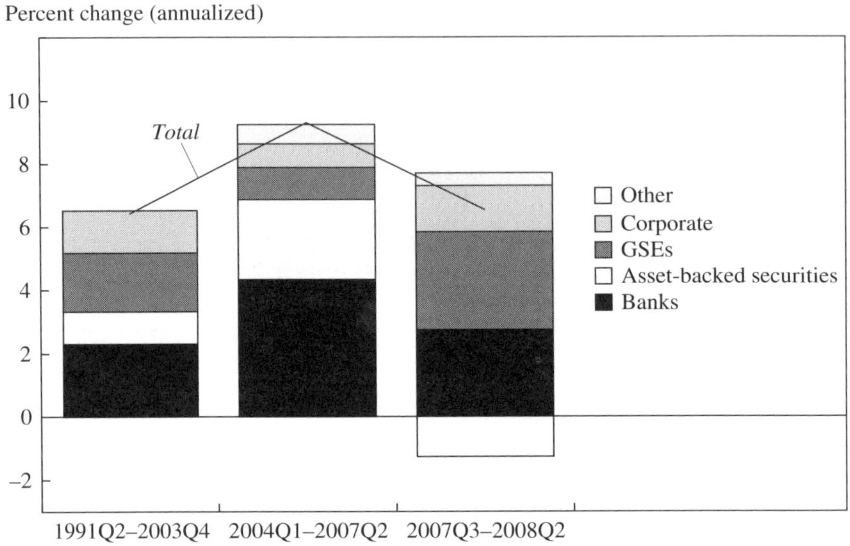

Source: Board of Governors of the Federal Reserve.

include mortgages held on a private sector balance sheet so long as the GSEs bear the credit risk.

—*Lending in the corporate bond and commercial paper markets* ($3.9 trillion). This figure again excludes assets held on the balance sheets of leveraged institutions.

—*Direct lending and holdings of securities by unleveraged entities* ($1.7 trillion). These include insurance companies, pension funds, and the government.

Figure 5 shows total private nonfinancial credit growth and its five components since 1991. Overall credit has grown at a compound annual rate of 7.1 percent, significantly faster than the 5.3 percent annual growth rate of nominal GDP over that period. By far the biggest contributor has been on-balance-sheet credit growth, which has contributed 2.7 percentage points, followed by GSE lending with 1.8 percentage points, corporate bonds with 1.2 percentage points, and the ABS markets with 1.1 percentage points.

However, the relative contributions of these different sectors have changed sharply over time. During the credit boom of the 2004–07 period, the surge in the private-label securitization markets contributed as much as 2.5 percentage points to overall credit growth. Since the start of the bust in mid-2008, however, this picture has changed dramatically, as the private-label ABS market has subtracted 1.3 percentage points from overall credit growth. In contrast, GSE-backed lending has accelerated sharply over the past year. During the boom, GSE-backed lending contributed 1.0 percentage point to credit growth, but since the bust started this number has increased to 3.1 percentage points. This acceleration has come despite the deterioration in the finances of Fannie Mae and Freddie Mac over that period.

Of particular interest in assessing the impact of the credit crisis are the first three sectors: leveraged institutions, private-label ABS markets, and the GSEs. The next subsection discusses the likely behavior of each of these in turn.

The Behavior of Leveraged Financial Institutions

The first shock to the supply of credit occurs through declining equity capital and declining leverage among financial institutions, including commercial banks, broker-dealers, savings institutions, credit unions, and finance companies. In what follows I refer to this entire group of leveraged institutions simply as "banks."

There are three key ingredients in this story, which follows GHKS in several important respects. First, the losses and writedowns cut into banks' equity capital base, despite offsets to these losses from recapitalization as well as lower corporate income taxes.[23] Second, the impact is magnified because banks appear to target a procyclical leverage ratio over the business cycle. This can be explained in terms of value-at-risk models that measure the approximate maximum daily loss ("approximate" in the sense that anything worse than this loss can only happen with some benchmark probability). Third, the impact of the first two factors on end-user credit—households and nonfinancial businesses—is dampened because some of the lost credit supply consists of claims on other banks.

To get an estimate of the impact on credit supply, one can summarize this story by means of the following equations:

(1) $$dA = \left[-C \times (1 - k - t) \times L\right] + (dL \times A)$$

(2) $$dY = dA \times Y/A,$$

23. The analysis of the offsets in this paper focuses only on private sector recapitalization. Government equity injections are discussed as part of the policy response in the final section.

Table 4. Worldwide Credit Losses by Type of Financial Institution since Mid-2007[a]
Billions of dollars

Type of institution	*United States*	*Europe*	*Rest of world*	*Total*
Investment banks	126.3	78.7	0.9	205.9
Commercial banks	370.3	112.4	14.2	496.9
Specialty finance	91.6	...	...	91.6
Insurance and asset management firms	38.8	6.6	...	45.4
Total	627.0	191.7	15.1	839.8

Sources: Company releases, Goldman Sachs Research.
a. Losses include writedowns, above-trend provisions, and equity in failed institutions.

where A is total bank assets (the total size of the unconsolidated balance sheet), Y is end-user credit (lending to private nonfinancial entities), C is the pre-tax credit loss suffered by banks, k is the percentage of pre-tax credit losses that is replaced by raising capital, t is the effective marginal corporate income tax rate, and L is leverage. To derive a benchmark for the contraction in total assets and nonfinancial private credit, I use the following numbers for the variables in equations 1 and 2:

Bank credit loss (C)	\$762 billion
Tax offset (t)	25 percent
Private recapitalization rate (k)	50 percent
Change in leverage (dL)	−10 percent
End-user credit ratio (Y/A)	63 percent.

I explain each of these assumptions in turn.

BANK CREDIT LOSS. For my illustrative calculation, I assume that home prices fall by another 15 percent (logarithmically) from mid-2008 to mid-2009, which, according to the model developed in the previous section, should result in a total credit loss on residential mortgages of \$750 billion. I assume that U.S. banks ultimately suffer 60 percent of this loss, or \$450 billion. Table 4 summarizes credit losses realized since the crisis began in the summer of 2007. Over the past year, financial institutions globally have written down or provisioned for a total of \$840 billion because of the credit crisis, mostly because of residential mortgages. (This figure includes about \$100 billion of equity capital lost in failed financial institutions.) U.S. commercial banks and investment banks account for \$497 billion (59 percent) of this total. My assumption that U.S. banks will bear 60 percent of the ultimate loss simply reflects their share in losses recognized to date.

In addition to the assumed \$450 billion in residential mortgage credit losses, banks are starting to see larger credit losses on other types of loans and ABSs, including commercial mortgages and consumer credit. To incorporate these into the analysis, I use the estimates provided by the International Monetary Fund (IMF).[24] Specifically, I use the midpoint of the IMF's ranges for bank losses on loans and securities exposures other than residential mortgages, residential MBSs, and residential ABS collateralized debt obligations. For loans, I assume that all bank losses are incurred by U.S. institutions; for securities, I assume that 60 percent of all bank losses are incurred by U.S. institutions. This results in additional estimated losses and writedowns for U.S. banks of $312 billion, for a total estimated loss, including residential mortgages, of $762 billion.

TAX OFFSET. The after-tax credit loss is likely to be lower than the pre-tax loss because most banks will be able to use their credit losses to lower their corporate income tax liability. However, the offset is likely to be below the statutory 35 percent corporate income tax rate. Banks that make losses for many years—or end up going out of business—will be unable to obtain this offset. Taking this into account, I assume that the average effective marginal tax rate offset is 25 percent.

PRIVATE RECAPITALIZATION RATE. So far during the crisis, U.S. commercial and investment banks have raised about 65 percent of the total pre-tax credit loss in new equity capital. More recently, however, the pace of private recapitalization has slowed as the crisis has intensified. I therefore assume a somewhat smaller ultimate private recapitalization ratio of 50 percent, in line with the central assumption in GHKS.

CHANGE IN LEVERAGE. GHKS show that leverage by commercial and investment banks is procyclical, rising in booms and declining in slumps. However, their paper does not provide much guidance with respect to the size of the potential leverage decline during the current crisis. To obtain a quantitative estimate, I therefore look at two other pieces of evidence: the history of the early 1990s, and recent disclosures by U.S. banks of changes in their balance sheet targets.

Figure 6 plots the aggregate leverage ratio of U.S. banks (both commercial and investment banks) since 1990.[25] It shows that leverage declined by 28 percent (from 17.0 to 12.3) in the four years from 1990 to 1994. If this

24. IMF (2008).

25. I define leverage as total assets divided by equity capital. The series is calculated from quarterly financial reports on the assets and equity capital of firms included in the following S&P 500 sectors: diversified banks (GICS code 40101010), regional banks (40101015), other diversified financial services (40201020), and investment banking and brokerage (40203020). The series is adjusted for two series breaks in June 2003 and April 2005.

Figure 6. Bank Leverage Ratios, 1990–2008

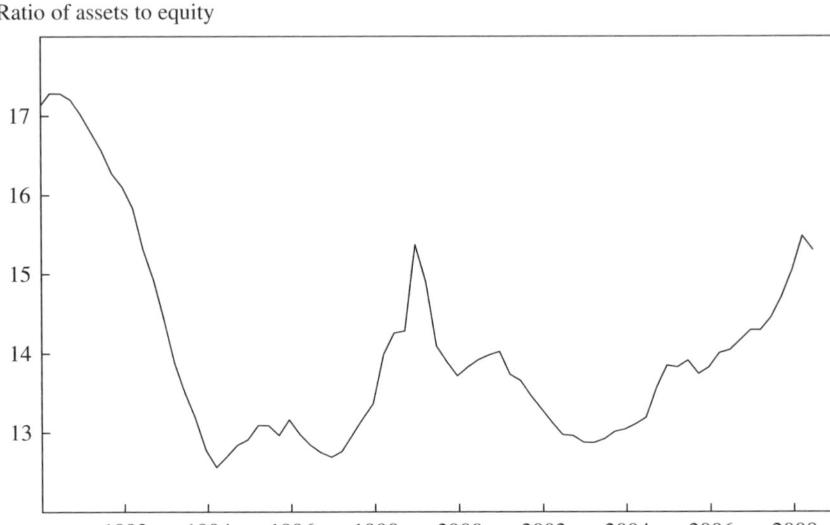

Sources: Standard & Poor's and author's calculations.
a. Data cover both commercial and investment banks.

were to be the template for the current crisis, it would imply a very large amount of deleveraging. However, the figure also shows that leverage in the banking system is now lower than it was in 1990. This suggests that the decline in leverage among banks could be a bit more muted.[26] Hence, I assume a decline in overall bank leverage of 10 percent, while acknowledging that the uncertainty about target leverage is sizable and that the risks are probably tilted in the direction of a larger decline.[27]

END-USER CREDIT RATIO. In the dataset for this paper, the ratio of end-user credit to total bank assets is 63 percent, calculated simply as the ratio of private nonfinancial credit to the total size of the unconsolidated

26. The analysis in this section excludes off-balance-sheet vehicles. However, the shrinkage of the off-balance-sheet ABS markets is discussed below.

27. In terms of the leverage ratio, I rely on the estimates in exhibit 4.5 in GHKS, rather than the bottom-up data in figure 6. Although the bottom-up data are suitable for assessing changes over time, they include S&P 500 firms only and exclude both finance companies and most savings institutions and are therefore considerably less comprehensive. When adjusted for the exclusion of the GSEs and imputed hedge fund figures from the leveraged sector, the GHKS data imply an aggregate leverage ratio of 10.9.

bank balance sheet. This is larger than the 42.7 percent share used in GHKS, which was estimated indirectly (and for a somewhat different set of institutions) from various accounting relationships in the U.S. banking sector. However, the 63 percent figure is similar to that reported in the recent study by Deutsche Bank, which estimates an end-user credit share of 67 percent for the European banking system.[28]

Armed with these assumptions, I can calculate benchmark figures for dA and dY as follows:

dA = [–\$762 billion × (1 – 0.50 – 0.25) × 10.9] – (0.1 × \$17.3 trillion) = –\$3.81 trillion

dY = –\$3.81 trillion × 0.63 = –\$2.40 trillion.

Thus, the above assumptions imply that banks could reduce the supply of credit to end users by \$2.4 trillion in response to credit losses and the change in their desired leverage ratios. This number is more than twice the \$1 trillion estimate in GHKS, for three main reasons. First, partly because of more adverse mortgage credit loss assumptions, and partly because I also consider nonmortgage credit losses, I assume considerably larger total credit losses for banks, although this difference is partly offset by the assumption that banks will use 25 percent of their losses to reduce their income tax liability. Second, I consider a decline in leverage of 10 percent rather than 5 percent. Third, I assume a larger end-user credit share.

One very important question is the time horizon over which the adjustment takes place. For purposes of quantifying the impact on real GDP growth, I assume that the impact occurs over a two-year period. This is based on the assumption that banks started to respond to the credit crisis in mid- to late 2007 and will have completed their response by mid- to late 2009, when home prices are assumed to bottom. Under this assumption, the combined effects of the losses and the deleveraging would subtract \$1.2 trillion from the annualized flow supply of end-user bank credit, relative to a baseline scenario in which there is no housing and credit crisis. In this baseline scenario, the most natural assumption is continued bank lending growth that matches the trend annual growth rate of nominal GDP of about 5 percent. Since this implies baseline bank lending of about \$500 billion a year (calculated as 5 percent × \$10.9 trillion), these calcula-

28. Deutsche Bank (2008).

tions imply an annualized shrinkage in the absolute flow supply of end-user bank credit of $700 billion during the crisis.[29]

ABS Market Disruptions

The second disruption to the supply of credit occurs through the ABS markets. The recent mortgage credit losses have brought the originate-and-distribute model underlying these markets into serious disrepute. That model is based on the idea that the bundling and structuring of small loans—most commonly residential or commercial mortgages, but also credit card debt, student loans, and a host of other loans—combined with an opinion from the major rating agencies can produce securities with risk characteristics comparable to those of traditional corporate bonds. However, the much higher than expected losses on these securities, especially subprime mortgage securities, have badly dented the reputation of the rating agencies and undermined the willingness of investors to purchase such securitized products from the financial institutions that bundle them. Without a respected third-party institution to assess the credit quality of ABSs, the model has broken down. As a result, gross issuance has fallen sharply.

Figure 7 shows the impact of this disruption on overall credit creation. It plots gross issuance of securitized nonconforming residential mortgages, commercial mortgages, credit cards, and automobile and student loans since early 2006, as well as the measure of net lending through the ABS markets discussed above. As gross issuance has fallen from around $1.3 trillion (annualized) in 2006 and the first half of 2007 to only around $500 billion (annualized) in the second half of 2007 and the first half of 2008, net credit extension through off-balance-sheet ABSs has swung from an average of around +$600 billion to –$300 billion. Hence, it appears that most of the drop in gross issuance has translated into a drop in net credit extension.

It is unlikely that ABS issuance will rebound until investors regain confidence in their ability to evaluate ABS credit quality. This could happen in

29. In apparent contrast to predictions of a credit slowdown, the Federal Reserve's weekly commercial bank balance sheet data point to a sharp *pickup* in bank credit growth since early September 2008. I believe that this pickup reflects a substantial increase in the demand for bank credit as other financing sources have dried up, and is therefore demand-rather than supply-driven. For example, a number of corporate borrowers have reportedly been shut out of the commercial paper markets and have therefore tapped backup credit lines. Despite the pickup in credit outstanding, the Federal Reserve's Senior Loan Officers' survey for 2008Q4 shows a clear increase in lending restraint by banks, consistent with the predictions of this analysis.

Figure 7. Issuance of Asset-Backed Securities, 2007–08

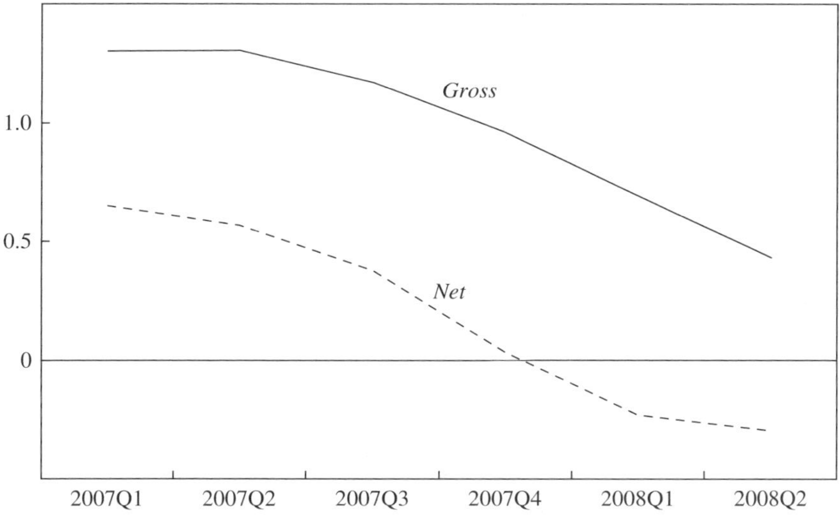

Sources: Board of Governors of the Federal Reserve, Securities Industry and Financial Markets Association, Bloomberg.

a. Sum of preceding four quarters.

one of two ways. Either the rating agencies regain the trust of investors, despite their failure to foresee the massive mortgage credit losses, or investors and issuers come up with alternative methods of monitoring credit quality in the ABS market. Neither development looks imminent, and so it is likely that gross ABS issuance will remain extremely low and net ABS issuance sharply negative. I therefore assume that net credit extension through the ABS markets will average –\$400 billion (annualized) in 2008 and 2009. Relative to a counterfactual trend of +\$125 billion (+5 percent of the outstanding stock of ABSs), this implies an impact of –\$525 billion.

The Behavior of Government-Sponsored Enterprises

The GHKS analysis includes the activity of Fannie Mae and Freddie Mac with that of other leveraged financial institutions. This seemed reasonable at the time because the GSEs are clearly among the most highly leveraged institutions in the U.S. financial system, and because they are more directly exposed to the housing market than any other. Now that the

Figure 8. Changes in GSEs' Mortgage Book of Business, 2004–08

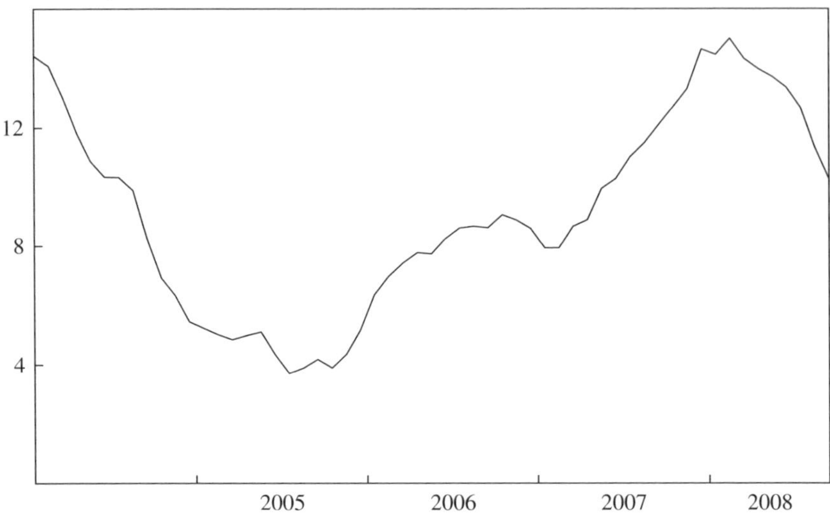

Sources: Freddie Mac, Fannie Mae.

GSEs have been taken into conservatorship by the federal government, however, they clearly need to be analyzed separately.

From the beginning of the financial crisis in August 2007 until about May 2008, the GSEs behaved very differently from other private financial institutions. As shown in figure 8, the GSEs grew their books of business at rates of up to 15 percent and provided a major offset to the tightening in the fully private financial sector. However, starting in June 2008, growth slowed sharply as the GSEs started to focus on capital preservation. The Treasury Department's decision in early September 2008 to take the GSEs into conservatorship raises the likelihood of a renewed pickup in growth. The present analysis assumes that the annualized contribution of the GSEs to overall credit growth will average $500 billion, or about 10 percent.

Implications for Overall Credit Supply

To sum up the discussion, table 5 shows my rough estimates of the net impact from the three sectors on the supply of nonfinancial private credit. This is done by adding up the estimated annualized reduction in the supply of bank credit, the annualized change in off-balance-sheet private-label ABSs relative to a counterfactual assumption of 5 percent annual growth,

Table 5. Projected Change in Credit Supply by Type of Financial Institution, 2008–09
Billions of dollars

Type of institution	*Change in credit from end-2007*	*Trend credit growth at 5 percent a year*	*Total change in credit supply*
Banks and other leveraged financial institutions[a]			−1,199
Asset-backed securities markets	−400	+125	−525
Government-sponsored enterprises	+500	+250	+250
Total			−1,474
Memorandum: change in credit as percent of total credit outstanding			−6.0

Source: Author's calculations.

a. Includes commercial banks, broker-dealers, savings institutions, credit unions, and finance companies.

and the annualized change in GSE-backed debt, also relative to a counterfactual assumption of 5 percent growth. These numbers sum to a total drag on nonfinancial private lending of \$1.47 trillion, equivalent to a 6.0-percentage-point drag on the growth rate of private nonfinancial debt. This is almost entirely due to the restraint on bank balance sheet growth from credit losses net of recapitalization and falling leverage.

The Link between Lending and Aggregate Economic Activity

To complete the analysis, I turn to the link between the supply of credit and aggregate economic activity. The effects of the credit losses on banks and off-balance-sheet ABS markets have led to a reduction in overall balance sheet capacity and therefore in the supply of credit to the real economy. A simple way to gauge the importance of this effect is to relate the volume of credit outstanding to a measure of cyclical fluctuation in overall economic activity, such as the growth rate of real GDP. However, since the causality between credit and economic activity clearly runs in both directions, it is important to look for instrumental variables that can be used to isolate the impact of an exogenous change in credit on activity. I use two survey measures of credit availability as instruments. The first is the perceived availability of credit to small businesses, as measured in the monthly survey of the National Federation of Independent Business (NFIB), and the second is the willingness of banks to extend consumer installment loans, as measured in the Federal Reserve's Senior Loan Officers' (SLO) survey.

Although an instrumental variables (IV) approach should reduce the endogeneity problem, there is also the risk that a tightening of credit availability may be due to a deterioration in the economy, which would render the instruments invalid.[30] The first-stage equation therefore uses only instruments lagged by two quarters or more. Even this does not entirely rule out endogeneity problems if banks are systematically able to predict a deterioration in the economy two quarters or more in the future and adjust their credit standards accordingly. Whether banks can do this, however, is open to question. The fact that the housing and credit crisis apparently caught many banks by surprise raises serious questions about their ability to forecast broader economic and market developments and reduces the concern about endogeneity in this analysis.

I start with a simple ordinary least squares regression of real GDP growth on real private domestic nonfinancial debt (PDNFD) growth, using quarterly data from 1974Q4 through 2008Q1:

$$\underset{}{\mathrm{d}GDP} = \underset{(1.93)}{0.0114} + \underset{(4.17)}{0.39309}\, \mathrm{d}PDNFD$$

$$\text{Adjusted } R^2 = 0.16,\ \text{SE} = 0.028,\ \text{D-W} = 1.56$$

where dGDP is the annualized log change in real GDP, d$PDNFD$ is the annualized log difference of real credit, and Newey-West t statistics are given in parentheses below the regression coefficients. SE is the standard error or the regression, and D-W is the Durbin-Watson statistic. There clearly is a reasonably strong correlation between credit growth and GDP growth, very much as expected.

Turning to the IV results, I start by presenting the results from an auxiliary first-stage regression of credit on the lagged survey variables:

$$\widehat{\mathrm{d}PDNFD} = \underset{(11.71)}{0.0752} - \underset{(4.83)}{0.005532}\, NFIB_{2\text{ to }4} + \underset{(1.70)}{0.00358}\, SLO_{2\text{ to }3}$$

$$\text{Adjusted } R^2 = 0.51,\ \text{SE} = 0.0226,\ \text{D-W} = 0.79$$

where $NFIB_{2\text{ to }4}$ is the average percentage of small businesses indicating in the NFIB survey that credit was harder to get from lags 2 to 4, and $SLO_{2\text{ to }3}$ is the average net percentage of banks reporting in the SLO survey an increased willingness to make consumer installment loans (seasonally adjusted using the Census X-12 algorithm) from lags 2 to 3. These

30. Mishkin (2008).

survey variables have substantial predictive power for future private credit growth.

Next, the second-stage IV regression is given by

$$dGDP = \underset{(1.10)}{0.002261} + \underset{(3.01)}{0.443059}\, d\widehat{PDNFD}$$

$$\text{Adjusted } R^2 = 0.16,\ \text{SE} = 0.0071,\ \text{D-W} = 1.55$$

where d*GDP* is the annualized log difference of real GDP. The equation implies that a supply-driven 1-percentage-point slowdown in real credit growth is associated with a 0.44-percentage-point slowdown in real GDP growth. This estimate is very similar to the results reported by GHKS, who estimate that a 1-percentage-point slowdown in credit growth lowers real GDP growth by 0.34 percentage point in the short run and 0.47 percentage point in the long run.

These regression results can be combined with the calculations in the prior section to estimate the approximate impact of the credit supply deterioration on economic activity. Recall that the estimate of supply-driven drag on credit growth was 6.0 percentage points per year. According to the IV estimates, this implies a drag on real GDP growth of 2.6 percentage points per year for a two-year period.

The above estimates should be interpreted as the shock to aggregate demand from the balance sheet tightening brought about by the increase in mortgage credit losses. The ultimate deviation of real GDP growth from trend could be larger or smaller than this estimate. It could be larger if there are substantial multiplier effects that amplify the initial shock. These multipliers could work through a deterioration in the labor market, a downturn in nonfinancial business investment in response to the original shock, or a U.S.-induced global economic slowdown that washes back onto U.S. shores through effects on international trade and investment. It could be smaller if economic policymakers react to the shock in a timely manner by cutting interest rates and loosening fiscal policy. In addition, the large-scale equity injections into the financial sector by the Treasury through the Troubled Asset Relief Program (TARP) have the potential to offset a significant part of the shock from reduced bank lending.

Conclusion

The analysis in this paper confirms that the decline in home prices and the associated increase in mortgage credit losses have been an important driver of the economic downturn through the disruptions in the financial system they have caused. These disruptions result not just from the impact of the losses on the lending capacity of banks, as emphasized by GHKS, but also from the sharp swing from positive into negative territory of net lending in the private-label ABS markets.

From a policy perspective, the analysis suggests that measures to boost the supply of credit are promising tools for softening the current economic downturn. One such measure is the $700 billion recapitalization of the financial system being undertaken by the Treasury Department through TARP. As of early November 2008, the Treasury had committed $250 billion in government capital injections into financial institutions through this program. Further injections could significantly soften the current credit squeeze.

Another possibility is to step up the supply of credit through Fannie Mae and Freddie Mac. The baseline assumption of this paper is that the GSEs will grow their book of business by 10 percent (at an annualized rate), or about $500 billion. This assumption is actually slightly more optimistic than the pace seen in the six months through September 2008, when the aggregate book of business grew by only 6.3 percent annualized. However, now that the Treasury essentially controls Fannie Mae and Freddie Mac, it could significantly boost the growth rate. The analysis in this paper implies that this would also soften the impact of the squeeze in the banking system and the ABS markets.

ACKNOWLEDGMENTS I am grateful to Charles Himmelberg, Donald Kohn, Nellie Liang, Edward McKelvey, Terence J. O'Neill, Andrew Tilton, and Dominic Wilson for helpful comments. Thanks are also due to Seamus Smyth for help with the models, and to Kent Michels and Shirla Sum for outstanding research assistance. The views expressed in this paper are solely those of the author and not necessarily those of Goldman Sachs. All errors are my own.

References

Bank of England. 2008. *Financial Stability Report.* No. 23. London (April).

Blundell-Wignall, Adrian. 2008. "The Subprime Crisis: Size, Deleveraging, and Some Policy Options." *OECD Financial Market Trends* 94, no 2008/1.

Deutsche Bank. 2008. "Unwinding Leverage." *Deutsche Bank Global Economic Perspectives* (July 28).

Foote, Christopher L., Kristopher Gerardi, Lorenz Goette, and Paul Willen. 2008a. "Subprime Facts: What (We Think) We Know about the Subprime Crisis and What We Don't." Federal Reserve Bank of Boston Public Policy Discussion Paper 08-2. Boston.

Foote, Christopher L., Kristopher Gerardi, and Paul Willen. 2008b. "Negative Equity and Foreclosure: Theory and Evidence." Federal Reserve Bank of Boston Public Policy Discussion Paper 08-3. Boston.

Freddie Mac. 2008. "Freddie Mac's Second Quarter 2008 Financial Results." Washington.

Goldman Sachs. 2007. "The Subprime Issue: A Global Assessment of Losses, Contagion, and Strategic Implications." November 20, 2007. New York.

Greenlaw, David, Jan Hatzius, Anil K Kashyap, and Hyun Song Shin. 2008. "Leveraged Losses: Lessons from the Mortgage Market Meltdown." In *Proceedings of the U.S. Monetary Policy Forum 2008.* Chicago: Initiative on Global Markets, University of Chicago Graduate School of Business.

International Monetary Fund. 2008. "Financial Stress and Deleveraging: Macrofinancial Implications and Policy." *Global Financial Stability Report.* Washington (October).

Judson, Ruth, and Ann L. Owen. 1997. "Estimating Dynamic Panel Data Models: A Practical Guide for Macroeconomists." Finance and Economics Discussion Series 97-3. Washington: Board of Governors of the Federal Reserve System.

Mishkin, Frederic S. 2008. "Comments [on 'Leveraged Losses: Lessons from the Mortgage Market Meltdown']." In *Proceedings of the U.S. Monetary Policy Forum 2008.* Chicago: Initiative on Global Markets, University of Chicago Graduate School of Business.

Muellbauer, John. 2007. "Housing, Credit, and Consumer Expenditure." In *Proceedings from the 2007 Jackson Hole Symposium.* Federal Reserve Bank of Kansas City.

Standard & Poor's. 2008. "Standard & Poor's Revises U.S. Subprime, Prime, and Alternative-A RMBS Loss Assumptions." New York (July 30).

STEPHEN MORRIS
Princeton University
HYUN SONG SHIN
Princeton University

Financial Regulation in a System Context

ABSTRACT The global financial crisis raises questions about the proper objectives of financial regulation and how best to meet them. Traditionally, capital requirements have been the cornerstone of bank regulation. However, the run on the investment bank Bear Stearns in March 2008 led to its demise even though Bear Stearns met the letter of its regulatory capital requirements. The risk-based capital requirements that underpin the Basel approach to bank regulation fail to distinguish between the inherent riskiness of an asset and its systemic importance. Liquidity requirements that constrain the *composition* of assets may be a necessary complement. A maximum leverage ratio—an idea that has gained favor in the United States and more recently in Switzerland—may also prove beneficial, deriving its rationale not from the traditional view that capital is a buffer against losses on assets, but rather from the importance of stabilizing liabilities in an interrelated financial system.

The global financial crisis of 2008 has raised fundamental questions about the conceptual foundations of financial regulation. Among a long list of momentous events has been the demise of stand-alone investment banks in the United States. At the beginning of the year, the U.S. broker-dealer sector was dominated by five such banks: Bear Stearns, Goldman Sachs, Lehman Brothers, Merrill Lynch, and Morgan Stanley. By the end of September, three of the five (Bear Stearns, Lehman Brothers, and Merrill Lynch) had either gone bankrupt or been taken over by commercial bank rivals after suffering varying degrees of distress. The remaining two (Goldman Sachs and Morgan Stanley) were allowed to convert themselves into bank holding companies, thereby coming under the Federal Reserve's bank supervision umbrella. In the space of a few months, the era of the stand-alone Wall Street investment bank thus came to an end, and the market-based financial system that they epitomized became the object of intense scrutiny for clues as to what went wrong.

Traditionally, capital requirements have been the cornerstone of bank regulation. Their rationale lies in maintaining the solvency of the regulated institution, thus protecting the interests of creditors—especially retail depositors.[1] As long as creditors are capable of monitoring a firm, they can protect their own interests by enforcing covenants and other checks on the actions of the firm's managers. However, the creditors of a traditional, deposit-funded bank are chiefly the small retail depositors, who face a coordination problem in monitoring the bank's managers and performing the other checks that large creditors are capable of. The purpose of bank regulation is seen as protecting the interests of depositors by putting into place, principally through capital requirements, the restrictions on the managers' actions that arise in normal creditor-debtor relationships.

This traditional rationale for capital regulation—protecting depositors by ensuring bank solvency—leads naturally to the conclusion that the key determinant of the size of the required capital buffer should be the riskiness of the bank's assets. After all, the degree to which solvency can be ensured depends on the likelihood that the realized value of the bank's assets will fall below the notional value of the creditors' claim. The original Basel capital accord of 1988 (Basel I, the first statement of bank regulatory principles to gain widespread international acceptance) introduced coarse risk classifications for bank assets. The Basel II rules, implemented in 2008, have taken the idea much further, refining the gradations of asset riskiness and fine-tuning the size of the capital buffer to the riskiness of the assets held by the bank.

However, the turmoil in the financial system witnessed in the current financial crisis poses a challenge to this traditional view of regulation. The Basel II regulations, which most of the world's developed economies are in the process of adopting, have largely been a bystander in the unfolding credit crisis that began with the subprime mortgage crisis in the United States.

In particular, recent events suggest that the traditional approach to financial regulation, based on institutional solvency and identifying solvency with equity capital, has come up short in its assigned task of ensuring system stability. The issue is highlighted in a recent open letter written

1. Dewatripont and Tirole (1994) discuss the underlying contract theory principles behind the prudential regulation of banks.

by Christopher Cox, the chairman of the Securities and Exchange Commission (SEC), explaining the background and circumstances of the run on Bear Stearns in March 2008:[2]

> The fate of Bear Stearns was the result of a lack of confidence, not a lack of capital. When the tumult began last week, and at all times until its agreement to be acquired by JP Morgan Chase during the weekend, the firm had a capital cushion well above what is required to meet supervisory standards calculated using the Basel II standard.
>
> Specifically, even at the time of its sale on Sunday, Bear Stearns' capital, and its broker-dealers' capital, exceeded supervisory standards. Counterparty withdrawals and credit denials, resulting in a loss of liquidity—not inadequate capital—caused Bear's demise.

Thus, Bear Stearns got into trouble not because it failed to meet the letter of its regulatory capital requirements, but because its lenders stopped lending. Put differently, the problem was on the *liabilities* side of the balance sheet, rather than on the asset side.

One possible counterargument by Basel traditionalists might be to question the sharp distinction between solvency and liquidity in the SEC chairman's letter. They might argue that the run was triggered by concerns over asset quality, and a rapid sale of assets to meet the run would have revealed that Bear Stearns was insolvent. The coordination failure scenario painted by John Bryant and by Douglas Diamond and Philip Dybvig in the 1980s raises the possibility of a sound bank succumbing to a self-fulfilling run,[3] but in practice, runs happen to weak banks. Strong banks, the counterargument goes, do not typically suffer runs, even though a run is always a logical possibility.

It is true that runs are typically associated with weak fundamentals. We will address this point in some detail in what follows. However, for policy purposes one needs to distinguish equilibrium outcomes from efficient outcomes. Even if it is difficult in practice to distinguish insolvent banks from illiquid banks, the distinction is nevertheless useful from a policy perspective, since one can then discuss the desirability of alternative policy measures to nudge the outcome in one direction or another.

Thus, the SEC chairman's point still needs to be addressed. Bear Stearns met the letter of its capital requirement, yet still suffered a run. We need to understand why, and whether better rules can be put in place.

2. Letter to the chairman of the Basel Committee on Banking Supervision, March 20, 2008 (www.sec.gov/news/press/2008/2008-48.htm).

3. Bryant (1980); Diamond and Dybvig (1983).

In this paper we will argue that if the purpose of financial regulation is to ensure the stability of the financial system as a whole, then the traditional approach to financial regulation built around risk-based capital requirements is inadequate. In a system context, actions taken by financial institutions have spillover effects that affect the interests of other financial institutions. System stability then takes on the attributes of a public good, and like any public good, it is undersupplied by the market. Actions that are individually rational for each market participant lead to an inefficient outcome overall. The market fails. The objective of financial regulation in a system context, then, is to levy the appropriate Pigovian tax that mitigates these externalities to the extent possible, and thereby move the financial system as a whole closer to an efficient outcome.

Of particular importance is that there is a difference between the *riskiness* of an asset and the *systemic importance* of that asset. Sometimes, as we will demonstrate shortly, even an asset that is deemed very safe under the Basel approach may have an important systemic impact that arises from the way that financial intermediaries' claims are interwoven, and how those intermediaries react to unfolding events.

The system approach to financial regulation suggests that the current capital regime needs to be overhauled to accommodate two additions to the regulatory toolkit:

—First, there is a case for liquidity regulation, which places limits on the *composition* of a financial institution's balance sheet, and not merely on the *size* of its equity relative to its total assets.

—Second, even assets that have traditionally been viewed as very safe may justifiably face a regulatory capital charge. Indeed, a simple leverage constraint that does not take account of the riskiness of assets may be a better way to ensure system stability than the traditional risk-based capital charge.

Both these additional regulatory elements have much in common with several recent proposals by others for the reform of financial regulation.[4] But besides some significant overlaps with these other proposals in terms of motivation, there are some differences in rationale and focus between those proposals and ours. Our discussion here is motivated by the debate on the regulation of the broker-dealer sector, and hence focuses on liquidity crises of the kind that undermined Bear Stearns, rather than on the general shortage of capital during a downturn. However, it is clear that the two

4. Such as that of Kashyap, Rajan, and Stein (2008).

issues should be considered together in a comprehensive agenda for regulatory reform. We begin with some general remarks on the importance of a system perspective in financial regulation.

A System Perspective

Financial stability is best viewed from a system perspective, rather than from the point of view of each individual financial institution. Andrew Crockett has argued for distinguishing between the *microprudential* dimension of financial stability and the *macroprudential* one.[5] The former has to do with the soundness of individual institutions, and the latter with the stability of the system as a whole. In his opening speech at the most recent Jackson Hole conference, Federal Reserve chairman Ben Bernanke argued for the superiority of the macroprudential perspective.[6]

A familiar truism holds that ensuring the soundness of each individual institution ensures the soundness of the system as a whole. Crockett makes the point that this statement is unhelpful, since it does not address *how* the soundness of all individual institutions is to be achieved simultaneously.[7] Actions that ensure the soundness of one institution may not be consistent with ensuring the soundness of another. Unless there are good reasons to believe that policies that ensure the soundness of a particular institution will invariably promote the overall stability of the system, the prescription is a vacuous one.

Figure 1 offers a simple example, in the spirit of Franklin Allen and Douglas Gale.[8] Bank 1 has borrowed from Bank 2. Bank 2 has other assets as well as its loans to Bank 1. Suppose that Bank 2 suffers credit losses on these other loans, but that the creditworthiness of Bank 1 remains unchanged. The loss suffered by Bank 2 depletes its equity capital. In the face of such a shock, a prudent course of action by Bank 2 is to reduce its overall exposure, trimming its asset book to a size that can be carried comfortably with the smaller equity capital.

The microprudential imperative is thus for Bank 2 to reduce its overall lending, including its lending to Bank 1. By doing so, Bank 2 achieves its microprudential objective of reducing its risk exposure. However, from Bank 1's perspective, Bank 2's reduction of its lending is a withdrawal of

5. Crockett (2000).
6. Bernanke (2008).
7. Crockett (2000).
8. Allen and Gale (2000).

Figure 1. Bank Balance Sheets in a Simple Interbank Loan

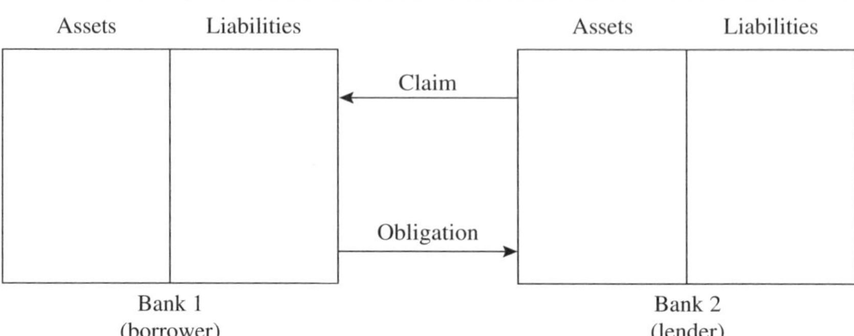

funding. Unless Bank 1 can find alternative sources of funding, it will have to reduce its own asset holdings, either by curtailing its lending or by selling marketable assets. If Bank 1 lacks alternative sources of funding, and if its assets are so illiquid that they can be sold only at fire-sale prices, then a large withdrawal of lending by Bank 2 will feel to Bank 1 no different from a run. In other words, a prudent shedding of exposures from the point of view of Bank 2 becomes a run from the point of view of Bank 1. Arguably, this type of run is what happened to the U.K. bank Northern Rock, which failed in 2007. The same perspective is useful in thinking about the run on Bear Stearns. In his March 2008 letter, SEC chairman Cox also says the following:

> It is worth noting, however, that net capital rules are designed to preserve investors' funds and securities in times of market stress, and they served that purpose in this case. This investor protection objective was amply satisfied by the current net capital regime, which—together with the protection provided by the Securities Investor Protection Corporation (SIPC) and the requirement that SEC-regulated broker-dealers segregate customer funds and fully-paid securities from those of the firm—worked in this case to fully protect Bear's customers.

Indeed, the run on Bear Stearns did help to protect its investors' funds. But it did so in a way that had the undesirable effect of undermining Bear Stearns itself. From a system perspective, the run is an undesirable outcome, even if it served the microprudential objectives of Bear Stearns' creditors.

The lesson is that the microprudential imperative of ensuring solvency at the level of the individual institution may not ensure the macroprudential objective of system stability. The truism that ensuring the solvency of each individual institution achieves overall system solvency is unhelpful as a policy prescription, since enhancing the solvency of one institution may conflict with maintaining the stability of the system as a whole. Therefore, as a practical matter, it is important for policy to be formulated from a system vantage point from the outset.

Thus, our starting point is the following proposition:

Proposition 1: Actions that enhance the soundness of an individual financial institution may undermine the stability of the system as a whole.

The system perspective has the virtue of opening up for scrutiny the motivation of the creditors to a bank suffering a run, as well as the fundamentals of the bank itself. Consider the situation depicted in figure 2, where Bank 0 has *N* creditors. These may include other banks, hedge fund clients who hold deposits at Bank 0, or money market mutual funds. For convenience, we label all creditors as "banks."

A run is associated with the self-confirming belief held by a creditor bank that when Bank 0's solvency comes into question, other creditors will take the prudent course of action and cut funding to Bank 0. This belief justifies cutting funding oneself. However, in practice, runs are associated with weak fundamentals on the part of the debtor bank and jitteriness on the part of creditors. If the debtor bank's fundamentals were stronger or its creditors more relaxed (or both), the run might be averted.

There is more at stake here than just the methodological point about finding the equilibrium. The hope is that if policymakers could engineer the initial conditions through appropriate regulation, so that the fundamentals of Bank 0 were stronger and the creditors less jittery, they could induce the stable, non-run outcome, instead of the run outcome.

A useful framework for thinking about this problem is provided by an example given by Lawrence Summers in his 2000 Ely Lecture. Summers proposed the following thought experiment:

> Imagine that everyone who has invested $10 with me can expect to earn $1, assuming that I stay solvent. Suppose that if I go bankrupt, investors who remain lose their whole $10 investment, but that an investor who withdraws today neither gains nor loses. What would you do? . . .
>
> Suppose, first, that my foreign reserves, ability to mobilize resources, and economic strength are so limited that if any investor withdraws I will go bankrupt. It would be a Nash equilibrium (indeed, a Pareto-dominant one) for everyone to remain, but (I expect) not an attainable one. Someone would reason that someone else would decide to be cautious and withdraw, or at least that someone would reason that someone would reason that someone would withdraw, and so forth. . . .

Figure 2. Bank Balance Sheets with Lending by Multiple Banks

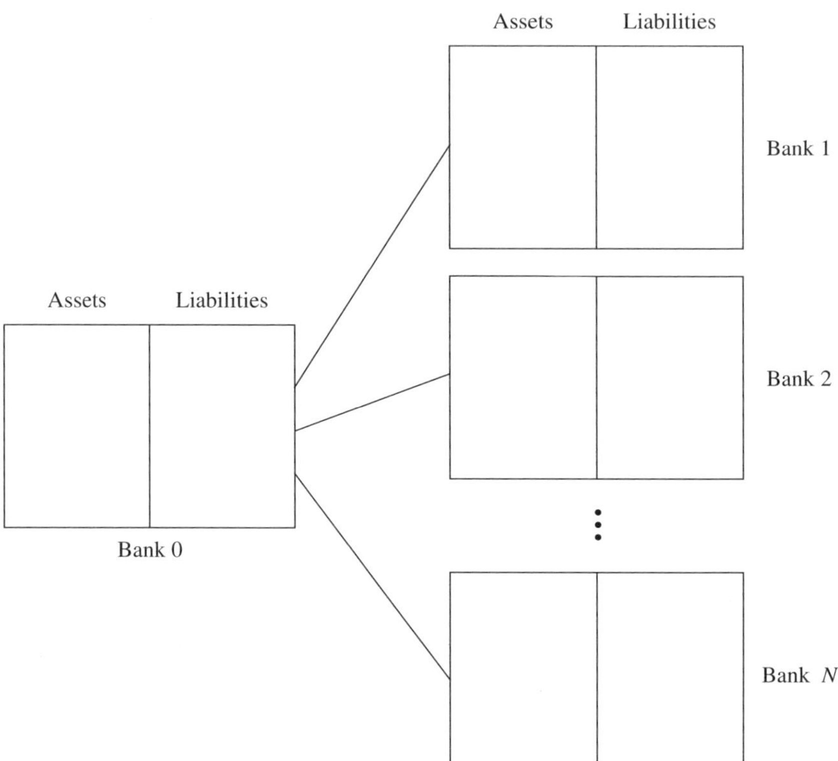

> Now suppose that my fundamental situation were such that everyone would be paid off as long as no more than one-third of the investors chose to withdraw. What would you do then? Again, there are multiple equilibria: everyone should stay if everyone else does, and everyone should pull out if everyone else does, but the more favorable equilibria seems much more robust.
>
> I think that this thought experiment captures something real. On the one hand, bank runs or their international analogues do happen. On the other hand, they are not driven by sunspots: their likelihood is driven and determined by the extent of fundamental weaknesses.[9]

The two dimensions to Summers' thought experiment are the same as in the example above: the strength of the fundamentals and the jitteriness of the creditors. But in Summers' formulation the first has to do with the threshold for the proportion of creditors who need to coordinate in order to

9. Summers (2000, p. 7).

Figure 3. Global Game Analysis of Bank Coordination to Avoid a Run

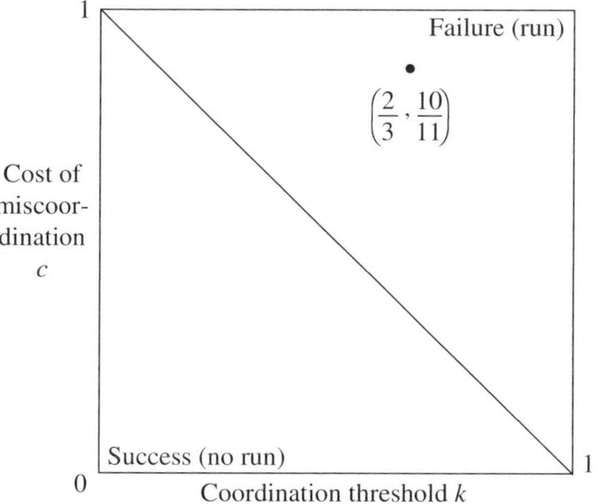

Source: Authors' model described in the text.

attain the good outcome. The weaker the fundamentals, the more fragile the borrower's balance sheet in the face of withdrawals. Summers appeals to our strong intuition that if the threshold value for coordination is close to one, coordination is very difficult to achieve. If the threshold is much less, coordination is easier.

The second dimension relates to the potential cost of miscoordination. In Summers' example the potential cost of failing to coordinate is losing one's stake of \$10, whereas the reward to successful coordination is \$11. The higher the cost of miscoordination, the more jittery the creditors will be. Again, our intuition would be that when the costs of miscoordination are high, coordination is more difficult to achieve.

It is possible to solve the Summers game using global game methods and verify that the two dimensions of the problem determine the unique equilibrium outcome.[10] This idea is depicted diagrammatically in terms of the unit square in figure 3. The horizontal axis plots the coordination threshold k, that is, the proportion of creditors who need to remain invested in order to achieve the good outcome. The vertical axis measures the cost of miscoordination c, expressed as a proportion of the payoff to successful coordination.

The global game analysis confirms the strong intuition articulated by Summers: successful coordination is achieved in the bottom left corner of

10. See Morris and Shin (2002).

the unit square (where the threshold for coordination is low and the cost of miscoordination is low), whereas in the opposite corner (where both the threshold for coordination and the cost of miscoordination are high) the good outcome cannot be achieved. The exact dividing line between the good and the bad regions depends on other parameters of the global game, but the benchmark dividing line is the straight line that cuts the unit square through the diagonal.

We can use this global game analysis to further test our intuitions. For the parameter values given by Summers in his thought experiment, the corresponding point in the unit square is (2/3, 10/11), since at least two-thirds of investors need to keep their money in, the cost of miscoordination is $10, and the payoff of the good outcome is $11. This point therefore lies in the failure region. The global game analysis thus suggests that Summers may have been too sanguine about the possibility of forestalling the run. But specific cases aside, the more general lesson is that coordination failure can be remedied by changes in the environment that make banks more robust to withdrawals, or by changes that lower the opportunity cost of miscoordination.[11]

In the banking context, if the debtor bank held more cash in place of illiquid assets, it could meet withdrawals more easily, thereby lowering the threshold k for coordination among the creditor banks. The cost of miscoordination c for the creditor banks could also be reduced if *they* held more cash, since they would then be less vulnerable to a run themselves. A more liquid creditor bank would be less jittery. It is thus possible to formalize within a global game the idea that greater cash holdings reduce the fragility of an institution's balance sheet to potential runs.[12]

Thus, to anticipate one of our conclusions, liquidity requirements on banks may reduce the potential for runs through two channels: they make debtor banks more robust to withdrawals, and they make creditor banks less trigger-happy. Recognition of the second channel is an insight that can only be gained in a system context.

11. This was a line of argument we pursued in our earlier paper on currency attacks (Morris and Shin, 1998).

12. In Morris and Shin (2008) we provide a formal decomposition of an institution's total credit risk into the risk of failure due to asset insolvency unrelated to a run by creditors, and the risk of failure purely due to a run. We examine how each of these components of credit risk depends on balance sheet composition and verify that greater cash holdings reduce total credit risk beyond the reduction attributable to the fall in the riskiness of the assets.

On the same theme, any institutional feature that constrains creditors in the direction of curtailing lending in reaction to events will undermine system stability. A prominent example in the context of Bear Stearns is the role of the triparty repurchase agreements (repos) that Bear Stearns entered into with certain money market mutual funds. In these agreements, Bear Stearns pledged illiquid securities as collateral, in return for which the money market funds provided Bear Stearns short-term funding. The transaction was overseen by a central counterparty that held the collateral and administered the payments.

The problem with this arrangement was that under their charters, most money market funds are prevented from holding illiquid securities of the type pledged by Bear Stearns. Thus, if Bear Stearns had become illiquid, and the assets pledged as collateral reverted to the money market funds, they would have been forced to sell those assets quickly, possibly at a large loss. This might have forced the funds to "break the buck"; that is, the value of their assets might have fallen below par value. Until Lehman Brothers' bankruptcy in September 2008, no money market fund had ever broken the buck. Therefore the Federal Reserve was concerned that such losses would have opened up the prospect of a run by retail investors on the entire money market mutual fund sector, by changing their perception of the funds' safety.

Some commentators have described the money market funds as extremely risk averse, but a more accurate description of their motivation is in terms of the cost of miscoordination. In effect, the cost of miscoordination c that these funds faced was extremely high. Hence, they heeded the imperative to be prudent and withdrew their funding to Bear Stearns. This in turn made other creditors, such as Bear Stearns' hedge fund clients, less willing to leave their money with the company as well.

The involvement of money market mutual funds in the triparty repo is an instance where institutional constraints made the run outcome more likely. It suggests that reform of institutional arrangements could change the underlying payoffs in the coordination game in the direction of making the system less fragile. We summarize this lesson as follows:

Proposition 2: A run is more likely when the coordination threshold is high or when the cost of miscoordination is high. Policies that lower the coordination threshold or the cost of miscoordination are likely to promote system stability.

The system perspective also raises an important distinction between the fundamental riskiness of an asset and its systemic importance. Even if an

Figure 4. Bank Balance Sheets with Reselling of Repo Securities

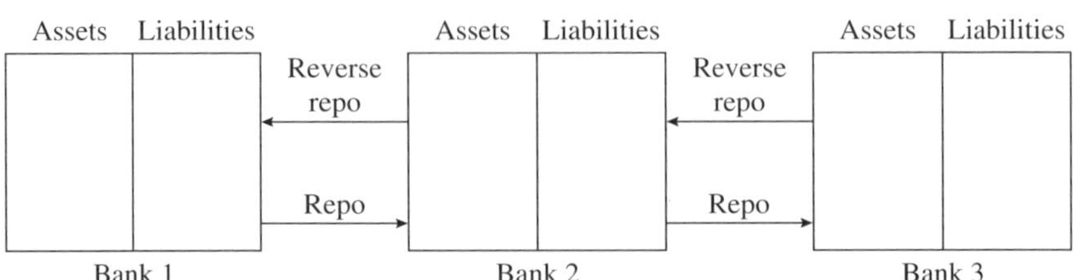

asset is very safe from the point of view of its credit risk profile, it may have a large impact on the stability of the system as a whole.

Consider the example illustrated in figure 4. Here Bank 1 holds mortgage-backed securities (MBSs) as its assets and finances this holding with overnight repos, in effect pledging the securities as collateral. In such an arrangement, Bank 1 actually sells the securities to another party (Bank 2 in this example) with the understanding that it will buy them back the next day at a prearranged price. Then, at the end of each day, the transaction is repeated. The repo thus enters as a liability on Bank 1's balance sheet and as a reverse repo on the asset side of Bank 2's balance sheet.

Bank 2, for its part, funds its lending to Bank 1 by pledging the same securities to another bank (Bank 3). Thus, Bank 2's balance sheet contains overnight reverse repos issued to Bank 1 on the asset side and overnight repos issued to Bank 3 on the liabilities side.

From Bank 2's perspective, its assets are extremely safe, for two reasons. First, the assets are short term, and so the range of possible realizations of their value is small. Second, the loan is fully collateralized, so that even if Bank 1 cannot repay, Bank 2's claim is protected. Furthermore, the maturity profiles of the two sides of Bank 2's balance sheet match perfectly. Both its assets and its liabilities involve overnight transactions. Hence, Bank 2 can react to any change in the environment by flexibly reducing the size of its balance sheet. By reducing the amount of the reverse repo to Bank 1 that it is willing to roll over, it can reduce its asset exposure. It is also in a good position to meet any run on its liabilities. If Bank 3 refuses for some reason to roll over the overnight repos, Bank 2 can immediately respond by refusing to roll over its reverse repos to Bank 1. In this sense Bank 2 is a very safe bank. The capital required of Bank 2 under Basel standards would be extremely low, and therefore Bank 2 could attain a very high degree of leverage. The Basel perspective justifies the high leverage by appealing to the safe nature of Bank 2's assets when viewed in isolation.

However, Bank 2's assets are also important from a system perspective, because they are the mirror image of Bank 1's liabilities. If Bank 1's assets are illiquid, such that they cannot realize much value in a fire sale, the impact on Bank 1's solvency of a run on its liabilities would be severe. If Bank 2 refused to roll over its overnight reverse repos issued to Bank 1, Bank 1 would be forced to sell its MBS assets unless it can find alternative sources of funding (say, from the central bank). Thus, even though they are very safe from the point of view of credit risk, Bank 2's assets have a high systemic impact. This leads to our third proposition:

Proposition 3: There is a distinction between risky assets and systemically important assets. Even safe assets can be systemically important.

The distinction between risky assets and systemically important assets takes on added significance in a market-based financial system built around the practice of secured lending through repos. One feature of a repo is that the "borrower" sells the securities today for a price below their current market price, because the understanding is that the borrower will later buy the securities back at a preagreed price. The difference between the current market price of the security and the price at which it is sold in the repo is called the "haircut."

The systemic impact of collateralized lending is especially strong when the haircut on the repo contract fluctuates in response to market conditions. The reason is that the haircut determines the maximum permissible leverage achieved by the parties involved. In terms of figure 4, suppose that the haircut on Bank 1's repos is 2 percent, so that Bank 1 receives \$98 for \$100 worth of securities sold. Then, to hold \$100 worth of securities, Bank 1 must come up with \$2 of equity. Thus, if the repo haircut is 2 percent, the maximum permissible leverage (ratio of assets to equity) is 50:1.

Suppose that Bank 1 leverages up to this maximum permitted level. Such action would be consistent with the objective of maximizing the return on equity, since leverage magnifies the return on equity. If a shock to the financial system then raises the haircut to, say, 4 percent, the permitted leverage falls by half, from 50:1 to 25:1. Bank 1 then must either raise new equity so that its equity doubles, or sell half its assets, or some combination of the two.

Times of financial stress are associated with sharply higher haircuts, which in turn entail substantial reductions in leverage, necessitating asset disposals or raising of new equity. Raising new equity is notoriously difficult in distressed market conditions, but selling assets in a depressed market is not much better. The evidence suggests that banks typically do the latter, leaving equity intact.[13] Thus, fluctuations in leverage are associated with pronounced fluctuations in the willingness to lend.

To the extent that the financial system as a whole holds long-term, illiquid assets financed by short-term liabilities, any tensions resulting from a sharp increase in repo haircuts will show up somewhere in the system. Even if some institutions can flexibly adjust their balance sheets downward in response to the greater stress, this action will itself expose pinch points in others.

These fluctuations in leverage in the context of widespread secured lending expose the myth of the "lump of liquidity" in the financial system. It is tempting to be misled by our use of language into thinking that "liquidity" refers to a fixed stock of available funding in the financial system, which will be redistributed to those who need it most. So, for instance, in the examples given in figures 1 and 2, the idea would be that when funding from one creditor dries up, the borrower can tap alternative sources. In reality, when liquidity dries up, it disappears altogether rather than being reallocated elsewhere. When haircuts rise, all balance sheets shrink in unison, leading to a generalized decline in the willingness to lend. Liquidity should therefore be understood in terms of the *growth* of balance sheets, that is, as a flow rather than as a stock.[14]

Indeed, the very term "secured lending" suggests that the assets are safe in terms of credit risk, since the loan is secured by collateral. However, funding conditions overall will vary substantially as haircuts fluctuate. Figure 4 illustrates the fact that fluctuations in Bank 2's assets have a systemic impact, even though Bank 2 is safe from credit risk. In this way the *riskiness* of an asset can diverge from its *systemic impact.* The Basel perspective, which focuses only on the credit risk of the asset, obscures this important distinction.

The distinction between risky assets and systemically important assets turns out to be crucial for broker-dealers, since many of the items on the balance sheet of an investment bank are precisely those that are collateralized and short term. Thus, as a prelude to our main discussion, we first examine the balance sheet characteristics of broker-dealers.

13. Adrian and Shin (2008, forthcoming).
14. Adrian and Shin (forthcoming); Fisher (2008).

Broker-Dealer Balance Sheets

Broker-dealers, a category of financial institutions that includes the major investment banks, differ sharply in the composition of their balance sheets from the archetypal deposit-funded bank. Figure 5 summarizes the balance sheet of Lehman Brothers as of November 30, 2007, the end of its financial year.

The two largest classes of Lehman Brothers' assets on that date were long positions in trading assets and other financial inventories, and collateralized loans. The latter reflect Lehman's role as prime broker to hedge funds and other borrowers and include reverse repos. Much of this lending was short term and therefore very safe from a credit risk perspective. Such loans are precisely the type of assets that could be systemically important even though their credit risk may be small.

The other remarkable feature of the asset side of Lehman Brothers' balance sheet is its small holding of cash: $7.3 billion out of a total balance sheet of $691 billion. However, this figure would be an underestimate of the cash that the company could have raised at short notice, if the securities holdings included liquid securities.

Lehman Brothers' liabilities, meanwhile, were largely short term. The largest component was collateralized borrowing, including repos. Short positions ("financial instruments and other inventory positions sold but not yet purchased") were the next largest component. Long-term debt made up only 18 percent of total liabilities.

One notable item, accounting for 12 percent of Lehman's balance sheet, was "payables," which included the cash deposits of Lehman's customers, especially its hedge fund clientele. These "payables" were much larger than the "receivables" on the asset side, which amounted to only 6 percent of the balance sheet. Hedge fund customers' deposits are subject to withdrawal on demand and hence may be an important source of funding instability. We will return to this issue when we discuss Bear Stearns' balance sheet and that company's more prominent reliance on payables to customers.

Finally, note that Lehman's equity ($22.5 billion) was only 3 percent of its total assets, implying a leverage ratio of 30.7:1. This is a much higher number than for commercial banks, which typically maintain a leverage ratio of 10:1 to 12:1. The higher leverage of investment banks reflects both the relatively low credit risk of the assets held and the short-term nature of much of their claims and obligations. Indeed, Lehman's end-2007 balance sheet as a whole consisted of precisely the types of assets and liabilities that have low credit risk but high systemic impact.

Figure 5. Composition of Lehman Brothers' Balance Sheet, November 30, 2007

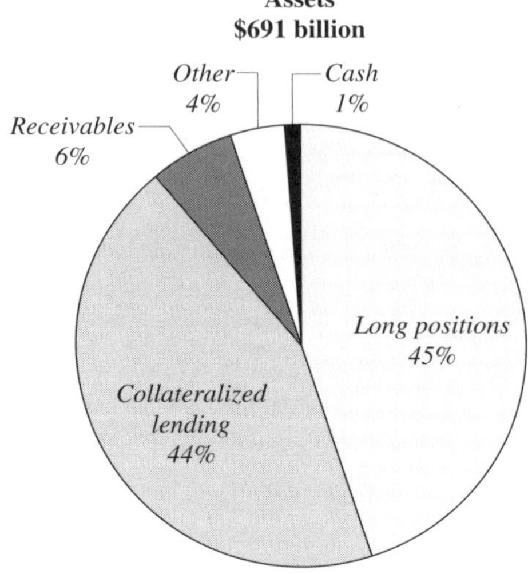

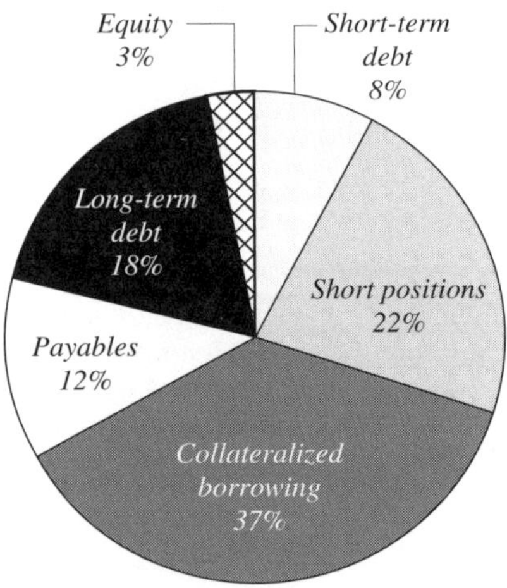

Source: Lehman Brothers 2007 annual report.

The balance sheet for Bear Stearns as of the same date (summarized in figure 6) shares many of the same characteristics noted for Lehman Brothers, but there are also some notable differences. As at Lehman, long positions in securities and collateralized lending formed the bulk of the company's assets. However, Bear Stearns' long positions also included the assets of special-purpose entities that were consolidated with Bear Stearns' own assets in accordance with standard accounting rules.[15] The liabilities of the special-purpose entities were also consolidated with those of the parent and were thus a counterpart to the asset holdings. Since these entities funded themselves mainly with short-term borrowing (such as commercial paper), the liability item "short-term debt" on Bear Stearns' balance sheet includes the liabilities of such entities.

One notable feature of Bear Stearns' balance sheet is the large proportion of funding—fully 22 percent of the total—consisting of payables. As with Lehman Brothers, the bulk of these payables were deposits of hedge fund customers, reflecting the importance of Bear Stearns' prime brokerage business. Also as at Lehman, they made Bear Stearns vulnerable to a classic run in the event of coordination failure among the hedge fund customers. Such a coordination failure might have reinforced whatever increase in repo haircuts already prevailed in the market.

In fact, during the run on Bear Stearns in March 2008, the defection of its hedge fund clients was one of the factors contributing to the funding shortage that eventually led to the company's request for Federal Reserve support. The *Wall Street Journal*'s special feature on Bear Stearns in May 2008 reported that several hedge funds and other customers had pulled their funds out of Bear Stearns at the height of the crisis in March.[16]

Figure 7, which plots the cash holdings of Bear Stearns in the days leading up to its demise, shows that in the three days from March 10 to March 13, these holdings dropped sharply, from $18 billion to only $2 billion. The speed with which the cash was exhausted shows the role played by the instability of liabilities in leading to the institution's failure. Thus, contrary to the traditional focus on credit risk on the asset side of the balance sheet, what mattered in the Bear Stearns case was the run on the liabilities side. To the extent that broker-dealer balance sheets

15. These rules stipulate that when the sponsor is the main beneficiary of the special-purpose entity and exercises substantial control over it, the entity should be considered as part of the sponsoring bank and their assets consolidated.

16. "The Fall of Bear Stearns: Fear, Rumors Touched Off Fatal Run on Bear Stearns," *Wall Street Journal,* May 28, 2008, p. A1.

Figure 6. Composition of Bear Stearns' Balance Sheet, November 30, 2007

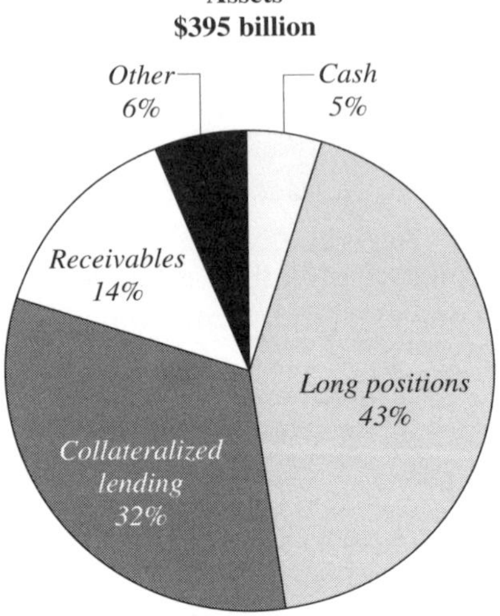

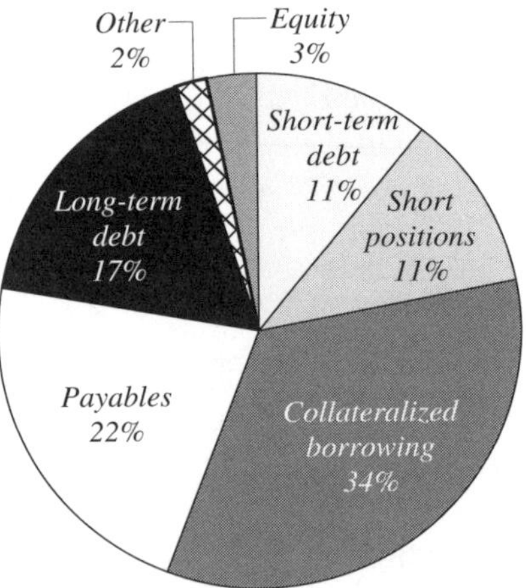

Source: Bear Stearns 10-K for fiscal 2007.

Figure 7. Bear Stearns' Cash Holdings, February 22–March 13, 2008

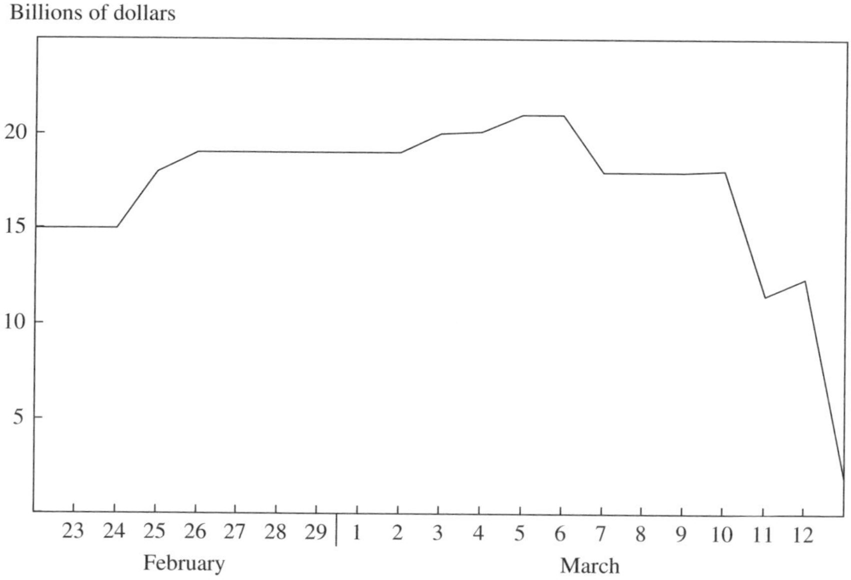

Source: Letter from SEC Chairman Christopher Cox to the Chairman of the Basel Committee on Banking Supervision, March 20, 2008.

consist primarily of such liquid and short-term claims and obligations, the run on Bear Stearns holds many useful lessons.

Implications for Financial Regulation: Liquidity Regulation

We now turn to the policy implications of our analysis so far. Our discussion is organized around the examples and propositions presented above. Returning to the case illustrated in figure 2, think of Bank 0 as a bank such as Northern Rock, the U.K. bank that failed in 2007, or as Bear Stearns, which financed its long-lived, illiquid assets by relying on short-term wholesale funding in the capital market. The exact identity of the lenders will differ from case to case, but the essence of the problem is this mismatch of maturities.

In this context, liquidity requirements on all banks, both debtors and creditors, might reduce the potential for runs through two channels: by making debtor banks more robust to withdrawals, and by making creditor banks less trigger-happy. Figure 8 illustrates this point using the Summers game described earlier. Point A on the parameter space is associated with a

Figure 8. Global Game Analysis of Bank Coordination with Liquidity Requirements

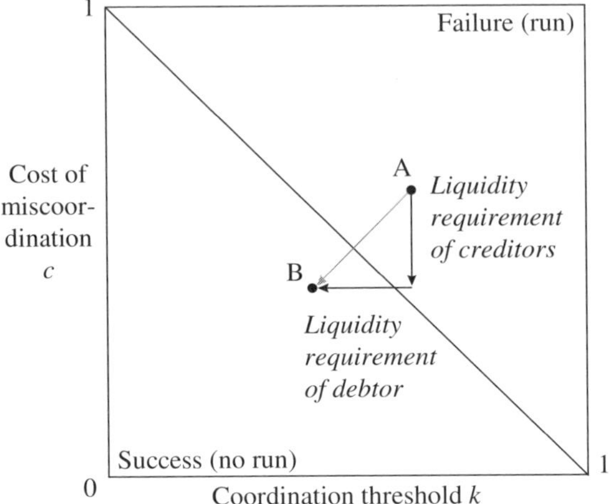

Source: Authors' model described in the text.

run outcome. It depicts a fragile arrangement where both the coordination threshold *k* and the cost of miscoordination *c* are high. A liquidity requirement on the debtor bank (Bank 0) would lower the critical threshold *k*, by making the debtor more robust to withdrawals, since moderately sized withdrawals can now be met by the debtor bank's liquid asset holdings. The liquidity requirement would also lower the cost of miscoordination *c* by making the creditor banks (Banks 1 to *N*) themselves less vulnerable to a deterioration of funding conditions.

The figure suggests that liquidity requirements might not have to be very onerous to be effective. Just as the fragility of the original arrangement sets in motion a vicious circle of reasoning that leads to the run, so the increased robustness achieved through higher liquidity would set in motion a virtuous circle of reasoning leading to a stable outcome. A more robust debtor bank would instill confidence in the creditor banks, which in any case will be more relaxed about the actions of other creditor banks in the face of worsening funding conditions.

How onerous the liquidity requirements must be to achieve the stable outcome would depend on the circumstances. A more systematic investigation, using both theoretical modeling and numerical simulations, would be worth pursuing. However, the important principle is that liquidity requirements would work by harnessing precisely those externalities that cause a run in the first place. The Summers game may oversimplify the comparison, but the same type of analysis can be brought to bear in an actual market context, as we have shown elsewhere.[17] In that analysis the model is set in a more complex environment with more parameters to be considered, such as the elasticity of the residual demand curve that absorbs concerted selling. However, the underlying principles are identical to those in the Summers game, and a unique outcome can be associated with each parameter configuration.

In addition, the underlying principle of distinguishing the credit risk of assets from their systemic impact seems important in any exercise of this sort, since the holding of cash buffers will affect the actions of interrelated players in subtle ways. As can be seen in figure 8, the (unique) equilibrium outcome can shift abruptly in response to small shifts in the underlying parameters of the problem that vary the susceptibility of the system to runs.

Recognizing the mutually reinforcing nature of banks' actions holds out some hope that the liquidity requirements sufficient to preclude a run might be rather modest, provided they are widely adopted. More systematic investigation will reveal precisely how onerous the liquidity requirements need to be to ensure stability. In such an exercise, there will be inevitable trade-offs between the size of the shocks contemplated and the liquidity requirements needed to meet those shocks. Numerical simulations will reveal the terms of that trade-off.

The actual cash holdings of U.S. broker-dealers have been relatively stable over the last 25 years or so, fluctuating between 2 and 4 percent of assets in recent years. Figure 9 traces this ratio for the whole of the U.S. broker-dealer sector since 1983, as given by the Federal Reserve's Flow of Funds Accounts. The sharp peak in 1987 and 1988 is associated with the stock market crash of 1987. Increases in cash holdings also occurred in 2000–02 (associated with the bursting of the dot-com bubble) and in the most recent couple of quarters (associated with the current credit crisis).

Interestingly, the relatively stable path for cash holdings for broker-dealers is not matched in the comparable series for U.S. commercial banks. As figure 10 shows, the ratio of cash assets (vault cash, cash items in process of collection, balances due from depository institutions, and balances at the Federal Reserve) to total financial assets of U.S. commercial banks has declined steadily in recent decades. As Tim Congdon has noted, the decline in cash holdings for U.K. banks has been, if anything, even

17. Morris and Shin (2004).

Figure 9. Cash Holdings of U.S.-Based Broker-Dealers, 1983Q2–2008Q1

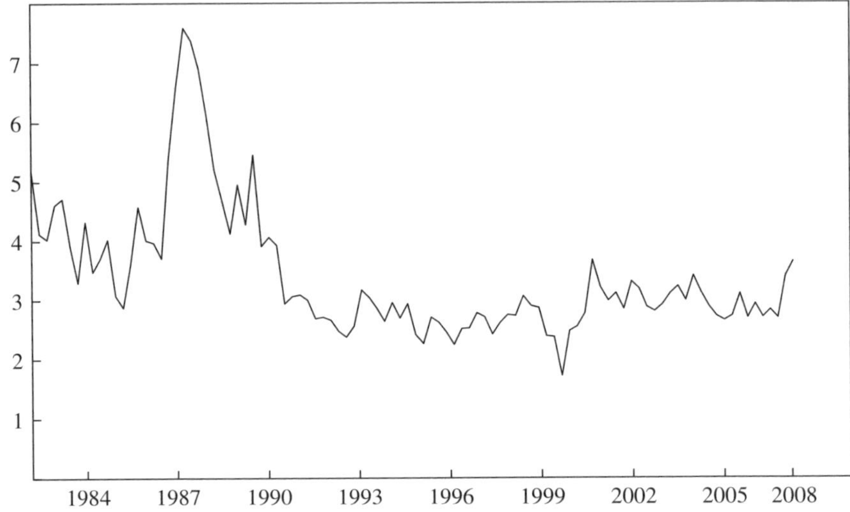

Source: Federal Reserve, Flow of Funds Accounts of the United States.
a. As of the end of the quarter.

Figure 10. Cash Holdings of U.S.-Based Commercial Banks, December 1981–June 2008

Source: Federal Reserve, "H.8 Assets and Liabilities of Commercial Banks in the United States: Historical Data."
a. As of the end of the month.

more dramatic.[18] In the 1950s it was typical for U.K. banks to hold as much as 30 percent of their assets in liquid form. However, Congdon reports that in the aggregate, their ratio of liquid assets to total assets has fallen to 1.0 percent in recent years. The Bank of England's Financial Stability Report of April 2008 charts bank liquidity ratios according to several definitions and confirms that the liquid asset holdings of U.K. banks have fallen sharply in recent decades.[19]

Although liquidity requirements might mitigate the potential for runs, the institutional constraints imposed on particular types of market players should also be taken into account. The triparty repo agreement involving money market mutual funds, discussed earlier, injects elements of greater fragility by involving players that are constrained to cut back on lending when financial conditions deteriorate.

We have already mentioned that money market mutual funds can be seen as creditors whose cost of miscoordination c is extremely high. Since the cost for these entities arises from the nature of the business and the charter that constrains their actions, liquidity requirements on them are unlikely to have much effect. This suggests a strong case for regulating their role in the triparty repo market.

Liquidity requirements would be complementary to other reforms of capital regulation to mitigate the cyclical nature of risk taking by financial intermediaries and the shortage of capital during a downturn. Although we have focused here on runs on the liability side, it is important to place such liquidity crises in the overall context of the credit cycle.

Anil Kashyap, Raghuram Rajan, and Jeremy Stein have recently proposed a regulatory scheme that would incorporate an element of funded capital insurance for banks. Banks would pay into a fund that holds safe securities in a "lockbox," to be opened in the event that certain defined aggregate thresholds of financial distress have been crossed.[20] The time necessary to verify that a threshold has been crossed makes the capital insurance scheme better suited for addressing a shortage of capital in the down phase of the financial cycle, and suggests that such a trigger mechanism could be seen as having a longer-term focus than the very short term acute liquidity shortages envisaged in a liquidity crisis. However, liquidity requirements and capital should be considered together in any reform of the regulatory framework.

18. Tim Congdon, "Pursuit of Profit Has Led to a Risky Lack of Liquidity." *Financial Times,* online edition, September 10, 2007. www.ft.com/cms/s/0/04ead7fc-5f36-11dc-837c-0000779fd2ac.html.

19. Bank of England (2008).

20. Kashyap, Rajan, and Stein (2008).

Implications for Financial Regulation: Leverage Constraints

We now turn our attention to another possible regulatory tool, namely, a constraint on the overall leverage of banks and brokers. We organize our discussion around the case illustrated in figure 4. The scenario we consider is one of a generalized increase in haircuts in the capital markets. Specifically, we assume that Bank 1 experiences funding problems that result from an increase in the haircut on its repo transactions with Bank 2. The increase in repo haircuts does damage because repo haircuts were previously very low and had encouraged all the banks in the system to increase their leverage.

Any discussion of proposed policies should be based on a clear set of objectives that those policies are intended to achieve. We will take as a working assumption that the purpose of financial regulation is to reduce the amplitude of financial booms and busts, and particularly the externalities generated by such a boom-and-bust dynamic.

One policy proposal that has already attracted considerable attention would impose a maximum leverage constraint on banks, *without* assigning any weights to the assets that figure in the leverage calculation. The United States has been at the forefront of such an initiative.[21] Although such constraints have been criticized as being too blunt, the system perspective provides a rationale. A leverage constraint has the potential to prevent the buildup in leverage that leaves the system vulnerable to a sudden reversal. The idea is that the maximum leverage constraint is a binding constraint on the upside of the cycle, when funding conditions are ample and banks can increase their leverage easily. The buildup of excessive leverage makes the system vulnerable to an increase in haircuts.

Note that an increase in haircuts does the most harm when starting from very low levels. For example, an increase from 1 to 2 percent means that leverage has to fall by half, from 100:1 to 50:1. But an increase from 20 to 21 percent, still only 1 percentage point, would have only a marginal effect, reducing leverage from 5.0:1 to about 4.8:1. In this sense the chasing of yield at the peak of the financial cycle is especially precarious, since the unwinding of leverage in the subsequent downturn will be that much more potent.

By preventing the buildup of leverage during good times, the leverage constraint could act as a dampener in the financial system. As with any constraint that threatens actually to bind, the banks will complain of being

21. See the speech by the chairperson of the Federal Deposit Insurance Corporation, Sheila Bair (2006).

prevented from pursuing higher profits. However, this is as it should be, since any Pigovian tax is just that—a tax.

The leverage constraint would work both at the level of the debtor and at the level of the creditor. In terms of figure 4, the constraint would prevent Bank 1 (the debtor) from building up excessive leverage, making it less susceptible to an uptick in the repo haircut. Meanwhile the constraint would also bind on Bank 2 during an upswing, so that when eventually the tide turns, some slack would remain available in Bank 2's balance sheet capacity. Hence, its lending to Bank 1 would suffer a smaller shock from any rise in repo haircuts. Thus, for both lender and borrower, the leverage constraint binds during boom times, so that the imperative to reduce leverage is less strong in the bust. Indeed, the bust may be averted altogether.

The fluctuations in leverage implied by the haircut in secured lending transactions suggest that banks and brokers expand their balance sheets to the maximum extent allowed by prevailing market conditions, only to cut back their balance sheets when funding conditions deteriorate. The imperative to maximize the return on equity could be one reason for such behavior. The externalities are manifested only in the down phase, but the potential for those externalities was created in the up phase. The rationale for a leverage constraint is that it binds during the expansion phase of the cycle, inviting the banks either to raise new equity or to slow balance sheet growth.

Also important to bear in mind is that the sharp increase in repo haircuts during a crisis episode is endogenous. The severity of the crisis depends on both the extent of the preceding boom and the actions of market participants.[22] When leverage unwinds, the force of the unwinding will be stronger when the boom has gone on longer and excesses have been allowed to persist. One of the desired effects of the leverage constraint is to dampen the fluctuations in repo haircuts themselves.

In effect, a leverage constraint can be considered a capital requirement that is not risk-sensitive: safe assets attract the same regulatory capital requirement as risky assets. It is important to emphasize the difference in rationale between the leverage constraint considered here and the traditional risk-based capital requirement. As discussed already, the credit risk of reverse repos is small, so that under Basel-style regulation, the required capital is likewise small. However, a leverage constraint would have the effect of mitigating the externalities generated by the fluctuations

22. Brunnermeier (2009) and Brunnermeier and Pedersen (forthcoming) describe the mechanisms at play when funding and market liquidity combine to amplify the financial distress.

in funding conditions in a market-based financial system built around secured lending. The focus is on the liabilities side of balance sheets, and on the potential spillover effects that result when financial institutions withdraw funding from each other, instead of on the asset side. Thus, it is raw assets, rather than risk-weighted assets, that matter.

The U.S. authorities have continued to impose a leverage constraint on regulated banks, a practice at variance with the minimum capital requirements laid down in pillar I of the Basel II capital requirements. Recently, however, the authorities in Switzerland have announced their intention to introduce a U.S.-style leverage constraint. This announcement has generated a fierce controversy.

The most commonly encountered criticism of a raw leverage constraint is that it does not take account of the riskiness of the assets. Basel II rules specify a very finely graduated capital requirement that depends on minute shifts in the measured risk of the asset portfolio. A simple leverage ratio is seen as throwing away all these finely calibrated calculations of asset risk. The *Financial Times* recently quoted the chief risk officer of Credit Suisse, speaking in reaction to an announcement by Philipp Hildebrand, the vice chairman of the Swiss central bank, as saying, "we manage banks according to Basel II, not Hildebrand I."[23] However, when viewed through the lens of systemic stability, the leverage ratio constraint has desirable properties that cannot be replicated by risk-based capital ratios alone.

Indeed, a leverage ratio constraint seems particularly appropriate for Switzerland. The country's two large banks, UBS and Credit Suisse, are both highly leveraged even by the standards of the U.S. investment banks, whose leverage ratios before the crisis were, as previously noted, around 30:1. (Commercial banks in the United States, also as previously noted, typically have much lower leverage ratios of 10:1 to 12:1.) The total assets of UBS at the end of 2007 were 2.27 trillion Swiss francs. With equity of only 42.5 billion Swiss francs, this implies a leverage ratio of 53:1. Although most of the assets on UBS's balance sheet are "safe" assets subject to a low capital requirement, we have seen that the credit risk weights do not always reflect the strength of the externalities in a financial system.

Two conceptual issues, however, need to be tackled in implementing a leverage ratio constraint; these have to do with the measurement of the two quantities involved in the definition of the leverage ratio. With regard to the numerator (total assets), the issue is what assets to include. In jurisdictions that apply the International Financial Reporting Standards (IFRS) of

23. "Taming Swiss Banks," *Financial Times*, online edition, July 1, 2008.

Figure 11. Composition of Northern Rock's Liabilities, June 1998–June 2007

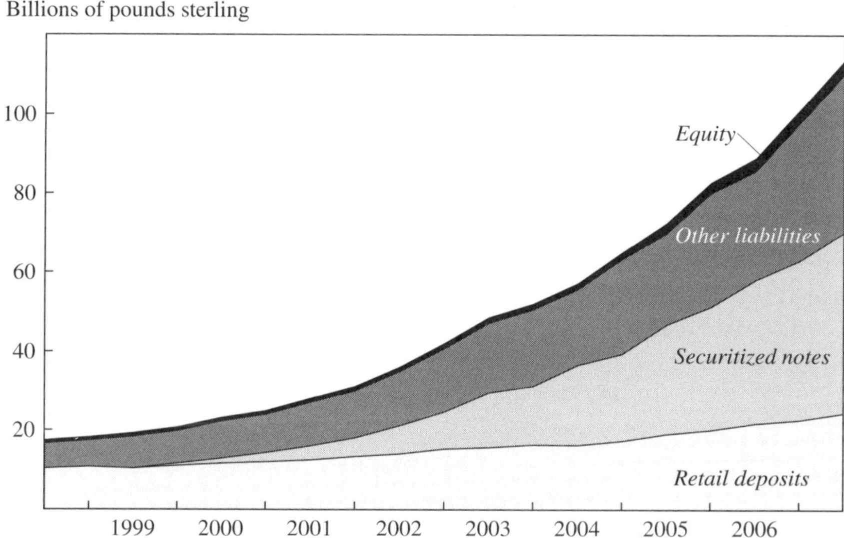

Source: Shin (forthcoming).

the International Accounting Standards Board, assets held in securitization vehicles are counted as part of the consolidated balance sheet. This raises the raw balance sheet size for European banks. (U.S. banks do not follow this standard.) For instance, figure 11 shows the liabilities side of Northern Rock's balance sheet in the 10 years from its demutualization in 1997 to its failure in 2007. Securitized assets accounted for much of the rapid increase in liabilities.[24] The rapid growth of Northern Rock's assets therefore reflects the active securitization it engaged in after demutualization.

Another accounting issue with regard to assets is how to assess the fair value of derivatives contracts. Under IFRS, both mark-to-market gains and mark-to-market losses are included in calculating the consolidated balance sheet, making it appear much larger than it would otherwise. The very high leverage of UBS is therefore partly an accounting phenomenon.[25]

The issue with regard to the denominator—that is, equity—is again what should be counted. Figure 12 plots Northern Rock's leverage ratio from June 1998 to December 2007 according to three different measures of equity, with very different results depending on whether preferred

24. See Yorulmazer (2008) for an empirical analysis of the U.K. banking sector at the time of the Northern Rock crisis.

25. See "Banks According to GAAP," *Financial Times,* online edition, July 29, 2008.

Figure 12. Northern Rock's Leverage under Various Definitions, 1998–2007

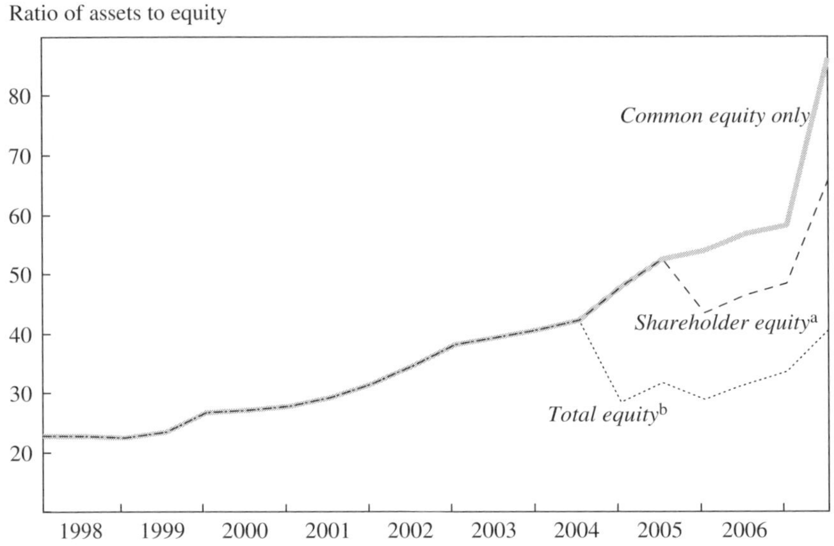

Source: Shin (forthcoming).

a. Includes preferred shares but not subordinated debt.

b. Includes preferred shares and subordinated debt.

shares and subordinated debt are included. Under the Basel approach to capital requirements, both count as bank capital, since they are buffers against loss. However, repo haircuts provide another interpretation of equity, as the stake that the controlling equity holder must have in order to borrow credibly from creditors who worry about moral hazard. Tobias Adrian and Shin, and Arvind Krishnamurthy, provide theoretical rationales for such an approach to the leverage calculation,[26] drawing on the work of Bengt Holmstrom and Jean Tirole.[27]

From this alternative viewpoint, subordinated debt holders and preferred shareholders are just another class of creditor to the bank, lacking the control of the bank's operations that common equity holders enjoy. For the purpose of calculating the permissible leverage in a moral hazard context, where the equity holders must have sufficient equity at stake to prevent moral hazard, it is the common equity that matters, not equity enhanced by subordinated debt or preferred shares.

26. Adrian and Shin (2008); Krishnamurthy (forthcoming).

27. Holmstrom and Tirole (1997).

Figure 12 shows that when leverage is interpreted strictly as the ratio of total assets to common equity, Northern Rock's leverage continued to climb throughout its history as a public company, from 22.8:1 in June 1998, just after its flotation, to 58.2:1 in June 2007, on the eve of its liquidity crisis. This is a very large number, even by the standards of U.S. investment banks that hold very liquid and short-term assets. Of course, Northern Rock's leverage rose even higher following the depletion of its common equity from losses suffered in the second half of 2007 and the run that ensued. The leverage on its common equity at the end of 2007 was 86.3.

Implications for Financial Regulation: System-Weighted Capital Requirements

If we take seriously the idea that the computation of leverage ratios is an exercise in computing Pigovian taxes to limit externalities, then a natural follow-up question is how to assess the impact of the negative externalities imposed by one bank on the financial system as a whole. In the textbook example of the smoky factory located next to the laundry, the externality is the factory's pollution, and a calculation of marginal costs will enter into the appropriate Pigovian tax on the factory.

In the case of the financial system, the negative externalities are those that one institution imposes on another through fluctuations in funding conditions. In the example in figure 4, Bank 2 imposes a negative externality on Bank 1 if it decides to curb its collateralized lending. However, the impact of a similar decision by Bank 3 can be even greater, since a reduction in its lending will cause a reduction in lending by Bank 2, which in turn will induce a reduction in lending by Bank 1. If Bank 1's assets are illiquid, the withdrawal of funding may cause even greater damage.

More generally, one can assign each bank in the financial system a "systemic impact factor" that corresponds to the degree of spillover that its actions have on other banks. The exact calculation of the systemic impact factor will depend on the network structure and on the nature of the assets held by each bank. However, the principle should be that any bank that lends heavily to other banks that have high systemic impact factors should itself have a high systemic impact factor.

Such a principle could be implemented through the type of fixed-point calculation used, for example, in rating the impact of scholarly papers by their citations in academic journals, or in calculating the impact weights that Google uses to rank websites. The impact weights for journals are designed such that a high-impact journal receives many citations from other high-impact journals. Similarly, Google's rankings give higher rank to a website the more links point to it from other high-ranking websites. Indeed, our use of the term "impact factor" is intended to underline this analogy with journal citations and Google webpage rankings.

In practice, however, complex calculations on impact factors would be difficult to implement in a financial regulatory regime. The lack of detailed balance sheet information on banks' cross exposures is an insurmountable hurdle. Even so, the principle of giving high systemic weight to institutions that have the potential to affect others' actions seems sound.

In any case, the impact factors associated with financial institutions in the same or similar categories may naturally be clustered. For example, a broker-dealer may have a higher impact factor than a small, locally based savings institution that deals primarily with retail customers and household borrowers. Thus, the fragmented way in which financial intermediaries in the United States have been regulated may turn out to have a deeper, unintended economic rationale. A given institution of a given type can be assumed to have characteristics similar to others of its type and can therefore be regulated similarly, and differently from other types of institutions. However the systemic impact factors are calculated, the principle of Pigovian taxation—that negative externalities should be taxed appropriately—can serve as a guide for our thinking.

An alternative approach in the practical implementation of system-weighted capital requirements would tie these requirements to summary statistical measures of spillovers, provided reliable summary measures could be obtained. A promising line of research is that reported in Adrian and Markus Brunnermeier, who consider the concept of "CoVar," defined as the value at risk of an institution's portfolio of assets conditional on some aggregate measure of distress.[28] Although some conceptual issues relating to aggregation and the endogeneity of the portfolios in response to incentives to game the regulatory system still need to be worked out, the approach is a promising one.

Concluding Remarks

The traditional approach to financial regulation based on risk-based capital requirements is not well suited to addressing the issue of the stability of the financial system as a whole. The truism that taking care of the solvency of

28. Adrian and Brunnermeier (2008).

each individual institution ensures the stability of the system is not useful, because it does not address spillover effects.

The most important distinction that the system perspective highlights is that between risky assets and systemically important assets. Even safe assets can be systemically important. Recognizing this distinction gives some rationale for two policy ideas that have attracted much attention: that of imposing a raw leverage constraint, and that of having a liquidity requirement that limits the composition of the asset portfolio, not merely its size. More systematic study will reveal how onerous the corresponding Pigovian taxes will have to be, but the severity of the current financial crisis suggests that the optimal Pigovian taxes will not be zero.

ACKNOWLEDGMENTS We are grateful to the participants at the Brookings Panel conference for their comments, and especially to our discussants Donald Kohn and Vincent Reinhart. We also thank Tobias Adrian and Charles Goodhart for comments on an earlier draft.

References

Adrian, Tobias, and Markus Brunnermeier. 2008. "CoVaR." Federal Reserve Bank of New York Staff Report 348. New York.

Adrian, Tobias, and Hyun Song Shin. Forthcoming. "Liquidity and Leverage." *Journal of Financial Intermediation.*

———. 2008. "Financial Intermediary Leverage and Value at Risk." Federal Reserve Bank of New York Staff Report 338. New York.

Allen, Franklin, and Douglas Gale. 2000. "Financial Contagion." *Journal of Political Economy* 108, no. 1: 1–33.

Bair, Sheila. 2006. Remarks at the Conference on International Financial Instability: Cross-Border Banking and National Regulation, sponsored by the Federal Reserve Bank of Chicago and the International Association of Deposit Insurers, October 5. www.fdic.gov/news/news/speeches/archives/2006/chairman/spoct0606.html.

Bank of England. 2008. *Financial Stability Report* no. 23. London (April). www.bankofengland.co.uk/publications/fsr/2008/fsrfull0804.pdf.

Bernanke, Ben. 2008. "Reducing Systemic Risk." Speech at the Federal Reserve Bank of Kansas City Symposium at Jackson Hole, Wyo., August 22. www.federalreserve.gov/newsevents/speech/bernanke20080822a.htm.

Brunnermeier, Markus. 2009. "Deciphering the 2007–08 Liquidity and Credit Crunch." *Journal of Economic Perspectives* 23, no. 1. Forthcoming.

Brunnermeier, Markus, and Lasse Pedersen. Forthcoming. "Market Liquidity and Funding Liquidity." *Review of Financial Studies.*

Bryant, John. 1980. "A Model of Reserves, Bank Runs and Deposit Insurance." *Journal of Banking and Finance* 4, no. 4: 335–44.

Crockett, Andrew. 2000. "Marrying the Micro- and Macro-Prudential Dimensions of Financial Stability." Bank for International Settlements, Basel. www.bis.org/review/rr000921b.pdf.

Dewatripont, Mathias, and Jean Tirole. 1994. *The Prudential Regulation of Banks.* Cambridge, Mass.: MIT Press.

Diamond, Douglas, and Philip Dybvig. 1983. "Bank Runs, Deposit Insurance, and Liquidity." *Journal of Political Economy* 91, no. 3: 401–19.

Fisher, Peter. 2008. "Role of Liquidity in Financial Crises." Commentary at the Federal Reserve Bank of Kansas City Symposium at Jackson Hole, Wyo., August 23. www.kc.frb.org/publicat/sympos/2008/fisher.09.01.08.pdf.

Holmstrom, Bengt, and Jean Tirole. 1997. "Financial Intermediation, Loanable Funds, and the Real Sector." *Quarterly Journal of Economics* 112, no. 3: 663–91.

Kashyap, Anil, Raghuram Rajan, and Jeremy Stein. 2008. "Rethinking Capital Regulation." Paper presented at the Federal Reserve Bank of Kansas City Symposium at Jackson Hole, Wyo., August 23. www.kc.frb.org/publicat/sympos/2008/KashyapRajanStein.09.15.08.pdf.

Krishnamurthy, Arvind. Forthcoming. "Amplification Mechanisms in Liquidity Crises." *American Economic Journal: Macroeconomics.*

Morris, Stephen, and Hyun Song Shin. 1998. "Unique Equilibrium in a Model of Self-Fulfilling Currency Attacks." *American Economic Review* 88, no. 3: 587–97.

———. 2002 "Measuring Strategic Uncertainty." Princeton University. www.princeton.edu/~hsshin/www/barcelona.pdf.

———. 2004. "Liquidity Black Holes." *Review of Finance* 8, no. 1: 1–18.

———. 2008. "Identifying the Illiquidity Component of Credit Risk." Working paper. Princeton University.

Shin, Hyun Song. Forthcoming. "Reflections on Northern Rock: The Bank Run that Heralded the Global Financial Crisis." *Journal of Economic Perspectives.*

Summers, Lawrence. 2000. "International Financial Crises: Causes, Prevention and Cures." *American Economic Review: Papers and Proceedings* 90, no. 2: 1–16.

Yorulmazer, Tanju. 2008. "Liquidity, Bank Runs and Bailouts: Spillover Effects during the Northern Rock Episode." Working paper. Federal Reserve Bank of New York.

Comments and Discussion

COMMENT BY

DONALD L. KOHN I appreciate the opportunity to comment on these three papers. They illuminate the sources and effects of the current financial market turmoil, and I learned a considerable amount from reading them and thinking about their implications. Instead of providing detailed comments on each paper, I would like to draw out the relationships among them and, in the process, comment a little on the papers and their implications. To foreshadow: I will be highlighting the role of leverage—in the household sector and in financial intermediaries—as a critical factor in understanding the buildup of excesses and their unwinding.

At the beginning of the chain of causation is the housing cycle in the United States. Karl Case points out the difference between this housing cycle and others over past decades and asks why the difference developed. One culprit he identifies is changes in the financial system that affected the way that mortgage credit is made available to borrowers. A key element of these changes, and one that accounts for a good part of the subsequent effects on the financial system and the economy, is the rise in leverage in housing finance. For several years mortgage indebtedness rose substantially relative to the value of owner-occupied housing. The willingness of lenders to tolerate—or, in some cases, encourage—huge increases in loan-to-value ratios added to the demand for housing, especially by people who normally might not have had the savings to enter the market, and contributed to the rise in home prices.

One reason for the loosening of standards was the expectation that home prices would continue to rise—and even more certainly that they

The views I express are my own and not necessarily those of other members of the Board of Governors of the Federal Reserve.

could not fall in all regions at the same time, supporting diversification through securitization. Rising prices would enable lenders to recoup their funds even if the borrower was unable to service the loan, mostly because the borrower would be able to obtain extra cash through refinancing. Expectations of home price appreciation facilitated and interacted with the increasing complexity of mortgage securities, including multiple securitizations of the same loan, which made it virtually impossible for ultimate lenders to monitor the creditworthiness of borrowers—a task they, in effect, had outsourced to credit rating agencies. The absence of investor caution and due diligence was especially noticeable for the highest-rated tranches of securitized debt.

Elevated leverage in housing markets has meant that as prices have fallen, lenders have had to absorb an unusually high proportion of the losses. As Case points out, foreclosures by lenders have added to the downward pressure on those prices. Conceptually, such price declines moving down the demand curve for housing services could accelerate and cushion the adjustment in activity necessitated by previous overbuilding.

The heavy involvement of financial intermediaries in amplifying the housing boom and the subsequent economic effects of the bust brings me to the paper by Stephen Morris and Hyun Song Shin, which raises a host of important issues related to the systemic aspects of financial intermediation and the lessons from the recent turmoil. As they emphasize, one of the important lessons has been the greater-than-expected vulnerability of secured financing when intermediaries are engaged in maturity, credit, and liquidity transformation. Recall that the turmoil first came onto the balance sheets of the banks through the collapse of the asset-backed commercial paper market in the fall of 2007, before it affected the funding of investment banks through the triparty repurchase agreement market. The new vulnerability results importantly from the extension of secured short-term financing to increasingly illiquid and riskier long-term assets. As the liquidity and creditworthiness of those assets—especially related to mortgage-backed securities—were called into question, lenders became more concerned about the possibility that they might end up owning the underlying assets, and they raised haircuts or simply refused to roll over loans.

Clearly, as Morris and Shin point out, what we have learned about various risks implies the need for intermediaries to build greater liquidity and capital buffers in good times, as well as to improve their abilities to manage their risks. And those larger buffers would help to offset the moral hazard that may have been created through the expansion of liquidity facilities at the Federal Reserve. Getting the microprudential piece right—having each institution adequately protected—would go a long way toward making the whole system more robust and resilient.

But Morris and Shin would go further; they would impose additional requirements on institutions to take account of the externalities for the system created when common shocks impair markets and credit availability by provoking widespread actions to preserve shareholder value. They would do this through a higher liquidity requirement and through the imposition of a leverage ratio on investment banks, which is already in place for commercial banks.

I agree with the authors, and with Federal Reserve Chairman Ben Bernanke, that we need to consider the level of buffers that is appropriate to ameliorate systemic risk. That said, a host of difficult judgments are inherent in how we establish such a system, and I will raise just a few on a very general level. One set concerns the size of the buffers. How far into the tail of the distribution of possible outcomes should intermediaries be required to insure themselves? Shouldn't the Federal Reserve take some of the liquidity tail risk, to facilitate intermediation of illiquid credits, as was intended at its founding? Moreover, the larger the regulatory tax, the more likely it is that activity will migrate to unregulated sectors in an environment of fluid and free capital movements. How can we gain better assurance of systemic stability when we are unlikely to be able to continuously extend the reach of regulation, and will it be sufficient to deepen the moats around the core institutions? In this regard, the leverage ratio gives incentives to move some activities away from regulated institutions.

A second question is, How we can structure these requirements and other aspects of regulation to damp, rather than reinforce, the natural procyclical tendencies of the financial system? Among the challenges will be encouraging firms and supervisors to comfortably allow buffers to be eroded in bad times. Interestingly, prompt corrective action under the Federal Deposit Insurance Corporation Improvement Act of 1991 was intended, in part, to induce an element of countercyclical behavior by banks. It gives banks an incentive to build excess capital—on both a risk-based and a leverage ratio basis—in good times to avoid the need for prompt corrective action when circumstances are less favorable. Now that we are in the latter state of the world, a study of how commercial banks are viewing capital ratios, including the leverage ratio, could inform consideration of the Morris and Shin proposal.

The Morris and Shin paper also provides a framework for thinking about the Federal Reserve's credit facilities. They note that liquidity makes borrowers feel more robust and lenders less likely to withdraw, raising the odds for a more stable equilibrium for the entire system. That is exactly what the Federal Reserve has been trying to do with its various discount lending facilities. The assurance of the availability of liquidity to sound institutions against good collateral should counter the greater uncertainty and risk aversion that have impaired normal arbitrage and intermediary functions, by making those institutions more willing to extend credit and take positions in the process of making markets. It should also assure other creditors of those institutions that illiquid markets will not impede the repayment of their loans, and therefore make them more willing to keep lending. A number of markets remain disrupted and illiquid. But I believe that they would have been even more illiquid, and the risk of disruptive runs even greater, without those various facilities; that is certainly what market participants are telling us.

The paper by Jan Hatzius tries to gauge the combined effects on aggregate spending of the losses generated by the effects of the decline in housing prices outlined in the Case paper and the impulse for deleveraging in the financial sector inherent in the processes discussed by Morris and Shin. To restore capital ratios depleted by mortgage losses and to raise those ratios even further in order to reduce leverage to the safer levels demanded by counterparties, banks and other lenders need to reduce assets. They do so by tightening terms and standards across a broad array of credit—and we at the Federal Reserve have seen this behavior reflected in our surveys of bank lending officers and in various spreads and other measures of risk perceptions, risk aversion, and reduced supply of credit at benchmark interest rates. In the current circumstances, some of the tightening we have seen has been in anticipation of possible adverse events in the economy and in confidence toward the financial sector. These types of actions not only move up the demand-for-credit curve, but also bolster profits going forward to cover potential write-offs and to attract new equity capital. Pressures on profits arise not only from write-offs, but also because some sources of earnings, like securitization of mortgages or leveraged loans, are no longer available.

In the steady state, lenders will get greater returns for taking risk than they did two years ago, intermediaries will be less leveraged and better capitalized, and the financial system will be more robust and resilient to shocks. The transition to the new steady state, however, as lenders deleverage and protect themselves against various downside risks, involves some overshooting—making terms and standards tighter than will be necessary over the long run.

This story is completely consistent with the one told in the Hatzius paper, which relies mostly on quantity relationships to gauge the possible effects on GDP. My instinct has been to go from the actual and expected indicators of tightening supply, such as the instrumental variables used in the paper, directly to estimates of the effects of that supply shift on GDP. Measures of flows would fall out of that exercise but would not be its focus. And I have questions about the stability and reliability of the debt-GDP relationship used in the forecasts at the end of the paper. But I will admit that we are in uncharted waters here, and the navigators should not discard any potential information about the location of the shoals.

The message of Hatzius's paper is that restraint on credit supplies is likely to persist because intermediaries have some way to go to rebuild their balance sheets. The process of adjustment to a safer, more resilient financial system is going to take a while. I agree with this observation.

COMMENT BY

VINCENT R. REINHART I appreciate the invitation to discuss these three fascinating papers focused on the important topic of the ongoing financial crisis. I will take this opportunity, first, to identify the commonality among them. Second, I will argue that a factor that is central to understanding recent financial market events is missing, both from these papers and in policymaking circles, at least judging from the actions of officials. Last, I will offer specific comments on each paper.

Over the past year, the chief impediment to aggregate spending in the United States and the major concern of policymakers has been that an adverse dynamic has taken hold. As can be seen working clockwise from the left of the simple schematic in my figure 1, the initiating economic loss came from building too many houses over the last decade. The efforts of builders to cope with bloated inventories have imposed a direct drag on spending. Home price declines, set in motion once this imbalance was recognized, have lowered wealth and consumption. The declines in home prices have also been associated with an elevated rate of mortgage foreclosures, which have strained the balance sheets of key financial intermediaries. The result has been that financial institutions are not supporting markets or making credit available, which further hampers spending and makes people less likely to buy houses.

Figure 1. Transmission of a Housing Market Shock

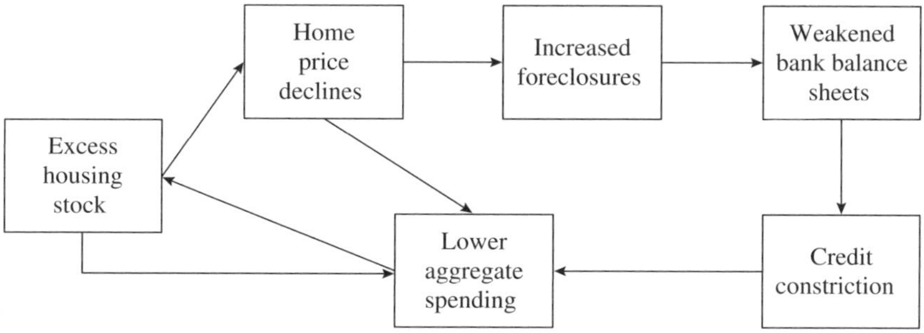

Source: Author's elaboration.

All three papers address this dynamic transmission mechanism, each focusing on a different aspect. Karl Case looks at the first part of that mechanism, namely, the relationship between the excess housing stock and home price declines. Jan Hatzius examines the macroeconomic mechanisms set in motion by home price declines. These include the restraint on spending through the direct wealth effect and the constriction of credit, that is, the financial accelerator. Finally, Stephen Morris and Hyun Song Shin address the interaction of financial institutions' balance sheets and credit constriction, and ask why the approximately $1 trillion loss from the surge of mortgage defaults has so impaired balance sheets and produced such a huge drag on an economy as large as the United States.

My central problem with these papers—and it is a problem shared by policymakers—is that they treat this map of the economics of home price adjustment as conceptually identical to a weather map. That is, they regard financial market problems as a force of nature imposed on the economy with a path invariant to policy. When the authors and policymakers talk about "the perfect storm" or "the hundred-year flood," they are revealing a belief that they have no influence on the route of the storm. These descriptions neglect the possibility that policy has itself shaped the contours of the crisis. Market activity and asset pricing have important expectational components. The determination of asset prices involves issues related to the coordination of beliefs and may tend toward multiple equilibriums.[1] As a result, even small policy actions can have large effects on the market. And the policy actions taken were not small.

1. A simple model of market activity addressing some of these issues is provided in Vincent R. Reinhart and Brian P. Sack, "The Economic Consequences of Disappearing Government Debt," *BPEA*, no. 2 (2000): 163–209.

In addition, policy interventions by the Federal Reserve and the Treasury in 2008, which were ambiguous in the scale and scope of the protections offered, created adverse incentives. The managers of firms with capital deficiencies were given the incentive to postpone adjustment. Creditors and short sellers were given the incentive to test the limits of government intervention. The net effect has been to deter private capital from flowing into an industry desperately in need of more capital.

Let me now turn to the individual papers. Karl Case assesses the economic loss that set the crisis in motion by examining the central role of home prices. The important message of that paper, although he does not put it exactly this way, is that home prices do not behave like other asset prices. This is evident in my figure 2. Each panel plots the quarterly return of an index of asset prices along the vertical axis against its own quarterly lagged return, over the period from 1991Q1 to 2008Q2. The top panel plots the change in the Case-Shiller national home price index. It shows that home prices are very predictable: last quarter's return sends a strong signal of what this quarter's return will be. That is nowhere near the case in the bottom panel, which plots the change in the S&P500 index against its own lag. Stock prices are more predictable than simple theory may suggest, but they are not very predictable.[2]

Why do home prices show such inertia? Sellers have discretion with respect to the listed price, advertising intensity, time on the market, and inclusion of amenities. Buyers have discretion on search intensities and time in the market. These are mechanisms that make prices sticky, but they are not the underlying reasons for this stickiness.

Two sets of insights from the macroeconomic literature may help in understanding the underlying source. This literature posits that prices can be inertial because of staggered contracting, menu costs, or sticky information. With respect to all three, price dynamics can be thought of as actual prices moving gradually toward a flexible shadow price. In the current environment, once the overhang of unsold homes became evident to the public, shadow prices fell. Now we are living through the inertial catch-up of transaction prices to those lower shadow prices. The relevant issue in explaining the overall economic adjustment is to determine which behaviors depend on shadow prices and which depend on transaction prices. Presumably, households' assessments of their own wealth, for instance,

2. James M. Poterba and Lawrence H. Summers, "Mean Reversion in Stock Prices: Evidence and Implications," Working Paper 2343 (Cambridge, Mass.: National Bureau of Economic Research, 1989), provide evidence of the modest predictability of stock returns over a long sample.

Figure 2. Correlations of Current with Lagged Changes in Asset Prices[a]

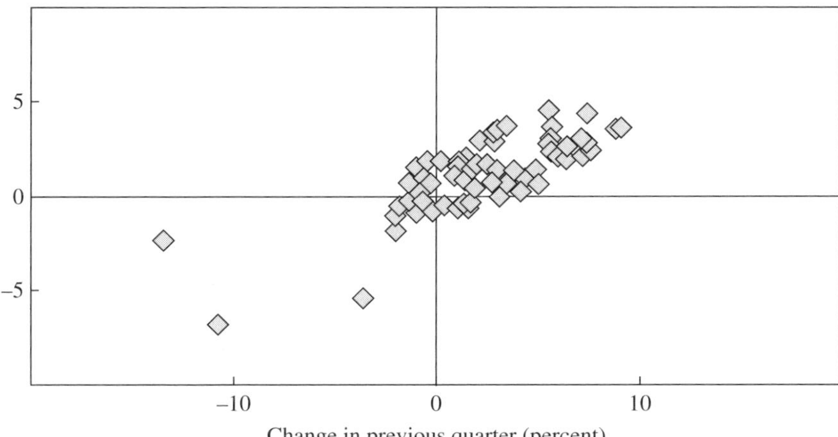

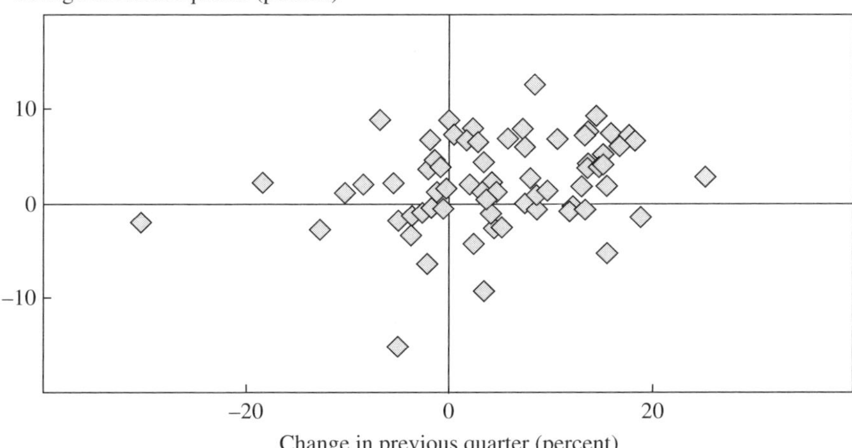

Sources: Standard & Poor's; author's calculations.

a. Quarterly changes in the S&P/Case-Shiller National Home Price Index (top panel) or the S&P500 index (bottom panel), 1991Q2–2008Q2.

Figure 3. OFHEO and Case-Shiller National Home Price Indexes, 1991Q1–2008Q2

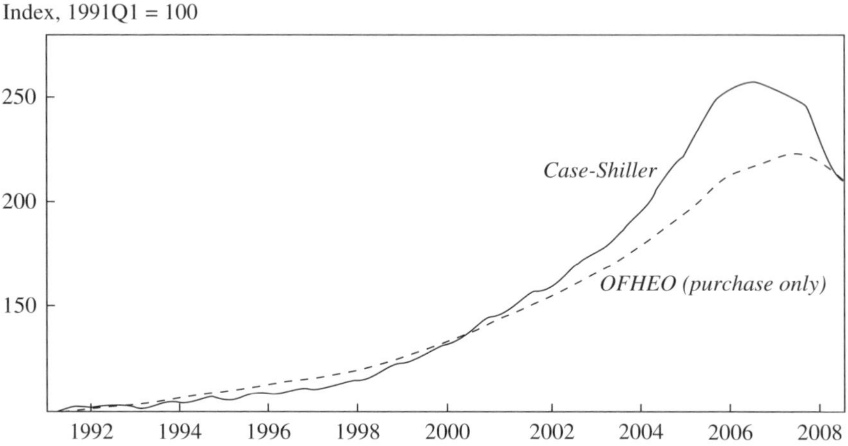

Sources: Office of Federal Housing Enterprise Oversight; Standard & Poor's.

relate to their beliefs about resale values, reflected in shadow prices. Credit constraints, in contrast, depend on the value of a home as collateral and, more likely operationally, are related to transaction prices. But that is an issue for macroeconomic theorists, and Case has provided many interesting empirical regularities for them to try to match.

Jan Hatzius addresses the broader economic consequences of declining home prices. His paper takes a careful, disaggregated approach, articulating the channels of influence that home prices have on macroeconomic activity. It takes advantage of regional variation in home prices, for which there is some precedent for the significant declines once thought impossible at the national level. It acknowledges, but does not always address, the econometric complications due to data limitations.

I would like to make three main points, from small to large, about Hatzius's paper. First, in his disaggregated description of the channels of the effects of home price changes, Hatzius uses auxiliary regressions to explain the change in the Office of Federal Housing Enterprise Oversight (OFHEO) state indexes with the change in the Case-Shiller national price index.[3] However, at the national level, as seen in my figure 3, the OFHEO

3. See Charles Calomiris, Stanley D. Longhofer, and William Miles, "The Foreclosure-House Price Nexus: Lessons from the 2007–2008 Housing Turmoil," Working Paper 14294 (Cambridge, Mass.: National Bureau of Economic Research, 2008), for a discussion of these price indexes.

and Case-Shiller price series begin and end at the same points 17 years apart. A change-on-change regression cannot explain this convergence. An error correction model, in contrast, would do a better job of explaining the two national series. This is more than an econometric nicety: it could have consequences for the long-run scenarios analyzed in the paper.

Second, a significant doctrinal history about the predictive relationship of debt on macroeconomic activity, which the paper also examines, has been part of Brookings Panel discussions over the past three decades. One reason that the Federal Reserve for some time had an aggregate debt measure, for instance, was the contributions made by Benjamin Friedman.[4] That literature discusses many aspects of the econometric difficulties in estimation and should be referenced.

Third, in calling attention to the critical role of the government-sponsored enterprises, the paper identifies an important public policy issue. If Fannie Mae and Freddie Mac are required to shrink their balance sheets along with everyone else, the macroeconomic losses will be considerably larger. Therein lies the uncomfortable choice for the Treasury. Were those two firms placed under conservatorship in order to bolster their creditworthiness, or in order to use their balance sheets to offset the unusual restraint in the mortgage market?

Morris and Shin study the effects of balance sheet adjustment, given the decline in home prices, on the financial system as a whole. They are to be credited for examining the issues in terms of first principles, offering a different perspective on the map of the ongoing economic adjustment. That perspective is especially important for understanding the aggregate consequences of individual behavior.

However, a risk of using a separate analytical framework to explain this adjustment is that it can become detached from the existing understanding of the underlying behavior that has led to market failure. It also invites bureaucratic capture of "systemic risk management," adding another layer between the regulators and market activity.

An example of the first risk can be seen in their proposition 1. Morris and Shin explain that "actions that enhance the soundness of an individual institution may undermine the stability of the system as a whole." This would have been much clearer to me had it been explained as a

4. See, for example, Benjamin M. Friedman, "Crowding Out or Crowding In? Economic Consequences of Financing Government Deficits," *BPEA,* no. 3 (1978): 593–641, and "The Roles of Money and Credit in Macroeconomic Analysis," Working Paper 831 (Cambridge, Mass.: National Bureau of Economic Research, 1981).

simple fallacy of composition, which is a concept as old as the field of macroeconomics.

Another example is their proposition 3, which distinguishes between risky assets and systemically important assets. The idea that an asset can serve multiple roles, and that its price can reflect those roles, is not new. For instance, Darrell Duffie has shown rigorously that the prices of Treasury securities incorporate their usefulness as collateral in repurchase transactions.[5] In that regard, price premiums on some Treasury securities serve as a "canary in the coal mine" indicating marked aversion to risk. Similarly, Lubos Pastor and Robert Stambaugh have shown that asset prices include a loading on the risk of illiquidity.[6] From this perspective, there is something that economists do not yet understand about expectation formation, the shape of the utility function, and coordination among agents that every so often puts a high price on this tail risk.

To sum up, these three papers provide a clear review of the channels through which home price declines affect the broader economy. They are essential reading for understanding the ongoing global financial crisis. However, absent from them is a discussion of an important role for expectations that could produce herding and self-fulfilling prophecies. In such an environment, policy matters for more than just shaping long-run incentives. Policy can influence immediate market outcomes, and not always for the best.

GENERAL DISCUSSION Martin Baily remarked that despite the common belief that the rise in home prices had been in large measure responsible for the current crisis, he himself placed much of the blame on the regulatory regime and the decline in lending standards. The sharp rise in foreclosure rates among more recent vintages of mortgages was evidence of such laxity, he argued.

Robert Hall noted that the impact of credit cutbacks has varied greatly across economic sectors: nonfinancial corporate businesses have remained largely unaffected so far, since the corporate sector, in the aggregate, has negative leverage. This would explain why real GDP continued to climb despite the credit crisis.

5. Darrell Duffie, "Special Repo Rates," *Journal of Finance* 51, no. 2 (1996): 493–526.

6. Lubos Pastor and Robert F. Stambaugh, "Liquidity Risk and Expected Stock Returns," *Journal of Political Economy* 111, no. 3 (2003): 642–85.

Paul Willen commented on the specification of regressions that include foreclosure rates. Changes in the foreclosure rates calculated by the Mortgage Bankers Association are driven both by changes in the numerator (the number of foreclosures of a given type of loan) and by changes in the denominator (the number of existing loans of that type); much of the recent volatility comes from volatility in the denominator. No new subprime loans are being made, and therefore the foreclosure rate for subprime loans is necessarily increasing. Thus, the recent movement in the foreclosure rate reflects mainly changes in the composition of the mortgage pool. Willen also mentioned that the level of, not the change in, home prices matters particularly with regard to the fraction of the population with negative equity: homeowners with negative equity who experience a negative shock to their ability to pay will go into foreclosure even if overall home prices have stabilized.

Olivier Blanchard suggested that rather than analyze home prices by themselves, one should look at the ratio of home prices to some other indicator, such as average rent. He also mentioned that price increases could have come from decreases in user costs, given that real interest rates and risk premiums were so low. He also wondered how much confidence one should have in the Case-Shiller futures data, which he viewed as alarming.

Andreas Lehnert mentioned several recent papers dealing with the issue of rent-to-price ratios. Several papers by Joshua Gallin at the Federal Reserve have established the tight link between rents and prices, and a paper that he himself had co-written had looked at trends in the rate of return on housing. He questioned the causal link between lending and GDP: he argued that projects with positive net present value should get funding unless quantity rationing or institutional distress limited lending. He also mused about the incredibly tight link between mortgage debt growth and home price growth. This link does not necessarily reflect a causal effect of borrowing on prices but may reveal less demand for credit when declining home prices make homes a less desirable investment. Lastly, he pointed out several institutional differences between housing markets in the United States and those in other countries and wondered about their implications and the reasons for the differences.

Benjamin Friedman observed that the impact of credit market stringency on the economy is likely to exceed that of declining household wealth. He also wondered whether the relationship between credit markets and the real economy will resemble in the future what it has been in the past. Lastly, he remarked that investment banks require high leverage ratios in order to be profitable. Should they be forced to deleverage, banks will have to develop new business models in order to stay profitable.

Bradford DeLong opined that one reason the crisis occurred was not that the market mistakenly accepted the triple-A ratings of risky tranches of subprime debt, but rather that the originators did not want to pay the rate that the market required to hold those tranches, and therefore required their own portfolio managers to hold those securities at par despite their institutions' high leverage ratios. He also wondered why the global financial markets did not mobilize the risk-bearing capacity of the global economy to spread the risk of a housing downturn.

Alan Blinder questioned the authors' downplaying of the importance of the role played by imprudent mortgage lending and the derivatives built on top of that lending. He also noted that the Basel capital standards have caused distortions and that measuring debt with a simple leverage ratio cannot be correct, since different forms of debt, such as Treasury bills, bank loans, or collateralized debt obligations, can produce the same leverage ratio.

Robert Gordon suggested that some of the ratios used in the papers should be rethought. For example, the population has doubled and the economy has grown by a factor of four or five over the past several decades. Thus, housing starts should be expressed as a ratio to the number of households. Additionally, it is not correct to deflate a home price index by real income per capita, because the income elasticity of housing quality is positive: households buy not only bigger but also better homes as their income rises. The Case-Shiller and OFHEO indices are inherently adjusted for quality because they consider repeat sales of the same homes. One could also look at real residential wealth per capita divided by real income per capita, or at the real value of residential construction divided by real income per capita. He also noted that movements in housing prices do not entirely explain the crisis. Declining lending standards are also to blame, as people were given mortgages that exceeded income constraints on monthly mortgage payments.

RAFAEL LA PORTA
Dartmouth College

ANDREI SHLEIFER
Harvard University

The Unofficial Economy and Economic Development

ABSTRACT In developing countries, informal firms account for up to about half of all economic activity. Using data from World Bank firm-level surveys, we find that informal firms are small and extremely unproductive compared with even the small formal firms in the sample, and especially relative to the larger formal firms. Formal firms are run by much better educated managers than informal ones and use more capital, have different customers, market their products, and use more external finance. Few formal firms have ever operated informally. This evidence supports the dual economy ("Wal-Mart") theory of development, in which growth comes about from the creation of highly productive formal firms. Informal firms keep millions of people alive but disappear as the economy develops.

In many developing countries, unofficial economic activity—that conducted by unregistered firms or by registered firms but hidden from taxation—accounts for between a third and a half of the total. This share declines sharply as the economy develops. Despite the sheer magnitude of unofficial activity, little is understood about its role in economic development, and in particular about how important "officializing" this hidden activity and the resources devoted to it might be for economic growth.

In this paper we attempt to shed some light on these issues by presenting some new facts about the unofficial (also called "informal") economy and interpreting them in light of various theories. We begin by reviewing the basic stylized facts: that the unofficial economy is huge, that it shrinks sharply in relative terms as the economy develops, and that various policy variables that determine the costs and benefits of becoming and staying official influence its size. This evidence is consistent with the generally accepted view that unofficial firms avoid paying taxes and adhering to regulations, but lose access to public goods and other benefits of official status, such as external finance. Much of the existing literature on the unofficial economy emphasizes these public policy aspects of the problem.[1]

Yet crucial as this perspective might be, it says little about the role of unofficial firms in development. There are three broad views of this role, which we refer to as the romantic view, the parasite view, and the dual economy ("dual" for short) view. According to the romantic view, which we associate with the work of Hernando de Soto,[2] unofficial firms are either actually or potentially extremely productive but are held back by government taxes and regulations, as well as by lack of secure property rights and access to finance. Pending the necessary legal reforms, "four billion people around the world are robbed of the chance to better their lives and climb out of poverty, because they are excluded from the rule of law."[3] If the barriers to official status were lowered and capital supplied through microfinance, unofficial firms would register, borrow, and take advantage of other benefits of official status, and by doing so expand and spark economic growth. The key aspect of this optimistic view is that unofficial firms are fundamentally similar to official ones but are kept down by policy. In particular, unofficial firms should look similar to official firms with respect to characteristics not affected by government policies, such as the characteristics of their entrepreneurs (for example, their education).

The other two views are more skeptical about unofficial firms and in particular see them as quite unproductive, not just because they are deprived of the benefits of official status, but also because they are run by entrepreneurs with lower human capital. In these alternative views, development comes about not so much from the unleashing of informal firms as from their displacement by efficient formal firms, usually run by totally different people. This is the "Wal-Mart" theory of development.

The latter two views differ in what they see as the benefits and the harms of the unofficial sector. The parasite view, associated primarily with the excellent empirical studies by the McKinsey Global Institute, sees unofficial firms primarily from the perspective of their illegality. These

1. This literature includes de Soto (1989), Loayza (1996), Johnson, Kaufmann, and Shleifer (1997), Friedman and others (2001), Djankov and others (2002), Almeida and Carneiro (2006), Dabla-Norris, Gradstein, and Inchauste (2008), and Russo (2008), as well as the recent work on Brazil by De Paula and Scheinkman (2008), Monteiro and Assunção (2006), and Fajnzylber, Maloney, and Montes Rojas (2006).

2. De Soto (1989, 2000).

3. United Nations (2008, p. 1).

firms need to stay small to avoid detection and therefore lack the necessary scale to produce efficiently. However, the "substantial cost advantage that informal companies gain by avoiding taxes and regulations more than offsets their low productivity and small scale."[4] This cost advantage allows unofficial firms to undercut the prices of official firms. Informal firms, then, hurt growth both because their small scale makes them unproductive and because they take away market share from bigger, more productive formal competitors. According to one McKinsey report, "The high proportion of small firms in service industries makes them particularly likely to operate informally, ignoring tax requirements, employee benefits, and other regulations. This is a much larger barrier to growth than most policymakers in emerging—and developed—economies acknowledge. Steps to reduce informality in local service sectors will be rewarded by rapid increases in their productivity, growth, and employment."[5] The first step in redressing the problems created by informal firms is to "add resources and beef up a government's audit capabilities."[6] More broadly, government policy should aim to eradicate informal firms by reducing tax evasion and increasing the enforcement of government regulations.

The dual view, associated in our minds with traditional development economics,[7] likewise emphasizes the inherent inefficiency of unofficial firms. This view is intimately related to the "big push" models of development economics, which see the coordinated transition from the informal, preindustrial economy to the formal, industrial one as the crucial strategy of economic development.[8] The earliest formal model of the unofficial economy is that of James Rauch,[9] who uses the framework of Robert Lucas to consider the allocation of talent between the unofficial and the official sectors.[10] In Rauch's framework, workers with lower human capital work in informal and smaller firms and receive lower wages, whereas those with higher human capital are allocated to the larger and more productive firms and receive higher wages.[11]

Unlike the romantic view, the dual view predicts that unofficial firms should look very different from official firms in their characteristics not

4. Farrell (2004, p. 28).

5. Baily, Farrell, and Remes (2005, p. 18).

6. Farrell (2004, p. 34).

7. Harris and Todaro (1970).

8. For example, Rosenstein-Rodan (1943); Rostow (1960); Murphy, Shleifer, and Vishny (1989).

9. Rauch (1991).

10. Lucas (1978).

11. See also Amaral and Quintin (2006) and de Paula and Scheinkman (2008).

affected by government policies. Productive entrepreneurs are willing to pay taxes and bear the cost of government regulation in order to advertise their products, raise outside capital, and access public goods. Such entrepreneurs find it more profitable to run the bigger, official firms than the smaller, unofficial ones. In contrast, the increase in firm value that less able entrepreneurs or managers could generate by operating formally is not large enough to offset the additional costs from taxes and regulations. The strong prediction of the dual view is that managers and assets are matched through a sorting process that results in low-ability managers being paired with low-quality assets.

Unlike the parasite view, the dual view does not see the unofficial firms as threatening the official ones, because they are hugely inefficient and hence unlikely to be able to charge lower prices for the same products. Indeed, official and unofficial firms operate largely in different markets and have different customers. The dual view sees the unofficial firms as providers of a livelihood to millions, perhaps billions, of extremely poor people,[12] and it cautions against any policies that would raise the costs of these firms. This view sees the hope of economic development in policies, such as human capital, tax, and regulatory policies, that promote the creation of official firms, letting the unofficial ones die as the economy develops. The official firms thus created will be new firms run by new people, not previously unofficial firms.[13]

To shed light on these alternative views, this paper follows the presentation of basic correlations with a comparative analysis of the characteristics and productivity of official and unofficial firms in several developing countries. We use three sets of surveys of both official and unofficial firms conducted recently by the World Bank. The first set, known as Enterprise Surveys, covers small, medium-size, and large registered firms in nearly 100 countries. We use these surveys largely for comparison. The second set, known as Informal Surveys, covers primarily unregistered, but also some registered, small firms in about a dozen countries. The third set, known as Micro Surveys, covers primarily registered, but also some unregistered, small firms in about a dozen countries (mostly different from those covered by the Informal Surveys). These surveys enable us to make comparative

12. Tokman (1992).

13. The sharp distinction we have drawn between the parasite and the dual views is too extreme. For example, informal firms may compete with formal ones in some industries and not in others, and they might pose a greater competitive threat at higher levels of economic development, when they perhaps become more similar to formal firms. We will return to the discussion of the relevance of the two views after presenting some of the data.

statements about the size, inputs, management characteristics, and—in a rough way—productivity of both official and unofficial firms.

We note from the start that the data we use have many problems, not least because we focus on firms that are by definition avoiding the government's notice. Nonetheless, our findings tend to favor the dual view over the romantic and the parasite views. The unofficial firms in the surveys tend to be small and unproductive compared even with the small but registered firms (which themselves are much less productive than larger registered firms). The unofficial firms also use lower-quality inputs and have less access to public goods and finance. Extremely few of the registered firms have ever operated as unregistered, again suggesting, as argued by Rauch,[14] that the two groups are very separate animals. The evidence points to a substantial difference between the registered and the unregistered firms in the human capital of their managers and suggests that this gap in human capital drives many other differences, including the quality of inputs and access to finance. The unregistered firms pay sharply lower wages to their employees, again consistent with the dual model.

As a final step, we consider how firms perceive their obstacles to doing business as reported in the three surveys. Informal firms see lack of access to markets and finance as their biggest problems. Formal firms also emphasize those, but taxes, tax administration, and problems with electricity supply as well. The legal system, regulations, and registration procedures rank lower as obstacles to doing business among both formal and informal firms. Finally, the surveys offer little evidence that the unregistered firms pose much of a competitive threat to the registered ones: the latter do not treat such competition (or unfair competition more generally) as a serious problem. This last result does not support the parasite view of the unofficial economy, which focuses on price undercutting by informal firms.

Over all, the evidence paints a relatively consistent picture. There is very little support for the romantic view, and indeed the differences in productivity between formal and informal firms are so large that it is hard to believe that simply registering unregistered firms would eliminate the gap. On the other hand, there is little support for the parasite view either, and the evidence suggests that subjecting unofficial firms to stronger enforcement would devastate the livelihood of millions of people surviving near subsistence. The evidence rather points to the dual view, with the fairly standard implication that the hope of economic development lies in the creation

14. Rauch (1991).

of large registered firms, run by educated managers and utilizing modern practices, including modern technology, marketing, and finance.

The Size of the Informal Economy and Its Determinants

Measuring the informal economy is inherently difficult. To start with, the informal economy encompasses very different phenomena. One is hidden firms. Such firms hide all of their output from the police, the tax authorities, or the regulators. Another phenomenon is hidden output. Output may be hidden even by registered firms to reduce their tax liability. Both phenomena occur in all developing countries. Indeed, the face of informality may change as the economy develops, from near-universal informality at earlier stages to mere tax avoidance as the economy grows richer.

Beyond these conceptual issues, there are serious practical problems in measuring hidden firms and output. Nevertheless, a variety of methods have been proposed. Since each method has its strengths and weaknesses, we gathered data on seven measures of the informal economy based on alternative methodologies and sources. All these measures of the informal economy are, if anything, likely to understate its true size.

Surveys are the most direct, although necessarily subjective, measure. We assembled data on two survey measures. The first is an indicator of unofficial or unregistered business activity from the World Economic Forum's *Global Competitiveness Report 2006–2007.*[15] Top business leaders from 125 countries were asked to estimate the size of the informal sector using a 1-to-7 scale, where 1 indicates that more than 50 percent of economic activity is unrecorded and 7 that all of it is registered. For comparability with the other measures, we rescaled this index on a scale from 0 to 50 percent of GDP. The 50 percent cutoff adopted by the *Global Competitiveness Report* is arbitrary and introduces a downward bias in this measure. The second survey measure is the percentage of total sales that a typical establishment reports for tax purposes, from the World Bank Enterprise Surveys. The respondents are the top managers of registered businesses in (mostly) developing countries. Accordingly, this measure of tax evasion likely understates the size of the informal economy, as entrepreneurs in the informal sector are not surveyed. This measure of tax evasion is available for 95 countries. Most countries have been surveyed twice, and we average the available observations between 2002 and 2006.

15. World Economic Forum (2007).

An alternative method infers the size of the informal economy from observable variables, such as the incidence of micro- and small enterprises, the male participation rate in the labor force, the fraction of workers contributing to social security, electricity consumption, and currency in circulation. We gathered data on three such indicators.

The first is the percentage of the active labor force that is self-employed, where self-employment is defined by the International Labour Office to include "jobs where the remuneration is directly dependent upon the profits derived from the goods and services produced,"[16] but not work by unpaid family workers, although the incidence of informality among the latter is probably high. This is admittedly a crude measure. In most developing countries there is a strong association between self-employment and informal activity, as most self-employed tend to be low-skilled, unregistered workers.[17] Of course, self-employment in developing countries may be high not only because informality is prevalent, but also because self-employment is common in agriculture. For this reason our second objective indicator is the percentage of workers in the nonagricultural sector who are self-employed. Other interpretations of self-employment are also possible. In particular, self-employment has been used as an indicator of entrepreneurial activity in the United States. However, the vast majority of self-employed workers in our data are, in fact, "own-account" workers who do not hire persons to work for them. Camilo Mondragón-Vélez and Ximena Peña-Parga show along these lines that the self-employed are rarely business owners in Colombia.[18] Data on self-employment are collected through population censuses as well as through household or labor force surveys.[19] Data on total and nonagricultural self-employment are available for 133 countries and 96 countries, respectively, from the International Labour Organization.

The third objective indicator is based on electricity consumption. For each country the ratio of electricity consumption to GDP for a base period is calculated and then extrapolated to the present, assuming that the elasticity of electricity consumption to GDP is one.[20] The size of the informal sector is then computed as the difference between GDP as estimated from

16. International Labour Office (2007).

17. Loayza and Rigolini (2006).

18. Mondragón-Vélez and Peña-Parga (2008).

19. There are two known biases in the self-employment data. First, OECD statistics relate to civilian employment and, as such, leave out the armed forces. Second, self-employment statistics in most Latin American countries relate to urban areas only. Both biases tend to understate the true size of self-employment.

20. Johnson and others (1997); Ernste and Schneider (1998).

this ratio and official GDP. This measure of the informal economy understates its size to the extent that informal activities are less electricity intensive than formal activities, and to the extent that technological progress allows for increased output per unit of electricity. This indicator is available for 57 countries from Eric Friedman and coauthors.[21]

Still another approach to measuring the informal economy models hidden output as a latent variable, using several indicator and causal variables. This is the approach followed by Friedrich Schneider to estimate a multiple indicators, multiple causes (MIMIC) model.[22] The indicator variables include the labor force participation rate among persons aged 18–64, annual GDP growth, and the change in local currency in circulation per capita. The causal variables are the tax-to-GDP ratio, the Heritage Foundation index of economic freedom, the unemployment rate, GDP per capita, and lagged values of the latent variable. This measure of the informal economy, which is available for 145 countries,[23] is only as good as the model that supports it. Later in this section we present evidence that the correlation between the size of the informal economy and variables such as tax rates is not particularly robust.

As a final robustness check, we gathered data on a direct measure of the *formal* economy: the number of registered businesses per 1,000 inhabitants. This measure, too, has problems. The number of firms per capita may increase with development, for example, as product variety expands. It may also be affected by cross-country differences in entrepreneurship. Finally, the data on total registered firms may be biased upward, especially in developing countries, because of underreporting of firms that have closed or exited. Data on the number of registered businesses are available for 83 countries from the World Bank's World Development Indicators dataset.

We group the determinants of the size of the unofficial economy into three broad categories: the cost of becoming formal, the cost of staying formal, and the benefits of being formal. As a proxy for the cost of becoming formal, we use the logarithm of the number of procedures required to legally start a business, from the 2002 paper by Simeon Djankov and coauthors and the World Bank's *Doing Business 2008.*[24] The costs of staying formal include paying taxes and obeying government regulations; we use six proxies for these costs. First, we use two measures of the cost of

21. Friedman and others (2001).
22. Schneider (2007).
23. Schneider (2007).
24. World Bank (2007); Djankov and others (2002).

paying taxes, from a 2008 paper by Djankov and coauthors:[25] total taxes (except for labor taxes) payable by businesses after accounting for deductions and exemptions; and the time it takes to prepare, file, and pay (or withhold) corporate income tax, value-added tax, and social security contributions, in hours per year. Second, we capture the cost of complying with labor laws with three variables: an index of the difficulty of hiring a new worker; an index of the difficulty and expense of firing a redundant worker; and the nonwage labor costs (payroll taxes and social security payments) associated with hiring a new worker as a percentage of the worker's salary. Data on complying with labor laws are from Juan Botero and coauthors and *Doing Business 2008.*[26] Third, we capture the cost of red tape using the percentage of senior management's time spent in dealing with requirements imposed by government regulations (such as taxes, customs, labor regulations, licensing, and registration); this includes time spent interacting with officials, completing forms, and other tasks. This variable is from the World Bank's Enterprise Surveys.

The benefits of being formal include expanded access to both public goods and finance. Regarding public goods, registered business may find it easier than unregistered ones to use the courts to enforce property rights and adjudicate disputes. We use two proxies for the efficiency of courts: the log of the number of steps required to collect on a bounced check, from the 2003 paper by Djankov and coauthors and *Doing Business 2008;*[27] and the efficiency of the bankruptcy procedure, from a recent paper by Djankov and coauthors.[28] We measure the quality of property rights using indices of corruption and the rule of law from Daniel Kaufmann, Aart Kraay, and Massimo Mastruzzi.[29] In addition, we use the density of the paved road network from World Development Indicators as a rough proxy for the scope of the domestic market. Finally, we measure the benefits of access to finance using three indicators of the size of financial markets. The first two indicators are standard: private credit and the market capitalization of domestic firms, both as a ratio to GDP. These two variables are also from the World Development Indicators. The third measure of the size of financial markets is a subjective indicator of the ease of access to credit, from the World Economic Forum's *Global Competitiveness Report 2006–2007.* The index ranges from 1 (impossible) to 7 (easy).

25. Djankov and others (2008b).
26. Botero and others (2004).
27. Djankov and others (2003).
28. Djankov and others (2008a).
29. Kaufmann, Kraay, and Mastruzzi (2005).

Table 1 presents our measures of the size of the informal economy. Countries are grouped into quartiles based on average income per capita at purchasing power parity (PPP) over the period 1996–2006. In practice, measures of the informal sector based on multiple indicators, energy consumption, self-employment, and the World Economic Forum survey are highly correlated with each other (see the correlation table in the appendix). In contrast, tax evasion and the number of registered businesses are less correlated with these other four indicators.

Two facts stand out. First, the informal economy in the average country in the sample is large, ranging from 22.5 percent of the total economy according to the tax evasion measure to 34.5 percent according to the multiple indicators approach. These numbers are especially large in light of the fact that our measures are likely biased down. About 26.5 percent of a country's workers, on average, are self-employed. That figure rises to 30.8 percent in the nonagricultural sector. Respondents to the World Economic Forum survey estimate that 27.6 percent of output is informal. Estimates based on electricity consumption suggest that 29.0 percent of output is informal. The various estimates thus suggest that, in an average country, roughly 30 percent of the economy is informal.

Second, the size of the informal economy is strongly negatively correlated with income per capita. Figure 1 illustrates this relationship, using the multiple indicators variable to measure the informal economy. The other measures also show the informal economy to be very large in poor countries, ranging from 29.0 percent according to the tax evasion measure to 57.3 percent according to the nonagricultural self-employment measure. The measure from the World Economic Forum survey suggests that the informal economy is 18 percentage points larger in poor countries than in rich ones. Estimates based on electricity consumption and multiple indicators suggest that the informal economy is between 21 and 24 percentage points larger, respectively, in poor countries than in rich ones. Even tax evasion by registered businesses—which is likely to understate tax evasion in poor countries—is 21 percentage points higher in poor countries than in rich ones. The self-employment statistics show that the fraction of self-employed workers rises from 13.3 percent in rich countries to 46.4 percent in poor ones. (Figure 2 illustrates the striking relationship between self-employment and income per capita.) The pattern for nonagricultural self-employment is even more extreme: self-employment as a share of nonagricultural employment rises by 44.8 percentage points as one moves from rich countries to poor ones. Consistent with this pattern, the number of registered businesses rises from 3.2 to 41.8 per thousand inhabitants as

Table 1. Size of the Informal Economy by Alternative Measures[a]

Percent except where stated otherwise

		Measure of informality						
						Informal share of GDP as estimated from		
Income quartile[a]	*GDP per capita at PPP (dollars)*	*Informal share of GDP as estimated by business leaders (WEF survey)*	*Tax evasion*[b]	*Self-employed as share of labor force*	*Self-employed as share of nonagricultural labor force*	*Electricity consumption*	*Multiple indicators*	*No. of registered firms per 1,000 population*
Bottom	429	35.4	29.0	46.4	57.3	38.9	42.3	3.2
Second	1,362	33.7	23.3	35.7	37.1	42.7	39.8	8.2
Third	4,002	27.6	19.7	23.1	24.6	31.3	34.1	28.7
Top	20,348	17.3	8.2	13.3	12.5	17.6	18.3	41.8
Sample mean	10,015	27.6	22.5	26.5	30.8	29.0	34.5	24.7
Difference between top and bottom quartiles	−19,919***	−18.1***	−20.8***	−33.1***	−44.8***	−21.4***	−23.9***	38.7***
No. of observations	185	125	95	133	96	57	145	83

Sources: World Bank, World Development Indicators; World Economic Forum (WEF; 2007); World Bank Enterprise Surveys; International Labour Organization; Friedman and others (2001); Schneider (2007).

a. Countries are grouped into quartiles by GDP per capita at purchasing power parity (PPP). Asterisks indicate statistically significantly different from zero at the *10 percent, **5 percent, and ***1 percent level.

b. Calculated as 1 minus the share of sales reported for tax purposes.

Figure 1. Size of the Informal Economy and GDP per Capita

Informal share of GDP, multiple indicators measure (percent)[a]

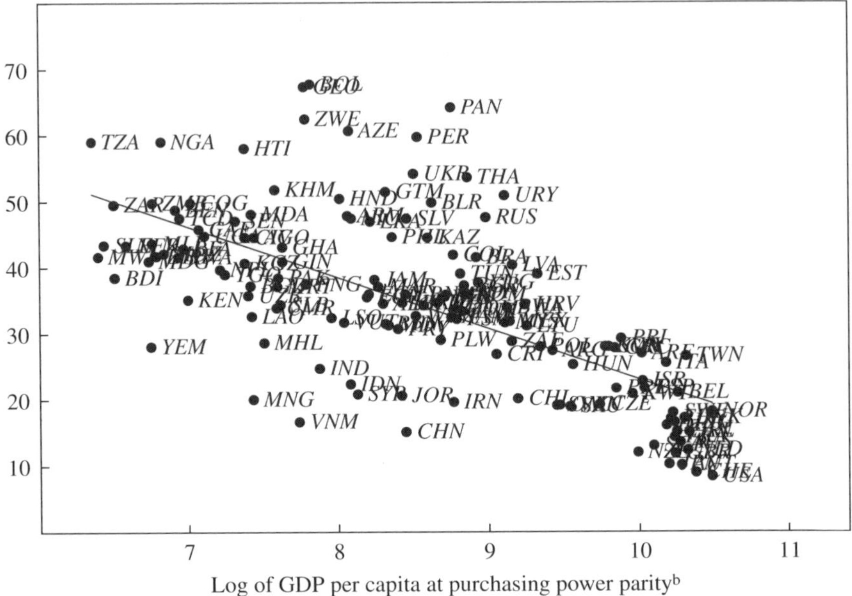

Sources: Schneider (2007); World Bank, World Development Indicators.
a. Average of the observations available for 1999–2004.
b. Average for 1996–2006.

one moves from poor to rich countries. These findings suggest that understanding the decline of informal firms as countries grow richer may be central to development economics.

Table 2 examines the determinants of the size of the informal sector. We present results first without (top panel) and then with GDP per capita (bottom panel) in the regression. The dependent variables are five of the above proxies for the size of the informal economy as well as the number of registered businesses per capita. (We omit the results using nonagricultural self-employment as they are qualitatively similar to those for total self-employment.) The independent variables are proxies for the cost of becoming formal and the costs and benefits of operating in the formal sector. Each cell in each panel presents the results from a single univariate regression (we do not report the constant).

The results in the top panel show the influence of policy variables. First, our proxy for the cost of becoming formal—the number of procedures necessary to start a business—is consistently associated with a larger

Figure 2. Self-Employment and GDP per Capita

Percent of active labor force that is self-employed[a]

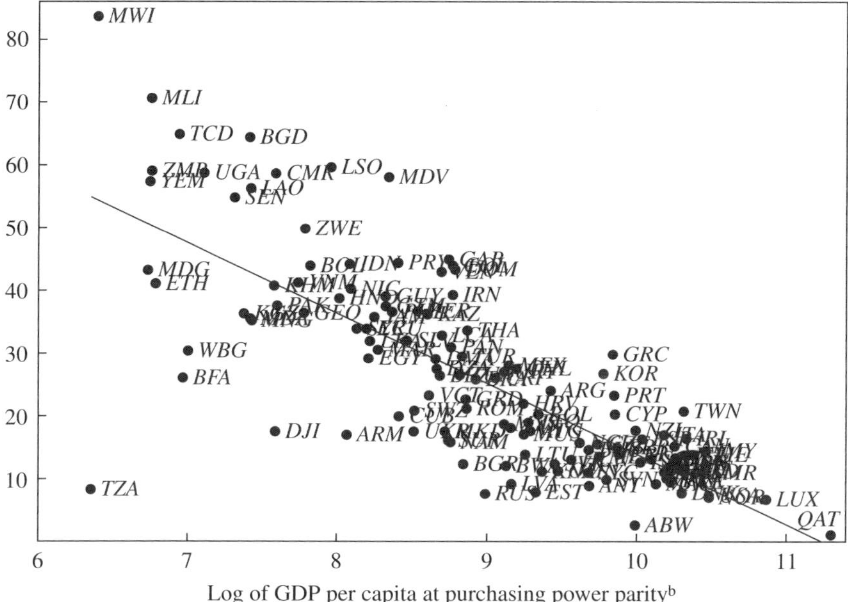

Sources: International Labour Office (2007); World Bank, World Development Indicators.
a. Data are as of the most recent year available.
b. Average for 1996–2006.

informal sector as well as with fewer registered firms. However, the economic effect is modest in size. For example, a 1-standard-deviation (equal to 0.4) increase in the log of the number of procedures is associated with a 4.8-percentage-point rise in the multiple indicators measure of the informal economy.

Second, the results for proxies for the cost of staying formal are mixed. All six proxies are statistically significant when the dependent variable is the measure from the World Economic Forum survey (first data column). On the other hand, none of the explanatory variables is significant when using the tax evasion proxy. Results for the other dependent variables are in between these two extremes. Among the explanatory variables in this category, the most consistently significant one is the time required to comply with taxes, which is significant for all dependent variables except tax evasion. Even then, increasing the time required to comply with taxes by 1 standard deviation (0.75) is associated with an increase of only 4.8 percentage points in the multiple indicators measure.

Table 2. Regressions Explaining the Size of the Informal Sector[a]

Independent variable	*Dependent variable*					
	Informal share of GDP as estimated by business leaders (WEF survey)	*Tax evasion*[b]	*Self-employed as share of labor force*	*Informal share of GDP as estimated from*		*No. of registered firms per 1,000 population*
				Electricity consumption	*Multiple indicators*	
	Regressions not controlling for GDP per capita					
Log of no. of procedures required to register a business	10.1815*** (1.2958)	14.7558*** (3.3801)	13.9296*** (2.6355)	11.3482*** (3.3149)	11.9328*** (2.1122)	−23.8551*** (4.4736)
Total taxes as percent of profits	0.0426** (0.0173)	0.0599 (0.0524)	−0.0408 (0.0995)	−0.1107 (0.0774)	0.0579*** (0.0182)	−0.2745** (0.1361)
Hours per year needed to comply with taxes	5.9038*** (0.8215)	−0.4877 (2.3969)	7.4048*** (1.8772)	8.4290*** (2.5841)	6.4492*** (1.4057)	−13.2818*** (3.4070)
Percent of management time spent dealing with regulations	0.5087*** (0.1069)	0.3931 (0.2941)	0.6275*** (0.2175)	0.4452 (0.3513)	0.3928 (0.2411)	−0.2511 (0.5630)
Index of difficulty of hiring a new worker	0.1096*** (0.0280)	0.0274 (0.0660)	0.0614 (0.0526)	0.0809 (0.0716)	0.1638*** (0.0387)	−0.0859 (0.0875)
Index of difficulty and expense of firing a worker	0.0942** (0.0371)	0.0079 (0.0599)	0.0996* (0.0574)	0.0558 (0.0971)	0.1147** (0.0530)	−0.2565** (0.1206)
Nonwage costs as percent of salary	0.1583*** (0.0494)	−0.2358 (0.1553)	0.0880 (0.0794)	0.0273 (0.1159)	−0.1008 (0.0980)	−0.2031 (0.1359)
Log of no. of steps required to collect on a bounced check	3.2047*** (0.8214)	1.3864 (1.5126)	3.3703*** (1.1305)	4.4214*** (1.5261)	5.4614*** (1.3257)	−5.0812 (3.2976)
Efficiency of bankruptcy procedure	−0.2207*** (0.0252)	−0.1832** (0.0757)	−0.2537*** (0.0347)	−0.2686*** (0.0677)	−0.2981*** (0.0352)	0.3117** (0.1175)

Log of paved roads per km^2	−0.0090***	−0.0334**	−0.0112***	−0.0137***	−0.0163***	0.0297***
	(0.0019)	(0.0130)	(0.0020)	(0.0023)	(0.0018)	(0.0109)
Corruption index	−7.4778***	−7.1143***	−10.8238***	−8.5364***	−9.4626***	11.9029***
	(0.3604)	(1.8722)	(0.9804)	(1.6594)	(0.5970)	(1.9284)
Rule of law index	−8.0286***	−6.0779***	−11.6845***	−9.1701***	−9.9850***	13.3112***
	(0.3697)	(1.7659)	(0.9440)	(2.0373)	(0.6170)	(2.0744)
Private credit as percent of GDP	−14.3709***	−14.8612***	−19.2173***	−11.7983***	−19.7457***	25.4301***
	(1.5940)	(5.2608)	(2.8056)	(3.5882)	(2.3164)	(8.9047)
Stock market capitalization as percent of GDP	−9.3152***	−6.9204	−10.5142***	−9.4449***	−13.8049***	10.2845**
	(1.7191)	(5.8906)	(2.5057)	(2.5483)	(3.0358)	(4.2383)
Access to credit	51.5059***	32.8132***	60.4548***	71.4457***	62.0713***	−13.1594
	(1.6596)	(5.3360)	(4.8082)	(7.8939)	(3.3155)	(9.7251)
			Regressions controlling for GDP per capita			
Log of no. of procedures required to register a business	3.9083***	12.1526***	1.4158	1.7380	3.6917*	−13.1812**
	(1.1217)	(3.5141)	(2.0266)	(3.2263)	(1.8926)	(5.2796)
Total taxes as percent of profits	−0.0039	0.0283	0.0389	−0.2306**	−0.0049	−0.3029***
	(0.0170)	(0.0563)	(0.0648)	(0.0866)	(0.0196)	(0.1019)
Hours per year needed to comply with taxes	3.1399***	−0.5181	2.6988*	2.5281	3.3539***	−6.9528**
	(0.6296)	(2.3814)	(1.5122)	(2.6397)	(1.2687)	(3.2654)
Percent of management time spent dealing with regulations	0.3950***	0.2007	0.2610	0.2312	0.2400	0.3767
	(0.0725)	(0.3011)	(0.1829)	(0.3418)	(0.1962)	(0.4977)
Index of difficulty of hiring a new worker	0.0485***	−0.0033	−0.0388	−0.0201	0.0777**	0.0537
	(0.0182)	(0.0631)	(0.0397)	(0.0526)	(0.0342)	(0.0682)
Index of difficulty and expense of firing a worker	0.0311	−0.0294	0.0170	−0.0469	0.0274	−0.1100
	(0.0275)	(0.0547)	(0.0420)	(0.0752)	(0.0470)	(0.1007)
Nonwage costs as percent of salary	0.0806**	−0.1075	−0.0405	−0.0966	0.0917	−0.0579
	(0.0311)	(0.1649)	(0.0571)	(0.0714)	(0.0769)	(0.1090)

(continued)

Table 2. Regressions Explaining the Size of the Informal Sector[a] (*Continued*)

	Dependent variable					
				Informal share of GDP as estimated from		
Independent variable	*Informal share of GDP as estimated by business leaders (WEF survey)*	*Tax evasion*[b]	*Self-employed as share of labor force*	*Electricity consumption*	*Multiple indicators*	*No. of registered firms per 1,000 population*
Log of no. of steps required to collect on a bounced check	1.7096***	2.2855	0.5051	−1.9308	3.3370***	−2.0003
	(0.5891)	(1.5024)	(0.8129)	(1.3614)	(1.0474)	(2.8724)
Efficiency of bankruptcy procedure	−0.0560	−0.0491	−0.0252	0.2044**	−0.0356	0.0752
	(0.0395)	(0.0863)	(0.0545)	(0.0895)	(0.0417)	(0.1736)
Log of paved roads per km^2	−0.0025	−0.0168*	−0.0029***	−0.0044**	−0.0051***	0.0175
	(0.0016)	(0.0088)	(0.0010)	(0.0018)	(0.0016)	(0.0119)
Corruption index	−5.6768***	−3.4956	−1.8315	0.3169	−6.9316***	3.8139
	(0.6844)	(3.0779)	(1.9129)	(3.1140)	(1.1440)	(3.7512)
Rule of law index	−6.4793***	−2.1094	−2.5183	1.6005	−7.7984***	4.9209
	(0.7095)	(3.0715)	(2.2886)	(3.9196)	(1.3920)	(3.3668)
Private credit as percent of GDP	−5.6811***	−6.1499	2.7131	9.3552**	−8.1961***	6.2312
	(1.6812)	(6.1198)	(2.3110)	(4.5279)	(3.1009)	(12.5764)
Stock market capitalization as percent of GDP	−3.3739***	−1.1785	0.5142	0.6396	−5.3196***	−3.5914
	(1.0313)	(5.7787)	(1.4782)	(2.0652)	(1.8352)	(8.0838)
Access to credit	68.5488***	−0.3639	125.7942***	164.0424***	99.0417***	−82.9238***
	(4.2760)	(1.7380)	(17.0908)	(21.0187)	(7.5245)	(14.1297)

Source: Authors' regressions.

a. Each cell reports the estimated regression coefficient for a single univariate regression. All regressions include a constant (not reported). Robust standard errors are in parentheses. Asterisks indicate statistical significance at the *10 percent, **5 percent, and ***1 percent level.

b. Calculated as 1 minus the share of sales reported for tax purposes.

Third, the proxies for the benefits of being formal are consistently associated with the size of the informal sector and the number of registered firms: the only two exceptions are court formalism (the number of steps necessary to collect on a bounced check) in the regressions for tax evasion and registered firms. The economic impact, in terms of the multiple indicators measure, of increasing these variables by 1 standard deviation ranges from 5.8 percentage points for court formalism to 9.6 percentage points for the rule of law. In sum, without controlling for income per capita, both the cost of becoming formal and the benefits of operating in the formal sector have a reliable but modest impact on the size of the informal economy. Our proxies for the cost of operating in the formal sector also have a modest effect but are less often significant.

Next, we rerun the previous regressions adding GDP per capita as an independent variable. The motivation is that the extent of the informal economy may be correlated with a country's development level. In poor countries the informal economy may provide subsistence income for workers unable to find formal employment. To the extent that informal firms avoid labor laws, the benefits of informality may be larger in the labor-intensive activities common in poor countries than in the capital-intensive activities common in rich countries. Along the same lines, informality may decline as more transactions are intermediated through the financial system. Finally, tax compliance may rise with income per capita as governments become more efficient at collecting taxes.

The bottom panel of table 2 shows the coefficients for the variables of interest when we control for GDP per capita. (As in the top panel, we do not report the constant. Nor do we report the coefficient for GDP per capita, but it is strongly significant in all regressions.) Most of the estimated coefficients fall in value and lose significance compared with the regressions without GDP per capita. Indeed, the coefficients remain consistently significant (11 of the 15 regressions) only for the World Economic Forum survey. Results for the other dependent variables are mostly insignificant. Our proxy for the cost of becoming formal remains significant in four of the six regressions (World Economic Forum survey, tax evasion, multiple indicators, and registered firms). Among the proxies for the cost of operating in the formal sector, the strongest variable is the time to comply with taxes, which is significant in four of the six regressions. Yet in contrast to the results on tax rates, nonwage costs are significant in only one regression. Finally, among the proxies for the benefits of operating in the formal sector, the strongest variables are road density (significant in four regressions) and the subjective assessment of access to credit (significant in five regressions).

The results using objective measures of the development of financial markets are mixed: private credit remains significant in three regressions, but market capitalization does so in only two regressions.

In sum, GDP per capita is the most robust predictor of the size of the informal economy. The most straightforward interpretation of the results in this section is that the informal economy is a manifestation of underdevelopment. It recedes as the economy develops, perhaps because public goods become better and financial markets larger, or because avoiding detection becomes harder. It remains a crucial, and open, question whether this decline of the informal sector results from the conversion of informal firms to official status, or from their death and replacement by formal firms.

An alternative interpretation is that we are overcorrecting by including GDP per capita. In particular, GDP per capita is strongly correlated (70 percent or better) with the efficiency of bankruptcy procedures, private credit, corruption, and the rule of law (see the correlation table in the appendix). Interestingly, variables that explicitly capture a country's economic structure (such as the share of agriculture in GDP; results not reported) leave much of the explanatory power of GDP per capita unchanged. Although GDP per capita is strongly correlated with some of the determinants of the size of the informal economy, multicollinearity is unlikely to explain why tax rates, nonwage costs, and labor laws work so poorly when we control for GDP per capita. We return to this issue below when we examine the productivity of informal firms, using micro data.

Although the cross-country evidence reveals some interesting patterns, it is merely suggestive and does not discriminate among the three views of the role of the informal economy. For this we need micro data, which we analyze next. Accordingly, the remainder of the paper is organized as follows. The next section describes our data on informal and formal firms. We ask such questions as: Are informal firms engines of growth as the romantic view would hold? For example, do informal firms grow quickly and over time join the formal sector? Is there evidence that—consistent with the parasite view—formal and informal firms operate in the same markets or that formal firms fear competition from informal firms? What evidence is there that—as predicted by the dual view—informal firms have inferior assets and management?

The third section is the heart of the paper. It presents evidence on the relative productivity of formal and informal firms. We ask five questions. First, are our data on productivity reliable? Second, how big are the differences in productivity between formal and informal firms? We want to know whether the prediction of the parasite view that informal firms have a cost advantage is borne out by the data. Third, what views of the informal economy are consistent with the observed differences in productivity? We want to examine whether it is plausible to believe—as in the romantic view—that all that is holding back informal firms are high taxes and bad government regulation. Fourth, what accounts for the difference in the productivity of formal and informal firms? The goal is to see whether differences in productivity can be traced to differences in inputs. Finally, what evidence is there that more-able managers run firms with better assets? Evidence of a strong selection effect would support the dual view and cast doubt on the prediction of the romantic view that relieving informal firms from oppressive taxes and regulation would put an end to poverty as we know it.

The fourth section focuses on obstacles to doing business, as reported by firms in all three surveys. We ask which of several problems, such as market access, financing, taxes, and regulations, but also unfair competition, are perceived as principal obstacles to doing business. These results shed light on the alternative theories but perhaps bear most directly on the parasite theory. The final section concludes with some implications of the evidence.

Characteristics of Informal Firms

In this section we describe our data and present simple descriptive statistics. Our basic approach is to compare, country by country, the relative performance of formal and informal firms. To do so, we combine data from three World Bank surveys of individual firms. The first survey—the Enterprise Survey—covers formal firms and is available for 105 countries. The other two surveys—the Informal and Micro Surveys—contain information on both informal and formal firms in a few poor countries. The Informal Survey is available for 13 countries: Bangladesh, Brazil, Cambodia, Cape Verde, Guatemala, India, Indonesia, Kenya, Niger, Pakistan, Senegal, Tanzania, and Uganda.[30] With the exception of Brazil, all these countries were below the world median income per capita in 2003 (equal to $5,322), and 7 out of 13 were below the 25th percentile (equal to $1,682). The Micro Survey is available for 14 mostly African countries: Angola, Botswana, Burundi, Democratic Republic of the Congo, The Gambia, Guinea, Guinea-Bissau, India, Mauritania, Namibia, Rwanda, Swaziland, Tanzania, and Uganda. With the exception of Botswana, all were below the world median

30. The World Bank also carried out an Informal Survey of Cameroon in 2006. However, data on sales are missing from that survey.

income per capita in 2006 (equal to \$6,224), and 9 out of 14 were below the 25th percentile (equal to \$1,965). The concept of informality used in the Informal and Micro Surveys focuses on registration (as we discuss below, there are several possible kinds of registration). Although questions about tax avoidance are asked, they are indirect. As discussed in the preceding section, this definition has both advantages and conceptual limitations.

Before describing the data in detail, we need to preempt a possible misconception about the nature of the firms in our data. In the context of poor countries, the term "informal firm" evokes the image of street hawkers selling goods out of baskets, or of eateries in front of homes. In fact, such an image is a good description of how the very poor make a living.[31] However, the informal firms in our sample do not fit that image. For example, firms accounting for roughly 85 percent of the observations in the Informal and Micro Surveys have, in addition to the entrepreneur, two employees or more. The informal firms in our sample are likely to be substantially more productive than the own-account workers described by Abhijit Banerjee and Esther Duflo.

Data

All three World Bank surveys have a similar structure and differ mainly in the firms that they sample. It is easiest to start by describing the Enterprise Survey, the source for our control group of *registered* or formal firms. It covers mainly manufacturing and certain services firms with five or more employees in 105 countries. The earliest available data are from 2002 and the latest from 2007. The initial step in carrying out an Enterprise Survey involves contacting the government statistical office of the relevant country to request a list of registered establishments. In some instances the World Bank supplements the government's list with firms registered with the chamber of commerce of the relevant country or listed by Dun & Bradstreet or by similar private vendors of business directories. Thus, although firms in the Enterprise Survey may hide some of their output, the government typically knows of their existence. We refer to these firms as "registered" and define the term below. The next step involves contacting the firms that will be sampled. Enterprise Surveys use either simple random sampling or random stratified sampling. A local World Bank contractor telephones each firm to set up an interview with the person who most often deals with banks or government agencies. At that stage, firms with fewer than five employees are dropped from the sample, as are government-owned establishments,

31. Banerjee and Duflo (2007).

cooperatives, and community-owned establishments. Typical final sample sizes range between 250 and 1,500 businesses per country. As described on the Enterprise Surveys website, "The core questionnaire is organized in two parts. The first part seeks managers' opinions on the . . . business environment. The second part focuses on productivity measures and is often completed with the help of the chief accountant or human resource manager."

The World Bank has also conducted separate surveys of informal firms to complement the Enterprise Survey in countries with large informal economies. Initially, data on the unofficial sector were collected through the "Informal Sector" questionnaire. Starting in 2005, the World Bank switched to the "Micro Sector" questionnaire while phasing out the Informal Sector questionnaire. Institutional amnesia makes it hard to ascertain the precise methodology followed with the Informal Sector questionnaire. Nevertheless, the basic outlines of what was done are clear. World Bank contractors identified neighborhoods perceived to have a large number of informal firms. These neighborhoods were then divided into enumeration blocks, which were then surveyed on foot.[32]

A similar methodology was followed to implement the Micro Sector questionnaire. A local contractor selected districts and zones within each district where, based on national information sources, there was a high concentration of establishments with fewer than five employees ("micro" establishments). The contractor then created a comprehensive list of *all* establishments in these zones. Finally, the contractor selected randomly from that list and went door to door to set up interviews with the top managers of the selected establishments. Although the Micro Survey targets establishments with fewer than five employees, larger establishments are not dropped from the sample. In fact, establishments with fewer than five employees account for only 50 percent of the Micro Survey sample.

Participation in the surveys is voluntary, and respondents are not paid to participate.[33] Respondents are asked sequentially about the business environment, infrastructure, government relations, employment, financing, and firm productivity. There is some variation in the response rate across questions. To illustrate, out of 6,466 Informal and Micro firms surveyed, we have the age of 6,412 firms, the number of employees of 6,416 firms, the sales of 6,136 firms, the fraction of investment financed internally of 5,689 firms, assessments of the fraction of taxes typically evaded by firms

32. Jorge Rodriguez Meza, World Bank, personal correspondence with the authors, June 27, 2008.

33. We lack detailed data on nonparticipation rates. In Mali, the only country for which we have data on nonparticipation, the refusal rate is 9 percent.

in their industry of 4,670 firms, and capacity utilization of 3,083 firms. Since Informal and Micro firms typically do not keep detailed records of their operations, some respondents may simply not have the information being asked. Unfortunately, we have no way of quantifying the biases, if any, from missing data.

Critically, the Informal and Micro Surveys cover registered firms as well as firms that exist without the government's knowledge ("unregistered" firms). In the remainder of this paper, we focus on informality understood in terms of hidden firms rather than hidden output. To compare the performance of registered and unregistered firms, we need to define what it means to be registered. The questions regarding the legal status of the firm are worded differently in the Informal and the Micro questionnaires. In the Informal Survey we rely on the respondent's answer to whether firms are "registered with any agency of the central government." In practical terms, firms are registered with an agency of the central government if they have obtained a tax identification number. In the Micro Survey, we rely on the respondent's answer to whether firms have either "registered with the Office of the Registrar . . . or other government institutions responsible for commercial registration" or "obtained a tax identification number from the tax administration or other agency responsible for tax registration."[34] Both surveys also keep track of whether firms are registered with "any local government agency" or with any "industry board or agency." We focus on registration with the central government because this form of registration is more directly relevant to avoiding taxes, enforcing contracts, and raising finance. We will also present statistics on municipal and industry board registration. In sum, the Informal and Micro Surveys allow us to examine the productivity of (small) registered and unregistered firms, whereas the Enterprise Survey provides information on the productivity of registered firms that have at least five employees.

Descriptive Statistics

Tables 3 and 4 list the countries surveyed and present the number of observations and average sales for the Informal and Micro samples, respectively. Most of the surveys (19 out of a total of 27) were carried out in African countries, but 6 surveys were done in Asia and 2 in Latin America. India, Uganda, and Tanzania were surveyed with both the Informal and the Micro questionnaires. As indicated earlier, most countries covered by the

34. We obtain very similar results if the definition of "registered" firms in the Micro Survey includes only firms that have a tax identification number.

Informal and Micro Surveys are poor. The average income per capita in current purchasing power terms is roughly $2,400 and ranges from $281 in Congo to $12,744 in Botswana.

The Informal Survey covered 13 countries. The surveys were typically carried out in 2003 and, on average, have 223 firms with nonmissing sales in each country. The Micro Surveys were carried out in 14 countries in 2006 and, on average, have 214 firms with nonmissing sales per country. The World Bank also carried out Enterprise Surveys in parallel with the relevant Informal and Micro Surveys. We use firms from the Enterprise Survey as the control group. The average number of firms in the control group with available sales data is 474 for the Informal sample and 554 for the Micro sample and ranges from 53 in Niger (table 3) to 3,860 in India (table 4).

Throughout the paper we emphasize productivity differences between registered and unregistered firms and between small and big firms. Critically, whereas firms in the Informal Survey are typically unregistered, firms in the Micro Survey are typically registered. The average Informal Survey has 31 *registered* firms out of a total of 223 firms, whereas the average Micro Survey has 137 *registered* firms out of a total of 214 firms. To examine differences in size, we group Enterprise Survey firms into three categories according to the number of employees: fewer than 20 ("small"), between 20 and 99 ("medium"), and 100 or more ("big"). When assessing some of our results on productivity, it is worth keeping in mind that the distribution of firms across these three categories is fairly uneven. For example, there is 1 big firm with nonmissing sales data (out of 93) in the control group for firms in Cape Verde, but there are 337 (out of 640) in the control group for firms in Indonesia (table 3). Perhaps because of the small number of observations, there are few extreme outliers in the data; these most likely result from errors in currency units. To mitigate the role of outliers, we cap at the 95th percentile the value of sales, sales per employee, and value added per employee in each country and in each survey. Capping does not qualitatively change the results we present.

The most striking fact in tables 3 and 4 is that the average annual sales of firms in the Informal and Micro Surveys are tiny even in comparison with those of small firms in the Enterprise Survey. Specifically, average sales are $24,671 for Informal Survey firms but $948,805 for small firms in the Enterprise Survey control group for those countries. Similarly, average sales are $50,853 for Micro Survey firms but $354,318 for small firms in that control group. Unregistered firms are even smaller than the average firm in the Informal and Micro Surveys. For example, in the Informal Survey

Table 3. Sales of the Informal Survey Sample and Its Control Group

Dollars at purchasing power parity except where stated otherwise

		Informal Survey sample					
		Unregistered firms		*Registered firms*		*All firms*	
Country	*Year*	*Sales*	*No. of observations*	*Sales*	*No. of observations*	*Sales*	*No. of observations*
Bangladesh	2003	19,794	195	48,856	2	20,089	197
Brazil	2003	32,528	218	51,227	126	39,377	344
Cambodia	2003	25,710	209	75,165	6	27,090	215
Cape Verde	2006	29,917	85	18,922	18	27,996	103
Guatemala	2003	16,339	183	23,604	10	16,716	193
India	2002	31,956	419	69,237	30	34,447	449
Indonesia	2003	29,237	276	. . .	. . .	29,237	276
Kenya	2003	20,297	149	30,712	36	22,323	185
Niger	2005	15,169	48	14,927	58	15,037	106
Pakistan	2003	15,435	210	7,805	3	15,327	213
Senegal	2004	24,944	153	29,827	41	25,976	194
Tanzania	2003	9,212	285	19,260	23	9,963	308
Uganda	2003	35,082	91	45,341	23	37,152	114
Average		23,509	194	36,240	31	24,671	223

	Enterprise Survey control group							
	Small firms (<20 employees)		*Medium-size firms (20–99 employees)*		*Big firms (>99 employees)*		*All firms*	
Country	*Sales*	*No. of observations*	*Sales*	*No. of observations*	*Sales*	*No. of observations*	*Sales*	*No. of observations*
Bangladesh	321,193	64	2,360,761	259	8,367,846	642	6,221,918	965
Brazil	767,484	252	3,419,992	811	24,100,000	406	8,683,195	1,469
Cambodia	167,574	193	979,849	40	3,260,287	26	603,488	259
Cape Verde	374,308	69	1,738,857	23	4,149,963	1	752,375	93
Guatemala	460,772	163	1,782,770	131	9,557,032	83	2,922,765	377
India	459,165	749	2,804,990	485	17,200,000	230	3,871,384	1,464
Indonesia	34,244	2	4,608,116	301	41,500,000	337	24,000,000	640
Kenya	1,675,268	49	6,070,552	65	31,800,000	41	11,500,000	155
Niger	4,999,650	34	4,416,983	16	14,700,000	3	5,371,892	53
Pakistan	2,066,015	7	4,316,266	66	9,332,258	33	5,729,247	106
Senegal	433,291	86	4,542,087	90	18,400,000	35	5,169,733	211
Tanzania	278,088	77	3,754,425	62	15,700,000	38	4,796,542	177
Uganda	297,418	107	3,222,021	58	10,700,000	28	2,681,279	193
Average	948,805	142	3,385,975	185	16,059,030	146	6,331,063	474

Sources: World Bank Informal and Enterprise Surveys; authors' calculations.

Table 4. Sales of the Micro Survey Sample and Its Control Group

Dollars at purchasing power parity except where stated otherwise

		Micro Survey sample					
		Unregistered firms		*Registered firms*		*All firms*	
Country	*Year*	*Sales*	*No. of observations*	*Sales*	*No. of observations*	*Sales*	*No. of observations*
Angola	2006	22,524	8	46,153	107	44,509	115
Botswana	2006	27,192	27	105,688	73	84,494	100
Burundi	2006	31,950	16	44,336	121	42,889	137
Congo, Dem. Rep.	2006	20,150	40	32,891	64	27,991	104
Gambia, The	2006	12,955	47	20,307	76	17,498	123
Guinea	2006	93,345	27	129,568	77	120,164	104
Guinea-Bissau	2006	22,532	29	48,451	108	42,965	137
India	2006	40,179	643	92,382	906	70,713	1,549
Mauritania	2006	56,070	69	38,977	53	48,644	122
Namibia	2006	5,392	49	31,419	47	18,134	96
Rwanda	2006	8,295	22	46,821	106	40,199	128
Swaziland	2006	5,658	34	52,230	83	38,696	117
Tanzania	2006	30,093	25	48,327	40	41,314	65
Uganda	2006	43,584	38	93,144	59	73,729	97
Average		29,994	77	59,335	137	50,853	214

	Enterprise Survey control group							
	Small firms (<20 employees)		*Medium-size firms (20–99 employees)*		*Big firms (>99 employees)*		*All firms*	
Country	*Sales*	*No. of observations*	*Sales*	*No. of observations*	*Sales*	*No. of observations*	*Sales*	*No. of observations*
Angola	219,543	353	440,131	64	826,909	6	261,533	423
Botswana	1,054,364	212	4,027,974	86	9,497,498	39	2,790,306	337
Burundi	262,566	219	1,313,305	43	2,923,213	8	508,740	270
Congo, Dem. Rep.	156,191	258	779,580	71	1,675,336	11	335,518	340
Gambia, The	191,976	118	975,985	47	3,564,678	7	543,472	172
Guinea	180,759	194	979,018	19	2,246,573	7	315,430	220
Guinea-Bissau	155,735	97	441,720	16	. . .	. . .	196,228	113
India	391,872	2,839	2,121,049	714	8,301,780	307	1,340,829	3,860
Mauritania	258,159	181	2,287,588	44	8,216,648	5	819,408	230
Namibia	665,167	225	2,917,353	82	9,329,198	17	1,689,759	324
Rwanda	344,204	143	2,071,016	53	7,671,968	16	1,328,946	212
Swaziland	391,593	207	2,418,694	55	6,982,505	32	1,488,191	294
Tanzania	326,825	259	3,430,273	111	16,400,000	44	2,866,305	414
Uganda	361,505	367	1,609,611	149	5,885,212	36	1,058,645	552
Average	354,318	405	1,843,807	111	6,424,732	41	1,110,236	554

Sources: World Bank Micro and Enterprise Surveys; authors' calculations.

sample, average sales for unregistered Brazilian firms are $32,528, compared with $51,227 for registered firms. Looking across countries, unregistered firms in the Informal Survey sample have average sales of $23,509, compared with $36,240 for registered firms. Similarly, unregistered firms in the Micro Survey sample have average sales of $29,994, compared with $59,335 for registered firms. It is natural to worry that the reported sales of unregistered firms may be low because respondents lie about their output. We address this issue in the third section of the paper.

What do unregistered firms do? Tables 5 and 6 shed light on some of the basic characteristics of firms in the Informal and Micro Surveys, respectively. The two tables have a similar—but not identical—structure, since there are only small differences between the two questionnaires. For each variable we present the mean for each group (for example, unregistered, registered, small, medium, and big) as well as the differences between the means for selected groups of interest (for example, small versus unregistered) and their statistical significance. So that the results are not driven by the countries with the most observations, we first average all observations within a country and then compute means and *t* statistics across countries.

The first block of variables in table 5 shows some general characteristics of the firms. Unregistered firms, although younger (9.9 years on average) than the average firm in the control group (17.8 years), have been operating for quite a long time. By definition, unregistered firms are not registered with the central government. Yet 34 percent of them are registered with a local government agency, and 7.2 percent are registered with an industry board or agency.

The next four variables describe the assets owned by firms in the Informal Survey. Unregistered firms own, on average, 52.3 percent of the land and 45.1 percent of the buildings that they occupy. Registered firms have comparable figures (55.5 percent and 48.1 percent). In contrast, firms in the Enterprise Survey control group own a significantly larger fraction of the land and buildings that they occupy (on average, 67.4 percent and 71.2 percent, respectively). The ownership of electric generators—a key asset in poor countries—shows a similar pattern. Few firms, unregistered or registered, in the Informal Survey own a generator (5.5 percent and 5.1 percent, respectively). In contrast, 20.1 percent of small firms and 77.0 percent of big firms in the Enterprise Survey own a generator. Capacity utilization rates vary little between unregistered Informal Survey firms and Enterprise Survey firms (61.9 percent versus 68.2 percent, respectively). The evidence also suggests that unregistered and registered firms may not share the same clients. In the Informal Survey, only 1.2 percent of the unregistered firms make the largest fraction of their sales to large firms. In contrast, large firms are the main client of 13.5 percent of registered firms—a percentage comparable to the average firm in the Enterprise Survey (15.1 percent).

The next block of variables describes the employees and their human capital in the Informal Survey. Unsurprisingly, unregistered firms have the smallest average number of employees (3.9). More interestingly, registered firms in the Informal Survey and small firms in the Enterprise Survey have very similar employment levels (9.8 and 10.3 employees, respectively). The key fact regarding informal firms is that—consistent with the dual view but not with the other two views—their top managers have low human capital. For example, the probability that the top manager of a firm has some college education is only 6.1 percent in the Informal Survey if the firm is unregistered, compared with 15.9 percent for registered firms in the same survey and 63.9 percent for all firms in the Enterprise Survey. To summarize the differences in human capital, we created an index ranging from 1 to 4 according to whether the top manager's highest level of education attended was primary school, secondary school, vocational school, or college. This index equals 1.6 for managers of unregistered firms and 3.3 for managers of Enterprise Survey firms. We constructed a similar index for the employees, with strikingly different results. Employees of Informal Survey firms have levels of education very similar to those of Enterprise Survey firms (indexes of 2.4 and 2.3, respectively).

Next, we turn to how firms are financed. All views of informality agree that greater access to finance is an important benefit of operating in the formal sector. In fact, roughly 75.1 percent of the unregistered Informal Survey firms have never even had a commercial loan. Instead, they finance 74.9 percent of investment with internal funds and 10.5 percent with help from the owner's family. The most striking fact about financing is that all small firms—not just unregistered ones—lack access to finance. In fact, small firms in the Enterprise Survey finance 67.8 percent of their investment with internal funds and 6.3 percent with family funds. Big firms in the Enterprise Survey have more access to external finance than small ones. For example, internal funds pay for 50.4 percent of the investment of big firms. Yet the fact that all small firms lack access to finance suggests that it may be misguided to put access to finance for unregistered firms at the center of the development agenda.

Finally, contrary to the romantic view, there is no evidence in the Informal Survey that unregistered firms are dynamic engines of employment creation. Two-year growth rates of employment are 5.2 percent for

Table 5. Attributes of Firms in the Informal Survey Sample

Percent except where stated otherwise

	Informal Survey sample			*Enterprise Survey control group*				*Difference*[a]			
Attribute	*Unregistered*	*Registered*	*All*	*Small*	*Medium*	*Big*	*All*	*Enterprise v. informal*	*Registered v. unregistered*	*Small v. unregistered*	*Big v. small*
General characteristics											
Age of the firm (years)	9.9	11.6	9.9	14.4	18.8	22.6	17.8	7.9***	1.7	4.5***	8.1***
Share of firms registered with a central government agency	0.0	100.0	14.9	...	...	...	...	...	100.0	...	...
Share of firms registered with a local government agency	34.0	47.2	37.0	...	...	...	...	...	13.2	...	...
Share of firms registered with an industry board or agency	7.2	14.8	8.9	...	...	...	...	...	7.6	...	...
Share of occupied land owned by the firm	52.3	55.5	53.9	59.0	70.9	70.8	67.4	13.5	3.2	6.7	11.8
Share of occupied buildings owned by the firm	45.1	48.1	44.9	60.8	74.8	79.3	71.2	26.2**	3.0	15.7	18.4**
Share of firms that own a generator	5.5	5.1	5.6	20.1	53.9	77.0	45.9	40.3***	–0.4	14.6***	56.8***
Average capacity utilization	61.9	65.8	62.4	66.5	68.0	71.2	68.2	5.8	3.9	4.5	4.7
Share of firms for which main customers are large firms	1.2	13.5	1.6	9.2	17.8	16.1	15.1	13.5***	12.3	8.0***	6.9
Employment and human capital											
Average number of employees	3.9	9.8	4.1	10.3	43.1	487.8	151.0	146.9***	5.9	6.4***	477.5***
Median number of employees	3.8	4.6	4.1	10.2	42.9	426.7	100.6	96.5***	0.9	6.4***	416.5***
Index of education of top manager (4 = attended college)	1.6	2.0	1.6	2.8	3.3	3.8	3.3	1.7***	0.4**	1.2***	1.0***

Share of top managers with indicated highest educational attendance:											
Primary	64.8	47.8	64.2	13.0	7.0	2.1	8.9	–55.3***	–17.0*	–51.8***	–10.9***
Secondary	19.3	20.8	18.6	34.8	19.5	5.9	18.1	–0.5	1.4	15.4*	–28.9***
Vocational	9.8	15.6	10.4	10.9	8.2	4.6	9.1	–1.3	5.8	1.0	–6.3*
College	6.1	15.9	6.8	41.4	65.2	87.5	63.9	57.0***	9.8**	35.3***	46.1***
Index of education of average employee (4 = attended college)	2.4	2.5	2.4	2.3	2.3	2.4	2.3	–0.1	0.1	–0.1	0.2
Share of employees with indicated highest educational attendance:											
Primary	59.0	50.0	58.2	52.3	51.5	45.2	47.9	–10.3	–9.1	–6.8	–7.1
Secondary	34.3	40.2	34.9	24.4	27.7	33.5	32.5	–2.4	5.9	–9.9	9.0
College	6.7	9.8	6.9	21.8	18.3	17.7	17.4	10.5***	3.2	15.1**	–4.0
Finance											
Share of firms that have ever had a commercial loan	24.9	35.6	26.0	. . .	. . .	. . .	. . .	. . .	10.7	. . .	. . .
Share of financing from:											
Internal funds	74.9	71.0	75.7	67.8	56.3	50.4	58.2	–17.5***	–3.9	–7.2	–17.4**
Trade	4.6	6.2	4.7	4.9	6.2	7.2	5.9	1.2	1.7	0.4	2.2
Owner's family	10.5	9.1	9.5	6.3	6.3	3.7	6.6	–2.9	–1.4	–4.2	–2.6
Banks	3.0	4.0	3.0	9.6	16.0	20.9	15.0	12.0***	1.1	6.6**	11.4***
Duration of last loan (months)	14.6	13.3	14.1	29.0	32.7	35.1	32.2	18.1**	–1.2	14.5**	6.1
Growth											
Annual growth in employment over previous two years	5.2	7.1	5.4	8.1	11.1	11.6	10.0	4.6*	1.9	2.9	3.5

Sources: World Bank Informal and Enterprise Surveys; authors' calculations.

a. Asterisks indicate significantly different from zero at the *10 percent, **5 percent, and ***1 percent level.

Table 6. Attributes of Firms in the Micro Survey Sample

Percent except where stated otherwise

	Micro Survey sample			Enterprise Survey control group				Difference[a]			
Attribute	*Unregistered*	*Registered*	*All*	*Small*	*Medium*	*Big*	*All*	*Enterprise v. micro*	*Registered v. unregistered*	*Small v. unregistered*	*Big v. small*
General characteristics											
Age of the firm (years)	7.0	8.2	7.8	9.2	14.3	18.3	10.7	3.0***	1.2	2.2***	9.1***
Share of firms registered with a central government agency	0.0	100.0	68.4	. . .	. . .	. . .	. . .	. . .	100.0	. . .	. . .
Share of firms registered with a local government agency	39.4	81.1	68.7	. . .	. . .	. . .	. . .	. . .	41.7***	. . .	. . .
Share of firms registered with an industry board or agency	5.0	30.7	20.0	. . .	. . .	. . .	. . .	. . .	25.7	. . .	. . .
Share of firms located in the owner's home	17.2	13.4	13.8	. . .	. . .	. . .	. . .	. . .	–3.9	. . .	. . .
Share of firms located in a permanent structure	71.4	80.4	77.0	. . .	. . .	. . .	. . .	. . .	9.0	. . .	. . .
Share of occupied land owned by the firm	21.7	20.1	20.1	28.4	54.3	71.0	36.2	16.1***	–1.6	6.7	42.7***
Share of firms forced to move last year because of lack of secure title	11.3	8.8	9.8	. . .	. . .	. . .	. . .	. . .	–2.5	. . .	. . .
Share of firms that own a generator	12.7	23.6	20.2	32.5	52.1	75.8	43.0	22.8***	10.9*	19.8***	43.3***
Share of firms with an electrical connection	60.0	79.2	73.6	. . .	. . .	. . .	. . .	. . .	19.2*	. . .	. . .
Share of firms that use their own transportation equipment	6.6	22.9	18.2	. . .	. . .	. . .	. . .	. . .	16.3***	. . .	. . .

Hours per week that the firm operates	64.8	64.6	64.9	59.4	60.9	79.8	62.2	–2.7	–0.2	–5.4	20.4***
Share of firms for which main customers are large firms	0.4	2.6	1.8	21.1	36.1	44.7	29.0	27.2	2.2***	20.7	23.6
Exports as share of sales	0.1	0.7	0.5	0.9	4.4	19.9	2.8	2.3***	0.7***	0.8***	19.0***
Share of firms that use e-mail to connect with clients	3.2	9.1	7.1	29.5	57.8	78.7	39.0	31.9***	5.9***	26.3***	49.1***
Share of firms that use a webpage to connect with clients	0.9	2.8	2.2	8.9	22.2	42.2	14.1	11.8***	2.0**	8.0***	33.3***
Employment and human capital											
Average number of employees	2.9	4.5	3.9	8.7	38.7	290.4	32.7	28.8***	1.5**	5.8***	281.6***
Median number of employees	2.7	3.7	3.5	8.7	39.4	253.2	29.1	25.6***	1.0**	5.9***	244.5***
Index of education of top manager (4 = attended college)	1.8	2.3	2.1	2.7	3.2	3.8	2.8	0.7***	0.4***	0.8***	1.1***
Share of top managers with indicated highest educational attendance:											
Primary	49.8	35.9	40.2	22.1	0.1	2.2	19.6	–20.6***	–13.9*	–27.7***	–19.9***
Secondary	27.8	26.2	26.2	25.3	0.1	5.5	21.6	–4.6	–1.7	–2.6	–19.8***
Vocational	10.2	13.4	12.4	17.0	0.1	6.9	15.7	3.3	3.2	6.8**	–10.1***
College	12.2	24.6	21.2	35.7	0.6	85.3	43.1	21.9***	12.4***	23.5***	49.7***
Index of education of average employee (4 = attended college)	2.3	2.3	2.3	2.5	2.5	2.8	2.5	0.2	0.0	0.1	0.3**
Share of employees with indicated highest educational attendance:											
Primary	48.7	46.1	46.4	47.8	0.4	31.2	44.8	–1.6	–2.7	–0.9	–16.5**
Secondary	40.2	41.2	41.3	42.9	0.5	52.8	45.8	4.5	1.0	2.7	9.9
College	4.0	5.7	5.3	9.3	0.1	16.0	9.4	4.1	1.7	5.3	6.6

(continued)

Table 6. Attributes of Firms in the Micro Survey Sample (*Continued*)

Percent except where stated otherwise

	Micro Survey sample			*Enterprise Survey control group*				*Difference*[a]			
Attribute	*Unregistered*	*Registered*	*All*	*Small*	*Medium*	*Big*	*All*	*Enterprise v. micro*	*Registered v. unregistered*	*Small v. unregistered*	*Big v. small*
Finance											
Share of firms that have ever had a commercial loan	7.3	12.5	10.9	. . .	. . .	. . .		. . .	5.1**	. . .	. . .
Share of financing from:											
Internal funds	81.9	76.9	78.9	75.5	64.4	59.1	72.4	−6.5*	−5.1	−6.4*	−16.4***
Trade	8.3	11.5	10.6	13.3	17.3	16.5	14.2	3.6	3.3	5.0*	3.2
Owner's family	6.6	6.7	6.2	4.6	3.1	0.9	4.1	−2.1	0.1	−2.0	−3.7***
Banks	0.4	2.0	1.5	4.1	11.3	18.5	6.4	4.9***	1.6***	3.7***	14.4
Duration of last loan (months)	13.2	29.9	26.8	30.5	39.3	55.5	37.6	10.8*	16.8**	17.4**	25.0**
Growth											
Annual growth in employment over previous two years	24.3	27.1	25.9	17.5	18.9	14.6	17.6	−8.3***	2.8	−6.8**	−2.9

Sources: World Bank Micro and Enterprise Surveys; authors' calculations.

a. Asterisks indicate significantly different from zero at the *10 percent, **5 percent, and ***1 percent level.

unregistered firms, 7.1 percent for registered firms, and 10.0 percent for all Enterprise Survey firms.

Firms in the Micro Survey sample show patterns very similar to those in the Informal Survey sample (table 6). We therefore discuss them only briefly, focusing on the questions that are available only on the Micro Survey questionnaire and on the few results that are different between the two questionnaires. The Micro questionnaire provides a bit more insight into the firms' assets. Only 17.2 percent of the unregistered firms and 13.4 percent of the registered ones are located in the owner's house. Most unregistered (71.4 percent) and registered (80.4 percent) firms occupy a permanent structure. However, there is evidence of hardship resulting from the lack of secure title:[35] 11.3 percent of unregistered firms and 8.8 percent of registered firms were forced to move in the previous year for this reason.

Much like their counterparts in the Informal Survey, unregistered firms in the Micro Survey sample are significantly less likely to own a generator than all other firms. This lack of generators is suggestive of insufficient capital, since unregistered firms are significantly less likely to have an electrical connection than registered ones (60 percent versus 79.2 percent). Furthermore, unregistered firms are much less likely to use their own transportation equipment than registered firms (6.6 percent versus 22.9 percent). Consistent with the view that unregistered firms and Enterprise Survey firms may serve different clients, big Enterprise Survey firms export 19.9 percent of their sales, whereas unregistered firms export only 0.1 percent of their sales. Finally, there is evidence that unregistered firms have less access to computers than do other firms. In particular, unregistered firms are less likely to use e-mail to communicate with their clients than either registered firms or Enterprise Survey firms (3.2, 9.1, and 39.0 percent, respectively). Similarly, unregistered firms are less likely to use a webpage to connect with clients than either registered firms or Enterprise Survey firms (0.9, 2.8, and 14.1 percent, respectively). Consistent with the dual view, unregistered firms tend to own low-quality assets.

Unregistered firms in the Micro sample—unlike their counterparts in the Informal sample—have a faster growth rate of employment than firms in the Enterprise Survey. Average annual employment growth among unregistered firms (24.3 percent), although not quite matching that of registered firms (27.1 percent), exceeds that of Enterprise Survey firms (17.6 percent). The fast employment growth rate of unregistered Micro Survey firms is consistent with the romantic view. However, this finding

35. De Soto (2000).

Table 7. Legal Status of Enterprise Survey Firms in Latin America

Country	*No. of observations*	*Percent of firms that registered upon formation*	*Percent not knowing when firm was registered*	*Firm age (years)*
Argentina	1,051	92.8	1.1	28.6
Bolivia	609	85.7	0.7	21.8
Chile	1,007	98.0	1.0	26.6
Colombia	995	89.0	0.5	17.0
Ecuador	652	91.6	0.9	21.3
El Salvador	683	77.7	1.4	21.4
Guatemala	511	90.4	2.1	20.9
Honduras	424	89.4	2.8	20.5
Mexico	1,439	94.9	2.8	18.5
Nicaragua	474	80.4	0.8	22.9
Panama	601	97.8	0.5	24.5
Paraguay	608	94.4	0.8	21.3
Peru	630	96.8	0.3	19.8
Uruguay	607	97.5	2.3	28.8
Average		91.2	1.3	22.4

Source: World Bank Enterprise Survey 2006.

needs to be interpreted cautiously, since these firms remain very small despite having been around for an average of 7 years.

To complement the evidence on growth rates, we examine, for a few countries, how often registered firms initially started operating as unregistered. The Enterprise Survey files for 14 Latin American countries include a question on whether firms were registered when they started operations and, if not, on whether they have since registered. As it turns out, all firms in this sample of 14 countries are registered. Table 7 shows the available data regarding the initial legal status of these firms. The fraction of firms that were registered from the outset ranges from 77.7 percent in El Salvador to 98 percent in Chile and averages 91.2 percent. Since 1.3 percent of the respondents did not answer the question, we estimate that only 7.5 percent of the firms registered after starting operations. Firms that start operations without being registered often register relatively quickly: 36.5 percent of the initially unregistered firms had registered by the end of the second year of operations (table 8). It is unclear whether those firms spent two years hiding from the government or, alternatively, started operations while their request for a permit was pending. Either way, firms rarely start as unregistered and later change their status. This is not the pattern that one would expect to see if the informal sector were a reservoir of entrepreneurial talent, as predicted by the romantic view. Nor is it the pattern that one would

Table 8. Delays in Registering by Enterprise Survey Firms in Latin America

Years[a]	*Frequency*	*Percent of total*	*Cumulative percent*
1	129	17.9	17.9
2	134	18.6	36.5
3	79	11.0	47.5
4	52	7.2	54.7
5	58	8.1	62.8
6	26	3.6	66.4
7	28	3.9	70.3
8	19	2.6	72.9
9	22	3.1	76.0
10	23	3.2	79.2

Source: World Bank Enterprise Survey 2006.
a. Year of operations in which the firm registered.

expect to see if entrepreneurs used entry into the informal sector as a way of acquiring information (for example, about demand for the firm's products) at a lower cost than entry into the formal sector.[36]

We conclude this section by presenting some data on the institutional environment in which firms operate. All views of informality agree on the basic trade-off faced by firms (the tax and regulatory burden versus access to public goods and finance). The previous literature has emphasized access to public goods as one of the main attractions of operating in the formal sector. Tables 9 and 10 present data on the institutional environment faced by firms in the Informal and the Micro Surveys, respectively, and how they operate in it.

Three facts stand out. First, consistent with all views of informality, unregistered firms enjoy tangible advantages. Managers of unregistered firms in the Informal sample estimate that a typical firm in their sector evades 74.8 percent of its tax liability. Tax evasion sharply decreases with firm size. For example, managers of small firms in the control group estimate that a typical firm in their sector evades 35.5 percent of its liability; tax evasion drops to 22.9 percent for big firms in the control group. Tax evasion by unregistered Micro Survey firms and by small firms in their control group follows a similar pattern (67.7 percent versus 44.4 percent, respectively).

Likewise, the regulatory burden increases rapidly with firm size. Whereas managers of unregistered firms in the Informal Survey sample report spending 5.6 percent of their time dealing with government regulations, that task requires 14.5 percent of the time of managers of big firms in the control group; the corresponding figures for the Micro Survey sample and

36. Bennett and Estrin (2007).

Table 9. Indicators of the Institutional Environment Facing Informal Survey Firms

Percent except where stated otherwise

Indicator	*Informal Survey sample*			*Enterprise Survey control group*				*Difference*[a]			
	Unregistered	*Registered*	*All*	*Small*	*Medium*	*Big*	*All*	*Enterprise v. informal*	*Registered v. unregistered*	*Small v. unregistered*	*Big v. small*
Compliance with government regulations											
Share of tax liability evaded by "typical" firm	74.8	53.5	72.2	35.5	28.6	22.9	30.3	–41.9***	–21.4*	–39.3***	–12.6
Share of management's time spent dealing with government regulations	5.6	6.8	5.3	9.8	15.4	14.5	12.9	7.6***	1.2	4.2*	4.7**
Share of sales a "typical" firm pays in informal gifts or payments to get things done	3.6	4.8	3.9	4.6	4.1	3.8	4.6	0.7	1.1	1.0	–0.8
Public goods											
Days last year with power outages	50.0	56.3	50.6	44.9	52.1	53.5	48.0	–2.6	6.3	–5.0	8.6

Days last year with water outages	33.6	31.3	34.3	22.5	24.4	24.2	23.5	−10.8	−2.4	−11.1	1.6
Days last year with telephone outages	4.1	19.3	14.2	13.1	10.6	11.8	11.7	−2.5	15.2	9.0	−1.3
Days last year with transportation outages	33.6	22.0	32.7	7.1	9.2	10.9	9.1	−23.6	−11.6	−26.5	3.8
Property rights											
Share of sales lost last year owing to theft	2.9	3.5	3.1	3.8	1.7	0.8	2.2	−0.9	0.6	0.9	−3.0
Share of sales spent on security expenses	1.8	1.2	1.6	2.2	2.3	2.5	2.3	0.6	−0.6	0.4	0.3
Share of sales spent on "protection payments"	1.0	0.5	1.0	0.5	0.8	0.7	0.7	−0.3	−0.5	−0.5	0.3
Share of incidents reported to police	14.1	26.2	19.1	36.0	38.0	54.0	42.6	23.5**	12.1	21.9**	18.1
Share of firms that had a payment dispute in last two years	21.5	0.0	21.3	. . .	. . .	. . .	. . .	. . .	−21.5	. . .	. . .
Days it took a typical court case to be resolved	60.9	90.3	66.2	67.9	56.1	68.3	61.9	−4.3	29.4	7.0	0.4

Sources: World Bank Informal and Enterprise Surveys; authors' calculations.

a. Asterisks indicate statistically significantly different from zero at the *10 percent, **5 percent, and ***1 percent level.

Table 10. Indicators of the Institutional Environment Facing Micro Survey Firms

Percent except where stated otherwise

	Micro Survey sample			*Enterprise Survey control group*				*Difference*[a]			
Indicator	*Unregistered*	*Registered*	*All*	*Small*	*Medium*	*Big*	*All*	*Enterprise v. micro*	*Registered v. unregistered*	*Small v. unregistered*	*Big v. small*
Compliance with government regulations											
Share of tax liability evaded by "typical" firm	67.7	54.2	58.3	44.4	33.7	32.5	41.6	−16.6**	−13.5	−23.3***	−11.9*
Share of management's time spent dealing with government regulations	1.5	4.2	3.5	8.2	9.3	10.5	8.5	5.0***	2.7***	6.6***	2.3*
Share of sales a "typical" firm pays in informal gifts or payments to get things done	4.0	3.5	3.3	6.6	7.1	5.6	6.6	3.2***	−0.5	2.6	−1.0
Public goods											
No. of power outages in last year	167.1	134.4	138.8	138.3	151.7	157.9	143.7	4.9	−32.7	−28.8	19.6
Days last year with water outages	. . .	. . .	. . .	57.9	56.4	51.8	51.9	. . .	. . .	. . .	−6.1
Days last year with telephone outages	. . .	. . .	. . .	3.7	4.8	3.5	4.0	. . .	. . .	. . .	−0.2

Property rights											
Share of sales lost last year owing to theft	0.5	0.5	0.5	2.6	1.8	1.6	2.4	1.8***	0.0	2.1***	−1.0
Share of sales spent on security expenses	3.4	2.8	2.9	2.3	2.1	1.2	2.1	−0.8*	−0.6	−1.1	−1.1***
Share of sales spent on "protection payments"	. . .	. . .	. . .	0.4	2.9	0.2	1.2	. . .	. . .	. . .	−0.1
Share of firms that had a payment dispute in last two years	6.0	8.4	7.5	9.5	16.6	19.4	11.4	4.0*	2.3	3.5	9.9***
Share of firms with payment dispute that used courts to resolve it	29.2	33.2	30.1	51.3	67.6	81.8	58.3	28.3***	4	22*	31.0***
Days it took a typical court case to be resolved	. . .	44.3	44.3	45.4	74.1	64.4	51.9	7.7	. . .	. . .	19.1

Sources: World Bank Micro and Enterprise Surveys; authors' calculations.

a. Asterisks indicate statistically significantly different from zero at the *10 percent, **5 percent, and ***1 percent level.

its control group are 1.5 and 10.5 percent, respectively. Finally, unregistered firms pay a smaller fraction of their sales in bribes than do firms in the control group. Managers of unregistered firms in the Informal Survey estimate that firms in their sectors pay 3.6 percent of their sales to "get things done." In contrast, managers of registered firms in the Informal Survey report that bribes equal 4.8 percent of sales, a percentage similar to that reported by firms in the control group (4.6 percent). Similarly, managers of unregistered firms in the Micro Survey estimate that firms in their sector pay 4.0 percent of their sales to "get things done"; the comparable figures are 3.5 percent for registered Micro Survey firms and 6.6 percent for firms in the control group. In sum, lower taxes and less regulation confer a clear cost advantage on unregistered firms.

Second, the quality of public goods in our sample is very low. In the Informal Survey, unregistered firms report that they experienced power outages on 50 days of the previous year. Firms in the Enterprise Survey fare only slightly better (48 days on average). On many days, firms experience multiple power outages. For this reason the number of power outages for the Micro Survey is dramatically higher than the number of days without power in the Informal Survey: unregistered firms in the Micro survey experienced 167.1 power outages in the previous year. Once again, Enterprise Survey firms do only marginally better (143.7 outages). In such an environment, only firms large enough to afford a generator can be productive. Outages of water, phones, and transportation are less frequent than power outages but nevertheless very common by the standards of developed countries. As a result, the performance of firms that are too small to provide substitutes for these public goods (their own transportation equipment, for example) may be severely impaired.

Third, outright theft is very prevalent in our sample, but small firms do not make much use of police or the courts. Theft affects all small firms, not just unregistered ones. Specifically, unregistered firms in the Informal Survey report that, in a typical year, losses from theft amount to 2.9 percent of annual sales. Registered firms in the same survey and small firms in the Enterprise Survey report even higher losses (3.5 percent and 3.8 percent, respectively). Somewhat surprisingly, losses as a result of theft appear to be lower for Micro Survey firms (0.5 percent) than for small firms in the control group (2.6 percent). To put these figures in context, note that Enterprise Survey respondents estimate losses as a result of theft equal to 0.54 percent of sales in Germany, 0.26 percent in Ireland, and 0.22 percent in Spain.

In response to theft, firms in our sample spend heavily on security and make "protection" payments to gangsters. For example, security and protection payments equal, respectively, 1.8 and 1.0 percent of the sales of unregistered firms in the Informal Survey sample. Firms in their control group spend a bit more on security and a bit less on protection, but their total expenditure is similar (3 percent). The police do not appear to play a central role in addressing theft. In fact, most theft is not even reported to the police. Only 14.1 percent of incidents suffered by unregistered firms in the Informal Survey were reported to the police. Registered firms in the same survey reported 26.2 percent of incidents—still a low figure. This pattern is consistent with the view that unregistered firms may have trouble protecting their property rights. Alternatively, the absolute value of the losses suffered by unregistered firms may be too low to justify filing a police complaint. Firm size does play a role in reporting theft to the police. However, even big firms in the control group for the Informal Survey sample report to the police only about half of theft incidents (54.0 percent).

Interestingly, small firms do not make much use of the courts to adjudicate disputes either. Only 29.2 percent of unregistered and 33.2 percent of registered firms in the Micro Survey sample used the courts to resolve commercial disputes during the previous year. In the control group, the use of the courts to solve commercial disputes rises quickly with firm size, from 51.3 percent for small firms to 81.8 percent for big firms. Surprisingly, the courts appear to work in a reasonably efficient manner. It takes roughly 62 days to resolve a commercial dispute in the Informal Survey countries and approximately 52 days in the Micro Survey countries. These figures are in line with the average length of court proceedings in Germany (35 days), Ireland (79 days), and Spain (91 days). The fact that unregistered firms and small firms in the control group behave similarly in solving commercial disputes suggests that inadequate access to courts is unlikely to explain differences in productivity between the two groups of firms. The same argument applies to lack of police protection.

The tentative picture that emerges from this section is inconsistent with the romantic view. Unregistered firms have been around for a long time (7 to 10 years on average), but their sales are still trivially small. Moreover, few registered firms started out unregistered. The small size of unregistered firms is symptomatic of uneducated management and low-quality assets. When public goods are unreliable, unregistered firms are too small to afford substitutes such as generators, computers, or transportation equipment. They do not have large firms as clients. They do not export. Despite de Soto's emphasis on access to credit as the key to igniting the growth of unregistered firms, lack of external finance appears to be an attribute of all small firms in poor countries, not just of unregistered firms. In sum, the limitations of unregistered firms appear to be far more severe than acknowledged by proponents of the romantic view.

Productivity of Unregistered Firms

In this section we examine the productivity of unregistered firms and present the key findings of the paper. In measuring the productivity of these firms, we face severe data limitations. In particular, we lack information on how much capital these firms have. The Informal and Micro questionnaires do not collect such information, since unregistered entrepreneurs typically lack detailed records to estimate the value of their assets. We thus have to measure productivity without capital.

To this end we use two crude measures of productivity: sales per employee and (gross) value added per employee, the latter defined as sales net of expenditure on raw materials and energy.[37] Thus, we define value added per employee for firm i in industry s as

$$VA_{si} = \frac{P_{si}Y_{si} - P_{m}M_{si} - P_{E}E_{si}}{L_{si}},$$

where $P_{si}Y_{si}$ is the level of sales, $P_{m}M_{si}$ is expenditure on raw materials, $P_{E}E_{si}$ is expenditure on energy, and L_{si} is the number of employees (including both full- and part-time but not seasonal workers). To the extent that seasonal employment is more prevalent in unregistered firms than in the formal sector, we overstate the productivity of unregistered firms. We use expenditure on production inputs (such as energy) as a crude proxy for capital invested.

This approach to productivity measurement has recently received considerable criticism, since the sales measure obviously combines physical output and prices. But in a competitive equilibrium, prices may vary inversely with efficiency exactly to eliminate any variation in productivity as measured by sales (or value added) per employee. The recognition of this problem in the absence of firm-specific price indices is credited to Tor Jakob Klette and Zvi Griliches;[38] several more recent studies seek to address the problem.[39] We follow the approach of Chang-Tai Hsieh and

37. Data on wages are unavailable for most countries in the Informal sample. For this reason we are unable to remove labor costs from our measure of value added.

38. Klette and Griliches (1996).

39. These include Bernard and others (2003); Katayama, Lu, and Tybout (2006); Foster, Haltiwanger, and Syverson (2008); Hsieh and Klenow (2007).

Peter Klenow,[40] which assumes that all firms in an industry use the same Cobb-Douglas production technology and that industry output is a constant-elasticity-of-substitution (CES) aggregate of the outputs of all the firms. They then show that, in a competitive equilibrium, physical productivity A_{si} (or real output per employee) can be estimated from nominal sales using the following formula:

$$A_{si} = \kappa_s \frac{(P_{si} Y_{si})^{\frac{\sigma}{\sigma - 1}}}{L_{si}},$$

where κ_s is an unobserved constant and σ is the elasticity of substitution of output. Although we do not observe κ_s, relative productivities are unaffected by setting κ_s equal to 1 for each industry *s*. Intuitively, goods sold by very productive firms must command lower prices to induce buyers to demand the higher output. Raising sales to the power $\sigma/(\sigma - 1)$ yields Y_{si}, making it possible to infer real output from nominal revenue. Since registered firms tend to have higher sales, productivity differences between registered and unregistered firms are increasing in σ. Empirically, estimates of σ range from 3 to 10. We follow Hsieh and Klenow and conservatively set σ equal to 3.[41]

Before turning to the results, we note the empirical finding of Lucia Foster and coauthors that the correlation between the sales-based and the corrected measures of productivity is incredibly high, well over 0.9.[42] Thus, although the theoretical objection to the traditional measures is compelling, its empirical significance appears minor. Indeed, Foster and coauthors have data on both prices and sales. The correlation that they report between nominal and real output is based on actual data rather than on a model.

Measurement Error

Even aside from the theoretical concerns, we need to deal with the fact that our sales numbers come from unofficial firms, raising concerns about measurement error. There is good reason to worry that our productivity measures may be biased, since unregistered entrepreneurs may choose to hide output not only from the government but also from the World Bank contractors. For example, Suresh de Mel, David McKenzie, and Christopher Woodruff find that microenterprises underreport profits by 30 percent

40. Hsieh and Klenow (2007).
41. Hsieh and Klenow (2007).
42. Foster and others (2008).

to researchers, although they attribute this more to lack of recall than to intentional understatement.[43]

We offer two pieces of evidence that support the view that such biases are unlikely to drive our main results. First, table 11 shows the available information regarding expenditure on various production inputs (scaled by sales). If unregistered entrepreneurs lied *only* about sales, inputs as a fraction of sales would be higher for unregistered firms than for other firms. In fact, expenditure on raw materials by small firms in the control group is 12.7 percentage points higher than for unregistered firms in the Informal sample, and 2.7 percentage points higher than for unregistered firms in the Micro sample. Moreover, expenditure on energy by unregistered firms is comparable to that by firms in the control group. Other variables show a mixed pattern. In particular, expenditure on labor by small firms in the control group is 8.1 percentage points higher than that by unregistered firms in the Informal sample, but 1.7 percentage points lower than that by unregistered firms in the Micro sample. Similarly, expenditure on machines by small firms in the control group is 14.8 percentage points higher than that by unregistered firms in the Micro sample, but equal to that by unregistered firms in the Informal sample. Finally, there is weak evidence that unregistered firms in the Informal Survey spend more on rent than do small firms in the control group. In sum, there is no evidence that unregistered firms consistently spend a larger fraction of their sales on inputs than do small firms in the control group, as would be the case if unregistered entrepreneurs lied only about their sales.

Second, table 12 shows the available data on wages per employee. Under the dual hypothesis, unregistered firms should pay low wages.[44] These low wages may be consistent with some on-the-job home production by workers in unregistered firms. Alternatively, workers in these firms may be less skilled than those in registered firms. Either way, the dual view predicts that the measured output of unregistered firms should be low relative to that of workers in the control group. In contrast, wages in the formal and informal sectors should be comparable if observed differences in productivity are due only to measurement error. The top panel of table 12 shows wages per employee in Cape Verde, the only country in the Informal sample with wage data. The bottom panel shows wages per employee for the countries covered by the Micro sample. Wages in both panels are scaled by income per capita.

43. De Mel, McKenzie, and Woodruff (2007).

44. Harris and Todaro (1970).

Table 11. Expenditure on Production Inputs by Informal and Micro Survey Firms

Percent of sales

Indicator	*Informal Survey sample*			*Enterprise Survey control group*				*Difference*[a]			
	Unregistered	*Registered*	*All*	*Small*	*Medium*	*Big*	*All*	*Enterprise v. informal*	*Registered v. unregistered*	*Small v. unregistered*	*Big v. small*
Raw materials	30.5	35.2	31.0	43.2	47.2	41.3	46.4	15.4***	4.7	12.7**	–1.9
Energy	6.3	6.8	6.8	6.8	6.8	6.8	6.8	0.0	0.0	0.0	0.0
Labor	13.4	21.8	14.9	21.5	17.8	17.3	18.9	4.0	8.4	8.1	–4.2*
Machines	0.1	0.1	0.1	0.1	0.1	0.0	0.1	0.0	0.0	0.0	0.0
Land	8.3	13.2	10.4	4.2	1.6	2.0	3.6	–6.8	4.9	–4.1	–2.2
Rent	7.5	9.7	7.9	3.9	2.2	1.3	2.8	–5.1***	2.3	–3.6**	–2.6**
Average difference								1.3	3.4	2.2	–1.8

Indicator	*Micro Survey sample*			*Enterprise Survey control group*				*Difference*			
	Unregistered	*Registered*	*All*	*Small*	*Medium*	*Big*	*All*	*Enterprise v. micro*	*Registered v. unregistered*	*Small v. unregistered*	*Big v. small*
Raw materials	38.5	39.7	39.6	41.3	44.4	49.3	42.6	3.0	1.2	2.7	8.0
Energy	3.6	2.9	2.9	4.2	3.8	4.6	4.1	1.2*	–0.7	0.6	0.4
Labor	23.3	21.0	21.5	21.6	19.7	17.7	20.9	–0.5	–2.3	–1.7	–3.9*
Machines	2.9	3.3	3.1	17.8	44.1	32.9	18.6	15.5	0.4	14.8	15.1
Land	. . .	. . .	. . .	0.7	0.7	0.7	0.7	. . .	. . .	. . .	0.0
Rent	7.4	8.3	8.0	6.7	3.5	2.3	5.8	–2.2*	0.9	–0.6	–4.4***
Average difference								3.4	–0.1	3.2	2.5

Sources: World Bank Informal, Micro, and Enterprise Surveys; authors' calculations.

a. Asterisks indicate statistically significantly different from zero at the *10 percent, **5 percent, and ***1 percent level.

Table 12. Ratio of Wages per Employee to GDP per Capita in Informal and Micro Survey Firms[a]

Country	Informal Survey sample			Enterprise Survey control group				Difference[b]			
	Unregistered	Registered	All	Small	Medium	Big	All	Enterprise v. informal	Registered v. unregistered	Small v. unregistered	Big v. small
Cape Verde	0.90	1.25	0.96	2.92	4.03	2.62	3.19	2.23***	0.35	2.03***	–0.30

Country	Micro Survey sample			Enterprise Survey control group				Difference			
	Unregistered	Registered	All	Small	Medium	Big	All	Enterprise v. micro	Registered v. unregistered	Small v. unregistered	Big v. small
Angola	1.35	2.23	2.17	3.26	3.02	1.51	3.20	1.03***	0.88*	1.91***	–1.74***
Botswana	0.35	0.58	0.52	0.89	1.05	1.03	0.95	0.43***	0.23***	0.54***	0.14
Burundi	1.76	3.13	2.97	5.84	7.29	4.82	6.04	3.07***	1.37*	4.08***	–1.02
Congo, Dem. Rep.	5.64	5.45	5.52	8.25	11.35	9.26	8.93	3.41***	–0.18	2.62***	1.01***
Gambia, The	0.54	1.04	0.85	1.52	2.41	1.92	1.78	0.94***	0.49***	0.98***	0.40
Guinea	0.83	1.23	1.13	1.30	1.13	0.91	1.27	0.15*	0.40**	0.47***	–0.39
Guinea-Bissau	6.11	7.21	6.97	9.64	6.92	. . .	9.25	2.29**	1.10	3.53*	. . .
India	1.31	1.43	1.39	1.54	1.82	1.62	1.64	0.25***	0.12***	0.22***	0.09
Mauritania	2.12	2.10	2.11	3.88	3.98	4.33	3.91	1.80***	–0.02	1.76***	0.44
Namibia	0.27	0.79	0.55	2.48	2.56	2.30	2.49	1.94***	0.51***	2.21***	–0.19
Rwanda	1.29	1.52	1.47	4.01	5.70	3.12	4.36	2.89***	0.23	2.72***	–0.89
Swaziland	0.50	1.20	1.05	1.92	2.21	1.88	1.97	0.92***	0.69***	1.42***	–0.04
Tanzania	1.44	1.59	1.53	3.59	5.07	5.72	4.21	2.68***	0.16	2.15***	2.13***
Uganda	3.08	3.93	3.60	4.32	4.90	3.91	4.45	0.85**	0.85	1.24**	–0.42
Average	1.90	2.39	2.27	3.75	4.24	3.26	3.89	1.62**	0.49	1.85**	–0.04

Source: World Bank Informal, Micro, and Enterprise Surveys; authors' calculations.

a. See tables 3 and 4 for the survey years for each country.

b. Asterisks indicate statistically significantly different from zero at the *10 percent, **5 percent, and ***1 percent level.

Three facts stand out. First, there is no clear correlation between firm size and wages within the control group. Big firms pay higher wages than do small firms in Congo and Tanzania. The reverse is true in Angola. On average, wages in big and small firms are essentially indistinguishable from each other. Second, unregistered firms consistently pay lower wages than do small firms in the control group. Cape Verde illustrates this point. Wages in unregistered firms there are 10 percent lower than income per capita. In contrast, wages in the control group of small firms are 2.92 times income per capita. On average, in the Micro sample, wages are 1.90 times income per capita in unregistered firms and 3.75 times income per capita in small firms in the control group. Third, although there is considerable heterogeneity across countries, the workers of unregistered firms are not the poorest among the poor. In India, for example, wages for the employees of unregistered firms exceed GDP per capita by 31 percent. Similarly, in the Micro sample, the average wage of unregistered workers is roughly twice GDP per capita. Taken at face value, the large wedge in wages between unregistered firms and the control group is strongly consistent with the dual view of unregistered firms. Of course, we cannot rule out the alternative interpretation that respondents shrewdly lie to the World Bank about sales, inputs, and wages. However, the findings on inputs and wages should allay some of the concerns regarding data quality.

As a final point, it seems to us that concerns about intentional understatement of revenues should not be exaggerated for our data. Firms participating in the surveys do so voluntarily. Virtually all of them answer questions about sales, even though they do not have to. They also give answers suggesting massive underpayment of taxes and bribe payments by "firms like theirs." This is not the behavior one would expect of those fearful that World Bank contractors will turn them in (or that the authorities would do anything about it if they did). Our view is that most informal firms operate in the open, that they have done so for years, that they pay the police and other authorities to leave them alone, and that fear of reprisals for truly reporting revenues to the World Bank is very far from most of their minds. This particular concern is a rich-country fear rather than a poor-country reality.

Productivity of Unregistered Firms

Tables 13 and 14 present the main findings of the paper. Table 13 shows estimates of log value added (top panel), log sales per employee (middle panel), and log real output per employee (bottom panel) for the Informal sample and its Enterprise Survey control group. Table 14 shows analogous data for the Micro sample. Three key facts stand out. First, registered

Table 13. Productivity of Firms in the Informal Sector Survey[a]

Log units

Country	*Informal Survey sample*			*Enterprise Survey control group*				*Difference*[b]			
	Unregistered	*Registered*	*All*	*Small*	*Medium*	*Big*	*All*	*Registered v. unregistered*	*Small v. unregistered*	*Big v. small*	*Big v. unregistered*
					Log of value added per employee						
Bangladesh	7.09	7.92	7.10	7.96	8.53	8.69	8.61	0.83	0.87**	0.73	1.60***
Brazil	8.30	8.77	8.47	9.22	9.58	10.36	9.74	0.48***	0.92***	1.14***	2.06***
Cambodia	7.19	8.01	7.22	. . .	. . .	. . .	. . .	0.82	. . .	. . .	. . .
Cape Verde	8.12	7.85	8.07	8.47	9.21	9.78	8.78	−0.27	0.35	1.30	1.65
Guatemala	7.37	8.59	7.48	8.95	9.39	9.42	9.21	1.22	1.57***	0.48***	2.05***
India	7.64	8.29	7.69	9.16	9.43	9.90	9.36	0.64***	1.52***	0.74***	2.26***
Indonesia	7.73	. . .	7.73	8.53	8.39	9.16	8.80	. . .	0.80	0.64	1.44***
Kenya	7.76	8.04	7.83	9.58	9.99	10.30	9.94	0.28	1.82***	0.71***	2.54***
Niger	9.32	7.16	8.24	11.44	10.01	9.98	10.83	−2.16	2.12	−1.46	0.66
Pakistan	7.21	6.59	7.20	9.78	9.76	9.18	9.58	−0.62	2.58***	−0.60	1.98***
Senegal	7.19	7.22	7.20	9.09	9.81	9.96	9.54	0.03	1.90***	0.87***	2.77***
Tanzania	6.23	. . .	6.23	8.65	9.51	9.83	9.40	. . .	2.43***	1.18	3.61***
Uganda	7.15	7.92	7.30	8.71	9.33	10.02	9.09	0.76	1.56***	1.31***	2.87***
Average	7.56	7.85	7.52	9.13	9.41	9.72	9.41	0.18***	1.54***	0.59**	2.12***
					Log of sales per employee						
Bangladesh	7.82	8.82	7.83	9.39	10.00	9.61	9.70	1.00	1.57***	0.22*	1.79***
Brazil	8.63	9.18	8.83	9.84	10.23	11.02	10.38	0.55***	1.21***	1.18***	2.40***
Cambodia	7.77	9.10	7.80	8.84	8.95	8.61	8.84	1.33***	1.08***	−0.24	0.84***
Cape Verde	8.35	8.33	8.34	9.82	10.35	9.94	9.96	−0.02	1.48***	0.12	1.60
Guatemala	7.80	8.12	7.81	9.70	10.14	10.19	9.96	0.32	1.90***	0.49***	2.39***

India	8.20	8.83	8.25	10.09	10.32	10.77	10.27	0.63***	1.89***	0.67***	2.56***
Indonesia	8.38	. . .	8.38	7.66	9.07	10.04	9.58	. . .	–0.72	2.38**	1.66***
Kenya	8.11	8.34	8.15	10.76	11.07	10.98	10.95	0.24	2.65***	0.22	2.87***
Niger	7.80	7.45	7.61	11.40	10.76	10.95	11.18	–0.35*	3.60***	–0.45	3.15***
Pakistan	7.73	7.30	7.73	10.73	10.83	10.17	10.62	–0.44	2.99***	–0.56	2.43***
Senegal	7.81	7.95	7.84	10.16	10.77	11.34	10.61	0.14	2.35***	1.19***	3.53***
Tanzania	7.26	8.08	7.32	8.96	10.28	10.68	9.79	0.82***	1.70***	1.73***	3.42***
Uganda	7.73	8.12	7.81	9.42	10.02	10.69	9.79	0.38	1.69***	1.27***	2.96***
Average	7.95	8.30	7.98	9.75	10.21	10.38	10.12	0.38**	1.80***	0.63**	2.43***
					Log of real output per employee						
Bangladesh	12.49	14.79	12.51	15.35	16.90	17.29	17.05	2.30**	2.86***	1.94***	4.80***
Brazil	13.49	14.34	13.80	16.12	17.21	19.25	17.59	0.85***	2.63***	3.13***	5.76***
Cambodia	12.56	14.66	12.62	14.23	15.26	16.00	14.57	2.10***	1.67***	1.77***	3.44***
Cape Verde	13.02	13.09	13.03	15.87	17.28	17.66	16.24	0.06	2.84***	1.80	4.64
Guatemala	12.46	13.00	12.49	15.74	17.04	18.15	16.72	0.54	3.28***	2.40***	5.69***
India	13.14	14.18	13.21	16.29	17.24	18.98	17.02	1.04***	3.15***	2.69***	5.84***
Indonesia	13.32	. . .	13.32	12.69	15.42	18.25	16.90	. . .	–0.62	5.55***	4.93***
Kenya	12.82	13.29	12.91	17.36	18.51	19.31	18.36	0.47	4.54***	1.95***	6.49***
Niger	12.27	12.01	12.13	18.31	18.10	19.16	18.29	–0.26	6.03***	0.85	6.88***
Pakistan	12.38	11.63	12.37	17.26	18.08	18.08	18.03	–0.75	4.88***	0.82	5.70***
Senegal	12.51	12.69	12.55	16.35	17.99	19.71	17.61	0.18	3.84***	3.36***	7.20***
Tanzania	11.55	12.85	11.65	14.55	17.28	18.72	16.40	1.30***	2.99***	4.17***	7.17***
Uganda	12.39	13.08	12.53	15.05	16.66	18.59	16.05	0.69	2.66***	3.54***	6.20***
Average	12.65	13.30	12.70	15.78	17.15	18.40	16.99	0.71***	3.14***	2.61***	5.75***

Source: World Bank Informal and Enterprise Surveys; authors' calculations.

a. See tables 3 and 4 for the survey years for each country.

b. Asterisks indicate statistically significantly different from zero at the *10 percent, **5 percent, and ***1 percent level.

Table 14. Productivity of Firms in the Micro Sector Survey[a]

Log units

Country	Micro Survey sample			Enterprise Survey control group				Difference[b]			
	Unregistered	*Registered*	*All*	*Small*	*Medium*	*Big*	*All*	*Registered v. unregistered*	*Small v. unregistered*	*Big v. small*	*Big v. unregistered*
				Log of value added per employee							
Angola	7.48	8.35	8.30	8.97	8.86	9.34	8.97	0.87***	1.50***	0.36	1.86***
Botswana	9.00	8.85	8.88	9.49	10.02	9.52	9.66	–0.15	0.48	0.03	0.51
Burundi	8.52	7.81	7.91	8.19	9.23	9.11	8.47	–0.72	–0.33	0.92**	0.59
Congo, Dem. Rep.	6.91	7.65	7.38	8.25	8.89	8.53	8.47	0.74**	1.34***	0.28	1.62***
Gambia, The	6.86	7.39	7.24	8.23	8.76	9.35	8.44	0.52*	1.37***	1.12	2.49***
Guinea	8.01	8.65	8.49	8.34	8.67	9.60	8.41	0.64*	0.33	1.26***	1.59**
Guinea-Bissau	7.78	8.39	8.31	8.28	8.47	. . .	8.32	0.61	0.50	. . .	. . .
India	8.05	8.40	8.25	8.75	8.99	9.44	8.93	0.35***	0.70***	0.68***	1.39***
Mauritania	8.43	7.50	8.16	8.69	9.23	9.34	8.92	–0.93**	0.26	0.66**	0.91*
Namibia	6.76	7.82	7.51	9.81	10.21	10.44	10.04	1.06**	3.05***	0.63**	3.68***
Rwanda	7.51	8.38	8.32	9.15	9.36	9.10	9.21	0.86	1.64***	–0.05	1.59*
Swaziland	7.63	8.64	8.54	9.83	9.55	9.62	9.67	1.00**	2.20***	–0.21	1.99***
Tanzania	7.88	8.21	8.09	8.92	9.74	10.37	9.32	0.33	1.05***	1.44***	2.49***
Uganda	8.13	8.40	8.30	8.66	8.92	9.71	8.80	0.27	0.52***	1.05***	1.57***
Average	7.78	8.17	8.12	8.83	9.21	9.50	8.97	0.39**	1.04***	0.63***	1.71***
				Log of sales per employee							
Angola	8.16	8.90	8.85	9.58	9.50	9.92	9.58	0.74***	1.43***	0.34	1.77***
Botswana	8.53	9.49	9.23	10.33	10.78	10.62	10.48	0.95***	1.80***	0.28	2.08***
Burundi	9.09	8.69	8.73	9.25	9.86	10.15	9.37	–0.40	0.16	0.91**	1.06**
Congo, Dem. Rep.	7.91	8.38	8.20	8.91	9.52	9.57	9.06	0.48*	1.01***	0.66**	1.67***

Gambia, The	7.42	8.02	7.79	8.76	9.41	10.30	9.00	0.60***	1.34***	1.55***	2.88***
Guinea	8.88	9.53	9.36	8.92	9.18	9.90	8.98	0.66**	0.05	0.98**	1.03
Guinea-Bissau	8.49	9.05	8.93	9.27	9.35	. . .	9.28	0.57*	0.79***	. . .	. . .
India	8.66	9.12	8.93	9.79	9.93	10.14	9.85	0.46***	1.13***	0.35***	1.48***
Mauritania	9.14	8.79	8.99	9.98	10.24	11.14	10.05	−0.35**	0.84***	1.17***	2.00***
Namibia	7.17	8.21	7.68	10.34	10.65	10.96	10.45	1.04***	3.16***	0.63***	3.79***
Rwanda	7.39	8.62	8.41	9.26	9.96	10.01	9.49	1.23***	1.87***	0.74**	2.61***
Swaziland	7.62	8.94	8.55	9.87	10.25	10.06	9.96	1.32***	2.25***	0.19	2.44***
Tanzania	8.51	8.93	8.77	9.36	10.21	11.12	9.77	0.42	0.85***	1.76***	2.61***
Uganda	8.66	9.17	8.97	9.32	9.69	10.36	9.49	0.50***	0.66***	1.04***	1.70***
Average	8.26	8.85	8.67	9.50	9.89	10.33	9.63	0.59***	1.24***	0.81***	2.09***
				Log of real output per employee							
Angola	12.97	14.13	14.05	15.57	15.94	17.27	15.65	1.16***	2.60***	1.71***	4.30***
Botswana	13.38	14.89	14.49	16.63	18.01	18.54	17.20	1.52***	3.25***	1.92***	5.16***
Burundi	14.20	13.67	13.73	14.96	16.58	17.71	15.30	−0.53	0.75	2.76***	3.51**
Congo, Dem. Rep.	12.44	13.32	12.98	14.46	16.02	16.92	14.87	0.88**	2.02***	2.46***	4.48***
Gambia, The	11.77	12.72	12.35	14.22	15.94	18.11	14.85	0.95***	2.46***	3.89***	6.35***
Guinea	14.06	15.02	14.77	14.47	15.55	17.57	14.66	0.96**	0.42	3.10***	3.51***
Guinea-Bissau	13.23	14.01	13.84	15.01	15.78	. . .	15.12	0.78*	1.78***	. . .	. . .
India	13.76	14.68	14.30	15.33	16.71	18.04	15.80	0.92***	1.57***	2.71***	4.28***
Mauritania	14.42	13.92	14.20	16.07	17.15	19.31	16.35	−0.49**	1.65***	3.24***	4.89***
Namibia	11.17	12.92	12.02	16.64	17.72	19.15	17.04	1.75***	5.47***	2.52***	7.99***
Rwanda	11.62	13.44	13.13	15.00	16.75	17.89	15.65	1.82***	3.38***	2.89***	6.27***
Swaziland	11.71	14.03	13.35	15.91	17.17	17.85	16.36	2.31***	4.20***	1.94***	6.14***
Tanzania	13.33	14.13	13.82	15.17	17.16	19.36	16.15	0.80*	1.84***	4.19***	6.03***
Uganda	13.79	14.72	14.36	15.14	16.33	18.28	15.66	0.94***	1.35***	3.15***	4.50***
Average	12.99	13.97	13.67	15.33	16.63	18.16	15.76	0.98***	2.34***	2.80***	5.19***

Sources: World Bank Micro and Enterprise Surveys; authors' calculations.

a. See tables 3 and 4 for the survey years for each country.

b. Asterisks indicate statistically significantly different from zero at the *10 percent, **5 percent, and ***1 percent level.

firms in both the Informal and the Micro Surveys are more productive than unregistered ones in the same survey. Firms in India in the 2006 Micro Survey illustrate this pattern. Value added per employee for registered firms is 35 percent higher than for unregistered firms (8.40 versus 8.05), sales per employee are 46 percent higher (9.12 versus 8.66), and real output per employee is 92 percent higher (14.68 versus 13.76). Most countries exhibit a similar pattern, although Burundi, Mauritania, Niger, and Pakistan are exceptions. On average, value added per employee for registered firms in the Informal and Micro samples is, respectively, 18 percent and 39 percent higher than for their unregistered counterparts. Differences in sales per employee are even larger: 38 percent for the Informal sample and 59 percent for the Micro sample. Differences between unregistered and registered firms are most extreme for real output per employee: 71 percent in the Informal Survey sample and 98 percent in the Micro Survey sample.

Second, these differences become much more dramatic when we compare Informal or Micro Survey firms with the Enterprise Survey firms. The productivity gap between unregistered firms and even the small firms in the control groups is truly enormous. Take the case of India in 2006 again. Value added per employee for small Enterprise Survey firms is 70 percent higher than for unregistered Micro Survey firms, and sales and real output per employee for small firms are 113 percent and 157 percent higher, respectively, than for unregistered ones. The example of India is representative of the results for other countries, except that value added and real output per employee in Burundi and sales per employee in Indonesia do not conform to this pattern. Bearing in mind that the observations are unevenly distributed across size groups (only two small firms in Indonesia have nonmissing sales), the consistency of the results across countries is striking. On average, based on the Informal sample, the productivity of small firms in the Enterprise Survey is around 154, 180, or 314 percent higher than for unregistered firms depending on whether we look at value added, sales per employee, or real output per employee, respectively. Similarly, based on the Micro sample, the productivity wedge between small firms in the Enterprise Survey and unregistered firms is 104, 124, or 234 percent depending on whether we look at value added, sales per employee, or real output per employee, respectively.

Third, big firms are significantly more productive than small ones. Continuing with the example of India in 2006, the productivity wedge between big and small firms in the control group for the Micro sample is 68 percent for value added, 35 percent for sales per employee, and 271 percent for real output per employee. This large heterogeneity in firm productivity is consistent with work by Hsieh and Klenow showing sizable gaps in the marginal products of labor and capital across plants within narrowly defined industries in China and India.[45] On average, depending on the measure and the sample, productivity of big firms is between 59 and 280 percent higher than that of small ones.

The cumulative effect of these productivity differences is large. Returning to the example of India in 2006, big firms are 139 to 428 percent more productive than unregistered firms. On average, the productivity wedge between big and unregistered firms in the Informal sample is 212 percent for value added, 243 percent for sales per employee, and 575 percent for real output per employee. The numbers for the Micro sample are of the same order of magnitude: 171 percent for value added, 209 percent for sales per employee, and 519 percent for real output per employee.

To illustrate what these differences in productivity mean in practice, consider the average unregistered Micro Survey firm in India. It has sales of $2,420 per employee and value added of $1,279 per employee. In contrast, an average small firm in the control group has sales of $12,285 per employee and value added of $4,335 per employee. If the unregistered firm could achieve the value added of a small Enterprise Survey firm simply by registering, would it choose to do that? By assumption, changing its legal status would generate $3,056 (= $4,335 – $1,279) in additional cash flow per employee. However, the firm would have to pay registration fees and taxes as well as comply with regulations. The registration fee—including the value of the entrepreneurs' time—would probably amount to roughly $400.[46] The firm would also need to pay labor taxes (17 percent of wages), corporate taxes (35 percent of profits), and value-added taxes (12.5 percent of profits).[47] Recall that our value-added estimates are based on expenditure on energy and materials and do not exclude labor costs. To keep things simple, assume that wages are 20 percent of sales ($2,457) and that there are no additional costs. Moreover, to bias the example against the firm choosing to register, assume that the firm would evade all taxes if unregistered but comply fully if registered. Under these assumptions, the firm would owe additional payments of $418 (= 0.17 × $2,457) in labor taxes, $657 in corporate taxes (= 0.35 × [$4,335 – $2,457]), and value-added tax of $235 (= 0.125 × [$4,335 – $2,457]), for a total of $1,710 per employee in taxes and fees. In this back-of-the-envelope calculation, the firm would pocket $1,346 (= $3,056 – $1,710) per employee by registering.

45. Hsieh and Klenow (2007).
46. Djankov and others (2002).
47. Djankov and others (2008b).

Of course, the gains would be even larger if the unregistered firm could, merely by registering, replicate the value added per employee of big firms in the control group. On average, such firms have value added per employee of $8,715 on sales per employee of $20,301. Calculations similar to the preceding ones suggest that the unregistered firm would gain $4,135 per employee if, simply by registering, it could replicate the value added per employee of big firms.

A similar set of calculations illustrates that unregistered entrepreneurs can simply not afford to pay taxes unless sales sharply increase from merely registering. Assuming wages equal 20 percent of sales ($484), the average unregistered firm has a pre-tax profit per employee of $795 (= $1,279 – $484) and owes taxes of $460 per employee.[48] Unless sales dramatically increased as a result of registering, the average unregistered firm would have considerable difficulty paying $400 to register.

In practice, these calculations mean that believers in the romantic view need to blame the precarious existence of unregistered firms on something beyond costly entry procedures and high tax rates. Given the very large difference in productivity between unregistered firms and the control group, the cost of complying with government regulations would have to be implausibly high to justify operating as an unregistered firm. A more realistic scenario is that—consistent with the dual view—unregistered firms would not be able to achieve the performance of small firms in the control group just by registering. Perhaps, for example, unregistered firms lack the human capital necessary to match the quality of the goods produced by formal firms. The image of unregistered firms that is consistent with their observed productivity is not that of predators but rather that of relics of the past.

What accounts for the large difference in productivity between unregistered firms and the control group? We begin by running simple ordinary least squares (OLS) regressions and discuss self-selection issues later. In principle, the productivity differences that we document in tables 13 and 14 could be driven by industry effects, by differences in inputs (including human capital), or by differences in size. The goal of these regressions is to examine whether unregistered firms remain unusually unproductive after we control for these factors. In simple terms, we interpret the estimated coefficient on the unregistered dummy as a measure of our ignorance regarding the production function of unregistered firms. Omitting the unregistered dummy would not mean that unregistered firms are as pro-

48. Such a firm would owe $82 in labor taxes (= 0.17 × $484), $278 in corporate taxes (= 0.35 × [$1,279 – $484]), and $99 in value-added taxes (= 0.125 × [$1,279 – $484]).

ductive as registered ones, but that differences in productivity are captured by differences in inputs, as in Rauch's selection story.[49]

All specifications include dummy variables equaling 1 under the following conditions: the firm is in the Informal Survey; the firm is registered and in the Informal Survey; the firm is in the Micro Survey; and the firm is registered and in the Micro Survey. Firms in the Enterprise Survey are the omitted category. We then add to the regression—one at a time—log income per capita, eight industry dummies, expenditure on raw materials, expenditure on energy, expenditure on machines, the index of manager education, and log sales.[50] All three expenditure variables are scaled by the number of employees.

Table 15 reports the results of OLS regressions in which log value added per employee is the dependent variable. Tables 16 and 17 show similar regressions for log sales and real output per employee, respectively. All three sets of results are qualitatively similar. We discuss the findings on value added in some detail and point out where the results for sales and real output per employee differ. The first regression reported in each table includes as independent variables only the dummies for whether the firm is in the Informal Survey sample or in the Micro Survey sample and the interactions between each of those two variables and whether the firm is registered.

The results confirm the findings in tables 13 and 14. The estimated coefficients in column 15-1 of table 15 are −1.78 for the Informal sample dummy and −1.29 for the Micro sample dummy. The coefficients for the interactions of the Informal and the Micro dummies with whether the firm is registered equal 0.81 and 0.35, respectively. All four dummies are highly statistically significant. Adding GDP per capita to the regression (column 15-2) does not change the basic pattern. Similarly, the estimated coefficients for the four dummies barely change as we add industry controls (column 15-3). The coefficients do change when we add expenditure on raw materials: the estimated coefficients for each of the four dummies are roughly cut in half (column 15-4). Adding expenditure on energy further lowers the estimated coefficients on the four dummies, but not significantly (column 15-5). The four coefficients barely change as we add expenditure on machinery (column 15-6). The coefficients for expenditure on raw materials, energy, and machines are not only statistically significant but also economically important. For example, increasing raw materials by

49. Rauch (1991).

50. Errors are clustered at the country level. We do not include country fixed effects since the frequency of unregistered firms in our sample may not reflect the incidence of unregistered firms in the population.

Table 15. Regressions Explaining Value Added per Employee[a]

	Regression							
Independent variable	*15-1*	*15-2*	*15-3*	*15-4*	*15-5*	*15-6*	*15-7*	*15-8*
Informal Survey dummy	−1.7788***	−1.7894***	−1.8135***	−0.8875***	−0.7075***	−0.6901***	−0.5574***	0.1247
	(0.1455)	(0.1265)	(0.1160)	(0.1788)	(0.1517)	(0.1543)	(0.1597)	(0.1225)
Informal Survey dummy × registered	0.8077***	0.6241***	0.5906***	0.3032**	0.1612	0.1705	0.1281	0.2948***
	(0.2476)	(0.1499)	(0.1204)	(0.1449)	(0.1223)	(0.1237)	(0.1226)	(0.0939)
Micro Survey dummy	−1.2910***	−1.2810***	−1.2488***	−0.7925***	−0.6626***	−0.5711***	−0.4746***	0.3720***
	(0.1464)	(0.0963)	(0.1035)	(0.1127)	(0.1256)	(0.1218)	(0.1133)	(0.0660)
Micro Survey dummy × registered	0.3454***	0.3763***	0.3115***	0.1821***	0.1510***	0.1387***	0.0986**	−0.0728
	(0.0368)	(0.0436)	(0.0330)	(0.0350)	(0.0467)	(0.0418)	(0.0398)	(0.0527)
Log of GDP per capita (at PPP)		0.3960***	0.4279***	0.3272**	0.2985**	0.2739**	0.2665**	0.0584
		(0.1164)	(0.1333)	(0.1184)	(0.1166)	(0.0983)	(0.0966)	(0.0760)
Log of expenditure on raw materials per employee				0.2873***	0.2140***	0.2034***	0.1977***	0.0381
				(0.0509)	(0.0491)	(0.0489)	(0.0483)	(0.0392)
Log of expenditure on energy per employee					0.2059***	0.1909***	0.1834***	0.1093***
					(0.0348)	(0.0317)	(0.0326)	(0.0303)
Log of expenditure on machines per employee						0.0570***	0.0544***	0.0078
						(0.0102)	(0.0100)	(0.0112)
Manager education (4 = attended college)							0.0986***	−0.0231
							(0.0292)	(0.0160)
Log of sales								0.4204***
								(0.0564)
Industry dummies	No	No	Yes	Yes	Yes	Yes	Yes	Yes
Constant	9.2615***	6.1996***	5.7435***	4.0303***	3.6547***	3.7987***	3.6445***	1.9736***
	(0.1389)	(0.9186)	(1.0810)	(0.9428)	(0.9646)	(0.8459)	(0.8393)	(0.6059)
Adjusted R^2 (percent)	24.19	28.07	29.90	43.13	46.83	47.94	48.47	64.00

Source: Authors' regressions.

a. Results of ordinary least squares regressions on data from the 27 countries covered by the Informal and Micro Surveys. The dependent variable is the logarithm of value added per employee at purchasing power parity. The number of observations in all regressions is 8,478. Standard errors are clustered at the country level and reported in parentheses. Asterisks indicate statistical significance at the *10 percent, **5 percent, and ***1 percent level.

Table 16. Regressions Explaining Sales per Employee[a]

Independent variable	Regression							
	16-1	*16-2*	*16-3*	*16-4*	*16-5*	*16-6*	*16-7*	*16-8*
Informal Survey dummy	−1.9768***	−1.9861***	−1.9875***	−0.5355***	−0.3742**	−0.3625**	−0.2536	0.3420**
	(0.1395)	(0.1190)	(0.1173)	(0.1783)	(0.1468)	(0.1442)	(0.1548)	(0.1349)
Informal Survey dummy × registered	0.7707***	0.6036***	0.5618***	0.1077	−0.0215	−0.0155	−0.0501	0.0916
	(0.2493)	(0.1560)	(0.1211)	(0.1797)	(0.1615)	(0.1601)	(0.1620)	(0.1069)
Micro Survey dummy	−1.4258***	−1.4163***	−1.3843***	−0.6690***	−0.5474***	−0.4840***	−0.4048***	0.3288***
	(0.1389)	(0.1087)	(0.1151)	(0.1002)	(0.1126)	(0.1107)	(0.1018)	(0.0515)
Micro Survey dummy × registered	0.4048***	0.4335***	0.3677***	0.1634***	0.1350***	0.1265***	0.0937***	−0.0554**
	(0.0447)	(0.0423)	(0.0532)	(0.0292)	(0.0326)	(0.0328)	(0.0314)	(0.0217)
Log of GDP per capita (at PPP)		0.3685***	0.4094***	0.2533***	0.2271***	0.2101***	0.2040***	0.0233
		(0.0903)	(0.1081)	(0.0762)	(0.0736)	(0.0605)	(0.0590)	(0.0420)
Log of expenditure on raw materials per employee				0.4536***	0.3835***	0.3759***	0.3713***	0.2300***
				(0.0509)	(0.0479)	(0.0478)	(0.0475)	(0.0449)
Log of expenditure on energy per employee					0.1934***	0.1829***	0.1768***	0.1126***
					(0.0331)	(0.0313)	(0.0322)	(0.0273)
Log of expenditure on machines per employee						0.0400***	0.0380***	−0.0031
						(0.0088)	(0.0086)	(0.0096)
Manager education (4 = attended college)							0.0807***	−0.0256
							(0.0247)	(0.0155)
Log of sales								0.3675***
								(0.0485)
Industry dummies	No	No	Yes	Yes	Yes	Yes	Yes	Yes
Constant	10.0297***	7.1802***	6.6180***	3.8967***	3.5466***	3.6473***	3.5206***	2.0659***
	(0.1430)	(0.7136)	(0.8958)	(0.6490)	(0.6878)	(0.6190)	(0.6062)	(0.3207)
Adjusted R^2 (percent)	28.95	32.20	34.72	68.86	70.06	70.60	70.94	82.59

Source: Authors' regressions.

a. Results of ordinary least squares regressions on data from the 27 countries covered by the Informal and Micro Surveys. The dependent variable is the logarithm of sales per employee at purchasing power parity. The number of observations in all regressions is 8,564. Standard errors are clustered at the country level and reported in parentheses. Asterisks indicate statistical significance at the *10 percent, **5 percent, and ***1 percent level.

Table 17. Regressions Explaining Real Output per Employee[a]

	Regression							
Independent variable	*17-1*	*17-2*	*17-3*	*17-4*	*17-5*	*17-6*	*17-7*	*17-8*
Informal Survey dummy	−3.9489***	−3.9681***	−3.9265***	−1.6477***	−1.3877***	−1.3577***	−1.0464***	0.3713**
	(0.2373)	(0.1678)	(0.1992)	(0.2838)	(0.2387)	(0.2307)	(0.2412)	(0.1343)
Informal Survey dummy	1.1202***	0.7732***	0.7754***	0.0627	−0.1455	−0.1301	−0.2290	0.1083
× registered	(0.3540)	(0.1764)	(0.1682)	(0.2821)	(0.2535)	(0.2387)	(0.2425)	(0.1122)
Micro Survey dummy	−3.1495***	−3.1298***	−3.1033***	−1.9807***	−1.7847***	−1.6211***	−1.3948***	0.3514***
	(0.2743)	(0.1637)	(0.1765)	(0.1908)	(0.2106)	(0.2069)	(0.1814)	(0.0486)
Micro Survey dummy	0.7682***	0.8279***	0.7794***	0.4588***	0.4130***	0.3911***	0.2974***	−0.0575**
× registered	(0.0945)	(0.0786)	(0.0972)	(0.0585)	(0.0580)	(0.0643)	(0.0663)	(0.0243)
Log of GDP per capita		0.7650***	0.7877***	0.5428***	0.5006***	0.4567***	0.4393***	0.0093
(at PPP)		(0.1502)	(0.1856)	(0.1343)	(0.1311)	(0.0987)	(0.0945)	(0.0399)
Log of expenditure on raw				0.7118***	0.5989***	0.5794***	0.5662***	0.2297***
materials per employee				(0.0820)	(0.0775)	(0.0769)	(0.0751)	(0.0459)
Log of expenditure on					0.3117***	0.2848***	0.2671***	0.1144***
energy per employee					(0.0538)	(0.0494)	(0.0515)	(0.0284)
Log of expenditure on						0.1032***	0.0973***	−0.0005
machines per employee						(0.0147)	(0.0151)	(0.0097)
Manager education							0.2307***	−0.0224
(4 = attended college)							(0.0595)	(0.0152)
Log of sales								0.8749***
								(0.0505)
Industry dummies	No	No	Yes	Yes	Yes	Yes	Yes	Yes
Constant	16.7985***	10.8838***	10.4597***	6.1889***	5.6246***	5.8843***	5.5221***	2.0591***
	(0.2667)	(1.2225)	(1.5417)	(1.1699)	(1.2260)	(1.0445)	(1.0103)	(0.3085)
Adjusted R^2 (percent)	28.95	32.20	34.72	68.86	70.06	70.60	70.94	82.59

Source: Authors' regressions.

a. Results of ordinary least squares regressions on data from the 27 countries covered by the Informal and Micro Surveys. The dependent variable is the logarithm of real output per employee at purchasing power parity. The number of observations in all regressions is 8,564. Standard errors are clustered at the country level and reported in parentheses. Asterisks indicate statistical significance at the *10 percent, **5 percent, and ***1 percent level.

1 standard deviation is associated with a 43 percent increase in value added per employee.[51] Similar increases in expenditure on energy and machines have somewhat smaller effects (32 and 16 percent, respectively). Coefficients fall another notch when we add manager education to the regression (column 15-7). Interestingly, ignoring selection issues, the estimated coefficient on manager education suggests that a top manager with some college education increases value added per employee by 27 percent (= 0.09 × 3) relative to a top manager with only some primary school education. Finally, there is no evidence that unregistered firms are unusually unproductive once we control for log sales: the estimated coefficients on both the Informal and the Micro dummies switch signs when we add log sales to the regression (column 15-8). In fact, the coefficient on the Micro dummy is not only positive but also significant. The interaction between the registration dummy and the Informal dummy is the only interaction term that remains statistically significant.

Again, the results on sales and real output per employee (tables 16 and 17, respectively) are very similar to those for value added. In the full specification, the estimated coefficients for both the Informal and the Micro dummies are positive and significant. The interaction between the registered and the Informal dummies is insignificant, whereas that between the registered and the Micro dummies takes a small—but statistically significant—negative value.

Selection

The OLS results in this section suggest that unregistered firms are not unusually unproductive once we take into account their expenditure on inputs, the human capital of their top managers, and their small size. Of course, these are all endogenous variables. In fact, a key distinguishing factor between the dual view and the other views of unregistered firms is the emphasis on the sorting process that matches able managers with good assets. High-quality managers are willing to pay taxes and bear the cost of government regulation in exchange for being able to advertise their products, raise outside capital, and access public goods. In contrast, low-quality managers avoid taxes and regulations, since the benefits of operating in the formal economy are less valuable for small firms.

Table 18 examines the sorting process. Specifically, we examine the relationship between the quality of the firm's assets and the human capital

51. The standard deviations for raw materials, energy, and machines are 2.11, 1.66, and 2.83, respectively.

Table 18. Probit and OLS Regressions Investigating Manager Ability and Self-Selection[a]

	Independent variables							
	Dummy for highest level of education attended by top manager							
Dependent variable	*Secondary*	*Vocational*	*College*	*Log of GDP per capita*	*Constant*	*No. of observations*	*Pseudo-*R^2 *or* R^2 *(percent)*	F-*test*[b]
			Probit regressions					
Firm is registered with	0.2064***	0.2090***	0.4096***	–0.0029	. . .	5,478	10.07	96.54***
central government	(0.0420)	(0.0452)	(0.0449)	(0.0555)	. . .			
Firm has ever had a	–0.0250	0.0115	–0.0521	0.0415	. . .	3,763	2.75	2.81
commercial loan	(0.0254)	(0.0369)	(0.0548)	(0.0379)	. . .			
Firm's main customers	0.0361***	0.0349***	0.0323**	0.0037	. . .	2,869	9.14	78.08***
are large firms	(0.0060)	(0.0110)	(0.0152)	(0.0054)	. . .			
Firm occupies a	0.0397	0.0954**	0.0778	–0.0762***	. . .	1,429	4.22	4.64
permanent structure	(0.0468)	(0.0434)	(0.0538)	(0.0265)		. . .		
Firm is located in	0.0561***	0.0868**	0.0076	–0.0258	. . .	1,439	2.31	36.87***
owner's house	(0.0210)	(0.0355)	(0.0249)	(0.0253)	. . .			
Firm owns building	0.0847	0.0863	0.1118**	0.0167	. . .	5,682	3.03	4.75
it occupies	(0.0527)	(0.0691)	(0.0542)	(0.0466)	. . .			
Firm owns land it	0.0497	0.0352	0.0982**	0.0197	. . .	11,760	5.82	6.11
occupies	(0.0453)	(0.0539)	(0.0490)	(0.0369)	. . .			
Firm uses its own	0.0031	0.1265**	0.1184***	0.0097	. . .	1,438	3.33	78.56***
transportation equipment	(0.0510)	(0.0574)	(0.0284)	(0.0216)	. . .			
Firm owns a generator	0.1280***	0.1390**	0.3675***	–0.1349***	. . .	12,794	13.01	75.84***
	(0.0455)	(0.0550)	(0.0454)	(0.0464)	. . .			

Firm uses e-mail to communicate with clients	0.1662***	0.2309***	0.4799***	0.1495**	. . .	11,081	21.62	158.61***
	(0.0460)	(0.0453)	(0.0438)	(0.0736)	. . .			
Firm uses website to communicate with clients	0.1159***	0.1676***	0.2574***	0.1358**	. . .	11,044	16.91	61.46***
	(0.0353)	(0.0361)	(0.0274)	(0.0648)	. . .			
Firm has electrical connection	0.1837***	0.1901***	0.2833***	−0.0200	. . .	1,439	12.82	33.1***
	(0.0503)	(0.0579)	(0.0597)	(0.0517)	. . .			
			OLS regressions					
Percent of investment financed with internal funds	0.9852	−2.9315	−10.1707***	−5.3383**	111.3720***	13,006	5.10	35.06***
	(3.6083)	(1.9982)	(2.1024)	(1.9468)	(14.7773)			
Expenditure on raw materials as percent of sales	0.0378***	0.0338**	0.0874***	−0.0080	0.4461***	11,966	3.83	11.32***
	(0.0130)	(0.0147)	(0.0193)	(0.0154)	(0.1340)			
Expenditure on energy as percent of sales	−0.0015	−0.0040	−0.0077	−0.0035	0.0747**	12,546	1.72	1.78
	(0.0039)	(0.0041)	(0.0047)	(0.0040)	(0.0302)			
Expenditure on machines as percent of sales	−0.0047	0.0162***	0.0019	−0.0023	0.0432	12,577	3.26	7.91***
	(0.0040)	(0.0052)	(0.0041)	(0.0046)	(0.0361)			
Capacity utilization (percent)	0.6230	1.0456	5.4810***	1.5761	57.7676***	9,380	4.18	7.15***
	(1.0430)	(1.8476)	(1.3208)	(1.1737)	(10.6062)			

Source: Authors' regressions.

a. Marginal effects of probit (top panel) or OLS (bottom panel) regressions on data from the 27 countries included in the Informal and Micro Surveys. All regressions include industry dummies. Robust standard errors are clustered at the country level and presented in parentheses. Asterisks indicate statistical significance at the *10 percent, **5 percent, and ***1 percent level.

b. Test of the null hypothesis that true coefficients on all three top-manager education dummies are zero.

of its top manager—our only proxy for managers' ability. The dependent variables fall into two categories: dummy variables (top panel, which reports probit regressions) and continuous variables (bottom panel, OLS regressions). The dummy variables include indicators for whether the firm is registered; the firm has ever had a loan; the firm's main customers are large firms; the firm occupies a permanent structure; the firm is located in the owner's house; the firm owns the building it occupies; the firm owns the land it occupies; the firm uses its own transportation equipment; the firm owns a generator; the firm uses e-mail to communicate with clients; the firm uses a website to communicate with clients; and the firm has an electrical connection. The five continuous variables are the percentage of investment that is financed internally; expenditure on raw materials as a fraction of sales; expenditure on energy as a fraction of sales; expenditure on machines as a fraction of sales; and capacity utilization. All regressions control for income per capita and include eight industry dummies.

Many—but not all—of the correlations in table 18 are consistent with sorting on managers' ability. Firms with more-educated managers are more likely to be registered, to sell mainly to large firms, to use their own transportation equipment, to own a generator, to communicate with clients through e-mail, to have a webpage, and to have an electrical connection. Along the same lines, managers who attended college are more likely to work for firms that own land and buildings. Firms with more-educated managers also use more raw materials and operate with higher capacity utilization. The economic significance of these coefficients is large. The probability of being registered increases by 41 percentage points if the top manager has some college education rather than only some primary school education. Having a top manager with some college education also has large effects on the probability of having a generator (+36.7 percentage points), the probability of using e-mail (+48.0 percentage points), the probability of having a webpage (+25.7 percentage points), and the probability of having an electrical connection (+28.3 percentage points). In contrast, the effect is moderate on the probability that the firm's main buyers are large firms (+3.2 percentage points), the probability of owning a building (+11.2 percentage points), the probability of owning land (+9.8 percentage points), and the probability of owning transportation equipment (+11.8 percentage points). Similarly, having a top manager with some college education increases expenditure on raw materials by a modest 8.7 percentage points (the standard deviation is 23.3 percent) and capacity utilization by 5.5 percentage points (the standard deviation is 21.4 percent).

The evidence on external finance is mixed. On the one hand, firms with more-educated managers rely more on external finance (bottom panel of table 18). On the other hand, the education of managers does not significantly affect the probability that the firm has ever had a loan (top panel). The evidence on investment in machines is also weak: in that regression the only significant coefficient is the one for vocational schooling. Nor is there evidence that expenditure on energy increases with managers' education. Only one regression has statistically significant coefficients with the "wrong" sign: the likelihood that the firm operates in the house of the owner is higher when managers have attended secondary or vocational school rather than primary school only.

These results suggest an explanation for the puzzlingly low productivity of unregistered firms. The productivity gap between registered firms and the control group disappears once we take into account crude proxies for physical and human capital and control for size. Of course, size is an endogenous variable. These results on manager selection are broadly consistent with the view that part of the reason that unregistered firms are small is that they are run by managers of low ability.[52] These managers do not find it worthwhile to pay the cost of running a formal firm. Unregistered firms are small because they are run by less able managers and, as such, face a high cost of capital, have few opportunities to advertise their products, and are of insufficient scale to own critical assets such as generators and computers.

Obstacles to Doing Business

As a final step, we present information on obstacles to doing business as reported by respondents in the Informal, Micro, and Enterprise Surveys. All obstacles are reported on a 0-to-4 scale for their perceived significance, with 0 representing "no obstacle," 1 "minor obstacle," 2 "moderate obstacle," 3 "major obstacle," and 4 "very severe obstacle." In table 19 we compare average responses about various obstacles for Informal Survey firms (top panel) and their Enterprise Survey counterparts, as well as for Micro Survey firms and their control group (bottom panel).

Starting with the Informal Survey, the most striking finding is the similarity in many responses between the registered Informal Survey firms and the Enterprise Survey firms. Both groups consider tax rates and tax administration their most significant problems. Registered Informal Survey firms,

52. Rauch (1991).

Table 19. Obstacles to Doing Business in the Informal and Micro Survey Samples

Index, 4 = very severe obstacle

	Informal Survey sample			Enterprise Survey control group				Difference[b]			
Obstacle[a]	*Unregistered*	*Registered*	*All*	*Small*	*Medium*	*Big*	*All*	*Enterprise v. informal*	*Registered v. unregistered*	*Small v. unregistered*	*Big v. small*
Access to or availability of markets	2.05	2.38	2.07	. . .	. . .	. . .	. . .	. . .	0.33	. . .	. . .
Tax rates	1.59	2.14	1.65	2.13	2.33	2.50	2.33	0.68**	0.55	0.54	0.37
Tax administration	1.40	2.05	1.46	1.79	2.14	2.37	2.05	0.59**	0.65*	0.39	0.58**
Cost of financing	2.19	2.37	2.25	1.99	2.25	2.30	2.20	–0.05	0.17	–0.20	0.31
Corruption	1.53	1.93	1.59	2.06	2.28	2.27	2.17	0.57**	0.40	0.53	0.21
Macroeconomic instability[c]	1.75	1.98	1.80	1.89	2.05	2.13	1.95	0.15	0.23	0.14	0.23
Electricity supply	1.74	1.70	1.74	1.85	1.94	2.12	1.92	0.18	–0.04	0.11	0.27
Anticompetitive or unfair practices by other businesses	1.74	2.16	1.78	1.74	1.98	2.11	1.94	0.16	0.42*	0.00	0.37
Economic policy uncertainty	1.72	1.96	1.75	2.08	2.20	2.10	2.07	0.33	0.24	0.36	0.02
Customs and trade regulations	1.00	1.51	1.06	1.24	1.61	2.09	1.53	0.46**	0.51	0.25	0.85***
Access to financing	2.29	2.46	2.32	1.95	1.92	1.83	1.83	–0.49**	0.17	–0.33	–0.12
Legal system, conflict resolution	1.04	1.33	1.07	1.10	1.47	1.78	1.24	0.17	0.29	0.06	0.67**
Labor regulations	0.84	1.20	0.91	0.99	1.27	1.75	1.17	0.26	0.36	0.15	0.76***
Crime, theft, and disorder	1.48	1.61	1.49	1.59	1.76	1.71	1.57	0.07	0.12	0.11	0.12
Skills and education of available workers	1.15	1.46	1.23	1.15	1.44	1.67	1.30	0.07	0.31	–0.01	0.52***
Transportation[d]	1.37	1.47	1.36	1.16	1.38	1.57	1.33	–0.04	0.11	–0.20	0.41**
Procedures to register firms, formalities, patents, etc.	1.26	1.64	1.49	1.20	1.21	1.42	1.12	–0.37	0.37	–0.06	0.23
Telephone, fax, e-mail	1.00	0.84	0.99	0.85	0.94	1.32	0.99	0.00	–0.16	–0.15	0.47**
Access to land	1.46	1.70	1.48	0.98	1.05	1.27	0.95	–0.53**	0.24	–0.47*	0.28
Postal services	0.07	0.00	0.06	. . .	. . .	. . .	. . .	. . .	–0.07	. . .	. . .

Obstacle[a]	*Micro Survey sample*			*Enterprise Survey control group*				*Difference*			
	Unregistered	*Registered*	*All*	*Small*	*Medium*	*Big*	*All*	*Enterprise v. micro*	*Registered v. unregistered*	*Small v. unregistered*	*Big v. small*
Electricity supply	1.96	1.99	1.98	2.24	2.43	2.69	2.30	0.32	0.03	0.27	0.45
Tax rates	1.35	1.69	1.59	1.75	1.90	1.84	1.78	0.19	0.34	0.40*	0.09
Access to financing	2.40	2.33	2.37	2.02	1.91	1.73	1.98	–0.39**	–0.06	–0.37	–0.29
Skills and education of available workers	0.51	0.63	0.60	0.92	1.17	1.64	1.02	0.41***	0.12	0.41***	0.72***
Macroeconomic instability[c]	1.38	1.67	1.63	1.47	1.51	1.53	1.50	–0.14	0.28	0.09	0.06
Tax administration	0.94	1.20	1.13	1.23	1.41	1.48	1.28	0.15	0.26	0.30*	0.25
Anticompetitive or unfair practices by other businesses	1.54	1.43	1.47	1.40	1.46	1.48	1.41	–0.06	–0.12	–0.14	0.08
Transportation[d]	1.34	1.30	1.31	1.23	1.25	1.40	1.25	–0.06	–0.04	–0.11	0.18
Corruption	1.09	1.06	1.07	1.20	1.46	1.37	1.27	0.20	–0.02	0.11	0.17
Crime, theft, and disorder	1.18	1.12	1.18	1.18	1.19	1.32	1.20	0.02	–0.06	0.01	0.14
Customs and trade regulations	0.55	0.82	0.76	0.79	1.20	1.22	0.91	0.15	0.27*	0.24*	0.43***
Cost of financing	. . .	. . .	. . .	0.99	1.02	1.12	1.01	. . .	. . .	. . .	0.14
Procedures to register firms, formalities, patents, etc.	1.22	1.11	1.10	1.00	1.08	1.00	1.01	–0.09	–0.12	–0.23	0.01
Labor regulations	0.34	0.33	0.34	0.49	0.74	0.99	0.57	0.24**	–0.01	0.15*	0.50***
Legal system, conflict resolution	0.38	0.44	0.43	0.55	0.68	0.98	0.60	0.17	0.07	0.17	0.43***
Economic policy uncertainty	0.88	0.92	0.96	1.02	1.11	0.96	1.05	0.08	0.04	0.14	–0.05
Access to land	1.44	1.14	1.22	1.06	0.90	0.89	1.02	–0.20*	–0.29	–0.38**	–0.17
Telephone, fax, e-mail	0.56	0.71	0.67	0.70	0.81	0.86	0.74	0.08	0.15	0.14	0.16

Sources: World Bank Informal, Micro, and Enterprise Surveys; authors' calculations.

a. All obstacles are reported on a 0-to-4 scale, with 0 indicating "no obstacle," 1 "minor obstacle," 2 "moderate obstacle," 3 "major obstacle," and 4 "very severe obstacle."

b. Asterisks indicate statistically significantly different from zero at the *10 percent, **5 percent, and ***1 percent level.

c. High inflation, exchange rate instability, etc.

d. Poor road quality, road blockages, difficulty finding ways to transport goods, etc.

like Enterprise Survey firms, regard the cost of financing and access to financing as major obstacles as well. Neither the Informal Survey firms nor the Enterprise Survey firms consider access to land, registration procedures, crime, low workforce skills, labor regulations (with the exception of big firms), or the legal system to be major obstacles to doing business (again with the exception of big firms).

There are some significant differences as well. Informal Survey firms consider access to or availability of markets to be a huge problem. The unregistered Informal Survey firms do not consider taxes or tax administration to be a huge problem, in obvious contrast to the registered firms. Corruption is a smaller problem for the unregistered firms than for the registered ones. Indeed, both tax administration and corruption are perceived as more serious obstacles by big firms than by small ones (but only differences in the perception of tax administration as an obstacle are statistically significant).

We can also use the information on obstacles to shed light on the parasite theory of the informal economy. Unfortunately, the question asked in the surveys is not ideal. Respondents assess on a 0-to-4 scale whether "anticompetitive and informal practices" are an obstacle to their business. Of course, anticompetitive practices can come not only from the informal firms, but also from formal firms with political or other connections. Nevertheless, several points emerge from these data. First, contrary to the parasite view, "anticompetitive and informal" practices are not among the key obstacles perceived by managers of firms in either the Informal Survey firms (the average score is 1.78) or their Enterprise Survey control group (1.94).[53] Second, the answer is only slightly higher for the Enterprise Survey firms than for the Informal Survey firms, which is not consistent with the view that the informal firms undercut the formal ones. Third, one might have guessed that it is the small registered firms in the Enterprise Survey that would be most severely affected by the informal firms. However, these firms perceive anticompetitive and informal practices to be a smaller problem, on average, than do the larger firms. None of this evidence is supportive of the parasite theory. The patterns in the Micro Survey are similar to those in the Informal Survey (except that some of the questions differ). Access to financing and electricity emerge as by far the greatest

53. Among big firms, concern over "anticompetitive or informal practices" ranks after concerns over tax rates, tax administration, cost of financing, corruption, macroeconomic instability, and electricity. On the other hand, it ranks ahead of, among other things, concerns over economic policy uncertainty, customs and trade regulations, access to financing, and crime, theft, and disorder.

obstacles to Micro Survey firms. These are also huge obstacles for their counterpart Enterprise Survey firms, along with tax rates. Finally, anti-competitive and informal practices are not among the top obstacles for firms in the Micro Survey.

A final piece of evidence comes from the Informal Survey, which only in Cape Verde asked respondents about the benefits of and obstacles to registering. The findings are summarized in table 20. The main benefits of registering are improved access to markets, to services, and to financing—findings broadly consistent with the previous findings about the obstacles to doing business faced by informal firms. Better property rights and lower need to pay bribes are not nearly as important. On the cost side, the main obstacles to registration are taxes and the cost of registering (along with

Table 20. Advantages and Obstacles to Registering in Cape Verde

Advantage or obstacle	*Percent of firms rating the advantage as very important or the obstacle as either major or extremely important*[a]
Advantages	
Better access to markets	44
Better access to services	39
Better access to financing	39
Better access to raw materials	34
Easier to bargain with formal enterprises	25
Easier to reduce theft by employees or others	23
Better access to government subsidies	20
More solid legal basis for property rights regarding real estate	20
Less turnover of employees or better product market competition	18
Less need to pay bribes	15
Obstacles	
Financial burden of taxes applicable to registered firms	43
Cost of registering	38
Difficulties in obtaining information about how to register	36
Minimum capital legally required to register	32
Administrative burden of complying with tax laws	32
Time necessary to register	19
Labor regulations applicable to registered firms	19
Other administrative burdens	18

Sources: World Bank Informal Survey for Cape Verde; authors' calculations.

a. Advantages are rated on a scale from 1 ("minor advantage") to 4 ("very important"). Obstacles are rated on a 0-to-4 scale, with 0 indicating "unimportant," 1 "minor obstacle," 2 "moderate obstacle," 3 "major obstacle," and 4 "extremely important."

the difficulty of obtaining information about how to register). Labor regulation and tax compliance are seen as much less important. Here as well, the picture that emerges is one in which the formal firms have better access to markets, services, and finance, and hence can be much more productive, but need to pay taxes. Presumably, for the Cape Verde firms in the Informal Survey, the tax price is too high to justify registration.

The evidence on obstacles further supports the dual theory and seems rather inconsistent with the parasite theory. Between their extreme inefficiency and their operation in very different markets, informal firms do not appear to pose much of a threat to formal firms, at least as perceived by the latter. Informal firms clearly recognize the many benefits of being official, including access to markets and to finance (although it is far from clear that they would gain the latter even if they registered). They do not seem to think that regulation and the cost of registration are the biggest obstacles to registration. On the other hand, they do see taxes as a huge problem. In this respect the results are consistent with the dual theory, as well as with the findings reported in the first section and by Djankov and coauthors.[54]

Conclusion

Our most basic finding is that high productivity comes from formal firms, and in particular from large formal firms. Productivity is much higher in small formal firms than in informal firms, and it rises rapidly with the size of formal firms. To the extent that productivity growth is central to economic development, the formation and growth of formal firms are necessary for economic growth.[55]

Formal firms appear to be very different animals from informal firms, and this fact accounts for their sharply superior productivity. Perhaps most important, they are run by much better educated managers. As a consequence, besides being larger, they tend to use more capital, have different customers, and market their products and use external finance to a greater extent than do informal firms. There is no evidence that informal firms tend to become formal as they grow. Rather, virtually none of the formal firms in our sample had ever been informal. Consistent with this result, Miriam Bruhn shows that business registration reform had a large effect on new registrations in Mexico, but that the new official entrants were former

54. Djankov and others (2008b).
55. See also Lewis (2004); Banerjee and Duflo (2005).

wage earners rather than informal entrepreneurs.[56] Similarly, Mondragón-Vélez and Peña-Parga find surprisingly little transition between self-employment and business ownership in Colombia.[57] It does not appear from the available evidence that informal firms would sharply increase their productivity if only they registered.

This interpretation raises the crucial question of what happens to informal firms as the economy develops. After all, the most basic fact about the informal economy is that its role diminishes sharply as incomes grow. How does this happen? Do informal firms register or do they die? We do not have a definitive answer to this question, but the evidence we have points in the direction of death rather than registration. It is still possible, of course, that a minority of informal firms, and especially the most productive ones, end up joining the formal economy, perhaps by supplying formal firms. But there is no evidence, at least in our data, that this is the typical story. The vast majority of informal firms appear to begin and end their lives as unproductive informal firms.

Informal firms nonetheless play a crucial role in developing economies, where they represent perhaps 30 to 40 percent of all economic activity and provide a livelihood to billions of poor people. Because these firms are so inefficient, taxing them or forcing them to comply with government regulations would likely put most of them out of business, with dire consequences for their employees and proprietors. If anything, strategies that keep these firms afloat and allow them to become more productive, such as microfinance, are probably desirable from the viewpoint of poverty alleviation. But these are not growth strategies: turning these unofficial firms into official ones is unlikely to generate substantial improvements in productivity.

Growth strategies, rather, need to focus on formal firms, especially the larger ones. Reducing the costs of formality, such as registration costs, is surely a good idea, but this is not the whole story. Likewise, some of the almost-standard proposals for development, such as improving land rights, the legal environment, and even the human capital of employees appear to address relatively minor factors, at least from the viewpoint of official entrepreneurs. The main obstacles to the operations of formal firms, according to our data, are three: taxation, uncertain supply of electricity, and lack of adequate access to finance.

To us, the most striking finding is the sharply higher education of managers of official than of unofficial firms, with no corresponding difference

56. Bruhn (2008).

57. Mondragón-Vélez and Peña-Parga (2008).

in the human capital of the employees. This suggests that educational policies, particularly those emphasizing secondary education, might be conducive to the formation of entrepreneurial talent that can run formal firms. We do not mean to suggest that formal education is either a necessary or a sufficient condition for entrepreneurial skills. But the data seem to indicate quite clearly that some aspects of management (for example, marketing and finance) require education. One can also think of other sources of human capital, such as immigration, as supplying the required entrepreneurial talent.

There is growing evidence that corporate income taxation deters investment and formal entrepreneurship. Using a new dataset of corporate income taxes in a large number of countries, Djankov and coauthors find strong evidence that these taxes reduce investment, foreign direct investment, and entrepreneurial activity.[58] Our evidence similarly shows that official firms perceive taxation as the top obstacle to doing business. To the extent that the formation and growth of official firms are the principal engines of development, this perception must be taken seriously. Needless to say, one needs to also think about alternative sources of public finance, as well as the size of government, in developing countries to determine whether corporate income tax cuts are warranted. But the evidence points to a potentially serious problem.

The evidence also suggests that official firms, just like unofficial ones, perceive lack of access to finance to be a serious obstacle to doing business. Recent research has pointed to a broad range of legal and regulatory reforms that can underpin the development of financial markets; in general these reforms seek to improve the legal rights of creditors and (in the case of very large firms) shareholders.[59] Unlike with tax cuts, there seem to be no compelling counterarguments to improving the laws and institutions that support financial markets.

Finally, the evidence indicates that problems with electricity supply, including disruptions, afflict unofficial as well as smaller official firms. This contrasts with an interesting lack of concern on the part of respondents with other limitations of infrastructure, such as transport, telephone, and mail. Most large firms have their own generators, whereas smaller official firms and unofficial firms do not and hence are more vulnerable.

The overall picture of economic development that emerges from this analysis is in many ways similar to the traditional pre-growth theory devel-

58. Djankov and others (2008b).

59. See La Porta, Lopez-de-Silanes, and Shleifer (2008) for a survey.

opment economics, although it is related to the modern reformulations of economic growth through the lens of development economics.[60] The recipe for productivity growth is the formation of official firms—the larger and the more productive, the better. Their formation must perhaps be promoted through tax, human capital, infrastructure, and capital markets policies, very much along the lines of traditional dual economy theories. From the perspective of economic growth, one should not expect much from the unofficial economy, with its millions of entrepreneurs, except to hope that it disappears over time. This "Wal-Mart" theory of economic development receives quite a bit of support from firm-level data.

ACKNOWLEDGMENTS We are grateful to Nicholas Coleman for excellent research assistance, to Jorge Rodriguez Mesa for help with the World Bank surveys, and to Charles Jones, Peter Klenow, James Rauch, Jeremy Stein, and William Nordhaus for helpful comments. This research was supported by the Kauffman Foundation.

60. Banerjee and Duflo (2005).

APPENDIX

Table A1. Correlations among the Main Variables[a]

Correlation coefficients

Variable	Informal share of GDP from WEF survey	Tax evasion[b]	Self-employed as share of labor force	Informal share of GDP estimated from: Electricity consumption	Informal share of GDP estimated from: Multiple indicators	Registered firms per 1,000 population	Procedures necessary to start a business	Taxes as percent of profits	Hours per year needed to comply with taxes	Management time dealing with regulations
Tax evasion[b]	0.25**									
Self-employed as share of labor force	0.70***	0.25**								
Informal share of GDP, from electricity	0.61***	0.35**	0.61***							
Informal share of GDP, multiple indicators	0.70***	0.17	0.47***	0.71***						
Registered firms per 1,000 population	−0.43***	−0.16	−0.46***	−0.21	−0.38***					
Procedures necessary to start a business	0.48***	0.32***	0.37***	0.30**	0.37***	−0.50***				
Taxes as percent of profits	0.16*	0.17*	−0.04	−0.13	0.16*	−0.19*	0.15*			
Hours per year needed to comply with taxes	0.50***	−0.02	0.34***	0.42***	0.37***	−0.42***	0.38***	0.22***		
Management time dealing with regulations	0.43***	0.14	0.26**	0.24	0.20*	−0.06	0.15	0.00	0.20*	
Index of difficulty of hiring a new worker	0.32***	0.05	0.10	0.13	0.34***	−0.10	0.26***	0.11	0.26***	0.24**
Index of difficulty of firing a worker	0.23**	0.01	0.14	0.08	0.20**	−0.25**	0.27***	0.20**	0.32***	0.28***
Nonwage costs as percent of salary	−0.10	−0.16	−0.26***	−0.20	−0.08	0.05	−0.01	0.18**	0.27***	0.02
Steps required to collect on a bounced check	0.36***	0.09	0.25**	0.30**	0.39***	−0.18	0.45***	0.27***	0.36***	0.46***
Efficiency of bankruptcy procedure	−0.64***	−0.32**	−0.59***	−0.46***	−0.57***	0.35***	−0.54***	−0.15	−0.37***	−0.35***

Log of paved roads per km²	−0.28***	−0.11	−0.24***	−0.22*	−0.20**	0.29***	−0.18**	−0.09	−0.33***	−0.03
Corruption index	−0.84***	−0.32***	−0.67***	−0.58***	−0.71***	0.48***	−0.57***	−0.23***	−0.43***	−0.26*
Rule of law index	−0.85***	−0.29***	−0.68***	−0.58***	−0.72***	0.49***	−0.59***	−0.26***	−0.44***	−0.29***
Private credit as percent of GDP	−0.67***	−0.28***	−0.49***	−0.38***	−0.60***	0.43***	−0.43***	−0.18*	−0.31***	−0.25*
Market capitalization as percent of GDP	−0.54***	−0.16	−0.39***	−0.37***	−0.51***	0.21*	−0.38***	−0.09	−0.36***	−0.19
Log of GDP per capita	−0.77***	−0.34***	−0.77***	−0.66***	−0.66***	0.52***	−0.45***	−0.27***	−0.30***	−0.13

Variable	*Index of difficulty of hiring a new worker*	*Index of difficulty of firing a worker*	*Nonwage costs as percent of salary*	*Steps required to collect on a bounced check*	*Efficiency of bankruptcy procedure*	*Log of paved roads per km²*	*Corruption index*	*Rule of law index*	*Private credit as percent of GDP*	*Market capitalization as percent of GDP*
Index of difficulty of firing a worker	0.36***									
Nonwage costs as percent of salary	0.21***	0.22***								
Steps required to collect on a bounced check	0.47***	0.38***	0.21*							
Efficiency of bankruptcy procedure	−0.37***	−0.15	−0.10	−0.56***						
Log of paved roads per km²	−0.12	−0.15*	−0.13	−0.26*	0.29***					
Corruption index	−0.23***	−0.21***	0.08	−0.37***	0.76***	0.29***				
Rule of law index	−0.25***	−0.25***	0.08	−0.39***	0.76***	0.31***	0.96***			
Private credit as percent of GDP	−0.26***	−0.21***	−0.03	−0.39***	0.61***	0.27***	0.74***	0.75***		
Market capitalization as percent of GDP	−0.24*	−0.17*	−0.08	−0.51***	0.52***	0.46***	0.62***	0.59***	0.71***	
Log of GDP per capita	−0.25***	−0.22***	0.21***	−0.22**	0.73***	0.27***	0.83***	0.84***	0.70***	0.52***

Source: Authors' calculations.

a. Asterisks indicate statistically significantly different from zero at the *10 percent, **5 percent, and ***1 percent level.

b. Calculated as 1 minus the share of sales reported for tax purposes.

References

Almeida, Rita, and Pedro Manuel Carneiro. 2006. "Enforcement of Regulation, Informal Labour, Firm Size and Firm Performance." Discussion Paper 5976. London: Centre for Economic Policy Research (December).

Amaral, Pedro, and Erwan Quintin. 2006. "A Competitive Model of the Informal Sector." *Journal of Monetary Economics* 53, no. 7: 1541–53.

Baily, Martin, Diana Farrell, and Jaana Remes. 2005. "Domestic Services: The Hidden Key to Growth." Washington: McKinsey Global Institute.

Banerjee, Abhijit, and Esther Duflo. 2005. "Growth Theory through the Lens of Development Economics." In *Handbook of Economic Growth,* vol. 1A, edited by Steve Durlauf and Philippe Aghion. Amsterdam: Elsevier Science.

———. 2007. "The Economic Lives of the Poor." *Journal of Economic Perspectives* 21, no. 1: 141–67.

Bennett, John, and Saul Estrin. 2007. "Informality as a Stepping Stone: Entrepreneurial Entry in a Developing Economy." Discussion Paper 2950. Bonn: Institute for the Study of Labor (July).

Bernard, Andrew, Jonathan Eaton, J. Bradford Jensen, and Samuel Kortum. 2003. "Plants and Productivity in International Trade." *American Economic Review* 93, no. 4: 1268–90.

Botero, Juan, Simeon Djankov, Rafael La Porta, Florencio Lopez-de-Silanes, and Andrei Shleifer. 2004. "The Regulation of Labor." *Quarterly Journal of Economics* 119, no. 4: 1339–82.

Bruhn, Miriam. 2008. "License to Sell: The Effect of Business Registration Reform on Entrepreneurial Activity in Mexico." Policy Research Working Paper 4538. Washington: World Bank.

Dabla-Norris, Era, Mark Gradstein, and Gabriela Inchauste. 2008. "What Causes Firms to Hide Output? The Determinants of Informality." *Journal of Development Economics* 85, no. 1: 1–27.

De Mel, Suresh, David J. McKenzie, and Christopher Woodruff. 2007. "Measuring Microenterprise Profits: Don't Ask How the Sausage Is Made." Policy Research Working Paper 4229. Washington: World Bank.

De Paula, Áureo, and José Scheinkman. 2008. "The Informal Sector." Working Paper 08-018. Philadelphia: Penn Institute for Economic Research (May).

De Soto, Hernando. 1989. *The Other Path: The Invisible Revolution in the Third World.* New York: Harper and Row.

———. 2000. *The Mystery of Capital: Why Capitalism Triumphs in the West and Fails Everywhere Else.* New York: Basic Books.

Djankov, Simeon, Rafael La Porta, Florencio Lopez-de-Silanes, and Andrei Shleifer. 2002. "The Regulation of Entry." *Quarterly Journal of Economics* 117, no. 1: 1–37.

———. 2003. "Courts." *Quarterly Journal of Economics* 118, no. 2: 453–517.

Djankov, Simeon, Oliver Hart, Caralee McLiesh, and Andrei Shleifer. 2008a. "Debt Enforcement around the World." *Journal of Political Economy* 116, no. 6: 1105–49.

Djankov, Simeon, Tim Ganser, Caralee McLiesh, Rita Ramalho, and Andrei Shleifer. 2008b. "The Effect of Corporate Taxes on Investment and Entrepreneurship." Working Paper 13756. Cambridge, Mass.: National Bureau of Economic Research (January).

Ernste, Dominik, and Friedrich Schneider. 1998. "Increasing Shadow Economies All Over the World—Fiction or Reality." Discussion Paper 26. Bonn: Institute for the Study of Labor (December).

Fajnzylber, P., W. F. Maloney, and G. V. Montes Rojas. 2006. "Does Formality Improve Microfirm Performance? Quasi-experimental Evidence from the Brazilian SIMPLES Program." World Bank, Washington.

Farrell, Diana. 2004. "The Hidden Dangers of the Informal Economy." *McKinsey Quarterly* 2004, no. 3: 26–37.

Foster, Lucia, John Haltiwanger, and Chad Syverson. 2008. "Reallocation, Firm Turnover, and Efficiency: Selection on Productivity or Profitability?" *American Economic Review* 98, no. 1: 394–425.

Friedman, Eric, Simon Johnson, Daniel Kaufmann, and Pablo Zoido-Lobaton. 2001. "Dodging the Grabbing Hand: The Determinants of Unofficial Activity in 69 Countries." *Journal of Public Economics* 76, no. 3: 459–93.

Harris, John, and Michael Todaro. 1970. "Migration, Unemployment and Development: A Two-Sector Analysis." *American Economic Review* 60, no. 1: 126–42.

Hsieh, Chang-Tai, and Peter Klenow. 2007. "Misallocation and Manufacturing TFP in China and India." Working Paper W13290. Cambridge, Mass.: National Bureau of Economic Research.

International Labour Office. 2007. *Key Indicators of the Labour Market,* 5th ed. CD-ROM version. Geneva.

Johnson, Simon, Daniel Kaufmann, and Andrei Shleifer. 1997. "The Unofficial Economy in Transition." *BPEA,* no. 2: 159–221.

Katayama, Hajime, Shihua Lu, and James Tybout. 2006. "Firm-level Productivity Studies: Illusions and a Solution." Penn State University.

Kaufmann, Daniel, Aart Kraay, and Massimo Mastruzzi. 2005. "Governance Matters IV: Governance Indicators for 1996–2004." Policy Research Working Paper 3630. Washington: World Bank (May).

Klette, Tor Jakob, and Zvi Griliches. 1996. "The Inconsistency of Common Scale Estimators When Output Prices Are Unobserved and Endogenous." *Journal of Applied Econometrics* 11, no. 4: 343–61.

La Porta, Rafael, Florencio Lopez-de-Silanes, and Andrei Shleifer. 2008. "The Economic Consequences of Legal Origins." *Journal of Economic Literature* 46, no. 2: 285–332.

Lewis, William. 2004. *The Power of Productivity: Wealth, Poverty, and the Threat to Global Stability.* University of Chicago Press.

Loayza, Norman. 1996. "The Economics of the Informal Sector: A Simple Model and Some Empirical Evidence from Latin America." *Carnegie-Rochester Conference Series on Public Policy* 45, no. 1: 129–62.

Loayza, Norman, and Jamele Rigolini. 2006. "Informality Trends and Cycles." Policy Research Working Paper 4078. Washington: World Bank (December).

Lucas, Jr., Robert E. 1978. "On the Size Distribution of Business Firms." *Bell Journal of Economics* 9, no. 2: 508–23.

Mondragón-Vélez, Camilo, and Ximena Peña-Parga. 2008. "Business Ownership and Self-employment in Developing Economies: The Colombian Case." Documentos CEDE. Universidad de los Andes.

Monteiro, Joana, and Juliano Assunção. 2006. "Outgrowing the Shadows: Estimating the Impact of Bureaucratic Simplification and Tax Cuts on Informality and Investment." Department of Economics, Pontifica Universidade Católica, Rio de Janeiro.

Murphy, Kevin, Andrei Shleifer, and Robert Vishny. 1989. "Industrialization and the Big Push." *Journal of Political Economy* 97, no. 5: 1003–26.

Rauch, James. 1991. "Modeling the Informal Sector Formally." *Journal of Development Economics* 35, no. 1: 33–47.

Rosenstein-Rodan, Paul. 1943. "Problems of Industrialization of Eastern and South-Eastern Europe." *Economic Journal* 53, no. 210/211: 202–11.

Rostow, Walt. 1960. *Stages of Economic Growth: A Non-Communist Manifesto.* Cambridge University Press.

Russo, Francesco. 2008. "The Cost of the Legal System and the Hidden Economy." Boston University.

Schneider, Friedrich. 2007. "Shadow Economies and Corruption All Over the World: New Estimates for 145 Countries." *Economics: The Open-Access, Open-Assessment E-Journal* 1 (2007–09). www.economics-ejournal.org/economics/journalarticles/2007–9.

Tokman, Victor. 1992. *Beyond Regulation: The Informal Economy in Latin America.* Boulder, Colo.: Lynne Rienner.

United Nations. 2008. "Making the Law Work for Everyone." Report of the Commission on Legal Empowerment of the Poor, vol. 1. New York.

World Bank. 2007. *Doing Business 2008.* Washington: World Bank.

World Economic Forum. 2007. *Global Competitiveness Report 2006–2007.* Geneva.

Comments and Discussion

COMMENT BY

CHARLES I. JONES This very nice paper is filled with interesting facts about firms in developing countries: about the size of the informal economy (around half that of the formal sector, on average); about the extent of theft among both small and large firms (less than 5 percent of sales); and about the number of days per year that firms face power outages (around 50, even for large firms). The tour through the extensive firm-level surveys across many countries is itself a valuable contribution. Indeed, but for the expert guidance provided by the authors, it would be easy to get lost along the way.

Rafael La Porta and Andrei Shleifer helpfully frame their discussion in terms of three "views" of the informal economy. The romantic view of Hernando de Soto and others suggests that the informal sector is an engine of growth just waiting to be released by giving informal firms property rights.[1] The parasitic view, associated with the McKinsey Global Institute,[2] sees the informal sector as a collection of firms that remain small (and unproductive) in order to avoid taxes and regulations, which allows them to inefficiently take away market share from more-productive formal firms. Finally, the dual economy view, associated with John Harris and Michael Todaro,[3] among others, suggests that informal firms are not so much a threat to formal firms as a social safety net that provides a livelihood for millions of very poor, uneducated people. In this view the informal economy is not so much a drag on development as it is a way station where people can

1. Hernando de Soto, *The Other Path: The Invisible Revolution in the Third World* (New York: Harper and Row, 1989).

2. For example, Martin Baily, Diana Farrell, and Jaana Remes, "Domestic Services: The Hidden Key to Growth" (Washington: McKinsey Global Institute, 2005).

3. John Harris and Michael Todaro, "Migration, Unemployment and Development: A Two-Sector Analysis," *American Economic Review* 60, no. 1 (1970): 126–42.

wait until development leads to the establishment of additional productive formal firms that can provide them with jobs.

After studying a wide range of correlations, facts, and survey responses in extensive firm-level surveys, La Porta and Shleifer conclude that the evidence is most consistent with the dual economy view. The main evidence against the romantic view is that informal firms look very different from formal ones—for example, the managers of informal firms are much less well educated—and the authors see very little evidence that growth occurs by informal firms eventually becoming large, productive formal establishments. The main evidence they offer against the parasitic view is that formal firms do not view competition from informal firms as a serious problem; they are much more concerned with access to markets, access to finance, and taxes.

A fact that emerges quite clearly from the data is that the informal sector is very large in the poorest economies and surely provides a kind of social safety net for many workers. By avoiding taxes and regulations, this sector can employ people who are not sufficiently productive to work in the formal sector. Given that this sector can encompass as much as half of the labor force, this is a substantial safety net. A question that naturally follows is whether or not this is the most effective way of providing it. What is the cost?

The firm-level surveys and a recent paper by Chang-Tai Hsieh and Peter Klenow suggest one way to make progress on this question.[4] Because this approach also provides some useful insights into the meaning of "value added per worker," I will outline a simple story along these lines in what follows.

WHAT DOES VALUE ADDED PER WORKER REALLY MEASURE? A recent and growing literature emphasizes the need for caution in interpreting measures of value added per worker, or "labor productivity." In particular, one seldom has access to firm-specific price deflators, so that measures of labor productivity actually measure *revenue per worker* rather than a real quantity—that is, they confound price and quantity.[5] La Porta and Shleifer recognize

4. Chang-Tai Hsieh and Peter Klenow, "Misallocation and Manufacturing TFP in China and India," Working Paper 13290 (Cambridge, Mass.: National Bureau of Economic Research, 2007).

5. Prominent examples from this literature include the following: Tor Jakob Klette and Zvi Griliches, "The Inconsistency of Common Scale Estimators When Output Prices Are Unobserved and Endogenous," *Journal of Applied Econometrics* 11, no. 4 (1996): 343–61; Andrew Bernard and others, "Plants and Productivity in International Trade," *American Economic Review* 93, no. 4 (2003): 1268–90; Hajime Katayama, Shihua Lu, and James Tybout, "Firm-Level Productivity Studies: Illusions and a Solution" (Penn State University, 2006); Lucia Foster, John Haltiwanger, and Chad Syverson, "Reallocation, Firm Turnover, and Efficiency: Selection on Productivity or Profitability?" *American Economic Review* 98, no. 1 (2008): 394–425; and Hsieh and Klenow, "Misallocation and Manufacturing TFP in China and India."

this in the published version of their paper and do a good job of incorporating some of the implications. In particular, they employ an insight from Hsieh and Klenow that says that if one knows the shape of the demand curve, one can infer price and quantity from revenue.

It is possible, however, to go even further. In particular, although "revenue labor productivity" is not a quantity measure, it contains very useful information about the nature of the distortions that affect firms. One can use these revenue measures to back out those distortions and consider the hypothetical question of how much higher output would be in their absence. To see how this works, consider the following benchmark model, which is a simplified version of the framework in Hsieh and Klenow, augmented to include a Harris-Todaro dual economy element.

THE MODEL: WAL-MART VERSUS A TRINKET SHOP. Suppose there are two highly substitutable goods in the economy: the output of a very productive, Wal-Mart-like store, y, and the output of a small and less productive informal trinket shop, x. Each good is produced using only labor. The total quantity of labor, $\bar{L}$, is fixed and can be either used for production or left unemployed (u is the endogenous fraction unemployed).

This setup is summarized in the following equations:

Utility	$U(x,y) = (\alpha x^{\rho} + \beta y^{\rho})^{1/\rho}$
Formal production	$y = A_y L_y$
Informal production	$x = A_x L_x$
Resource constraint	$L_x + L_y = (1-u)\bar{L}.$

Assume that resources are allocated according to perfect competition, subject to several distortions. First, each sector faces a firm-specific sales tax, at rates τ_x and τ_y, respectively. (One can think of the informal sector facing a tax rate of $\tau_x = 0$ as a special case.) Second, a combination of minimum wage laws and regulations leads to a wedge between the wage in the formal sector and that in the informal sector, such that the formal sector wage is $1 + \mu$ times the informal sector wage. This wage differential leads to queueing for the formal jobs, generating unemployment as in the Harris-Todaro model.

Profit maximization by the two kinds of firms ensures that labor is hired until the after-tax marginal revenue product of labor equals the wage:

$$p_y(1-\tau_y)A_y = w_y = w_x(1+\mu) \tag{1}$$

$$p_x(1-\tau_x)A_x = w_x. \tag{2}$$

On the household side, utility maximization delivers the following conditions for demand and the allocation of labor:

$$\frac{U_y}{U_x} = \frac{p_y}{p_x} \tag{3}$$

$$w_x = w_y(1-u) \Rightarrow u^* = \frac{\mu}{1+\mu}. \tag{4}$$

When these equations are combined, the allocation of labor to the formal and informal sectors satisfies

$$\frac{L_x^*}{L_y^*} = \left[\frac{\alpha}{\beta} \times \frac{1-\tau_x}{1-\tau_y} \times (1+\mu)\right]^{\frac{1}{1-\rho}} \left(\frac{A_x}{A_y}\right)^{\frac{\rho}{1-\rho}}. \tag{5}$$

According to equation 5, the informal sector is larger when

—the informal sector faces lower distortions or lower taxes (τ_x is smaller),

—the formal sector faces higher distortions or higher taxes (τ_y is larger),

—the wage premium μ in the formal sector is higher, or

—the informal sector is more productive relative to the formal sector (A_x / A_y is greater).

VALUE ADDED PER WORKER. Now suppose that Wal-Mart-specific and trinket store–specific price indexes are unavailable, and instead all firms' revenues are deflated by a common retail sector price deflator. What does a comparison of "value added per worker" reveal in this case? Recall the first-order conditions in equations 1 and 2, which can be rearranged to yield

$$\frac{p_y y}{L_y} = \frac{w_x(1+\mu)}{1-\tau_y} \tag{6}$$

and

$$\frac{p_x x}{L_x} = \frac{w_x}{1-\tau_x}. \tag{7}$$

Notice that differences in "revenue" labor productivity across firms reflect differences in the distortions (τ_y, τ_x, μ) and say nothing about differences in "true" productivity (A). Marginal revenue products are equated across firms, apart from any distortions that are present. At some level, everyone knows this already: more-productive firms will charge lower prices, so sales revenue will not reveal which firm has higher productivity.

I have developed this point in the context of labor productivity. But exactly the same point applies to multifactor productivity measures.

Although this result is well known at some level, it is also ignored quite often in studies of firm-level productivity. One prominent example is the draft of the La Porta and Shleifer paper presented at the Brookings Panel conference, but these authors are certainly in extremely good company—nearly every study of firm-level productivity until recently likely suffers from the same criticism.

From this point there are two useful directions in which to proceed. First, one can seek better price deflators or other clever means to recover the true underlying productivities. Second, one can consider what is to be learned from revenue labor productivity itself. I will consider each of these in turn.

MEASURING TRUE PRODUCTIVITY. Recovering true productivity requires some measure of prices. In some (perhaps only a few) cases, such a price measure can be obtained directly.[6] Alternatively, one can use information about the demand elasticity to recover prices and quantities from firm revenue. For example, in the simple model here,

$$\frac{y}{x} = \text{constant} \times \left(\frac{p_y y}{p_x x} \right)^{\frac{1}{\rho}}. \tag{8}$$

Knowledge of the curvature parameter ρ (or of the elasticity of substitution) allows one to infer relative quantities. Hsieh and Klenow discuss this second approach in more detail, and this is the approach followed by La Porta and Shleifer, for example in the bottom panels of their tables 13 and 14.

An interesting and surprising finding that seems to be emerging from this literature—it is a feature in the La Porta and Shleifer paper as well as in others[7]—is that revenue labor productivity and "true" labor productivity are highly correlated. That is, even though there is no reason a priori to expect revenue labor productivity to provide any information about true labor productivity, the two seem to be closely related. One interpretation of this—explored in the next section—is that revenue labor productivity reveals something important about the pattern of distortions, namely, that more-productive firms face greater distortions. I have to confess to a

6. This is the approach taken in Foster, Haltiwanger, and Syverson, "Reallocation, Firm Turnover, and Efficiency."

7. Foster, Haltiwanger, and Syverson, "Reallocation, Firm Turnover, and Efficiency"; Hsieh and Klenow, "Misallocation and Manufacturing TFP in China and India."

nagging worry that it might reflect something else, but what exactly it is I am not sure.

STUDYING DISTORTIONS. As I noted above in discussing equations 6 and 7, even if revenue labor productivity says nothing about true productivity, it can still be quite informative about the distortions that affect the allocation of resources. Indeed, the results reported in tables 13 and 14 in this paper allow one to back out estimates of the distortions faced by firms. In particular, the ratio of firms' revenue labor productivities provides an estimate of $(1 + \mu)(1 - \tau_x) / (1 - \tau_y)$. This can be summarized in a measure of an "effective tax rate"—the tax rate that would apply if all of the distortions were embodied in τ_y itself. This effective tax rate is then equal to $1 - (1/RLP)$, where *RLP* denotes the ratio of revenue labor productivity across the two groups of firms. An example of results of this kind is summarized in table 1 below.

Apparently, big firms—which turn out to be the firms with the highest "true" productivity—have a marginal revenue product of labor that is 8.33 times that of unregistered firms. Part of this difference could come from big firms employing higher-quality labor; however, table 12 of the paper shows that big firms pay only somewhat higher wages than unregistered firms and actually pay lower wages than small firms. Instead, the interpretation suggested by the Hsieh-Klenow approach outlined here is that big firms face much larger distortions than unregistered firms.

The implication is that moving labor from the unregistered sector into big firms would have a large effect on total output. Hsieh and Klenow perform calculations along these lines (for China and India) to see by how much output could be raised if marginal revenue products were equated across firms.

A similar calculation could be done using the results in this paper, not across individual firms but across groups of firms: by how much would out-

Table 1. Effective Tax Rates Faced by Formal Firms

Comparison	*Log difference*[a]	*Factor [exp(logdiff)]*[b]	*Effective tax rate*[c]
Registered v. unregistered firms	0.18	1.20	0.17
Small v. unregistered firms	1.54	4.66	0.79
Big v. unregistered firms	2.12	8.33	0.88

Source: Author's calculations.

a. "Average" log difference for value added per employee, in log units, from La Porta and Shleifer, this volume, table 13.

b. Exponential of the difference in the first column.

c. Tax rate on formal firms that would apply if τ_x and μ were zero.

put be raised if labor were reallocated across unregistered, small, medium-size, and big firms so as to equate the marginal revenue products? I have done some simple calculations along these lines, and the results suggest that output could be increased by a factor of between 3.1 and 3.5 (of which a factor of 2 comes from the Harris-Todaro distortion associated with μ). A more careful calculation would be interesting and would help to shed some light on the important question of how costly it is to use the informal sector to provide social insurance. If those costs turn out to be high, it would suggest the need to think about more-efficient ways of providing that insurance.

COMMENT BY

WILLIAM D. NORDHAUS This paper by Rafael La Porta and Andrei Shleifer discusses the importance of the unofficial economy in economic development. They emphasize the different views of informal sector firms in development economics, but in parallel there has been a growing recognition of the innovational importance of small or nascent firms in developed countries. Work by Hernando de Soto and the awarding of the Nobel Peace prize to Muhammad Yunus, the founder of microfinance, are symptoms of the view that the smallest economic entities may be crucially important.

To begin, what does one mean by the "unofficial" (or "underground" or "informal") economy? I know of at least five possible definitions: unlawful economic activity, activity not reported on financial statements, activity not reported on tax statements, activity not measured in the national accounts, and activity by businesses not registered with government agencies. The paper discusses all of these, but I think the last one (or, more specifically, activity by businesses not registered with *central* government agencies) comes closest to describing the object of their analysis.

It is worth noting that even in the United States, where the data are good relative to those from developing countries, on which the paper must rely, most "businesses" are not registered in any meaningful sense. There were around 30 million tax returns of a business nature in 2005. Perhaps 6 million of these were from corporations, which would be registered. It is unclear how many of the other 24 million "businesses" are registered, although they do file tax returns. The government estimates that there are 20 million nonemployer firms. I would guess that the actual number of unregistered small businesses with receipts of more than $100 a year is as large as the number that file tax returns.

Which of the above five categories do these tens of millions of unofficial firms fall into? Most are unlikely to be engaged in unlawful activities, although the value of illegal drugs (circa $100 billion a year) is not far from the Internal Revenue Service's estimate of underreporting on tax returns (on the order of $130 billion). At the other extreme, most are unlikely to be required to register with governments. But they are likely to be included in the national accounts because of the multiple sourcing and imputations. It is not clear to me that the unofficial economies discussed in the paper are any larger in proportion to their national economies than the unofficial economy in the United States.

Let me turn to the question of the importance of the unofficial sector. The authors draw a rather extreme conclusion from their analysis: "From the perspective of economic growth, one should not expect much from the unofficial economy, with its millions of entrepreneurs, except to hope that it disappears over time." However, the paper does not discuss in any detail the characteristics of "unofficiality" that are critical to economic performance. Nonregistration per se is not obviously important. At the very least, it should be unlawful nonregistration. There is no way to know whether firms are not registered because they are small, or small because they are not registered.

As a rhetorical exercise, the paper is appealing. It distinguishes three views of the unofficial economy: the romantic view, the parasitic view, and the dual economy view. Aside from the names, however, which are probably self-explanatory, there is little to the paper's analysis of the different views. The first two are actually more similar to each other than to the third. The romantic view holds that bad laws, barriers to entry, and excessive regulation are holding back the vast pool of entrepreneurship among people in the informal sector. The parasitic view is in a sense the mirror image. It holds that implicit subsidies to unregistered small or microscopic enterprises give them advantages relative to the formal sector, and that this process undermines productivity and entrepreneurship in the formal sector. The dual view, in contrast, is that the informal sector is essentially another world—it goes about its business repairing shoes and the like but has little linkage with or, for good or bad, influence on the formal sector.

The paper provides some impressionistic evidence to back the authors' view. It discusses multiple indicators of informality, which turn out to be correlated with GDP per capita. However, the causal structure is so complex and the problems of measurement are so great that I take this just as an interesting correlation. Many of the variables tested, such as access to electric power and the number of employees in firms, are only tangentially related to the informal economy. The most important missing variable is the industry in which a given firm operates. If the dual economy view is the correct one, there should be a big disconnect between the preferred industries of the two sets of firms, whereas under the other two views the firms should be in the same industries.

The paper uses three interesting datasets compiled by the World Bank to investigate the characteristics of informal firms. We learn a fair amount about these characteristics, but the paper provides no analytical structure, no central hypothesis, and little in the way of genuinely exogenous variables on which to base any analysis. One example of where the analysis is uninformative is in the productivity analysis. The authors do not measure productivity in the sense of real output per unit of real input—their "output" measures are nominal. If the small firms tend to have low-wage workers (as the authors indicate they do), then it would follow that value added per worker will be relatively low. The authors' defense of their use of nominal output would apply if those outputs referred to the same industries over time, or if they could control for industrial composition, but since the measures have only the crudest of industry controls, there is no convincing evidence that they measure real productivity growth accurately.

This point can be seen as follows. The budget identity for firms is $pQ \equiv wL/s$, where p is price, Q is quantity, w is the wage rate, L is labor inputs, and s is the share of compensation in the value of nominal output. I suppress any subscripts for time, country, industry, formality, and so forth for simplicity. Taking logarithms, $\ln(pQ) = \ln(L) + e$, where the residual e is equal to $\ln(w) - \ln(s)$. This is essentially the equation fitted by La Porta and Shleifer. Differences across firms reflect only differences in the share of compensation and in relative wages across firms. If the shares of compensation are equal, then the only difference is the relative wage rate. *The level of labor productivity or total factor productivity does not even enter the empirical estimate.*

One test that could be helpful would be to compare the incidence of self-employment in different sectors. For example, in the United States, ratios of self-employed to employed workers vary from (in rough figures) 100 percent in agriculture, through 24 percent in construction, to 2½ percent in manufacturing, to zero in utilities. It would be a demanding project, but I would think that looking at differential employment trends by industry would provide a better test than a selection of proxies and indicators such as the level of freedom.

Let me close with a comment on the romantic view of the informal sector. I am mindful of the observation, attributed to many, that "Anyone under 30 who is not romantic has no heart, and anyone over 30 who is romantic has no head." With that in mind, what is the hard-headed romantic's take on all this? The role of small enterprises is, fundamentally, to provide radical new approaches to economic activity. The authors claim that virtually no informal firms make it into the formal sector. This is akin to saying that almost no storms become hurricanes and destroy major American cities. Out of the millions of small enterprises, it does not take more than a handful of tiny innovational hurricanes causing creative destruction to make a major contribution to economic growth.

GENERAL DISCUSSION Chang Hsieh interpreted the paper's evidence as clearly supporting the view of the informal sector as parasitic: the observed differences in output per worker indicate that the marginal product of labor is lower in the informal than in the formal sector. He wondered whether, in addition to the difference in the productivity of labor between the formal and informal sectors, one could also look at the productivity of capital in both sectors to determine the weighted average of the marginal products of capital and labor in the two sectors.

Paul Romer noted that the paper's conclusion seemed to imply that although the dual economic structure induces some distortions, it serves the goal of income redistribution and thus can be left alone. That idea seemed to him inefficient or even perverse. He suggested a model consisting of an informal sector in which output rises linearly with the labor input, and a formal sector with Cobb-Douglas output based on educated labor and unskilled labor, the latter of which can also be used in the informal sector. A tax on the formal sector ends up being a tax on human capital and thus serves to redistribute income. However, if foreign direct investment makes the supply of human capital elastic, such a tax could have large efficiency costs. The result could be that after-tax wages for less skilled workers are lower than if they were taxed directly. Romer remarked that the paper itself makes a similar statement, which is inconsistent with other comments in the paper. He also discussed the difference between catch-up growth and growth at the frontier: although start-up firms may be key to the development and dispersion of new technology in the United States, established firms like Nike might be better at raising wages quickly in developing countries like Vietnam, because of differences in industrial structures and dynamics between developing and developed countries.

Lawrence Summers proposed a distinction between two types of formal versus informal sector dualism, which he called right-wing and left-wing.

Under right-wing dualism, as exemplified by Charles Jones's comment on the paper, there are interferences in markets that restrict the size of the formal sector, making it the smaller of the two sectors and with higher measured productivity. Left-wing dualism, as articulated by the late W. Arthur Lewis and possibly Michael Todaro, posits a modern sector that has figured out how to be more productive. Workers in that sector share in the increased productivity, and therefore everyone would like to work in that sector. However, because the sector can expand only so fast, it may persistently remain too small, with high wages for the few workers it employs.

Martin Baily, drawing on his own investigations into the informal sector at the McKinsey Global Institute, offered several examples of interactions between the formal and informal sectors and particular industry concentrations in the informal sector. He cited Brazil's retail grocery sector as an example of the parasitic view (although he objected to the term): a large number of small, informal supermarkets compete directly with larger, formal supermarkets; the formal sector chains often acquire the informal stores as part of an expansion strategy. In Russia, in contrast, the informal sector deals in moonshine liquor and smuggled goods and thus competes with the formal sector little if at all. In many of these countries, large government bureaucracies essentially create the informal sector by necessitating very high taxes for their support. Tax and regulatory structures need to be reformed and downsized to bring them more in line with what the public wants, so that the formal sector can expand more easily.

Eduardo Engel added that the generous subsidies that some governments provide to the informal sector limit growth of the formal sector just as high taxes do. Examples are Mexico's social programs for day care, pensions, and health care, which are paid for by taxes on the formal sector. He cited a paper by Santiago Levy, a former Mexican cabinet member and currently the chief economist at the Inter-American Development Bank, which argues that these programs were a major source of Mexico's low productivity growth in the past few decades.

DANI RODRIK
Harvard University

The Real Exchange Rate and Economic Growth

ABSTRACT I show that undervaluation of the currency (a high real exchange rate) stimulates economic growth. This is true particularly for developing countries. This finding is robust to using different measures of the real exchange rate and different estimation techniques. I also provide some evidence that the operative channel is the size of the tradable sector (especially industry). These results suggest that tradables suffer disproportionately from the government or market failures that keep poor countries from converging toward countries with higher incomes. I present two categories of explanations for why this may be so, the first focusing on institutional weaknesses, and the second on product-market failures. A formal model elucidates the linkages between the real exchange rate and the rate of economic growth.

Economists have long known that poorly managed exchange rates can be disastrous for economic growth. Avoiding significant overvaluation of the currency is one of the most robust imperatives that can be gleaned from the diverse experience with economic growth around the world, and one that appears to be strongly supported by cross-country statistical evidence.[1] The results reported in the well-known papers by David Dollar and by Jeffrey Sachs and Andrew Warner on the relationship between outward orientation and economic growth are largely based on indices that capture the degree of overvaluation.[2] Much of the literature that derives policy recommendations from cross-national regressions is now in disrepute,[3] but it

1. Razin and Collins (1997); Johnson, Ostry, and Subramanian (2007); Rajan and Subramanian (2006).
2. Dollar (1992); Sachs and Warner (1995); Rodriguez and Rodrik (2001).
3. Easterly (2005); Rodrik (2005).

is probably fair to say that the admonishment against overvaluation remains as strong as ever. In his pessimistic survey of the cross-national growth literature,[4] William Easterly agrees that large overvaluations have an adverse effect on growth (although he remains skeptical that moderate movements have determinate effects).

Why overvaluation is so consistently associated with slow growth is not always theorized explicitly, but most accounts link it to macroeconomic instability.[5] Overvalued currencies are associated with foreign currency shortages, rent seeking and corruption, unsustainably large current account deficits, balance of payments crises, and stop-and-go macroeconomic cycles, all of which are damaging to growth.

I will argue that this is not the whole story. Just as overvaluation hurts growth, so undervaluation facilitates it. For most countries, periods of rapid growth are associated with undervaluation. In fact, there is little evidence of nonlinearity in the relationship between a country's real exchange rate and its economic growth: an increase in undervaluation boosts economic growth just as powerfully as a decrease in overvaluation. But this relationship holds only for developing countries; it disappears when the sample is restricted to richer countries, and it gets stronger the poorer the country. These findings suggest that more than macroeconomic stability is at stake. The relative price of tradable goods to nontradable goods (that is, the real exchange rate) seems to play a more fundamental role in the convergence of developing country with developed country incomes.[6]

I attempt to make the point as directly as possible in figure 1, which depicts the experience of seven developing countries during 1950–2004: China, India, South Korea, Taiwan, Uganda, Tanzania, and Mexico. In each case I have graphed side by side my measure of real undervaluation (defined in the next section) against the country's economic growth rate in the same period. Each point represents an average for a five-year window.

To begin with the most fascinating (and globally significant) case, the degree to which economic growth in China tracks the movements in my index of undervaluation is uncanny. The rapid increase in annual growth of GDP per capita starting in the second half of the 1970s closely parallels the increase in the undervaluation index (from an overvaluation of close to

4. Easterly (2005).

5. See, for example, Fischer (1993).

6. Recently, Bhalla (forthcoming), Gala (2007), and Gluzmann, Levy-Yeyati, and Sturzenegger (2007) have made similar arguments.

Figure 1. Undervaluation and Economic Growth in Selected Developing Countries, 1950–2004

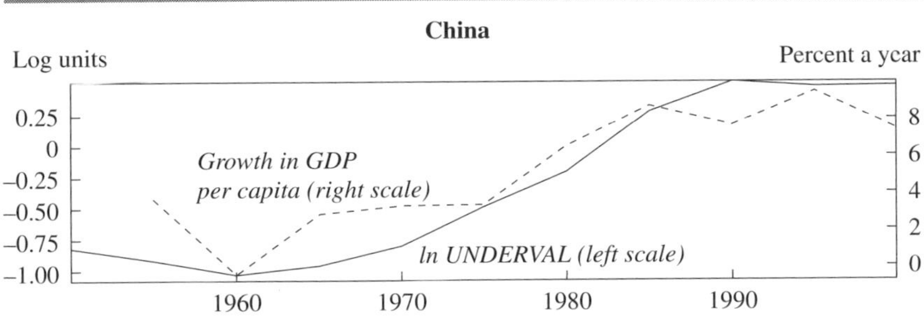

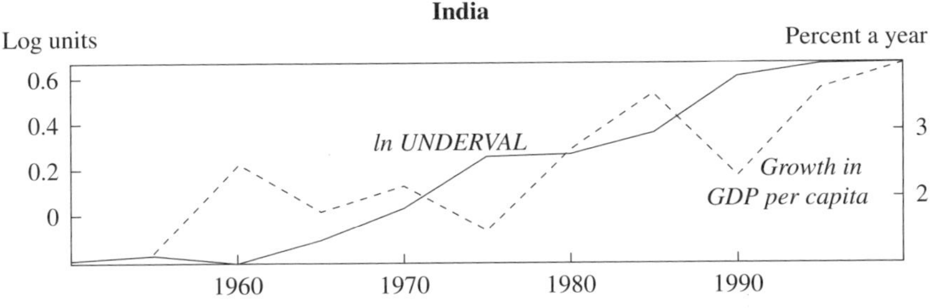

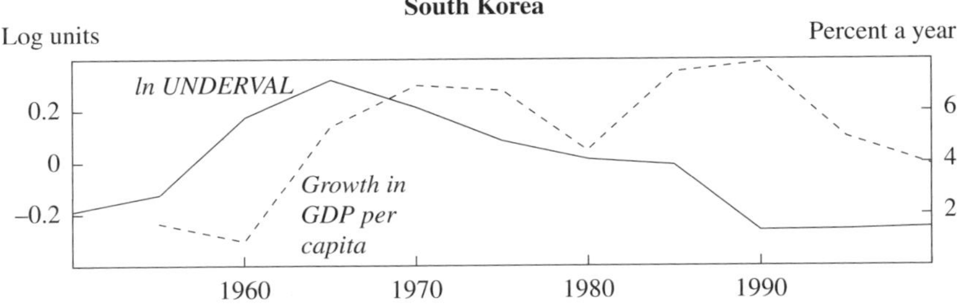

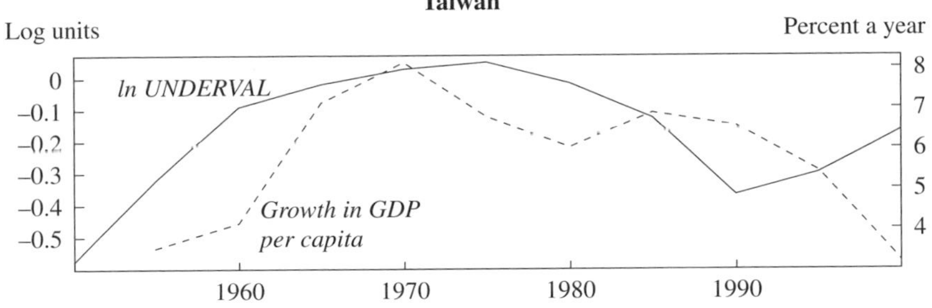

(*continued*)

Figure 1. Undervaluation and Economic Growth in Selected Developing Countries, 1950–2004 (*Continued*)

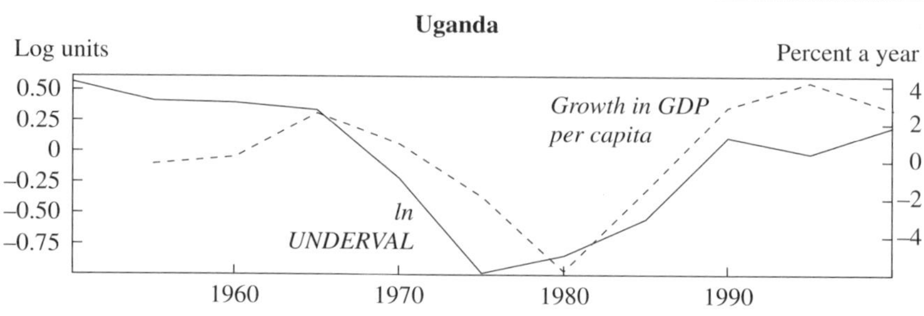

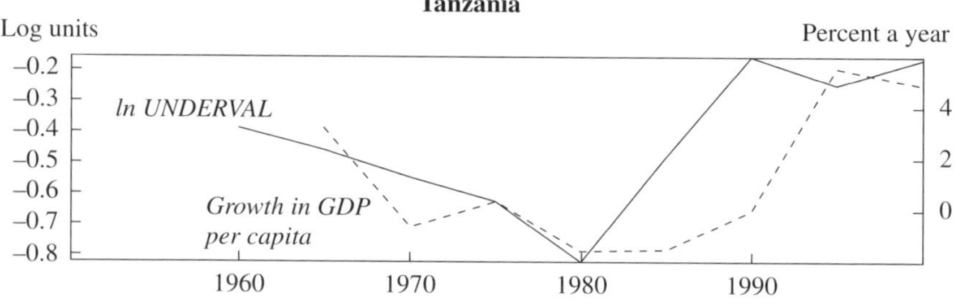

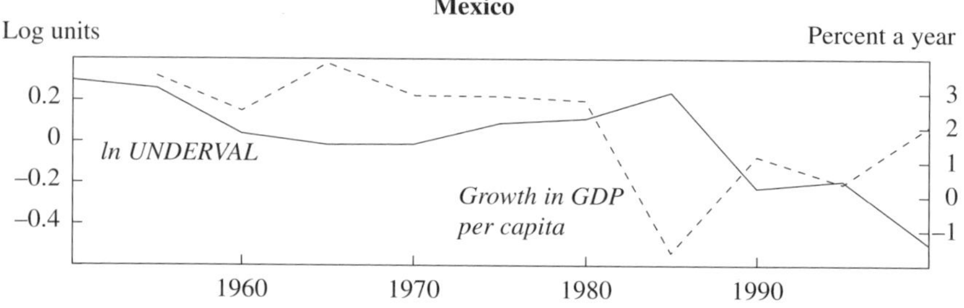

Sources: Penn World Tables version 6.2, and author's calculations.

100 percent to an undervaluation of around 50 percent[7]), and both undervaluation and the growth rate plateau in the 1990s. Analysts who focus on global imbalances have, of course, noticed in recent years that the yuan is undervalued, as evidenced by China's large current account surplus. They have paid less attention to the role that undervaluation seems to have played in driving the country's economic growth.

7. Recent revisions in purchasing power parity indices are likely to make a big difference to the levels of these undervaluation measures, without greatly affecting their trends over time. See the discussion below.

For India, the other growth superstar of recent years, the picture is less clear-cut, but the basic message is the same as that for China. India's growth in GDP per capita has steadily climbed from slightly above 1 percent a year in the 1950s to 4 percent by the early 2000s, while its real exchange rate has moved from a small overvaluation to an undervaluation of around 60 percent. In the case of the two East Asian tigers depicted in figure 1, South Korea and Taiwan, what is interesting is that the growth slowdowns in recent years were in each case preceded or accompanied by increased overvaluation or reduced undervaluation. In other words, both growth and undervaluation exhibit an inverse-U shape over time.

These regularities are hardly specific to Asian countries. The next two panels in figure 1 depict two African experiences, those of Uganda and Tanzania, and here the undervaluation index captures the turning points in economic growth exceptionally well. A slowdown in growth is accompanied by increasing overvaluation, and a pickup in growth is accompanied by a rise in undervaluation. Finally, the last panel of figure 1 shows a somewhat anomalous Latin American case, that of Mexico. Here the two series seem quite a bit out of sync, especially since 1981, when the correlation between growth and undervaluation turns negative rather than positive. Those familiar with the recent economic history of Mexico will recognize this to be a reflection of the cyclical role of capital inflows in inducing growth in that country. Periods of capital inflows in Mexico are associated with consumption-led growth booms and currency appreciation; when the capital flows reverse, the economy tanks and the currency depreciates. The Mexican experience is a useful reminder that there is no reason a priori to expect a positive relationship between growth and undervaluation. It also suggests the need to go beyond individual cases and undertake a more systematic empirical analysis.

In the next section I do just that. First, I construct a time-varying index of real undervaluation, based on data from the Penn World Tables on price levels in individual countries. My index of undervaluation is essentially a real exchange rate adjusted for the Balassa-Samuelson effect: this measure of the real exchange rate adjusts the relative price of tradables to nontradables for the fact that as countries grow rich, the relative prices of nontradables as a group tend to rise (because of higher productivity in tradables). I next show, in regressions using a variety of fixed-effects panel specifications, that there is a systematic positive relationship between growth and undervaluation, especially in developing countries. This indicates that the Asian experience is not an anomaly. I subject these baseline results to a series of robustness tests, employing different data sources, a range of alternative undervaluation indices, and different estimation methods. Although ascertaining causality is always difficult, I argue that in this instance causality is likely to run from undervaluation to growth rather than the other way around. I also present evidence that undervaluation works through its positive impact on the share of tradables in the economy, especially industry. Hence developing countries achieve more rapid growth when they are able to increase the relative profitability of their tradables.

These results suggest strongly that there is something "special" about tradables in countries with low to medium incomes. In the rest of the paper I examine the reasons behind this regularity. What is the precise mechanism through which an increase in the relative price of tradables (and therefore the sector's relative size) increases growth? I present two classes of theories that would account for the stylized facts. In one, tradables are "special" because they suffer disproportionately (that is, compared with nontradables) from the institutional weakness and inability to completely specify contracts that characterize lower-income environments. In the other, tradables are "special" because they suffer disproportionately from the market failures (information and coordination externalities) that block structural transformation and economic diversification. In both cases, an increase in the relative price of tradables acts as a second-best mechanism to partly alleviate the relevant distortion, foster desirable structural change, and spur growth. Although I cannot discriminate sharply between the two theories and come down in favor of one or the other, I present some evidence that suggests that these two sets of distortions do affect tradable activities more than they do nontradables. This is a necessary condition for my explanations to make sense.

In the penultimate section of the paper, I develop a simple growth model to elucidate how the mechanisms I have in mind might work. The model is that of a small, open economy in which the tradable and nontradable sectors both suffer from an economic distortion. For the purposes of the model, whether the distortion is of the institutional and contracting kind or of the conventional market failure kind is of no importance. The crux is the relative magnitude of the distortions in the two sectors. I show that when the distortion in tradables is larger, the tradable sector is too small in equilibrium. A policy or other exogenous shock that can induce a real depreciation will then have a growth-promoting effect. For example, an outward transfer, which would normally reduce domestic welfare, can have the reverse effect because it increases the equilibrium relative price of tradables and can thereby increase economic growth. The model clarifies how changes in relative prices can produce growth effects in the presence of distortions that affect the two sectors differently. It also clarifies the sense in which the real exchange rate is a "policy" variable: changing its level requires complementary policies (here the size of the inward or outward transfer).

I summarize my findings and discuss some policy issues in the concluding section of the paper.

Undervaluation and Growth: The Evidence

I will use a number of different indices in what follows, but my preferred index of under- or overvaluation is a measure of the domestic price level adjusted for the Balassa-Samuelson effect. This index has the advantage that it is comparable across countries as well as over time. I compute this index in three steps. First, I use data on exchange rates (*XRAT*) and purchasing power parity conversion factors (*PPP*) from the Penn World Tables version 6.2 to calculate a "real" exchange rate (*RER*):[8]

$$\ln RER_{it} = \ln\left(XRAT_{it} / PPP_{it}\right),$$

where i indexes countries and t indexes five-year time periods. (Unless specified otherwise, all observations are simple averages across years.) *XRAT* and *PPP* are expressed as national currency units per U.S. dollar.[9] Values of *RER* greater than one indicate that the value of the currency is lower (more depreciated) than indicated by purchasing power parity. However, in practice nontradable goods are also cheaper in poorer countries (through the Balassa-Samuelson effect), which requires an adjustment. So in the second step I account for this effect by regressing *RER* on GDP per capita (*RGDPCH*):

$$\ln RER_{it} = \alpha + \beta \ln RGDPCH_{it} + f_t + u_{it}, \tag{1}$$

where f_t is a fixed effect for time period and u is the error term. This regression yields an estimate of β ($\hat{\beta}$) of –0.24 (with a very high t statistic of around 20), suggesting a strong and precisely estimated Balassa-Samuelson effect: when incomes rise by 10 percent, the real exchange rate falls by around 2.4 percent. Finally, to arrive at my index of undervaluation, I take the difference between the actual real exchange rate and the Balassa-Samuelson-adjusted rate:

8. The Penn World Tables data are from Heston, Summers, and Aten (2006).

9. The variable p in the Penn World Tables (called the "price level of GDP") is equivalent to *RER*. I have used p here as this series is more complete than *XRAT* and *PPP*.

$$\ln UNDERVAL_{it} = \ln RER_{it} - \ln \widehat{RER_{it}},$$

where $\ln \widehat{RER_{it}}$ is the predicted value from equation 1.

Defined in this way, *UNDERVAL* is comparable across countries and over time. Whenever *UNDERVAL* exceeds unity, it indicates that the exchange rate is set such that goods produced at home are relatively cheap in dollar terms: the currency is undervalued. When *UNDERVAL* is below unity, the currency is overvalued. In what follows I will typically use the logarithmic transform of this variable, ln *UNDERVAL,* which is centered at zero and has a standard deviation of 0.48 (figure 2). This is also the measure used in figure 1.

My procedure is fairly close to that followed in recent work by Simon Johnson, Jonathan Ostry, and Arvind Subramanian.[10] The main difference is that these authors estimate a different cross section for equation 1 for each year, whereas I estimate a single panel (with time dummies). My method seems preferable for purposes of comparability over time. I emphasize that my definition of undervaluation is based on price comparisons and differs substantially from an alternative definition that relates to the external balance. The latter is typically operationalized by specifying a small-scale macro model and estimating the level of the real exchange rate that would achieve balance of payments equilibrium.[11]

One issue of great significance for my calculations is that the World Bank's International Comparison Program has recently published revised PPP conversion factors for a single benchmark year, 2005.[12] In some important instances, these new estimates differ greatly from those previously available and on which I have relied here. For example, price levels in both China and India are now estimated to be around 40 percent above the previous estimates for 2005, indicating that these countries' currencies were not nearly as undervalued in that year as the old numbers suggested (15 to 20 percent as opposed to 50 to 60 percent). This is not as damaging to my results as it may seem at first sight, however. Virtually all my regressions are based on panel data and include a full set of country and time fixed effects. In other words, as I did implicitly in figure 1, I identify the growth effects of undervaluation from changes within countries, not from differences in levels across a cross section of countries. So my results

10. Johnson, Ostry, and Subramanian (2007).

11. See Aguirre and Calderón (2005), Razin and Collins (1997), and Elbadawi (1994) for some illustrations.

12. International Comparison Program (2007).

Figure 2. Distribution of the Undervaluation Measure

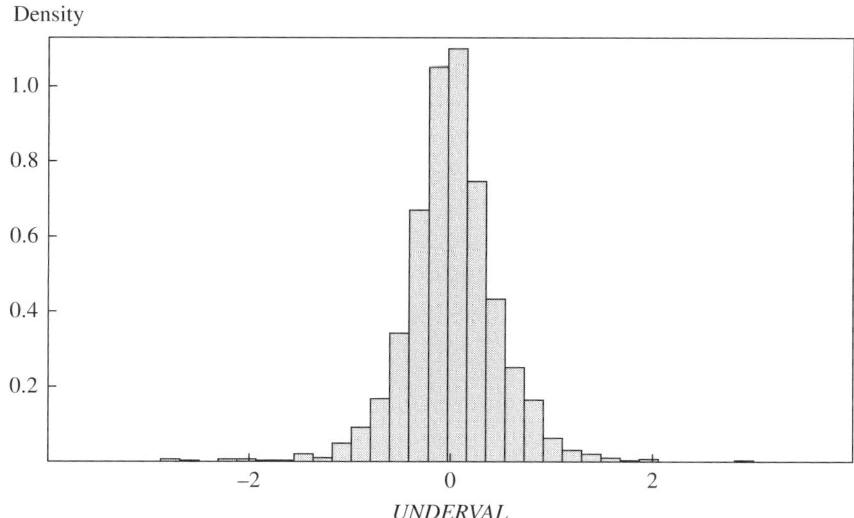

Source: Author's calculations.

should remain unaffected if the revisions to the PPP factors turn out to consist of largely one-time adjustments to the estimated price levels of individual countries, without greatly altering their time trends. Even though the time series of revised PPP estimates are not yet available, preliminary indications suggest that this will be the case.

In fact, the revised data yield a cross-sectional estimate of β for 2005 that is virtually the same as the one presented above (–0.22, with a *t* statistic of 11). In other words, the magnitude of the Balassa-Samuelson effect is nearly identical whether estimated with the new data or the old.

The Baseline Panel Evidence

My dataset covers a maximum of 188 countries and 11 five-year periods from 1950–54 through 2000–04. My baseline specification for estimating the relationship between undervaluation and growth takes the following form:

$$(2)\ growth_{it} = \alpha + \beta \ln RGDPCH_{i,t-1} + \delta \ln UNDERVAL_{it} + f_i + f_t + u_{it},$$

where the dependent variable is annual growth in GDP per capita. The equation thus includes the standard convergence term (initial income per capita, $RGDPCH_{i,t-1}$) and a full set of country and time dummies (f_i and f_t).

My primary interest is in the value of $\hat{\delta}$. Given the fixed-effects framework, what I am estimating is the "within" effect of undervaluation, namely, the impact of changes in under- or overvaluation on changes in growth rates within countries. I present regressions with additional covariates, as well as cross-sectional specifications, in a later subsection.

Table 1 presents the results. When estimated for the panel as a whole (column 1-1), the regression yields a highly significant $\hat{\delta}$ of 0.017. However, as columns 1-2 and 1-3 reveal, this effect operates only for developing countries. In the richer countries in the sample, $\hat{\delta}$ is small and statistically indistinguishable from zero, whereas in the developing countries $\hat{\delta}$ rises to 0.026 and is highly significant. The latter estimate suggests that a 50 percent undervaluation—which corresponds roughly to one standard deviation in *UNDERVAL*—is associated with a boost in annual growth of real income per capita during the same five-year period of 1.3 percentage points (0.50 × 0.026). This is a sizable effect. I will discuss the plausibility of this estimate later, following my discussion of robustness tests and theoretical explanations.

The results in column 1-4 confirm further that the growth impact of undervaluation depends heavily on a country's level of development. When *UNDERVAL* is interacted with initial income, the estimated coefficient on the interaction term is negative and highly significant. The estimated coefficients in column 1-4 indicate that the growth effects of a 50 percent undervaluation for Brazil, China, India, and Ethiopia at their current levels of income are 0.47, 0.60, 0.82, and 1.46 percentage points, respectively. The estimates also imply that the growth effect disappears at an income per capita of $19,635, roughly the level of Bahrain, Spain, or Taiwan.

Interestingly, the estimated impact of undervaluation seems to be independent of the time period under consideration. When I split the developing country data into pre- and post-1980 subperiods (columns 1-5 and 1-6), the value of $\hat{\delta}$ remains basically unaffected. This indicates that the channel or channels through which undervaluation works have little to do with the global economic environment; the estimated impact is, if anything, smaller in the post-1980 era of globalization, when markets in rich countries were considerably more open. So the explanation cannot be a simple export-led growth story.

Robustness: Sensitivity to Outliers

As noted in the introduction, the literature on the relationship between exchange rate policy and growth has focused to date largely on the delete-

Table 1. Baseline Panel Regressions of Economic Growth on the Undervaluation Measure[a]

	Sample					
Independent variable	*All countries, 1950–2004* *1-1*	*Developed countries,*[b] *1950–2004* *1-2*	*Developing countries, 1950–2004* *1-3*	*All countries, 1950–2004* *1-4*	*Developing countries, 1950–79* *1-5*	*Developing countries, 1980–2004* *1-6*
ln initial income	−0.031***	−0.055***	−0.039***	−0.032***	−0.062***	−0.065***
	(−6.67)	(−6.91)	(−5.30)	(−7.09)	(−3.90)	(−4.64)
ln *UNDERVAL*	0.017***	0.003	0.026***	0.086***	0.029***	0.024***
	(5.21)	(0.49)	(5.84)	(4.05)	(4.20)	(3.23)
ln initial income × ln *UNDERVAL*				−0.0087***		
				(−3.39)		
No. of observations	1,303	513	790	1,303	321	469

Source: Author's regressions.

a. The dependent variable is annual growth in GDP per capita, in percent. Observations are five-year averages. All regressions include time and country fixed effects. Countries with extreme observations for *UNDERVAL* (Iraq, Laos, and North Korea) have been excluded from the samples. Robust *t* statistics are in parentheses. Asterisks indicate statistical significance at the *10 percent, **5 percent, or ***1 percent level.

b. Developed country observations are those with real GDP per capita exceeding $6,000.

Figure 3. Growth and Undervaluation in the Developing Country Sample

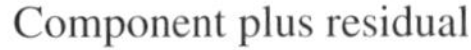

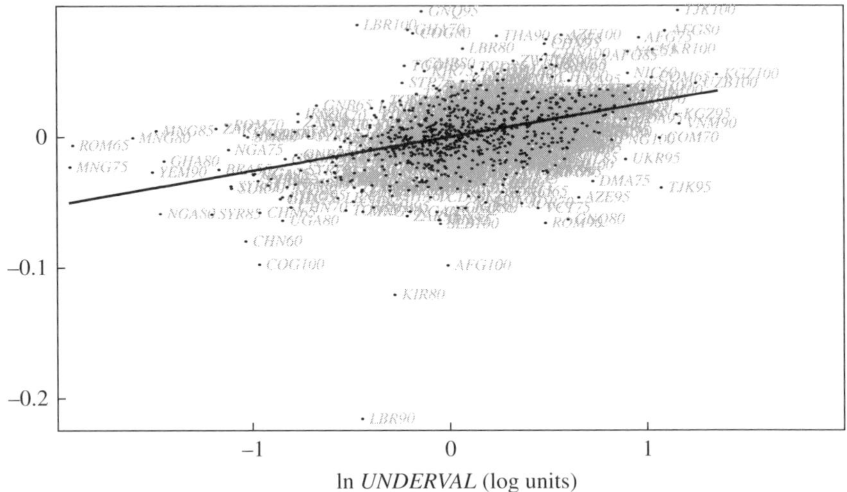

Sources: Penn World Tables version 6.2, and author's calculations.

rious consequences of large overvaluations. In his survey of the cross-national growth literature, Easterly warns against extrapolating from large black market premiums for foreign currency, for which he can find evidence of harmful effects on growth, to more moderate misalignments in either direction, for which he does not.[13] However, the evidence strongly suggests that the relationship I have estimated does not rely on outliers: it is driven at least as much by the positive growth effect of undervaluation as by the negative effect of overvaluation. Furthermore, there is little evidence of nonlinearity in either direction.

Figure 3 presents a scatterplot of the data used in column 1-3 of table 1 (that is, developing countries over the entire sample period). Inspection suggests a linear relationship over the entire range of *UNDERVAL* and no obvious outliers. To investigate this more systematically, I ran the regression for successively narrower ranges of *UNDERVAL*. The results are shown in table 2, where the first column reproduces the baseline results from table 1, the second excludes all observations with *UNDERVAL* < –1.50 (that is, overvaluations greater than 150 percent), the third excludes observations with *UNDERVAL* < –1.00, and so on. The final column

13. Easterly (2005).

Table 2. Impact of Excluding Extreme Observations of the Undervaluation Measure[a]

		Range of UNDERVAL *included in sample*				
	Baseline	*Greater than −150%*	*Greater than −100%*	*Greater than −50%*	*Greater than −25%*	*Between 50% and −50%*
Coefficient on ln *UNDERVAL*	0.026	0.029	0.034	0.034	0.028	0.030
t statistic	(5.84)	(6.31)	(7.28)	(5.46)	(4.32)	(3.72)
No. of observations	790	786	773	726	653	619

Source: Author's regressions.

a. See table 1 for details of the specification. All estimated coefficients are statistically significant at the 1 percent level.

restricts the range to undervaluations or overvaluations that are smaller than 50 percent. The remarkable finding is that these sample truncations affect the estimated coefficient on ln *UNDERVAL* very little. The coefficient obtained when I eliminate all overvaluations greater than 25 percent is nearly identical to that for the entire sample, and the coefficient obtained when I eliminate all under- and overvaluations above 50 percent is still highly significant. Unlike Álvaro Aguirre and César Calderón, and Ofair Razin and Susan Collins, I find little evidence of nonlinearity in the relationship between undervaluation and economic growth.[14]

Robustness: Different Real Exchange Rate Measures

There are some potential concerns with relying exclusively on *UNDERVAL* as a measure of under- or overvaluation. One issue is the uncertain reliability of the price-level measures in the Penn World Tables. As I mentioned above, the most recent revisions have revealed the estimates to be problematic in quite a few countries (even though the implications for changes over time within countries may not be as severe). This suggests the need to check the validity of my results using real exchange rate series constructed from other data sources.

Another worry relates to my adjustment for the Balassa-Samuelson effect. Although this adjustment is proper and introduces no bias when there is a direct feedback from incomes to price levels as indicated in equation 1, it may be problematic under some other circumstances. For example,

14. Aguirre and Calderón (2005); Razin and Collins (1997). I have also tried entering the square of *UNDERVAL*, distinguishing between positive and negative values of *UNDERVAL*. I find some evidence that extreme overvaluations (large negative values of *UNDERVAL*) are proportionately more damaging to growth, but the effect is not that strong, and the main coefficient of interest remains unaffected.

if the Balassa-Samuelson effect is created by a third variable ("productivity") that affects both income per capita and the price level, the coefficient estimates on *UNDERVAL* may be biased upward (as discussed by Michael Woodford in his comment on this paper). This suggests the need to employ alternative measures of the real exchange rate that do not incorporate the Balassa-Samuelson adjustment. Even though estimates from regressions that use such alternative measures are in turn likely to be biased downward (in the presence of Balassa-Samuelson effects that operate over time within countries), such estimates are still useful insofar as they provide a lower bound on the growth effects of undervaluation.

I therefore use four additional real exchange rate indices in the regressions that follow, to complement the results obtained with *UNDERVAL* above. First, I simply use the inverse of the index of the price level from the Penn World Tables, without the Balassa-Samuelson adjustment:

$$\ln RER_{PWT} = \ln\left(\frac{XRAT}{PPP}\right).$$

This measure has all the problems of the Penn World Tables, since it is constructed from that source, but for purposes of robustness testing it has the virtue that it is not subject to the sort of bias just mentioned. Next I use the real effective exchange rate index of the International Monetary Fund (IMF), $\ln REER_{IMF}$, which is a measure of the value of home currency against a weighted average of the currencies of major trade partners divided by a price deflator or index of costs. This is a multilateral measure of competitiveness and is available for a large number of industrial and developing countries, although the coverage is not nearly as complete as that of the Penn World Tables. The third index is a simple bilateral measure of the real exchange rate with the United States, constructed using wholesale price indices:

$$\ln RER_{WPI} = \ln\left(\frac{E \times PPI_{US}}{WPI}\right),$$

where E is the home country's nominal exchange rate against the U.S. dollar (in units of home currency per dollar), PPI_{US} is the producer price index for the United States, and *WPI* is the home country's wholesale price index. All of the data are from the IMF's International Financial Statistics (IFS). Since the IFS does not report wholesale price indices for many countries, I use as my final index a bilateral real exchange rate constructed using consumer prices:

$$\ln RER_{CPI} = \ln\left(\frac{E \times PPI_{US}}{CPI}\right),$$

where *CPI* is the home country's consumer price index. Note that the levels of the last three measures are not comparable across countries, but this is of no consequence for the panel regressions, which track the effects of changes in real exchange rates within countries.

Table 3 reports the results, for the full sample and the developing country sample separately, of rerunning the baseline specification from table 1 (columns 1-1 and 1-3), substituting in turn each of the above measures for *UNDERVAL*. The numbers tell a remarkably consistent story, despite the differences in data sources and in the construction of the index. When the regression is run on the full sample, the growth impact of a real depreciation is small and often statistically insignificant. But when the sample is restricted to developing countries (again defined as those with real GDP per capita below $6,000), the estimated effect is strong and statistically significant in all cases. (Only the estimate using $REER_{IMF}$ misses the 5 percent significance threshold, and that narrowly.) The coefficient estimates range between 0.012 and 0.029 (using RER_{CPI} and RER_{WPI}, respectively) and bracket the estimate with *UNDERVAL* reported earlier (0.026). Note in particular that the coefficient estimate with RER_{PWT} is highly significant and, as expected, smaller than the estimate with *UNDERVAL* (0.016 versus 0.026). It is hard to say how much of this difference is due to the lack of correction for the Balassa-Samuelson effect (and hence a downward bias in the estimation when using RER_{PWT}) and how much to the correction of a previous bias in the estimation with *UNDERVAL*. Even if the "correct" estimate is the lower one of 0.016, it still establishes a strong enough relationship between real undervaluation and economic growth to command attention: a 50 percent undervaluation would boost annual growth of income per capita by 0.8 percentage point.

Robustness: Additional Covariates

The specifications reported thus far are rather sparse, including only a convergence factor, fixed effects, and the undervaluation measure itself. Of course, the fixed effects serve to absorb any growth determinants that are time-invariant and country-specific, or time-specific and country-invariant. But it is still possible that some time-varying country-specific determinants correlated with *UNDERVAL* have been left out. The regressions reported in table 4 therefore augment the baseline specification with additional covariates. I include measures of institutional quality ("rule of

Table 3. Panel Regressions of Economic Growth on Undervaluation Using Alternative Real Exchange Rate Measures[a]

	Real exchange rate measure and sample							
	ln RER_{PWT}[b]		*ln* $REER_{IMF}$[c]		*ln* RER_{WPI}		*ln* RER_{CPI}	
Independent variable	*All countries*[d]	*Developing countries*[e]	*All countries*	*Developing countries*	*All countries*[d]	*Developing countries*	*All countries*[d]	*Developing countries*
ln initial income	−0.029***	−0.033***	−0.041***	−0.049**	−0.041***	−0.031	−0.033***	−0.033***
	(−6.02)	(−4.43)	(−3.63)	(−2.51)	(−5.32)	(−1.63)	(−7.37)	(−4.81)
ln *UNDERVAL*	0.006**	0.016***	0.005	0.015*	0.003	0.029***	0.003*	0.012***
	(1.97)	(3.74)	(0.94)	(1.92)	(1.54)	(2.95)	(1.72)	(2.83)
No. of observations	1,293	790	476	206	440	162	987	557

Source: Author's regressions.

a. The dependent variable is annual growth in GDP per capita, in percent. Observations are averages over five-year periods. All regressions include time and country fixed effects. Robust *t* statistics are in parentheses. Asterisks indicate statistical significance at the *10 percent, **5 percent, or ***1 percent level.

b. Sample excludes Iraq, Laos, and North Korea, which have extreme observations for *UNDERVAL*.

c. Sample excludes Nicaragua, which has extreme observations for *UNDERVAL*.

d. Sample excludes the United States, as it is the base country with an invariant real exchange rate index.

e. Developed country observations are those with real GDP per capita exceeding $6,000.

Table 4. Panel Regressions of Economic Growth on Undervaluation and Additional Covariates, Developing Countries Only[a]

	Regression						
Independent variable	*4-1*[b]	*4-2*	*4-3*	*4-4*	*4-5*	*4-6*	*4-7*
ln initial income	−0.039***	−0.015***	−0.037***	−0.033***	−0.036***	−0.045***	−0.046***
	(−5.30)	(−6.40)	(−5.17)	(−4.51)	(−5.06)	(−6.65)	(−4.33)
ln *UNDERVAL*	0.026***	0.063***	0.025***	0.021***	0.018***	0.019***	0.016***
	(5.84)	(3.33)	(4.51)	(4.01)	(3.66)	(4.06)	(2.87)
Rule of law[c]		0.007					
		(0.010)					
Government consumption as percent of GDP[d]			−0.076**	−0.042			
			(−2.00)	(−1.32)			
ln terms of trade[d]				0.013*	0.005		
				(1.93)	(0.71)		
ln (1 + inflation rate[d])					−0.030***	−0.027***	−0.023***
					(−3.23)	(−3.34)	(−3.16)
Gross domestic saving as percent of GDP[d]						0.099***	0.124***
						(4.34)	(4.40)
Average years of education × 100[e]							0.030
							(0.87)
No. of observations	790	191	626	546	478	529	335

Source: Author's regressions.

a. The dependent variable is annual growth in GDP per capita, in percent. Observations are averages over five-year periods. All regressions include time and country fixed effects. Robust *t* statistics are in parentheses. Asterisks indicate statistical significance at the *10 percent, **5 percent, or ***1 percent level.

b. Baseline estimate from table 1, column 1-3.

c. From Kaufmann, Kraay, and Mastruzzi (2008). Higher values indicate stronger rule of law.

d. From World Bank, World Development Indicators.

e. From Barro and Lee (2000).

law"), government consumption, the external terms of trade, inflation, human capital (average years of education), and saving rates.[15] One limitation here is that data for many of the standard growth determinants are not available over long stretches of time, so that many observations are lost as regressors are added. For example, the "rule of law" index starts only in 1996. Therefore, rather than include all the additional regressors simultaneously, which would reduce the sample size excessively, I tried various combinations, dropping those variables that seem to enter insignificantly or cause too many observations to be lost.

The bottom line is that including these additional regressors does not make much difference to the coefficient on *UNDERVAL*. The estimated coefficient ranges somewhat widely (from a high of 0.063 to a low of 0.016) but remains strongly significant throughout, with the *t* statistic never falling below 2.8. The variation in these estimates seems to derive in any case as much from changes in the sample as from the effect of the covariates. Indeed, given the range of controls considered and the significant changes in sample size (from a low of 191 to a high of 790), the robustness of the central finding on undervaluation is quite striking. Note in particular that *UNDERVAL* remains strong even when the regression controls for changes in the terms of trade or government consumption (or both together), or for saving rates, three variables that are among the main drivers of the real exchange rate (see below).

Robustness: Cross-Sectional Regressions

As a final robustness check, I ran cross-sectional regressions using the full sample in an attempt to identify the growth effects of undervaluation solely through differences across countries. The dependent variable here is the growth rate of each country averaged over a twenty-five-year period (1980–2004). Undervaluation is similarly averaged over the same quarter century, and initial income is GDP per capita in 1980. Regressors include all the covariates considered in table 4 (except for the terms of trade) along with dummies for developing country regions as defined by the World Bank.

The results (table 5) are quite consistent with those in the vast empirical literature on cross-national growth. Economic growth over long time horizons tends to increase with human capital, quality of institutions, and

15. The data source for most of these variables is the World Bank's World Development Indicators. Data for the "rule of law" come from the World Bank governance dataset (Kaufmann, Kraay, and Mastruzzi, 2008), and those for human capital (years of education) from Barro and Lee (2000).

Table 5. Cross-Sectional Regressions of Economic Growth on Undervaluation and Other Variables[a]

Independent variable	Regression 5-1	5-2	5-3	5-4	5-5	5-6	5-7
ln initial income[b]	−0.014***	−0.013***	−0.013***	−0.016***	−0.018***	−0.017***	−0.013***
	(−4.20)	(−3.59)	(−3.51)	(−6.18)	(−6.00)	(−7.74)	(−6.80)
ln *UNDERVAL*	0.022***	0.021***	0.020***	0.022***	0.021***	0.020***	0.019***
	(5.95)	(4.45)	(4.32)	(5.31)	(4.93)	(5.12)	(5.32)
Average years of education × 100	0.250**	0.210*	0.224*	0.143	0.114		
	(2.06)	(1.67)	(1.75)	(1.57)	(1.18)		
Rule of law	0.019***	0.021***	0.020***	0.020***	0.020***	0.020***	0.021***
	(8.19)	(8.09)	(6.40)	(8.28)	(6.91)	(7.34)	(7.90)
Government consumption as percent of GDP		−0.060*	−0.063*				
		(−1.82)	(−1.89)				
ln (1 + inflation rate)			−0.008				
			(−0.92)				
Gross domestic saving as percent of GDP				0.072***	0.070***	0.053***	
				(3.52)	(3.12)	(3.93)	
Sub–Saharan Africa dummy					−0.004	−0.014***	−0.009**
					(−0.87)	(−3.28)	(−2.08)
Latin America dummy					0.002	−0.006	−0.002
					(0.35)	(−0.16)	(−0.43)
Asia dummy[c]					0.000	−0.009**	−0.001
					(0.06)	(−2.22)	(0.16)
R^2	0.57	0.56	0.57	0.68	0.69	0.55	0.48
No. of observations	104	102	102	102	104	147	155

Source: Author's regressions.

a. The dependent variable is average annual growth in income per capita over 1980–2004. World regions are as defined by the World Bank. Robust *t* statistics are in parentheses. Asterisks indicate statistical significance at the *10 percent, **5 percent, or ***1 percent level.

b. Initial income is GDP per capita in 1980.

c. "Asia" is East Asia and South Asia.

saving, and to decrease with government consumption and inflation. The Africa dummy tends to be negative and statistically significant. Interestingly, the Asia dummy is negative and significant in one regression that controls for saving rates (column 5-6) and not in the otherwise identical regression that does not (column 5-7). Most important for purposes of this paper, the estimated coefficient on *UNDERVAL* is highly significant and virtually unchanged in all these specifications, fluctuating between 0.019 and 0.022. It is interesting—and comforting—that these coefficient estimates and those obtained from the panel regressions are so similar.

Given the difficulty of controlling for all the country-specific determinants of growth, there are good reasons to distrust estimates from cross-sectional regressions of this kind. That is why panels with fixed effects are my preferred specification. Nevertheless, the results in table 5 represent a useful and encouraging robustness check.

Causality

Another possible objection to these results is that the relationship they capture is not truly causal. The real exchange rate is the relative price of tradables to nontradables in an economy and as such is an endogenous variable. Does it then make sense to put it (or some transformation) on the right-hand side of a regression equation and talk about its effect on growth? Perhaps it would not in a world where governments did not care about the real exchange rate and left it to be determined purely by market forces. But we do not live in such a world: except in a handful of developed countries, most governments pursue a variety of policies with the explicit goal of affecting the real exchange rate. Fiscal policies, saving incentives (or disincentives), capital account policies, and interventions in currency markets are part of the array of such policies. In principle, moving the real exchange rate requires changes in real quantities, but economists have long known that even policies that affect only nominal magnitudes can do the trick—for a while. One of the key findings of the open-economy macroeconomic literature is that except in highly inflationary environments, nominal exchange rates and real exchange rates move quite closely together. Eduardo Levy-Yeyati and Federico Sturzenegger have recently shown that sterilized interventions can and do affect the real exchange rate in the short to medium term.[16] Therefore, interpreting the above results as saying something about the growth effects of different exchange rate management strategies seems plausible.

16. Levy-Yeyati and Sturzenegger (2007).

Of course, one still has to worry about the possibility of reverse causation and about omitted variables bias. The real exchange rate may respond to a variety of shocks besides policy shocks, and these may confound the interpretation of δ. The inclusion of some of the covariates considered in tables 4 and 5 serves to diminish concern on this score. For example, an autonomous reduction in government consumption or an increase in domestic saving will both tend to produce a real depreciation, ceteris paribus. To the extent that such policies are designed to move the real exchange rate in the first place, they are part of what I have in mind when I talk of "a policy of undervaluation." But to the extent they are not, the results in tables 4 and 5 indicate that undervaluation is associated with faster economic growth even when those policies are controlled for.

A more direct approach is to treat *UNDERVAL* explicitly as an endogenous regressor; this is done in table 6. Note first that a conventional instrumental variables approach is essentially ruled out here, because it is difficult to think of exogenous regressors that influence the real exchange rate without plausibly also having an independent effect on growth. I will report results of regressions on the determinants of *UNDERVAL* in table 10; all of the regressors used there have been used as independent variables in growth regressions. Here I adopt instead a dynamic panel approach using the generalized method of moments (GMM) as the estimation method.[17] These models use lagged values of regressors (in levels and in differences) as instruments for right-hand-side variables and allow lagged endogenous (left-hand-side) variables as regressors in short panels.[18] Table 6 presents results for both the "difference" and the "system" versions of GMM. As before, the estimated coefficients on *UNDERVAL* are positive and statistically significant for the developing countries (if somewhat at the lower end of the range reported earlier). They are not significant for the developed countries. Hence, when *UNDERVAL* is allowed to be endogenous, the resulting pattern of estimated coefficients is quite in line with the results reported above, which is reassuring.

It is worth reflecting on the sources of endogeneity bias a bit more. Many of the plausible sources of bias that one can think of would induce a negative relationship between undervaluation and growth, not the positive relationship I have documented. So to the extent that endogenous mechanisms are at work, it is not clear that they generally create a bias that works

17. I follow here the technique of Arellano and Bond (1991) and Blundell and Bond (1998).

18. See Roodman (2006) for an accessible user's guide.

Table 6. Generalized Method of Moments Estimates of the Effect of Undervaluation on Growth[a]

	Full sample		*Developed economies only*		*Developing economies only*	
Independent variable	*Two-step difference*	*Two-step system*	*Two-step difference*	*Two-step system*	*Two-step difference*	*Two-step system*
Lagged growth	0.187***	0.308***	0.273***	0.271***	0.200***	0.293***
	(4.39)	(5.45)	(5.34)	(4.48)	(3.95)	(4.55)
ln initial income	−0.038***	0.001	−0.043***	−0.016***	−0.037***	−0.006**
	(−4.86)	(1.17)	(−5.21)	(−4.11)	(−4.72)	(−2.34)
ln *UNDERVAL*	0.011	0.011**	0.017	0.005	0.014**	0.013**
	(1.74)	(2.14)	(1.55)	(0.60)	(2.28)	(2.26)
No. of countries	156	179	79	89	112	125
Average no. of observations per country	6.04	6.27	6.22	5.18	6.07	5.29
Hansen test of overidentifying restrictions, $p > \chi^2$	0.067	0.101	0.893	0.762	0.332	0.253

Source: Author's regressions.

a. The dependent variable is annual growth in GDP per capita, in percent. Observations are averages over five-year periods. Results are generated using the xtabond2 command in Stata, with small sample adjustment for standard errors, forward orthogonal deviations, and assuming exogeneity of initial income and time dummies (see Roodman 2005). All regressions include time fixed effects. Extreme observations are excluded as noted in table 1. Robust *t* statistics are in parentheses. Asterisks indicate statistical significance at the *10 percent, **5 percent, or ***1 percent level.

against my findings. Economic growth is expected to cause a real appreciation on standard Balassa-Samuelson grounds (which I control for by using *UNDERVAL*). Shocks that cause a real depreciation tend to be shocks that are bad for growth on conventional grounds—a reversal in capital inflows or a terms of trade deterioration, for example. Good news about the growth prospects of an economy is likely to attract capital inflows and thus bring about a real appreciation. So, on balance, it is unlikely that the positive coefficients reported here result from the reverse effect of growth on the real exchange rate.

Evidence from Growth Accelerations

A different way to look at the cross-national evidence is to examine countries that have experienced noticeable growth accelerations and ask what happened to *UNDERVAL* before, during, and after these episodes. This way of parsing the data throws out a lot of information but has the virtue that it focuses attention on a key question: have those countries that managed to engineer sharp increases in economic growth done so on the back of undervalued currencies?[19]

Ricardo Hausmann, Lant Pritchett, and I identified 83 distinct instances of growth acceleration in which annual growth in GDP per capita rose by 2 percentage points or more and the spurt was sustained for at least eight years.[20] Figure 4 shows the average values of *UNDERVAL* in each of these episodes for a 21-year window centered on the year of the acceleration (the 10-year periods before and after the acceleration plus the year of the acceleration). The figure shows some interesting patterns in the trend of *UNDERVAL* but is especially telling with respect to the experience of different subgroups.

For the full sample of growth accelerations, a noticeable, if moderate, decline in overvaluation occurs in the decade before the onset of the growth spurt. The increase in *UNDERVAL* is on the order of 10 percentage points and is sustained into the first five years or so of the episode. Since these growth accelerations include quite a few rich countries in the 1950s and 1960s, figure 4 also shows results for only those growth accelerations in the sample that occurred after 1970. There is a much more distinct trend in *UNDERVAL* for this subsample: the growth spurt takes place after a decade of steady increase in *UNDERVAL* and immediately after the index reaches its peak value (at an undervaluation of 10 percent). Finally, figure 4 also

19. A similar exercise was carried out for a few, mostly Asian, countries by Hausmann (2006).

20. Hausmann, Pritchett, and Rodrik (2005).

Figure 4. Relative Timing of Undervaluations and Growth Accelerations

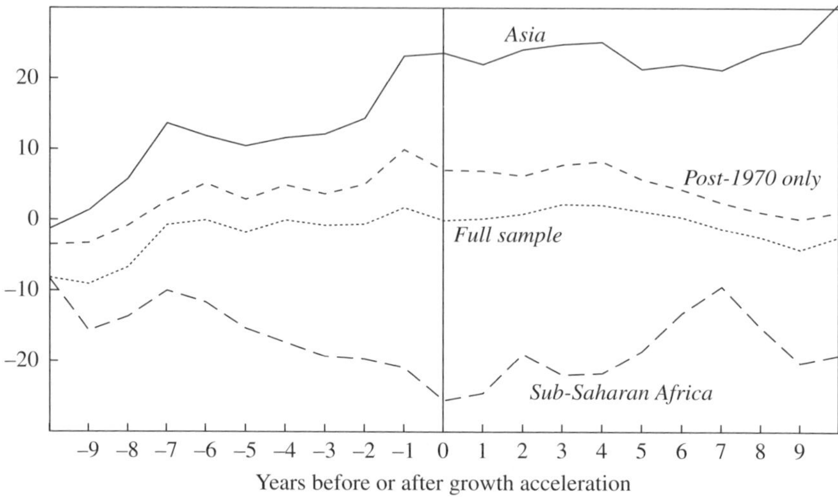

Source: Author's calculations.

shows results for the Asian and Sub-Saharan African countries separately. The Asian countries reveal the most pronounced trend, with an average undervaluation of more than 20 percent at the start of the growth acceleration. Moreover, the undervaluation is sustained into the growth episode, and in fact it increases further by the end of the decade. In the African growth accelerations, in contrast, the image is virtually the mirror opposite. Here the typical growth acceleration takes place after a decade of increased overvaluation, and its timing coincides with the peak of the overvaluation. As is well known, the Asian growth accelerations have proved significantly more impressive and lasting than African ones. The contrasting behavior of the real exchange rate may offer an important clue as to the sources of the difference.

Size of the Tradable Sector as the Operative Channel

The real exchange rate is a relative price, the price of tradable goods in terms of nontradable goods:

$$RER = P_T / P_N.$$

An increase in *RER* enhances the relative profitability of the tradable sector and causes it to expand (at the expense of the nontradable sector).

I now provide some evidence that these compositional changes in the structure of economic activity are an important driving force behind the empirical regularity I have identified. I show two things in particular. First, undervaluation has a positive effect on the relative size of the tradable sector, and especially of industrial economic activities. Second, the effects of the real exchange rate on growth operate, at least in part, through the associated change in the relative size of tradables. Countries where undervaluation induces resources to move toward tradables (again, mainly industry) grow more rapidly.

The first four columns in table 7 report standard panel regressions where five-year-average sectoral shares (in real terms) are regressed on income, a complete set of fixed effects, and my measure of undervaluation. I initially lumped agriculture and industry together in constructing the dependent variable, since both are nominally tradable, but as these regressions show, they have quite a different relationship with real exchange rates. Whether measured by its share in GDP or its share in employment, the relative size of industry depends strongly and positively on the degree of undervaluation as shown in the first two columns.[21] Simply put, undervaluation boosts industrial activities. Agriculture, on the other hand, does not have a positive relationship with undervaluation. Its GDP share actually depends negatively on the undervaluation measure (third column). This difference may reflect the prevalence of quantitative restrictions in agricultural trade, which typically turn many agricultural commodities into nontradables at the margin.

The last two columns of table 7 report results of two-stage panel growth regressions (with, as before, a full set of fixed effects) that test whether the effect of undervaluation on growth operates through its impact on the relative size of industry. The strategy consists of identifying whether the component of industrial shares directly "caused" by undervaluation—that is, industrial shares as instrumented by undervaluation—enters positively and significantly in the growth regressions. The answer is affirmative. These results indicate that undervaluation causes resources to move toward industry and that this shift in resources in turn promotes economic growth.[22]

21. Blomberg, Frieden, and Stein (2005) report some evidence that countries with larger manufacturing sectors have greater difficulty in sustaining currency pegs. But it is not immediately evident which way this potential reverse causality cuts.

22. See also the supporting evidence in Rajan and Subramanian (2006), who find that real appreciations induced by aid inflows have adverse effects on the relative growth rate of exporting industries as well as on the growth rate of the manufacturing sector as a whole. Rajan and Subramanian argue that this is one of the more important reasons why aid fails to

Table 7. Panel Regressions Estimating the Effect of Undervaluation on Tradables[a]

	Dependent variable					
Independent variable	*Industry share in GDP*	*Industry share in employment*	*Agriculture share in GDP*	*Agriculture share in employment*	*Growth (TSLS estimation)*[b]	*Growth (TSLS estimation)*[b]
ln current income	0.079*** (9.99)	0.025 (1.51)	−0.110*** (−12.50)	−0.128*** (−4.94)		
ln initial income					−0.134*** (−8.33)	−0.071*** (−4.39)
ln *UNDERVAL*	0.024*** (3.62)	0.042*** (4.87)	−0.016** (−2.25)	−0.010 (−0.48)		
Industry share in GDP					1.716*** (7.59)	
Industry share in employment						1.076*** (6.15)
No. of observations	985	469	985	469	938	459

Source: Author's regressions.

a. Observations of the dependent variable are five-year averages. All regressions include time and country fixed effects. Robust *t* statistics are in parentheses. Asterisks indicate statistical significance at the *10 percent, **5 percent, or ***1 percent level.

b. Industry shares, in constant local currency units, are regressed on ln *UNDERVAL,* ln income, and lagged ln income in the first stage of a two-stage least squares (TSLS) regression.

The estimates in table 7 also provide a useful check on the quantitative magnitudes involved. They break the undervaluation-growth relationship into two separate links, one from undervaluation to the size of tradables (that is, industry) and the other from the size of industry to economic growth. If undervaluation has a potent effect on growth, that is because each of these two links is estimated to be quite strong. A 50 percent undervaluation is estimated to increase the share of industry in total employment by 2.1 percentage points (0.042×0.50), which is quite large given that the typical share of industry in total employment in developing countries is around 20 percent. An increase in the industrial employment share is in turn estimated to raise growth roughly one for one.

Understanding the Importance of the Real Exchange Rate

Why might an increase in the relative price of tradables and the associated expansion of tradable economic activities have a causal impact on economic growth, as my results suggest? There is no generally accepted theory that would explain these regularities in the data.[23] Any such theory would have to explain why tradables are "special" from the standpoint of growth. That is the sense in which my results open an important window on the mechanisms behind the growth process. If the role that tradables play in driving growth can be understood, it may be possible to identify policies that will promote (and those that will hamper) growth.

Although any of a large number of stories might account for the role of tradables, two clusters of explanations deserve attention in particular. One focuses on weaknesses in the contracting environment, and the other on market failures in modern industrial production. Both types of explanation have been common in the growth and development literature, but in the present context something more is needed. One has to argue that tradables

induce growth in recipient countries. Gluzmann, Levy-Yeyati, and Sturzenegger (2007), by contrast, find little role for the tradables channel and argue that real undervaluations promote growth through redistributions of income that raise domestic saving (and ultimately investment). However, their argument seems to require that the current account be invariant to the real exchange rate, which is contradicted by considerable evidence. See also Galvarriato and Williamson (2008) on the role played by favorable relative prices in the rapid industrialization of Latin American countries such as Brazil and Mexico after 1870, and Freund and Pierola (2008) on the significance of currency undervaluation in stimulating export surges.

23. In Rodrik (1986) I argued that manipulating the real exchange rate could play a welfare-enhancing role if this served to improve the internal terms of trade of sectors subject to dynamic learning externalities. Gala (2007) suggests that undervaluation is good for growth because activities subject to increasing returns tend to be located in the tradable rather than the nontradable sector.

Figure 5. Undervaluation as a Second-Best Mechanism for Alleviating Institutional Weakness

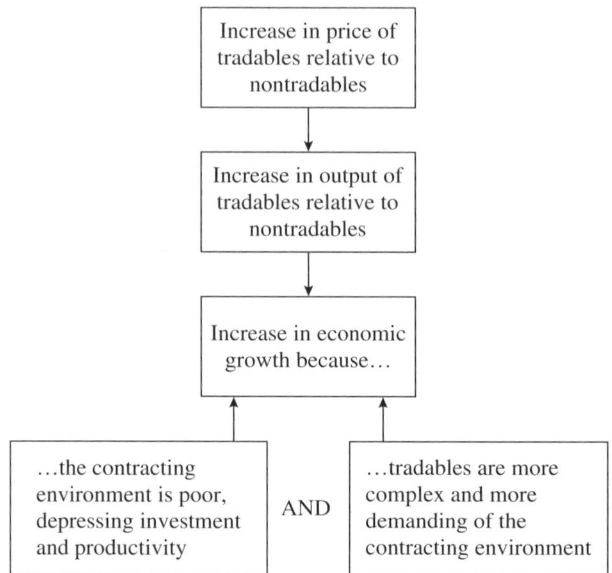

Source: Author's model described in the text.

suffer disproportionately from these shortcomings, so that absent a compensating policy, developing economies devote too few of their resources to tradables and thus grow less rapidly than they should. Real undervaluation can then act as a second-best mechanism for spurring growth of tradables and for generating more rapid overall economic growth.

The two clusters of explanations are represented schematically in figures 5 and 6. I discuss them in turn in the rest of this section. The mechanics of how changes in relative prices can generate growth in the presence of sectorally differentiated distortions is discussed in the following section.

Explanation 1: Bad Institutions "Tax" Tradables More

The idea that poor institutions keep incomes low and explain, at least in part, the absence of economic convergence is by now widely accepted.[24] Weak institutions reduce the ability of private investors to appropriate the returns on their investment through a variety of mechanisms: contractual

24. North (1990); Acemoglu, Johnson, and Robinson (2001).

Figure 6. Undervaluation as a Second-Best Mechanism for Alleviating Market Failure

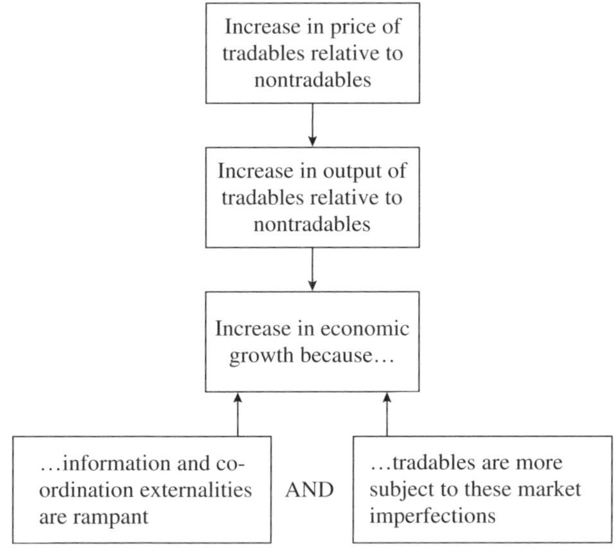

Source: Author's model described in the text.

incompleteness, hold-up problems, corruption, lack of property rights, and poor contract enforcement. The resulting wedge between private and social returns in turn blunts the incentives for capital accumulation and technological progress alike.

Now suppose that this problem is more severe in tradables than in nontradables. This is a plausible supposition since production systems tend to be more complex and roundabout in tradables, placing a greater premium on the ability to specify contracts and on reliable third-party enforcement of contracts. A barber needs to rely on little more than a few tools, a chair, and his skill and ingenuity to sell his services. A manufacturing firm needs the cooperation of multitudes of suppliers and customers, plus financial and legal support. When the institutions that foster these relationships are weak, the result is to impose a higher "tax" on tradables—especially modern tradables. This results in both a static misallocation of resources that penalizes tradables, and a dynamic distortion in the form of investment in tradables that is lower than socially optimal. An increase in the relative price of tradables can improve static efficiency and enhance growth in second-best fashion by eliciting more investment in tradables at the margin (as I will show in the following section).

A fair amount of empirical work, both across countries and across industries, presents suggestive evidence on the disproportionate cost borne by tradables—as a whole or in part—in the presence of weak institutions:

—Across countries, lower quality of institutions (as measured by indices of the rule of law, contract enforcement, or control of corruption) is associated with lower ratios of trade to GDP ("openness").[25]

—Across different categories of tradable goods, more "institution-intensive" tradables are prone to larger effects. Pierre-Guillaume Méon and Khalid Sekkat find that the relationship they identify holds for manufactured exports but not for nonmanufactured exports; Priya Ranjan and Jae Young Lee find that the effect is stronger for differentiated goods than for homogeneous goods.[26]

—Institutional weakness interacts with the contract intensity of goods to play a role in determining comparative advantage. Andrei Levchenko; Daniel Berkowitz, Johannes Moenius, and Katharina Pistor; and Nathan Nunn find that countries with poor institutions have comparative disadvantage in products that are more institutions-intensive, more complex, or more relationship-intensive.[27]

To provide more direct evidence, I used unpublished data kindly provided by Nathan Nunn to compare directly the contract-intensiveness of tradables and nontradables. Nunn investigated whether differences in institutional quality across countries help determine patterns of comparative advantage.[28] He reasoned that relationship-specific intermediate inputs, defined as inputs that are not sold on exchanges or do not have reference prices,[29] are more demanding of the contractual environment. Nunn used measures of relationship specificity for tradables alone, since his main concern was with comparative advantage. But he collected similar data for services as well, which are what I use to carry out the tradables-nontradables comparison.

The top panel of table 8 shows the shares of intermediate goods that are relationship-specific in tradables and nontradables industries. (These numbers are based on the U.S. input-output tables.) At first sight, these numbers seem to conflict with what my argument requires, in that they show that the

25. See, for example, Anderson and Mercouiller (2002), Rodrik, Subramanian, and Trebbi (2004), Rigobon and Rodrik (2005), Méon and Sekkat (2006), Berkowitz, Moenius, and Pistor (2006), and Ranjan and Lee (2004).

26. Méon and Sekkat (2006); Ranjan and Lee (2004).

27. Levchenko (2004); Berkowitz, Moenius, and Pistor (2006); Nunn (2007).

28. Nunn (2007).

29. As in Rauch (1999).

Table 8. Illustrative Calculations on the Importance of Relationship Specificity of Inputs for Traded and Nontraded Goods
Percent

	Tradables	*Nontradables*
Tradables use intermediate goods that tend to be less relationship specific . . .		
Share of intermediates not sold on exchanges and not reference-priced[a]	49.6	75.1
Share of intermediates not sold on exchanges[a]	87.3	96.4
. . . but tradables rely more on intermediate inputs . . .		
Share of intermediates in total output[b]	64.3	35.1
Share of interindustry sales in total output[b]	58.4	29.4
. . . so, on balance, relationship-specific intermediate goods account for a much larger share of output in tradables.		
Share in gross output of intermediates not sold on exchanges and not reference-priced[c]	17.9	7.5
Share in gross output of intermediates not sold on exchanges[c]	31.5	9.7

Source: Author's calculations.
a. Unweighted averages, from the U.S. input-output tables, calculated using data provided by Nathan Nunn, based on Nunn (2007).
b. From the Brazilian input-output tables for 1996, available on the website of the OECD Directorate for Science, Technology, and Industry (www.oecd.org/sti).
c. Sums of the products of the underlying data in the top two panels weighted by U.S. value-added shares.

inputs used in tradables are less relationship-specific, and hence less demanding of the institutional environment. But this is misleading because it overlooks the fact that tradables tend to have much higher intermediate input shares in gross output. This is shown in the middle panel of the table (this time relying on Brazil's input-output tables). Putting the two pieces together yields the results in the bottom panel of table 8, which show that, on balance, tradable goods rely on relationship-specific inputs to a much greater extent. The numbers for the two sets of goods differ by a factor of between two and three.

Hence the evidence that institutional and contracting shortcomings, the bane of every developing society, impose a higher "tax" on the tradable sector than on the nontradable sector is fairly compelling. But if this story is correct, its implications should also be evident in the growth regressions. Specifically, the growth impact of undervaluation should be greater in those countries where this "taxation" is greatest, namely, the countries with the weakest institutions. Although GDP per capita does track institutional quality closely, it is not a perfect proxy. So the question is whether one can detect the differential impact in settings with different institutional environments.

To attempt this more direct test, I used the World Bank governance indices to divide the countries in the full sample into three subgroups based on their "adjusted" institutional quality (above average, around average, and below average).[30] The exercise was conducted as follows. For each country I took a simple average of the World Bank's rule of law, government effectiveness, regulatory quality, and corruption indices over 1996–2004 (starting from the earliest year for which these indices are available). I then regressed these indices on log GDP per capita, generating a predicted value based on this cross section. Taking the difference between actual and predicted values, I ranked countries according to their "adjusted" levels of institutional quality. I then divided the sample into three subgroups of equal size.

The middle three columns of table 9 show the results of my benchmark specification when the regression is run for each subgroup separately. (For comparison, the first column repeats the baseline results from column 1-1 of table 1.) The results are broadly consistent with the theoretical expectation. The positive effect of undervaluation is strongest in the below-average group and virtually nil in the above-average group. In other words, when initial income is taken into account, undervaluation works most potently in those countries where institutions perform the least well. In the last column in table 9, I instead interact dummies for the subgroups with *UNDERVAL* (taking the above-average group as the omitted category), and the results are very similar.

The analytics of how institutional weakness interacts with undervaluation to influence growth will be developed further in the next section. But first I turn to the second category of explanations.

Explanation 2: Market Failures Predominate in Tradables

The second hypothesis for why the real exchange rate matters is that tradables are particularly prone to the market failures with which development economists have long been preoccupied. A short list of such market failures would include

—learning externalities: valuable technological, marketing, and other information spills over to other firms and industries;

30. For the latest version of these indices see Kaufmann, Kraay, and Mastruzzi (2008).

Table 9. Institutional Quality and the Impact of Undervaluation on Growth[a]

Independent variable	*Baseline (all countries)*	*Countries where institutional quality is*			*Interactions with group dummies (all countries)*
		Above average	*Around average*	*Below average*	
ln initial income	−0.031***	−0.036***	−0.017**	−0.060***	−0.031***
	(−6.67)	(−5.59)	(−2.32)	(−4.73)	(−6.90)
ln *UNDERVAL*	0.017***	0.004	0.022***	0.028***	0.005
	(5.21)	(1.17)	(3.98)	(4.42)	(1.45)
ln *UNDERVAL* × around-average institutions					0.019***
					(2.86)
ln *UNDERVAL* × below-average institutions					0.019**
					(2.36)
No. of observations	1,303	513	434	356	1,303

Source: Author's regressions.

a. The dependent variable is annual growth in GDP per capita, in percent. Observations are five-year averages. All regressions include time and country fixed effects. Robust t statistics are in parentheses. Asterisks indicate statistical significance at the *10 percent, **5 percent, or ***1 percent level.

—coordination externalities: getting new industries off the ground requires lumpy and coordinated investments upstream, downstream, or sideways;

—credit market imperfections: entrepreneurs cannot finance worthwhile projects because of limited liability and asymmetric information;

—wage premiums: monitoring, turnover, and other costs keep wages above market-clearing levels, and employment remains low.

These and similar problems can plague all kinds of economic activity in developing countries, but arguably their effects are felt much more acutely in tradables. If so, output and investment in tradables will be suboptimal. A real depreciation would promote capacity expansion in tradables and increase growth. Note that once again this is a second-best argument for undervaluation. First-best policy would consist of identifying distinct market failures and applying the appropriate Pigovian remedies. Undervaluation is in effect a substitute for industrial policy.

What is the evidence? By their very nature, the types of market failures listed above are difficult to identify, and so it is practically impossible to provide direct evidence that some kinds of goods are more prone to these market failures than others. But the basic hypothesis is quite plausible, and a close look at the processes behind economic development yields plenty of indirect and suggestive evidence. Economic development consists of structural change, investment in new activities, and the acquisition of new productive capabilities. As countries grow, the range of tradable goods that they produce expands.[31] Rich countries are rich not just because they produce traditional goods in greater abundance, but also because they produce different goods.[32] The market failures listed above are likely to be much more severe in new lines of production—those needed to increase economy-wide productivity—than in traditional ones. New industries require "cost discovery,"[33] learning-by-doing, and complementary economic activities to get established. They are necessarily risky and lack track records. These features make them fertile ground for learning and coordination externalities. The recent findings of Caroline Freund and Martha Pierola are particularly suggestive in this connection: currency undervaluation appears to play a very important role in inducing producers from developing countries to enter new product lines and new markets, and this seems to be the primary mechanism through which they generate export surges.[34]

Discussion

Unfortunately, it is not easy to distinguish empirically between the two broad hypotheses I have outlined. In principle, if one could identify the goods that are most affected by each of these two categories of imperfections—contractual and market failures—one could run a horse race between the two hypotheses by asking which goods among them are more strongly associated with economic growth. Nunn's data are a useful beginning for ranking goods by degree of contract intensity.[35] Perhaps an analogous set of rankings could be developed for market failures using the commodity categorization in Hausmann and Rodrik,[36] which are loosely based on the prevalence of learning externalities. But ultimately I doubt that one can make a sufficiently fine and reliable distinction among goods to allow discrimination between the two stories in a credible manner. Rich countries differ from poor countries both because they have better institutions and because they have learned how to deal with market imperfections. Producers of tradable goods in developing economies suffer on both counts.

31. Imbs and Wacziarg (2003).
32. Hausmann, Hwang, and Rodrik (2007).
33. Hausmann and Rodrik (2003).
34. Freund and Pierola (2008).
35. Nunn (2007).
36. Hausmann and Rodrik (2003).

A Simple Model of Real Exchange Rates and Growth

I argued in the previous section that when tradables are affected disproportionately by preexisting distortions, a real depreciation can be good for growth. I now develop a simple model to illustrate the mechanics behind this hypothesis. I will consider an economy in which there exist "taxes" on both the tradable and the nontradable sectors that drive a wedge between the private and the social marginal benefits. When the tax on tradables is larger (in ad valorem terms) than the tax on nontradables, the economy's resources will be misallocated, the tradable sector will be too small, and growth will be suboptimal. Under these circumstances a real depreciation can promote growth.

Consumption and Growth

In the model, consumers consume a single final good, which as shown below is produced using a combination of tradable and nontradable inputs. Their intertemporal utility function is time-separable and logarithmic and takes the form

$$u = \int \ln c_t e_t^{-\rho} dt,$$

where c_t is consumption at time t and ρ is the discount rate. Maximizing utility subject to an intertemporal budget constraint yields the familiar growth equation

$$\dot{c}_t / c_t = r_t - \rho, \tag{3}$$

where r is the real interest rate (or the marginal product of capital). The economy's growth is increasing in r, and this is the feature that I will exploit in the rest of this section.

Production

I assume that the economy produces the single final good using tradable and nontradable goods (y_T and y_N, respectively) as the sole inputs. Production of the final good (y) is a Cobb-Douglas aggregate of these two inputs. In addition, to allow for endogenous growth (while maintaining perfect competition throughout), I assume that capital produces external economies in the production of the final good. With these assumptions, the production function of the representative final-good producer can be written as follows:

$$y = \bar{k}^{1-\varphi} y_T^{\alpha} y_N^{1-\alpha}, \tag{4}$$

where k is the economy's capital stock at any point in time (treated as exogenous by each final-goods producer), and α and $1 - \alpha$ are the shares of tradable and nontradable goods, respectively, in the production costs of the final good ($0 < \alpha < 1$). For convenience, I choose the exponent on k to be a parameter $(1 - \varphi)$ that will make aggregate output linear in capital—as will be shown shortly—and which therefore considerably simplifies the comparative dynamics of the model. I also omit time subscripts to simplify the notation.

Tradables and nontradables are in turn produced using capital alone and subject to decreasing returns to scale. These production functions take the following simple form:

$$q_T = A_T k_T^{\varphi} = A_T \left(\theta_T \bar{k}\right)^{\varphi} \tag{5}$$

$$q_N = A_N k_N^{\varphi} = A_N \left[\left(1 - \theta_T\right)\bar{k}\right]^{\varphi}, \tag{6}$$

where k_T and k_N denote the capital stock employed in the tradables and the nontradables sectors, respectively; θ_T is the share of total capital employed in tradables and $0 < \theta_T < 1$; and $0 < \varphi < 1$. To justify decreasing returns to capital in the sectoral production functions (that is, $\varphi < 1$), one can suppose that there are other, sector-specific factors of production employed in each sector that are fixed in supply.

By definition, nontradables that are used as inputs in the final-goods sector can only be sourced domestically. And since nontradables do not enter consumption directly,

$$q_N = y_N. \tag{7}$$

With respect to tradables, I allow the economy to receive a transfer from the rest of the world (or to make a transfer to it). Let b stand for the magnitude of the inward transfer. Then the material-balances equation in tradables is given by

$$q_T + b = y_T.$$

It will be more convenient to express b as a share γ of total domestic demand for tradables. That is, $b = \gamma y_T$. The equality between demand and supply in tradables then becomes

$$\frac{1}{1-\gamma} q_T = y_T. \tag{8}$$

When the economy makes an outward transfer, γ will be negative. I will use γ as a shifter that alters the equilibrium value of the real exchange rate.

Using equations 4 through 8, one can express the aggregate production function as

$$y = (1-\gamma)^{-\alpha} A_T^{\alpha} A_N^{1-\alpha} \theta_T^{\alpha\varphi} (1-\theta_T)^{(1-\alpha)\varphi} \bar{k}. \tag{9}$$

Net output $\tilde{y}$ differs from gross output insofar as the economy makes a payment to the rest of the world for the transfer b (or receives a payment from it if b is negative). I express this payment in general form, assuming that it is a share σ of the transfer's contribution to gross output; that is, $\sigma \times (\partial y/\partial b) \times b = \sigma \times (\partial y/\partial y_T) \times \gamma y_T = \sigma \times (\alpha/y_T)y \times \gamma y_T = \sigma\alpha\gamma y$. Net output $\tilde{y}$ equals $y - \sigma\alpha\gamma y = (1 - \sigma\alpha\gamma)y$. Therefore, using equation 9,

$$\tilde{y} = (1-\sigma\alpha\gamma)(1-\gamma)^{-\alpha} A_T^{\alpha} A_N^{1-\alpha} \theta_T^{\alpha\varphi} (1-\theta_T)^{(1-\alpha)\varphi} \bar{k}. \tag{10}$$

This way of expressing the payment for the transfer allows a wide variety of scenarios. The transfer's contribution to net output is maximized when $\sigma = 0$, that is, when b is a pure transfer (a grant). The contribution becomes smaller as σ increases.

Note that the production function ends up being of the *Ak* type, that is, linear in capital. This results in an endogenous growth model with no transitional dynamics. The (net) marginal product of capital r is $\partial\tilde{y}/\partial\bar{k}$, or

$$r = (1-\sigma\alpha\gamma)(1-\gamma)^{-\alpha} A_T^{\alpha} A_N^{1-\alpha} \theta_T^{\alpha\varphi} (1-\theta_T)^{(1-\alpha)\varphi}, \tag{11}$$

which is independent of the capital stock but depends on the allocation of capital between tradables and nontradables, θ_T, as well as on the net value of the transfer from abroad.

Since the economy's growth rate will depend on r, it is important to know precisely how r depends on θ_T. Log-differentiating equation 11 with respect to θ_T yields

$$\frac{d \ln r}{d\theta_T} \propto \left[\left(\frac{\alpha}{\theta_T}\right) - \left(\frac{1-\alpha}{1-\theta_T}\right)\right],$$

with

$$\frac{d \ln r}{d\theta_T} = 0 \Leftrightarrow \theta_T = \alpha.$$

In other words, the return to capital is maximized when the share of the capital stock that the economy allocates to tradables (θ_T) is exactly equal to the input share of tradables in final production (α). This rate of return, and ultimately the economy's growth rate, will be suboptimal when tradables receive a smaller share of capital. I next analyze the circumstances under which such inefficiencies obtain.

Sectoral Allocation of Capital

The allocation of capital between the tradable and the nontradable sectors will depend both on the relative demand for the two goods and on the relative profitability of producing them. Consider the latter first. In equilibrium, capital will be allocated such that its (private) value marginal product is equalized in the two sectors. As discussed previously, I presume that each sector faces an "appropriability" problem, arising from either institutional weaknesses or market failures or both. I model this by assuming that private producers can retain only a share $1 - \tau_i$ of the value of producing each good $i = T, N$. In other words, τ_T and τ_N are the effective "tax" rates faced by producers in their sector. Let the relative price of tradables p_T/p_N be denoted by R. This is my index of the "real exchange rate." The equality between the value marginal product of capital in the two sectors can then be expressed as

$$(1-\tau_T)R\varphi A_T(\theta_T\bar{k})^{\varphi-1} = (1-\tau_N)\varphi A_N[(1-\theta_T)\bar{k}]^{\varphi-1},$$

which simplifies to

$$\left(\frac{\theta_T}{1-\theta_T}\right)^{\varphi-1} = \left(\frac{1-\tau_N}{1-\tau_T}\right)\frac{1}{R}\frac{A_N}{A_T}. \qquad (12)$$

This is a supply-side relationship which says that the share of capital allocated to tradables increases with the relative profitability of the tradable sector. This relative profitability in turn increases with R, τ_N, and A_T and decreases with τ_T and A_N (remember that $\varphi - 1 < 0$). The SS schedule is positively sloped between θ_T and R, as is shown in figure 7.

Now turn to the demand side. In view of the Cobb-Douglas form of the production function for the final good, the demands for the two intermediate goods are given by

$$\alpha y = p_T y_T = p_T\left(\frac{1}{1-\gamma}\right)q_T = p_T\left(\frac{1}{1-\gamma}\right)A_T(\theta_T\bar{k})^{\varphi}$$
$$(1-\alpha)y = p_N y_N = p_N q_N = p_N A_N[(1-\theta_T)\bar{k}]^{\varphi}.$$

Taking the ratios of these two expressions and rearranging terms,

Figure 7. Allocation of Capital and the Real Exchange Rate in Equilibrium

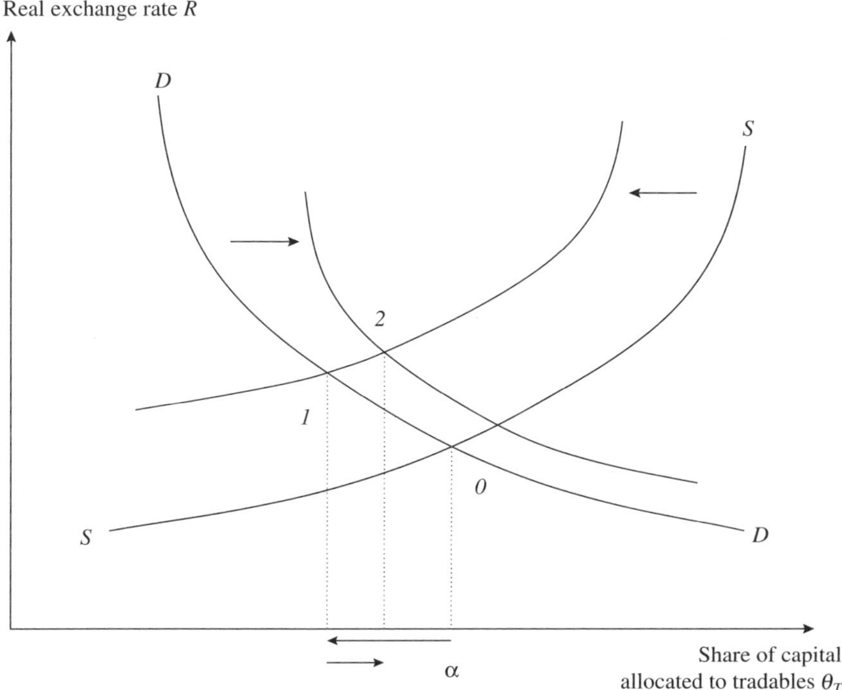

Source: Author's model described in the text.

(13) $$\left(\frac{\theta_T}{1-\theta_T}\right)^{\varphi} = (1-\gamma)\left(\frac{\alpha}{1-\alpha}\right)\frac{1}{R}\frac{A_N}{A_T}.$$

This is a demand-side relationship between θ_T and R and is shown as the DD schedule in figure 7. This schedule is negatively sloped since an increase in R makes tradables more expensive and reduces the demand for capital in that sector. Note that a reduction in γ (a smaller inward transfer) shifts this schedule to the right: it increases θ_T at a given R or increases R at a given 0_T.

Equilibrium and Implications

The equilibrium levels of θ_T and R are given by the point of intersection of the SS and DD schedules. Several things should be noted about the nature of this equilibrium. To begin with, suppose that the economy is at an initial position where there is no transfer from abroad ($\gamma = 0$). If there are no appropriability problems in either of the intermediate-goods sectors, such that $\tau_T = \tau_N = 0$, then it is relatively easy to confirm that the equilibrium is one where $\theta_T = \alpha$ (point 0 in figure 7). This ensures that the returns to capital and growth are maximized. Now suppose that τ_T and τ_N are positive but that their magnitude is identical ($\tau_T = \tau_N > 0$). One can see from equation 11 that the equilibrium remains unaffected. As long as the distortion affects tradables and nontradables equally, θ_T remains at its growth-maximizing level.

Things are different when $\tau_T \neq \tau_N$. Suppose that $\tau_T > \tau_N$, which I have argued is the more likely situation. Relative to the previous equilibrium, this entails a leftward shift in the SS schedule. In the new equilibrium (point 1 in figure 7), θ_T is lower (and R is higher). Because $\theta_T < \alpha$, the economy pays a growth penalty as a result of the tradable sector being too small. Note that the endogenous real depreciation plays a compensatory role, but only a partial one.

Starting from this new equilibrium (where $\tau_T > \tau_N$ and $\theta_T < \alpha$), it is entirely possible that a negative transfer would improve the economy's growth. That is because a reduction in γ leads to an increase in the equilibrium level of the real exchange rate and moves θ_T closer to α. In terms of figure 7, a fall in γ shifts the DD schedule to the right and causes both R and θ_T to rise (point 2). Whether growth also increases ultimately remains uncertain, because the reduction in γ also has a direct negative effect on growth (see equation 11). But if σ is sufficiently high, one can always generate cases where this is on balance growth promoting. In such cases, the real depreciation generated by the negative external transfer becomes a second-best instrument to offset the growth costs of the differential distortion of tradables.

Policy Implications

The main point of this paper can be stated succinctly. Tradable economic activities are "special" in developing countries. These activities suffer disproportionately from the institutional and market failures that keep countries poor. A sustained real depreciation increases the relative profitability of investing in tradables and acts in second-best fashion to alleviate the economic cost of these distortions. It speeds up structural change in the direction that promotes growth. That is why episodes of undervaluation are strongly associated with more rapid economic growth.

Are my quantitative estimates of the growth effects of undervaluation plausible? For developing countries my estimates of $\hat{\delta}$ range from 0.063

(albeit in a highly reduced sample, in column 4-2 of table 4) to 0.012 (in the last column of table 3) and cluster around 0.020. If one takes the last number as a central estimate, the implication is that an undervaluation of, say, 20 percent boosts annual growth by 0.4 percentage point. Can the channel I have focused on deliver effects of this magnitude? Remember that the mechanism that generates growth here is structural change. So the answer obviously depends on the size of the gaps between social marginal products in tradable (especially industrial) and nontradable sectors. I have already given some reasons for why these gaps can be quite large. A long tradition of thought on economic dualism in developing countries takes the persistence of large differences between marginal products in the advanced, "formal" parts of the economy (such as industry) and marginal products elsewhere as the very essence of underdevelopment. Detailed industry studies carried out recently by the McKinsey Global Institute provide some striking, if indirect, evidence on the magnitude of these gaps.[37] They find that productivity levels in the most advanced firms and sectors of developing economies are not too distant from the frontier in the rich economies. Since average productivity in these developing economies is a fraction of that prevailing in the rich economies, the implied intersectoral differences within developing economies are quite large. This paper's distinction between tradable and nontradable sectors maps directly onto this dualistic structure, since most (nonagricultural) tradable activities in a typical developing country are formal whereas most nontradable activities (except for public services) are informal.[38]

There is an obvious parallel between the argument I have developed here and the results presented in a recent paper by Eswar Prasad, Raghuram Rajan, and Arvind Subramanian,[39] who note that fast-growing developing countries have tended to run current account surpluses rather than deficits.

37. See, for example, McKinsey Global Institute (2001, 2003).

38. A simple finger exercise can be helpful here. Denote the productivity premium in industry by ψ and the share of employment in industry by λ_I. Some straightforward algebra can establish that the growth effect of reallocating labor to industry in the amount $d\lambda_I$ is given by growth impact = $[\psi/(1+\psi\lambda_I)]d\lambda_I$. A reasonable assumption on the industrial premium (at the margin) would be that ψ = 50 percent, and a typical industrial share of labor is $\lambda_I = 0.20$. Note from the second column of table 7 that a 20 percent undervaluation would be associated with an increase of 0.84 percentage point in industry's share of total employment ($d\lambda_I = 0.042 \times 0.2 = 0.0084$). Applying the formula, an increase in the industrial labor share of 0.84 percentage point would be expected to generate additional growth equal to 0.38 percentage point, which is virtually identical to the result obtained using the coefficient estimates from the growth regressions (0.4 percentage point).

39. Prasad, Rajan, and Subramanian (2007).

This runs counter to the view that developing countries are constrained by external finance, and to the presumption that capital inflows supplement domestic saving and enable more rapid growth.[40] One of the explanations that Prasad and his coauthors advance is that capital inflows cause a real appreciation and hurt growth through reduced investment incentives in manufactures. They also provide some evidence on this particular channel. Even though these authors focus on the costs of overvaluation rather than the benefits of undervaluation, their concern with the real exchange rate renders their paper complementary to this one.

A maintained hypothesis in this paper thus far has been that the real exchange rate is a policy variable. Strictly speaking, this is not true, as the real exchange rate is a relative price and is determined in general equilibrium along with all other relative prices. But governments have a variety of instruments at their disposal to influence the real exchange rate, and the evidence is that they use them. Maintaining a real undervaluation requires either higher saving relative to investment or lower expenditure relative to income. This can be achieved through fiscal policy (a large structural surplus), incomes policy (redistribution of income to high savers through real wage compression), saving policy (compulsory saving schemes and pension reform), capital account management (taxation of capital account inflows, liberalization of capital outflows), or currency intervention (building up foreign exchange reserves). Experience in East Asia as well as elsewhere (for example, Tunisia) shows that countries that target the real exchange rate (that is, follow a policy of "competitiveness") can have a fair amount of success.

Table 10 presents some systematic evidence on how policy choices feed into the real exchange rate and undervaluation. The table shows the results of regressing *UNDERVAL* on a series of independent variables in a panel with fixed effects. The baseline specification (column 10-1) includes the following regressors: the terms of trade, government consumption (as a percent of GDP), an index of capital account liberalization (*KAOPEN*), and a set of dummy variables capturing the exchange rate regime in force. *KAOPEN* comes from Menzie Chinn and Hiro Ito and is a continuous variable designed to capture the extent and intensity of capital controls.[41] It increases as a country's capital account regime becomes more liberal. The exchange rate regime indicators come from Ethan Ilzetzki, Carmen Reinhart, and Kenneth Rogoff and are entered as separate dummy vari-

40. Rodrik and Subramanian (forthcoming).

41. Chinn and Ito (2006).

Table 10. Panel Regressions of Undervaluation on Selected Policy and Other Variables[a]

Independent variable	*Regression* 10-1	10-2	10-3	10-4
ln terms of trade	–0.139***	–0.164***	–0.167***	–0.115***
	(–3.52)	(–4.14)	(–4.09)	(–2.86)
Government consumption as share of GDP	–0.793***	–0.680***	–0.519***	–0.045
	(–4.35)	(–3.53)	(–2.61)	(–0.23)
Capital account openness (*KAOPEN*)[b]	–0.031***	–0.029***	–0.026***	–0.031***
	(–5.70)	(–5.39)	(–4.56)	(–5.98)
Exchange rate regime dummies:[c]				
Crawl or managed float	0.068***	0.065***	0.065***	0.071***
	(4.86)	(4.64)	(4.47)	(4.87)
Float	0.027	0.028	0.058*	0.026
	(0.85)	(0.89)	(1.83)	(0.82)
Currency in free fall	0.161***	0.158***	0.172***	0.162***
	(4.97)	(4.86)	(5.21)	(4.80)
Dual market with missing parallel market data	0.065	0.067	0.063	0.021
	(1.12)	(1.19)	(1.17)	(0.39)
Gross domestic saving as share of GDP		0.310***	0.355***	0.492***
		(3.55)	(3.80)	(5.10)
FDI inflows as share of GDP			–0.376***	–0.382***
			(–3.11)	(–3.04)
ln (1 + inflation rate)				0.039
				(1.10)
No. of observations	3,153	3,147	2,994	2,757

Source: Author's regressions.

a. The dependent variable is ln *UNDERVAL*. All regressions include time and country fixed effects. See the text for definitions and sources of capital account openness and classifications of exchange rate regimes. Extreme observations are excluded as noted in table 1. Robust *t* statistics are in parentheses. Asterisks indicate statistical significance at the *10 percent, **5 percent, or ***1 percent level.

b. From Chinn and Ito (2006). Higher values indicate greater openness.

c. Classification of exchange rate regimes is from Ilzetzki, Reinhart, and Rogoff (2008). Countries with a rigid exchange rate regime are the excluded category.

ables identifying distinct regimes.[42] So, for example, the "Crawl or managed float" dummy takes the value of one when the country is classified as having a currency regime with a preannounced crawl, a de facto crawl, or a managed float and is zero otherwise. The excluded category is the set of observations with a rigid exchange rate (a fixed peg, a currency board, or a currency union).[43] The remaining columns in the table augment the base-

42. Ilzetzki, Reinhart, and Rogoff (2008). The data for the indicators are available at www.economics.harvard.edu/faculty/rogoff/files/ERA_Background_Material.htm.

43. "Crawl or managed float" corresponds to categories 2 and 3 in Ilzetzki, Reinhart, and Rogoff's (2008) "coarse" classification, and "rigid" corresponds to their category 1.

line specification by adding domestic saving, inflation, and foreign direct investment (FDI) inflows as regressors. Among the variables considered, government consumption, capital account openness, the exchange rate regime, and inflation can be considered direct policy variables, whereas domestic saving and FDI inflows are indirectly affected by policy. The terms of trade are exogenous for most countries but are expected to have a determinate effect on the real exchange rate.

The results in table 10 are quite strong. As expected, positive terms of trade shocks are bad for undervaluation. More important for the present discussion, fiscal policies, capital account policies, and the choice of exchange rate regime all have quite significant effects on undervaluation. Increases in government consumption tend to produce a real appreciation, as do policies that liberalize the capital account. The coefficient on *KAOPEN* implies that going from the Chinese level of capital account restrictions in 2006 (*KAOPEN* = −1.13) to the Mexican level (*KAOPEN* = 1.19) is associated with a decrease in *UNDERVAL* of around 7 percent. (Note that these effects are identified in these regressions from the variation within countries, not across countries, and are therefore more credible.) The operative channel, presumably, is that opening up the capital account invites inflows, which in turn cause the real appreciation.

The coefficients on the exchange rate regime dummies are also quite interesting The central finding here is that regimes in which the exchange rate is actively managed—crawling pegs or managed floats—produce larger undervaluations than do fixed-rate regimes, with a difference of around 7 percent. Unsurprisingly, periods in which the currency is in a "free fall" as defined by Ilzetzki, Reinhart, and Rogoff are also good for undervaluation.[44] A pure float, by contrast, does not seem to generate significantly different levels of undervaluation.

The results in table 10 also show that high saving is good for undervaluation, whereas FDI inflows are bad. Both of these findings are in line with theoretical expectations. Finally, the level of inflation does not have a strong association with undervaluation, indicating that undervaluation need not come at the cost of inflation. In short, policy choices, particularly on the fiscal and external fronts, matter, and they do so in the manner suggested by straightforward economic logic.

44. Ilzetzki, Reinhart, and Rogoff (2008). It is worth noting that the growth effects of undervaluation, as detailed earlier in the paper, do not seem to depend on the type of exchange rate regime the country happens to have at the time. In particular, the results remain unchanged when the countries whose currencies are in a "free fall" are excluded from the sample.

It is worth emphasizing once again that real exchange rate policy is only second-best in the context of the economic distortions discussed here. One of the side effects of maintaining a real overvaluation is a surplus on the current account (or a smaller deficit). This obviously has effects on other countries. Were all developing countries to follow this strategy, the developed countries would have to accept living with the corresponding deficits. This is a major issue of contention in U.S.-China economic relations at present. Moreover, when some developing countries (for example, the Asian economies) follow this strategy while others do not, the growth penalty incurred by the latter becomes larger as their tradable sector shrinks even further under the weight of Asian competition.

Conceptually, the first-best strategy is clear, if fraught with practical difficulties: eliminating the institutional and market failures in question would do away with the policy dilemmas. But recommending this strategy amounts to telling developing countries that the way to get rich is to get rich. A more practical approach is to subsidize tradables production directly, rather than indirectly through the real exchange rate. Real undervaluation is equivalent to a production subsidy plus a consumption tax on tradables. The direct strategy of subsidizing production of tradables achieves the first without the second. Hence it avoids the spillovers to other countries. A production subsidy on tradables boosts exports and imports simultaneously (provided the exchange rate, or wages, or both are allowed to adjust to equilibrate the current account balance) and therefore need not come with a trade surplus.

However, it goes without saying that production subsidies have their own problems. Fine-tuning them to address the perceived distortions would amount to a highly intricate form of industrial policy, with all the attendant informational and rent-seeking difficulties. Even if that were not a problem, the strategy would come into conflict with existing World Trade Organization rules that prohibit export subsidies. There is, it appears, no easy alternative to exchange rate policy.

ACKNOWLEDGMENTS I thank the Center for International Development for partial financial support, and David Mericle, Olga Rostapshova, and Andres Zahler for expert research assistance. I also thank Nathan Nunn for sharing his unpublished data with me. The paper has greatly benefited from the comments of Ricardo Hausmann, Arvind Subramanian, John Williamson, Michael Woodford, Peter Henry, and other Brookings panelists.

References

Acemoglu, Daron, Simon Johnson, and James A. Robinson. 2001. "The Colonial Origins of Comparative Development: An Empirical Investigation." *American Economic Review* 91, no. 5 (December): 1369–1401.

Aguirre, Álvaro, and César Calderón. 2005. "Real Exchange Rate Misalignments and Economic Performance." Working Paper 315. Santiago: Central Bank of Chile, Economic Research Division (April).

Anderson, James E., and Douglas Mercouiller. 2002. "Insecurity and the Pattern of Trade: An Empirical Investigation." *Review of Economics and Statistics* 84, no. 2: 342–52.

Arellano, Manuel, and Stephen Bond. 1991. "Some Tests of Specification for Panel Data: Monte Carlo Evidence and an Application to Employment Equations." *Review of Economic Studies* 58, no. 2: 277–97.

Barro, Robert J., and Jong-Wha Lee. 2000. "International Data on Educational Attainment: Updates and Implications." CID Working Paper 42. Center for International Development, Harvard University (April).

Berkowitz, Daniel, Johannes Moenius, and Katharina Pistor. 2006. "Trade, Law, and Product Complexity." *Review of Economics and Statistics* 88, no. 2: 363–73.

Bhalla, Surjit S. Forthcoming. "Second among Equals: The Middle Class Kingdoms of India and China." Washington: Peterson Institute for International Economics.

Blomberg, S. Brock, Jeffry Frieden, and Ernesto Stein. 2005. "Sustaining Fixed Rates: The Political Economy of Currency Pegs in Latin America." *Journal of Applied Economics* 8, no. 2 (November): 203–25.

Blundell, Richard, and Stephen Bond. 1998. "Initial Conditions and Moment Restrictions in Dynamic Panel Data Models." *Journal of Econometrics* 87, no. 1: 115–43.

Chinn, Menzie, and Hiro Ito. 2006. "What Matters for Financial Development? Capital Controls, Institutions, and Interactions." *Journal of Development Economics* 81, no. 1 (October): 163–92.

Dollar, David. 1992. "Outward-Oriented Developing Economies Really Do Grow More Rapidly: Evidence from 95 LDCs, 1976–1985." *Economic Development and Cultural Change* 40, no. 3: 523–44.

Easterly, William. 2005. "National Policies and Economic Growth: A Reappraisal." In *Handbook of Economic Growth,* edited by Philippe Aghion and Steven Durlauf. Amsterdam: Elsevier.

Elbadawi, Ibrahim. 1994. "Estimating Long-Run Equilibrium Real Exchange Rates." In *Estimating Equilibrium Exchange Rates,* edited by John Williamson. Washington: Institute for International Economics.

Fischer, Stanley. 1993. "The Role of Macroeconomic Factors in Growth." *Journal of Monetary Economics* 32, no. 3: 485–512.

Freund, Caroline, and Martha Denisse Pierola. 2008. "Export Surges: The Power of a Competitive Currency." World Bank, Washington (October).

Gala, Paulo. 2007. "Real Exchange Rate Levels and Economic Development: Theoretical Analysis and Econometric Evidence." *Cambridge Journal of Economics* 32, no. 2: 273–88.

Galvarriato, Aurora Gómez, and Jeffrey G. Williamson. 2008. "Was It Prices, Productivity or Policy? The Timing and Pace of Latin American Industrialization after 1870." NBER Working Paper 13990. Cambridge, Mass.: National Bureau of Economic Research (May).

Gluzmann, Pablo, Eduardo Levy-Yeyati, and Federico Sturzenegger. 2007. "Exchange Rate Undervaluation and Economic Growth: Díaz Alejandro (1965) Revisited." Kennedy School of Government, Harvard University.

Hausmann, Ricardo. 2006. "Economic Growth: Shared Beliefs, Shared Disappointments?" Speech at the G-20 Seminar on Economic Growth in Pretoria, South Africa, August 2005. CID Working Paper 125. Center for International Development, Harvard University (June).

Hausmann, Ricardo, and Dani Rodrik. 2003. "Economic Development as Self-Discovery." *Journal of Development Economics* 72, no. 2 (December): 603–33.

Hausmann, Ricardo, Jason Hwang, and Dani Rodrik. 2007. "What You Export Matters." *Journal of Economic Growth* 12, no. 1: 1–25.

Hausmann, Ricardo, Lant Pritchett, and Dani Rodrik. 2005. "Growth Accelerations." *Journal of Economic Growth* 10, no. 4: 303–29.

Heston, Alan, Robert Summers, and Bettina Aten. 2006. "Penn World Table Version 6.2." Center for International Comparisons of Production, Income and Prices at the University of Pennsylvania (September). pwt.econ.upenn.edu/php_site/pwt_index.php.

Ilzetzki, Ethan O., Carmen M. Reinhart, and Kenneth Rogoff. 2008. "Exchange Rate Arrangements Entering the 21st Century: Which Anchor Will Hold?" University of Maryland and Harvard University.

Imbs, Jean, and Romain Wacziarg. 2003. "Stages of Diversification." *American Economic Review* 93, no. 1 (March): 63–86.

International Comparison Program. 2007. "2005 International Comparison Program Preliminary Results." World Bank, Washington (December 17).

Johnson, Simon, Jonathan Ostry, and Arvind Subramanian. 2007. "The Prospects for Sustained Growth in Africa: Benchmarking the Constraints." IMF Working Paper 07/52. Washington: International Monetary Fund (March).

Kaufmann, Daniel, Aart Kraay, and Massimo Mastruzzi. 2008. "Governance Matters VII: Aggregate and Individual Governance Indicators, 1996–2007." World Bank Policy Research Working Paper 4654. Washington: World Bank (June 24).

Levchenko, Andrei. 2004. "Institutional Quality and International Trade." IMF Working Paper 04/231. Washington: International Monetary Fund.

Levy-Yeyati, Eduardo, and Federico Sturzenegger. 2007. "Fear of Floating in Reverse: Exchange Rate Policy in the 2000s." World Bank, Harvard University, and Universidad Torcuato di Tella.

McKinsey Global Institute. 2001. *India: The Growth Imperative.* San Francisco: McKinsey & Co.

———. 2003. *Turkey: Making the Productivity and Growth Breakthrough*. Istanbul: McKinsey & Co.

Méon, Pierre-Guillaume, and Khalid Sekkat. 2006. "Institutional Quality and Trade: Which Institutions? Which Trade?" Working Paper DULBEA 06-06.RS. Brussels: Université Libre de Bruxelles, Department of Applied Economics.

North, Douglass C. 1990. *Institutions, Institutional Change and Economic Performance*. Cambridge University Press.

Nunn, Nathan. 2007. "Relationship-Specificity, Incomplete Contracts and the Pattern of Trade." *Quarterly Journal of Economics* 122, no. 2 (May): 569–600.

Prasad, Eswar, Raghuram G. Rajan, and Arvind Subramanian. 2007. "Foreign Capital and Economic Growth." *BPEA*, no. 1: 153–209.

Rajan, Raghuram G., and Arvind Subramanian. 2006. "Aid, Dutch Disease, and Manufacturing Growth." Peterson Institute for International Economics, Washington (August).

Ranjan, Priya, and Jae Young Lee. 2004. "Contract Enforcement and the Volume of International Trade in Different Types of Goods." University of California, Irvine.

Rauch, James E. 1999. "Networks versus Markets in International Trade." *Journal of International Economics* 48, no. 1: 7–35.

Razin, Ofair, and Susan M. Collins. 1997. "Real Exchange Rate Misalignments and Growth." Georgetown University.

Rigobon, Roberto, and Dani Rodrik. 2005. "Rule of Law, Democracy, Openness and Income: Estimating the Interrelationships." *Economics of Transition* 13, no. 3 (July): 533–64.

Rodriguez, Francisco, and Dani Rodrik. 2001. "Trade Policy and Economic Growth: A Skeptic's Guide to the Cross-National Evidence." *NBER Macroeconomics Annual 2000* 15:261–325.

Rodrik, Dani. 1986. " 'Disequilibrium' Exchange Rates as Industrialization Policy." *Journal of Development Economics* 23, no. 1 (September): 89–106.

———. 2005. "Why We Learn Nothing from Regressing Economic Growth on Policies." Kennedy School of Government, Harvard University (March). ksghome.harvard.edu/~drodrik/policy%20regressions.pdf.

Rodrik, Dani, and Arvind Subramanian. Forthcoming. "Why Did Financial Globalization Disappoint?" International Monetary Fund *Staff Papers*.

Rodrik, Dani, Arvind Subramanian, and Francesco Trebbi. 2004. "Institutions Rule: The Primacy of Institutions over Geography and Integration in Economic Development." *Journal of Economic Growth* 9, no. 2 (June): 131–65.

Roodman, David. 2005. "xtabond2: Stata Module to Extend Xtabond Dynamic Panel Data Estimator." Center for Global Development, Washington. econpapers.repec.org/software/bocbocode/s435901.htm.

———. 2006. "How to Do xtabond2: An Introduction to 'Difference' and 'System' Gmm in Stata." Working Paper 103. Center for Global Development, Washington (December).

Sachs, Jeffrey, and Andrew Warner. 1995. "Economic Reform and the Process of Global Integration." *BPEA*, no. 1: 1–95.

Comments and Discussion

COMMENT BY

PETER BLAIR HENRY The real exchange rate is one of the most important prices in open-economy macroeconomics. In this paper Dani Rodrik provides a provocative analysis that links this key variable to the all-important issue of economic growth. In the process of doing so, the paper delivers at least two central messages. The first is empirical: real exchange rates exert a significant impact on economic growth, and developing countries that systematically undervalue their currencies in real terms grow faster than their counterparts that do not. The second message provides a theoretical explanation for the first: developing countries that systematically undervalue grow faster because undervaluation raises the rate of return to capital employed in the production of tradable goods by an amount sufficient to overcome the wide range of institutional problems that disproportionately affect that sector of the economy.

The paper contains a lot of fertile ground for a discussant: measurement issues, modeling assumptions, and implications of undervaluation for inflation and monetary policy, to name a few. My comment will focus primarily on the persuasiveness of the main results, their interpretation, and their policy implications.

Regarding the results, let me first offer a general statement about the paper's empirical contribution. In their article on exchange rate regimes and growth, Eduardo Levy Yeyati and Federico Sturzenegger demonstrate that developing countries with fixed nominal exchange rate regimes grow, on average, 0.7 percentage point per year more slowly than other countries.[1] In theory, a fixed nominal exchange rate need not translate into a

1. Eduardo Levy Yeyati and Federico Sturzenegger, "To Float or to Fix: Evidence on the Impact of Exchange Rate Regimes on Growth," *American Economic Review* 93, no. 4 (2003): 1173–93.

real overvaluation, but with rare exceptions that is the reality, so Rodrik's documentation that countries with overvalued currencies grow more slowly is not particularly novel.

What is new about the Rodrik paper is the demonstration that countries with undervalued currencies systematically grow faster. A 50 percent undervaluation is associated with a five-year growth rate that is about 1.3 percentage points above the country-specific mean.

The paper tries hard to disentangle causation from correlation. Building on his previous work with Ricardo Hausmann and Lant Pritchett,[2] Rodrik examines the relationship between growth accelerations and undervaluation, asking the following question: Conditional on experiencing a growth acceleration, have countries done so with the help of an undervalued currency? In general, I applaud the use of an episodic approach to the data, but the problem with the question being asked is that it selects episodes on the basis of the desired outcome. Cutting the data in this way throws out important information about the number of times that large real depreciations occurred without any growth acceleration following in due course.

Instead of picking growth acceleration episodes and examining undervaluation relative to the beginning of those episodes, why not turn the analysis on its head? Using an appropriate definition, one could identify episodes of large sustained real depreciations and examine the time path of economic growth and the allocation of real resources after the onset of the depreciation. If the real exchange rate does indeed exert a causal effect, one should observe faster growth and a shift of resources from the nontradable to the tradable sector.

Cutting the data on episodes of large real depreciations would also focus attention on the important issue of levels versus changes. It is one thing to say that countries grow faster when the real exchange rate is at an undervalued *level.* But such a statement reveals nothing about the optimal way to *change* the real exchange rate to reach a level at which robust growth can occur. It would be useful to know if the way in which a country's currency becomes undervalued seems to matter for subsequent growth outcomes.

For instance, the words "nominal devaluation" do not appear anywhere in the paper. Yet a large nominal devaluation is one of the quickest ways of achieving a real depreciation. In fact, Ilan Goldfajn and Rodrigo Valdes have shown that most countries exit episodes of overvaluation not through

2. Ricardo Hausmann, Lant Pritchett, and Dani Rodrik, "Growth Accelerations," *Journal of Economic Growth* 10, no. 4 (2005): 303–29.

adjustments in the price level, but through large nominal devaluations of the currency.[3] Of course, wage and price compression can do the job without a devaluation. Disinflation reduces the domestic price level relative to the international price level, but this process can take a long time and exact a heavy cost in terms of lost output and higher unemployment.

The issue of how to change the real exchange rate raises the question of why undervaluation produces faster growth in the first place. One's natural inclination is to think that a competitive real exchange rate generates growth through an improvement in the trade balance. But Rodrik argues that the statistical relationship he uncovers between undervaluation and growth is not simply a story of export-led growth. To explain why undervaluation has an impact on growth, he therefore introduces an intermediate goods version of the dependent economy model. The logic of the model is straightforward. Absent any frictions, the real exchange rate settles at a level that equalizes the marginal return of resource allocation in the tradable and the nontradable sectors, thereby maximizing their contribution to growth. Associated with this optimality condition are the fractions of resources that get devoted to the production of tradable and nontradable goods.

The story changes in the presence of distortions, and the paper introduces two of them: a tax that reduces producers' rate of return to capital in the tradable sector, and another tax that reduces the return to capital in nontradables. We are told to think of these taxes as proxies for poor institutions. When the institutional tax on tradable and nontradable returns is the same, no real consequences ensue, as the fraction of resources devoted to the tradable sector remains at its growth-maximizing level. The key to the model, then, is that the institutional tax on returns in each sector not be the same. For Rodrik's story to work, one has to believe that poor institutions are much more costly for the producers of traded goods.

It is not clear that this is true across the board. Although it is easy to believe that a poor contracting environment hurts manufacturers more than barbers, the comparison between manufacturing and construction, for example, is less obvious. A major builder relies on many of the same factors as a manufacturer: suppliers, subcontractors, customers, and financial and legal support. Even if one accepts Rodrik's story that poor institutions have a disproportionately large negative effect on tradable goods, the analysis comes up flat, because the paper does not provide a way of

3. Ilan Goldfajn and Rodrigo Valdes, "The Aftermath of Appreciations," *Quarterly Journal of Economics* 114, no. 1 (1999): 229–62.

quantifying just how important (or trivial) the distortion is for production over all.

Without a means of quantifying the negative impact of distortions in the contracting environment (or the positive impact of undervaluation), it is not clear what policy conclusions to draw from the paper's results. More generally, although Rodrik demonstrates that temporarily faster growth is one benefit of undervaluation, the paper does not provide a welfare analysis. This is important, because undervaluation has costs as well as benefits. To draw reliable policy conclusions, one needs to know more about the costs of undervaluation and how they compare with the benefits of faster growth. There are at least two potential costs of real undervaluation.

First, undervaluation subsidizes producers in the tradable goods sector at the expense of consumers. In the context of this model, which, as mentioned, never really discusses the nominal exchange rate, one can think of undervaluation as roughly equivalent to a policy of forced saving. Therefore, the critical question is whether one can conclude that faster growth in this context is welfare enhancing. In other words, given the population's rate of time preference, are people made better off by consuming less today than they would otherwise choose? The answer is far from clear, and I would add that this is more than a theoretical consideration. If one is considering the impact on growth of a policy change such as trade liberalization or the removal of capital controls, it is possible to write down models in which strange, counterintuitive things happen and aggregate welfare falls. But one has to try very hard to do that, because when one moves from a scenario in which people have fewer choices (closed markets) to one where they have more choices (open markets), people are usually made better off. Introducing distortions, on the other hand, generally reduces utility. In this case the distortion is that real undervaluation interferes with the price signal that drives the relative production and consumption of tradable and nontradable goods. Although it is true that the distortion occurs in a second-best world, I do not think one can conclude that welfare improves. Again, to make that case, one needs to know just how great the benefits of undervaluation are relative to the costs it imposes.

A second, well-known cost of a real undervaluation is that it generates destabilizing pressure on the balance of payments and attendant inflationary pressure. Suppose that Mexico chooses to undervalue the peso vis-à-vis the dollar. With Mexico's nominal exchange rate, in terms of pesos per dollar, set higher than the market clearing rate, Mexico will run a chronic surplus in tradable goods. Those surpluses will generate a commensurately large inflow of dollars to the central bank. Since the exchange rate is not allowed to adjust, the quantity of currency in circulation will rise in concert with the excess demand for Mexican tradables. If there is no adjustment in the exchange rate, over time the imbalance gets reflected in rising reserves and inflation, unless the central bank is able to successfully sterilize the inflow.

Some of Rodrik's other research actually highlights the potentially large welfare cost associated with accumulating excess foreign reserves.[4] Since a policy of undervaluation is isomorphic to a policy of excess reserve accumulation, I am surprised that the paper does not try to reconcile the apparent inconsistency between the arguments in favor of undervaluation in this paper with Rodrik's earlier stance that emerging economies are overaccumulating reserves.

It is also worth emphasizing that although small, open economies may safely ignore the worldwide externalities of their policy choices, the same cannot be said for large countries. For example, if Barbados were to choose a policy of grossly undervaluing its currency, it could safely assume that its policy choice would have a negligible impact on the world balance of trade. The same assumption would be invalid for a large country. Furthermore, policies that are benign when implemented by a single country may be harmful if pursued by many countries simultaneously. From an individual country's point of view, a policy of undervaluation promotes export growth. But we all know very well the terrible externalities associated with a world in which everyone tries to undervalue at once. Whether this is done through a cascading series of competitive devaluations or through tighter fiscal policy, the consequences are largely the same. Rodrik likes to argue that countries need policy space. Such space is often appropriate and beneficial, but negative externalities of the type just mentioned are precisely the reason we have international organizations that try to encourage mutually beneficial exchange rate policies.

Turning from costs back to benefits, one implication of the model is that an outward transfer depreciates the currency. This real depreciation raises the rate of return to capital in the nontradable sector, improves resource allocation, and therefore acts as a second-best strategy for alleviating the implicit tax associated with poor institutions. Rodrik justifies this policy prescription on the grounds that foreign capital inflows do not contribute to growth. The support for such a claim comes, in part, from the paper by

4. Dani Rodrik, "The Social Cost of Foreign Exchange Reserves," *International Economic Journal* 20, no. 3 (2006): 253–66.

Eswar Prasad, Raghuram Rajan, and Arvind Subramanian that I discussed in these pages about eighteen months ago.[5] There I outlined several reasons why the data did not support the authors' claims about the impact of foreign capital on growth.

I will not repeat that discussion today. But I will say that the assertion that capital inflows do nothing but fuel consumption booms does not stand up to scrutiny. An article I published in the December 2007 issue of the *Journal of Economic Literature* documents the mounting body of evidence that foreign resource flows into developing countries reduce their cost of capital, stimulate investment, and raise GDP per capita.[6] Similarly, in a recent working paper, Diego Sasson and I document the large, positive impact of capital account liberalization on real wages and productivity.[7]

None of this is to say that capital account liberalization is the secret to faster growth. In fact, I agree that the impact of capital inflows on the real exchange rate can be a major source of concern for small, open economies. Thailand's struggle with the real appreciation of the baht—roughly 20 percent against the dollar in 2006–07—provides an important case in point. Furthermore, I agree with the argument that Rodrik has made elsewhere, that emerging economies tend to rely too heavily on short-term debt. But if the problem is an overreliance on short-term debt, the real exchange rate is a rather indirect and blunt instrument for dealing with it. The principle of policy targeting suggests that it is much more efficient to address directly the imperfections in the international financial system that give market participants the incentive to accumulate large quantities of short-term debt that are privately optimal but carry large negative consequences for the general public.

Rodrik acknowledges that eliminating the institutional and market failures in question would be preferable to adopting policies that drive the real exchange rate away from its equilibrium value. He argues, however, that encouraging developing countries to improve their institutions amounts to telling them that the way to get rich is to get rich.

5. Eswar Prasad, Raghuram G. Rajan, and Arvind Subramanian, "Foreign Capital and Economic Growth." *BPEA,* no. 1 (2007): 153–209; Peter Blair Henry, "Comment [on Prasad, Rajan, and Subramanian]," *BPEA,* no. 1 (2007): 217–23.

6. Peter Blair Henry, "Capital Account Liberalization: Theory, Evidence and Speculation," *Journal of Economic Literature* 45, no. 4 (2007): 887–935.

7. Peter Blair Henry and Diego Sasson, "Capital Account Liberalization, Real Wages, and Productivity," Working Paper 13880 (Cambridge, Mass.: National Bureau of Economic Research, 2008).

This line of argument feels paternalistic. A few years ago, economists engaged in much hand wringing over the problem of "original sin," with some claiming that elaborate financial engineering schemes were needed to help developing countries avoid the problem of accumulating dollar-denominated debt.[8] Developing countries, it was said, would need decades to achieve the level of institutional development necessary to enable them to issue debt denominated in their own currency. I argued that this view not only was far too pessimistic but implicitly assumed that developing countries are incapable of helping themselves. I also said that once developing country governments demonstrated a sustained commitment to sound policies, they would have no trouble issuing local currency-denominated debt.[9]

Time has been kind to my prediction. A recent report by the Bank for International Settlements (BIS) demonstrates just how much progress has been made on the development of local-currency bond markets.[10] According to the BIS, in 2000 the total stock of international emerging market bonds outstanding was $498 billion; by 2005 that stock was $618 billion. Subtracting the first number from the second gives a rough estimate of the cumulative amount of new international debt issued by emerging markets from 2000 to 2005: $120 billion.

To gauge just how much the world has changed since 2000, consider the analogous figures for local-currency-denominated emerging market bonds. The BIS report tells us that at the end of 2000 the total stock of internationally issued emerging market bonds denominated in local currency was $20 billion. By 2006 that stock had grown to $102 billion, which implies that emerging markets issued $82 billion in such bonds between 2000 and 2006. In other words, almost 70 percent ($82 billion divided by $120 billion) of the internationally issued bonds of emerging market countries between 2000 and 2005 were denominated in local currency. This is a remarkable increase given that the market for such instruments was previously nonexistent.

A big reason behind the shift is the improved macroeconomic environment in emerging markets. In the words of the Committee on the Global

8. See, for example, Barry Eichengreen, "Financial Instability," in *Global Crises, Global Solutions*, edited by Bjørn Lomborg (Cambridge University Press, 2004).

9. Peter Blair Henry, "Perspective Paper on Financial Instability," in *Global Crises, Global Solutions*, edited by Bjørn Lomborg (Cambridge University Press, 2004).

10. Committee on the Global Financial System, "Financial Stability and Local Currency Bond Markets," CGFS Papers 28 (Basel: Bank for International Settlements, 2007). www.bis.org/publ/cgfs28.htm.

Financial System, "With the support of better domestic macroeconomic policies, reliance on foreign currency debt has indeed been reduced in almost all emerging market economies. . . . Issuance of local currency bonds has expanded substantially and domestic bond markets have deepened."[11]

Policies matter. There is no inherent conflict between persuading countries not to overvalue their currencies and encouraging them to enhance their institutional environments. Improving the material existence of millions of people around the world inevitably requires that governments do both.

COMMENT BY

MICHAEL WOODFORD In this paper Dani Rodrik offers a provocative argument for policies that seek to maintain an "undervalued" currency in order to promote economic growth. The key to his argument is the empirical evidence that he presents, indicating the correlation of his measure of undervaluation with economic growth in cross-country panel regressions.

Rodrik does not really discuss the measures that should be undertaken to maintain an undervalued currency or whether it is likely that a country that pursues undervaluation as a growth strategy should be able to maintain that undervaluation over time. For example, he remarks (as justification for interest in the question of a causal effect of undervaluation on growth) that "one of the key findings of the open-economy macroeconomic literature is that . . . nominal exchange rates and real exchange rates move quite closely together." But although this is true, and although it is widely interpreted as indicating that monetary policy can affect real exchange rates (since it can obviously move nominal rates), it hardly follows that monetary policy alone can maintain a weak real exchange rate for long enough to serve as part of a long-run growth strategy.

Indeed, conventional theoretical models with short-run price stickiness that are perfectly consistent with the observed short-run effects of monetary policy on real exchange rates also imply that monetary policy should *not* have long-run effects. Rodrik also cites evidence showing that sterilized interventions in the foreign exchange market can affect real exchange rates. But economic theory suggests that interventions not associated with

11. Committee on the Global Financial System, p. 89.

any change in current or subsequent monetary policy should have even more transitory effects. And the experiences of countries that have sought to use devaluation to boost economic growth have often found that the real exchange rate effect of a nominal devaluation is not long-lasting. The case of South Korea, discussed below, is an example.

Nonetheless, the point of Rodrik's paper is to provide evidence that undervaluation favors growth, on the assumption that policies to maintain undervaluation are available, and it is that central contention that I shall examine here. I find the evidence less persuasive than the paper suggests, for two reasons. First, I believe that the paper exaggerates the strength and robustness of the association between the real exchange rate and growth in the cross-country evidence. And second, even granting the existence of such a correlation, a causal effect of real exchange rates on growth is hardly the only possible interpretation.

HOW STRONG IS THE ASSOCIATION OF UNDERVALUATION WITH ECONOMIC GROWTH? Rodrik's key result is the panel regression reported in his table 1, in which the coefficient in a regression of growth on his *UNDERVAL* measure is found to be significantly positive and substantial in magnitude. The relationship, he argues, is in fact confined to developing countries, as the coefficient is near zero when the sample is restricted to countries with GDP per capita greater than \$6,000 a year; for the sample consisting only of countries with incomes less than \$6,000 a year, the coefficient is both larger and has an even larger *t* statistic.

However, it is quite possible that Rodrik's measure of undervaluation exaggerates this association. Apart from the constant and fixed-effect terms, his measure of undervaluation is equal to

$$\ln UNDERVAL_{it} = \ln RER_{it} + 0.24 \ln RGDPCH_{it}. \tag{1}$$

But since lagged income per capita is also included as a regressor in Rodrik's table 1 regressions, and since *t* refers to a five-year period in these regressions, so that

$$growth_{it} \equiv (1/5)\left[\ln RGDPCH_{it} - \ln RGDPCH_{i,t-1}\right],$$

his specification is *equivalent* to a regression of the growth rate (for each country-date pair) on the variable ln RER_{it} + 1.2 $growth_{it}$ and lagged income per capita, and $\hat{\delta}$ (the estimated coefficient on ln *UNDERVAL* in his regression) would be the coefficient on the "growth-adjusted real exchange rate" in the alternative specification. This way of viewing Rodrik's regression specification makes it evident that a positive estimate of $\hat{\delta}$ need not indicate any association between real exchange rates and growth at all—it may simply reflect the positive correlation between the growth rate *and itself.*

Rodrik defends the use of his constructed measure *UNDERVAL* on the ground that it is necessary to correct for the Balassa-Samuelson effect. One should expect a lower real exchange rate (more-expensive nontraded goods) for higher-income countries, owing to this effect; Rodrik then defines "undervaluation" as the degree to which a country's real exchange rate is higher than expected given the country's income per capita. The latter prediction is made by regressing ln RER_{it} on ln $RGDPCH_{it}$ in a panel regression with time effects but no country fixed effects, so that the correlation between countries' average real exchange rates and their average incomes can be used to estimate the relationship. The coefficient on income per capita in this first-stage regression is (the negative of) the 0.24 appearing in equation 1 above.

However, two objections must be raised to this argument. First, Rodrik's panel regressions in his table 1 already include country fixed effects. Hence, average differences in the level of the real exchange rate associated with particular countries (for example, the developing countries with low real exchange rates, for the reason explained by Balassa and Samuelson) would have no consequences for the regression coefficient $\hat{\delta}$, even in the absence of Rodrik's proposed "adjustment" of the real exchange rate measure. A further adjustment is needed only if the Balassa-Samuelson effect is expected to create a higher-frequency correlation between income and the real exchange rate as well—that is, if the five-year periods in which a country's income per capita is relatively higher are ones in which it should correspondingly have a relatively lower exchange rate. The fact that the Balassa-Samuelson effect is well established as a factor explaining long-run average differences between countries does not make it obvious that such a high-frequency effect should be important. (As a theoretical matter, this should be true only to the extent that it is also true at higher frequencies that variations in the rate of productivity growth in the production of tradables are an important source of variation in both aggregate output growth, on the one hand, and the relative price of tradables, on the other.)

Second, even supposing that the high-frequency Balassa-Samuelson effect exists, the proposed correction will not necessarily be the correct one and will generally introduce an upward bias in the estimated coefficient $\hat{\delta}$. The reason is that the Balassa-Samuelson effect is not a direct causal effect of income on the real exchange rate (or equivalently, on the relative price of tradables). Instead, it is a mechanism according to which both income and the relative price of tradables are affected by a third variable (the rate of productivity growth in the tradable sector), which creates a negative correlation between the two variables (to the extent that other factors do not also simultaneously affect both variables).

The correction proposed by Rodrik would be appropriate if one believed that income and the real exchange rate were determined by a structural model of the form

$$E = -\beta Y + P + u \tag{2}$$

$$Y = dE + v, \tag{3}$$

where I now simply write E for the log of the real exchange rate and Y for the log of income per capita, P is a policy variable (treated as exogenous), and u and v are additional exogenous disturbances. Here equation 2 is a structural model of real exchange rate determination, in which the term $-\beta Y$ represents the (high-frequency) "Balassa-Samuelson effect" for which Rodrik apparently wishes to correct, and the term P indicates the kind of policy that can influence the degree of undervaluation, the effects of which upon growth Rodrik wishes to determine. Equation 3 is a structural model of income determination, in which the term dE represents the growth effect of the real exchange rate as such (that is, independent of what has caused the exchange rate to vary) hypothesized by Rodrik. Although no such model is spelled out or defended, something of this form is implicit in Rodrik's empirical strategy.

Suppose that equations 2 and 3 are a correct model, and suppose further that one has a strategy that allows one to identify the correct value of β (say, from the countries' long-run differences in incomes and in real exchange rates, on the supposition that there are no long-run cross-country differences in the terms P or u).[1] Under these assumptions, the "adjusted" real exchange rate

$$\tilde{E} \equiv E + \beta Y \tag{4}$$

1. To simplify the discussion, I shall abstract from the problems created by the use of a generated regressor and treat the true value of β as known with certainty.

will provide a measure of the composite disturbance $\tilde{u} \equiv u + P$. Under the further simplifying assumption that v is orthogonal to $\tilde{u}$, the coefficient $\hat{\delta}$ from a regression of Y on $\tilde{E}$ will be a consistent estimator of

$$(5) \qquad \delta \equiv \frac{d}{1+\beta d} = \frac{\partial Y}{\partial P}.$$

This is precisely the interpretation that Rodrik wishes to give to his estimate of $\hat{\delta}$.

But among the several assumptions required for this approach to yield a consistent estimate of $\partial Y / \partial P$, note that the "Balassa-Samuelson effect" is treated as a direct effect of Y on E in equation 2. In fact, this is not the nature of the Balassa-Samuelson theory. Even if one considers the theory as referring to purely instantaneous and static effects (which therefore have the same quantitative form at all frequencies), the model should instead be one of the form

$$(6) \qquad E = -aT + P + u$$

$$(7) \qquad Y = cT + dE + v,$$

where T is a measure of productivity in the tradable sector and, according to the Balassa-Samuelson theory, the coefficients a and c are both positive. Here P is again a policy that is hypothesized to directly affect the exchange rate, and dE again indicates the hypothesized effect of exchange rate variations (from whatever source) on national income. I shall suppose that T is an exogenous disturbance, independent of all of the factors P, u, and v.

Suppose now that the true structural model is of the form in equations 6 and 7, but that one is able to correctly estimate the elasticity of the real exchange rate with respect to variations in income per capita *due purely to variations in productivity of the tradable sector,* which is what one needs for the Balassa-Samuelson adjustment proposed by Rodrik. That is, suppose that one has a correct estimate of the coefficient

$$\beta \equiv -\frac{\partial E / \partial T}{\partial Y / \partial T} = \frac{a}{c - ad}.$$

(This could be estimated by a cross-country regression of long-run average real exchange rates on long-run average levels of income per capita, under the assumption that there are no cross-country differences in the long-run average values of either $\tilde{u}$ or v.) And again suppose that one constructs an "adjusted" real exchange rate, defined as in equation 4. What will be the economic interpretation of the coefficient $\hat{\delta}$ obtained by regressing Y on $\tilde{E}$? In particular, will it provide a consistent estimate of $\partial Y / \partial P$?

Under the assumption that β is correctly estimated, $\tilde{E}$ will be a measure of "undervaluation" that has been purged of any effects of variations in the productivity of the tradable sector; specifically,

$$\tilde{E} = \frac{c}{c - ad}\tilde{u} + \frac{a}{c - ad}v.$$

In this sense one has controlled for variations in the real exchange rate due to the Balassa-Samuelson effect. But this does *not* suffice to make $\hat{\delta}$ a consistent estimate of $\partial Y / \partial P$. Even under the assumption (for simplicity) that v is orthogonal to $\tilde{u}$, $\hat{\delta}$ is in this case a consistent estimate of

$$\delta + \frac{1}{\beta^2}\frac{(a/c)\sigma_v^2}{(c/a)^2\sigma_{\tilde{u}}^2 + \sigma_v^2}, \tag{8}$$

where δ is again defined as in equation 5 and σ^2 is the variance. But this quantity is not equal to

$$\frac{\partial Y}{\partial P} = d,$$

for two distinct reasons. Even if $\sigma_v^2 = 0$, expression 8 will equal δ rather than d, but because the Balassa-Samuelson effect is *not* a direct effect of income on the exchange rate (as represented in equation 2), the policy-relevant elasticity is d rather than δ. But, likely more important, if $\sigma_v^2 > 0$, the second term in expression 8 represents an upward bias in $\hat{\delta}$. One would find a positive estimate for $\hat{\delta}$ even if the true policy elasticity d were equal to zero.

Not only is the coefficient obtained from a regression on $\tilde{E}$ likely to be biased; it is far from obvious that this should be a more reliable estimate than would be obtained by simply regressing on the unadjusted real exchange rate. Assuming again that v is orthogonal to $\tilde{u}$, my simple model implies that the coefficient $\hat{d}$ obtained by regressing Y on E should be a consistent estimator of the quantity

$$\frac{d\sigma_{\tilde{u}}^2 - \beta^{-1}a^2\sigma_T^2}{\sigma_{\tilde{u}}^2 + a^2\sigma_T^2}.$$

This will be an underestimate of the true policy elasticity d (if $\beta > 0$ and $\sigma^2_{\tilde{T}} > 0$), owing to the failure to correct for the Balassa-Samuelson effect. But the bias will be relatively small as long as

$$a^2\sigma^2_{\tilde{T}} << \sigma^2_{\tilde{u}},$$

which is to say, as long as productivity growth in the tradable sector accounts for a relatively small share of total high-frequency variation in the exchange rate. This last assumption seems a fairly reasonable one, except over quite long periods.

How dependent are Rodrik's results on the use of the *UNDERVAL* measure? His table 3 presents results for corresponding panel regressions using a variety of simple real exchange rate measures instead of his "adjusted" measure. In most cases the measure of undervaluation is no longer a significant explanatory factor when the entire sample of countries is used. Rodrik instead stresses that when one restricts attention to the sample of developing countries, the coefficient on the measure of undervaluation remains significantly (at the 5 percent level or better) positive in three out of the four cases (albeit substantially smaller than when *UNDERVAL* is used).

These results indicate that within the sample of lower-income countries, there is a positive association between the level of the real exchange rate and growth, after one controls for country effects and time effects; Rodrik's basic finding is not purely an artifact of the way in which his preferred measure of undervaluation is constructed. Nonetheless, if one were to emphasize the results using the real exchange rate (as I would prefer), one would not only obtain a smaller estimated effect, but have more reason for concern for the robustness of the finding as well.

For example, when one uses the real exchange rate as the measure of undervaluation, it becomes more important to restrict attention to the sample of "developing" countries in order to find evidence of the association between undervaluation and growth. But this in turn leads to questions about what should define the sample of countries that are included. Table 1 illustrates the consequences for the value of the estimated coefficient $\hat{\delta}$ of alternative choices of the set of countries included in the sample. Here the measure of undervaluation used is the real exchange rate measure from the Penn World Tables (the one used in the first two columns of Rodrik's table 3).[2] The first line of the table essentially replicates the result in

2. Note that among the real exchange rate measures that Rodrik considers in table 3, this is the one that results in the most significant positive value for $\hat{\delta}$ when the sample is restricted to countries with income per capita less than $6,000.

Table 1. Estimates of the Coefficient on Rodrik's Undervaluation Measure for Different Samples

Sample limited to countries with income per capita	*Coefficient*	*Standard error*	t *statistic*
Less than $6,000	0.0144	0.0038	3.77
Less than $8,000	0.0091	0.0037	2.50
Between $1,000 and $8,000	0.0077	0.0040	1.91

Source: Author's calculations.

Rodrik's table 3.[3] The second line shows, however, that the estimated coefficient is reduced by one-third if the income cutoff is raised from $6,000 to $8,000.[4] It is not obvious that only countries with income per capita less than $6,000 should be regarded as developing countries; in particular, if the justification for expecting to observe the hypothesized relationship only in lower-income countries is that these countries have weaker institutions, it is not obvious that countries with incomes per capita between $6,000 and $8,000 do not also suffer from many of the institutional weaknesses that are common in the developing world.[5] But the evidence for a positive association between the real exchange rate and growth is considerably weaker when these additional countries are included in the set of "developing" countries. Moreover, the evidence becomes weaker still if the lowest-income countries (those with income per capita less than $1,000) are excluded from the sample. (One is surely not much interested in using the experiences of these desperate countries as illustrations of a successful growth strategy.) When these countries are dropped from the sample (third line of table 1), the estimated effect is only about half as large as for the "developing" sample used by Rodrik and no longer significant at the 5 percent level.

DOES THE CORRELATION INDICATE CAUSALITY? Even granting the existence of a positive correlation between a country's real exchange rate and its growth rate, is it legitimate to interpret this as evidence of a *causal effect* of the exchange rate on growth? In particular, is it evidence of a causal mechanism that can be relied upon in predicting the effects of a policy of seeking to maintain a depreciated currency?

3. Rodrik reports a slightly larger coefficient (0.016) and a *t* statistic of 3.74.

4. As in Rodrik's regressions, the income level used in this classification is average real income per capita over the period 1950–2004, where real GDP per capita is taken from the Penn World Tables.

5. The countries in this set are Bulgaria, Chile, Kazakhstan, Mauritius, Poland, South Africa, South Korea, Swaziland, Taiwan, Turkmenistan, Uruguay, and Venezuela.

I should begin by admitting that I suspect that at least some of the positive association found in the data does reflect episodes in which policies that manipulate the exchange rate have had significant consequences for growth—specifically, examples of a familiar sort, in which policies that maintain an *overvalued* currency create distortions that stifle economic activity. But Rodrik stresses that this well-known lesson is not the *only* connection between exchange rate policy and growth; the declared purpose of his paper is to establish that policies leading to *undervaluation* are *beneficial* to growth. Yet much of the evidence that he presents (and the only evidence using unadjusted measures of the real exchange rate) consists of correlations that might largely reflect cases of overvaluation. Beneficial effects of undervaluation on growth can hardly be established merely by observing that countries are able to reduce their growth rates by intervening to maintain an overvalued currency. For example, the policies used to maintain a severe overvaluation typically involve rationing of access to foreign exchange, and one may suppose that it is these controls, rather than the level of the exchange rate as such, that account for much of the reduction in economic performance; but if so, one can hardly argue on this ground that other types of interference with free convertibility will instead increase efficiency, as long as the controls keep the currency undervalued rather than overvalued. One might instead expect growth to be favored by a policy that does not create distortions of either sign.

Rodrik offers several comments on the issue of causality. The first is an assertion that although an inference of causality from real exchange rate depreciation to growth would be problematic "in a world where governments did not care about the real exchange rate and left it to be determined purely by market forces," in fact "most governments pursue a variety of policies with the explicit goal of affecting the real exchange rate." But there is a great leap between the observation that real exchange rates are affected by policy and an assumption that the real exchange rate is *purely determined* by policy, and by policies that are *exogenous* with respect to the state of the economy at that. Yet only under the assumption that the real exchange rate is an exogenous policy choice can one sidestep the issue of causality.

In fact, Rodrik admits that endogeneity of the real exchange rate is an issue, and he proposes two ways of dealing with it. One is an extension of his regression model to include additional explanatory variables, such as the inflation rate, government consumption as a share of GDP, and gross domestic saving as a share of GDP. Inclusion of additional variables lowers the coefficient $\hat{\delta}$ on the *UNDERVAL* variable, but the coefficient remains significantly positive;[6] this is taken to suggest that undervaluation does indeed have a positive effect on growth, even after one has controlled for possible sources of endogenous variation in the real exchange rate. In fact, Rodrik suggests that some of the endogenous variation in the exchange rate that has been controlled for ought really to be counted as policy-induced variation: "To the extent that [policies that reduce government consumption or increase saving] are designed to move the real exchange rate in the first place, they are part of what I have in mind when I talk of 'a policy of undervaluation.'" This last point, however, is hardly convincing: if it is shown that policies that increase saving, for example, increase economic growth even when policymakers adopt them because of their anticipated consequences for the real exchange rate, it would hardly follow that policymakers should therefore be advised to attempt to depreciate *by whatever means possible,* for the growth effect of the increased saving might occur through other channels than the effect on the real exchange rate. Moreover, the mere fact that one has controlled for *some* possible kinds of endogeneity of the real exchange rate is hardly a proof that the remaining variation is exogenous.

Rodrik's final argument is an assertion that "many of the plausible sources of bias . . . would induce a negative relationship between undervaluation and growth, not the positive relationship I have documented." This, in his view, makes an interpretation of the positive value of $\hat{\delta}$ as reflecting omitted-variable bias implausible. Accordingly, it is perhaps worth discussing a simple example of how endogeneity of the real exchange rate could result in a positive correlation between the real exchange rate and growth, even under circumstances where devaluation would not stimulate economic activity at all.

I shall illustrate my point using a purposely oversimplified model of equilibrium real exchange rate determination.[7] Consider a two-period ($t =$ 1, 2) small, open economy model with two sectors ($j = T, N$) producing tradables and nontradables, respectively. I assume a competitive world market for the T good (which will also be the numeraire) and a world real

6. Of course, this robustness of the significantly positive coefficient may reflect the bias resulting from use of the *UNDERVAL* measure, discussed above.

7. In particular, my use here of a model in which monetary policy cannot affect the real exchange rate does not mean that I believe that, in reality, monetary policy cannot influence the real exchange rate, at least for a time. My point is simply to show that a positive empirical correlation between the real exchange rate and real activity need not imply anything about the magnitude of the growth effects of exchange rate policy, and that point is made most simply with a model in which there is no scope at all for monetary policy to affect real variables, even in the short run.

interest rate $r > 0$ (in terms of the T good, between periods 1 and 2) that is unaffected by the net capital flows of the small country. Let the production technology in each sector j and each period t be of the Cobb-Douglas form,

$$Y_{jt} = K_{jt}^{1-a_j} H_{jt}^{a_j},$$

where K_{jt} is the capital stock in sector j, H_{jt} is hours of labor in that sector, and the coefficient $0 < \alpha_j < 1$ may be sector specific. The initial capital stocks K_{j1} of both sectors are given as parameters, and I assume that K_{N2}, the capital stock of the N sector in the second period, is given exogenously as well. (To simplify, I shall assume a constant exogenous value, $K_{Nt} = K_N$, for both periods t.) The second-period capital stock of the tradable sector instead depends on investment spending I, according to the law of motion

$$K_{T2} = I + (1 - \delta) K_{T1},$$

where $0 < \delta < 1$ is the rate of depreciation of capital in the T sector.

I assume that the representative household in the small economy seeks to maximize

$$U = U_1 + \beta U_2,$$

where the contribution to utility U in period t is of the form

$$U_t = \gamma \log C_{Nt} + (1 - \gamma) \log C_{Tt} - \frac{\lambda}{1 + v} H_t^{1+v},$$

in which expression C_{jt} is consumption in period t of the sector j good, H_t is hours worked, and the preference parameters satisfy λ, $v > 0$ and $0 < \beta$, $\gamma < 1$. For simplicity I assume competitive domestic spot markets each period for both labor and the N good, neither of which is traded internationally. Finally, the government sets the nominal exchange rate each period, which then determines the domestic-currency price of the T good in that period (by the law of one price). I shall suppose that the government also imposes a proportional tax τ on savings in period 1, so that the real return received by domestic savers is $(1 - \tau)(1 + r)$. I abstract from government consumption; the government revenue raised by the tax is assumed to be simply rebated as a lump sum to households.

In any period t, given values for (K_{Tt}, Y_{Tt}), one can solve uniquely for equilibrium values of H_{Tt}, H_{Nt}, $Y_{Nt} = C_{Nt}$, C_{Tt}, w_t, and P_{Nt}, where both the wage w_t and the price of nontradables P_{Nt} are quoted in units of the T good. (Thus, w_t is a real wage and P_{Nt} is actually the relative price of nontradables.) One can easily show that there is a unique, differentiable solution for each of these variables and that the solution functions satisfy (among other properties)

$$\frac{\partial C_T}{\partial Y_T} < 0, \quad 0 < \frac{\partial \log C_T}{\partial \log K_t} < -\frac{\partial \log C_T}{\partial \log Y_T},$$

$$\frac{\partial Y_N}{\partial Y_T} < 0, \quad 0 < \frac{\partial \log Y_N}{\partial \log K_T} < -\frac{\partial \log Y_N}{\partial \log Y_T},$$

$$\frac{\partial GDP}{\partial Y_T} \equiv 1 + P_N \frac{\partial Y_N}{\partial Y_T} > 0$$

$$\frac{\partial P_N}{\partial Y_T} < 0, \quad 0 < \frac{\partial \log P_N}{\partial \log K_T} = -\frac{\partial \log Y_N}{\partial \log Y_T}.$$

Using these solution functions, an *intertemporal equilibrium* can then be described as a set of values for the endogenous variables (Y_{T1}, K_{T2}, Y_{T2}) that satisfy the following three equilibrium conditions:

$$(9) \quad C_T(K_{T1},Y_{T1}) + [K_{T2} - (1-\delta)K_{T1}] + \frac{C_T(K_{T2},Y_{T2})}{1+r} = Y_{T1} + \frac{Y_{T2}}{1+r}$$

$$(10) \quad C_T(K_{T2},Y_{T2}) = \tilde{\beta}(1+r)C_T(Y_{T1})$$

$$(11) \quad (1-\alpha_T)Y_{T2} = (1+r)K_{T2},$$

given values of the exogenous parameters (K_{T1}, r, $\tilde{\beta}$), where $\tilde{\beta} \equiv \beta(1-r)$.

Here equation 9 is the requirement that there be intertemporal balance in the country's capital account (assuming zero net foreign assets at the beginning of period 1); equation 10 is the Euler equation for an optimal saving decision by the representative household; and equation 11 is the first-order condition for profit-maximizing investment demand, stating that the anticipated marginal product of capital in period 2 must equal 1 plus the required real rate of return.[8] One can again show that there is a unique solution to these three equations for the endogenous variables as differentiable functions of the exogenous parameters.

Consider now the consequences of an exogenous increase in the composite parameter $\tilde{\beta}$, which implies an increase in domestic households'

8. Note that since period 2 is the last period of the model, there is effectively 100 percent depreciation of capital in this period.

willingness to save, as a result of either a change in preferences (an increase in β) or a change in policy that increases incentives for saving (a reduction in τ). Total differentiation of the system of equations 9, 10, and 11 reveals that

$$\frac{\partial Y_{T1}}{\partial \tilde{\beta}} > 0,$$

which implies in turn that

$$\frac{\partial GDP_1}{\partial \tilde{\beta}} > 0, \quad \frac{\partial P_{N1}}{\partial \tilde{\beta}} < 0, \quad \frac{\partial \left(Y_{T1} - C_{T1}\right)}{\partial \tilde{\beta}} > 0.$$

Hence an increase in the willingness to save in period 1 (whether due to changing attitudes or to changing incentives) will simultaneously increase the production of tradables (Y_{T1}), the small country's exports ($Y_{T1} - C_{T1}$), and its real GDP (GDP_1), while reducing the relative price of nontradables (P_{N1}) and hence increasing the real exchange rate.

Note that this equilibrium scenario resembles the phenomenon often interpreted as "export-led growth": a real depreciation coincides with an increase in exports and an increase in total GDP (hence an increase in the growth rate). Moreover, if one were to compare a panel of small, open economies, to each of which the above model applies, with identical parameter values except for cross-country variation in the value of $\tilde{\beta}$, one would observe a positive correlation between a country's real exchange rate in period 1 and its growth rate in that period.[9] Yet the high-growth countries would not be in this situation because of their exchange rate policies; their higher growth rates would be due to other factors (factors that favor a higher saving rate) that happen to lead *both* to a lower equilibrium real exchange rate and to higher GDP growth. Moreover, the model is one in which if a country were to use monetary policy to depreciate its currency in nominal terms, this would not affect growth (or any other real variables, including the real exchange rate); it would only raise the nominal domestic prices of both tradables and nontradables (without affecting their relative price).

It is true that there *is* a policy intervention, in the simple model, that would depreciate in real terms, namely, a reduction in the tax rate on sav-

9. The exogenous parameters taking identical values for the different countries are assumed to include GDP in the period immediately before period 1, with respect to which the period 1 growth rate is calculated.

ings τ, which is one of the factors determining the value of $\tilde{\beta}$. And such a policy change would increase GDP (through its effect on saving) in the same way that an increase in households' patience would. But it does not really make sense to call this a demonstration that a deliberate policy of exchange rate depreciation can be used to stimulate growth, since the most obvious example of a policy with that intent would be completely ineffective.[10]

The example shows that it is certainly possible for an omitted variable to move both the real exchange rate and GDP in the same direction, so that this is a potential interpretation of a positive coefficient $\hat{\delta}$ in Rodrik's panel regression. But is this theoretical possibility likely to be of practical relevance? Here it is worth noting that the regressions reported in Rodrik's table 10 show that a country's ratio of gross domestic saving to GDP has a significant positive effect on his *UNDERVAL* measure; and of course, a higher saving rate is also correlated with higher growth, as many authors have noted, and as Rodrik's panel regressions in tables 4 and 5 show. (The latter regressions show that the saving rate is a significant variable in explaining differences in growth across country-time pairs, even when the undervaluation measure is also included in the regression, and that inclusion of the saving rate as an explanatory variable reduces the estimated coefficient on the undervaluation measure.)

Rodrik notes that the inclusion of the saving rate in the growth regressions does not completely eliminate the significance of *UNDERVAL* as an explanatory variable, and he concludes from this that endogeneity resulting from factors of the kind illustrated in the simple example do not fully account for the association between undervaluation and growth. But the fact that inclusion of a single proxy for factors of the kind represented by the simple example eliminates only part of the association between *UNDERVAL* and growth hardly establishes that endogenous mechanisms of this kind are not responsible for the correlation—in particular, for the cases in which undervaluation coincides with strong growth, as opposed to the cases in which overvaluation coincides with weak growth.[11]

10. Moreover, some other policies that would result in a real depreciation as a byproduct would lower rather than raise GDP growth.

11. Again, it is only the association of *UNDERVAL* with growth that is shown to be robust to inclusion of the saving rate in the regression, not the association between simple measures of the real exchange rate and growth. One should not expect the association between *UNDERVAL* and growth to be completely eliminated by the inclusion of any number of regressors representing determinants of the real exchange rate, because *UNDERVAL* also reflects the economy's growth rate, as explained above.

The simple example also illustrates another important point. The mere existence of a positive correlation between the real exchange rate and growth (across some class of developing countries) need not be evidence of any *greater distortions* in the tradable sector that can in turn justify policies that essentially subsidize that sector. Ultimately, this is Rodrik's argument for the pursuit of undervaluation: one would like to subsidize the production of tradables, but for political economy reasons it may be most practical to do so by manipulating the exchange rate rather than through industrial policy. The main evidence Rodrik offers for the hypothesis of an inefficiently small relative size of the tradable sector in developing economies is the evidence for a stimulative effect of a real depreciation. Yet in the simple model, a positive correlation exists between the real exchange rate and growth—and faster growth is associated with a shift of resources from the nontradable to the tradable sector—but this does not mean that the equilibrium production of tradables is suboptimal. In the case that $\tau = 0$, the intertemporal equilibrium maximizes the welfare of the representative household (subject to the constraint that trade with the rest of the world must satisfy intertemporal balance of the capital account), and the introduction of a subsidy for the production of tradables would *reduce* welfare, relative to that optimum. Similarly, the introduction of other sorts of market distortions that represent indirect ways of subsidizing the tradable sector would most likely reduce welfare, whether or not they would increase GDP.

A CASE STUDY: SOUTH KOREA. Ultimately, the issue of causality is unlikely to be settled using panel regressions of the kind that constitute Rodrik's main results, owing to a lack of suitable instruments for exogenous changes in exchange rate policy. Case studies can often be more illuminating in this regard. Here I consider only one, that of South Korea, which is one of the countries Rodrik cites to illustrate the association of growth with undervaluation (see his figure 1). One can obtain a more complete picture of the degree to which the Korean case supports Rodrik's thesis by looking at higher-frequency data (his figure 1 uses five-year averages) and at additional variables.

My figure 1 plots annual data for both the (official) nominal won-dollar exchange rate and the implied real exchange rate, as well as Korean prices relative to U.S. prices.[12] The figure shows the several large won devaluations of the 1950s and 1960s—in particular, those

12. The data are from the Penn World Tables and are the same data used by Rodrik in constructing the *UNDERVAL* measure that he plots.

Figure 1. South Korea: Exchange Rates and Relative Prices, 1953–2004[a]

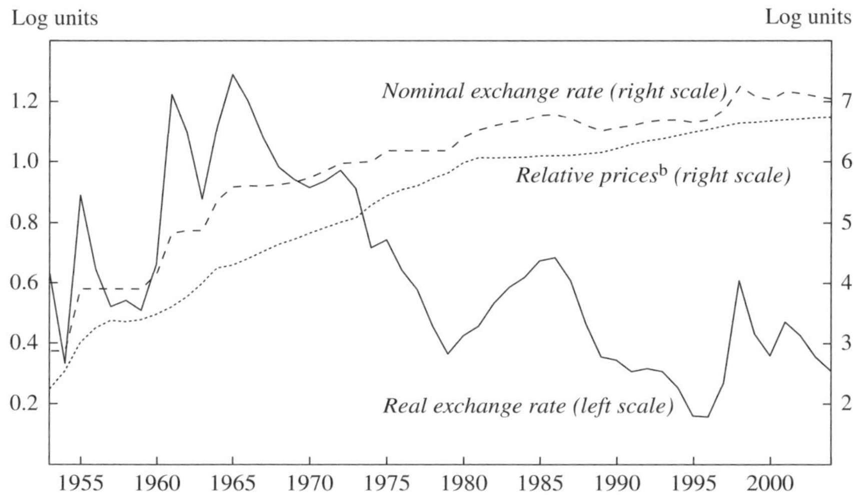

Source: Penn World Tables.
a. Exchange rates are against the dollar; a rise indicates a depreciation of the won.
b. Korean prices relative to U.S. prices.

of 1955, 1960, 1961, and 1964.[13] Each of these did result (at least temporarily) in a substantial real depreciation, providing clear evidence that at least some of the relatively high frequency variation in the real exchange rate in South Korea represents effects of exchange rate policy. But the figure also makes clear that devaluations need not have any long-lasting effect on the real exchange rate: much of the effect of the 1955 and 1961 devaluations had already been undone by increased inflation two years later. Indeed, this fact explains why the Korean government found additional large devaluations to be necessary so soon after the previous ones.

The 1964 devaluation might appear to have been more successful: for the next decade, Korea maintained a real exchange rate that was substantially weaker than it had been during most of the 1950s. Of course, this was also the decade over which Korea's real GDP growth accelerated to a rate of 6 to 8 percent a year (figure 2), which Rodrik interprets as supporting the view that an undervalued currency was the key to the Korean growth

13. A 30 percent devaluation in February 1960 was followed by another 100 percent devaluation in February 1961; the annual data are not of high enough frequency to show this as two distinct episodes.

Figure 2. South Korea: Exchange Rates, Saving, and Economic Growth, 1953–2004

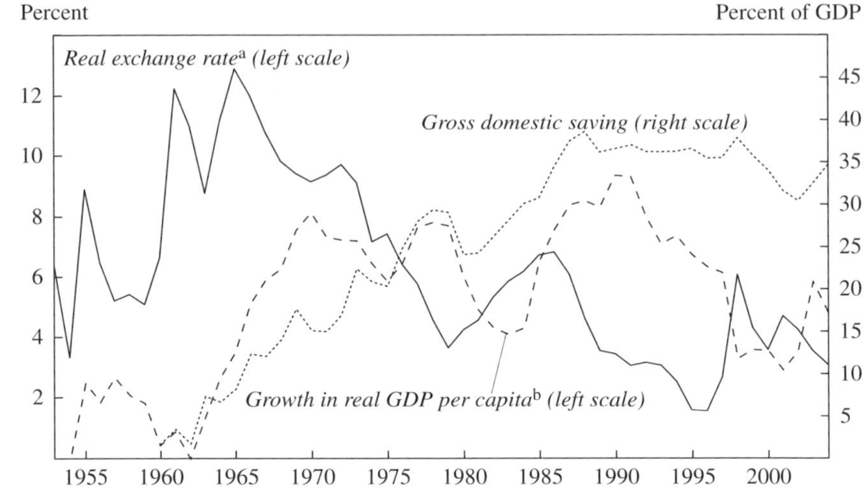

Percent | Percent of GDP

Real exchange rate[a] (left scale)

Gross domestic saving (right scale)

Growth in real GDP per capita[b] (left scale)

Source: Penn World Tables.

a. Logarithm of the real exchange rate from figure 1, divided by 10.

b. Five-year moving average.

"miracle." But in order to attribute the sustained real depreciation to the 1964 devaluation, one must explain why earlier devaluations did not have similarly long-lasting effects.

An obvious interpretation would be as follows: the earlier devaluations were not associated with any change in the *equilibrium* real exchange rate, and therefore monetary policy could weaken the real exchange rate only temporarily; in contrast, the 1964 devaluation coincided with a weakening of the equilibrium real rate, so that the devaluation, rather than resulting in a true undervaluation, facilitated a shift in the real exchange rate that would have had to occur in any event. Why might the equilibrium real exchange rate have weakened? A clue is provided by the fact that gross domestic saving surged after the early 1960s, as figure 2 also shows.

Before 1965, ceilings on bank deposit rates in South Korea depressed household saving, since (under the high inflation of the time) the implied real interest rates on deposits were negative. Instead, households lent funds to the informal financial sector, where interest rates were quite high. By raising interest rate ceilings in 1965 and at the same time reducing inflation, the government brought household savings back into the banking system, and so reduced the cost of capital for businesses through more efficient intermediation.[14] In addition, tighter fiscal policy increased public saving, further contributing to the sharp increase in overall domestic saving.

This increase in saving, which coincided fairly closely with the acceleration of economic growth, was likely an important cause of the growth miracle. Moreover, the simple model presented above shows that increased incentives for saving can also increase the equilibrium real exchange rate. This may be one of the reasons that Korea's equilibrium real exchange rate was higher in the late 1960s and early 1970s than earlier, so that the effects of the 1964 devaluation on the real exchange rate were not quickly reversed. Indeed, Kwang Suk Kim argues that Korea's persistent current account deficit and buildup of external debt in the decade after 1965 point to overvaluation, not undervaluation, of the won in this period (providing, incidentally, a further reason to doubt the accuracy of Rodrik's *UNDERVAL* measure).[15]

Of course, my interpretation of the Korean case does not imply that exchange rate policy is completely irrelevant to a country's development strategy. Overly tight regulation of financial flows can be an important impediment to growth, as seems to have been the case in Korea before the 1960s, and policies that seek to maintain an overvalued currency will often require extensive controls. Hence the creation of conditions conducive to growth will mean, among other things, refraining from attempts to maintain a seriously overvalued currency. Moreover, the Korean case shows that the process of development may involve a reduction in the equilibrium real exchange rate (that is, that which would result from fully flexible wages and prices and an absence of impediments to capital flows). In such a case, a nominal devaluation can be valuable as a way of allowing the necessary real depreciation to occur without the more painful process of forcing wages and prices down in response to insufficient aggregate demand. But such a policy is not correctly described as the pursuit of an "undervalued" currency; rather, it is again an example of the wisdom of avoiding overvaluation, with the important proviso that the equilibrium exchange rate, with respect to which overvaluation must be defined, can easily change as the economic structure changes.

14. Kim, Kwang Suk, "The 1964–65 Exchange Rate Reform, Export-Promotion Measures, and Import-Liberalization Program." In *Economic Development in the Republic of Korea: A Policy Perspective,* edited by Lee-Jay Cho and Yoon Hyung Kim (Honolulu: East-West Center, 1991, p. 137).

15. Kim, "The 1964–65 Exchange Rate Reform," p. 132.

GENERAL DISCUSSION Lawrence Summers commented that if the findings of the paper are correct, the implications are striking: mercantilism is the right economic strategy for developing countries seeking faster growth. According to the paper, certain sectors of the economy are likely to generate externalities and contribute to growth in ways different from other sectors, and therefore policies that support those sectors are likely to be preferred. This argument is directly at odds with economists' traditional opposition to most forms of industrial policy. But Summers raised two problems that prevented him from being persuaded by the paper's results. First, he questioned whether the externalities in the tradable goods sector could be so large relative to those in the nontradable goods sector as to account for the estimated growth effect. Second, he doubted that all the benefits of such externalities would be realized within just five years, as the paper's empirical approach implied. Summers also criticized Rodrik's use of both time fixed effects and five-year measurement periods, on the grounds that they would likely obscure the longer-term impact. He argued that omitting the country fixed effects would allow a closer examination of permanent differences in the structure of national economies.

Richard Cooper broadly agreed with Rodrik's conclusion but observed that it was not a new idea: many of the Asian countries had adopted it in the second half of the twentieth century. Those countries followed a policy of currency undervaluation for two reasons: to promote reliable demand for their exports, and to encourage capital imports. Cooper disagreed with Summers that such a policy constituted mercantilism: mercantilism focuses on restricting imports, whereas this policy acts primarily on exports. On a more technical note, Cooper expressed reservations about the use of purchasing power parity–adjusted prices in determining over- or undervaluation, given that those numbers are subject to significant revision.

Linda Goldberg commended the paper for attempting to grapple with the distortions limiting growth in developing countries, particularly those falling disproportionately on the industrial sector. However, she objected to the paper's exclusive focus on the real exchange rate as the mechanism for dealing with those distortions, since the real exchange rate is correlated with other policies and macroeconomic variables. She suggested looking instead at natural experiments directly related to industrial policy and focusing specifically on the sectors most affected by the distortions.

Pierre-Olivier Gourinchas cautioned against the use of the Penn World Tables as the main data source. Given the large changes in the most recent revision of the data, he suggested, as a robustness test, rerunning the paper's regressions using earlier versions of the Penn tables. Gourinchas also questioned the practice of defining the real exchange rate as the relative price of goods in the tradable and the nontradable sectors, since other literature has shown that movement in the real exchange rate is not driven by movements in these relative prices. He added that he would like to see more empirical evidence in support of the paper's main argument.

Kathryn Dominguez agreed with previous speakers about the role of undervaluation in overcoming distortions but added that maintaining a real undervaluation is a costly policy. She requested that Rodrik provide an explanation of how undervaluation should be achieved so that it is actually beneficial.

Frederic Mishkin discussed other possible mechanisms for encouraging growth, focusing primarily on improvements in institutions. A shift in output toward tradable goods creates incentives to improve institutions, particularly in the financial sector, to meet the need for additional capital. Such improvement leads to growth in other sectors as well, as previous literature has shown.

BROOKINGS The Brookings Institution is a private nonprofit organization devoted to research, education, and publication on important issues of domestic and foreign policy. Its principal purpose is to bring the highest quality independent research and analysis to bear on current and emerging policy problems. The Institution was founded on December 8, 1927, to merge the activities of the Institute for Government Research, founded in 1916, the Institute of Economics, founded in 1922, and the Robert Brookings Graduate School of Economics and Government, founded in 1924. Interpretations or conclusions in Brookings publications should be understood to be solely those of the authors.